AMAZING TEMPLES OF THE WORLD

AMAZING TEMPLES OF THE WORLD

MICHAEL KERRIGAN

amber BOOKS

Published by
Amber Books Ltd
United House
North Road
London N7 9DP
United Kingdom
www.amberbooks.co.uk
Instagram: amberbooksltd
Facebook: amberbooks
Twitter: @amberbooks
Pinterest: amberbooksltd

Project Editor: Michael Spilling
Designer: Mark Batley
Picture Research: Terry Forshaw

ISBN: 978-1-83886-094-3

Printed in China

Contents

Introduction

We take our word 'temple' from the Latin *templum*, which in its earliest Indo-European etymological ancestry denoted a space or stretch of ground – here, one specially marked out for religious ceremony. Also measured out in stretches by the Romans was time, hence the coincidence by which this came to have so similar a Latin name: *tempus*.

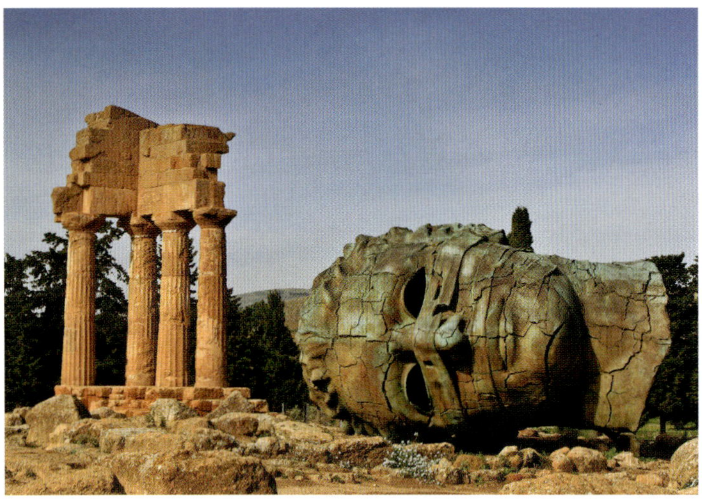

The connection is fitting because a temple contains all time: as a memorial to the past; a place of worship in the present; and a repository of hopes and intentions for the future. Even as it also embodies a set of aesthetic ideals in its architecture and decoration and communicates the spiritual values of those it serves.

Actually, it serves all of us, regardless of our faith – or lack of it. A temple is a monument to yearning; a testament to the human impulse to reach beyond the present moment, to aspire to something higher, better. And, that is something in which every one of us can believe.

ABOVE:
Valle dei Templi, Agrigento, Sicily
This bronze head, from what was once a colossal statue, lies behind the ruins of what is traditionally held to have been the Temple of the Dioscuri – Castor and Pollux, twin sons of the beautiful Leda after she'd been raped by Zeus in the form of a swan.

OPPOSITE:
Banteay Srei, Siem Reap, Cambodia
Sculpted sentries guard the doors to this great temple raised up in honour of the Hindu deity, Lord Shiva, in 967 CE by counsellors to King Rajendravarman II.

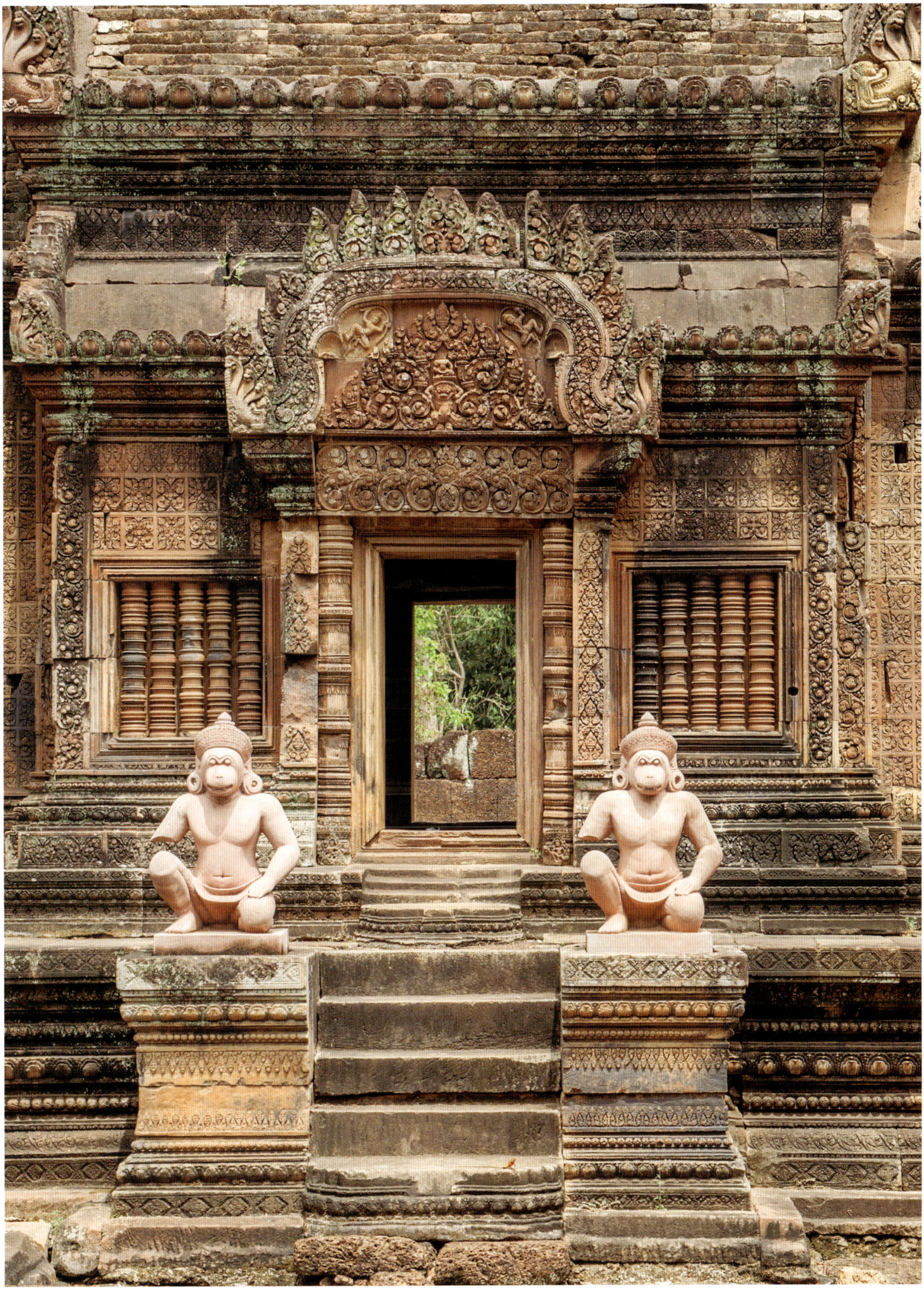

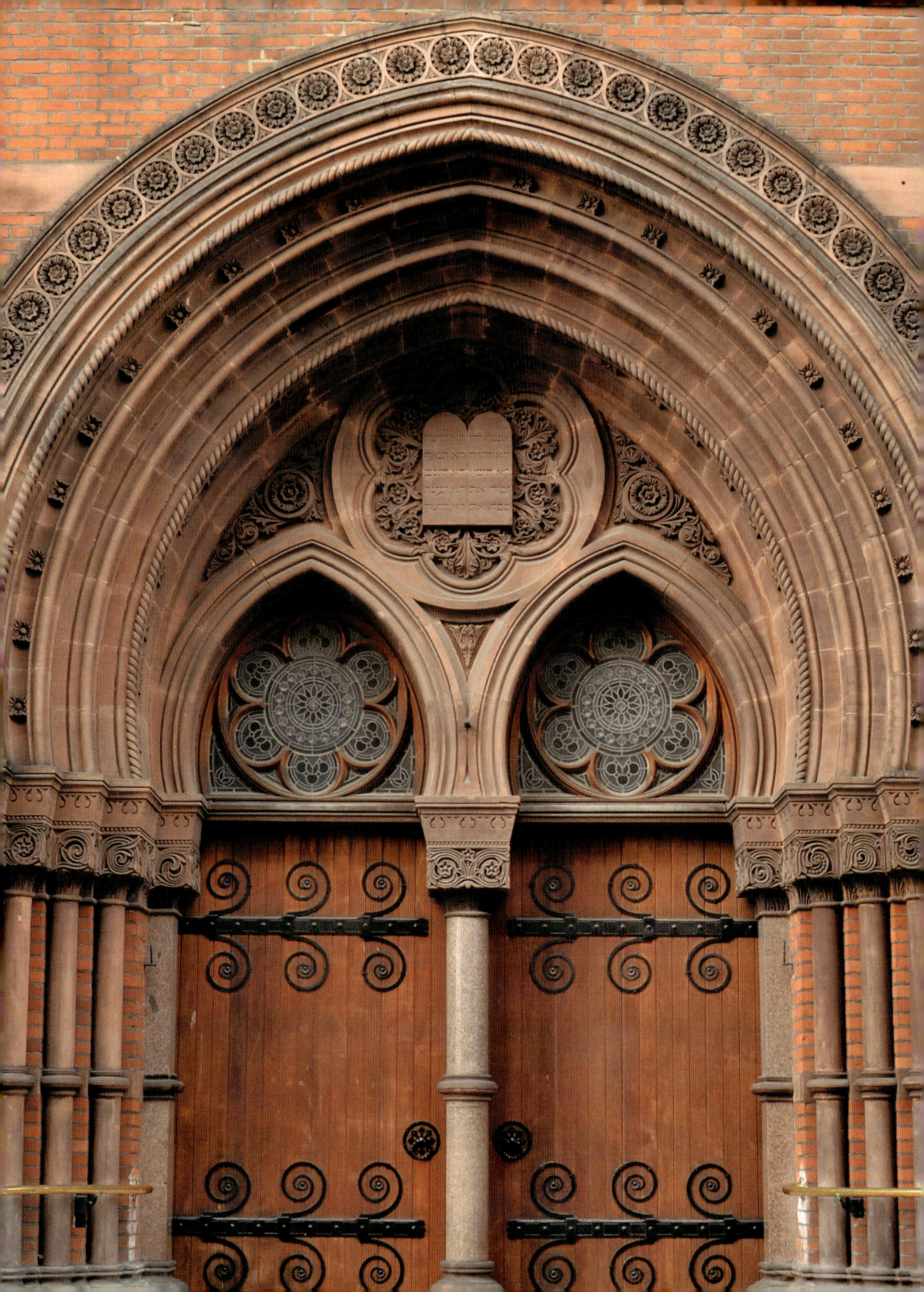

Europe

For the best part of 2000 years now, Christianity has held sway in Europe, its ascendancy essentially unquestioned. Viewed up-close of course, its history has been one of turbulence, dissent and schism, attended by cruel persecution and vicious war. Even so, it's been Christianity all the way.

Inevitably, this has meant a near-monopoly in religious architecture. Despite a decline in church attendance that's seen many made over into nightclubs or community centres, the UK has over 40,000 churches. Paris alone has 200, and the story's been the same across the continent as a whole.

In such a context, the sight of a temple is likely to be at least a little startling. Beautiful it may be in its classical symmetries, but a Greek or Roman temple is also an abrupt intrusion by a remote, and often forgotten, pagan past into the present. A Hindu temple or a Buddhist pagoda is a sudden reminder that there's a world outside, a world to which generations of immigration have opened an exciting door. Either way, it's an arresting sight that expands our horizons – historically, geographically or culturally; a sight that spurs us to consider new possibilities, different ways of thinking and imagining.

OPPOSITE:
New West End Synagogue, London, England
Strictly speaking, a synagogue is not a temple – it can't be, that title being reserved for the Temple in Jerusalem destroyed by the Romans in 70 CE. We've included synagogues here because they're clearly intended to reproduce the functions of that first temple for the Jewish diaspora. London's leading synagogue was opened in 1879.

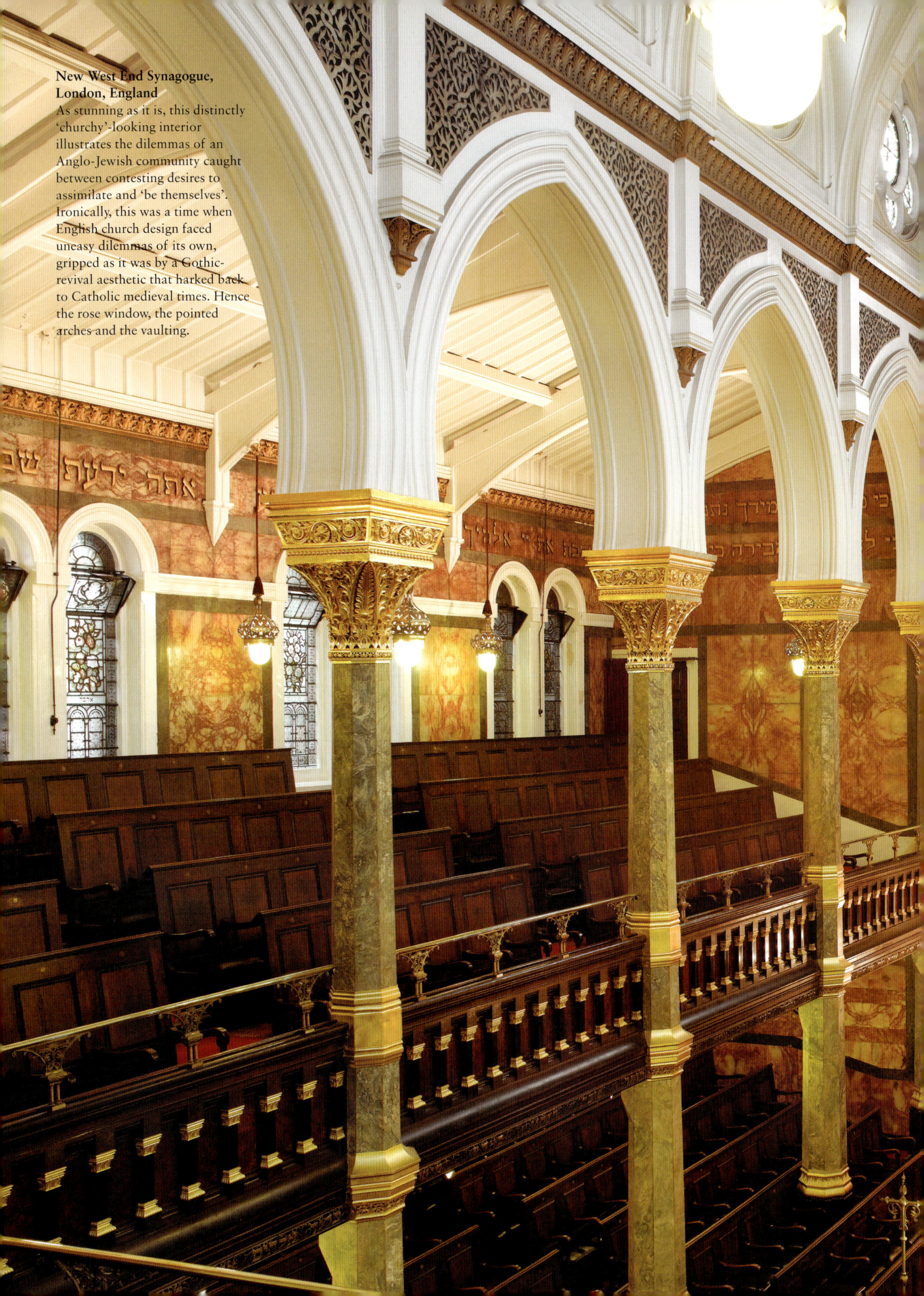

New West End Synagogue, London, England
As stunning as it is, this distinctly 'churchy'-looking interior illustrates the dilemmas of an Anglo-Jewish community caught between contesting desires to assimilate and 'be themselves'. Ironically, this was a time when English church design faced uneasy dilemmas of its own, gripped as it was by a Gothic-revival aesthetic that harked back to Catholic medieval times. Hence the rose window, the pointed arches and the vaulting.

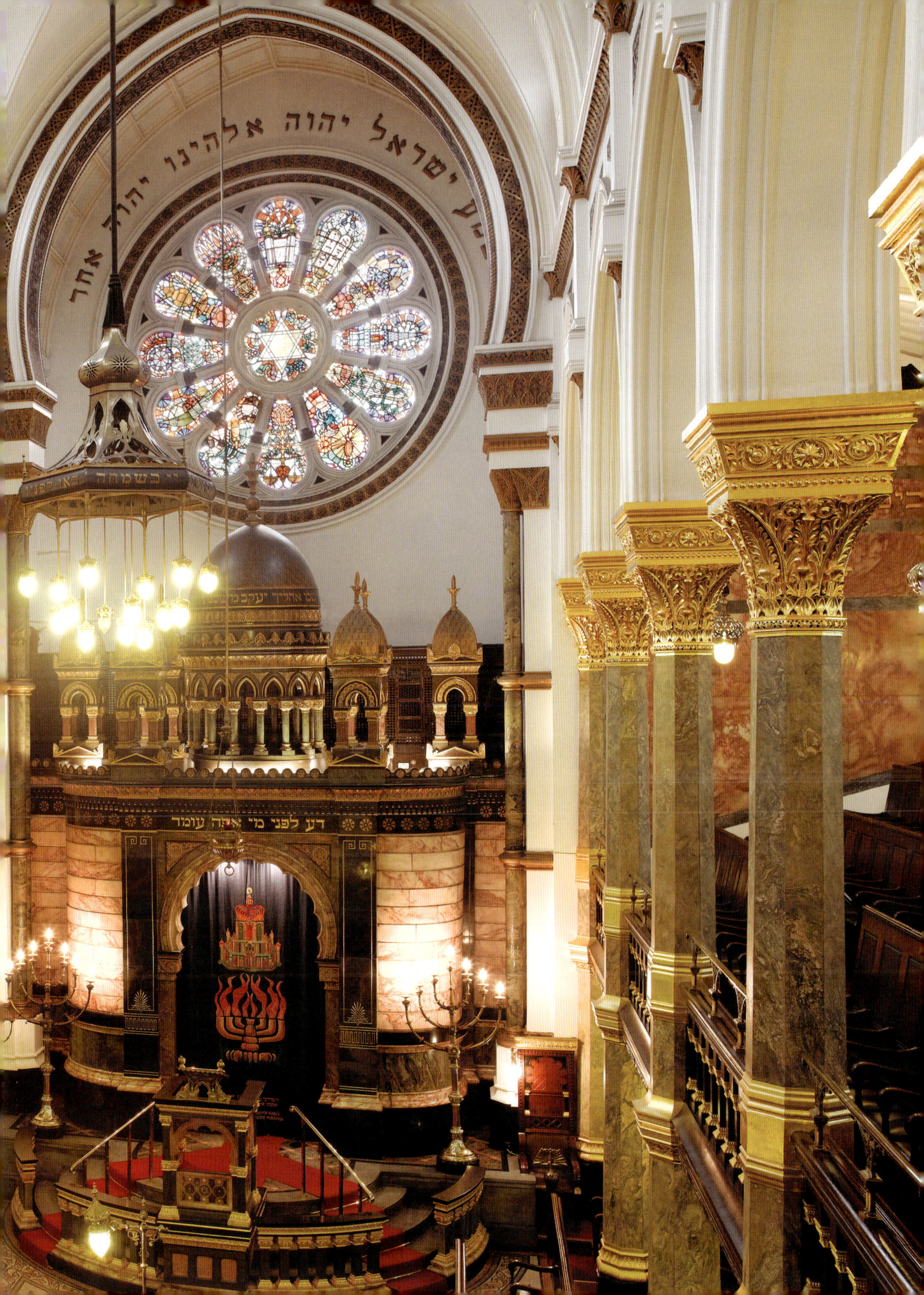
ישראל יהוה אלהינו יהוה אחד
דע לפני מי אתה עומד

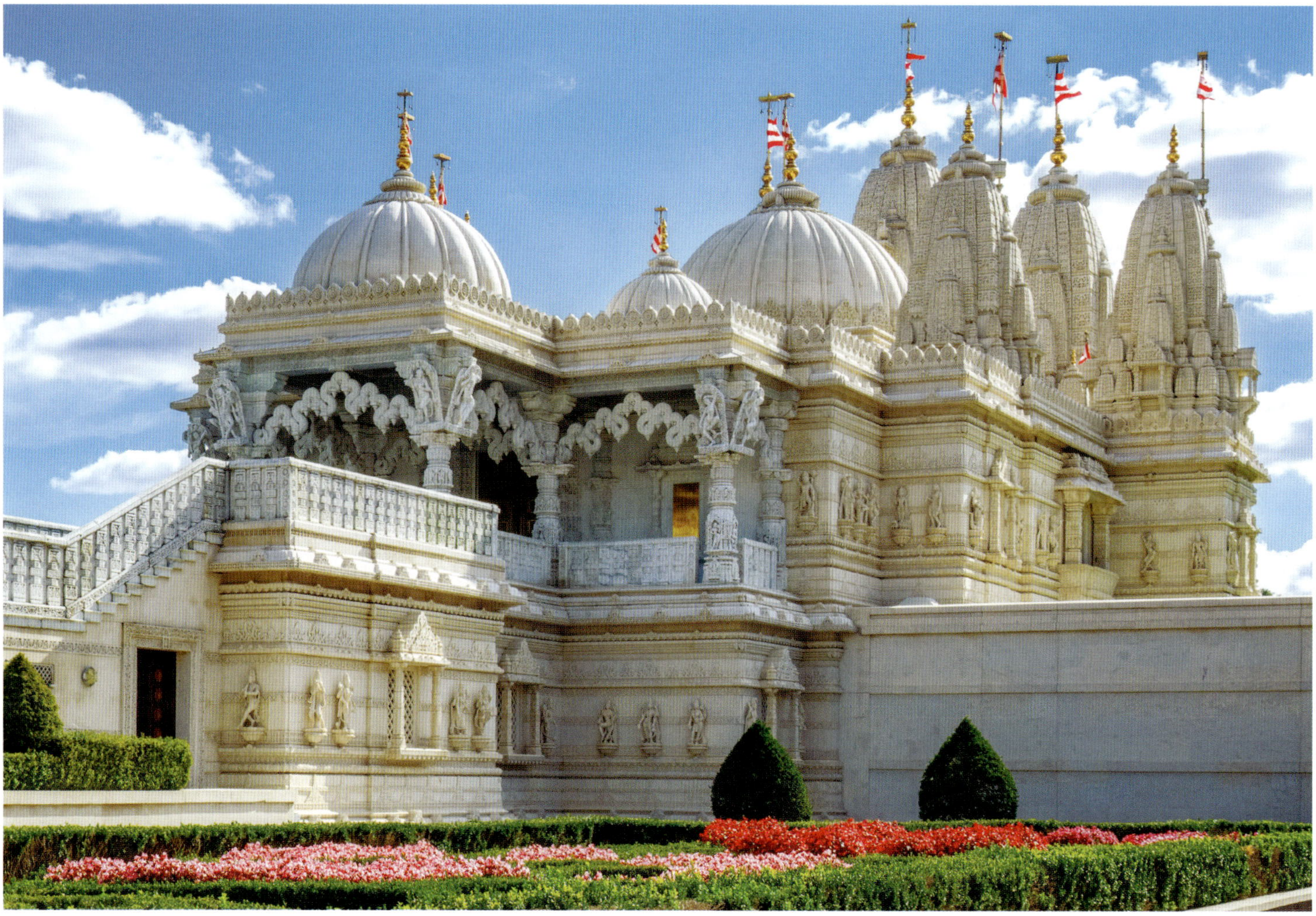

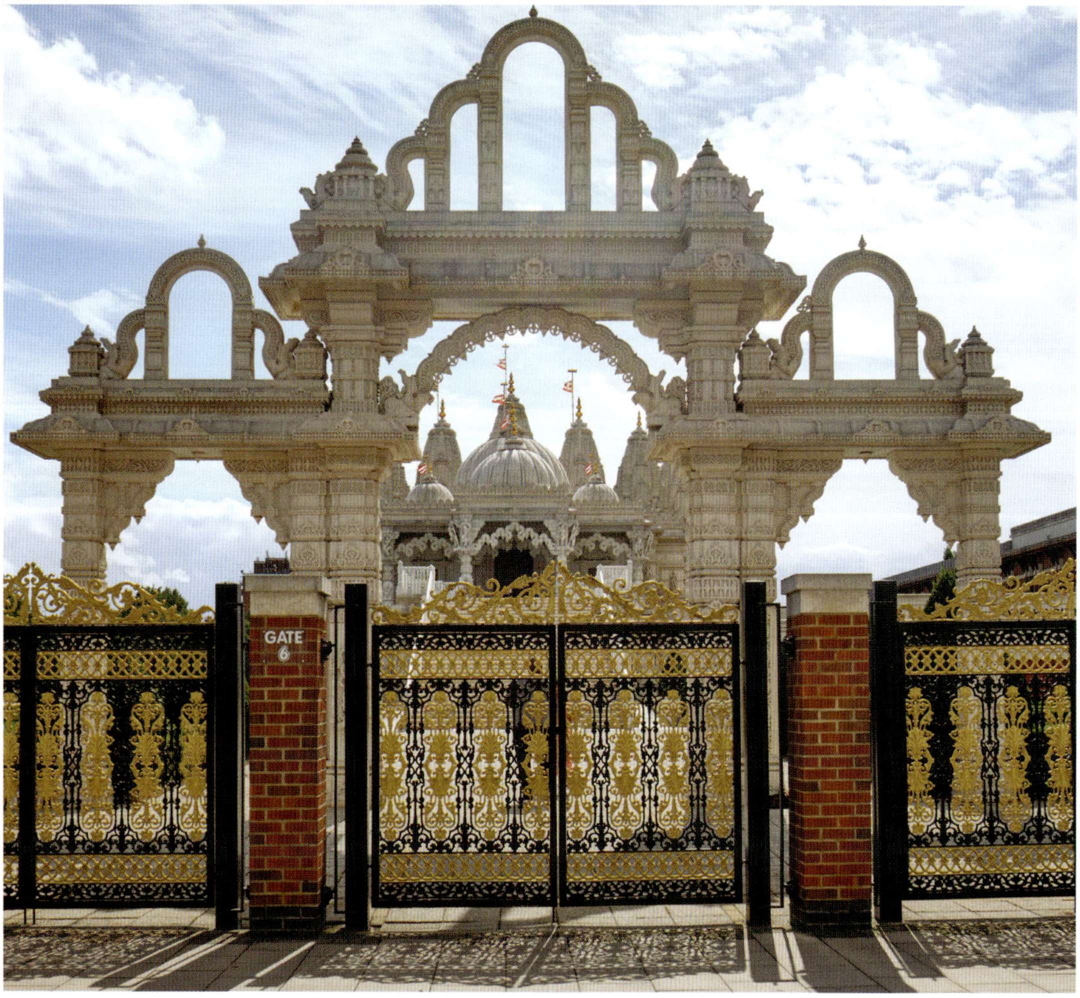

ALL PHOTOGRAPHS:

Shri Swaminarayan Mandir, Neasden, London, England

Whatever faith or denomination it represents, a place of worship is never solely that. However heartfelt its spiritual purpose, it's also an emblem, an assertion. Inaugurated in 1995, the so-called 'Neasden Temple' is not just a religious, cultural and social centre for London's Hindus, but a public proclamation by an immigrant community: 'We are here.' And, at the same time: 'We are proud of who we are.'

Shri Swaminarayan Mandir wasn't just built using traditional materials and methods, Italian marble was actually shipped to India to be worked in readiness before being brought to England for construction.

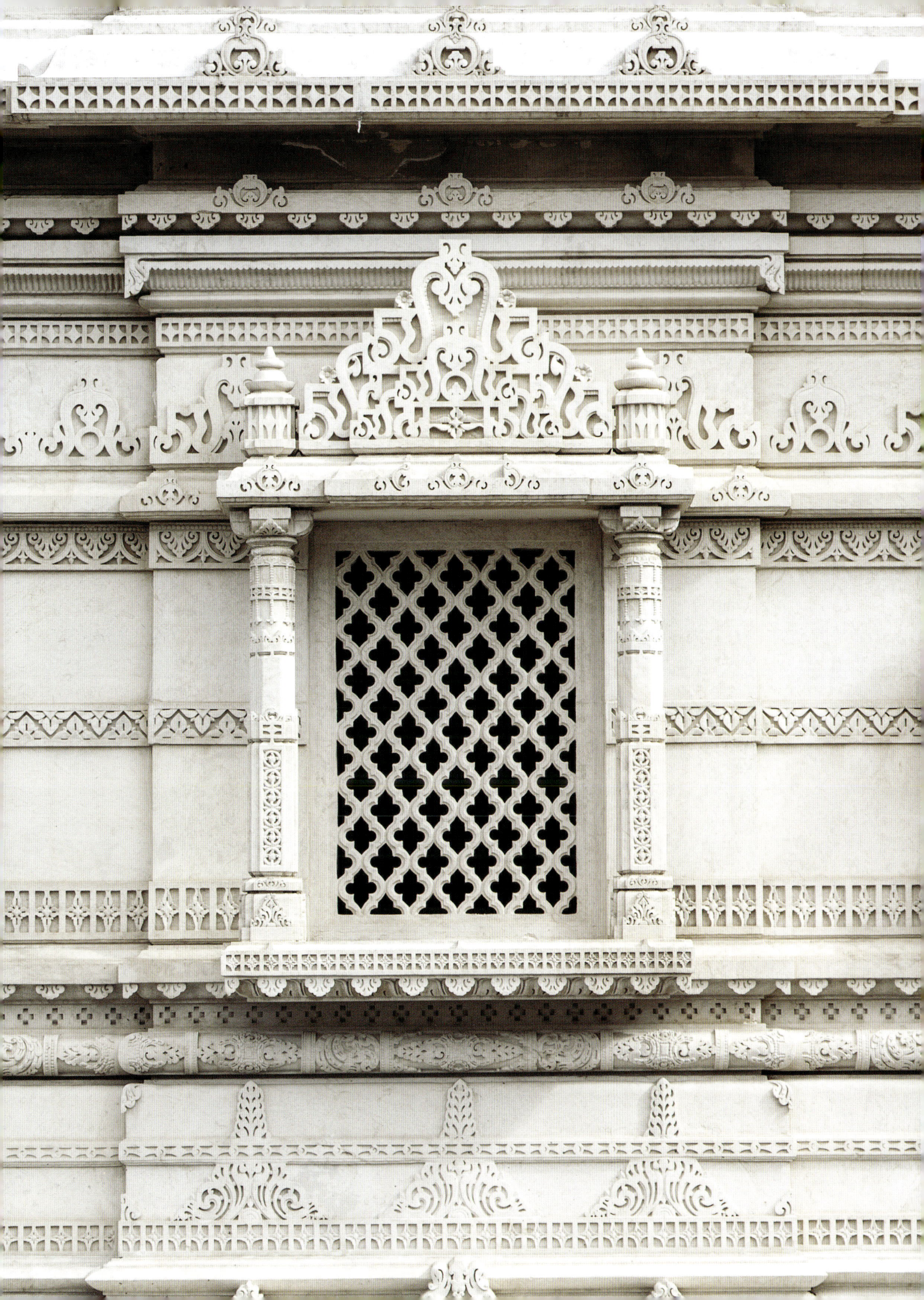

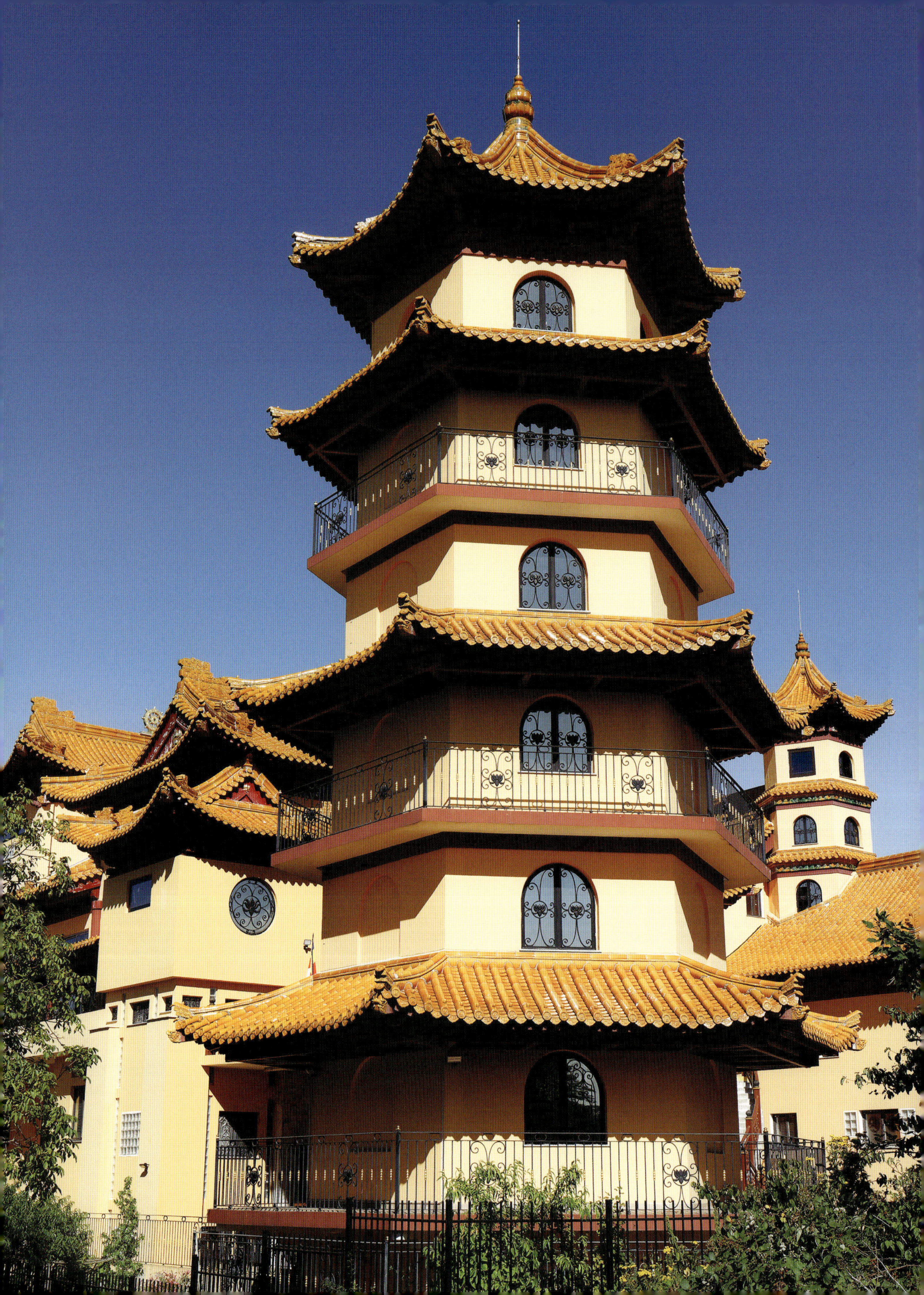

OPPOSITE:

Pagode Khánh-Anh, Évry, France

Construction of this Buddhist temple at Évry, south of Paris, was largely funded by France's Vietnamese community, and the wider diaspora forced to flee from Vietnam after the conclusion of the war there, from 1978 through to the 1990s.

RIGHT AND BELOW:

Paldenshangpa La Boulaye, Burgundy, France

La France doesn't get much more *profonde* than the commune of La Boulaye. You wouldn't normally expect to encounter a pagoda here. Paldenshagpa was founded by a Tibetan lama in 1974. It boasts brightly coloured paintings and Buddha statues.

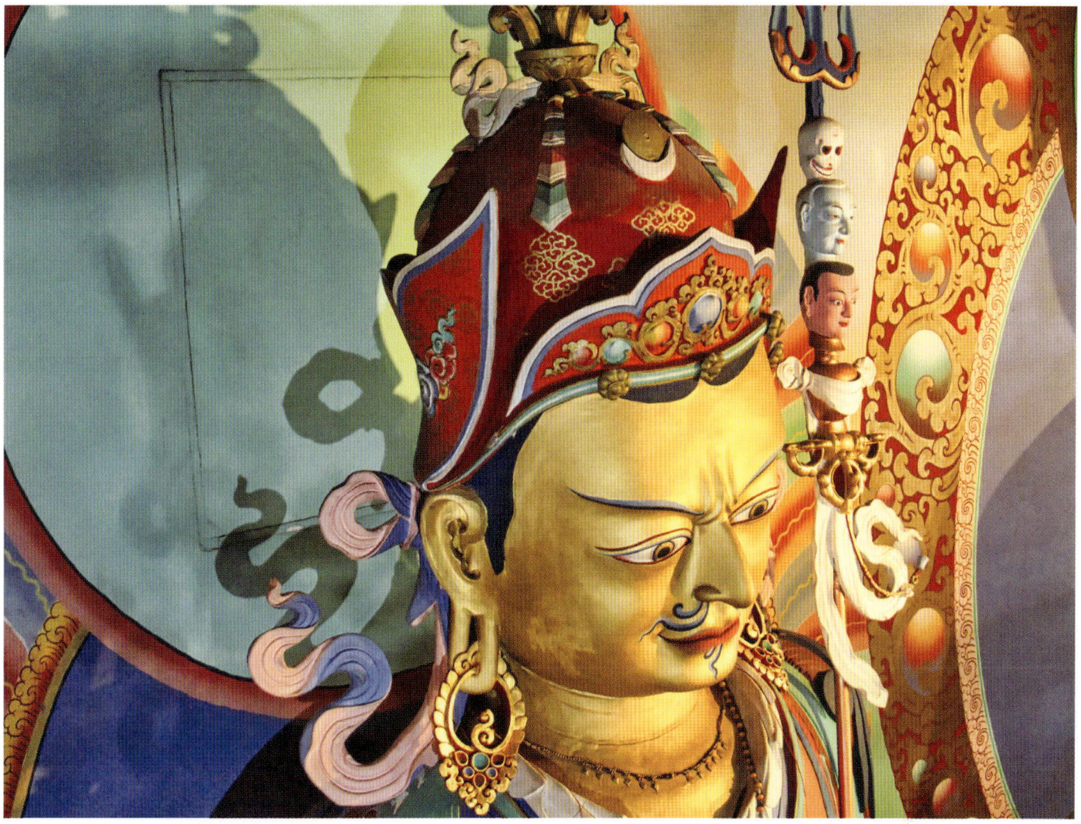

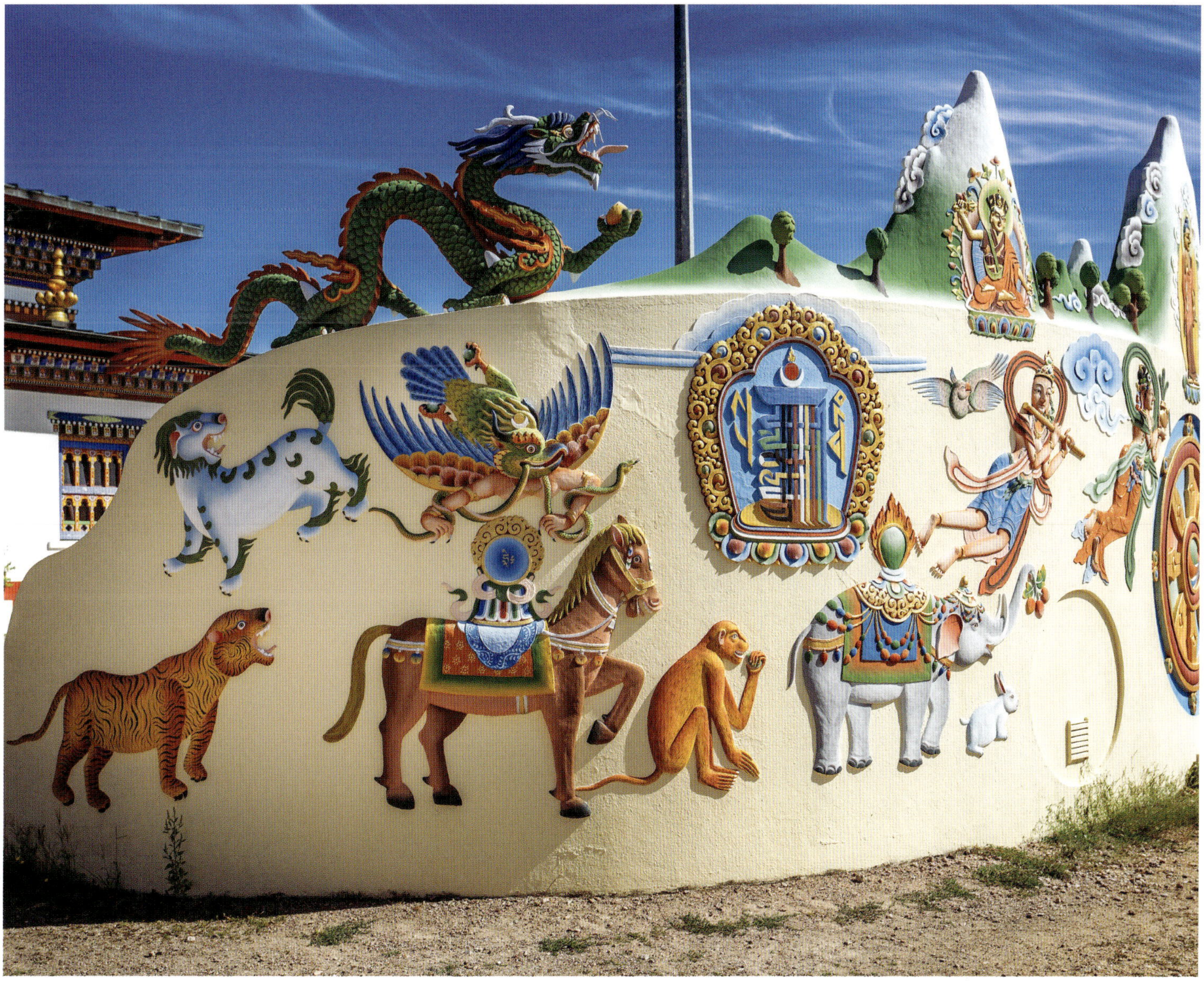

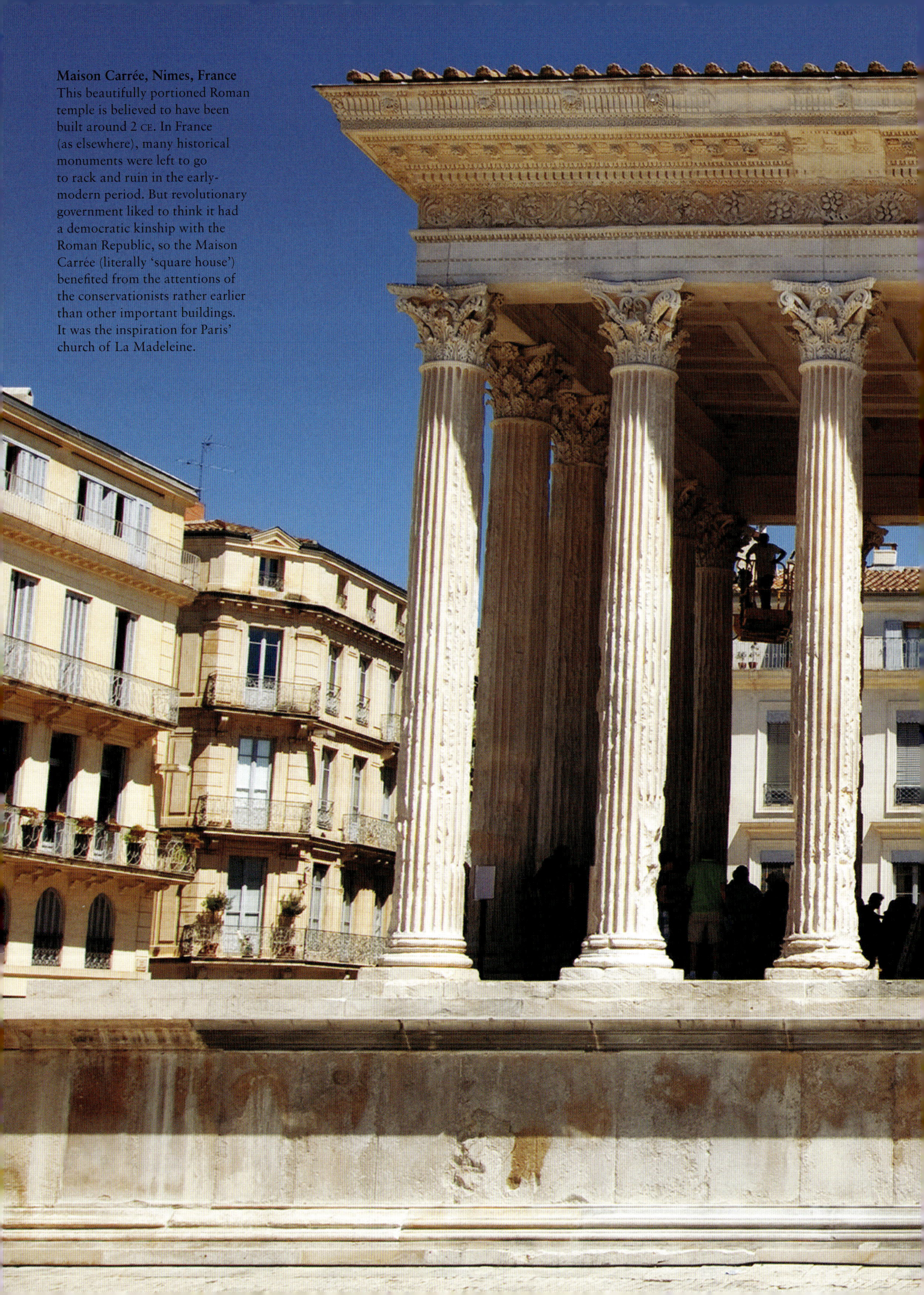

Maison Carrée, Nimes, France
This beautifully portioned Roman temple is believed to have been built around 2 CE. In France (as elsewhere), many historical monuments were left to go to rack and ruin in the early-modern period. But revolutionary government liked to think it had a democratic kinship with the Roman Republic, so the Maison Carrée (literally 'square house') benefited from the attentions of the conservationists rather earlier than other important buildings. It was the inspiration for Paris' church of La Madeleine.

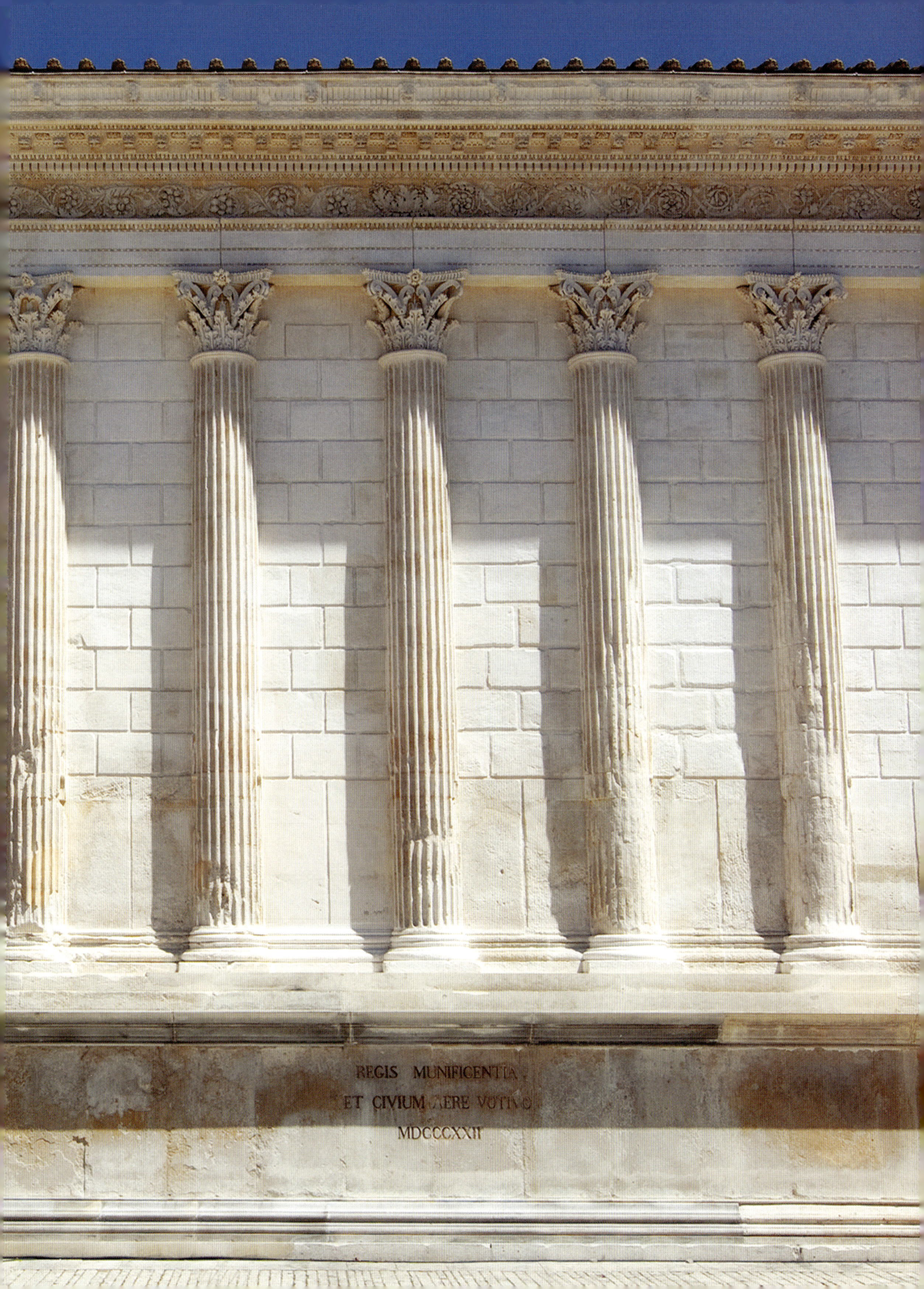
REGIS MUNIFICENTIA
ET CIVIUM AERE VOTIVO
MDCCCXXII

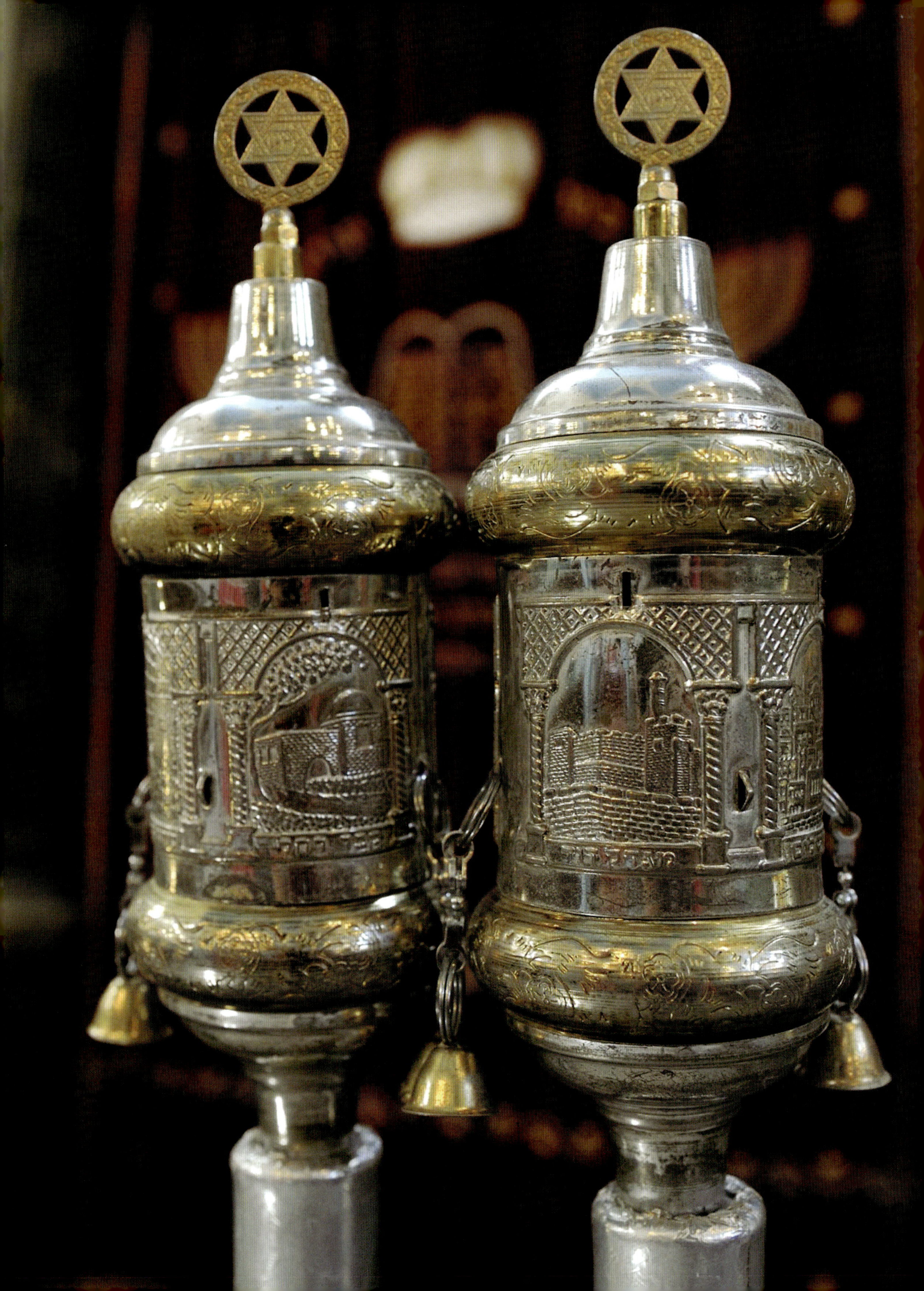

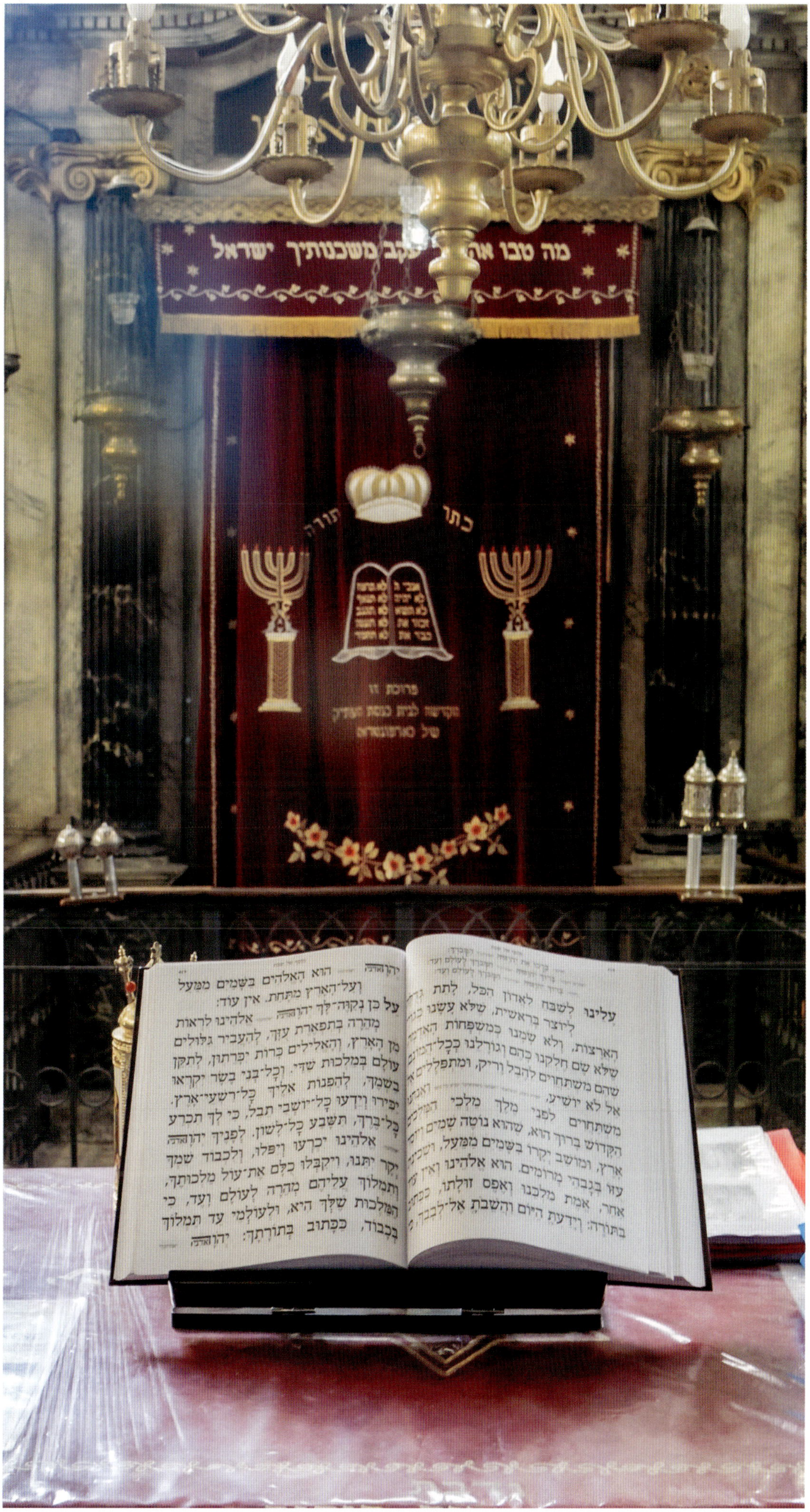

OPPOSITE AND LEFT:

Synagogue of Carpentras, France

France's oldest synagogue was designated in 1367. By then there had been a Jewish community in this Provençal city for a couple of centuries but they'd been persecuted (and at times expelled) by the local church. In 1306, King Philip IV (1268–1314) expelled the Jews from France completely, but excepted Carpentras (with Avignon, Cavaillon and L'Isle-sur-la-Sorgue). The lands here were owned by the Pope, who exacted rents from local Jews.

OVERLEAF:

Ulm Synagogue, Germany

The experience of the Jews in Nazi Germany was not of course a happy one. Ulm's Old Synagogue was destroyed in the violence of *Kristallnacht* (1938). The community which had worshipped here was subsequently rounded up and sent for extermination. Several hundred Jews live here now, many of them immigrants from the former Soviet Union. The new synagogue doesn't just meet a social and spiritual need: it's a declaration of confidence and an act of faith.

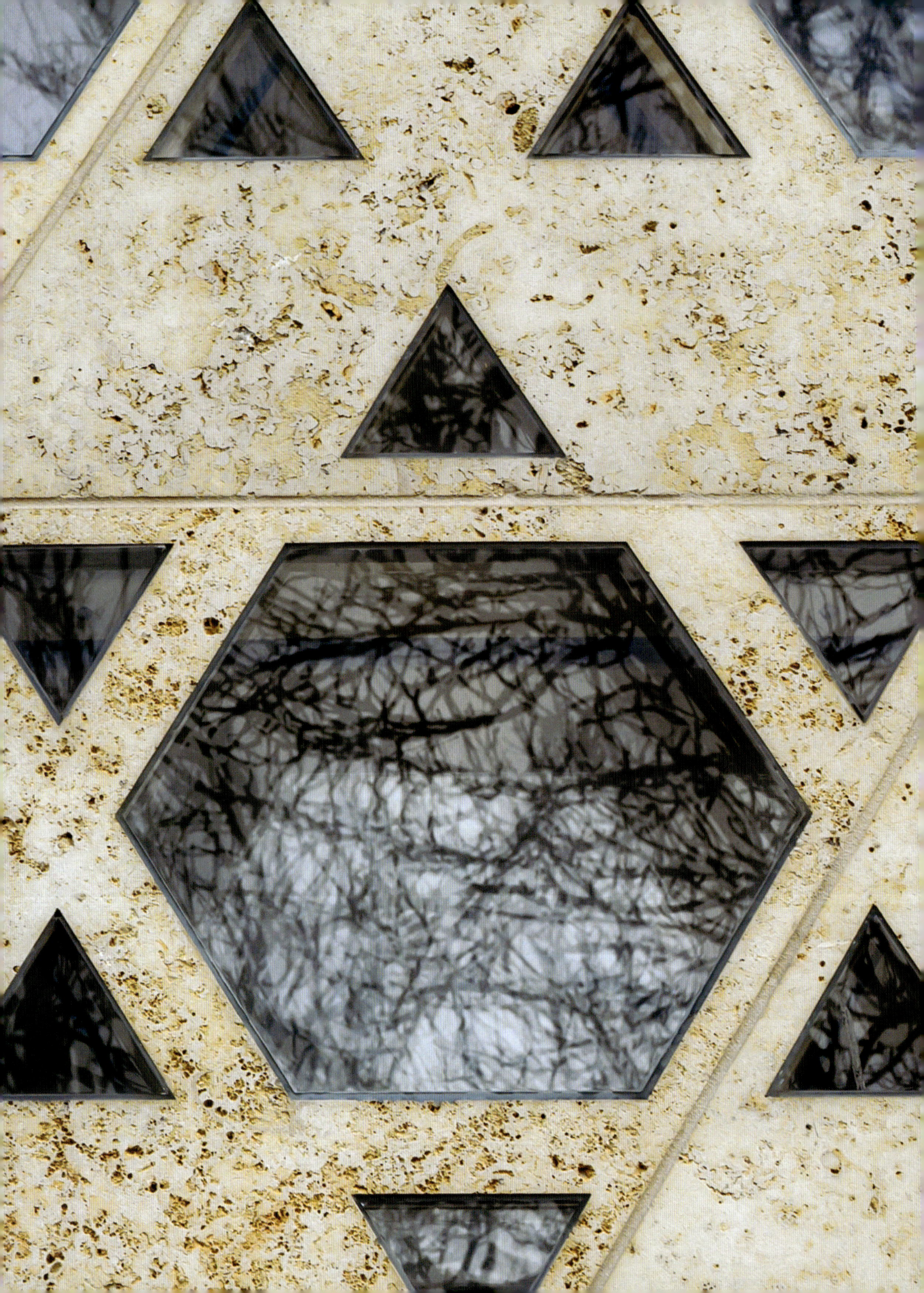

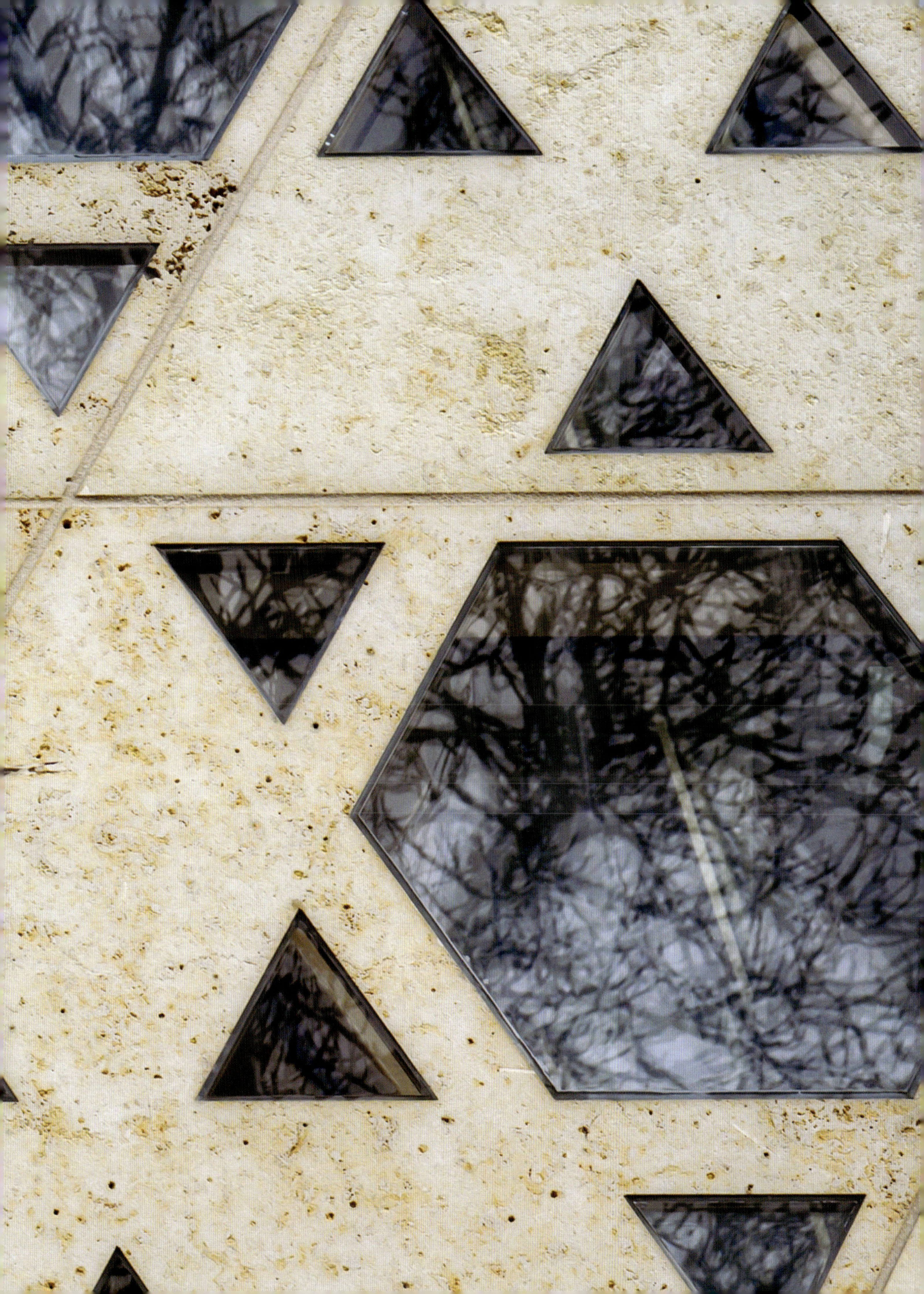

New Synagogue, Berlin, Germany
Only relatively 'new', this synagogue dates from 1866, though it had to be substantially rebuilt. Between Nazi vandalism and Allied bombing, it was all but destroyed. The Communist authorities in East Berlin made impressive efforts to refurbish historic monuments, including churches, in the post-war period, but the plight of this particular building (a Moorish-Revival masterpiece) was ignored. The bulk of the restoration work had to wait until after 1989 when Germany was at last reunified.

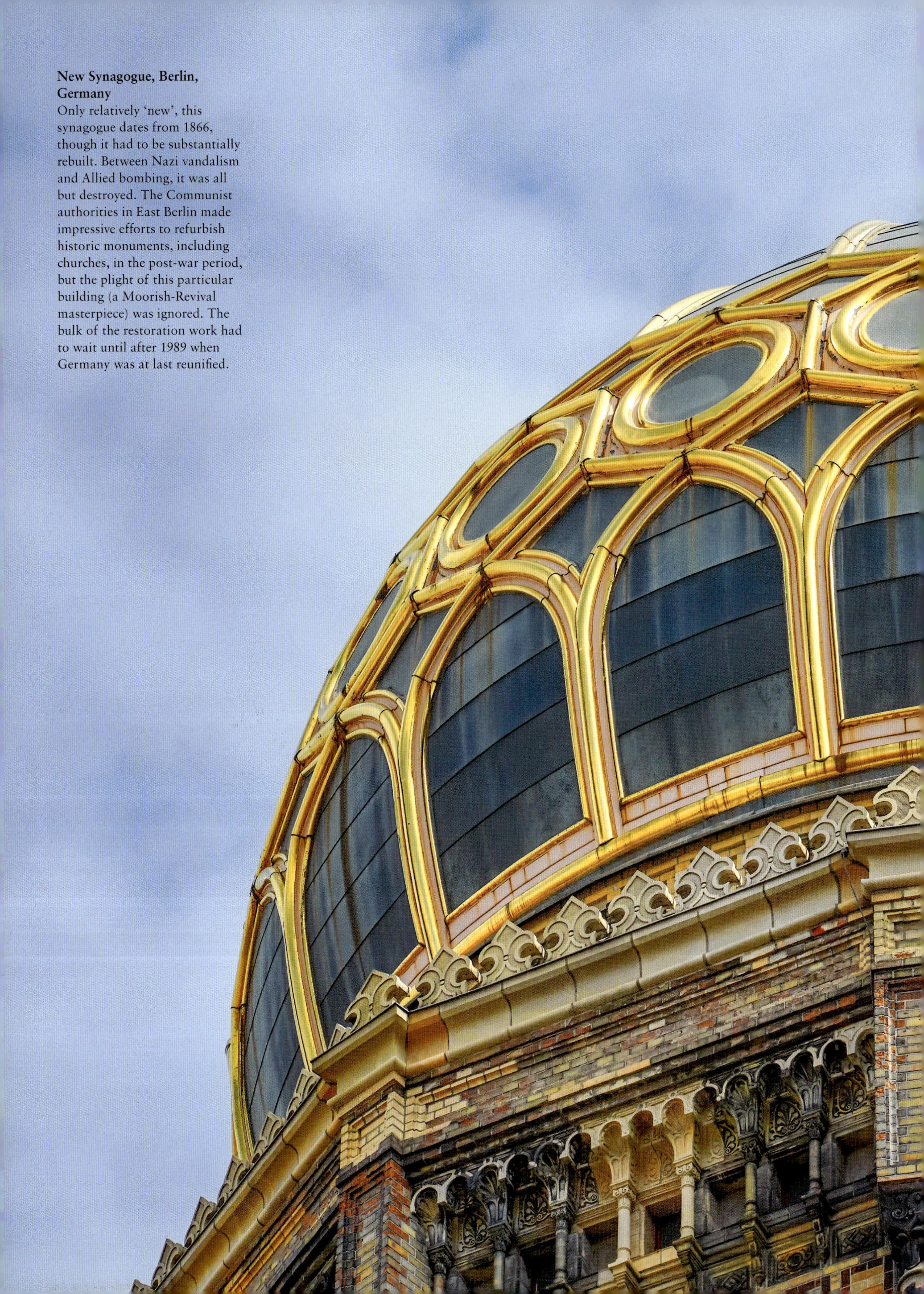

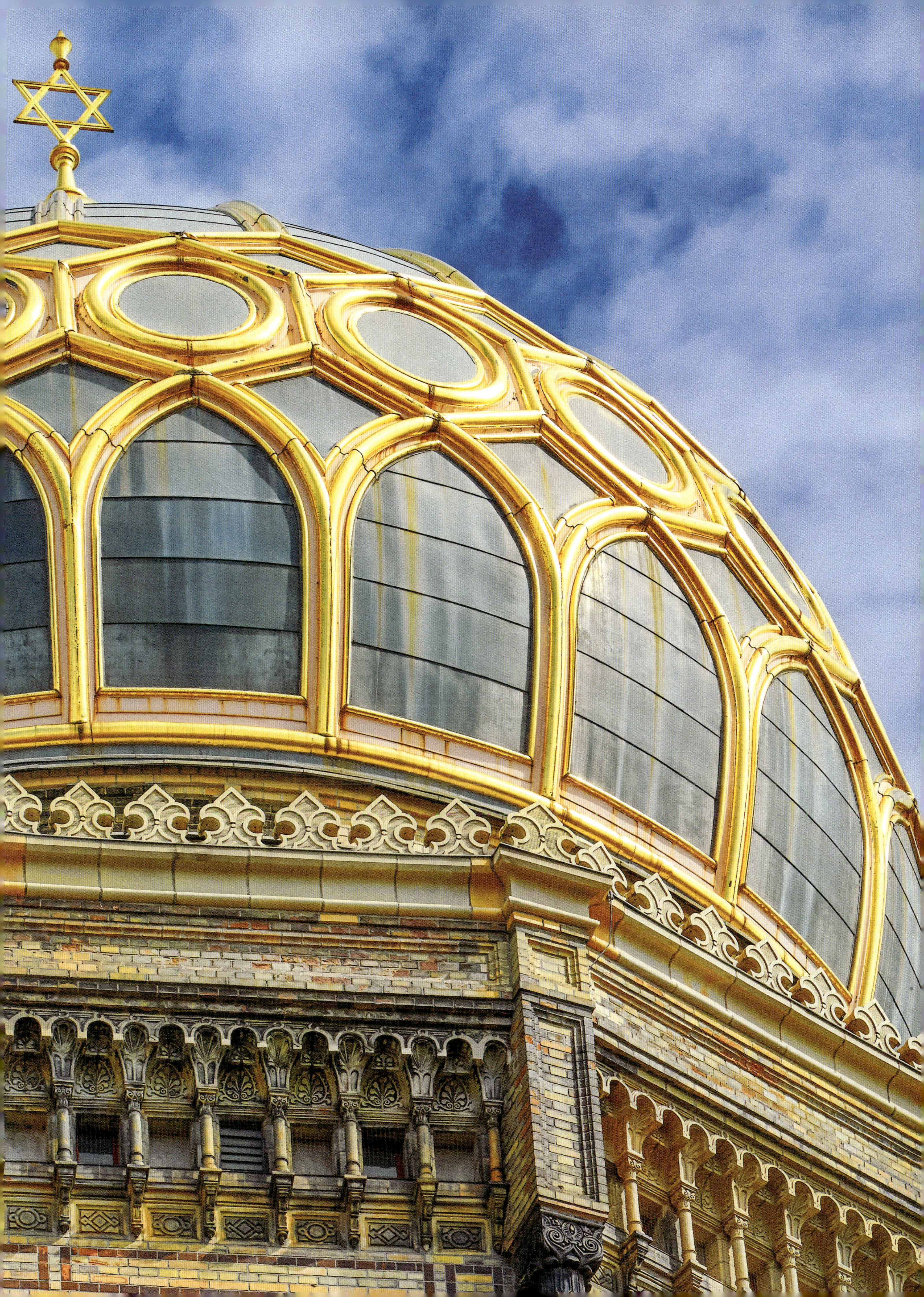

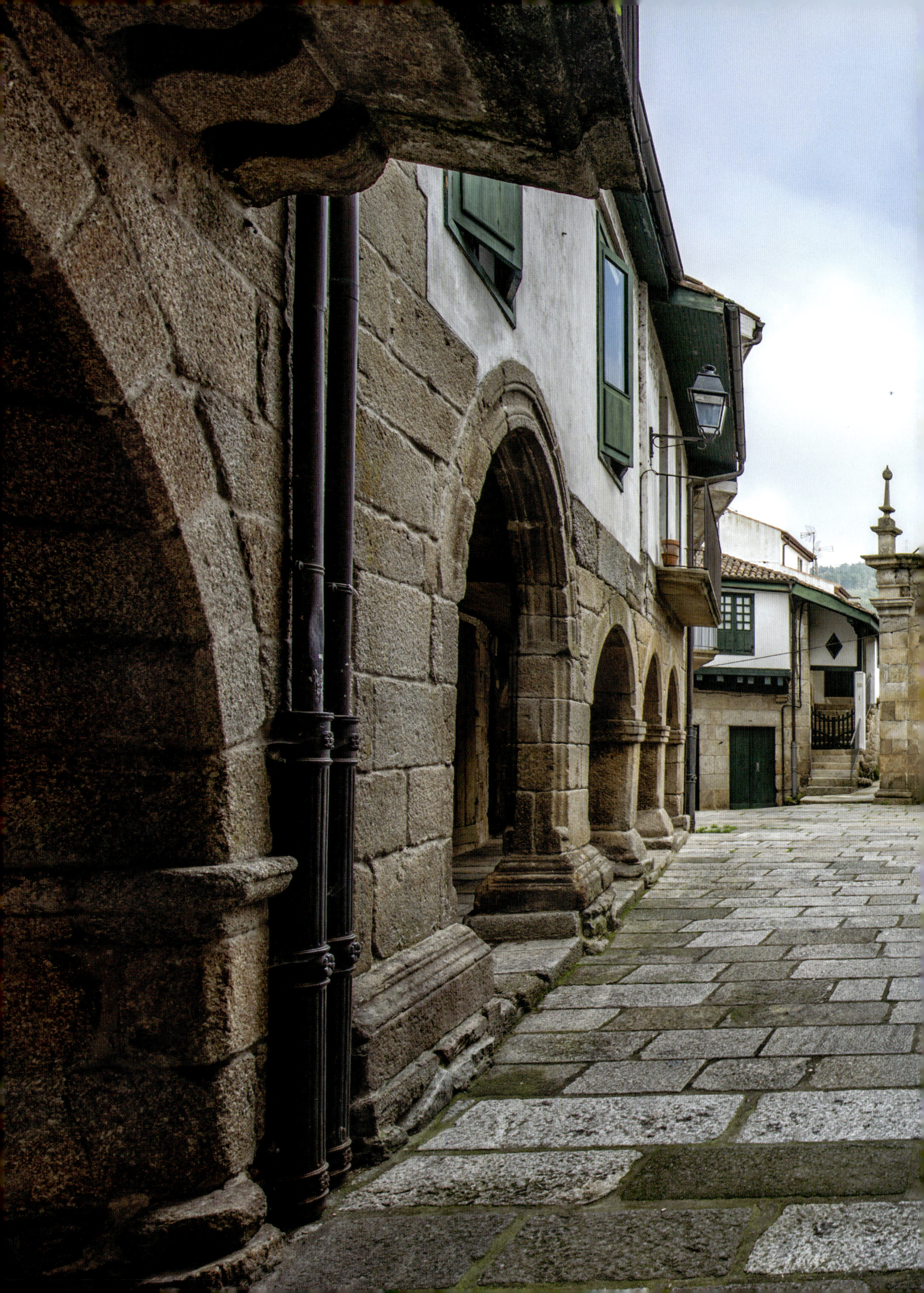

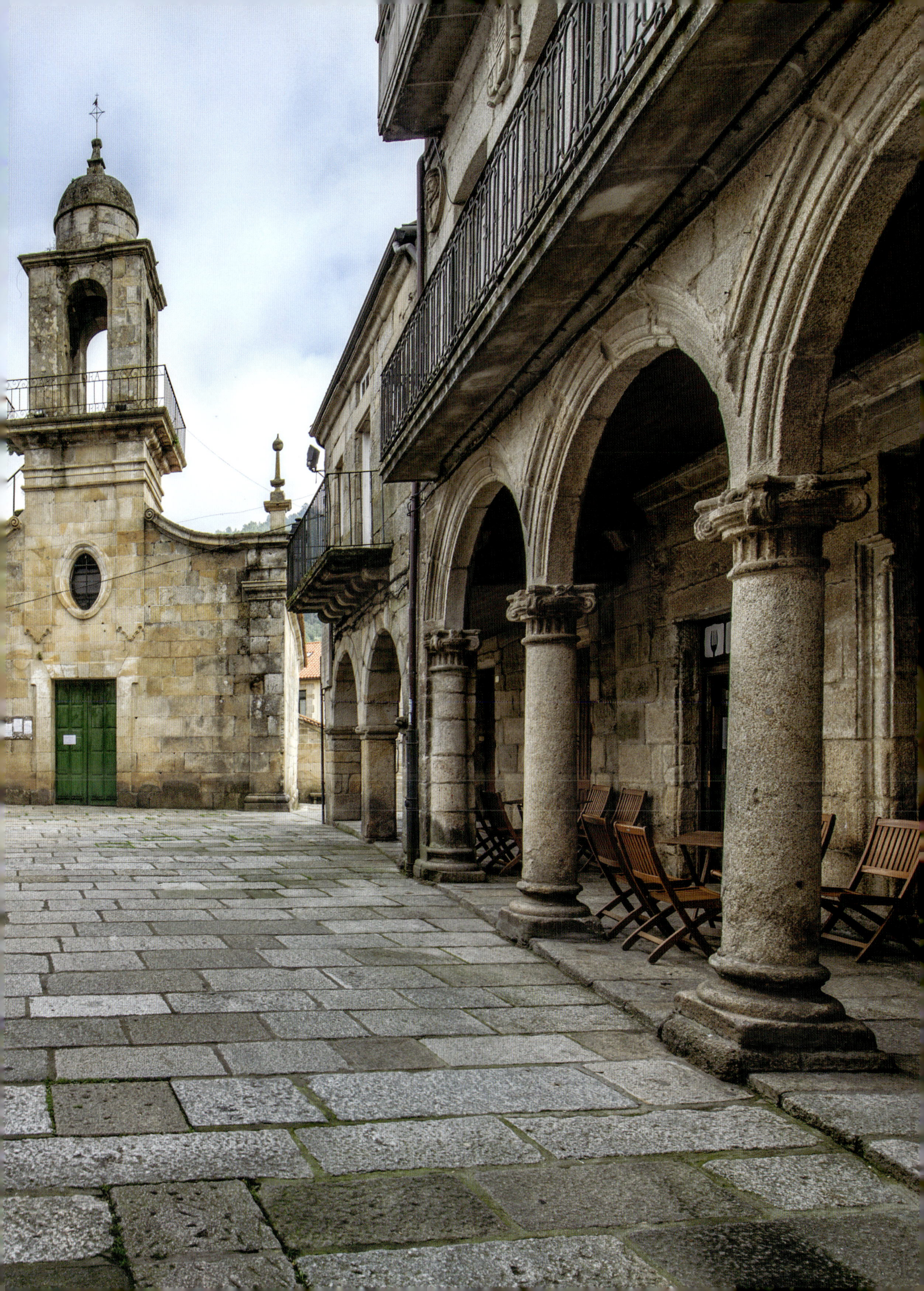

PREVIOUS PAGES:

Ribadavia Synagogue, Galicia, Spain

Spain's Jews were expelled en masse in 1492, though the quarters they had lived in would endure in many towns. The sleepier the better, in this remotest corner of the country's secluded province, there was no rage to redevelop, and little changed. Few Jews live in Ribadavia now, and none claim descent from the old Sephardic community, but there's increasing interest in this aspect of the place's past.

RIGHT:

Temple of Debod, Madrid, Spain

Europe's museums abound in ancient artefacts secured during the colonial period in ways that seem quite controversial now. This 2200-year-old temple is different: snatched to safety by the Egyptian authorities as the waters rose behind the Aswan High Dam in 1960, it was sent to Spain as an official gift.

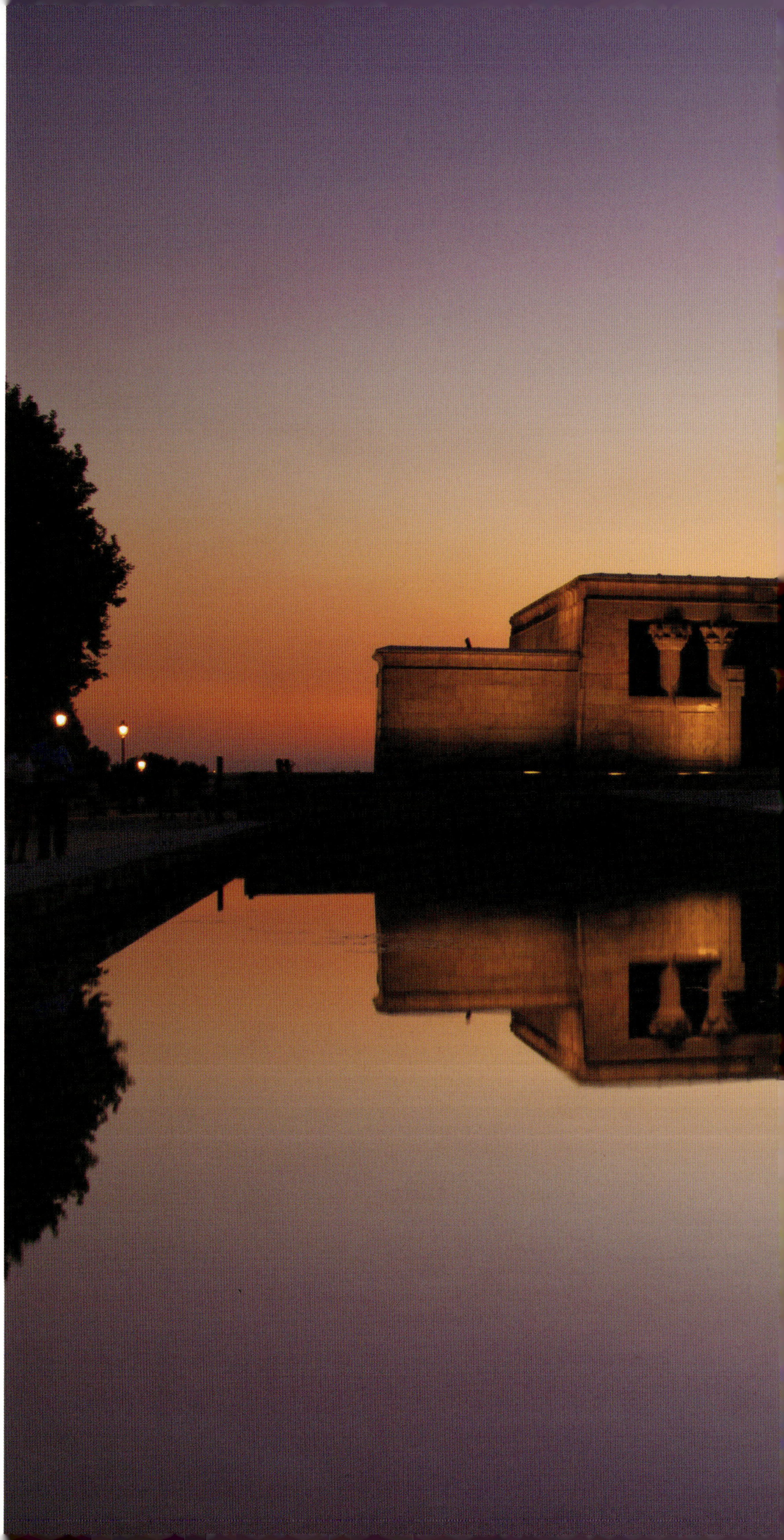

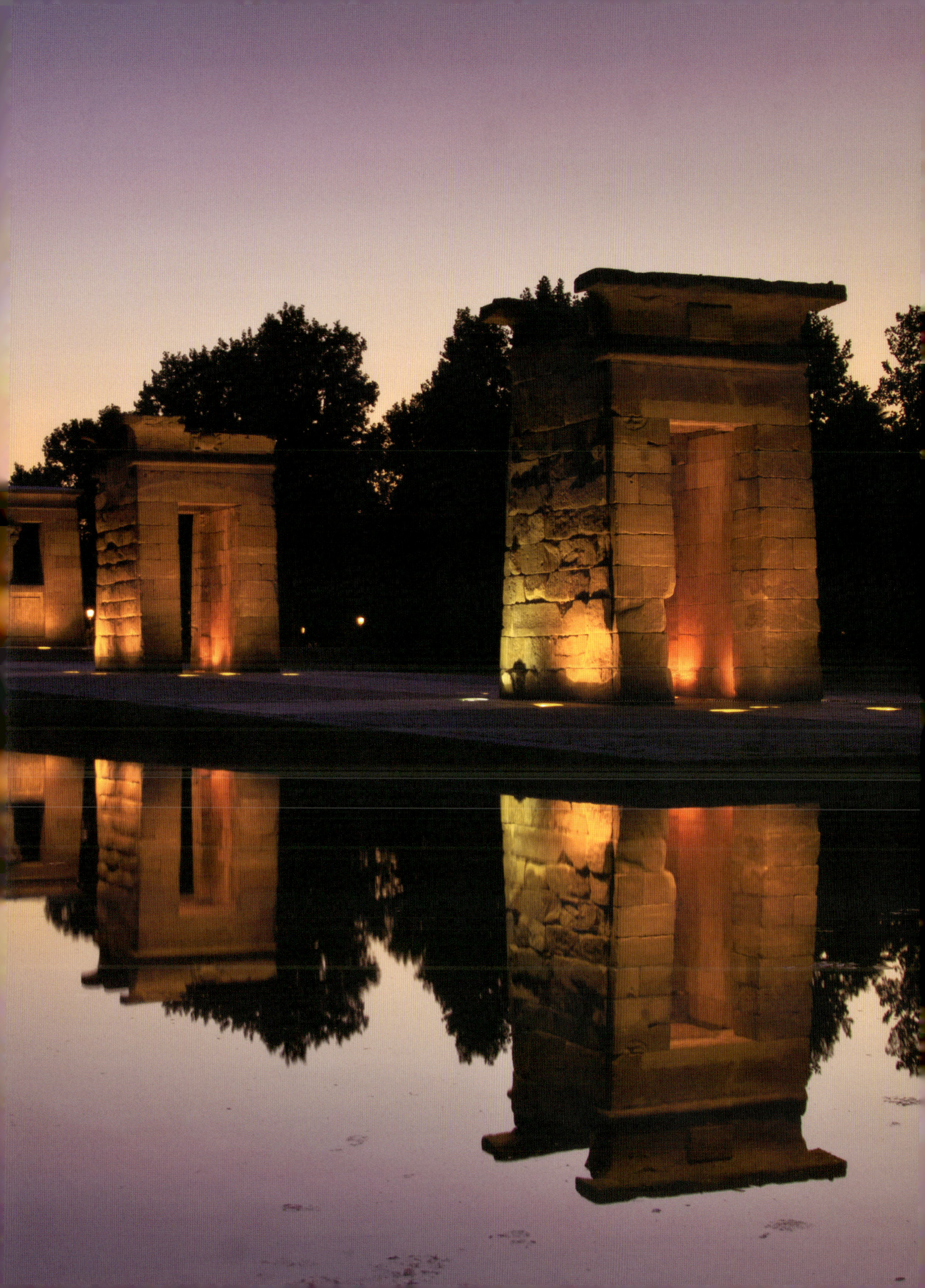

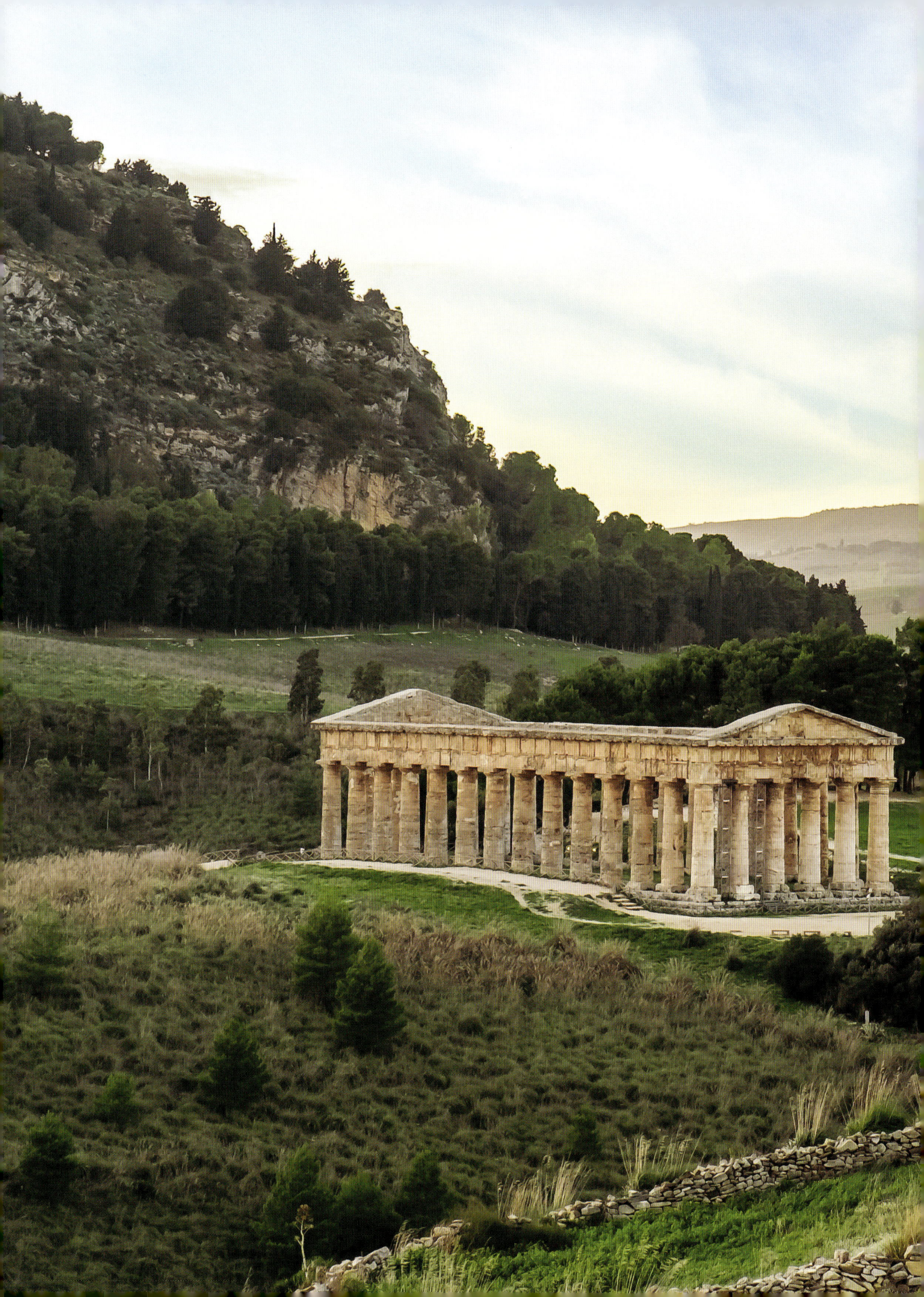

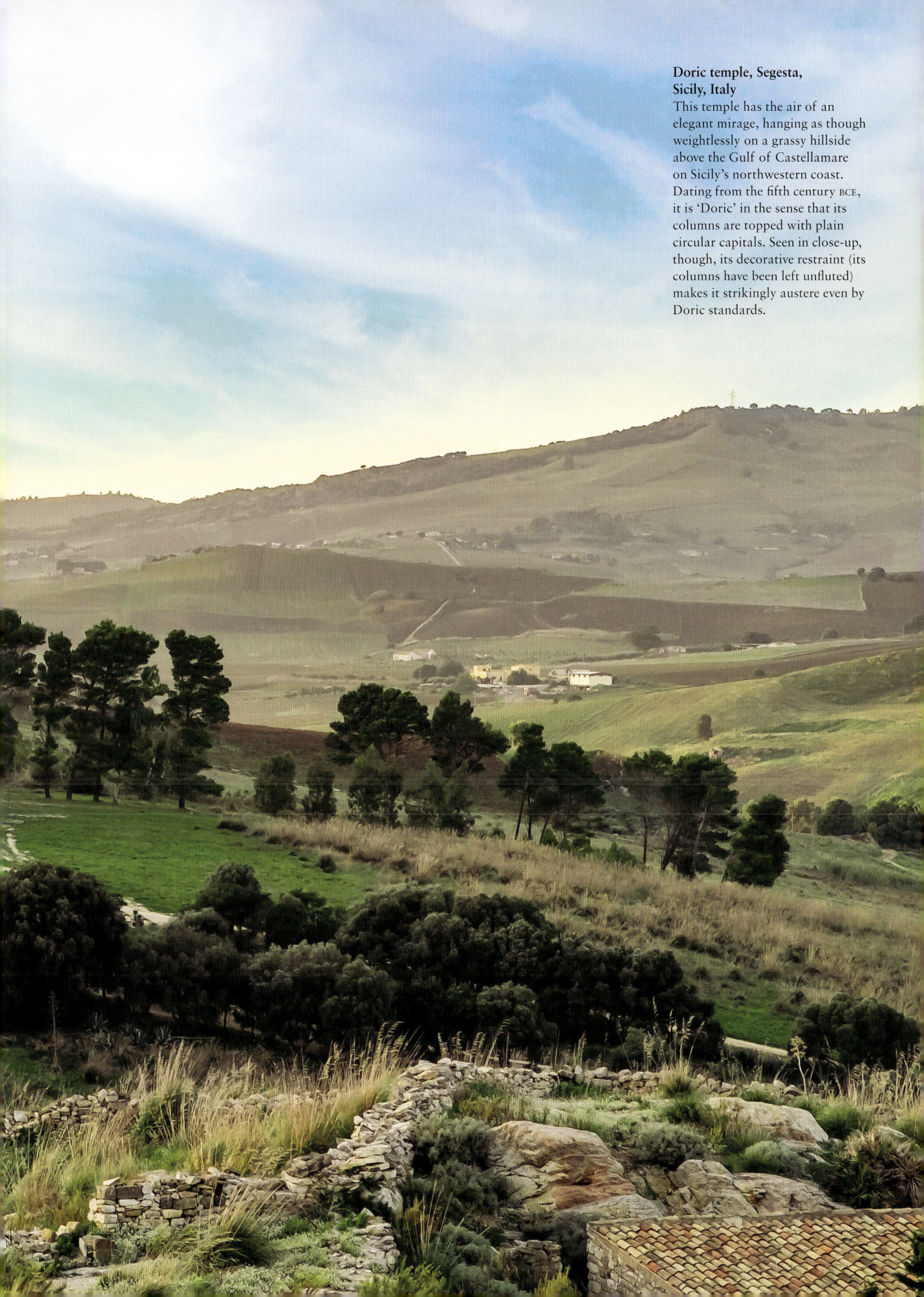

Doric temple, Segesta, Sicily, Italy
This temple has the air of an elegant mirage, hanging as though weightlessly on a grassy hillside above the Gulf of Castellamare on Sicily's northwestern coast. Dating from the fifth century BCE, it is 'Doric' in the sense that its columns are topped with plain circular capitals. Seen in close-up, though, its decorative restraint (its columns have been left unfluted) makes it strikingly austere even by Doric standards.

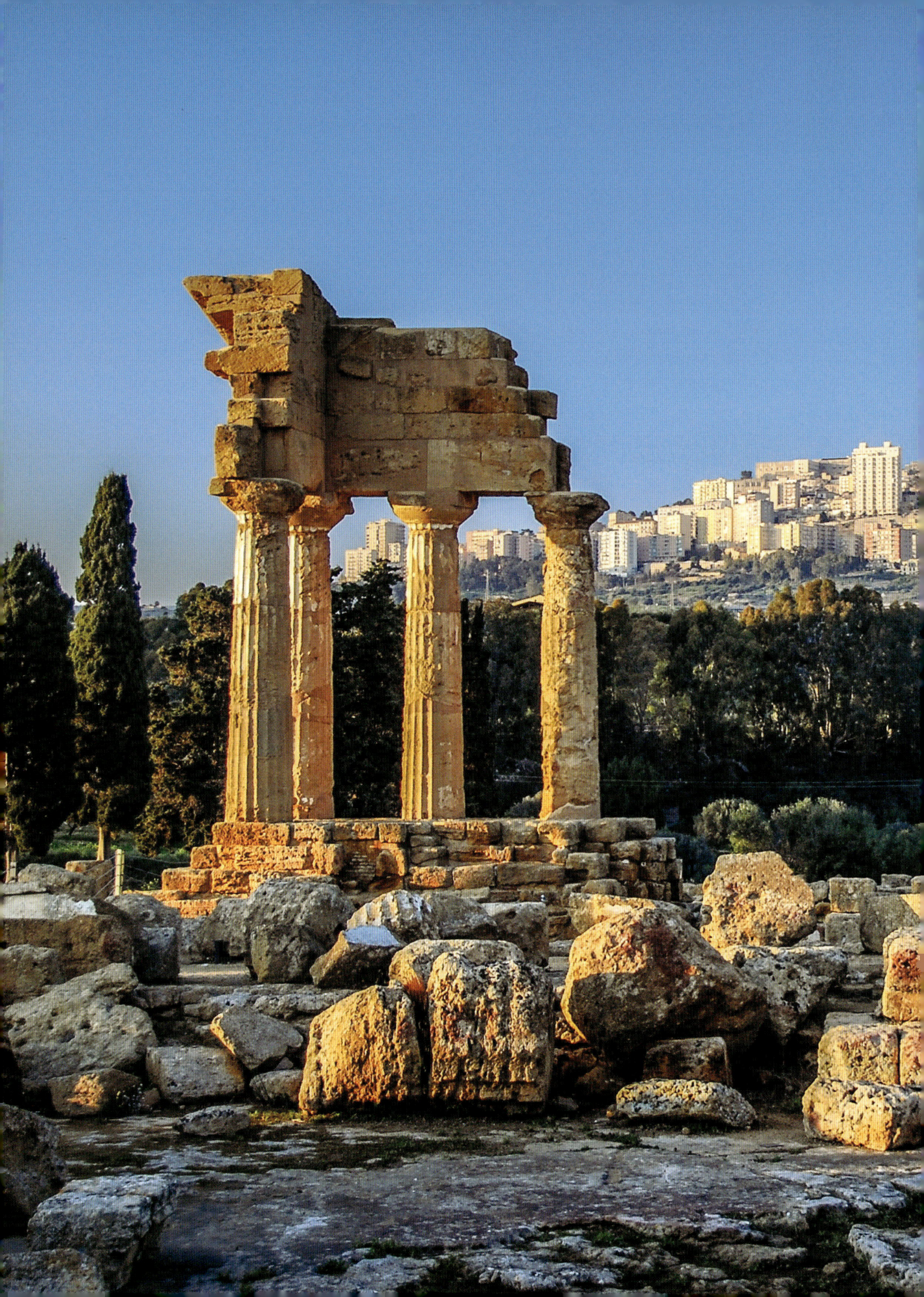

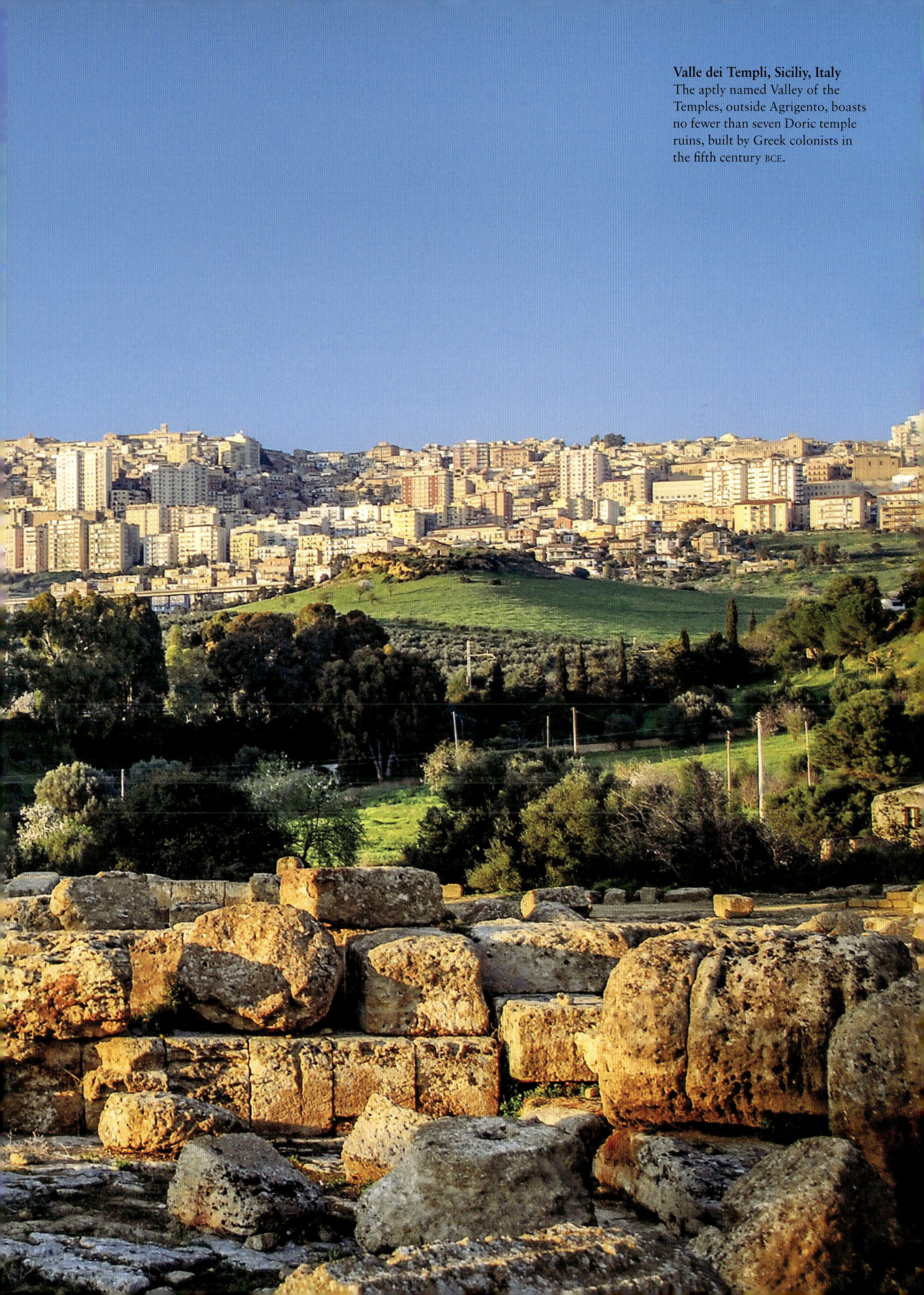

Valle dei Templi, Siciliy, Italy
The aptly named Valley of the Temples, outside Agrigento, boasts no fewer than seven Doric temple ruins, built by Greek colonists in the fifth century BCE.

Temple of Apollo, Pompeii, Italy
Along with the rest of the city in which it stood, this Roman temple was buried in volcanic ash when Mount Vesuvius erupted in 79 CE. Built in the Doric style, it was dedicated in 120 BCE and formed the eastern side of the ancient Forum. Associated with the sun, Apollo was the god of prophecy, poetry, music and healing. This statue was pieced together from fragments found during excavations in the nineteenth century.

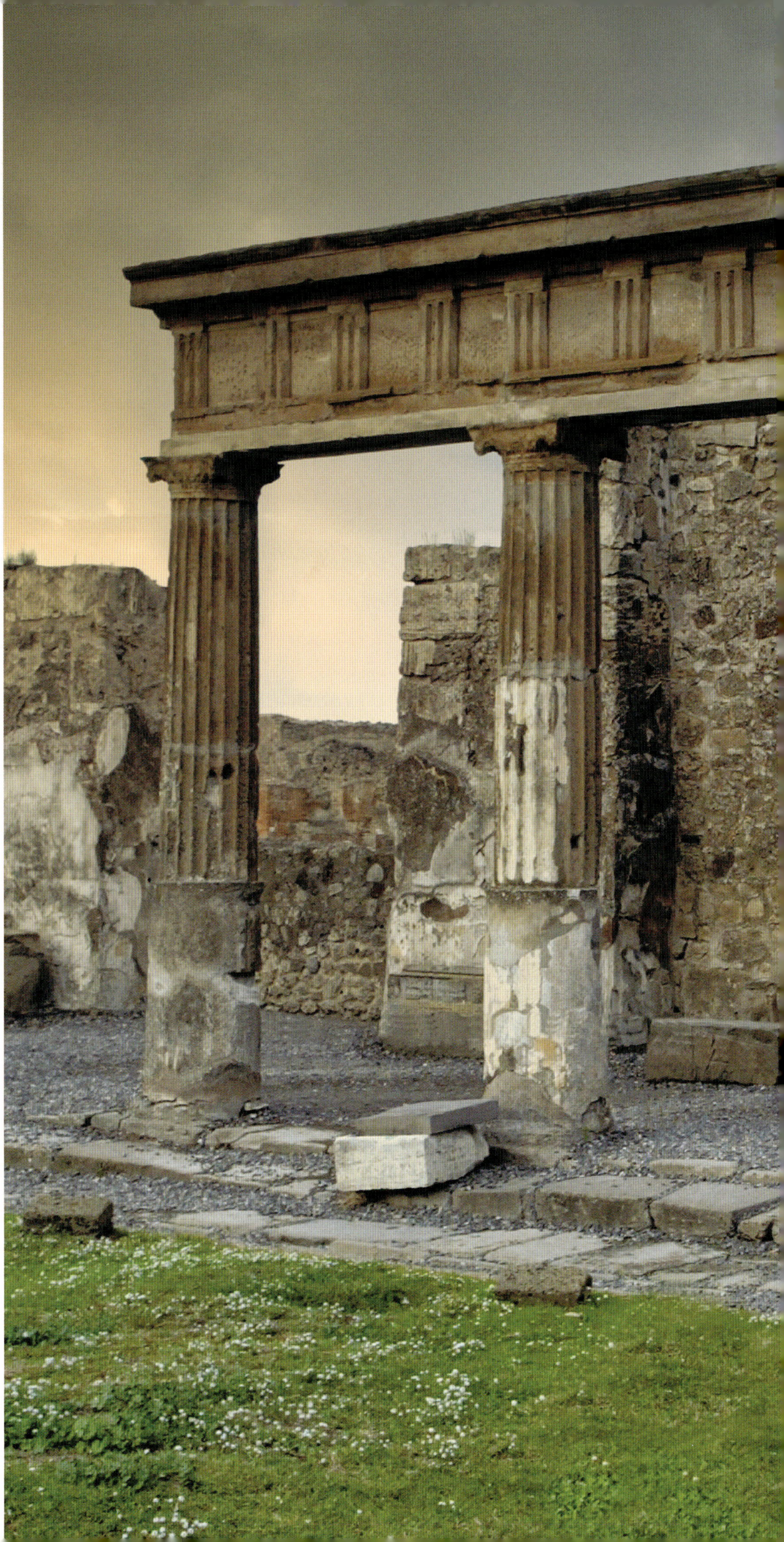

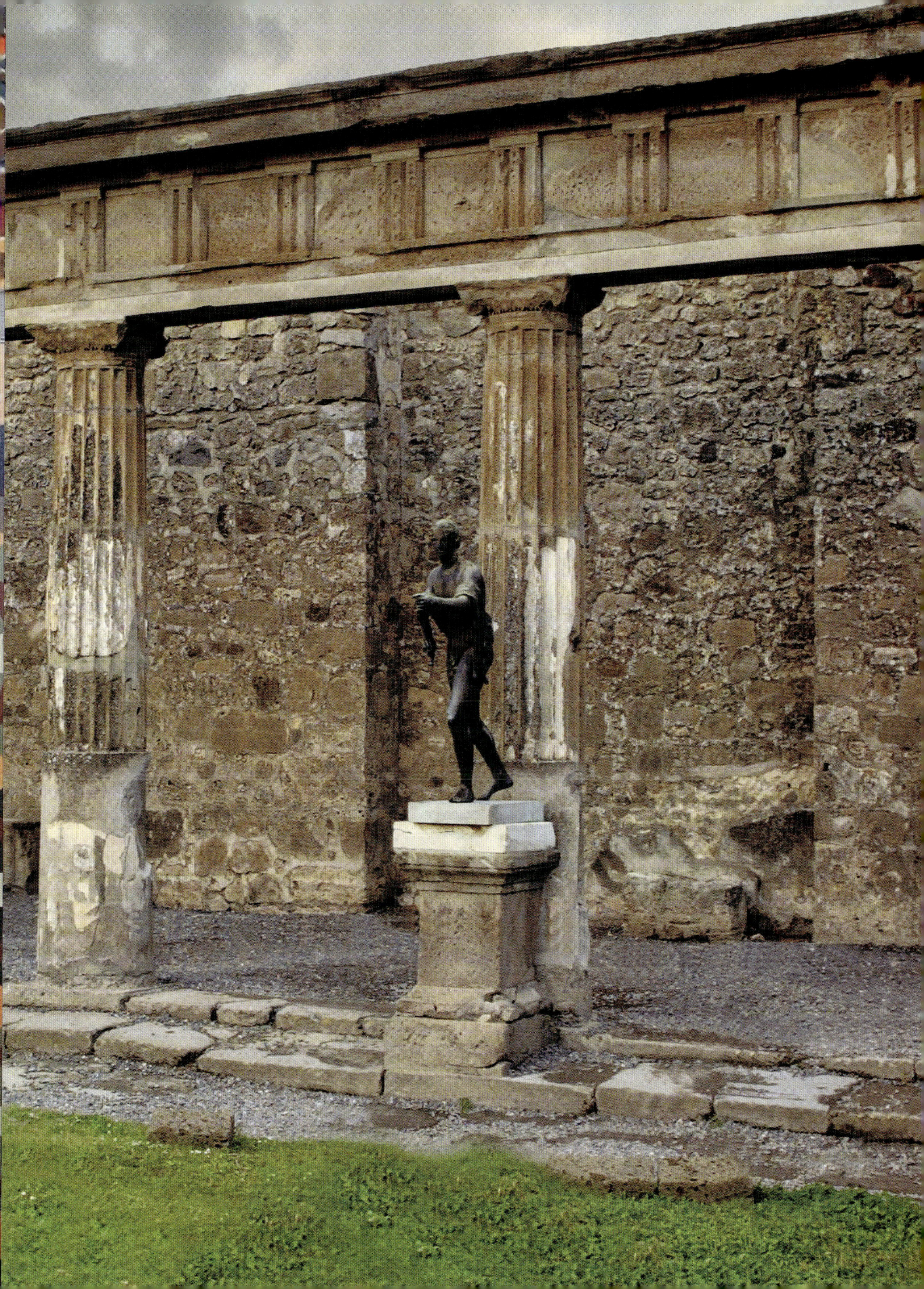

Tempio Maggiore, Florence, Italy

The interior of the Tempio Maggiore maintains the Moorish theme. In overarching form, it shows the influence of Hagia Sophia in Istanbul – a Byzantine church, but the inspiration for the classic mosque design. Its walls are covered in decorative designs, again in an Islamic-influenced style. Horseshoe arches drive the Moorish message home. During World War II, German soldiers carried off artworks and committed acts of vandalism here. Forced into retreat by the approaching Allies, they tried to blow it up completely but were thwarted in this by local partisans.

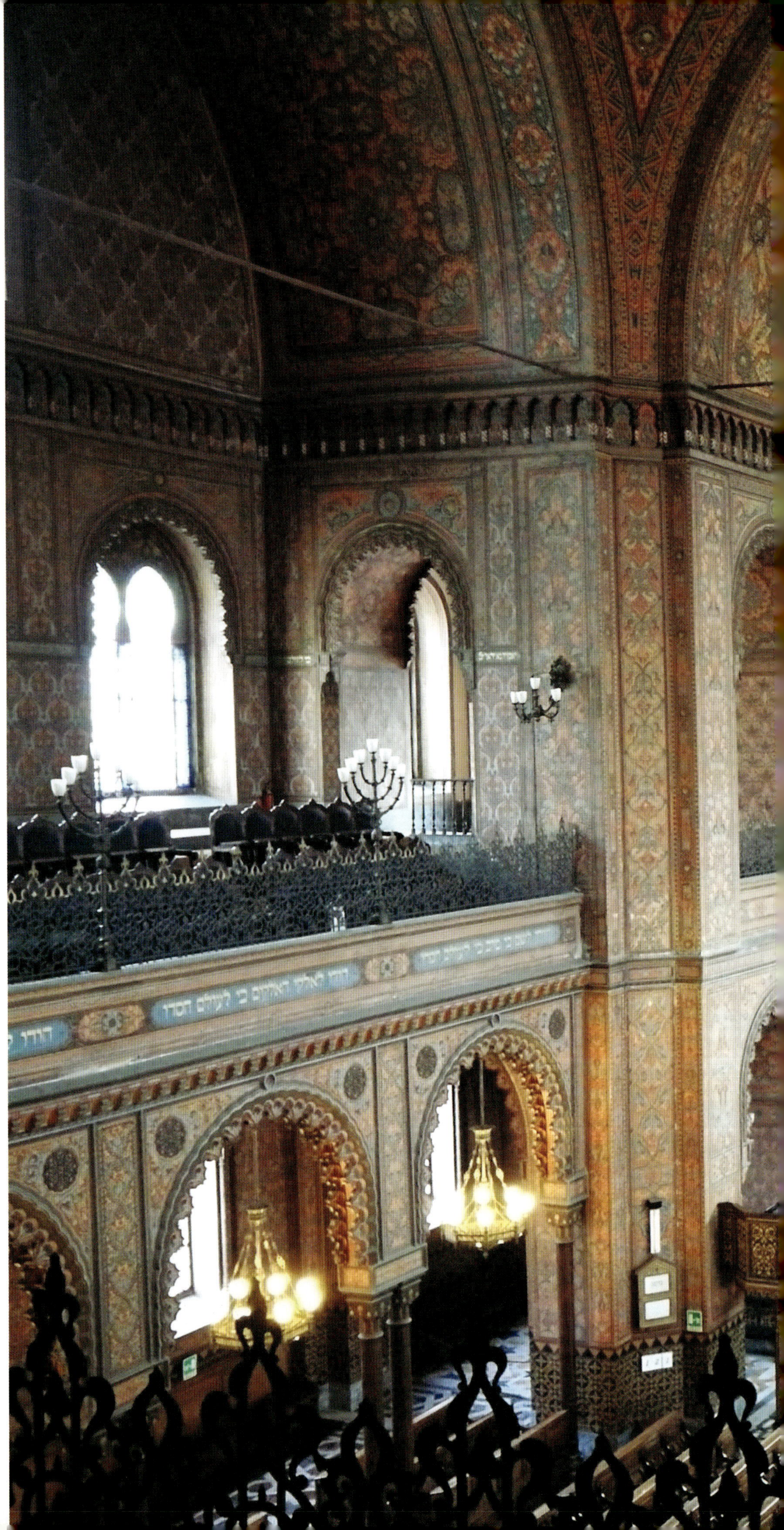

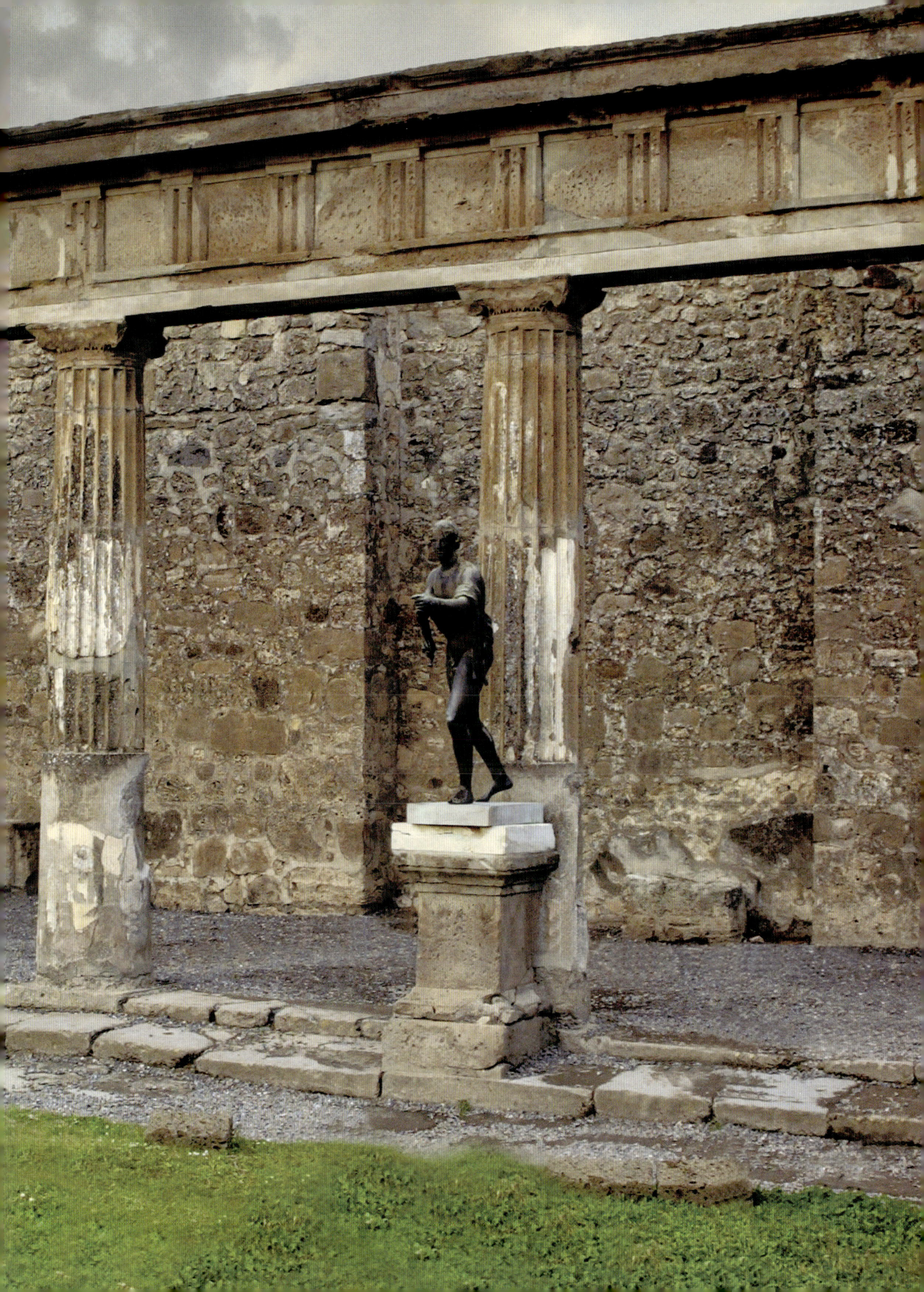

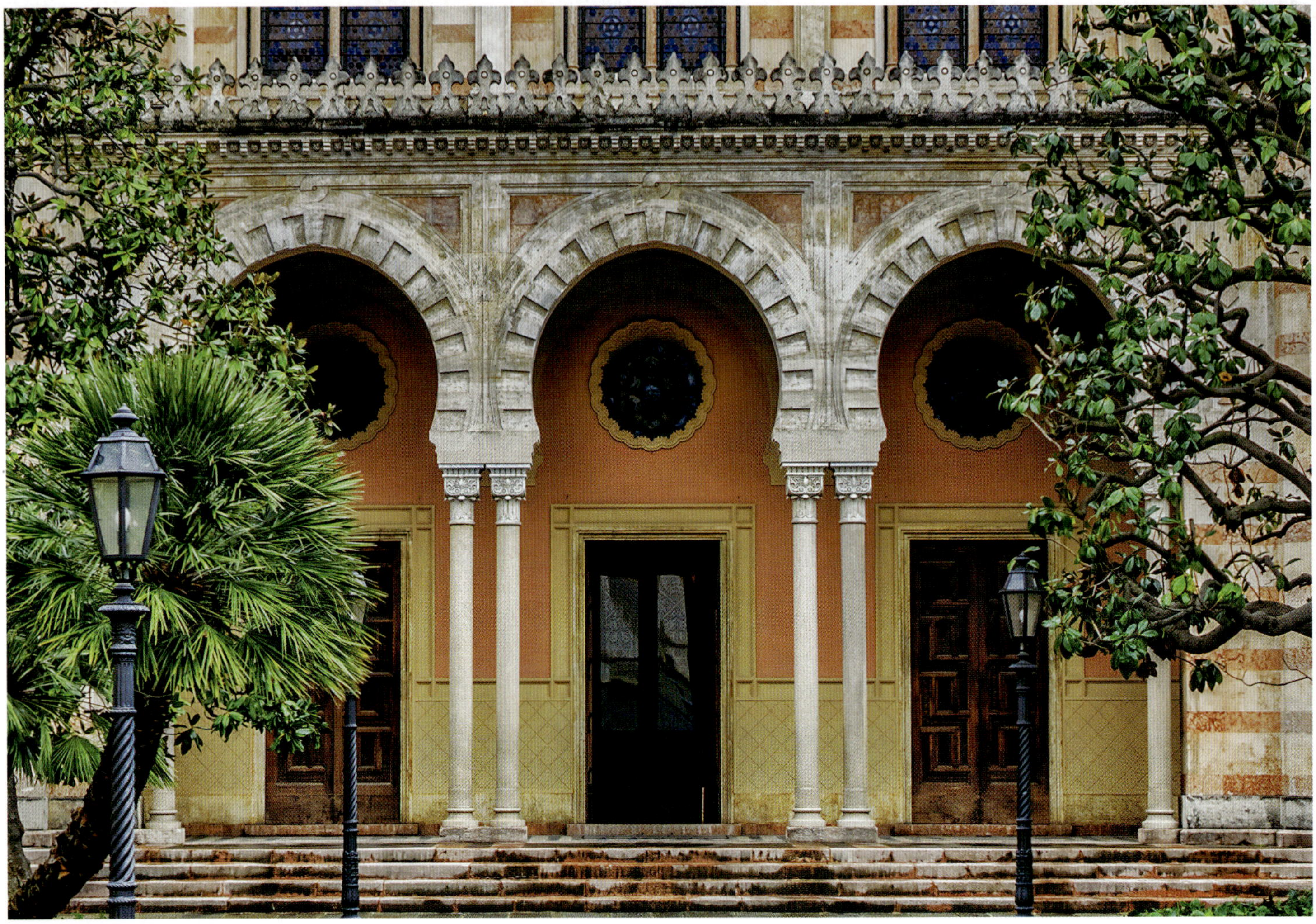

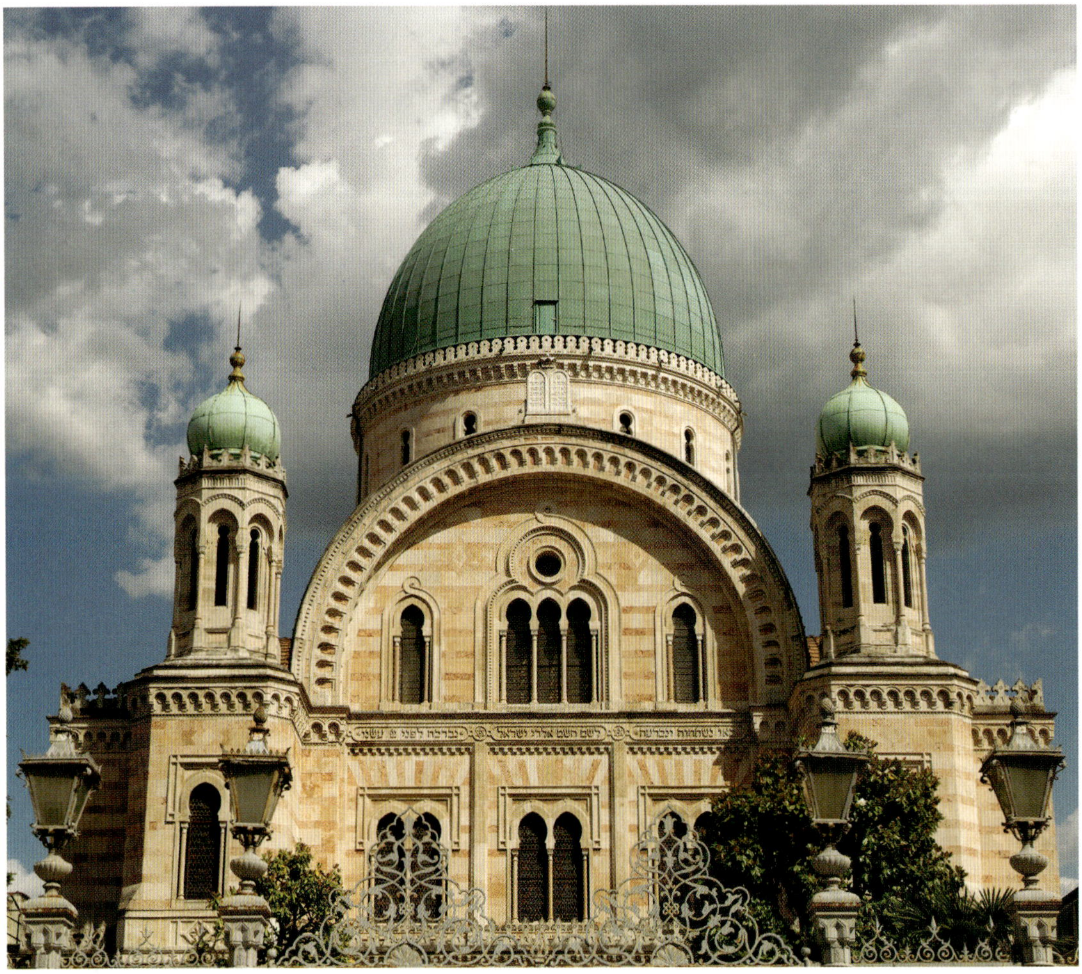

ALL PHOTOGRAPHS:
Tempio Maggiore, Florence, Italy
Tuscany's Jewish community were granted civil rights by the Duchy in 1848; Napoleon had allowed them these in 1799, but they'd been rescinded since. The completion of Italian Unification in 1871 saw their rights as citizens cemented and three years later, the construction of this Great Synagogue began. The work was completed in 1882. Unlike the architects of London's New West End Synagogue, the designers of this one steered well clear of Christian influences, acknowledging the Sephardic strand in European Jewry's heritage and embracing their 'exoticism' with this majestic building in the Spanish Moorish style.

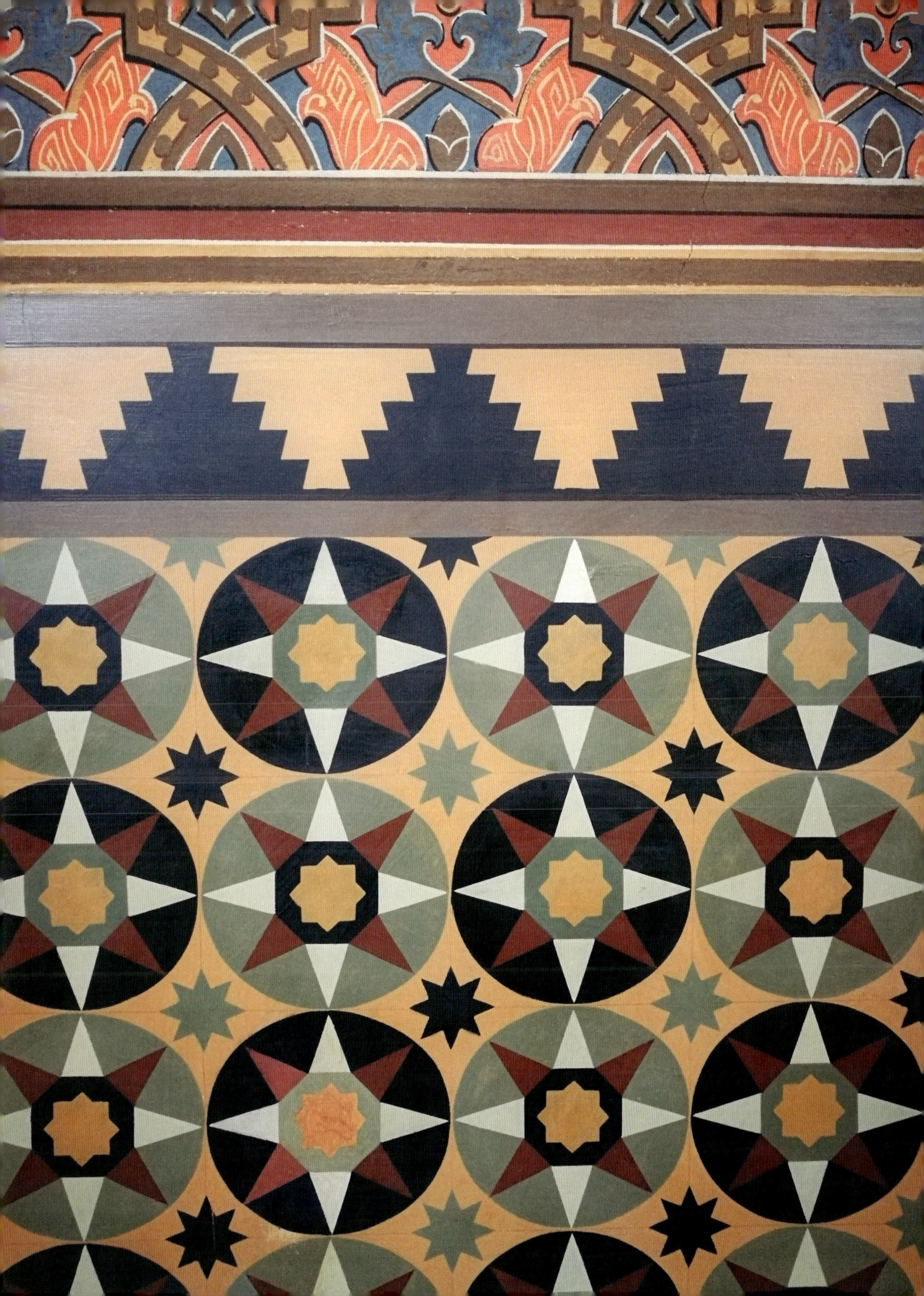

Tempio Maggiore, Florence, Italy

The interior of the Tempio Maggiore maintains the Moorish theme. In overarching form, it shows the influence of Hagia Sophia in Istanbul – a Byzantine church, but the inspiration for the classic mosque design. Its walls are covered in decorative designs, again in an Islamic-influenced style. Horseshoe arches drive the Moorish message home. During World War II, German soldiers carried off artworks and committed acts of vandalism here. Forced into retreat by the approaching Allies, they tried to blow it up completely but were thwarted in this by local partisans.

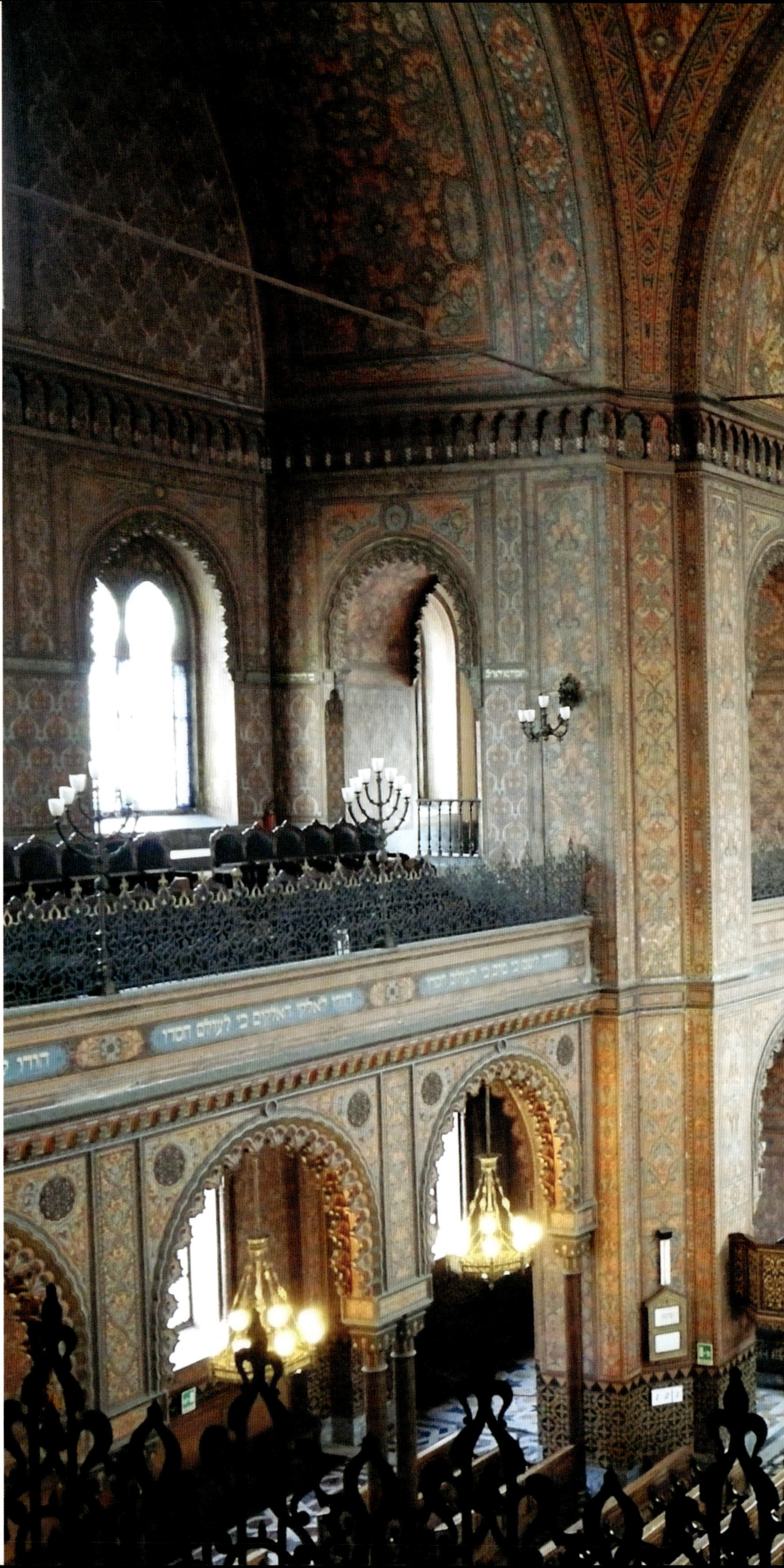

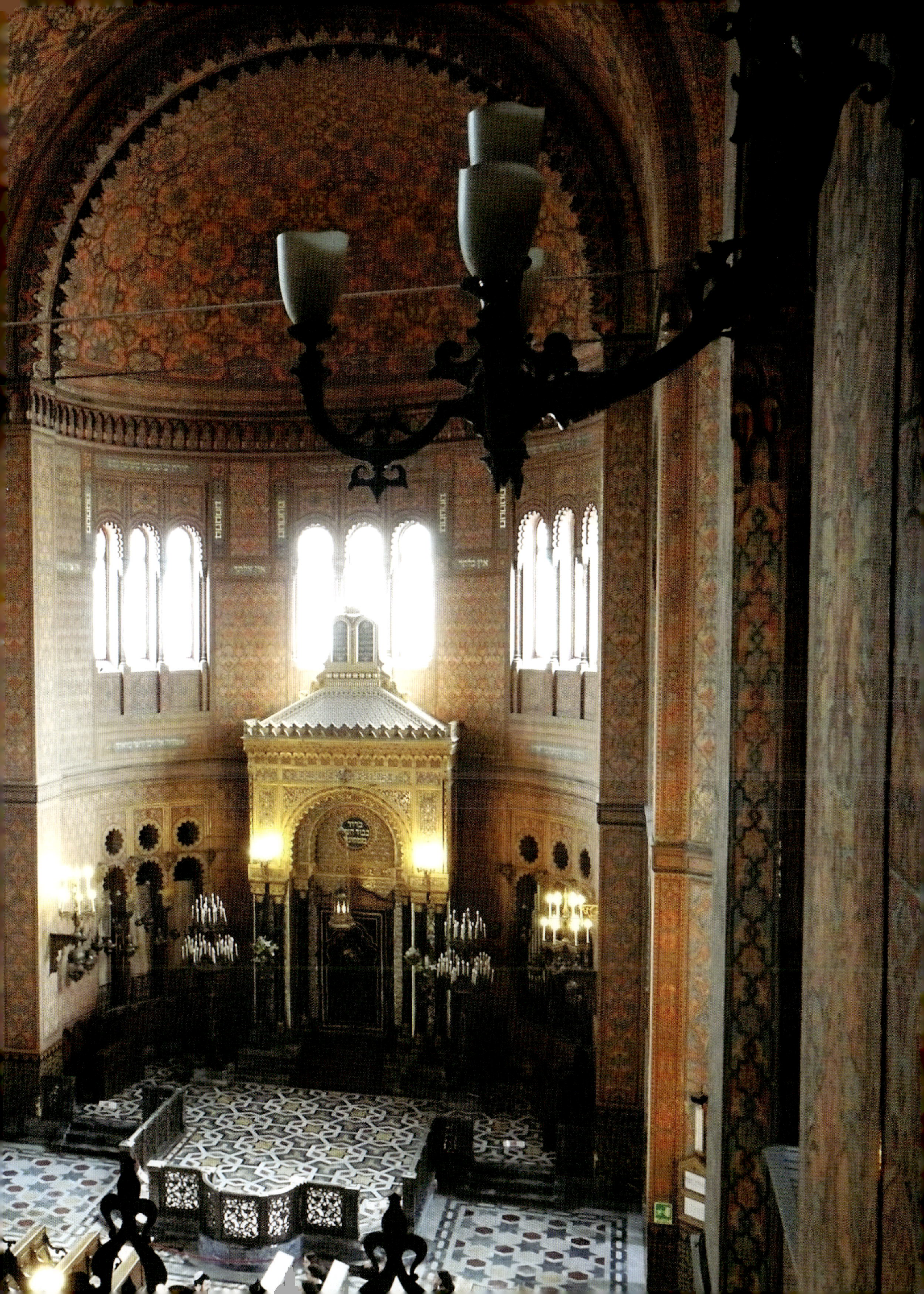

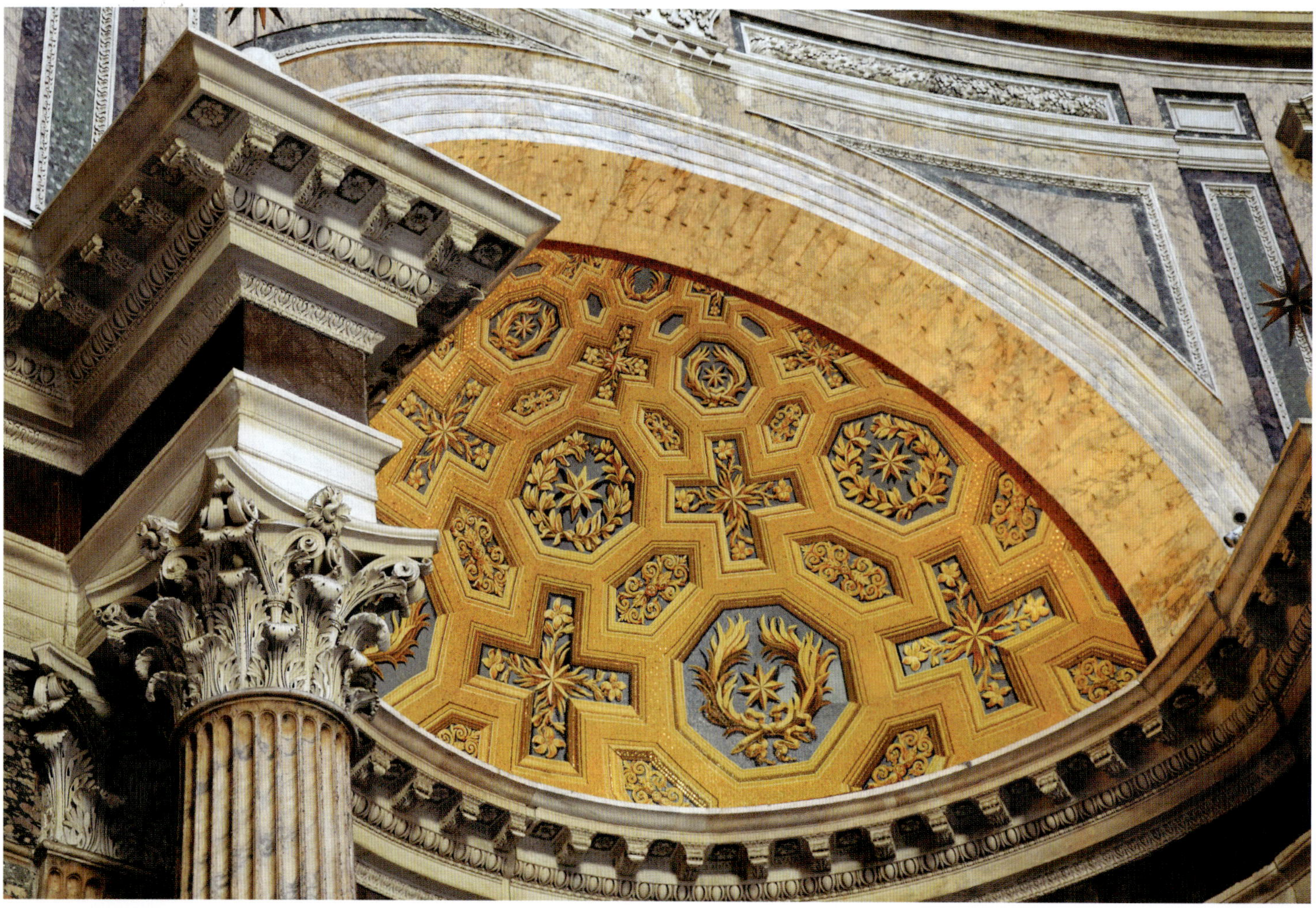

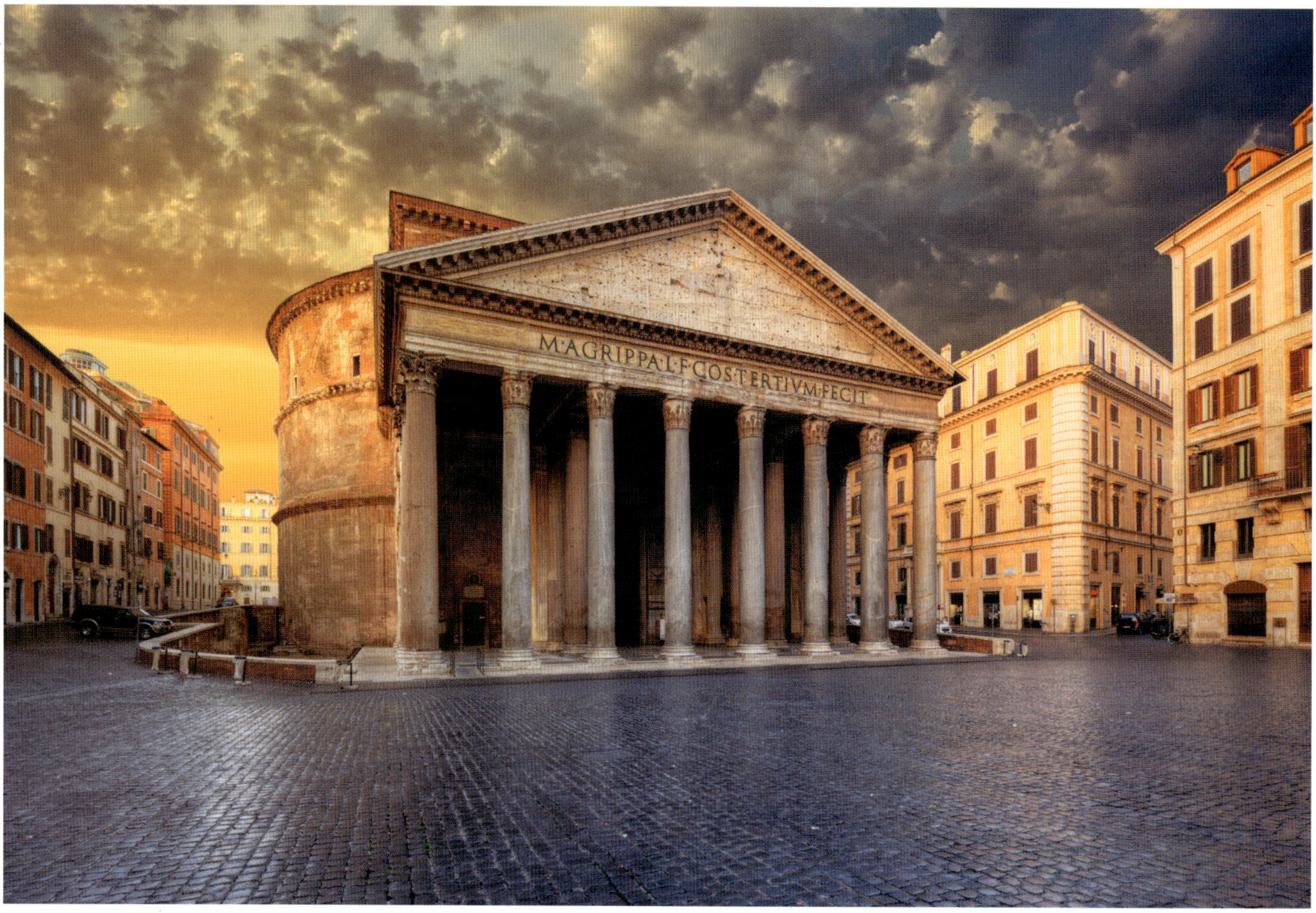
M·AGRIPPA·L·F·COS·TERTIVM·FECIT

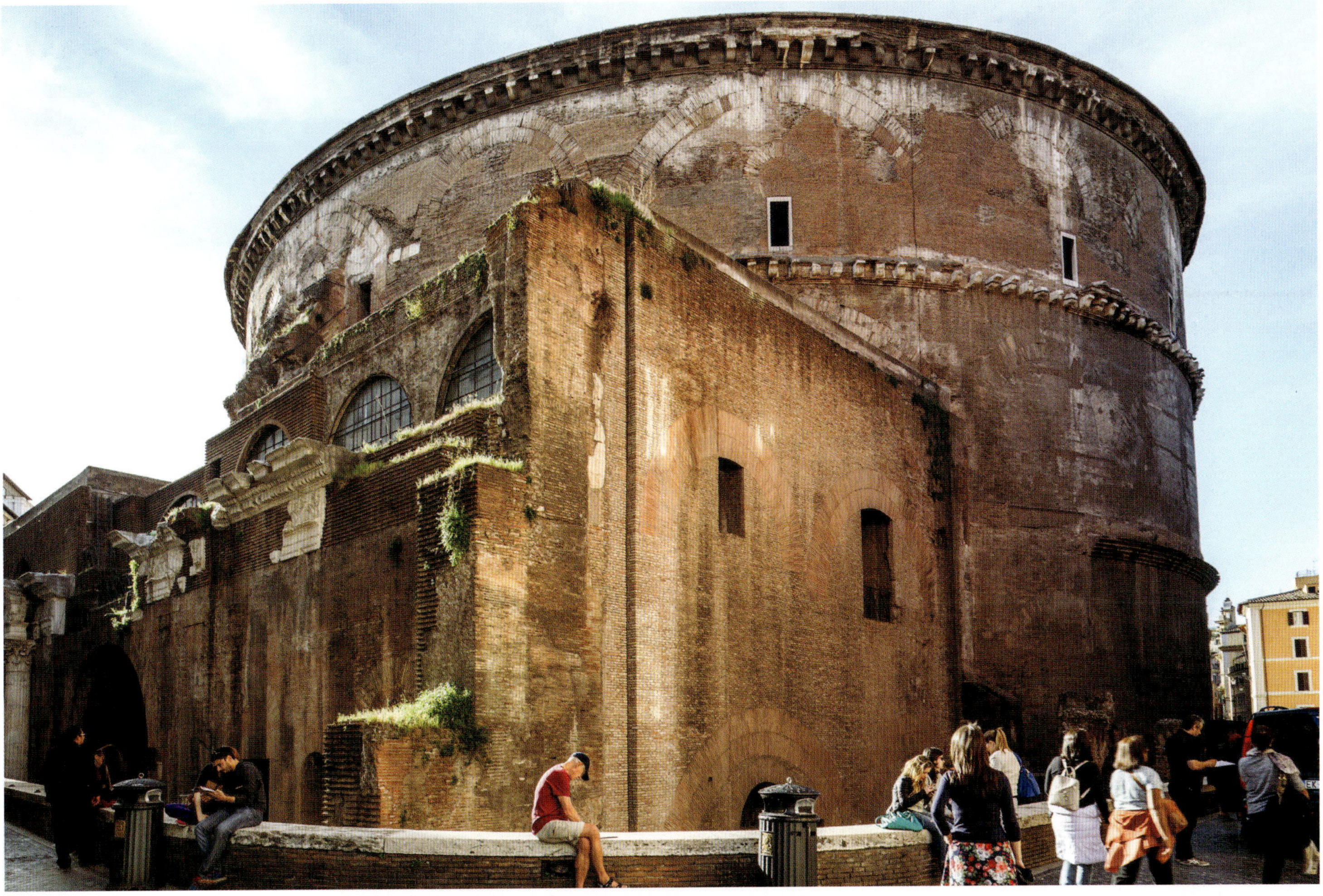

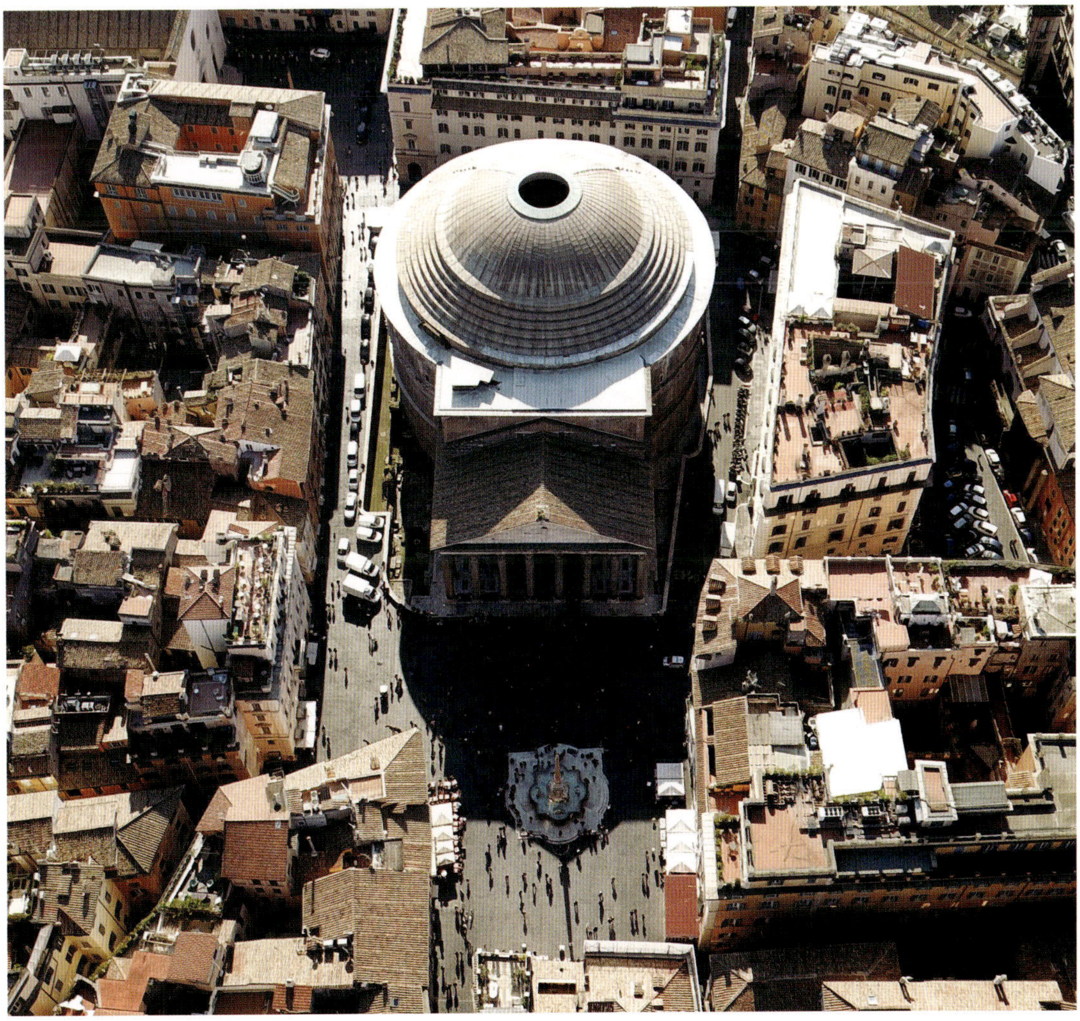

ALL PHOTOGRAPHS AND OVERLEAF:
Pantheon, Rome, Italy
Completed in 125 CE, this 'Temple of All the Gods' has held on to its own little place in architectural history for its status in having what remains the world's largest unreinforced concrete dome. Filippo Brunelleschi (1377–1446) took it as his model in 1446 when he designed the *duomo* for Florence – and, many feel, fired the starting gun on the Renaissance.

The Pantheon was originally commissioned by the general Marcus Vipsanius Agrippa (c. 64–12 BCE), a supporter of Octavian (subsequently the Emperor Augustus), in celebration of his naval victory over Mark Antony and Cleopatra at the Battle of Actium in 31 BCE. Agrippa's temple was destroyed by fire: it isn't clear how far the present Pantheon reflects his founding vision and how far it is a completely different building raised on the same site. Since the seventh century, it's been used as a Catholic church – consecrated to the Blessed Virgin Mary and the Martyrs.

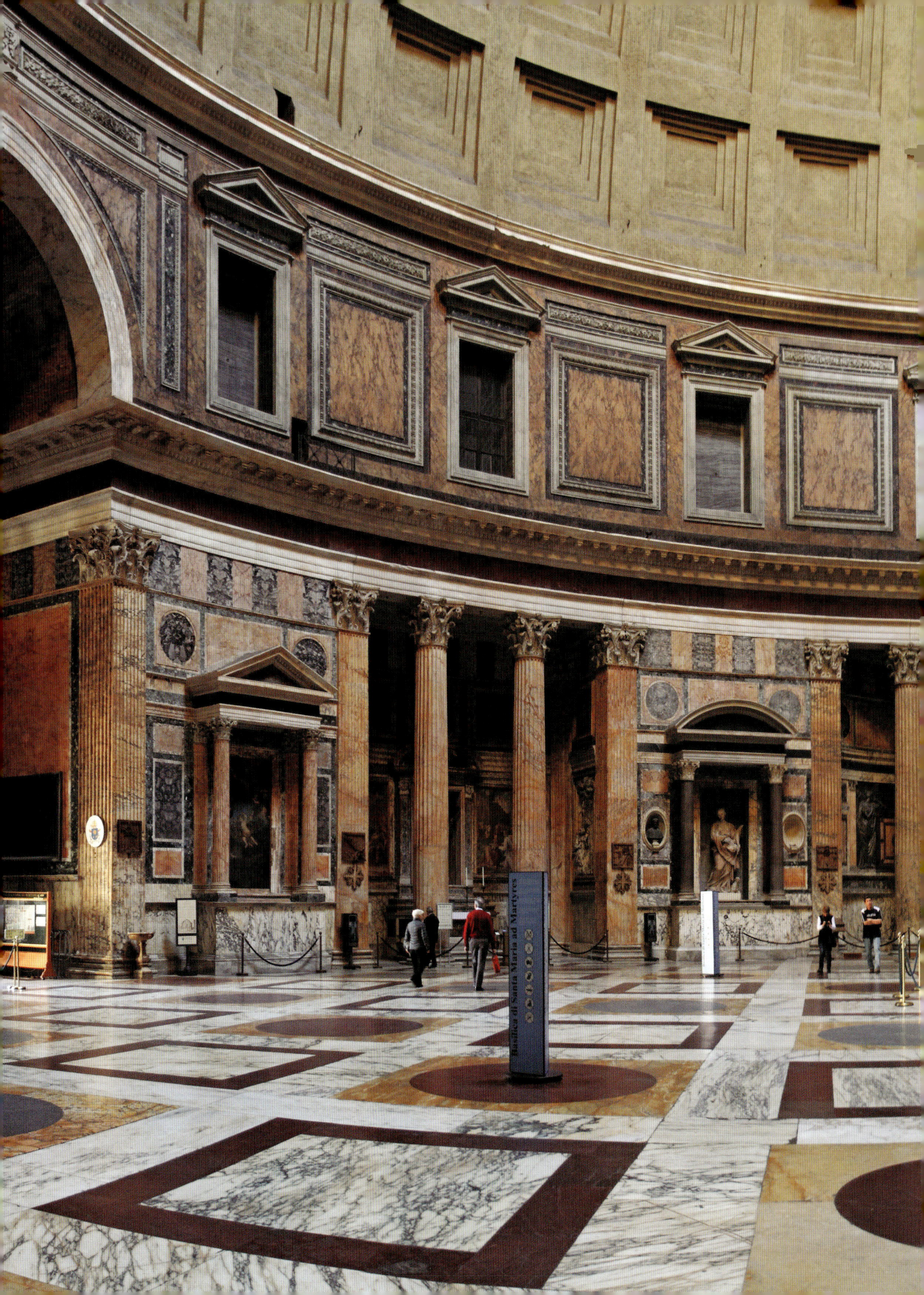
Basilica di Santa Maria ad Martyres

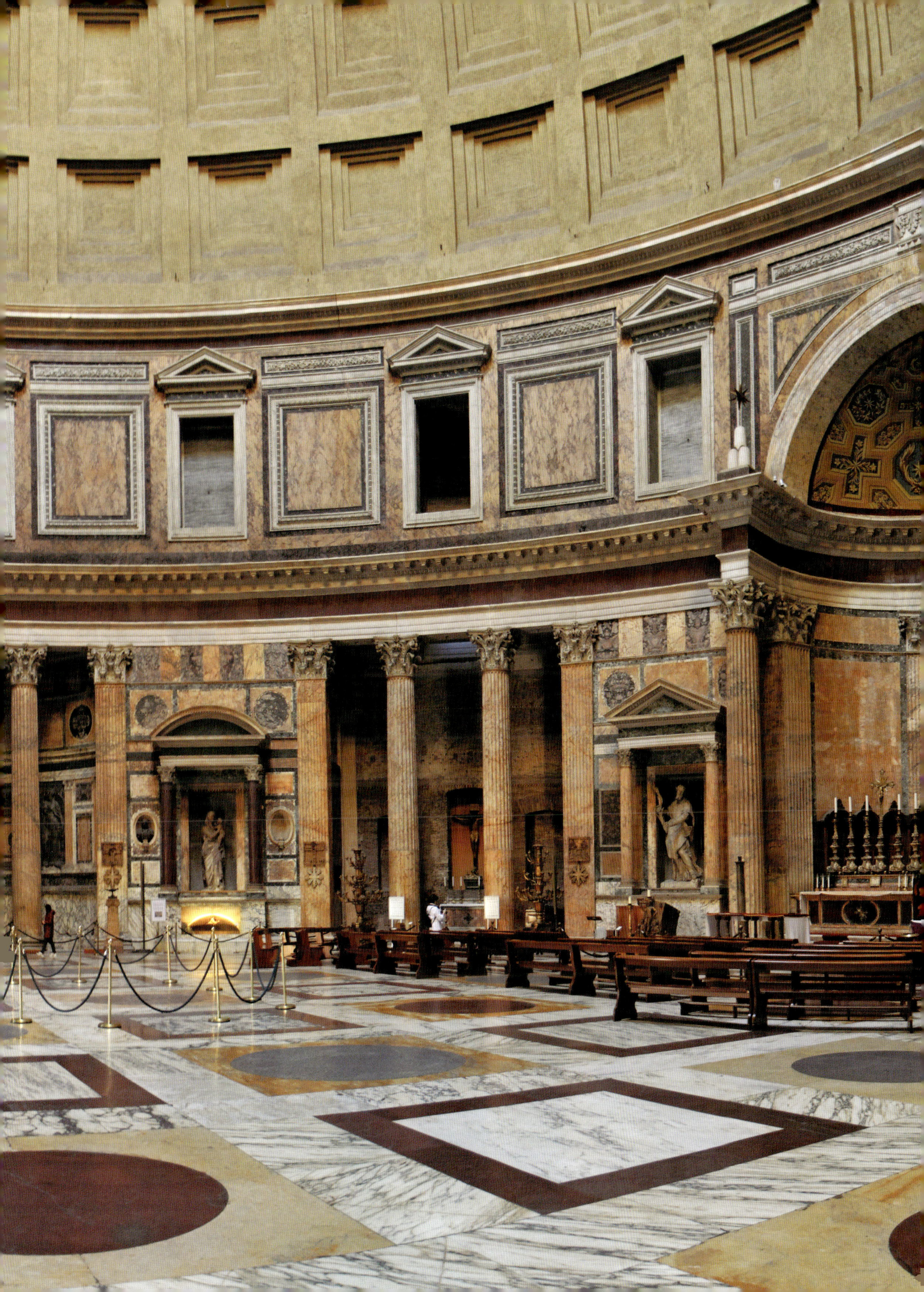

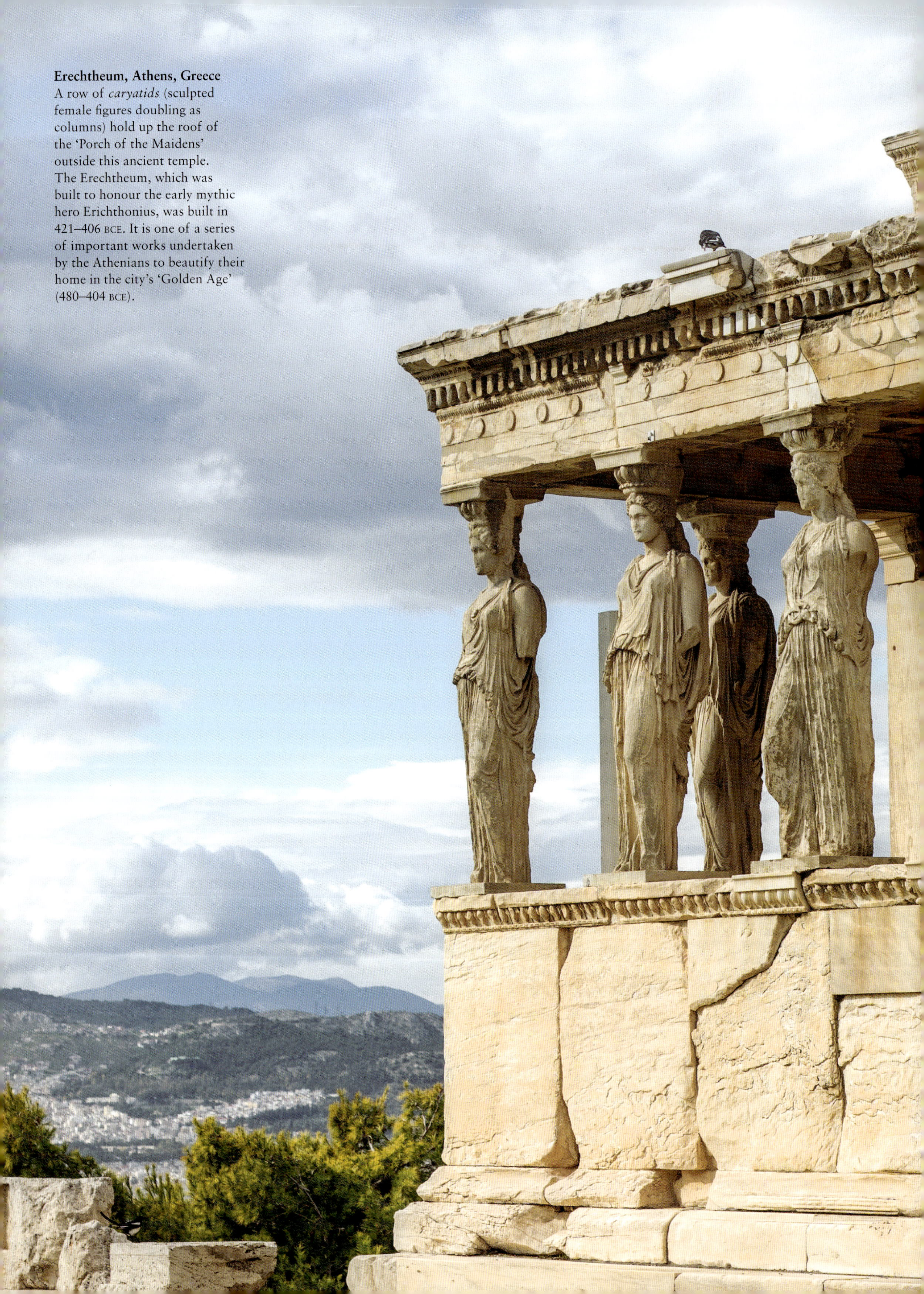

Erechtheum, Athens, Greece
A row of *caryatids* (sculpted female figures doubling as columns) hold up the roof of the 'Porch of the Maidens' outside this ancient temple. The Erechtheum, which was built to honour the early mythic hero Erichthonius, was built in 421–406 BCE. It is one of a series of important works undertaken by the Athenians to beautify their home in the city's 'Golden Age' (480–404 BCE).

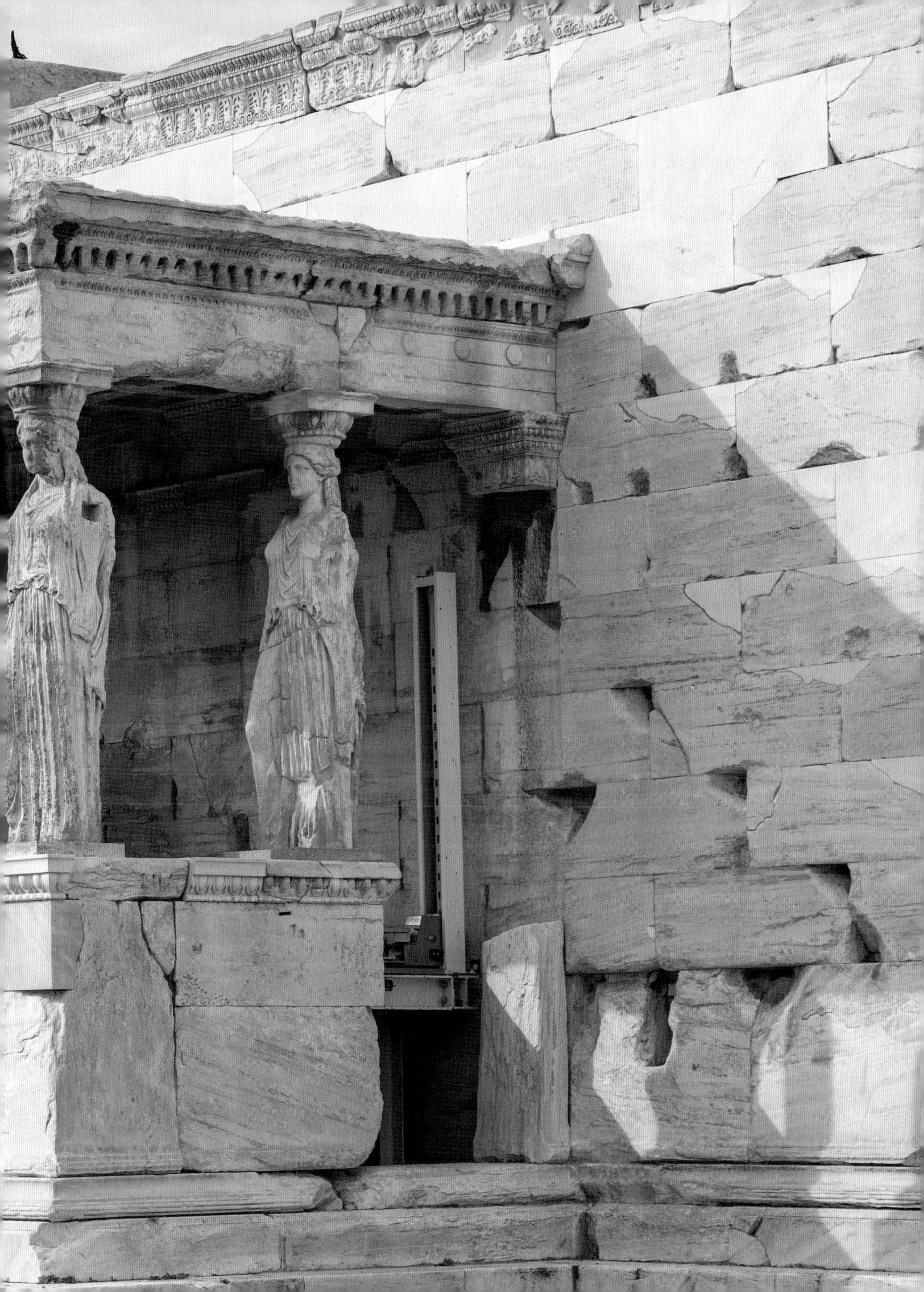

Temple of Hephaestus, Athens, Greece

Another monument to Athens' 'Golden Age', this shrine to Hephaestus, the god of fire and technology, was completed in around 415 BCE. Construction began as part of the programme of improvements called for by Pericles (c. 495–29 BCE), who wanted to assert Athens' supremacy over the other Greek cities as head of the so-called Delian League – an unequal alliance in which Athens took the lead.

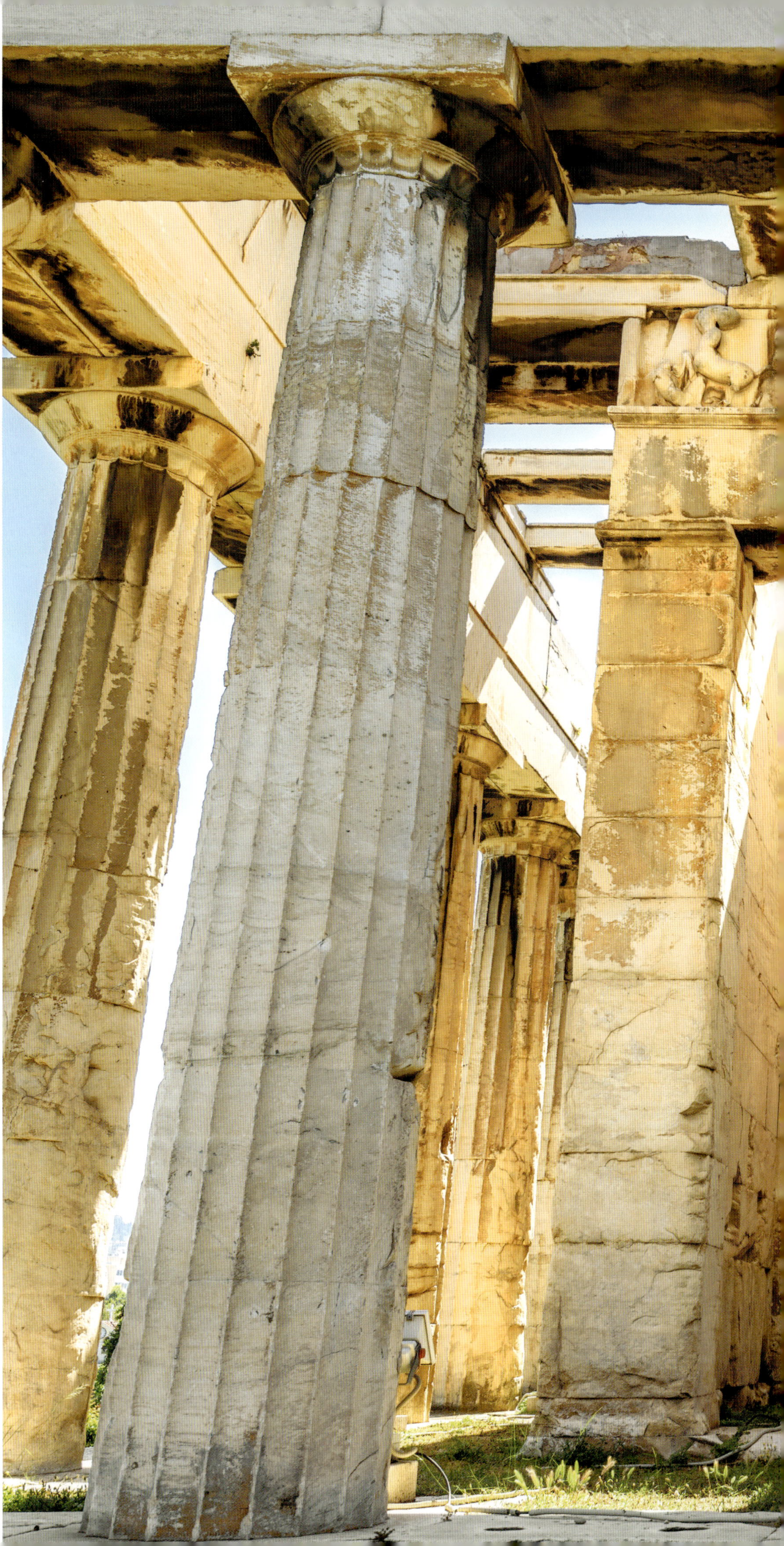

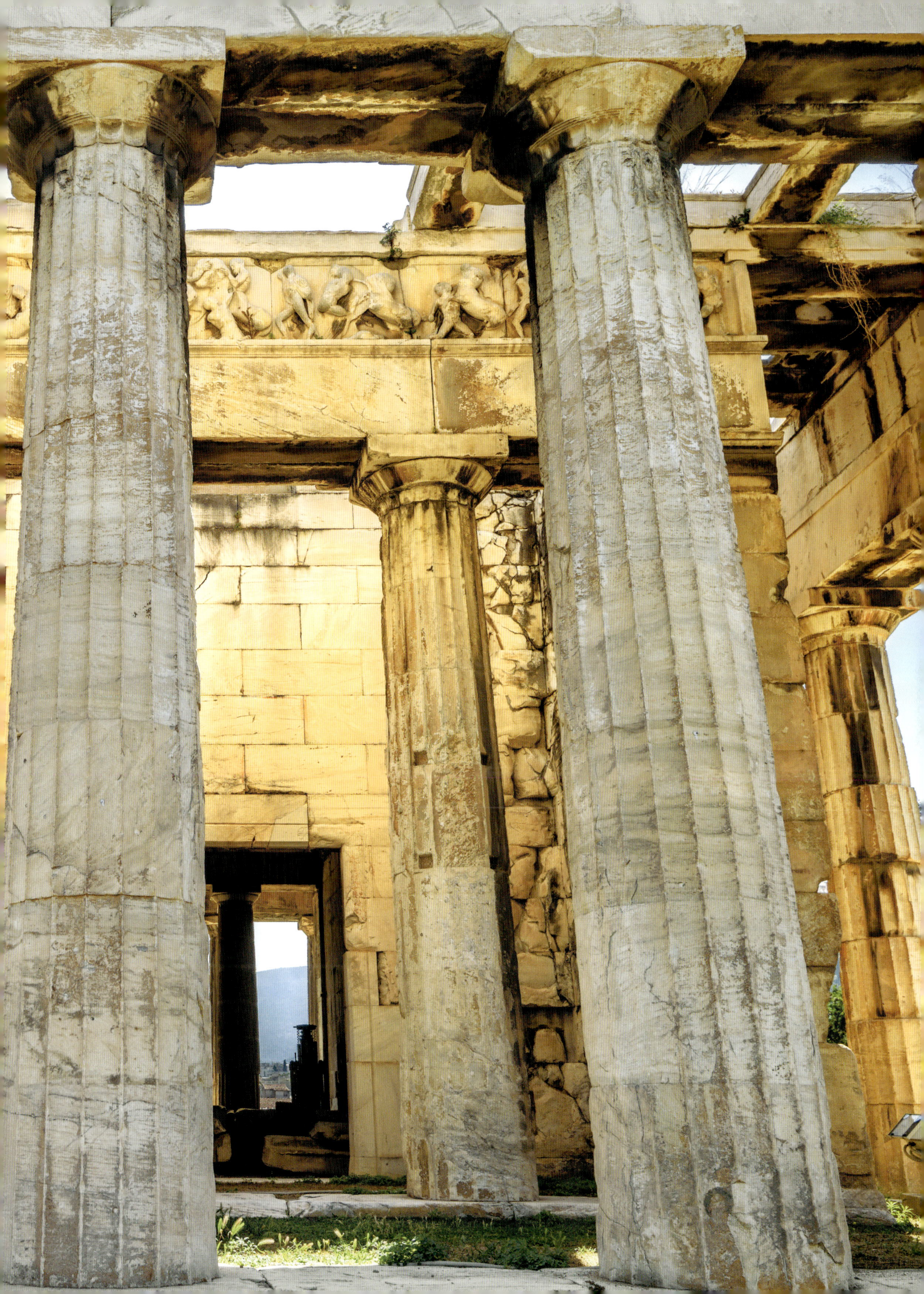

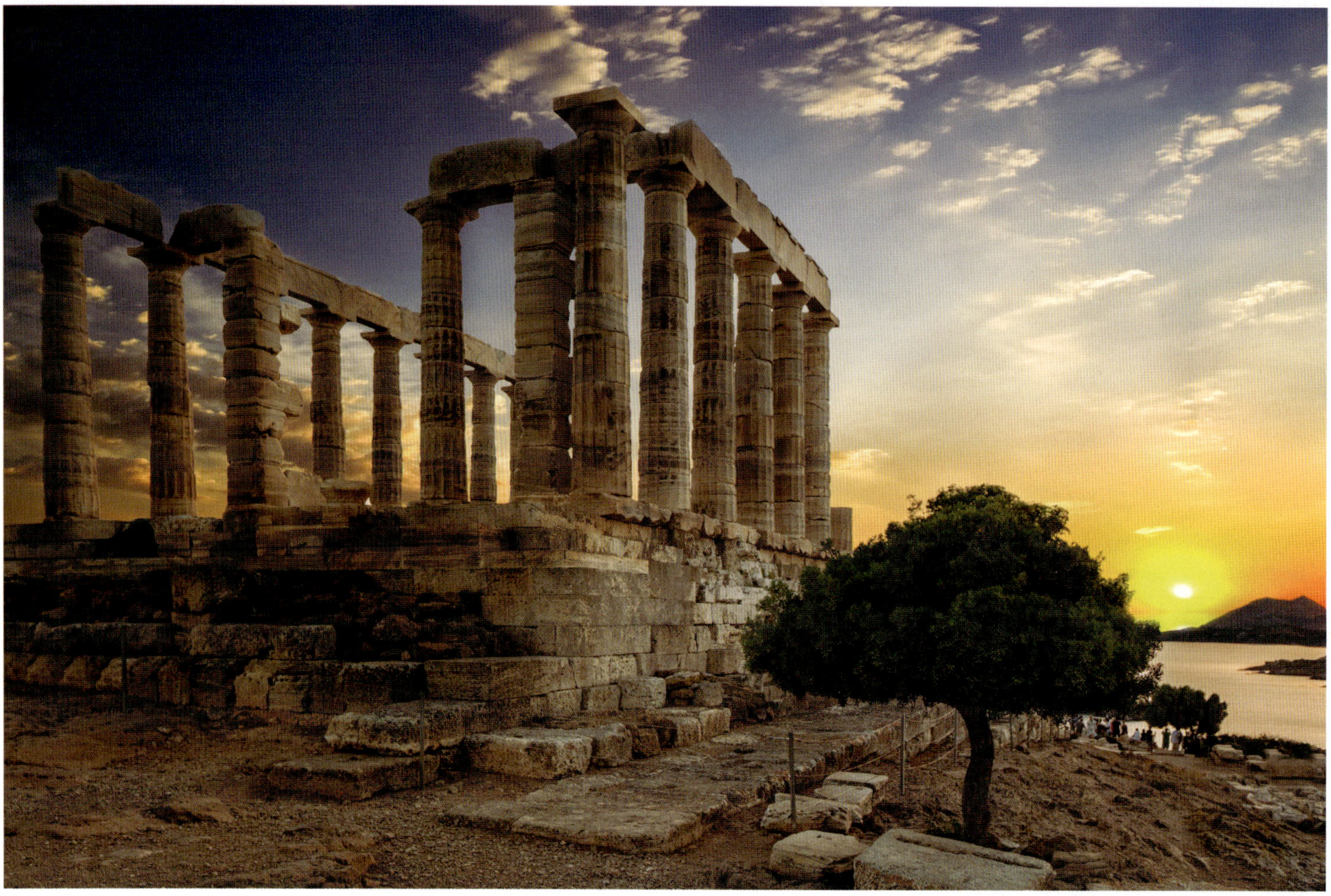

ALL PHOTOGRAPHS AND OVERLEAF:

Temple of Poseidon, Cape Sounion, Greece

Though it stands some way south of the city itself, the Temple of Poseidon – ancient Greek god of the sea – is another monument to Athens' 'Golden Age'. Dramatically situated atop Cape Sounion, it commanded the all-important shipping lanes that linked Athens with the outside world and were the basis of its wealth and power. Its appeal to tourists is understandable and was already apparent in the nineteenth century when many visitors (including the poet Lord Byron, 1788–1824) left graffiti here. Long after the ancient civilization that built these classical temples had vanished and its religious rituals and beliefs had been forgotten, a place like this still has the power to stir the soul.

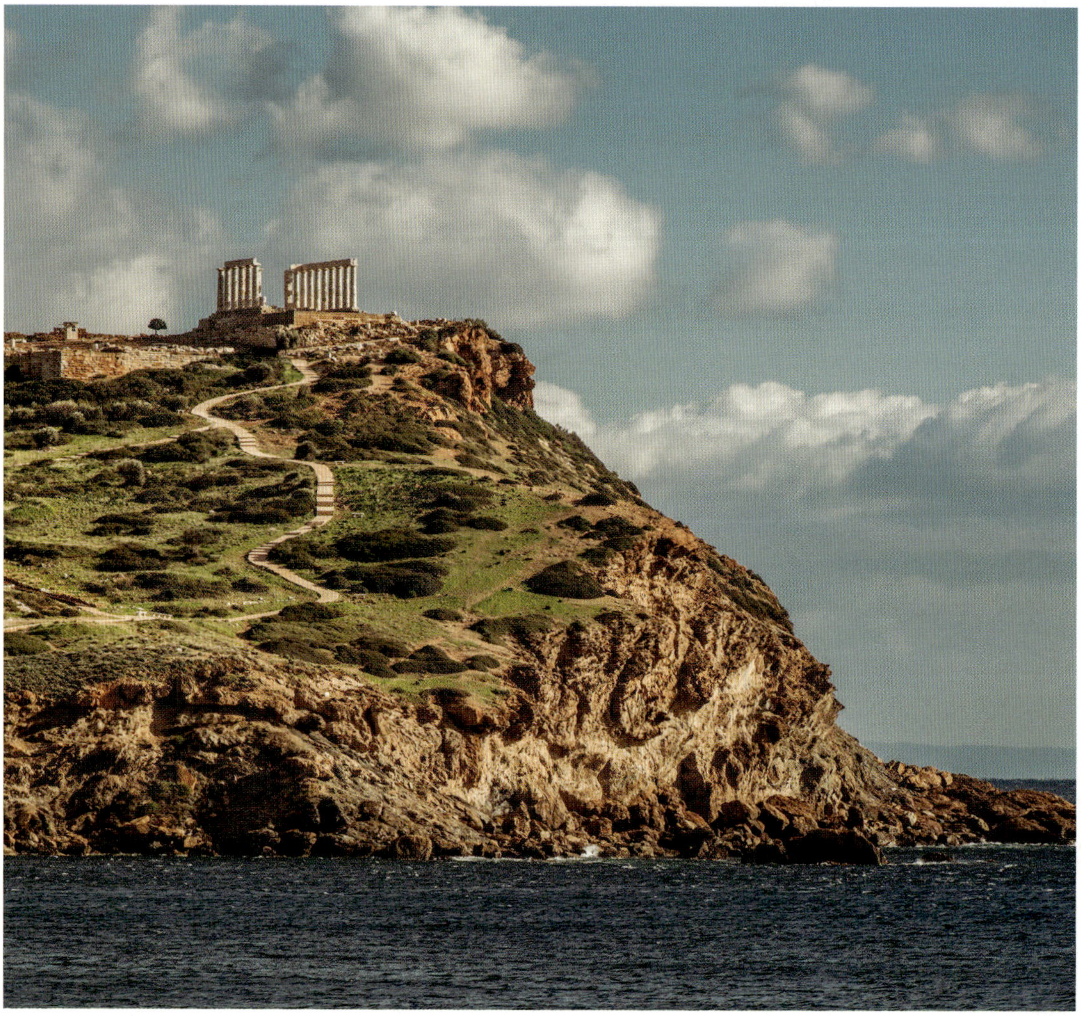

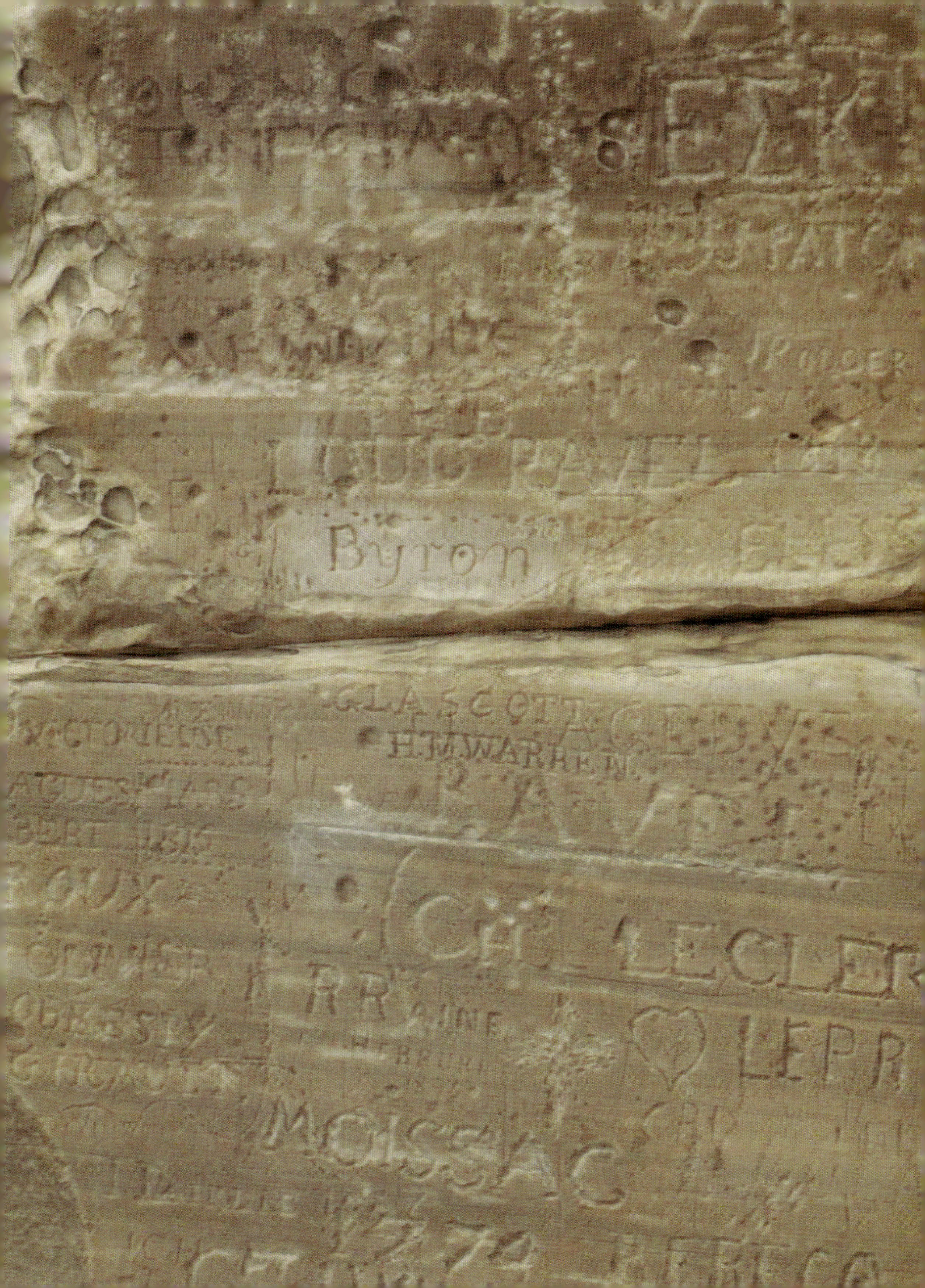
Byron
GLASCOTT
H.M.WARREN
LECLER
MOISSAC

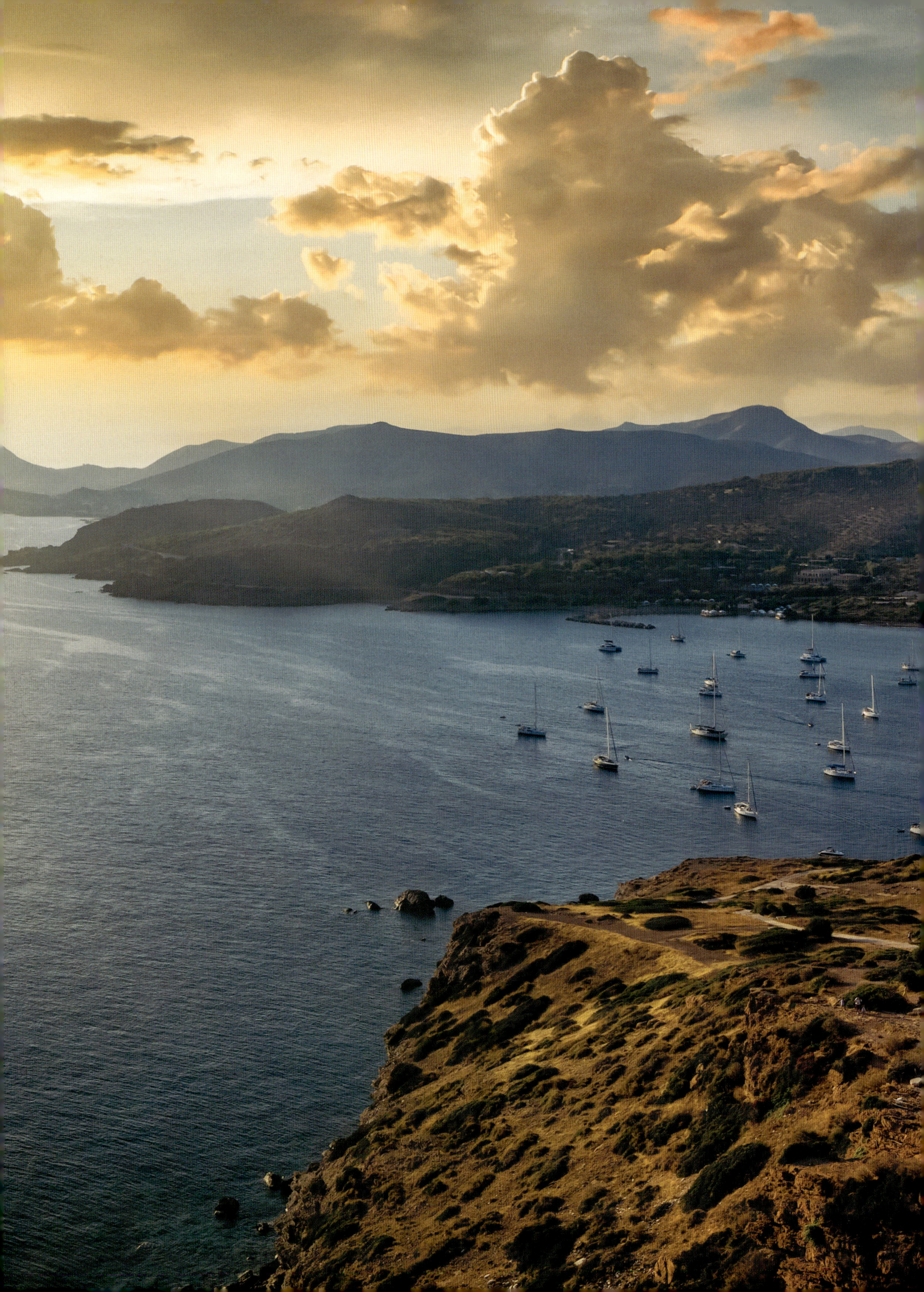

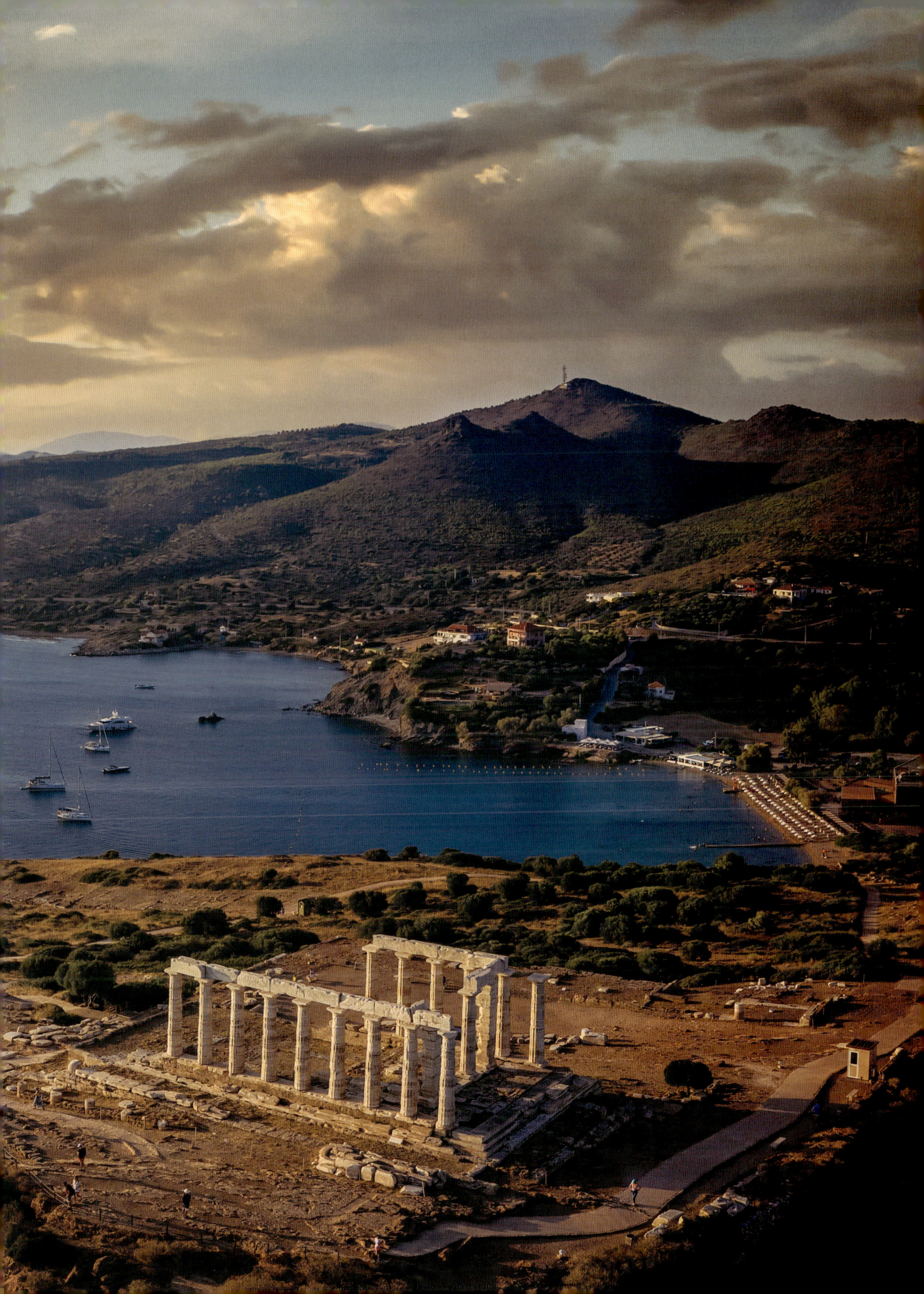

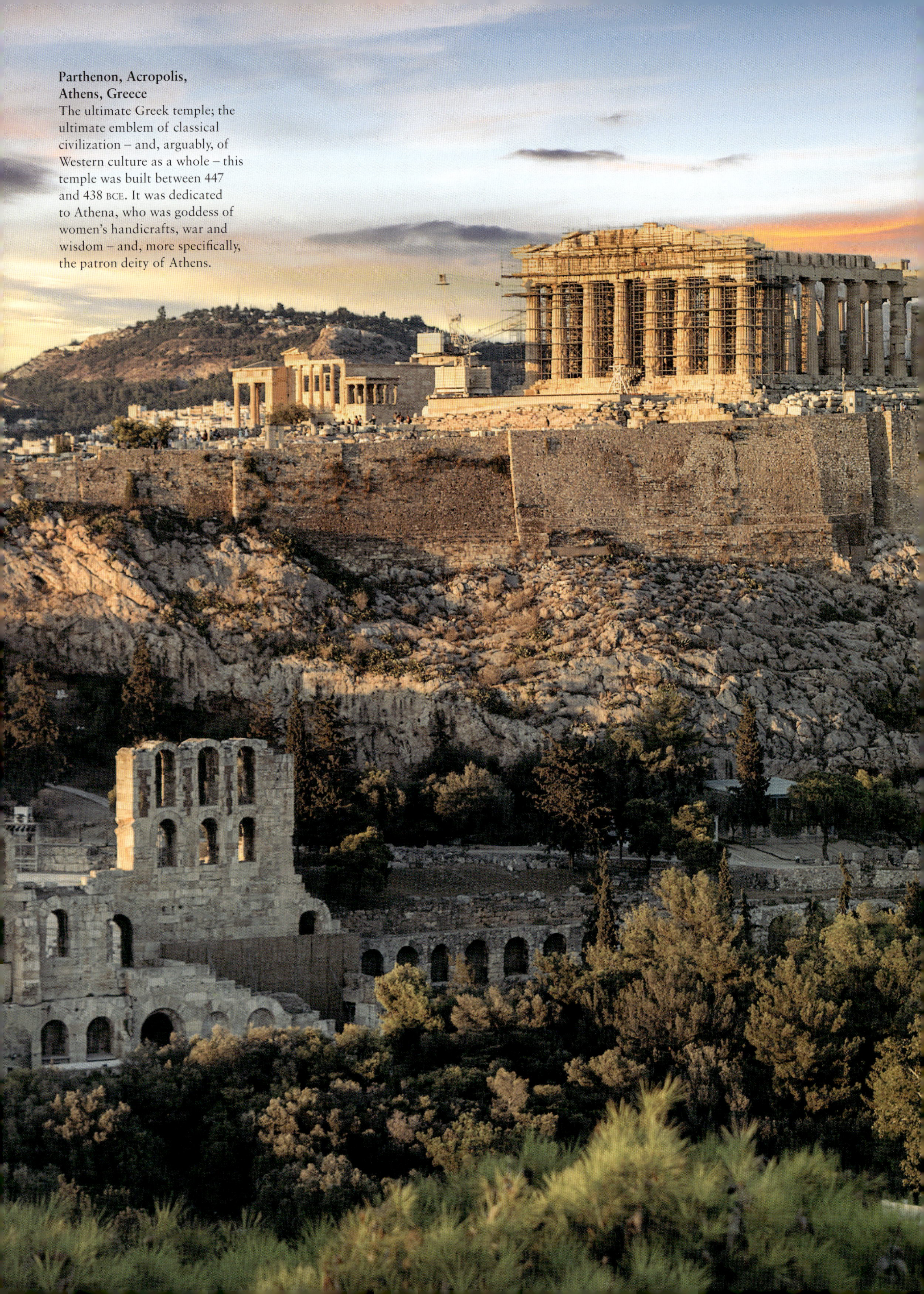

Parthenon, Acropolis, Athens, Greece
The ultimate Greek temple; the ultimate emblem of classical civilization – and, arguably, of Western culture as a whole – this temple was built between 447 and 438 BCE. It was dedicated to Athena, who was goddess of women's handicrafts, war and wisdom – and, more specifically, the patron deity of Athens.

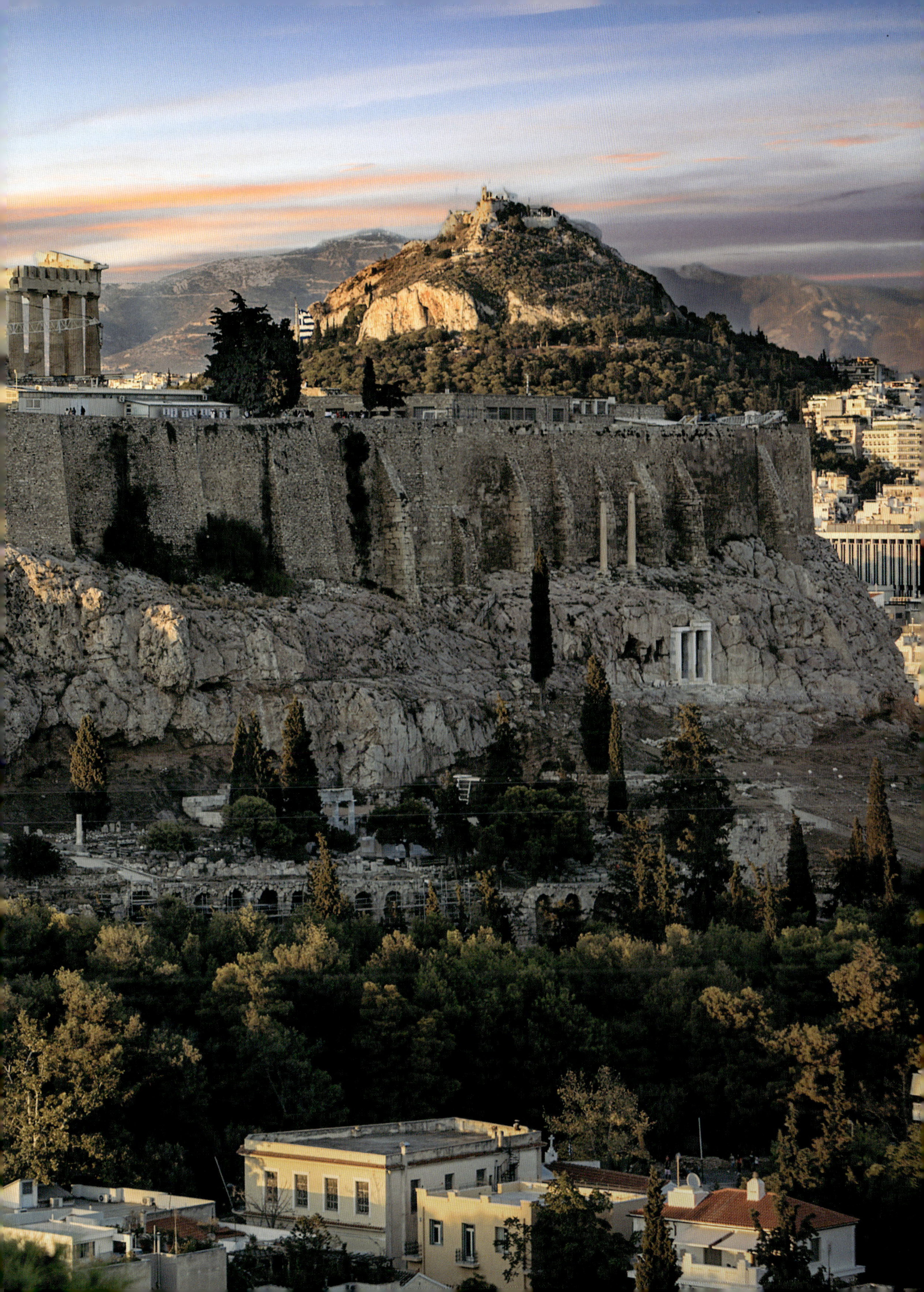

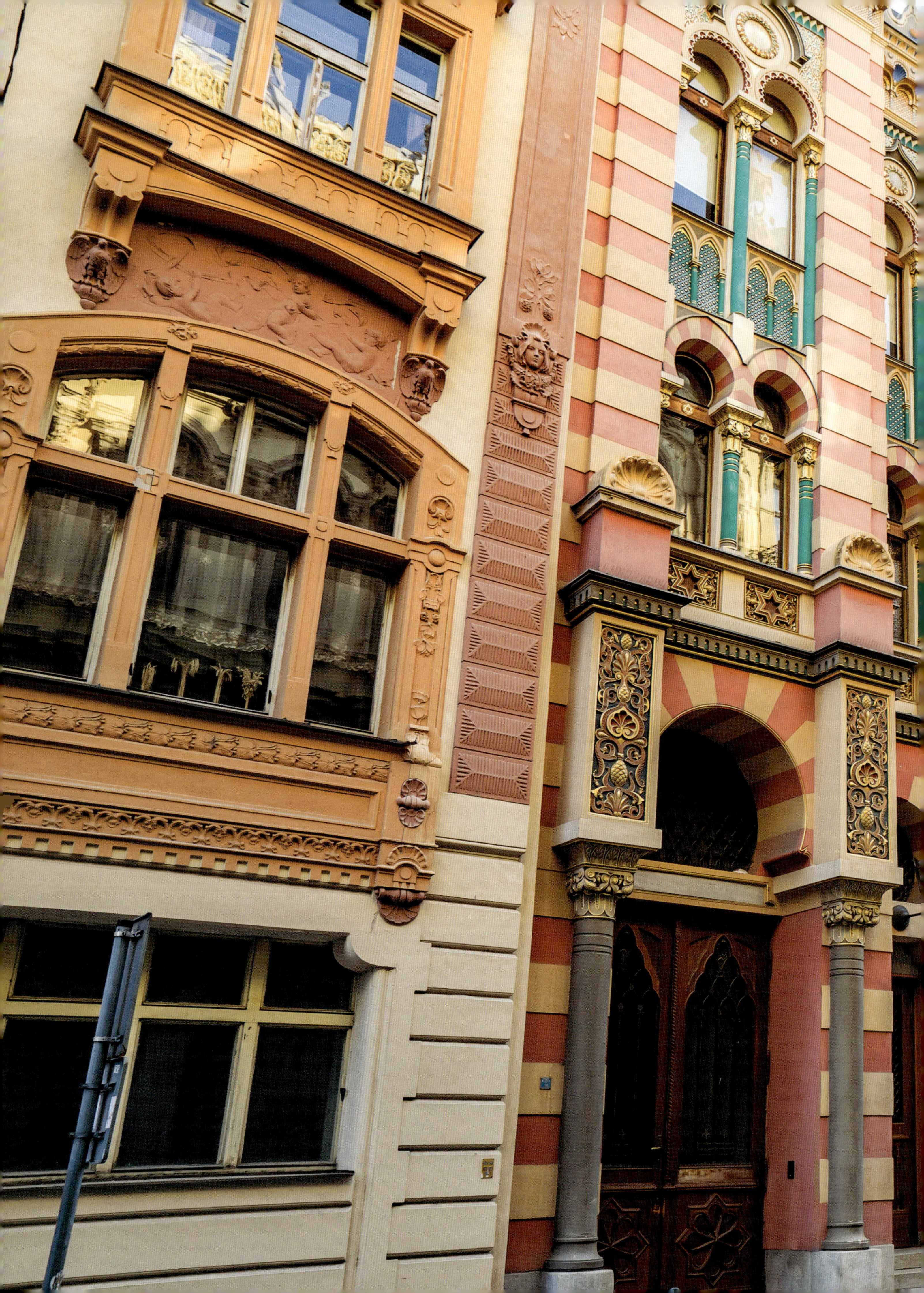

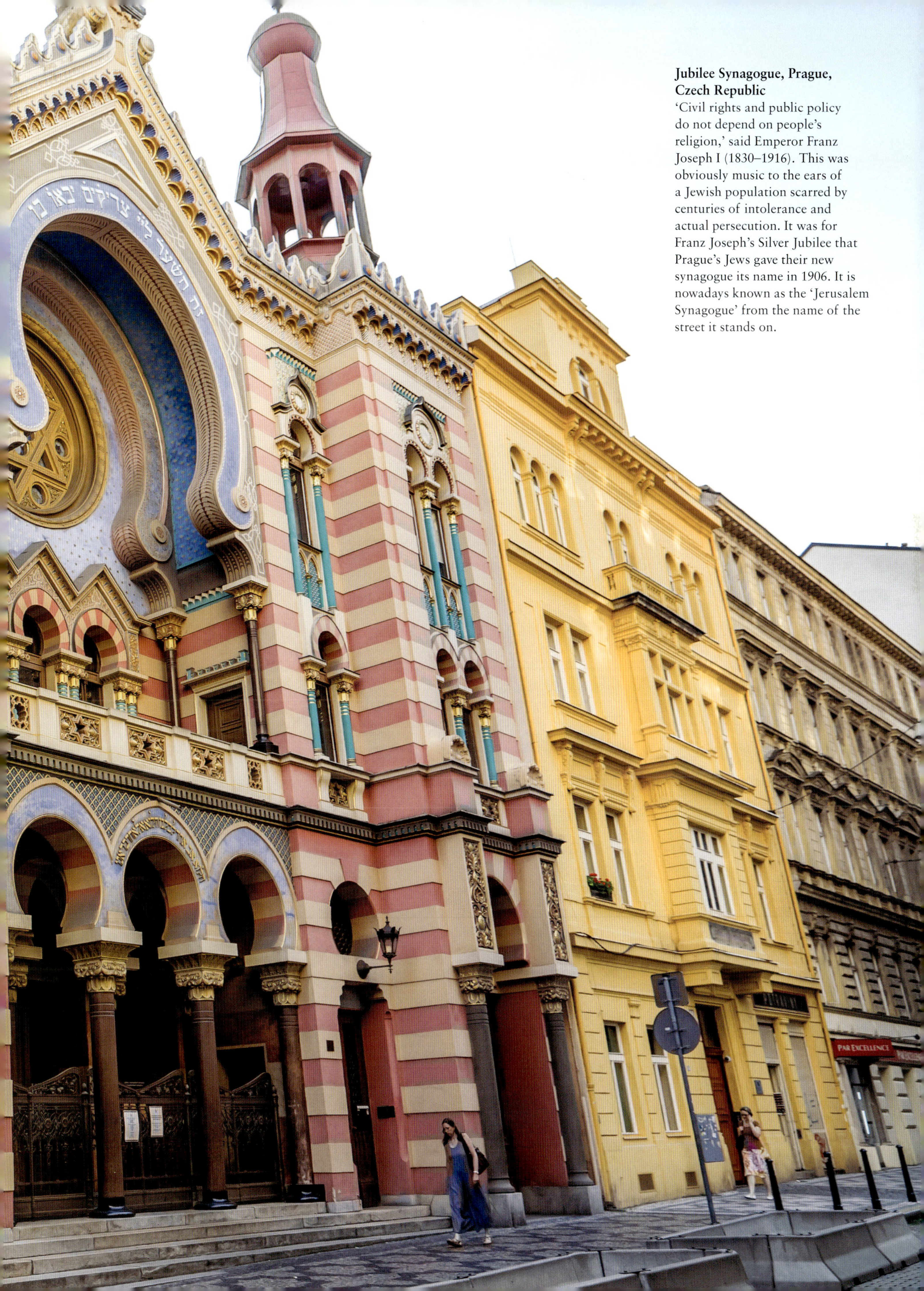

Jubilee Synagogue, Prague, Czech Republic
'Civil rights and public policy do not depend on people's religion,' said Emperor Franz Joseph I (1830–1916). This was obviously music to the ears of a Jewish population scarred by centuries of intolerance and actual persecution. It was for Franz Joseph's Silver Jubilee that Prague's Jews gave their new synagogue its name in 1906. It is nowadays known as the 'Jerusalem Synagogue' from the name of the street it stands on.

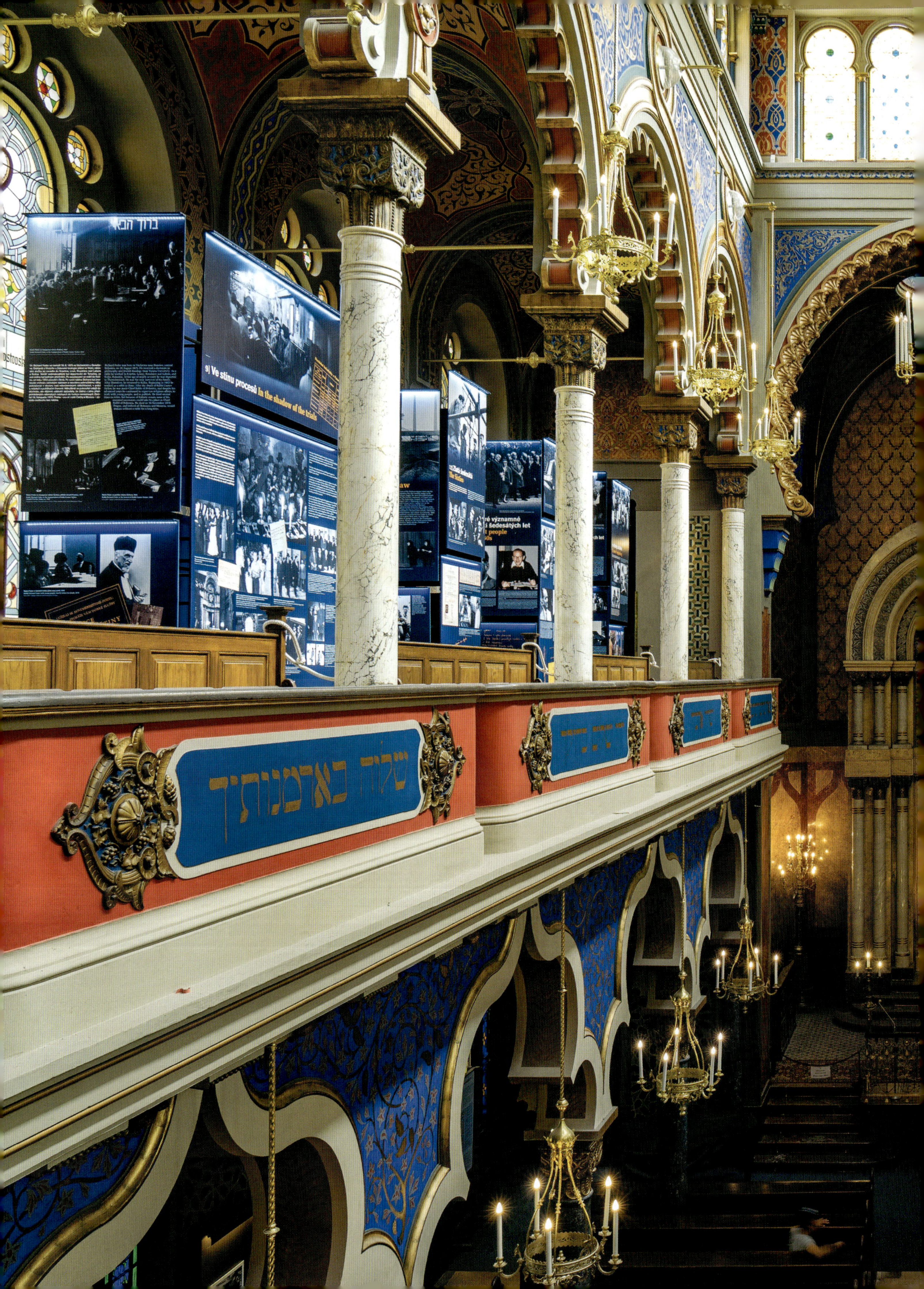
9) Ve stínu procesů In the shadow of the trials

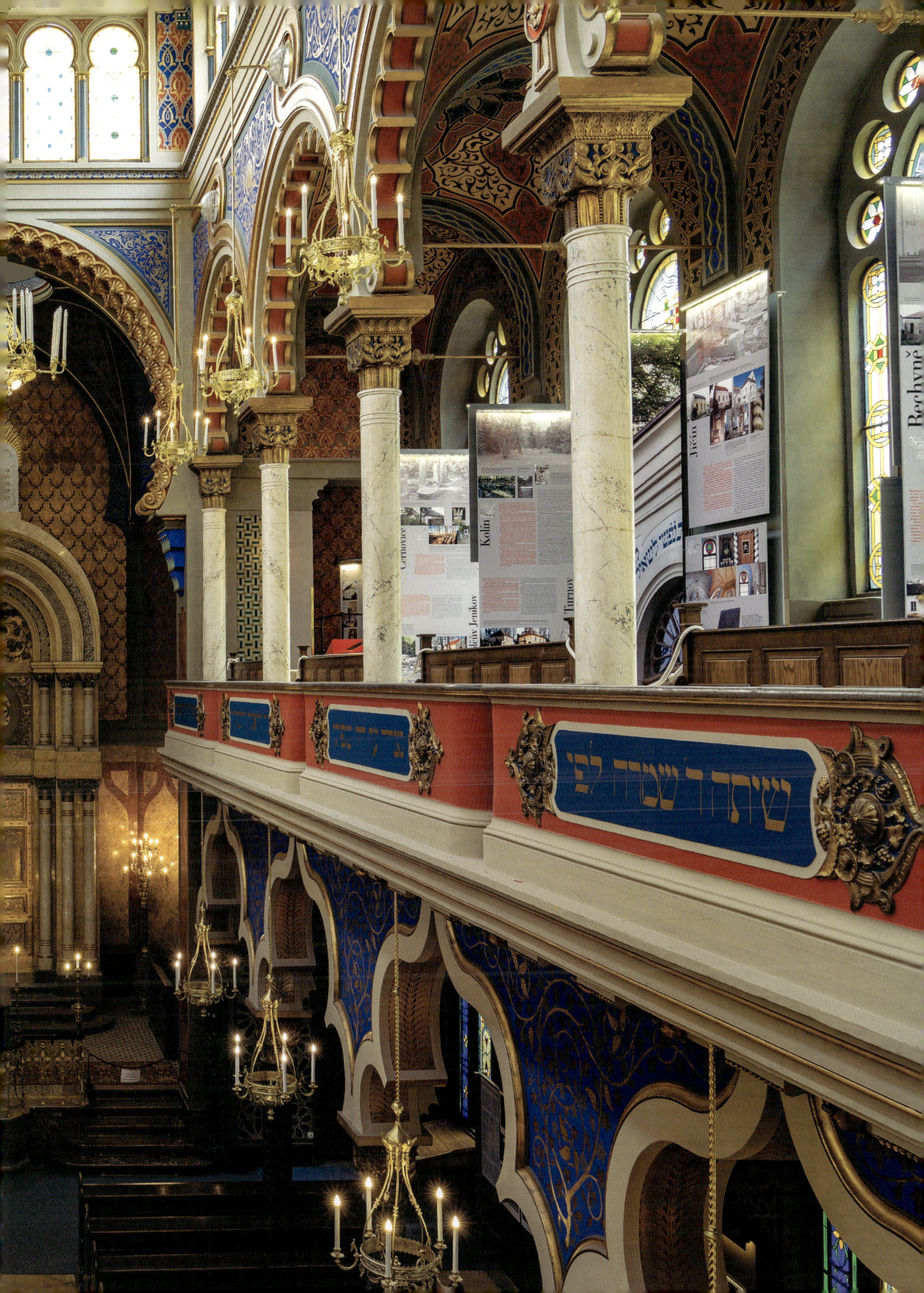
Jičín
Kolín
Turnov
Bechyně

PREVIOUS PAGES:

Jubilee Synagogue, Prague, Czech Republic

Art Nouveau meets Moorish Revival here – and to gorgeous effect. From a twenty-first-century perspective, perhaps, it makes no sense for a synagogue to model itself on a Muslim example. Like those of Berlin and Florence, however, Prague's Jews seem at this time to have been ready to accept – even embrace – the 'oriental' foreignness they knew they had in European eyes.

RIGHT AND OVERLEAF:

Old New Synagogue, Prague, Czech Republic

An 'Old Old' Synagogue was cleared away in the nineteenth century. Prague also has an all-new synagogue; hence the title given to this medieval foundation, an active synagogue since 1270 – so possibly Europe's oldest. The original Golem – a miraculously animated figure of clay – is said by some to be kept in the attic here. Certainly, it's a beautiful and atmospheric place.

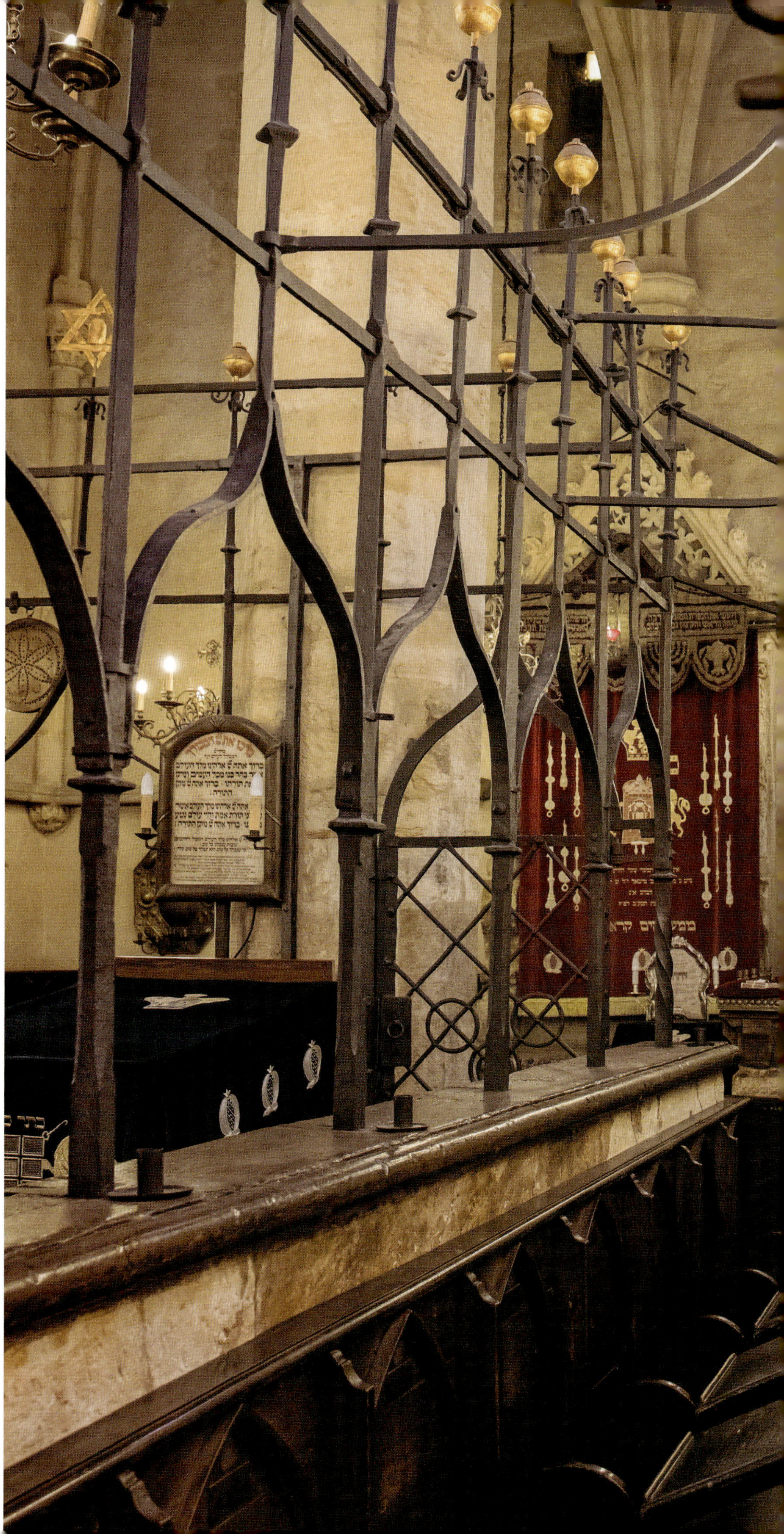

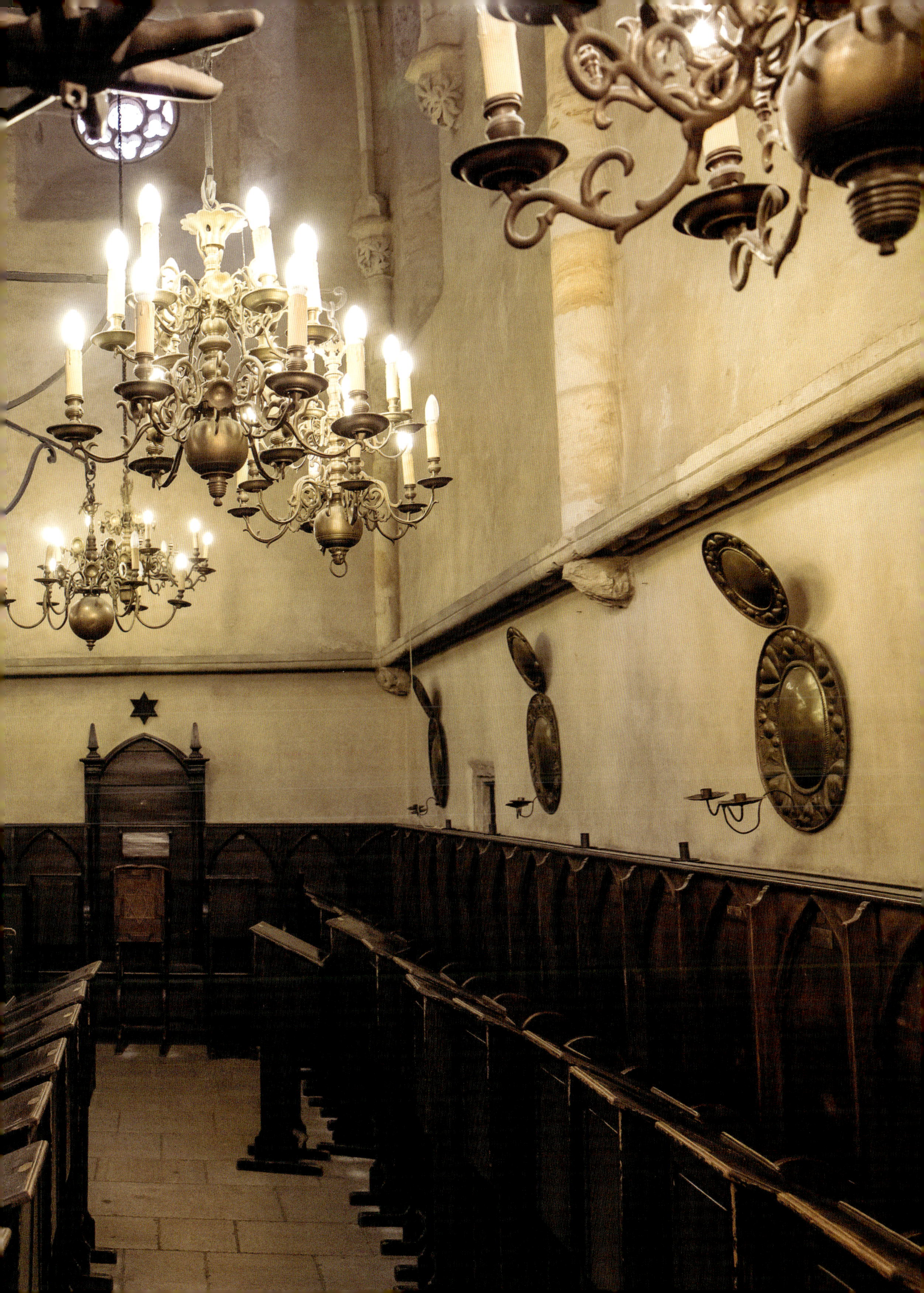

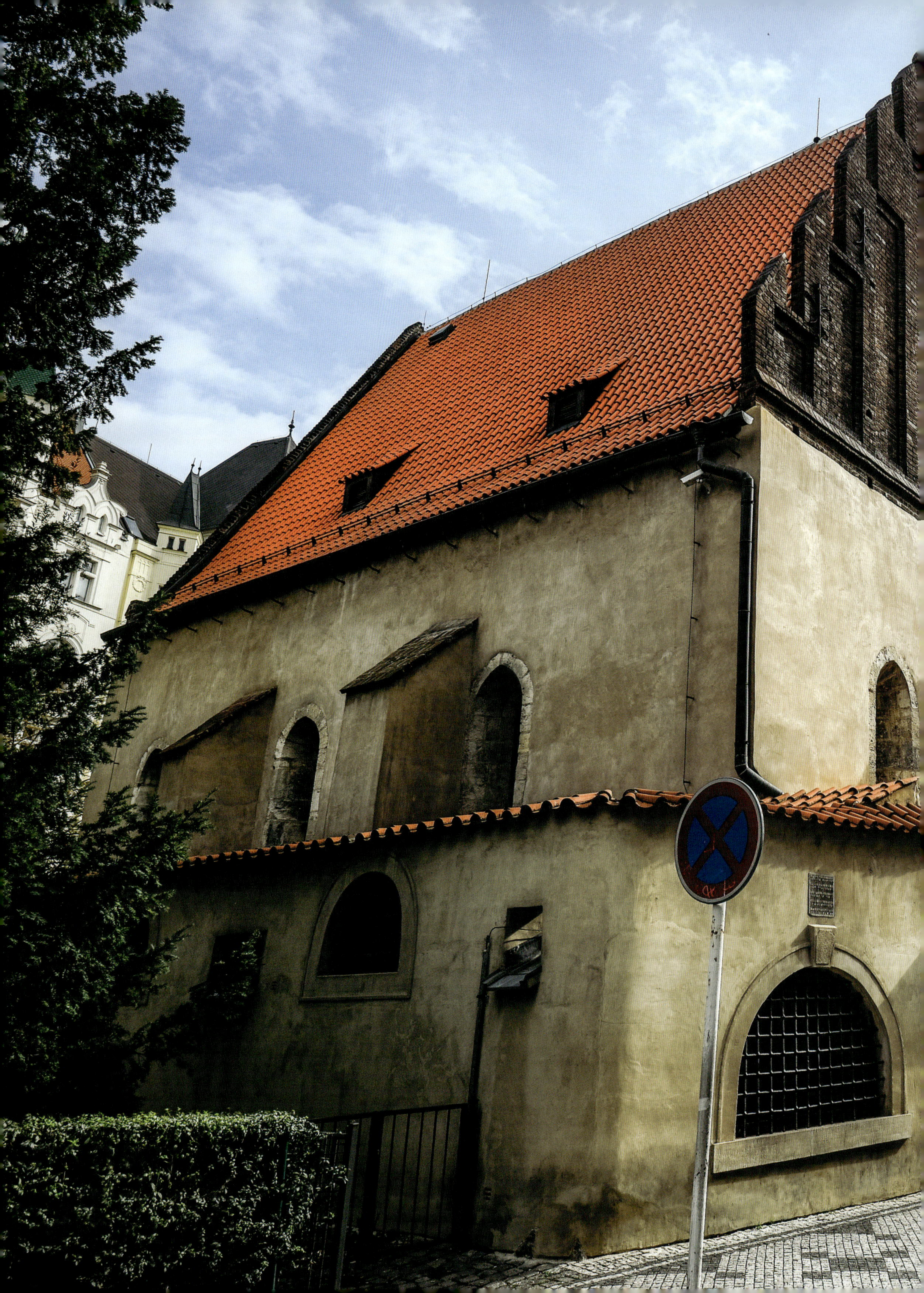

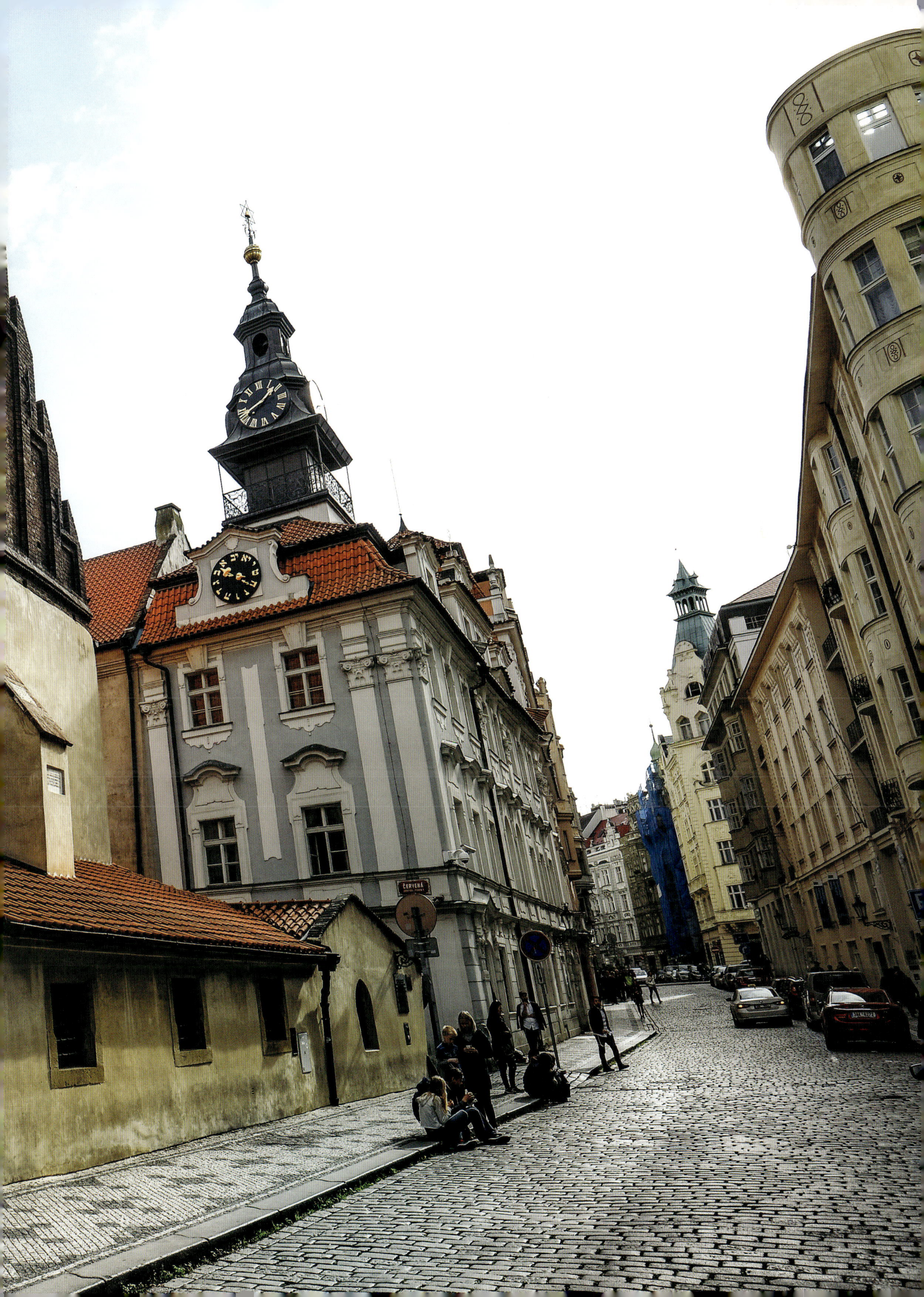
ČERVENÁ

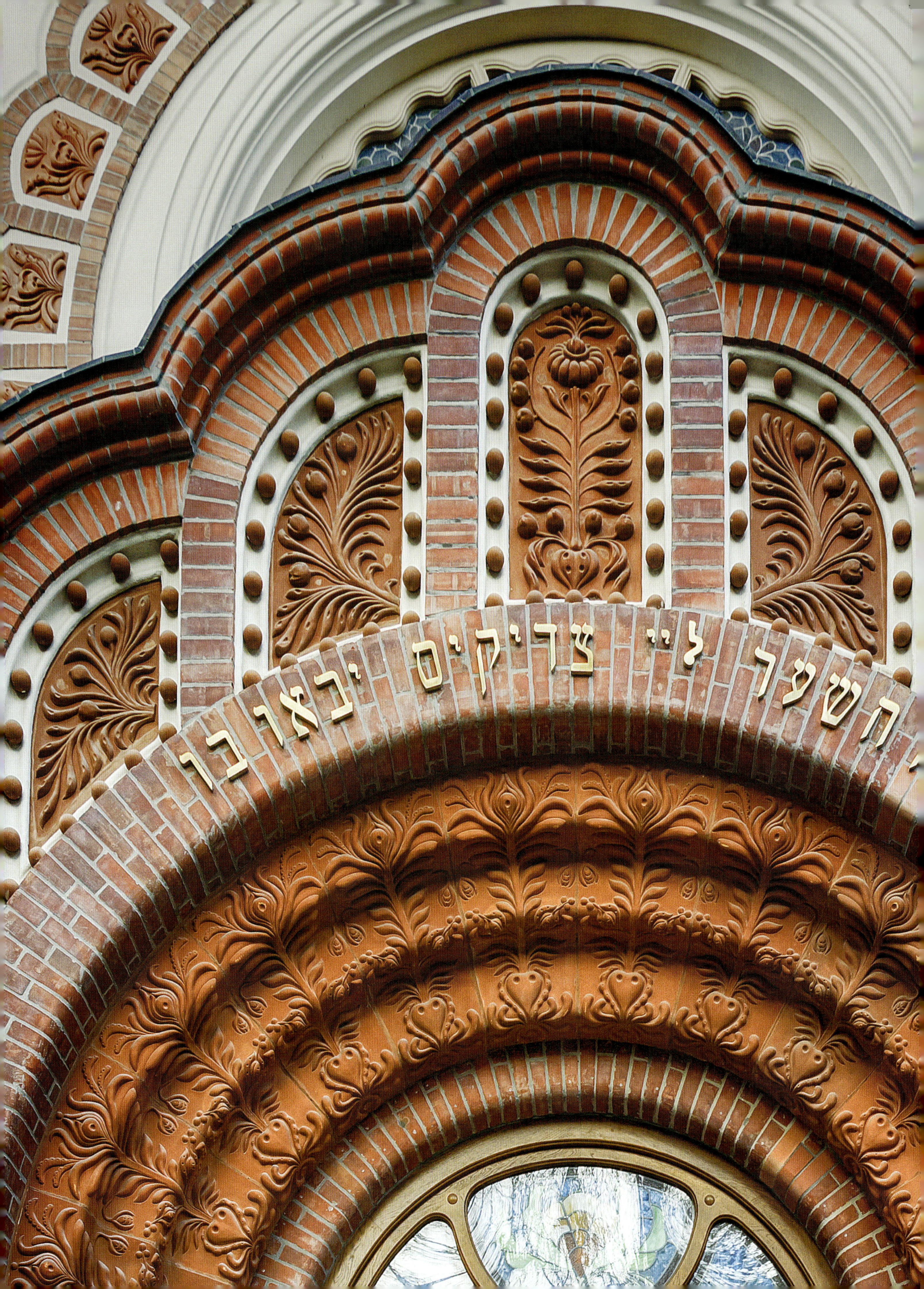
השער ליי צדיקים יבאו בו

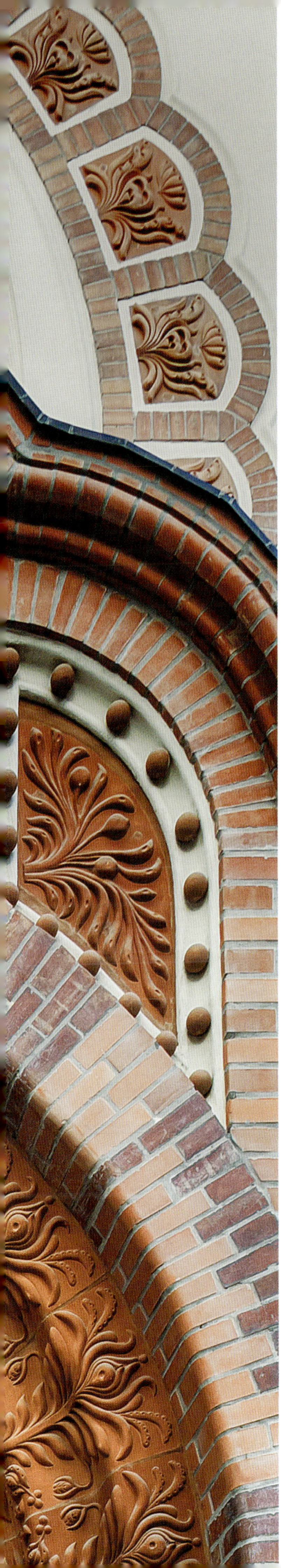

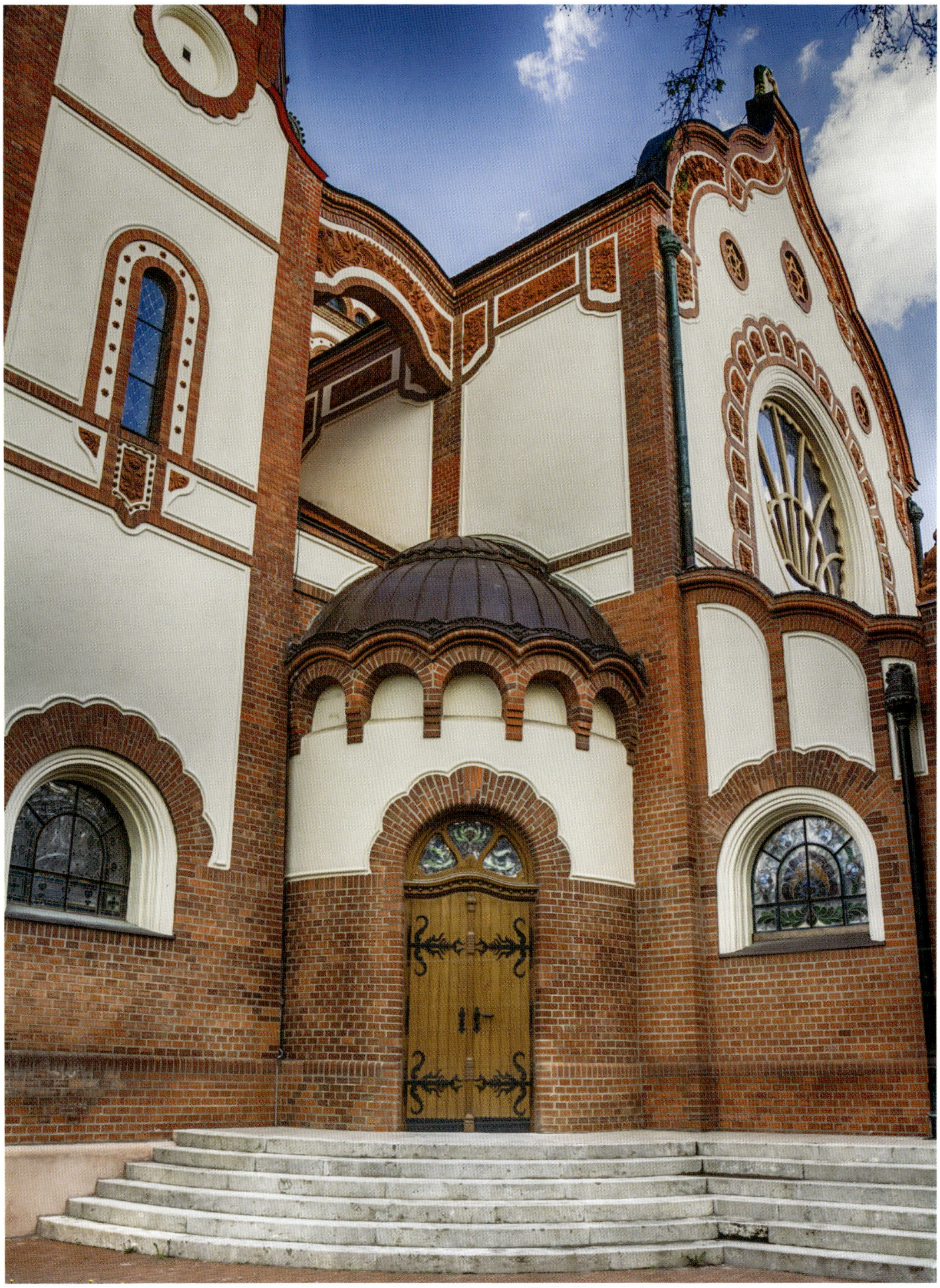

ALL PHOTOGRAPHS:

Subotica Synagogue, Serbia

Dedicated in 1903, Europe's second-largest synagogue now, by tragic irony, serves a population it could accommodate several times over. There were 6000 Jews in what was then a Hungarian city when local Fascists, subcontracted by the Nazis, set about seizing them in 1941. Some were killed immediately and others sent to the death camps. Of the few hundred survivors after World War II, most left to make a new life in Israel.

Today, it is as much a state memorial as a place of worship. The building is a work of awe-inspiring beauty, though, evidently influenced by Art Nouveau. In contrast with contemporary synagogues elsewhere in Europe, and in a manner more like that of London's New West End Synagogue, it makes a point of meeting the local Christian culture halfway.

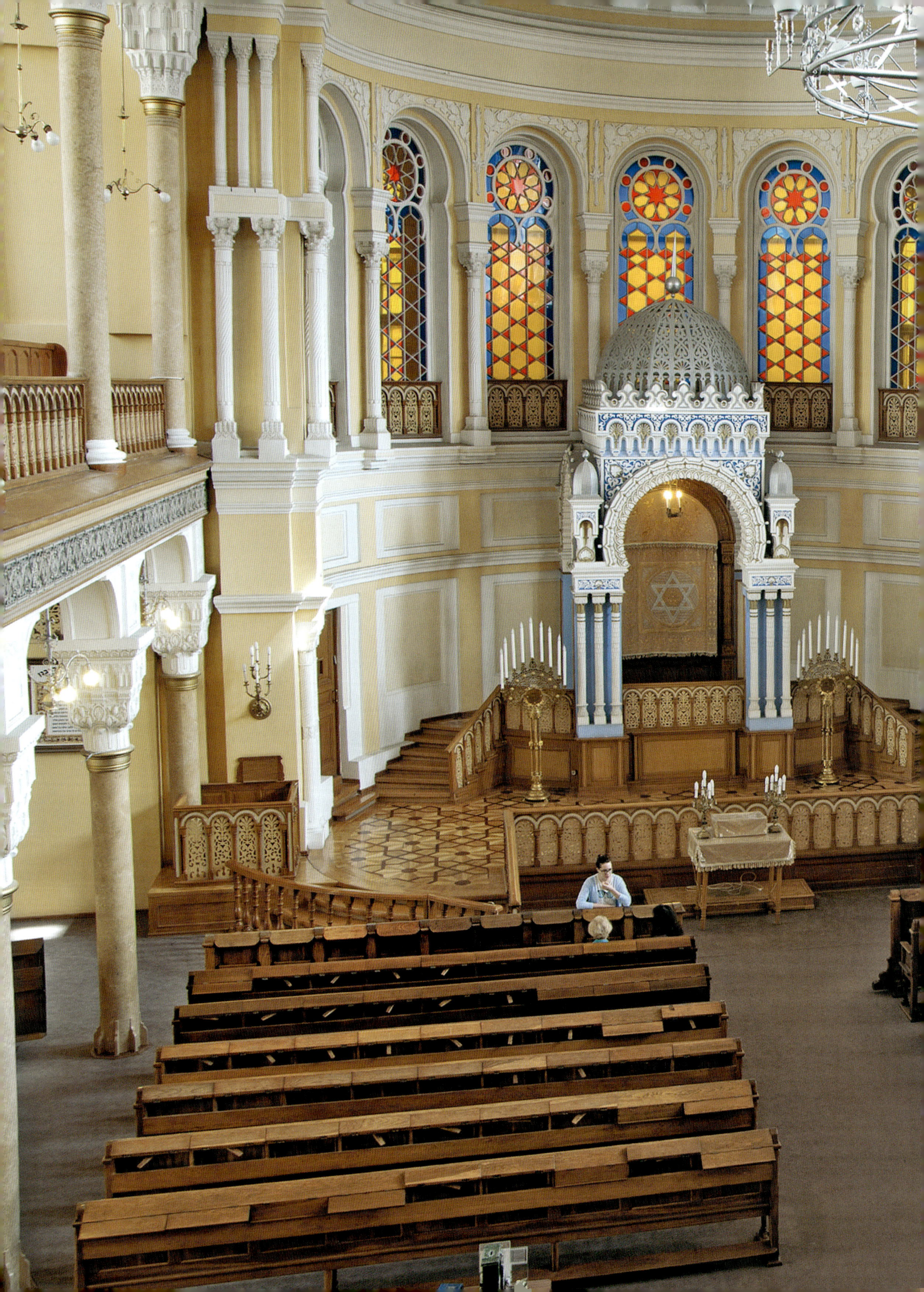

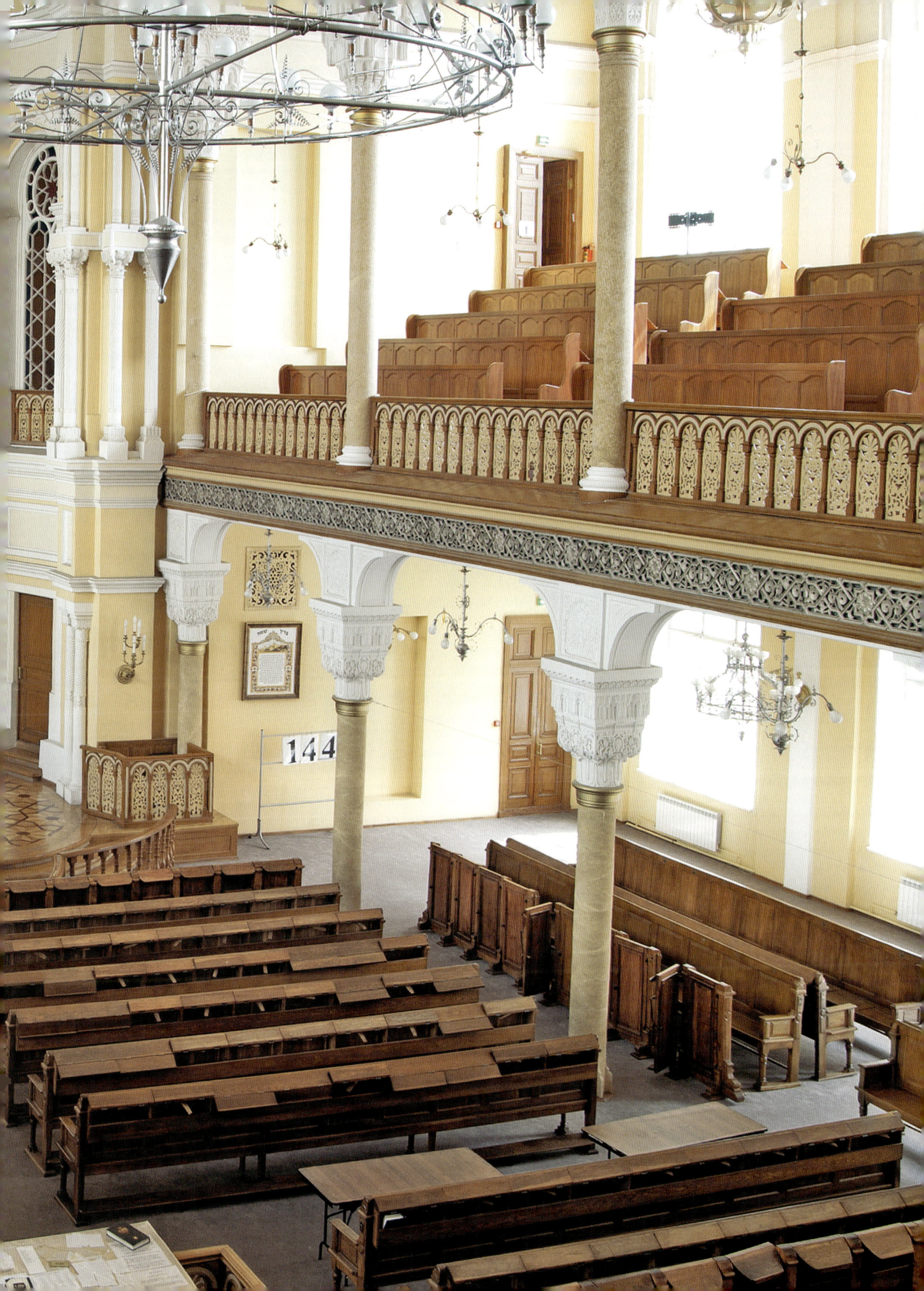
144

PREVIOUS PAGES:
Grand Choral Synagogue, St Petersburg, Russia
Intended as a fitting venue for Russia's Jews to worship in what was then their country's capital, this synagogue was opened in 1893. Like several other synagogues of this time, its exterior combines features of the Byzantine and Moorish styles. Its interior décor is, however, much more chaste. Starved of support during the Soviet era (and all but obliterated by German bombs during the Siege of Leningrad, 1941–44) this synagogue has been much-restored in recent years.

RIGHT:
Choral Temple Synagogue, Bucharest, Romania
Romania's fascist 'Iron Guard' destroyed this synagogue in a pogrom in 1941; they also murdered over 120 Jews. This was just a prelude to the atrocities a few months later after Romania entered World War II on the Axis side. It became a point of honour for the post-war Communist state to restore the synagogue, though by this time it scarcely had a congregation left.

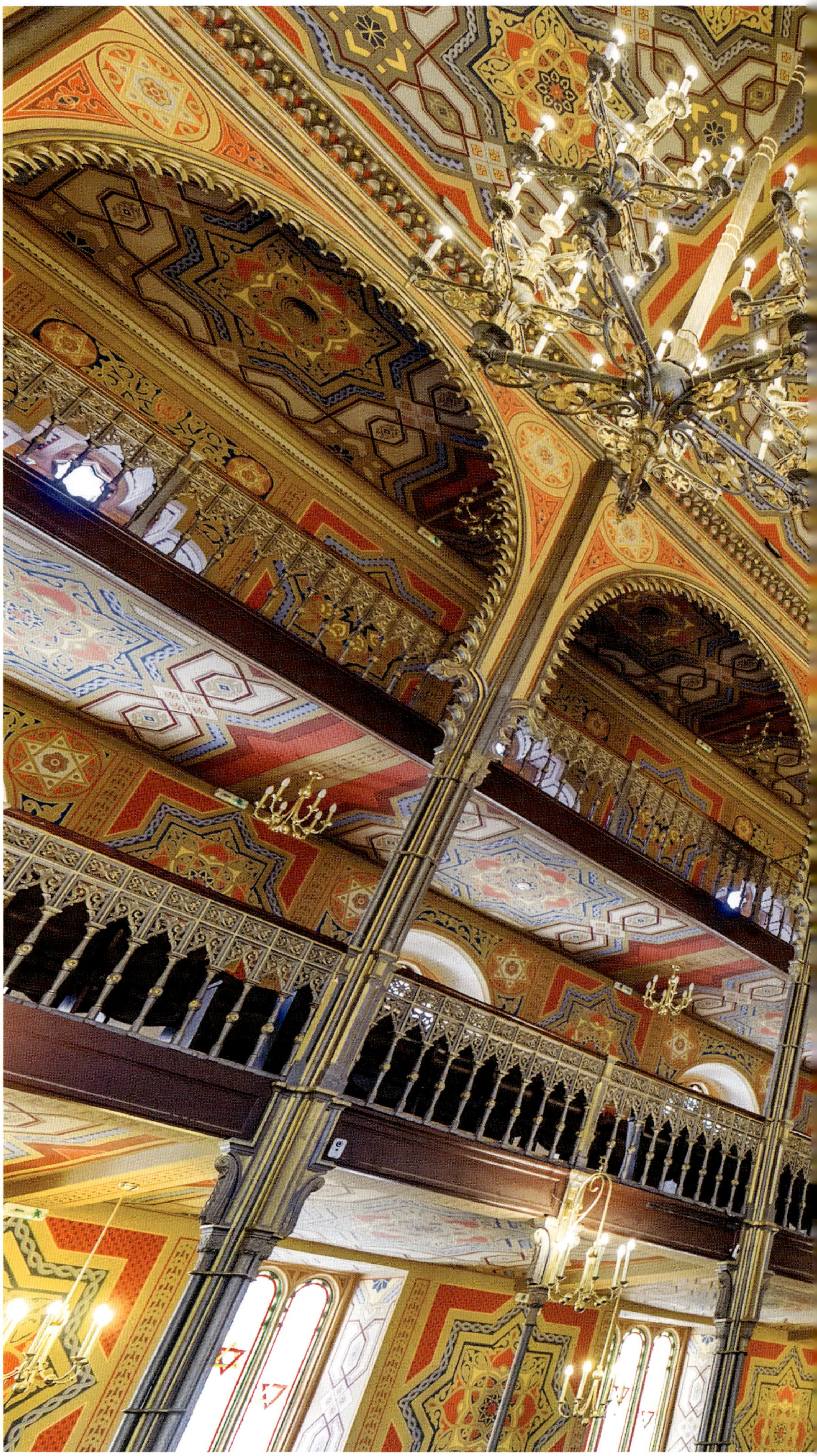

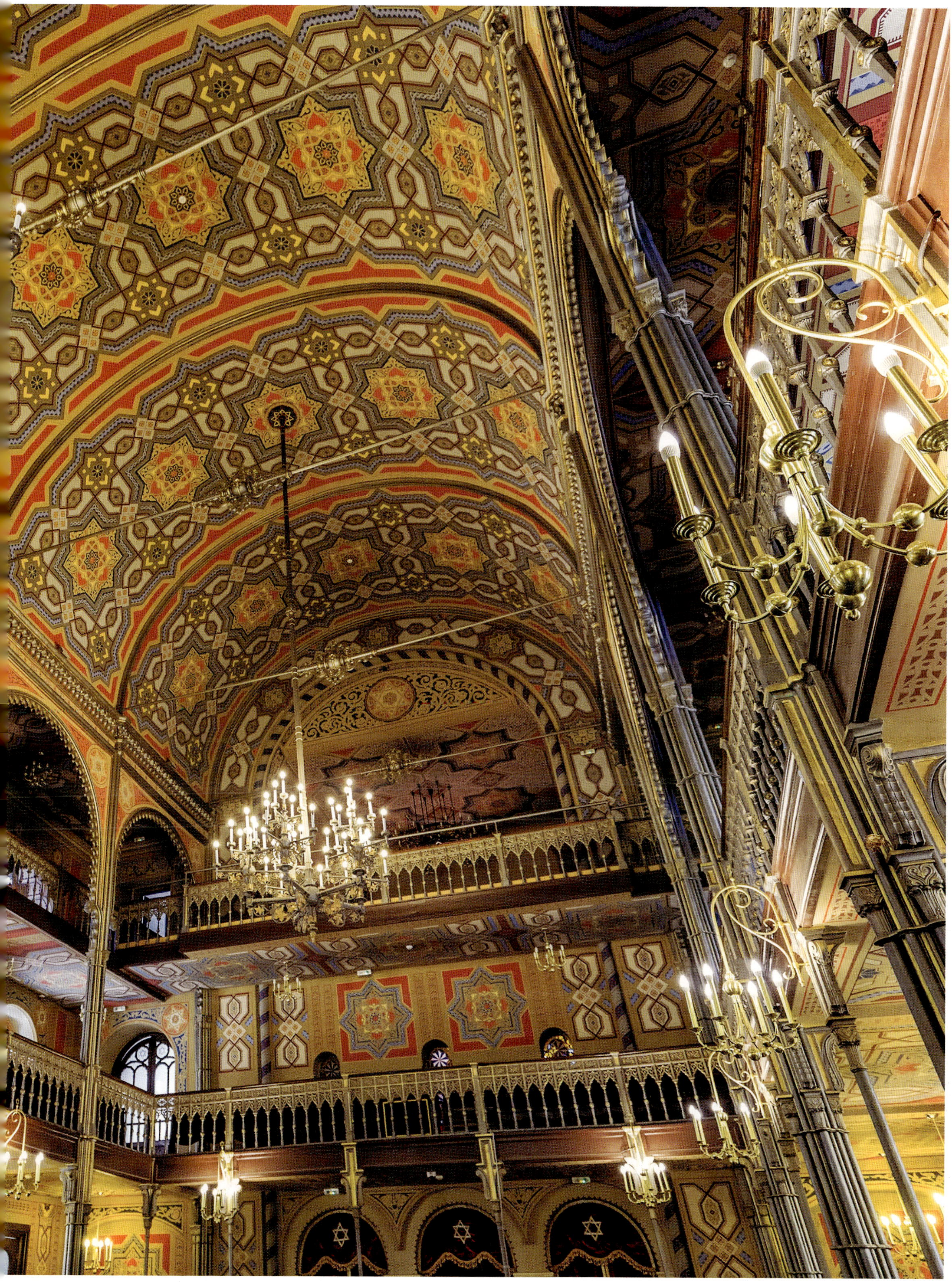

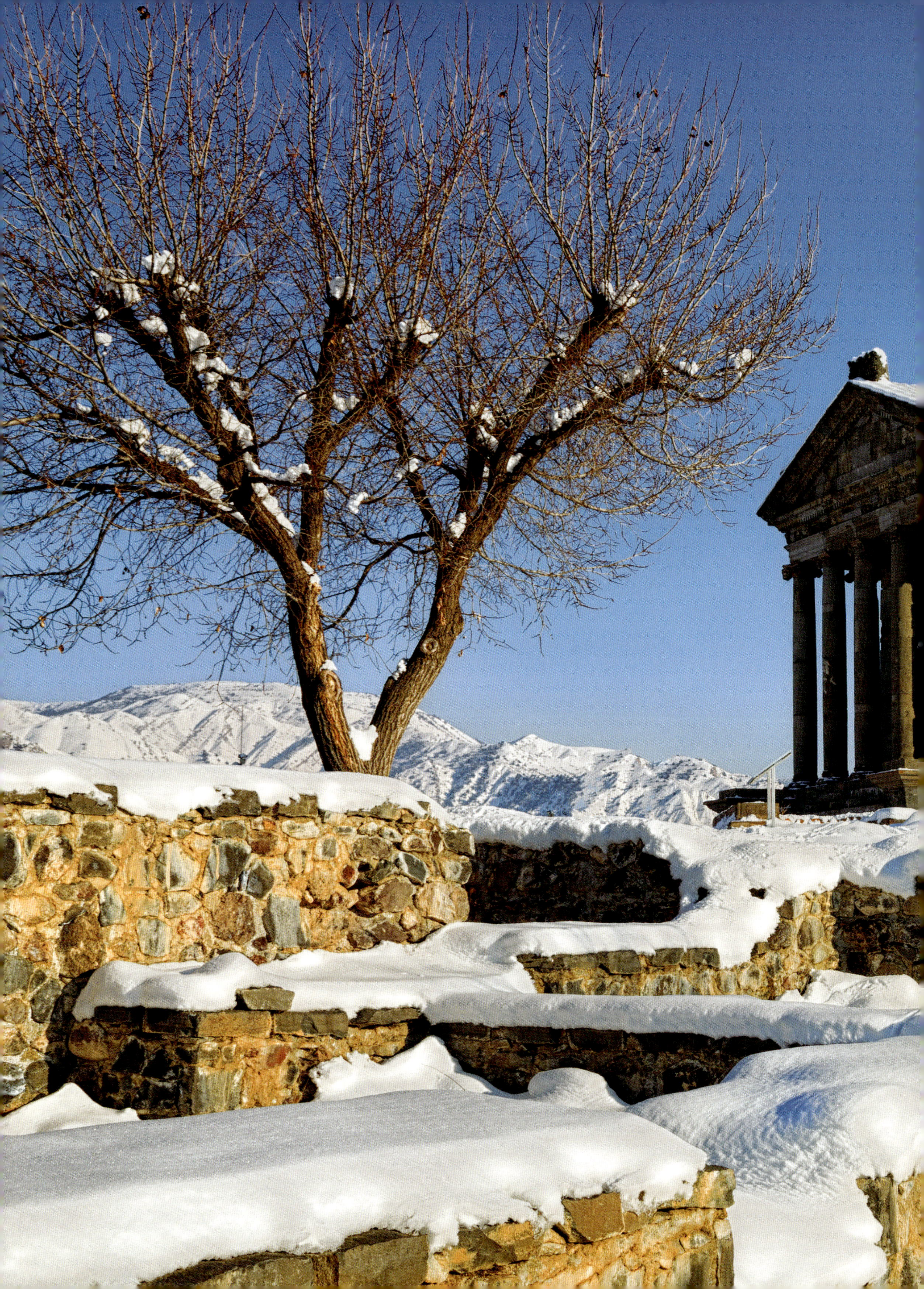

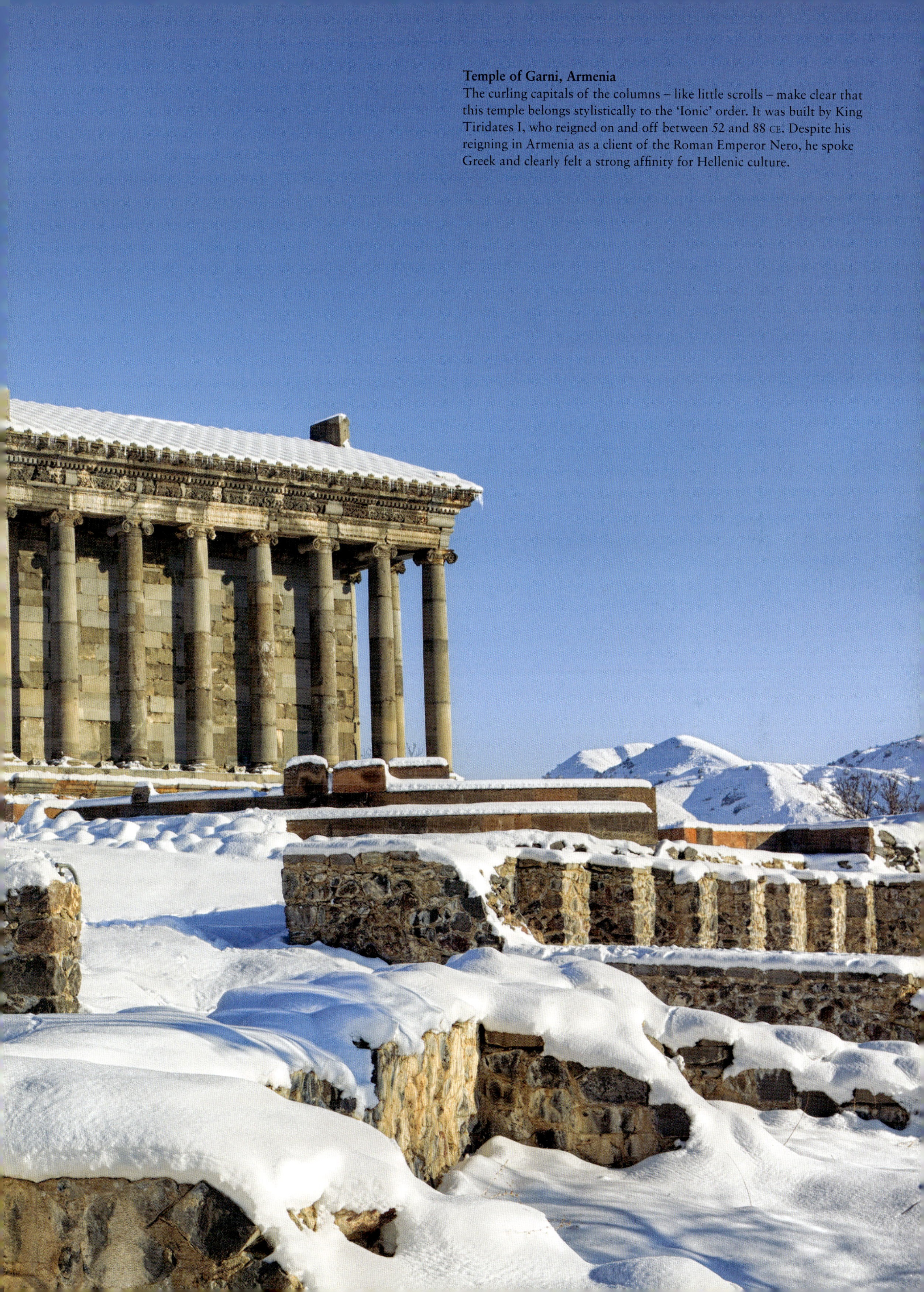

Temple of Garni, Armenia
The curling capitals of the columns – like little scrolls – make clear that this temple belongs stylistically to the 'Ionic' order. It was built by King Tiridates I, who reigned on and off between 52 and 88 CE. Despite his reigning in Armenia as a client of the Roman Emperor Nero, he spoke Greek and clearly felt a strong affinity for Hellenic culture.

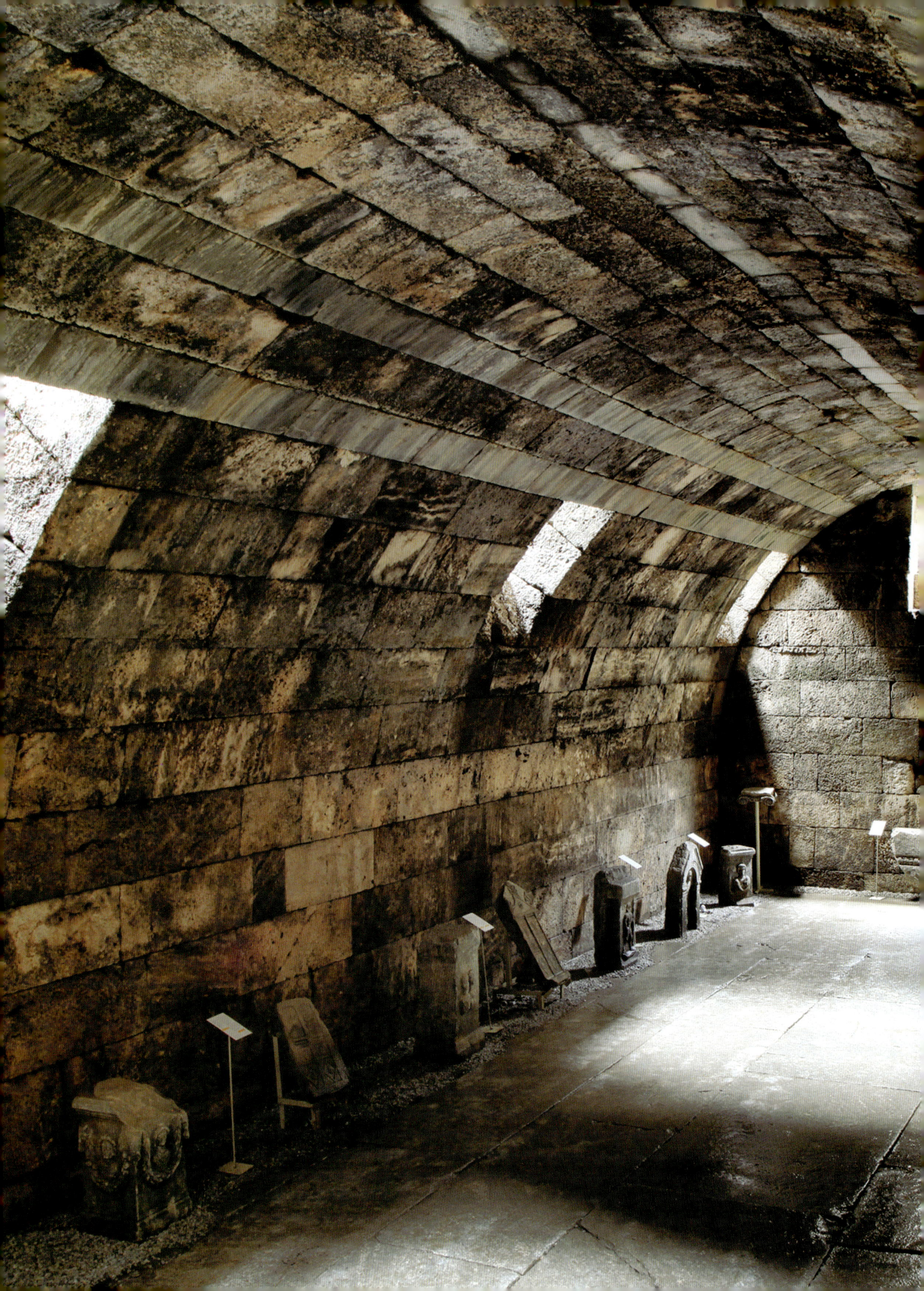

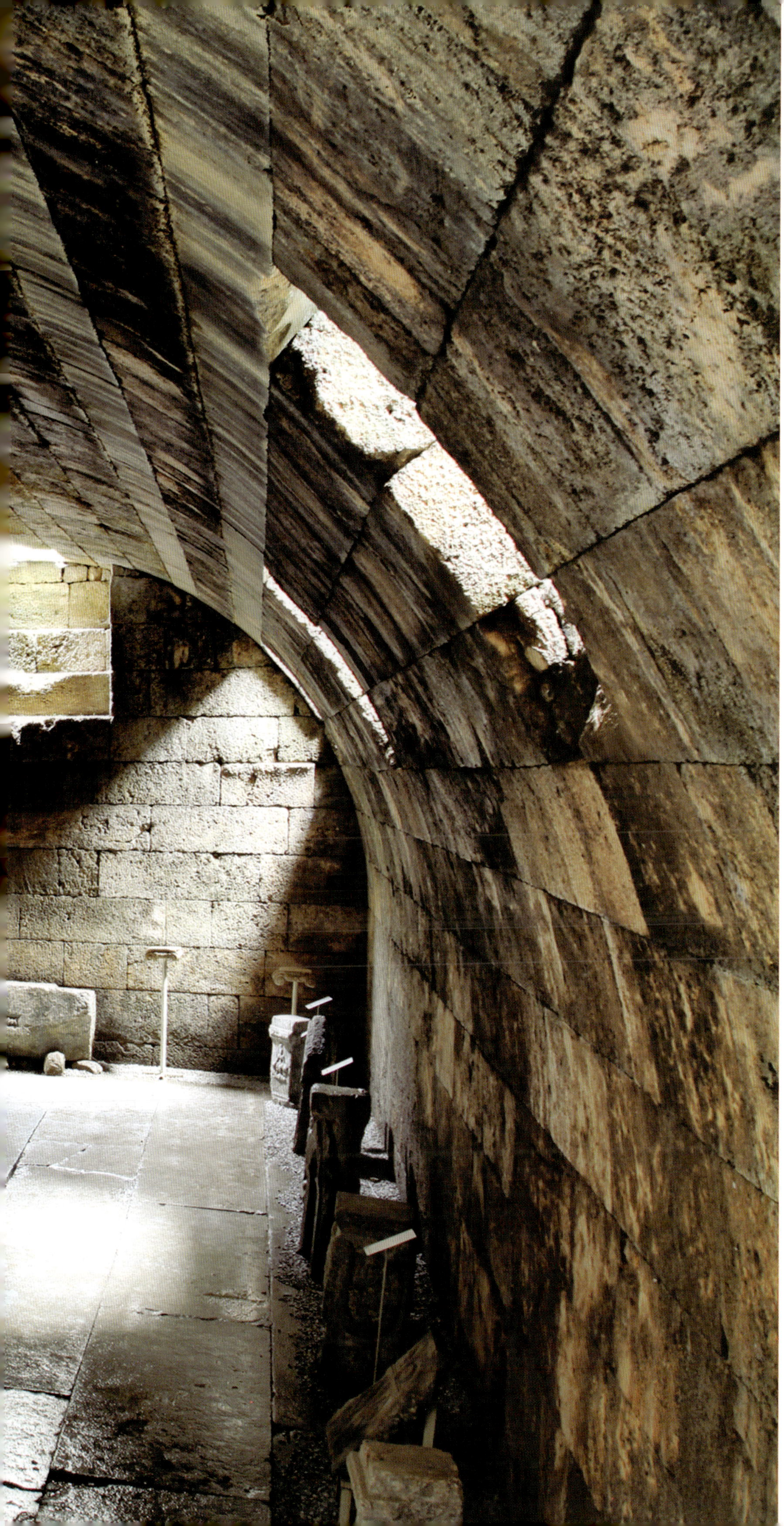

Temple of Zeus, Aizanoi, Turkey
Aizanoi was a Greek colony in what is now Turkey, near the present-day city of Kütahya. The Temple of Zeus is an impressive ruin, though its most intriguing feature is this womb-like underground chamber. It is believed to have been used for ritual offerings to Cybele, an ancient Anatolian mother-goddess, associated with the earth, whom the settlers seem to have adopted as their own.

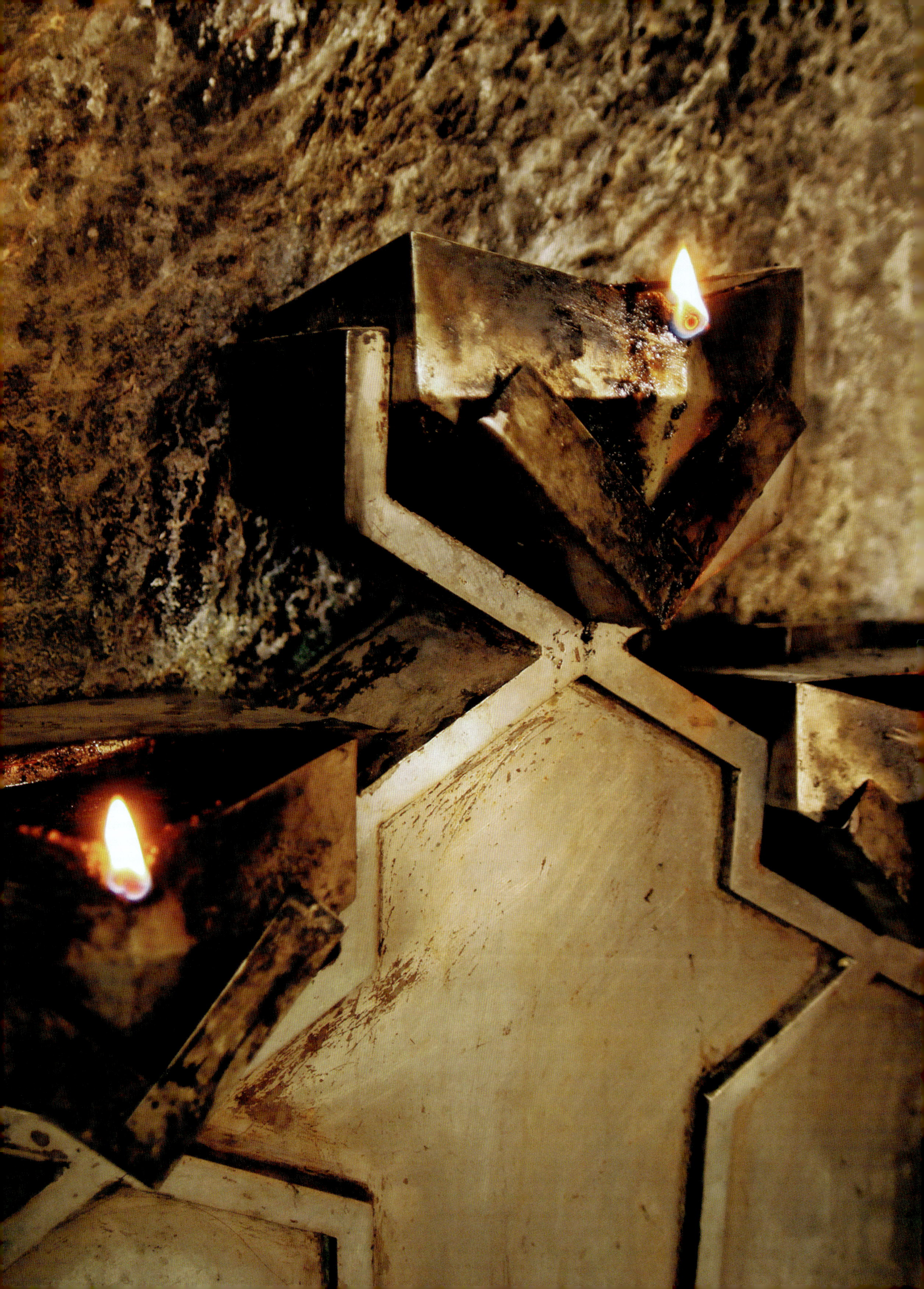

Africa and the Middle East

The Middle East is metaphor-central: having started out as the so-called 'Cradle of Civilization', it went on to be the 'Crossroads of the Ancient World'. Both these age-old identities are still evident in its surviving heritage of religious architecture – whether as working modern temples or as stately but abandoned ruins. The region's Greek and Roman sites represent a relatively recent strand in the history of a region that boasts important shrines from Mesopotamia's early cultures. Of the great world religions that started here, Christianity and Islam are both beyond the scope of this book: neither churches nor mosques can truly be described as temples. Nor, strictly speaking, can synagogues. The Great Temple of Jerusalem was of course all but obliterated by the Romans in 70 CE. It remains present-as-an-absence at the heart of Judaism. So it is important to Jews that their synagogues should not be seen as replacements for a building they hope one day to raise up again.

Africa's ancient temples recall a time before modern European culture could 'other' it as a 'Dark Continent'. (What civilization has ever shone more brightly than Pharaonic Egypt?) Newer constructions here hold out the hope of a more open-minded era in which non-European ways aren't automatically seen as second-best.

OPPOSITE:
Chak Chak, Yazd, Iran
Flames flicker everlastingly in this, one of Zoroastrianism's most important shrines. Pilgrims come here in their thousands every year. Zoroastrianism pivots upon the dualistic opposition of light and darkness, good and evil, so naturally living fire, with its warming glow, is its most sacred sign.

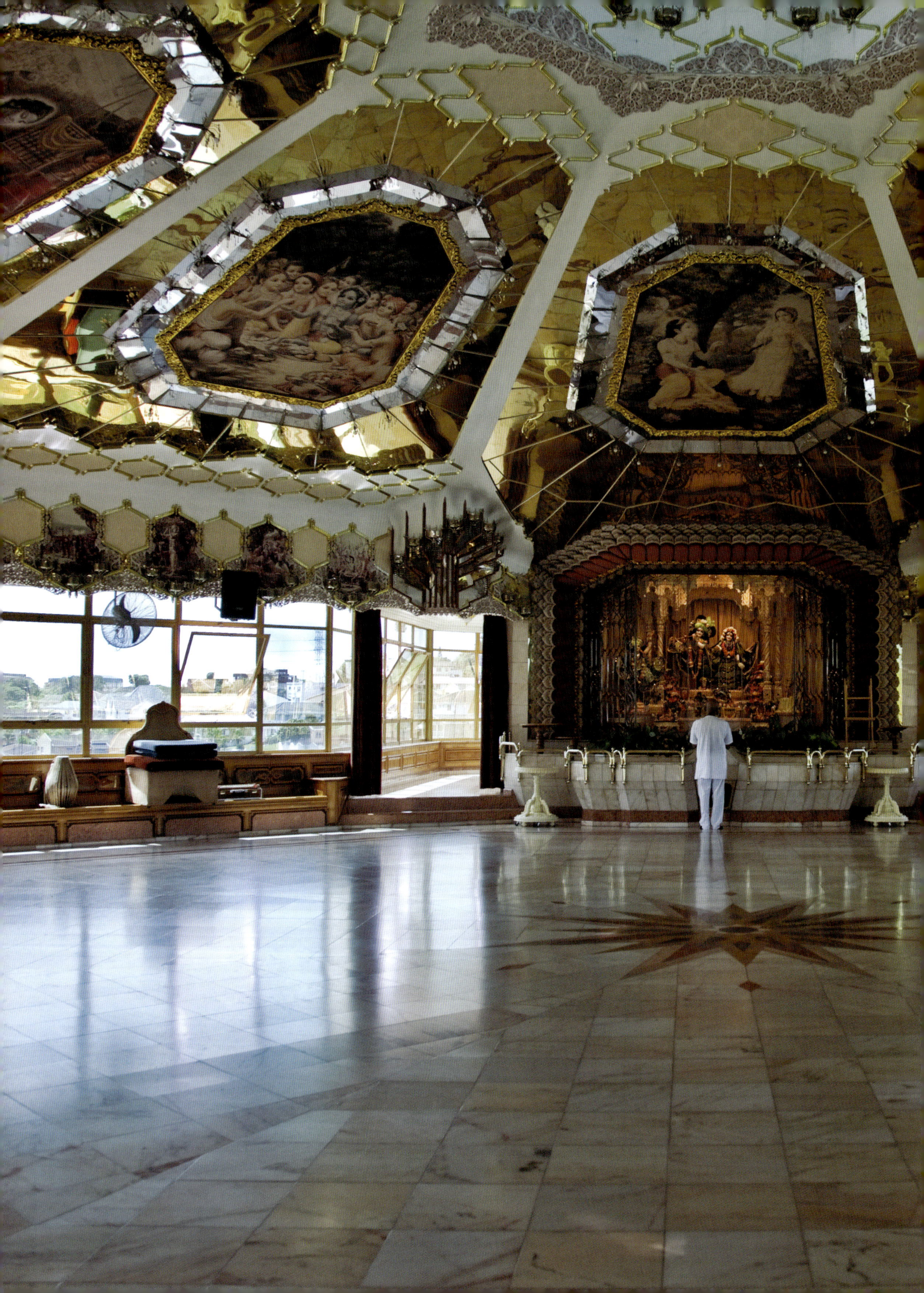

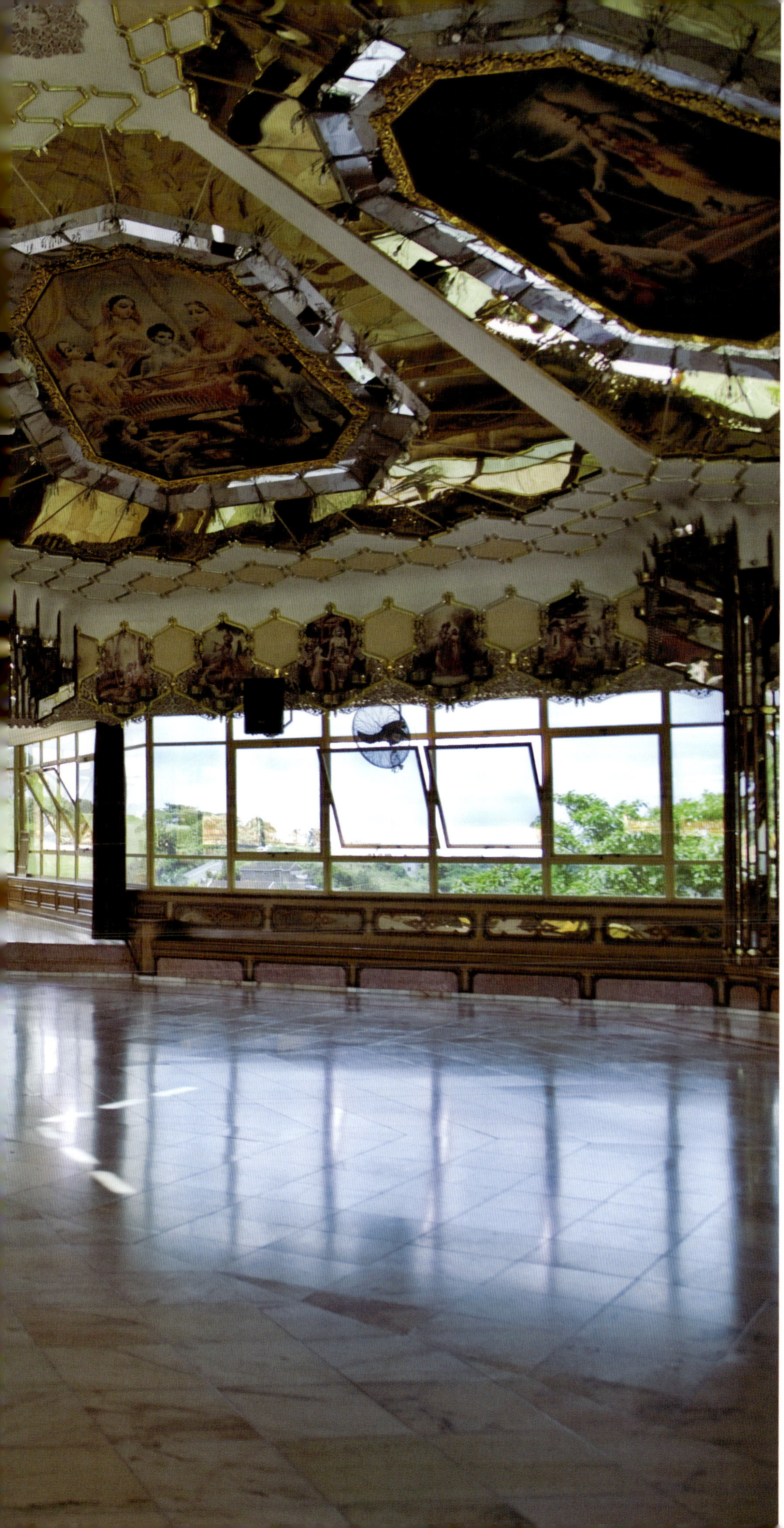

Krishna Temple, Durban, South Africa
In the apartheid era, Chatsworth, west of Durban, was the designated home of the city's Indian population, with white suburbs to the north and black townships on its southern side. Its black population has increased since then, but it is still closely-identified with an Indian Hindu community for whom this temple, built in the 1980s, has become an emblem.

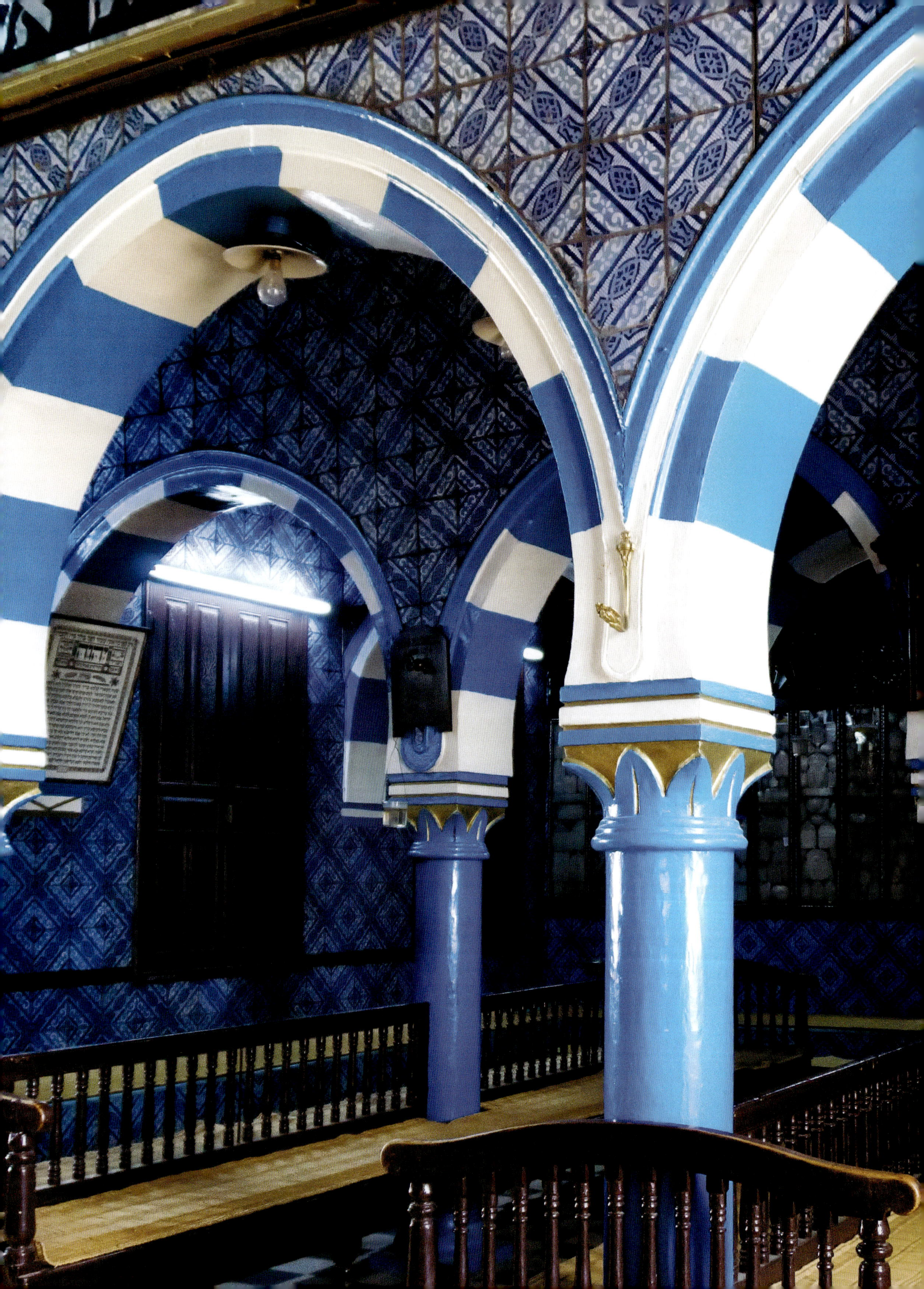

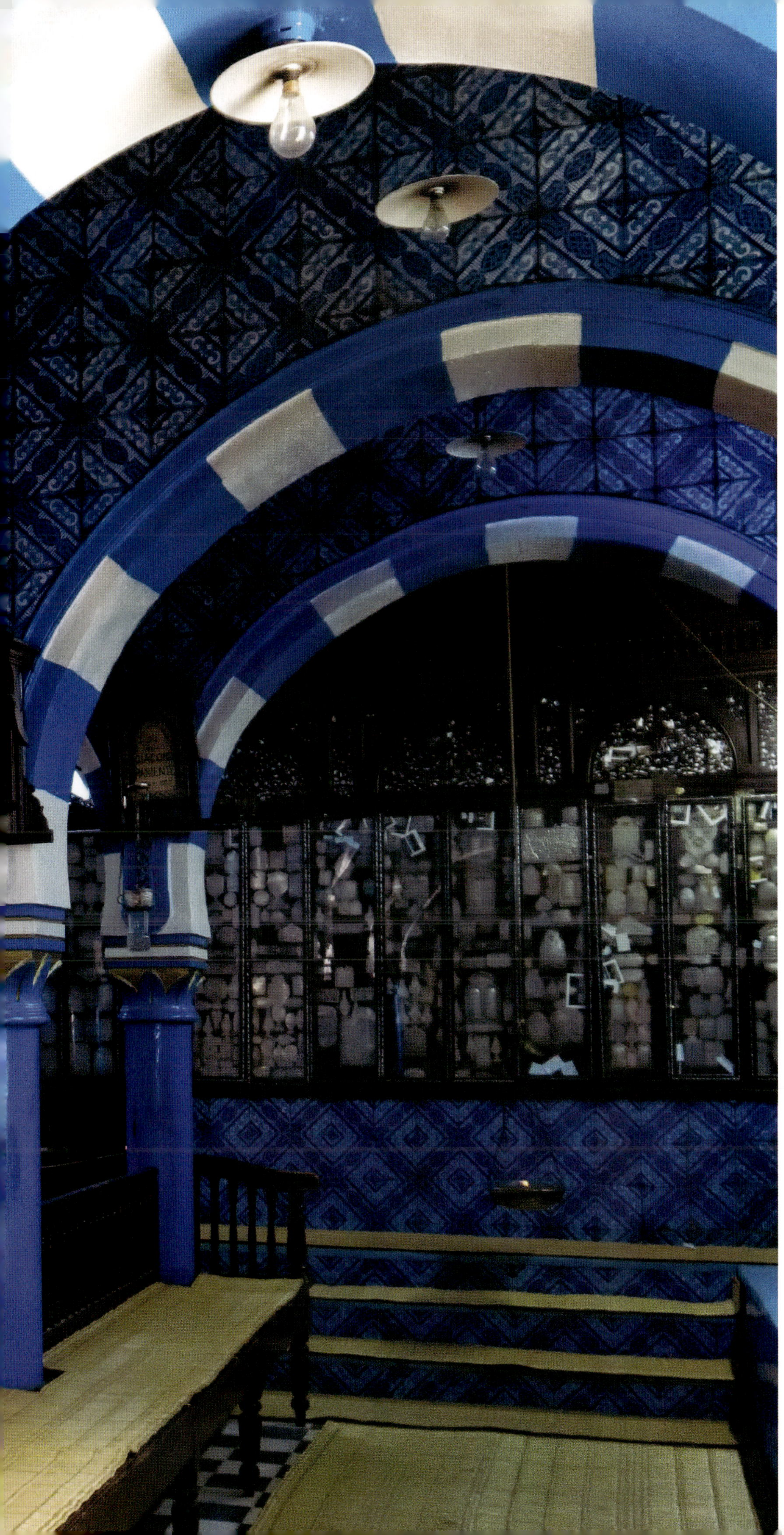

LEFT AND OVERLEAF:

El Ghriba Synagogue, Djerba, Tunisia

An island off Tunisia's coast, Djerba has, since ancient times, been home to a community of over a thousand Jews. Whilst their synagogue dates back only to the end of the nineteenth century, popular opinion is that it's supposed to have been built around fragments recovered from the ruins of the Temple in Jerusalem.

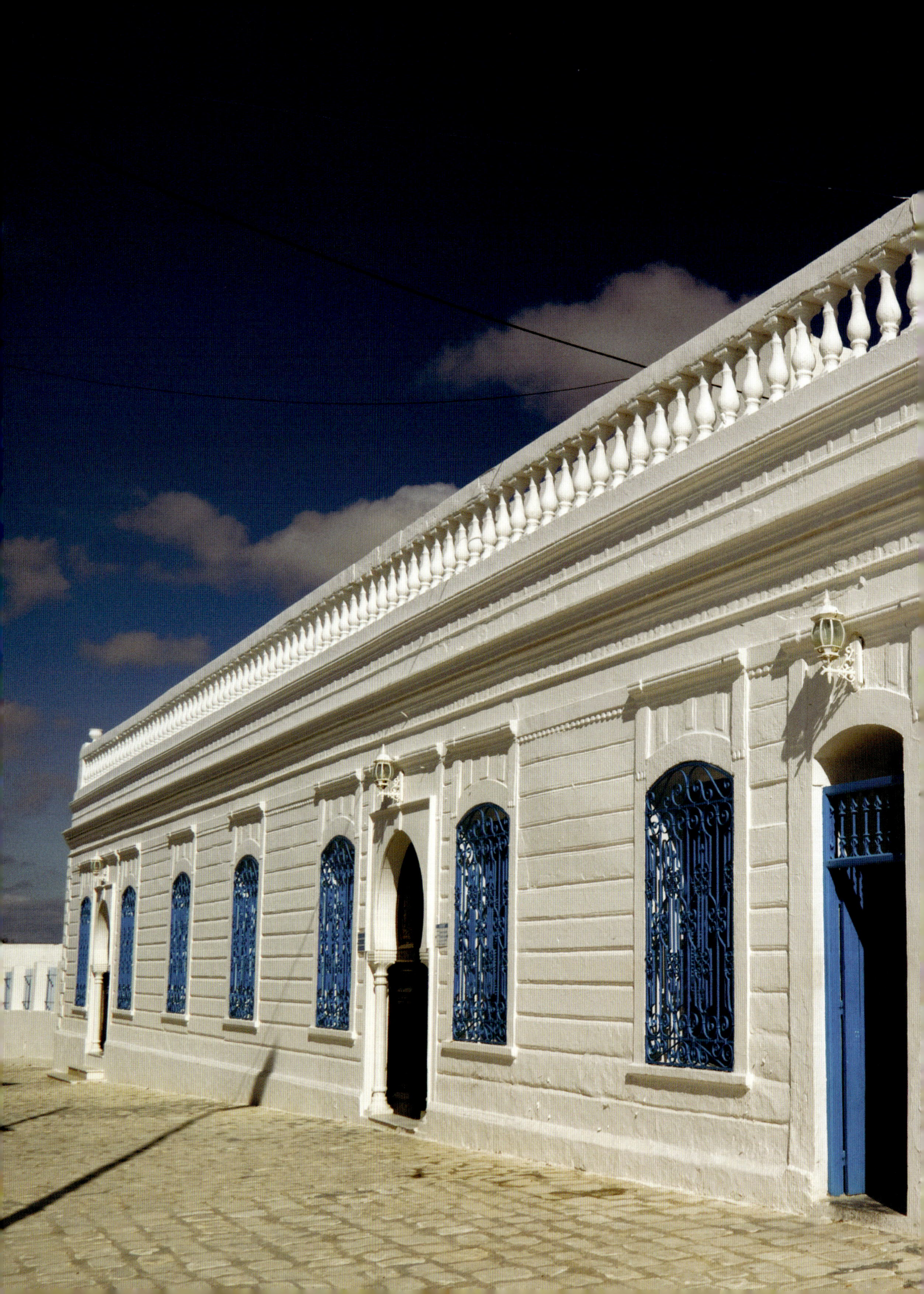

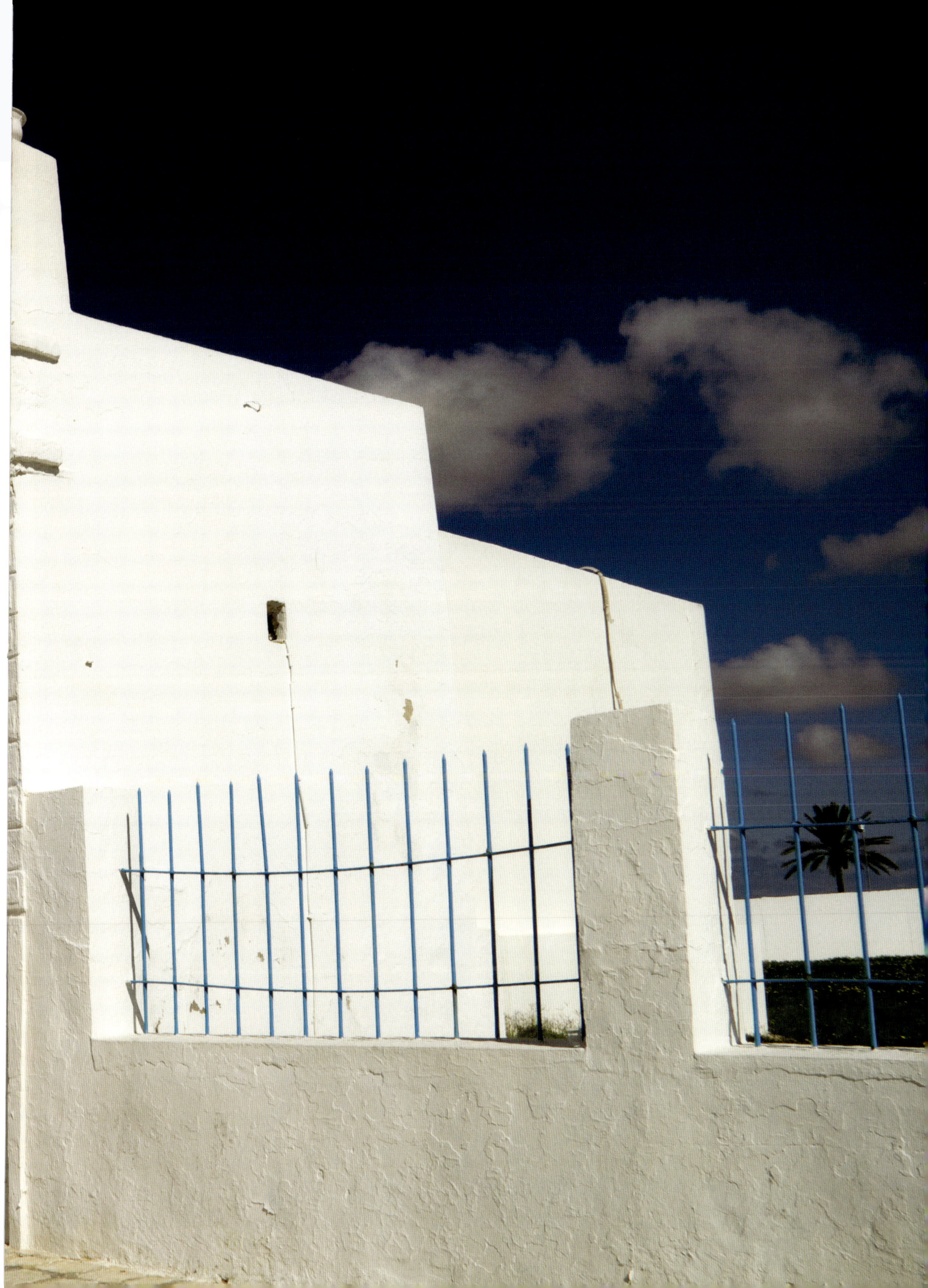

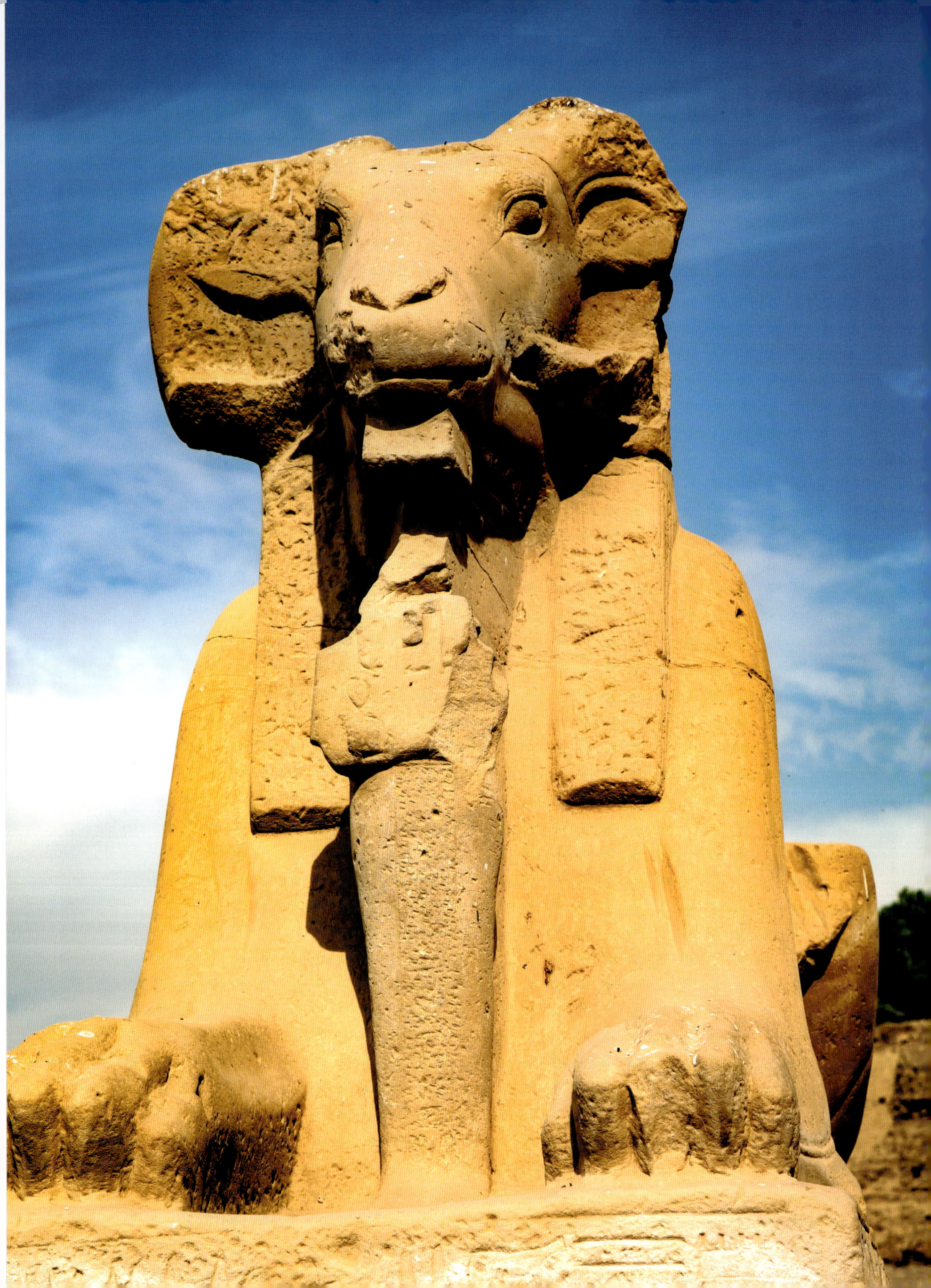

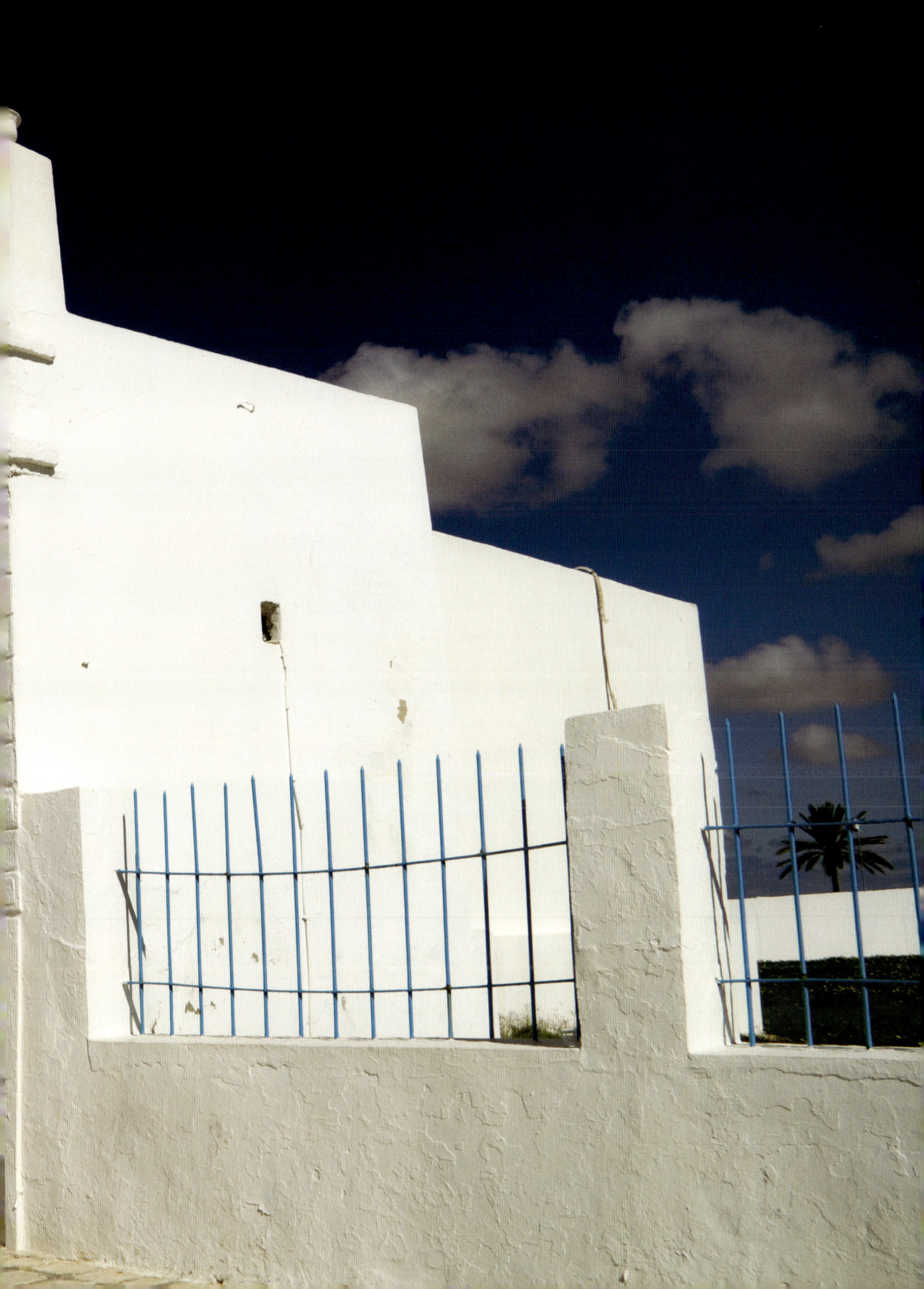

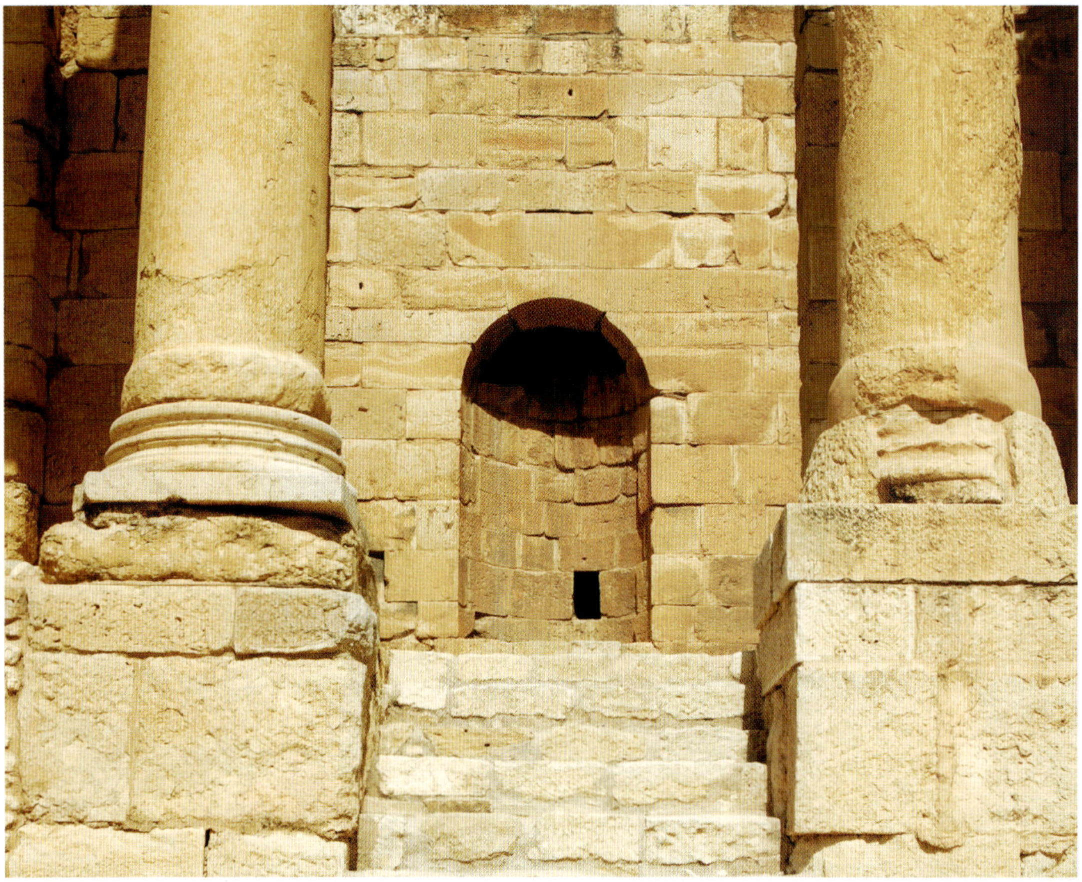

ALL PHOTOGRAPHS:

Three temples, Sbeitla, Tunisia

Sufetula, the Romans called it. Now three temples, dedicated to Minerva, Jupiter and Juno (*left to right, below*), have pride of place beside a beautifully-preserved forum or public square. Jupiter, god of the heavens, was married to Juno, goddess of marriage; their daughter, Minerva, represented wisdom, and skill in arts and crafts. Typically, this 'holy family' would have been represented by a single shrine. This arrangement placed a clearer spotlight on the female deities. A close-up view of Minerva's temple (*left and opposite*) shows the kind of care and skill that were lavished upon these buildings, in tribute to the deities – and the community's civic pride.

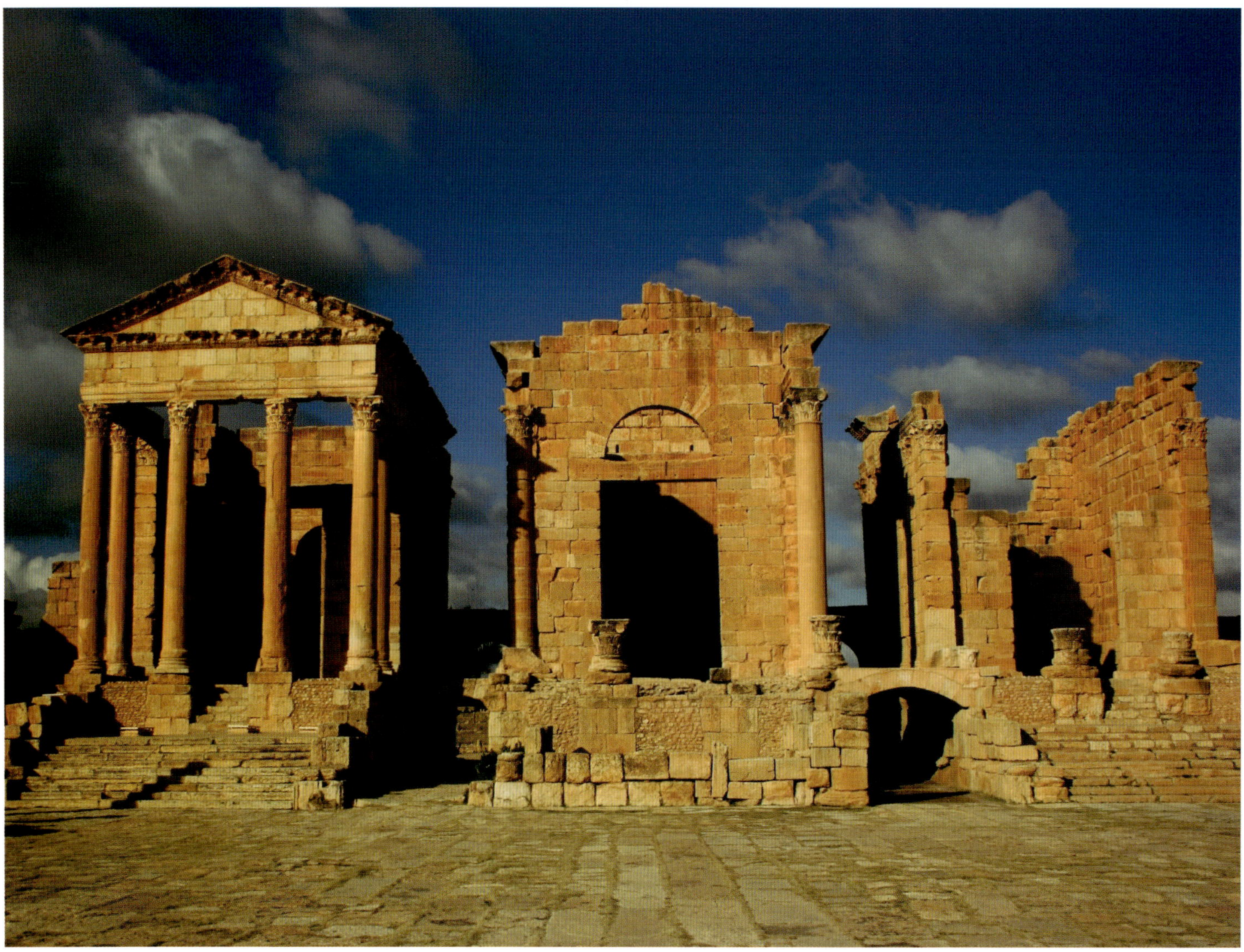

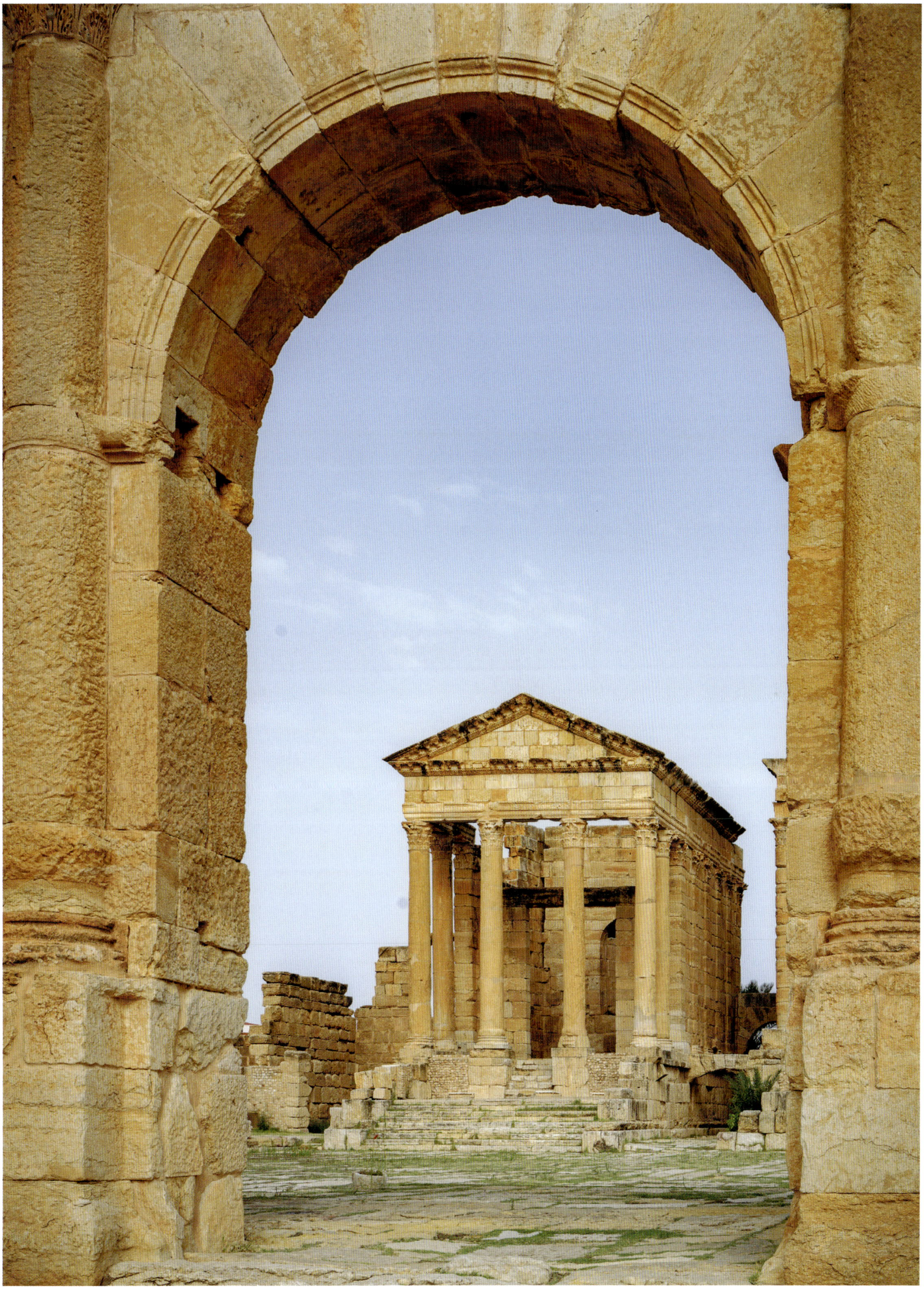

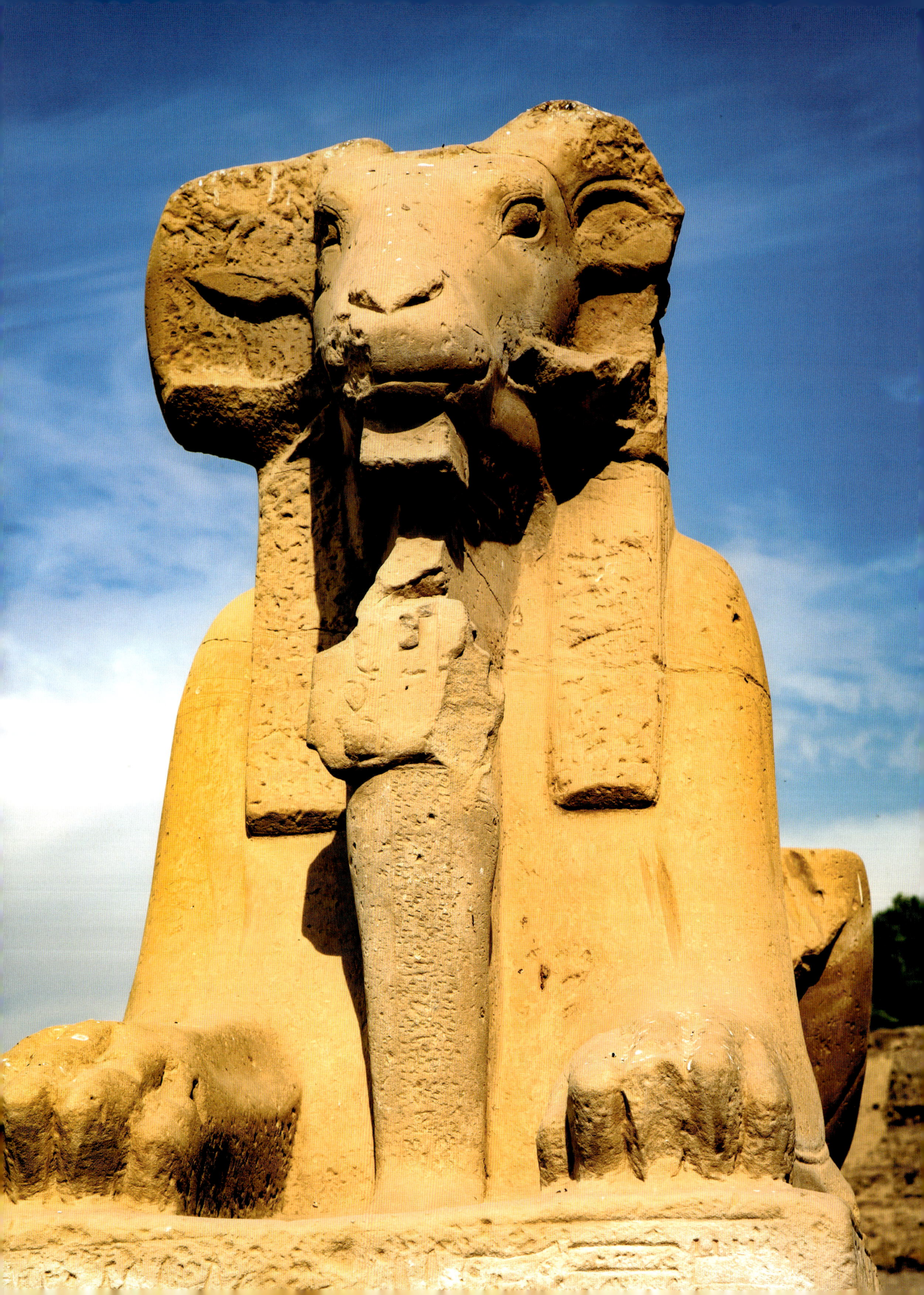

OPPOSITE:

Sphinx statue, Karnak, Luxor, Egypt

An important sacred complex on the Upper Nile, believed to have had its heyday during the New Kingdom (sixteenth–eleventh centuries BCE), Karnak belongs to the ancient city of Thebes and is rich in ruined temples. Among the deities worshipped here were Amun-Re (the sun-god), his wife the mother-goddess Mut and their son Montu. Conventionally, the sphinx has the body of a lion, with an eagle's wings. Its head (like that of the Giza Sphinx) is human.

RIGHT:

Great Hypostyle Hall, Karnak, Luxor, Egypt

Ramses II (c. 1303–1213 BCE) plucks the fruit of knowledge from the tree of life in this relief. The 'Hypostyle Hall' is so-called because its roof is held up by columns.

BELOW:

Great Temple of Hatshepsut, Karnak, Luxor, Egypt

Hatshepsut (1507–1458 BCE) was the most famous of several female pharaohs, reigning for over 20 years. She commissioned extensive restoration work on several buildings at the Karnak complex, but also had this temple specially constructed as an enduring monument to her reign.

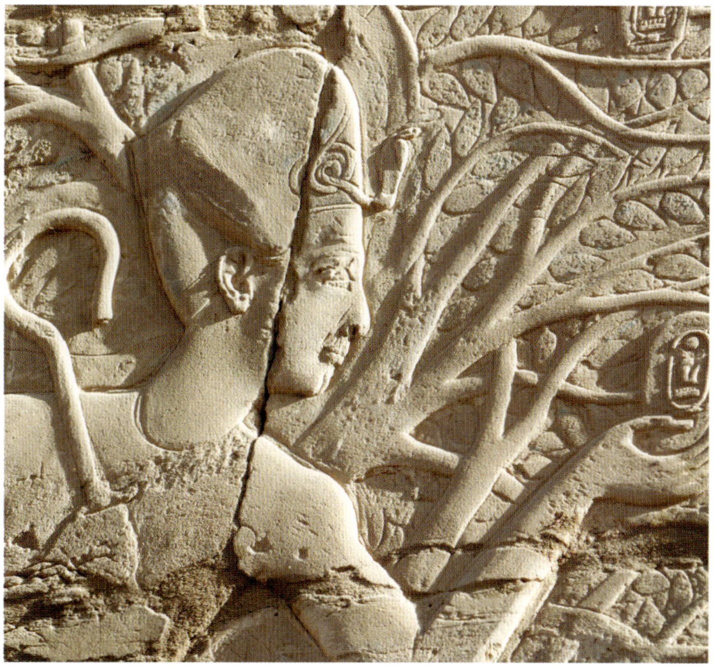

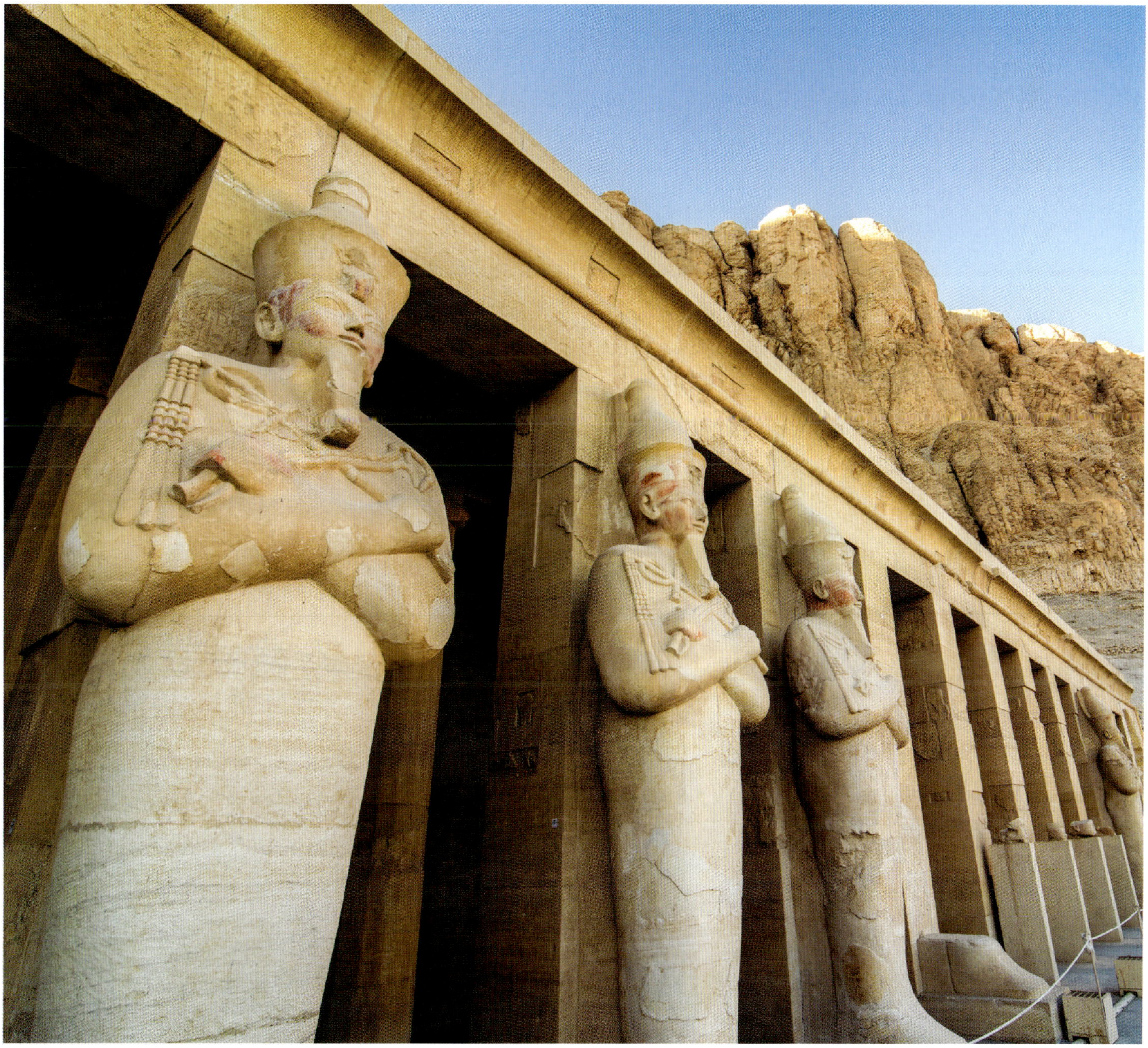

RIGHT:

Hathor Temple, Dendera, Egypt

Just downriver from Karnak on the Upper Nile, the temple complex at Dendera was the headquarters of the cult of Hathor, an Egyptian sky goddess and feminine counterpart to the sun god Ra. Her temple boasts a basement crypt, but it also has a great many ingeniously concealed chambers and passages within its walls, enhancing the air of mystery that imbues the site.

OVERLEAF:

Mortuary Temple of Hatshepsut, Deir el-Bahari, Luxor, Egypt

The Egyptians had a 'death cult' precisely because they believed the departed didn't leave forever but were liable to return to look after (and to judge) their mortal descendants. Hence their elaborate embalming rituals; the pyramids of the Old Kingdom and the colossal tombs built during the New Kingdom. Hatshepsut was not actually interred in her mortuary temple but in the Valley of Kings, not far away.

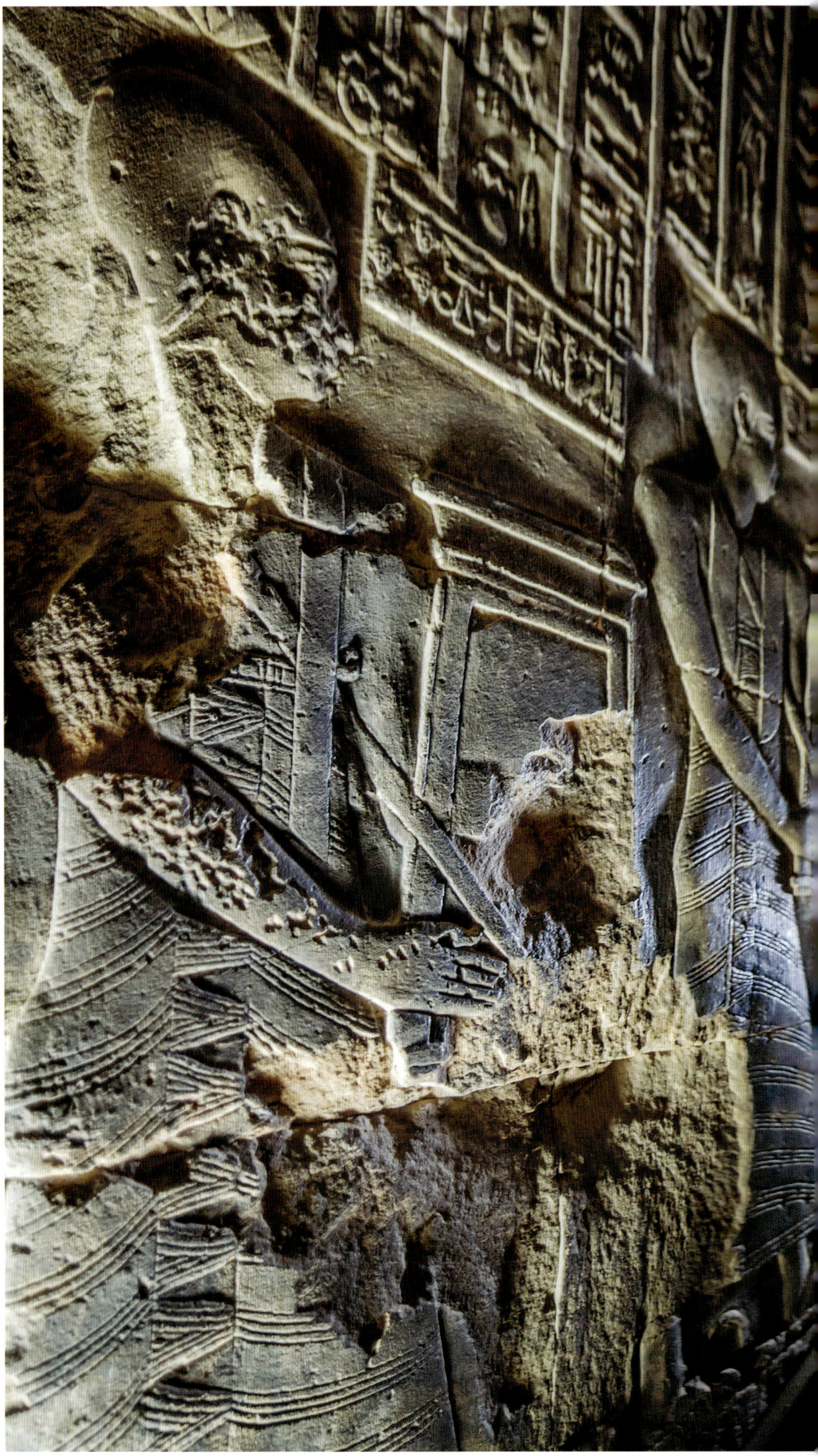

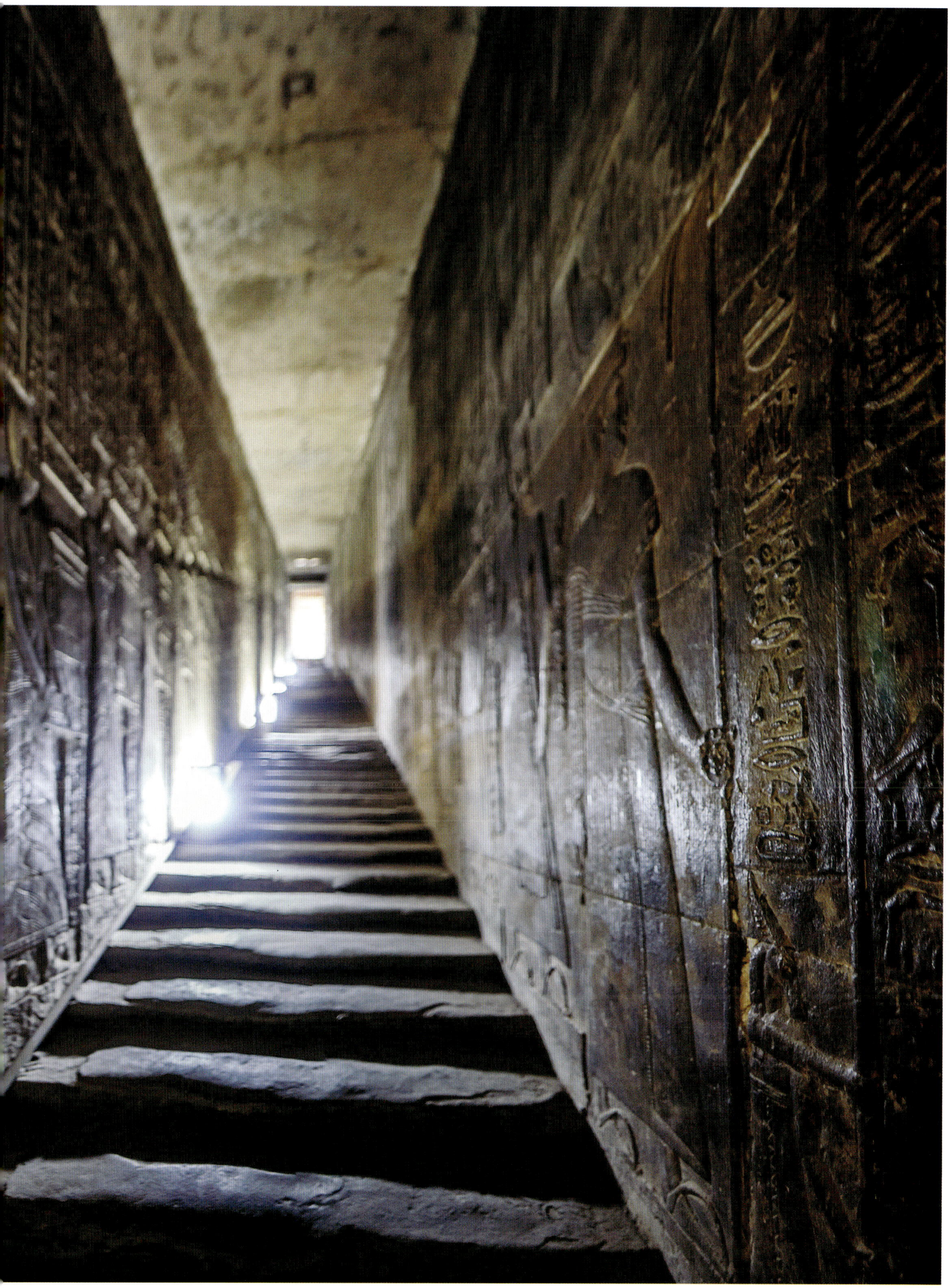

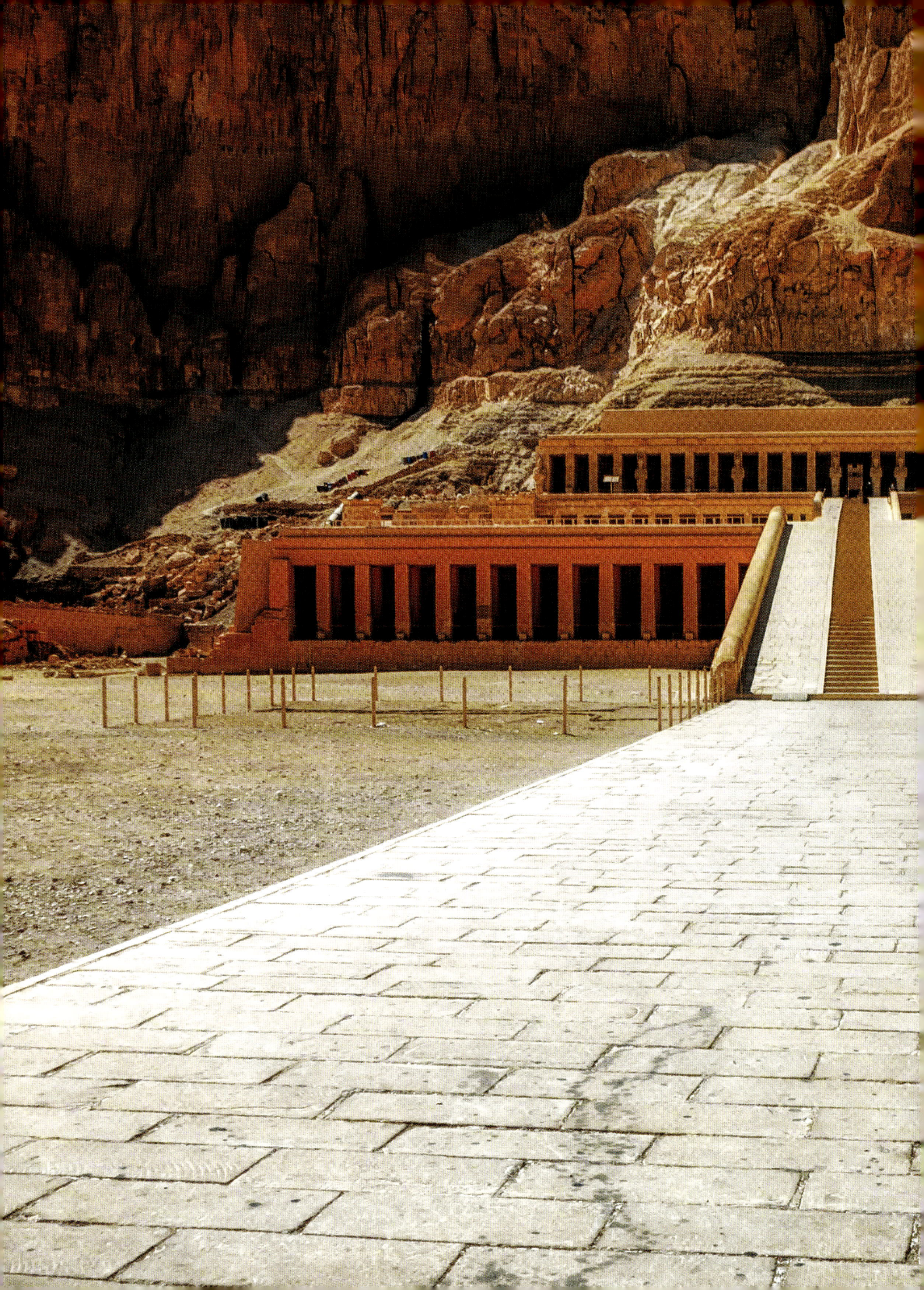

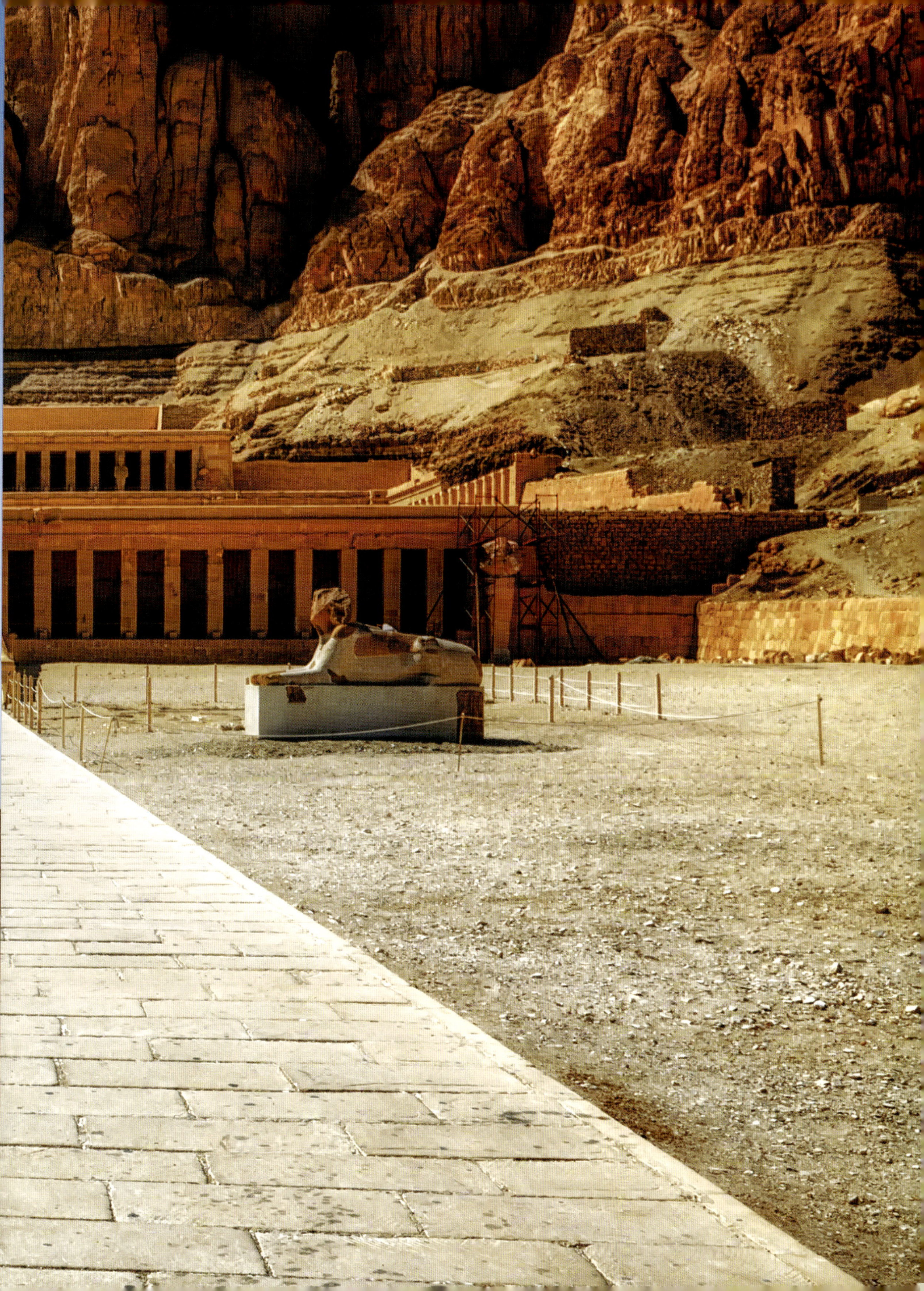

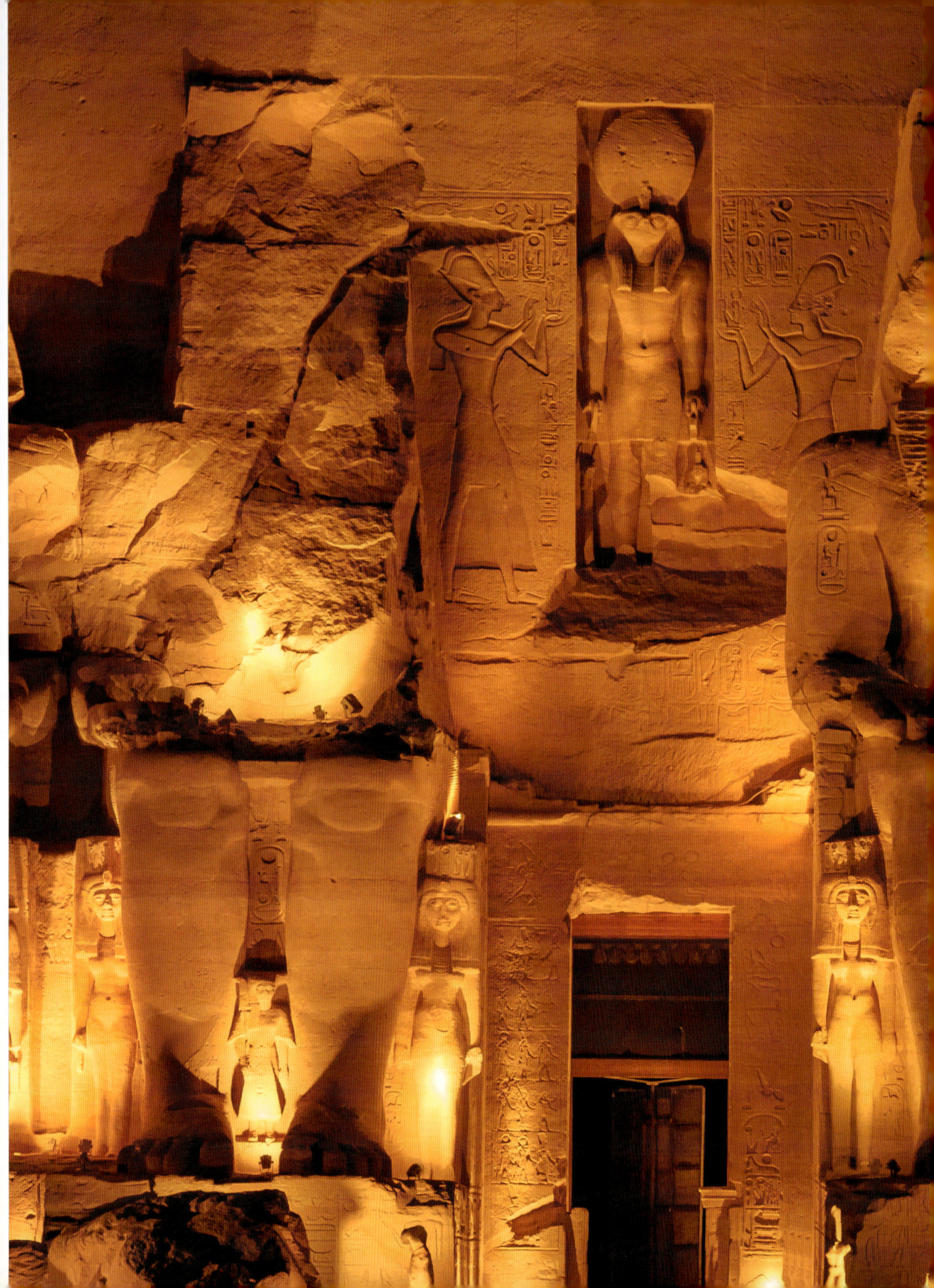

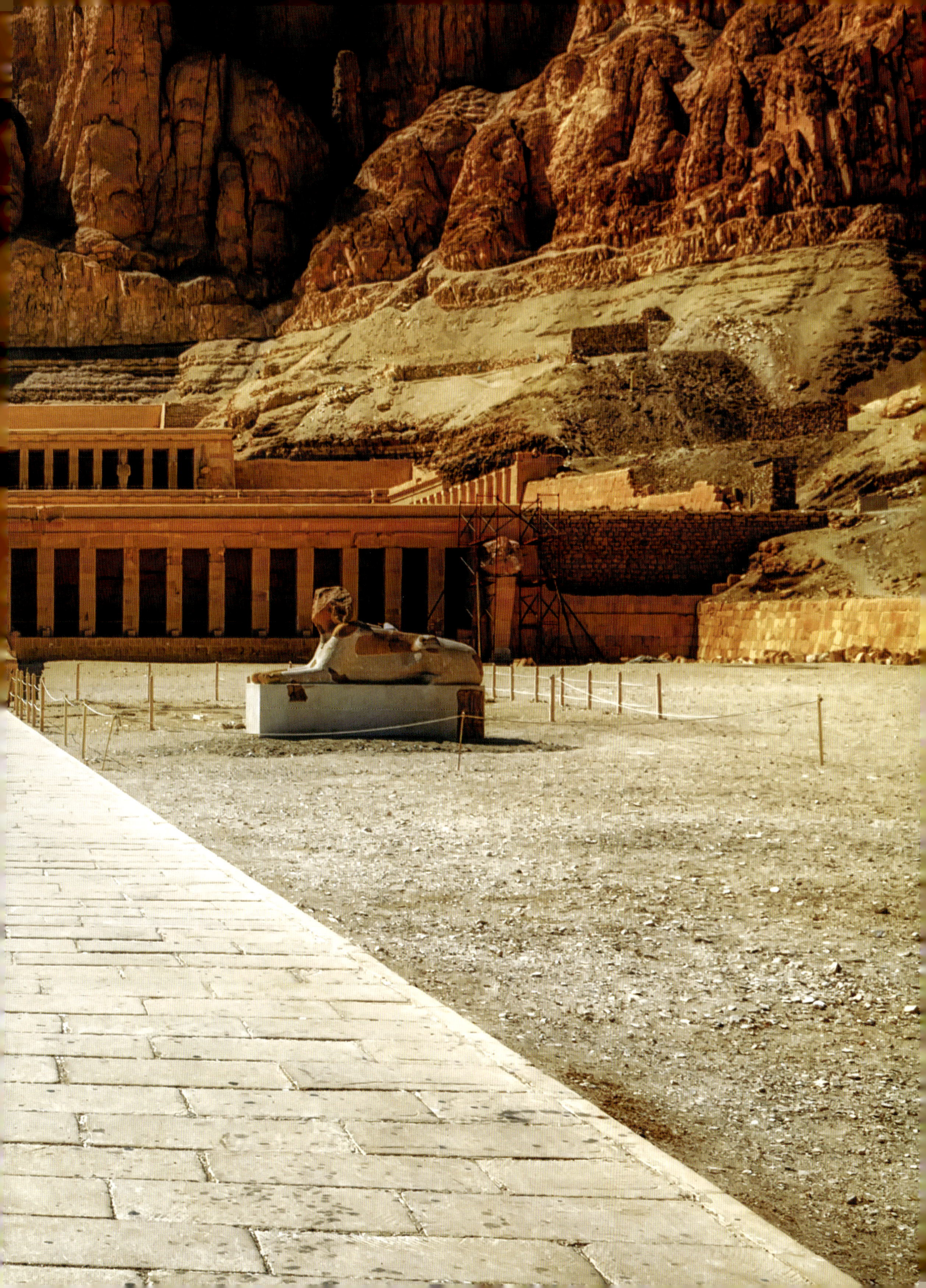

Statue of Ramses II, Luxor Temple, Thebes, Egypt
The spectacular scale of the 'Ramesseum' reminds us that the Egyptian Pharaoh was regarded as not just a ruler, but a god. Ramses II (c. 1303–1213 BCE) was a great military leader, guiding his armies to a string of dazzling victories and bringing Egypt new territories both to the north (in modern Libya) and to the south, in Nubia, now Sudan. His mortuary temple is appropriately grandiose.

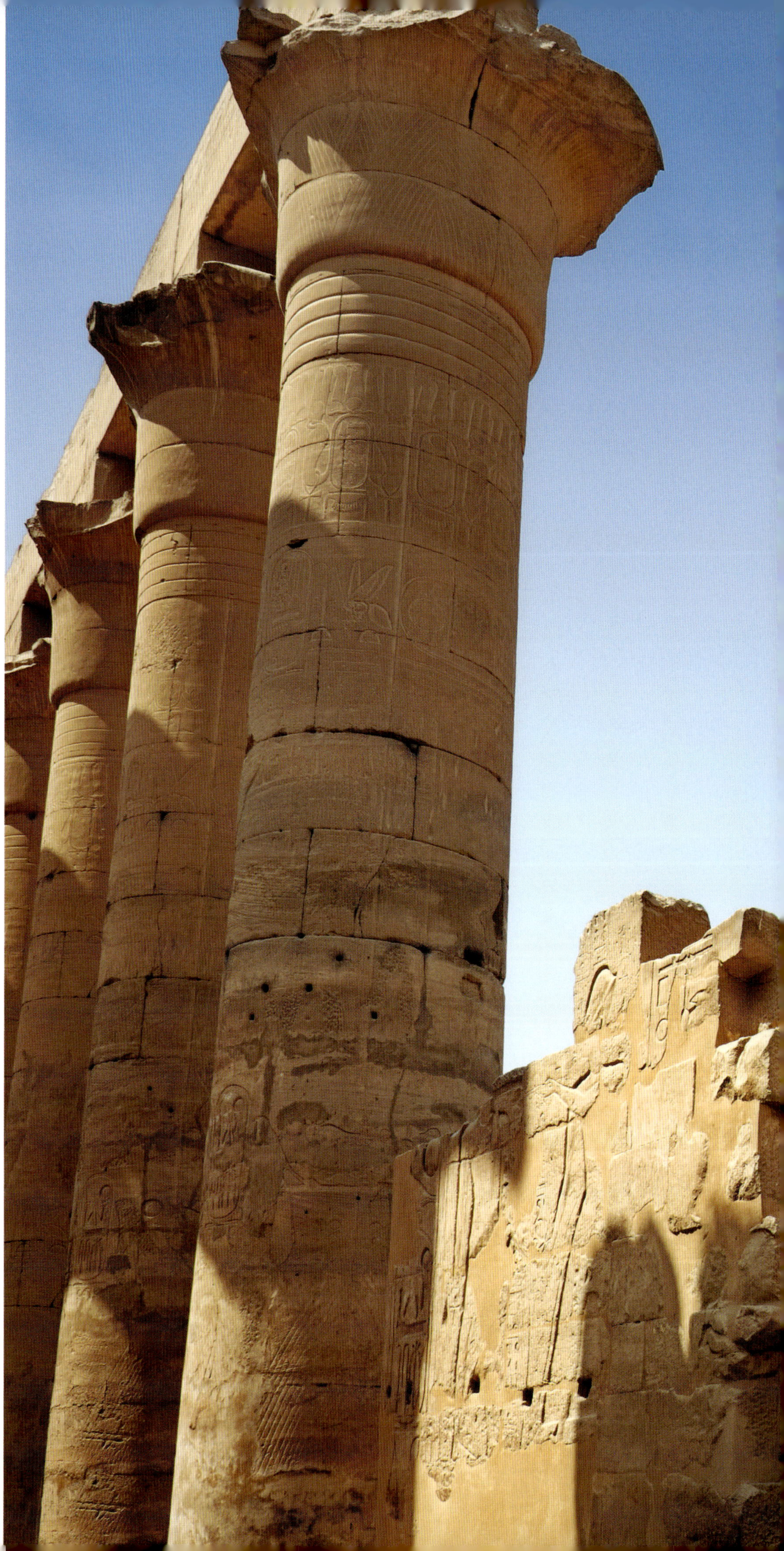

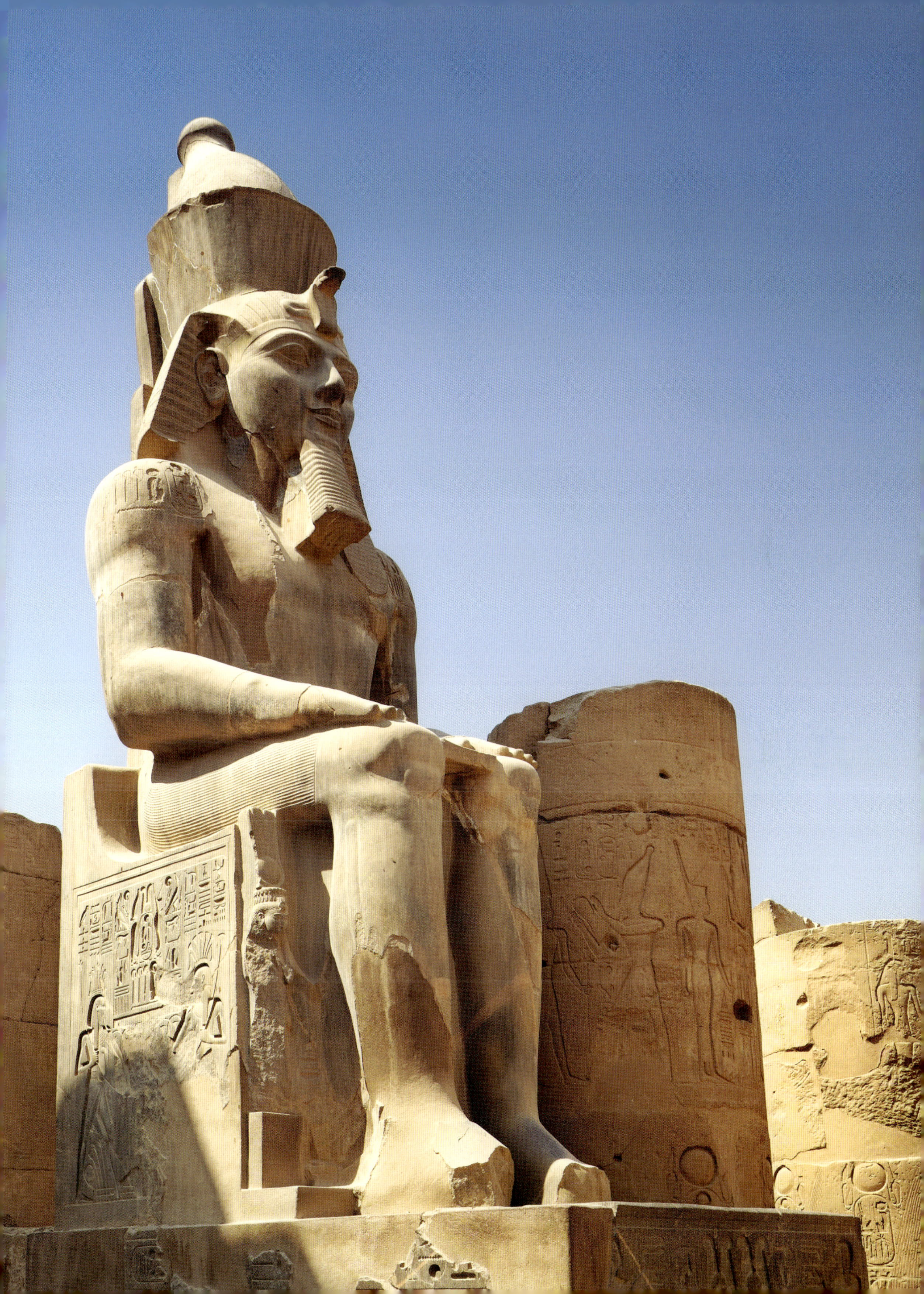

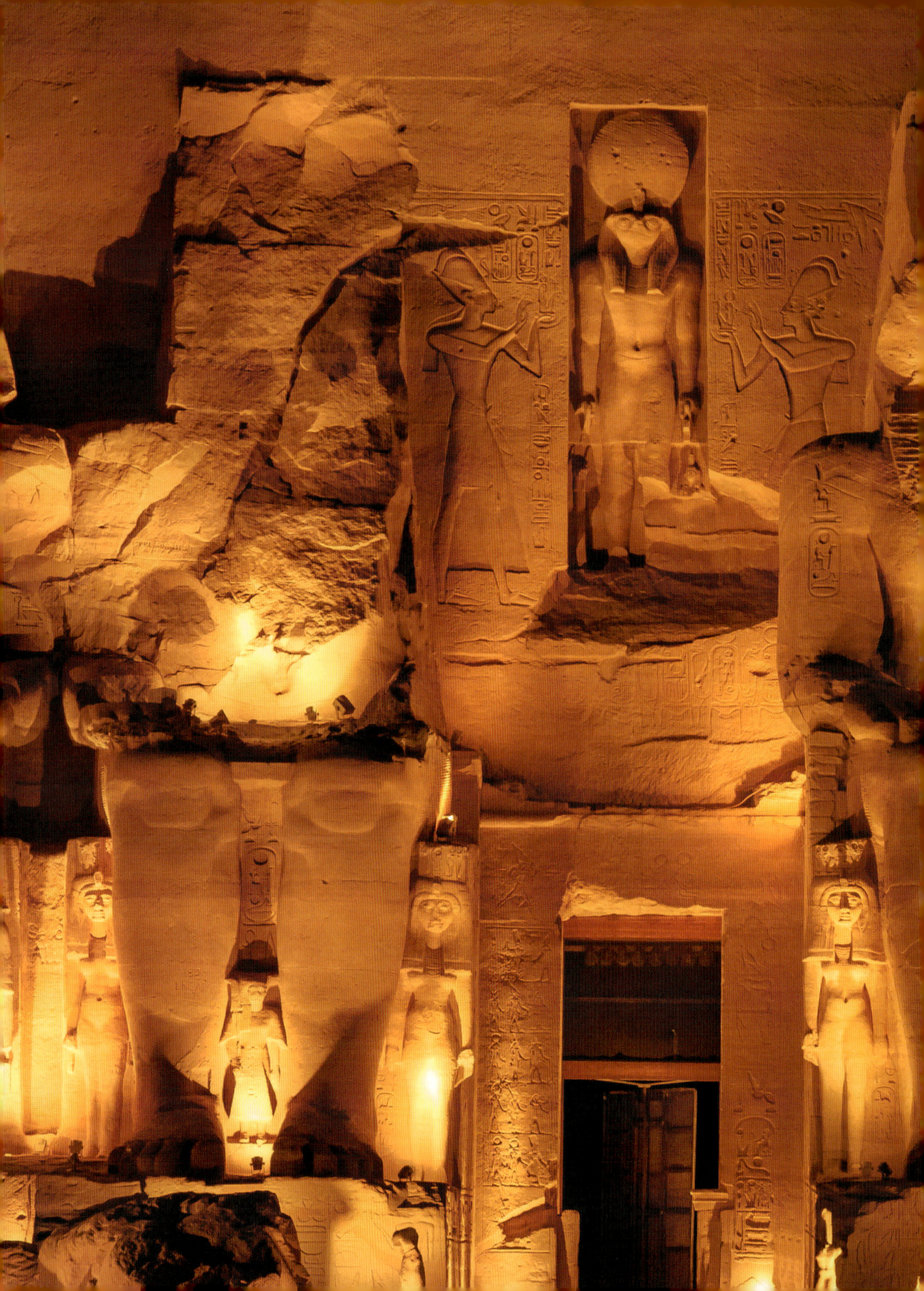

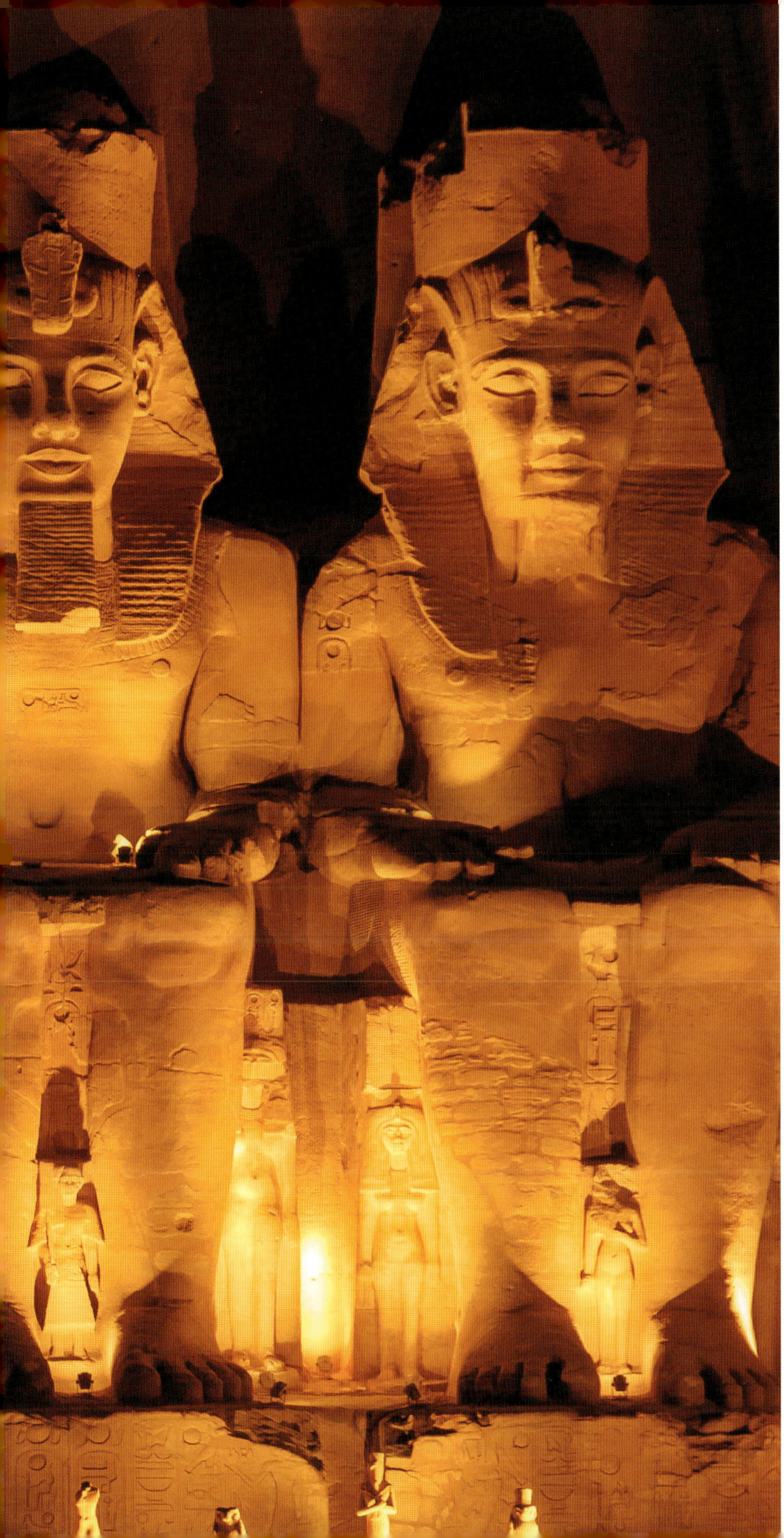

The Great Temple, Abu Simbel, Egypt
Far upriver, near the modern border between Egypt and Sudan, the Abu Simbel temples were built during the reign of Ramses II to commemorate his victory over the Hittites at Kadesh (1274 BCE). The entire complex was moved in 1968 to ensure its safety above the rising waters after the construction of the nearby Aswan Dam.

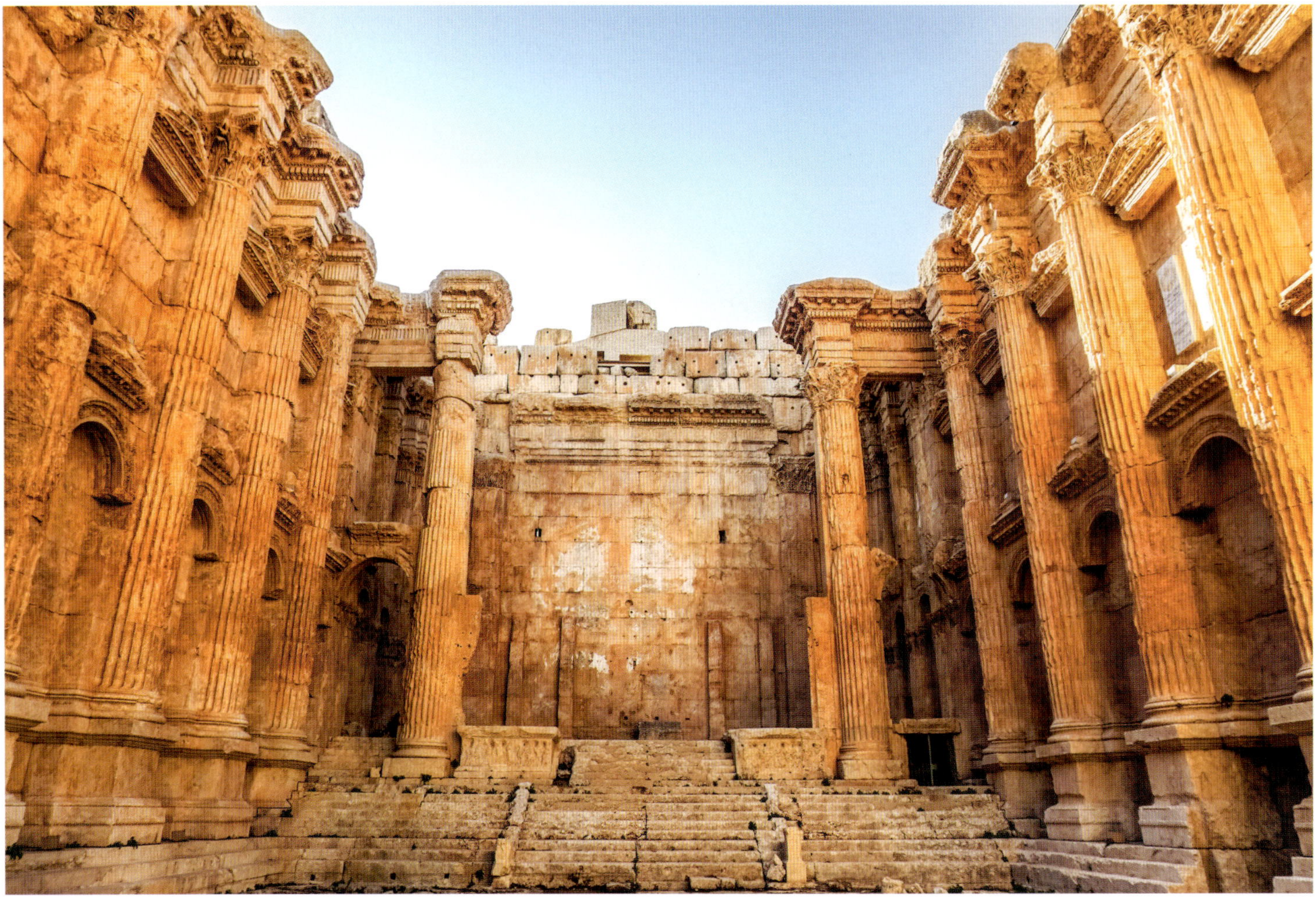

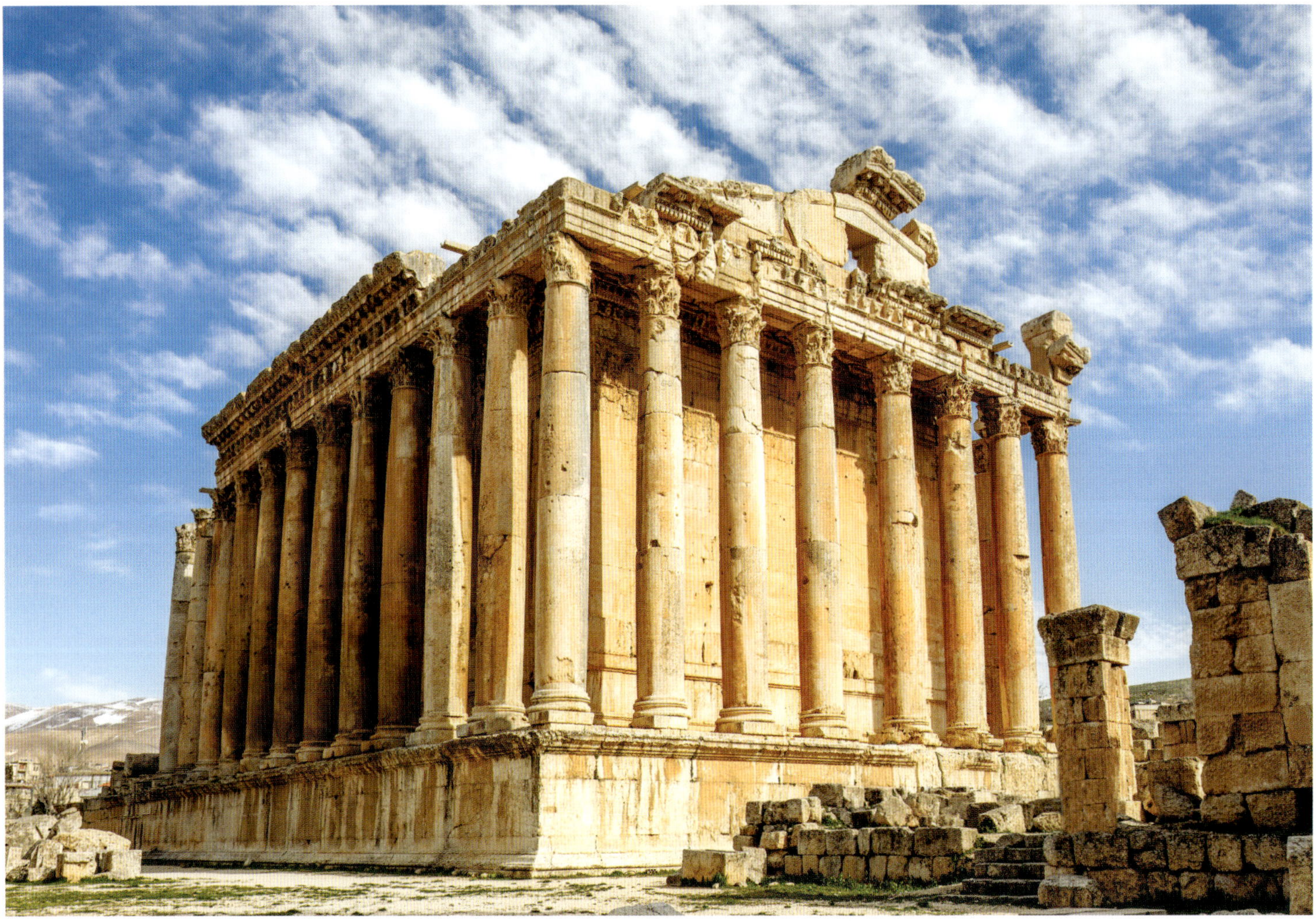

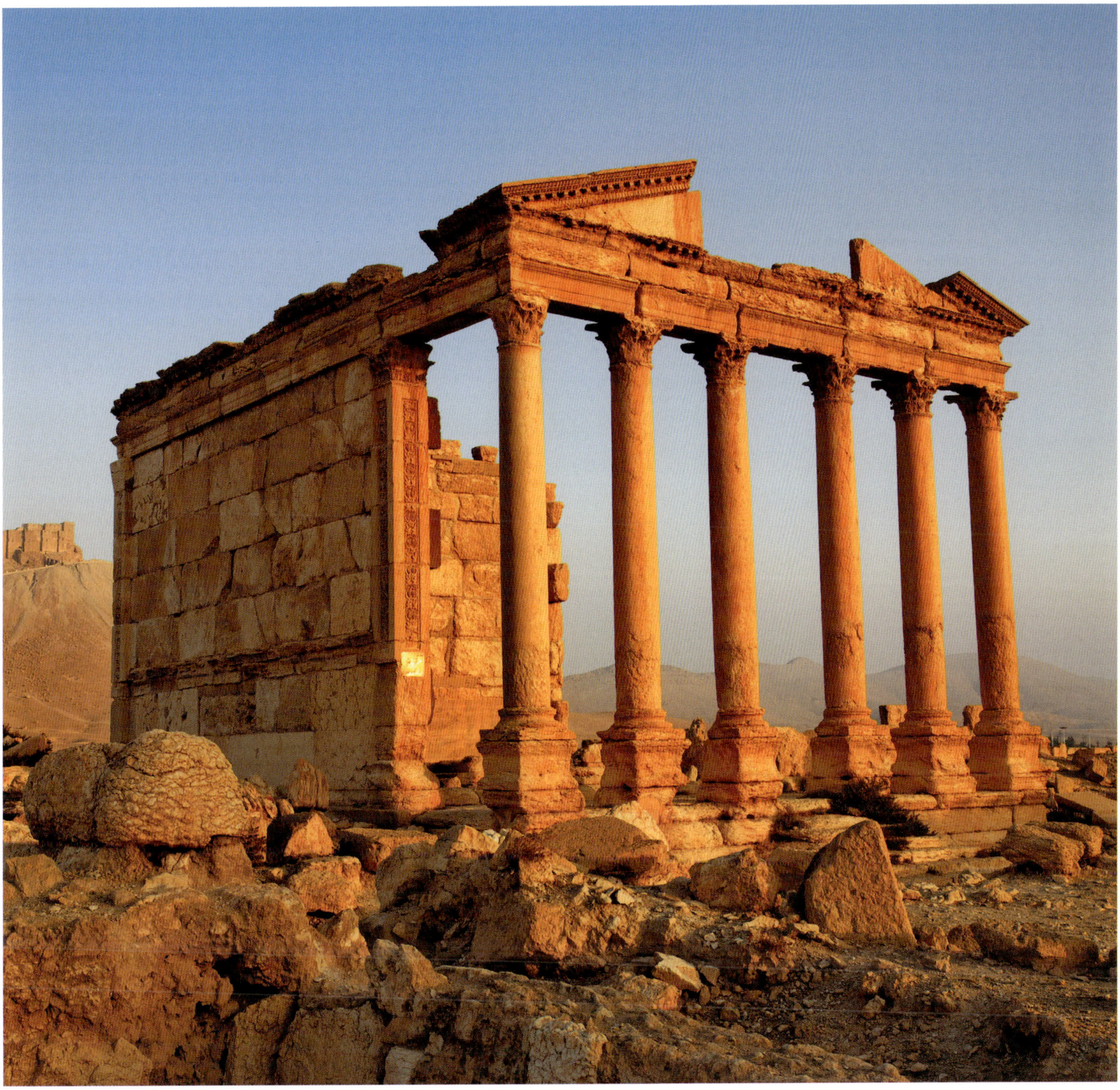

OPPOSITE (BOTH PHOTOGRAPHS):
Temple of Bacchus, Baalbek, Lebanon
Bacchus was the Roman god of wine, fertility and fun. His temple here was built around the middle of the second century CE. The Bekaa Valley was hotly contested in the Lebanese Civil War of 1975–90 and an already ruined temple was further damaged, but extensive restoration work has been done since.

ABOVE:
Funerary Temple, Palmyra, Syria
Palmyra had been sacred to a range of Semitic deities long before the Hellenistic Greeks and then the Romans got here. This structure – the unromantically entitled 'Funerary Temple no. 86' – dates from the third century CE, so towards the end of the Roman era. It stands above a staircase leading down into a crypt in which the bodies of local rulers were laid to rest.

OVERLEAF:
Ziggurat of Ur, Iraq
Ur, near Nasiriyah, on the Euphrates is believed to have been one of the world's very oldest cities. By tradition, it was the birthplace of the biblical patriarch, Abraham. This great monumental temple, terraced in its construction, was built in mud-brick in the twenty-first century BCE, by King Ur-Nammu, then restored by the neo-Babylonian King Nabonidus in the sixth century BCE.

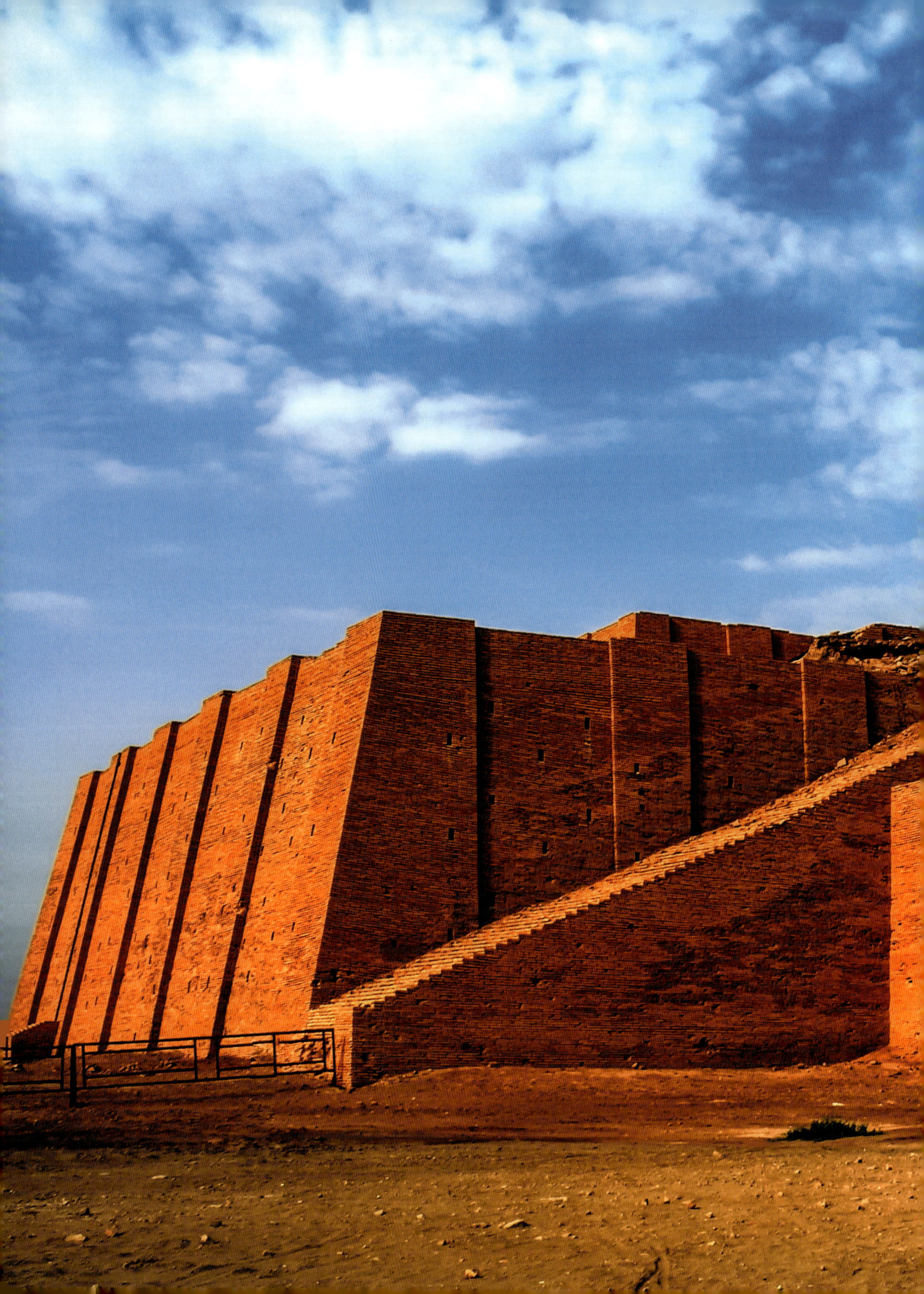

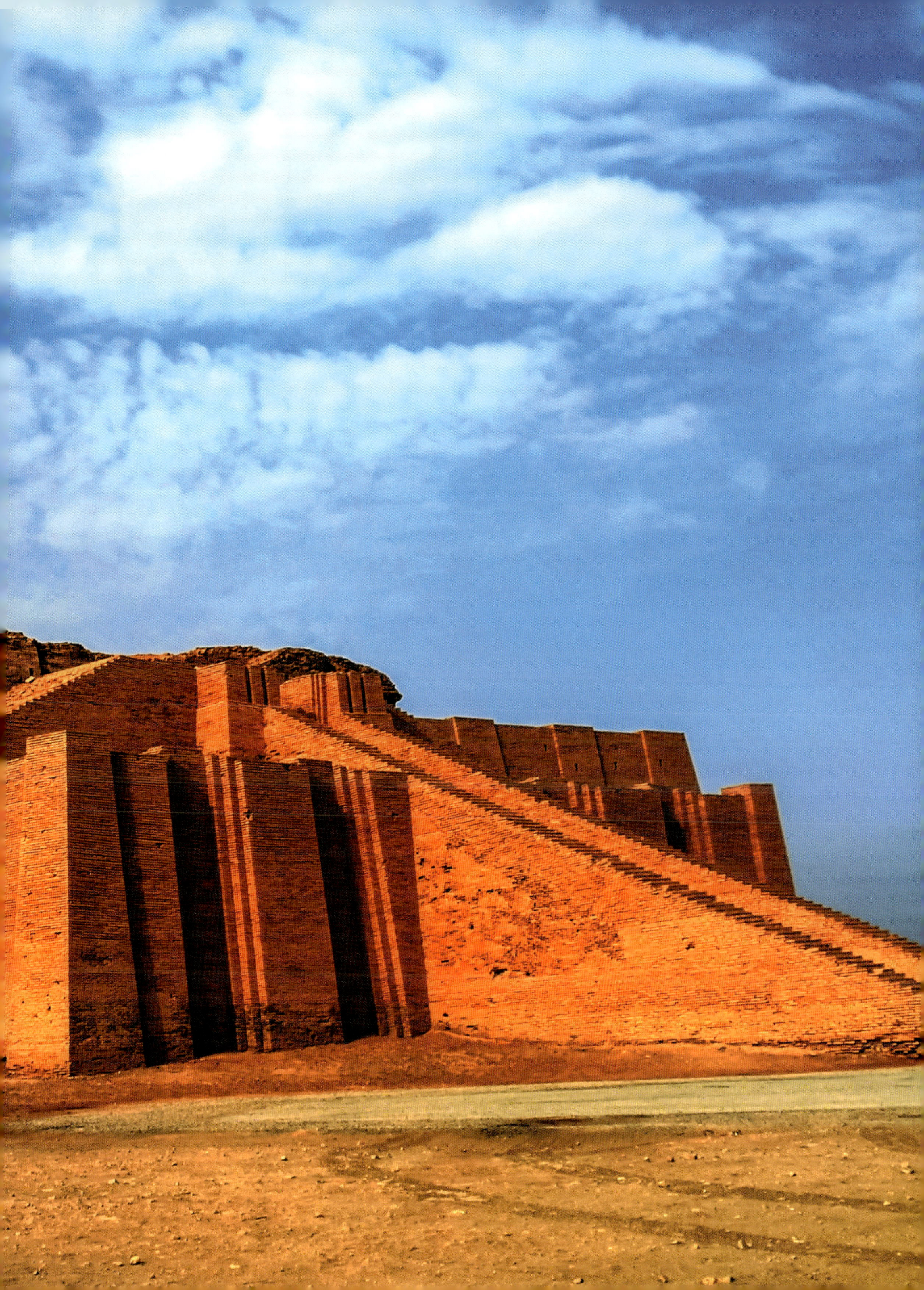

RIGHT:

Eternal Fire, Fire Temple of Yazd, Iran

A millennium and a half and counting … If not literally 'eternal', this flame has been burning constantly since it was first lit in 470 CE. For Zoroastrians, fire is the ultimate emblem of light and life; this temple is Zoroastrianism's ultimate shrine. Its importance was underlined at the time of the Arab invasions of the seventh century when the mountains opened up to shelter and protect the local ruler, Princess Nikbanou.

BELOW:

Dome, Fire Temple of Yazd, Iran

Roofing over the eternal fire, the *gumbad* ('dome') doesn't just look beautiful: it makes the whole temple into a stylized version of the oven in which bread – the stuff of life – is baked.

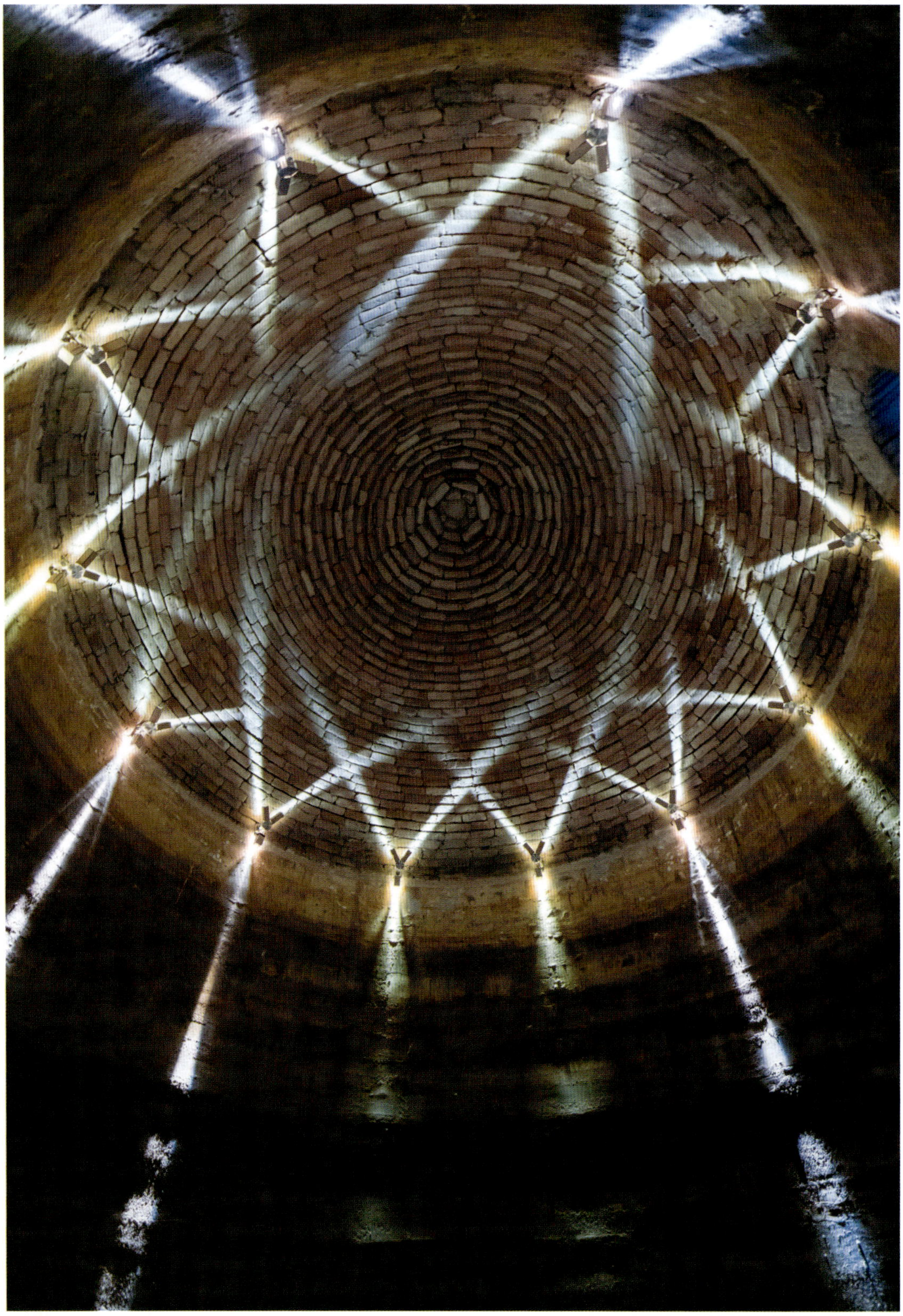

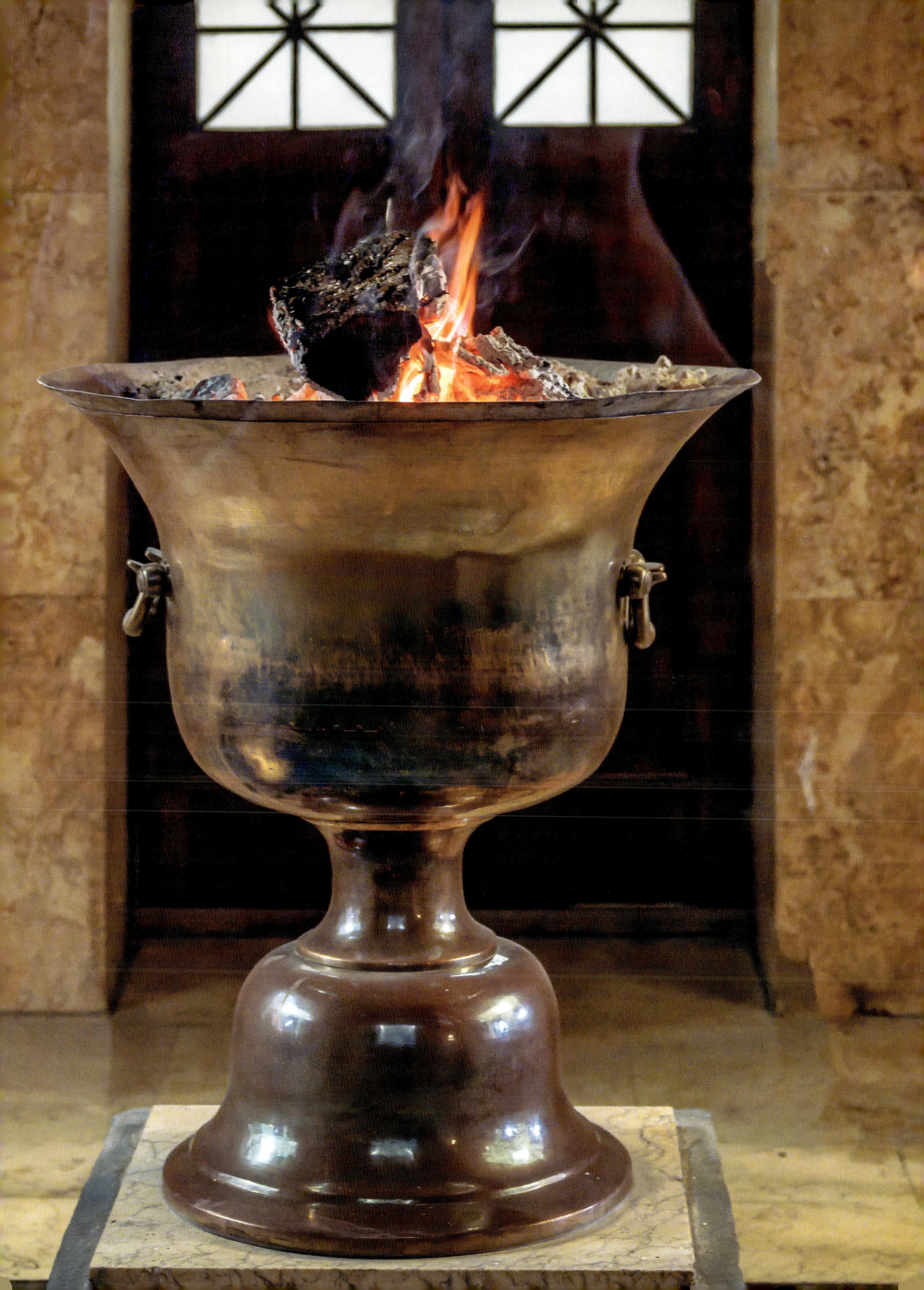

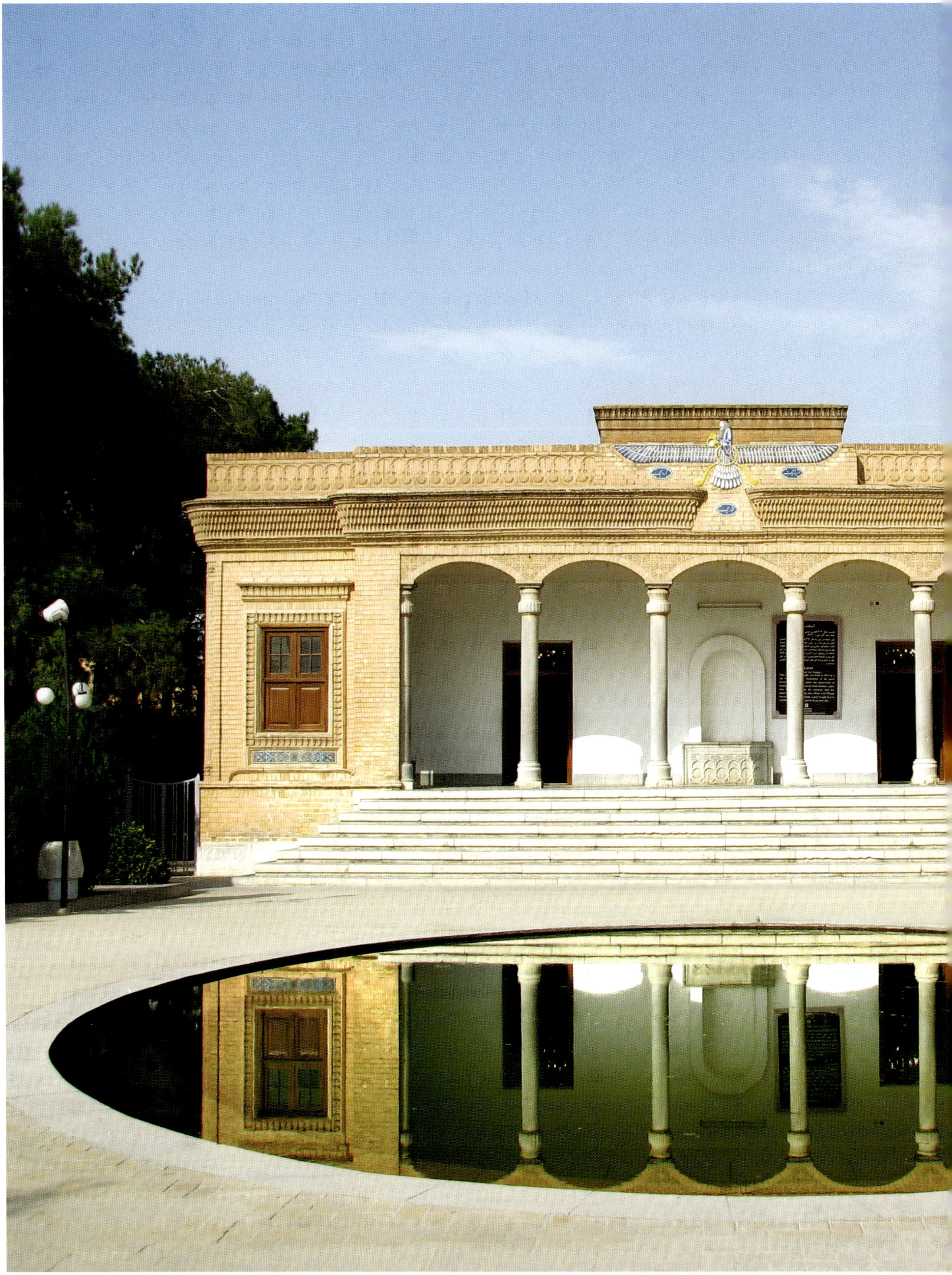

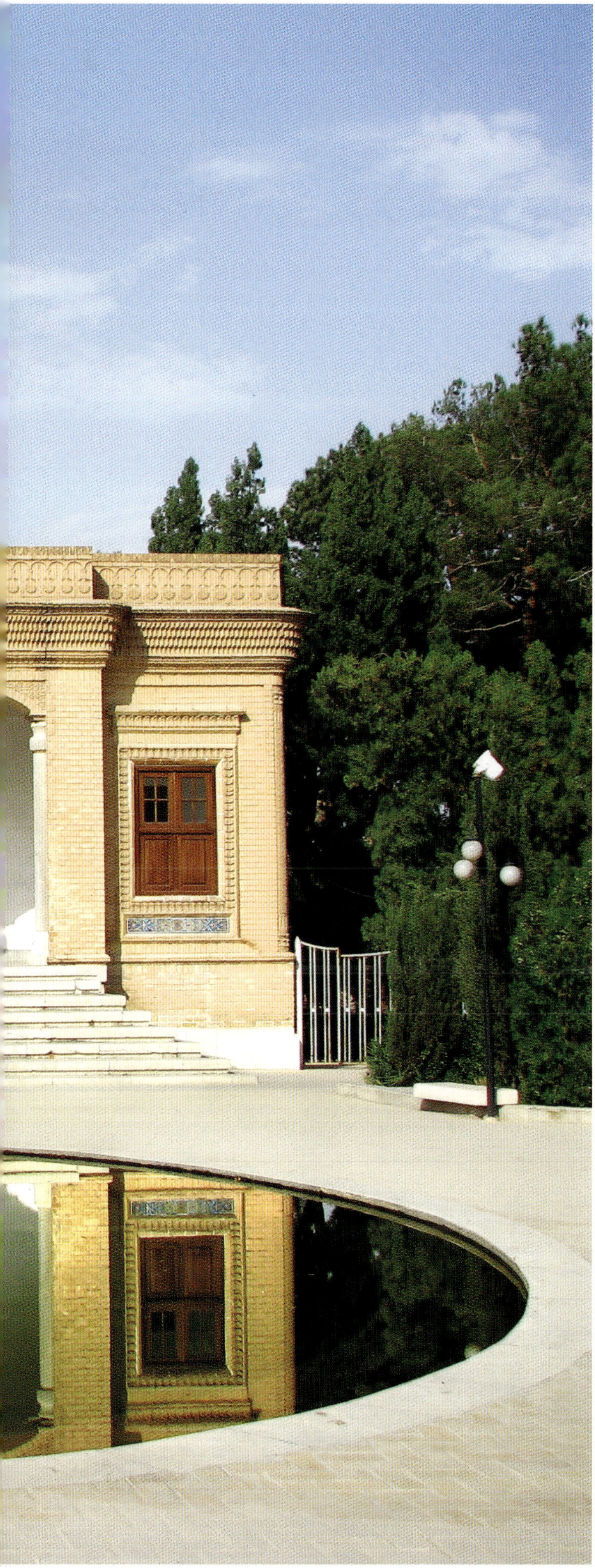

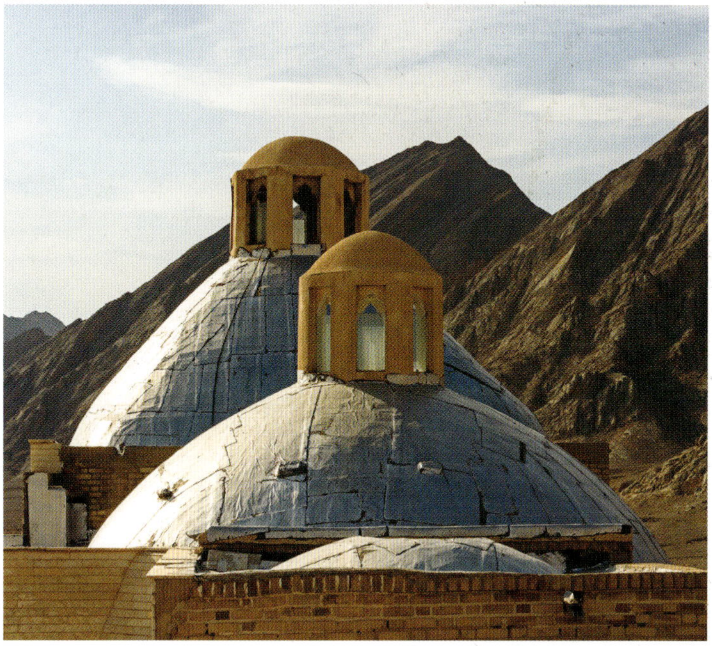

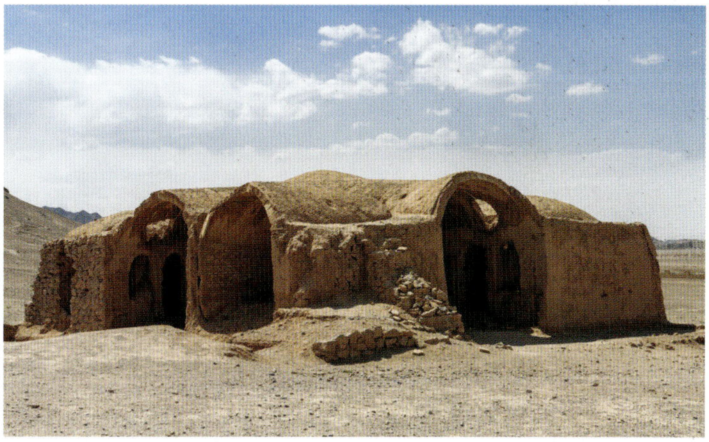

LEFT:
Fire Temple of Yazd, Iran
As much as they prize fire, the Zoroastrians recognize that it has its place in a universal cosmos with three other basic elements: the earth, the air and water. Hence the presence, before this stone-built shrine, beneath a vast and empty sky, of a beautifully laid-out pool of limpid water. Though seen in the modern western view as antithetical to fire, water was in this scheme a balancing force, the second most important element.

ABOVE TOP:
Zarjow Fire Temple, Yazd, Iran
The main fire temple in Yazd is relatively modern, and clearly classical in inspiration. Older examples are more rough-and-ready, but still impressive. Persia's Zoroastrians pioneered the use of the dome, long before the Muslim Arabs had discovered its possibilities.

ABOVE BOTTOM:
Dakhmeh Towers of Silence, Yazd, Iran
By Zoroastrian tradition, the dead were not to be buried in the earth but exposed to the air – and the attentions of scavenging birds. Special temples, 'towers of silence', were built for just this purpose. Cadavers were placed carefully on the flattened roof.

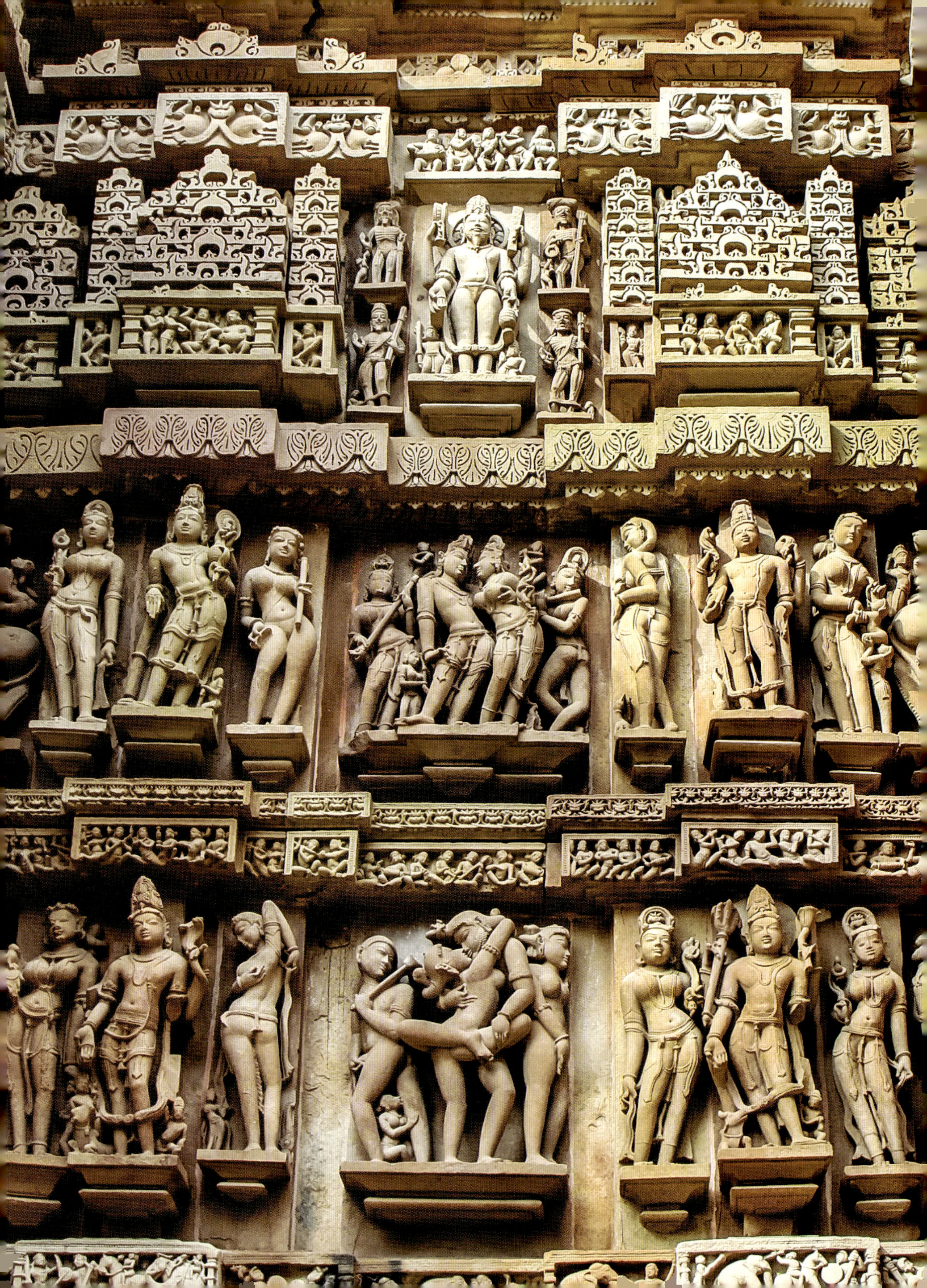

Asia

Hinduism, Buddhism, Sikhism, Judaism, Christianity, Islam, Jainism, Bahá'i, Confucianism, Taoism ... It's hard to think of a major religion that doesn't have its roots in Asia, however widely it may be practiced in modern times. That heritage has made its mark in Asia in the shape of some of the world's most spectacular religious monuments; and some of its most extravagantly interesting historic shrines.

Spiritual leaders of all faiths have been eager to stress that the true temple is in the believer's soul, but the need for some sort of physical structure has still been there. A home for ritual observance, for individual contemplation and collective worship, the temple is also an expression of pride in tradition and identity, an architectural emblem of belonging, rich in cultural (and, sometimes, political) associations.

Asia's religious traditions date back many thousands of years, during which time they've weathered enormous turbulence and change. Empires have risen and fallen within Asia itself while, more recently, the whole continent has had to deal with the impact of western colonialism, and of nationalist and communist revolution in the twentieth century. A book like this could never hope to do justice to the immense complexity of this heritage: we can, though, offer at least a taster of the wonderful variety of Asia's temples.

OPPOSITE:
Kandariya Mahadeva Temple, Madhya Pradesh, India
This big and beautiful Hindu temple was built in the eleventh century by rulers of the Chandela dynasty, who held sway over much of central India. Built from sandstone on a granite base, its walls are adorned with stunning statuary representing a range of divinities and mortal figures.

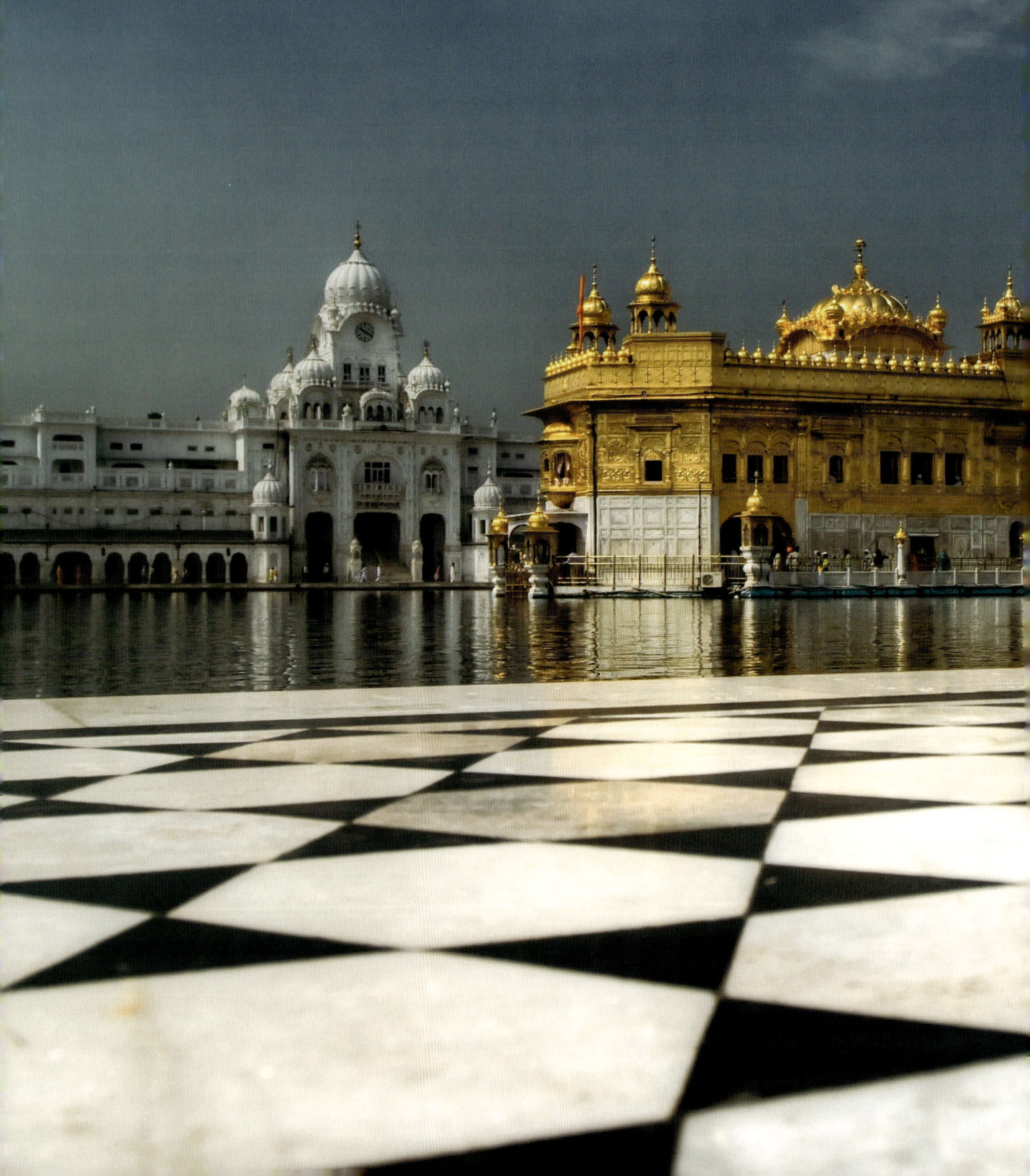

Harmandir Sahib (Golden Temple), Amritsar, India
Sikhism's most important shrine stands beside an artificial *sarovar* or sacred pool. Its main building is sumptuously gilded, hence its name. It was first constructed in the sixteenth century. The Muslim Mughals sacked it in the eighteenth century after the Sikhs set up their own independent confederacy with its centre at Amritsar. Though it was rebuilt afterwards, history repeated itself 300 years later. Indian government forces destroyed the temple again in 1984, after Sikh insurgents took refuge from the authorities here. Once again, it was rebuilt and lavishly restored.

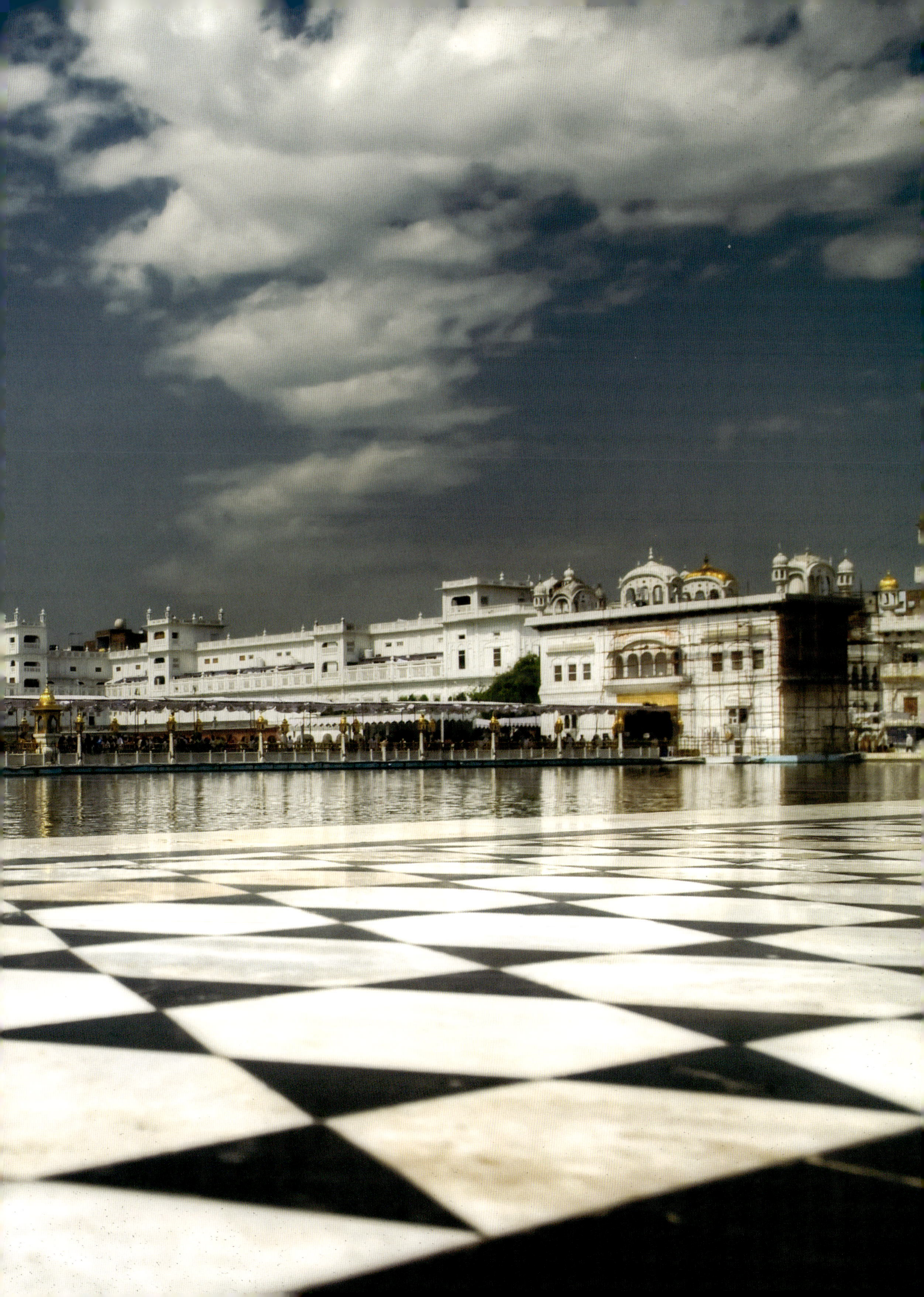

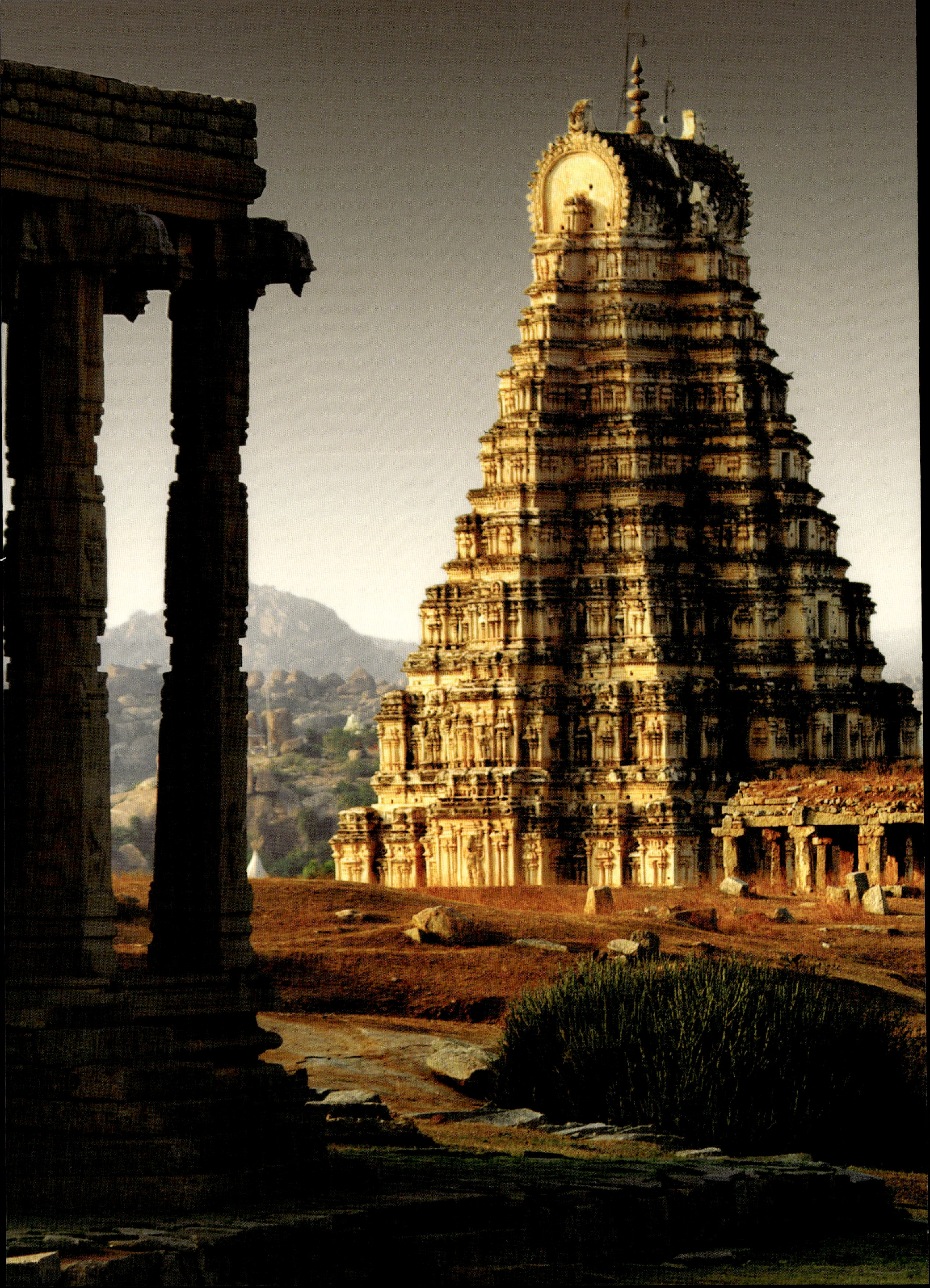

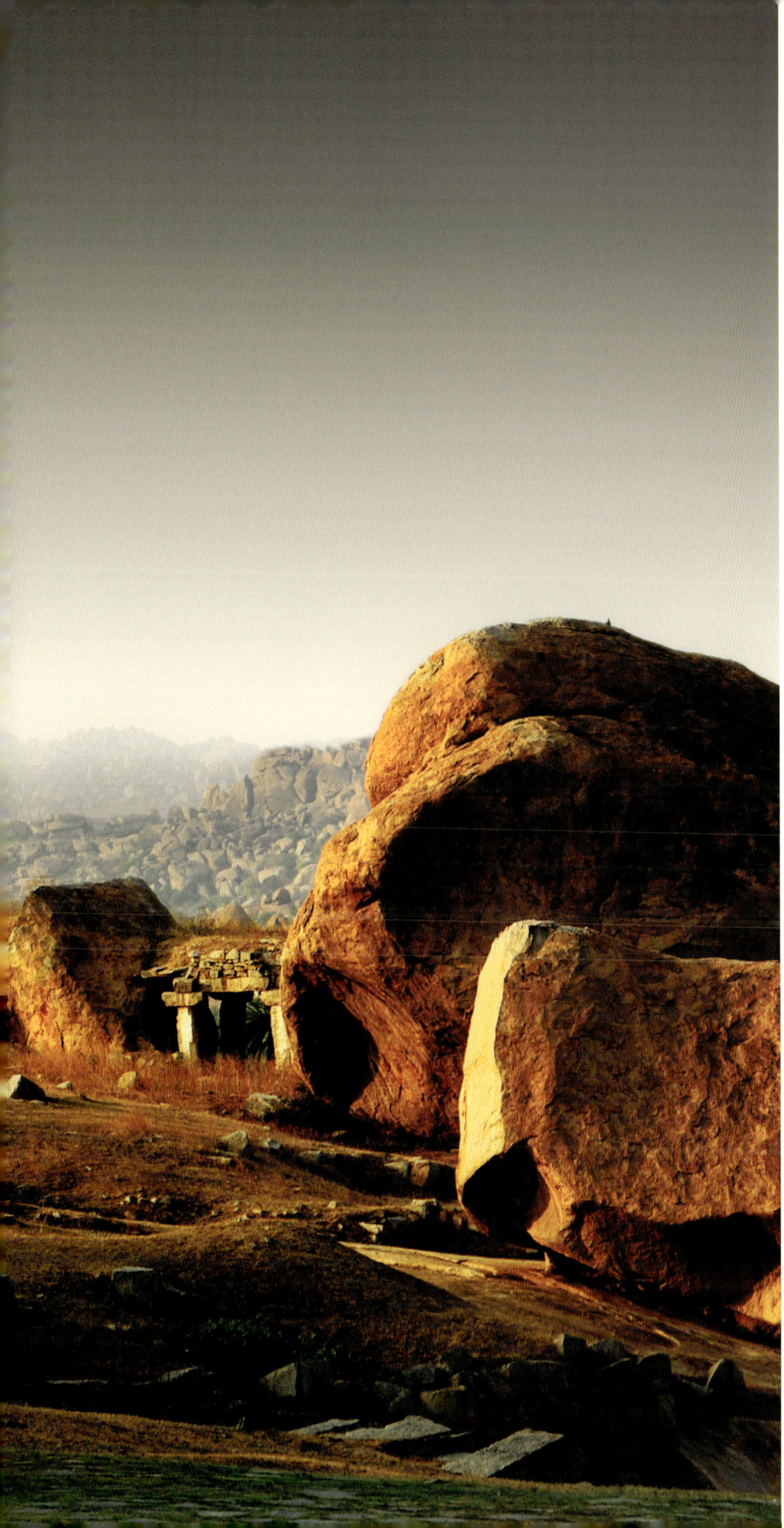

Virupaksha Temple, Hampi, India

Towering high above the hills of Ballari, in southwest India's Karnataka state, this complex was constructed in the fourteenth century. But, the place had already been a pilgrimage centre for centuries by that time. It was dedicated to Virupaksha, a locally-revered incarnation of Lord Shiva, one of Hinduism's foremost gods. Unlike the modern western religions, Hinduism has traditionally had innumerable different deities – often honoured very locally – though at the same time an overall 'oneness' of life and existence is recognized.

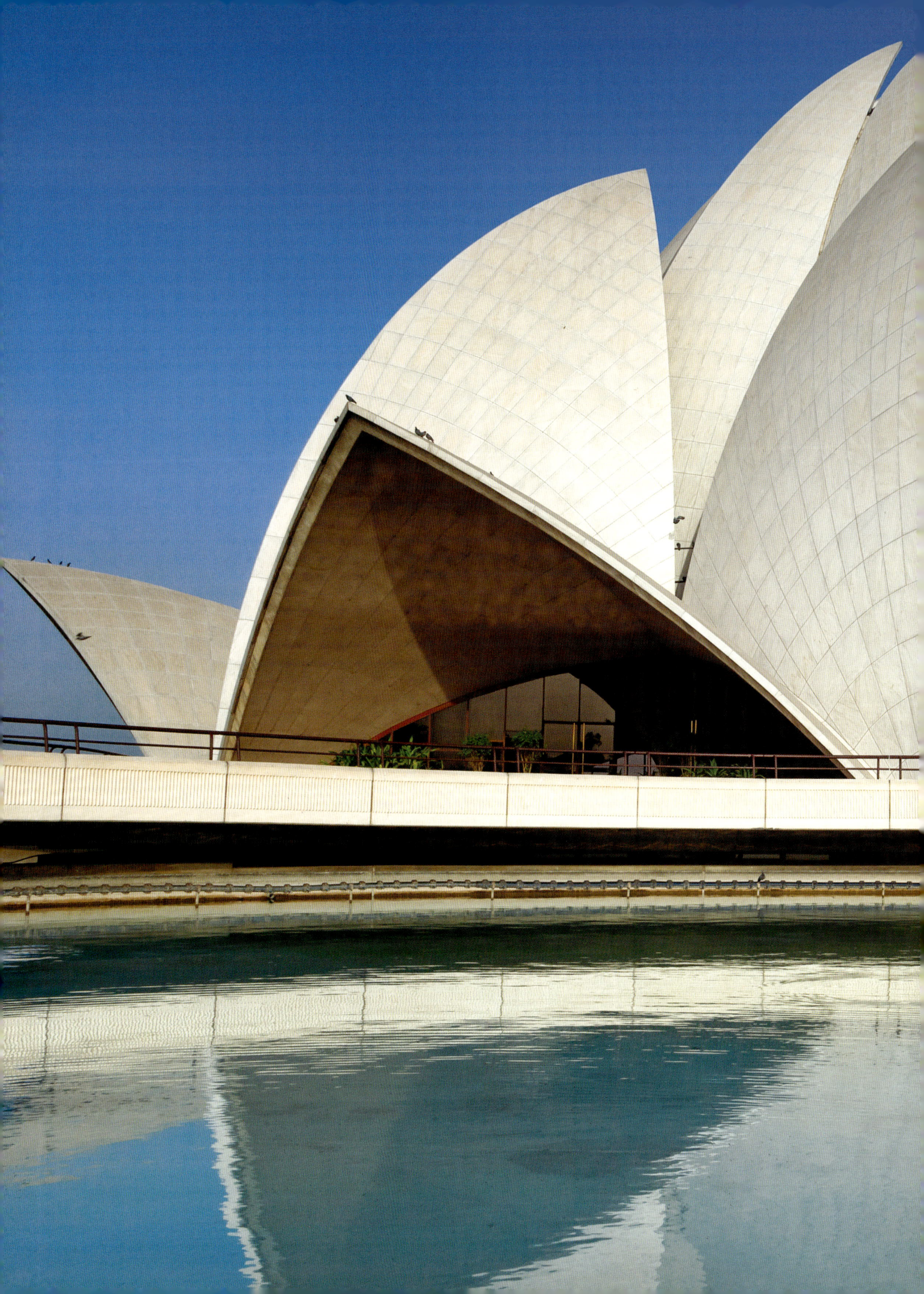

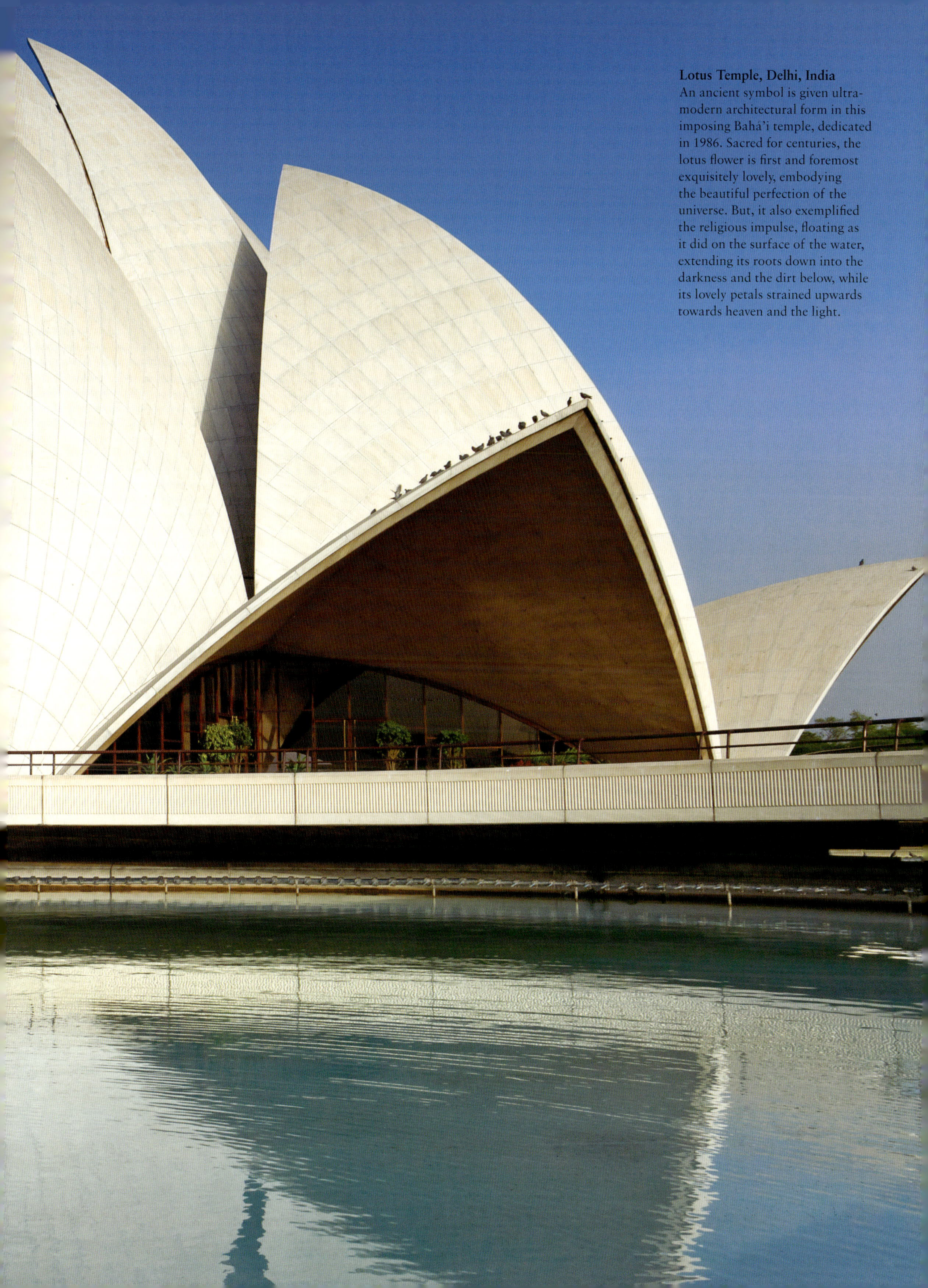

Lotus Temple, Delhi, India
An ancient symbol is given ultra-modern architectural form in this imposing Bahá'í temple, dedicated in 1986. Sacred for centuries, the lotus flower is first and foremost exquisitely lovely, embodying the beautiful perfection of the universe. But, it also exemplified the religious impulse, floating as it did on the surface of the water, extending its roots down into the darkness and the dirt below, while its lovely petals strained upwards towards heaven and the light.

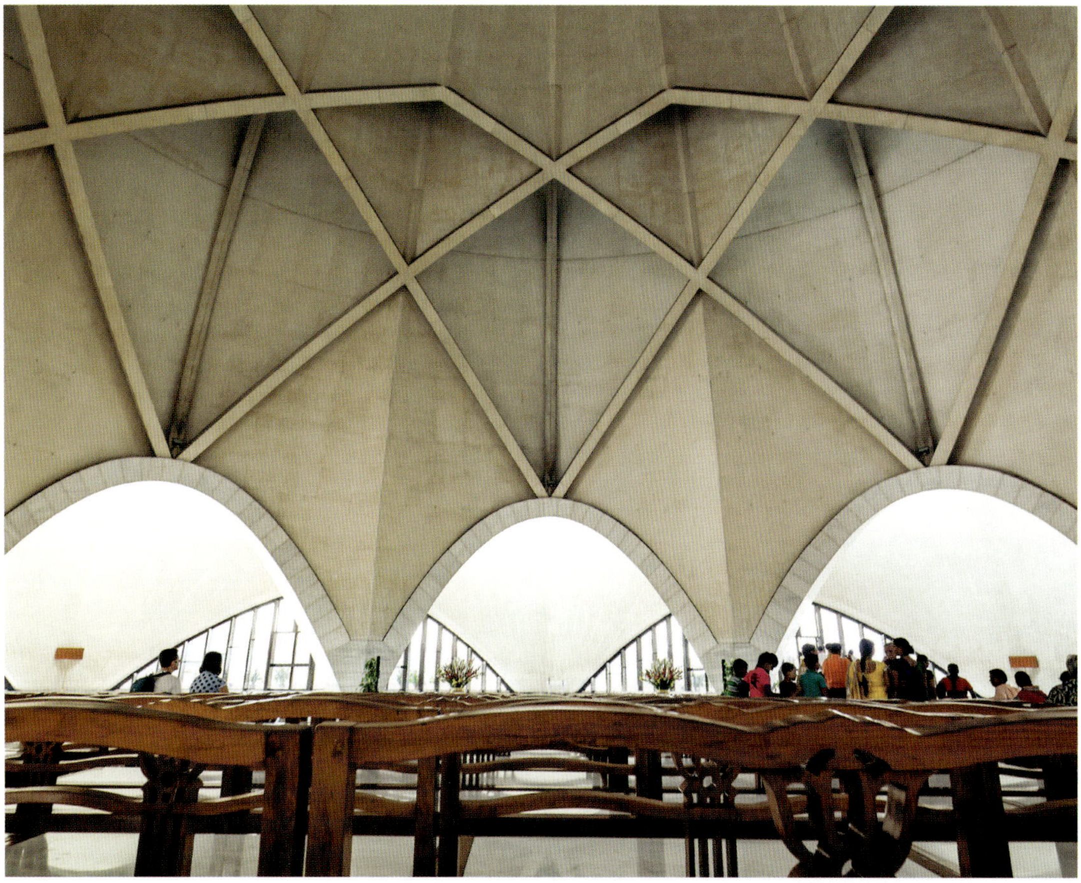

ALL PHOTOGRAPHS:

Lotus Temple, Delhi, India

This extraordinary temple was built in the 1980s to a design by the Iranian-American architect Fariborz Sahba (1948–). Bahá'i is a modern faith, founded by the Persian prophet Bahá'u'lláh (1817–92) in the 1860s, though it draws on older creeds from Buddhism and Christianity to Islam. It is, indeed, essentially something of a synthesis of these earlier spiritualities, setting out to unify all humanity in a single faith. The result is a comparatively rarefied, intellectualized approach to religion which we see exemplified in the geometric shapes and abstract patterns here. In keeping with Bahá'i's principles, the Lotus Temple is open to all; pilgrims and sightseers flock here in their thousands every year.

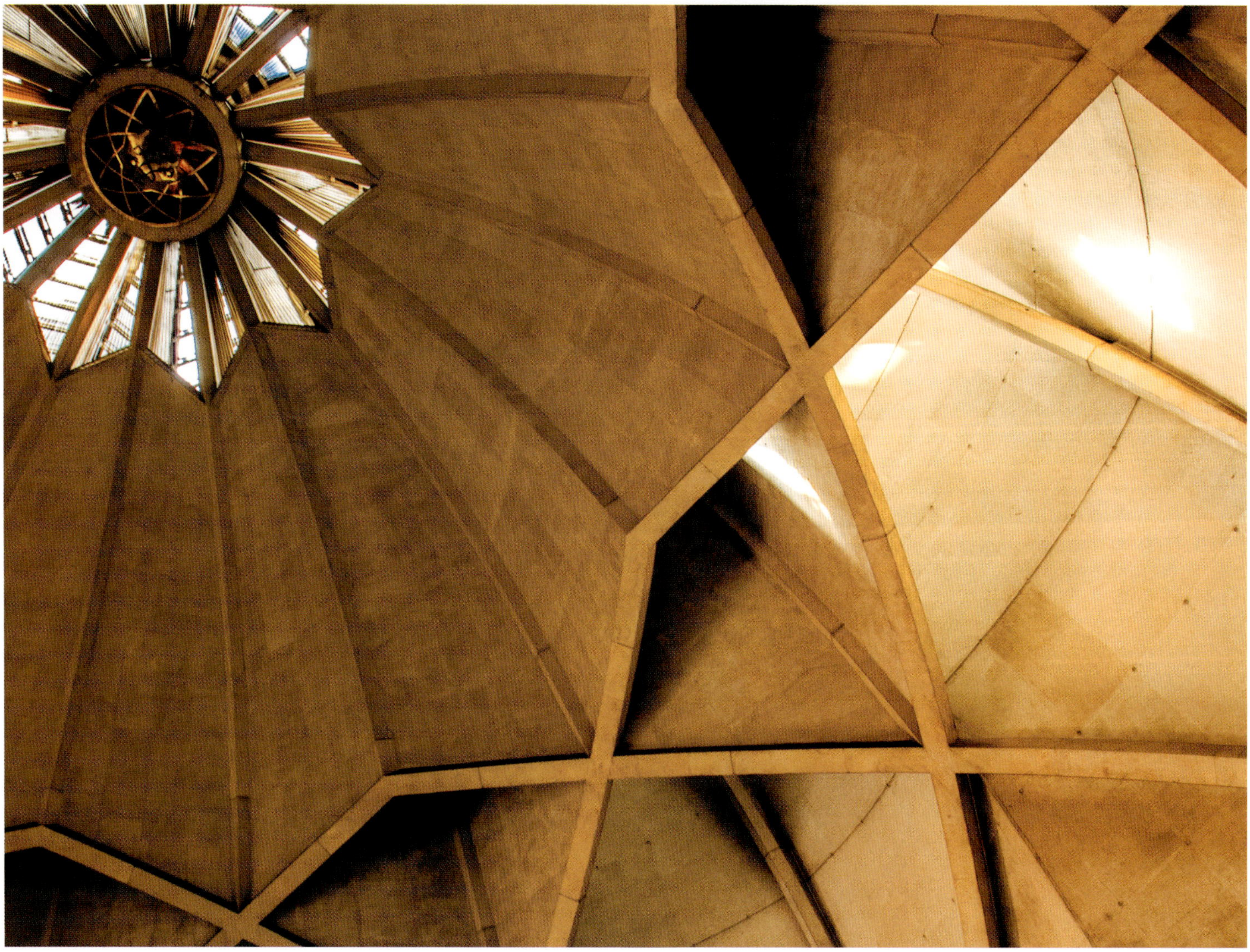

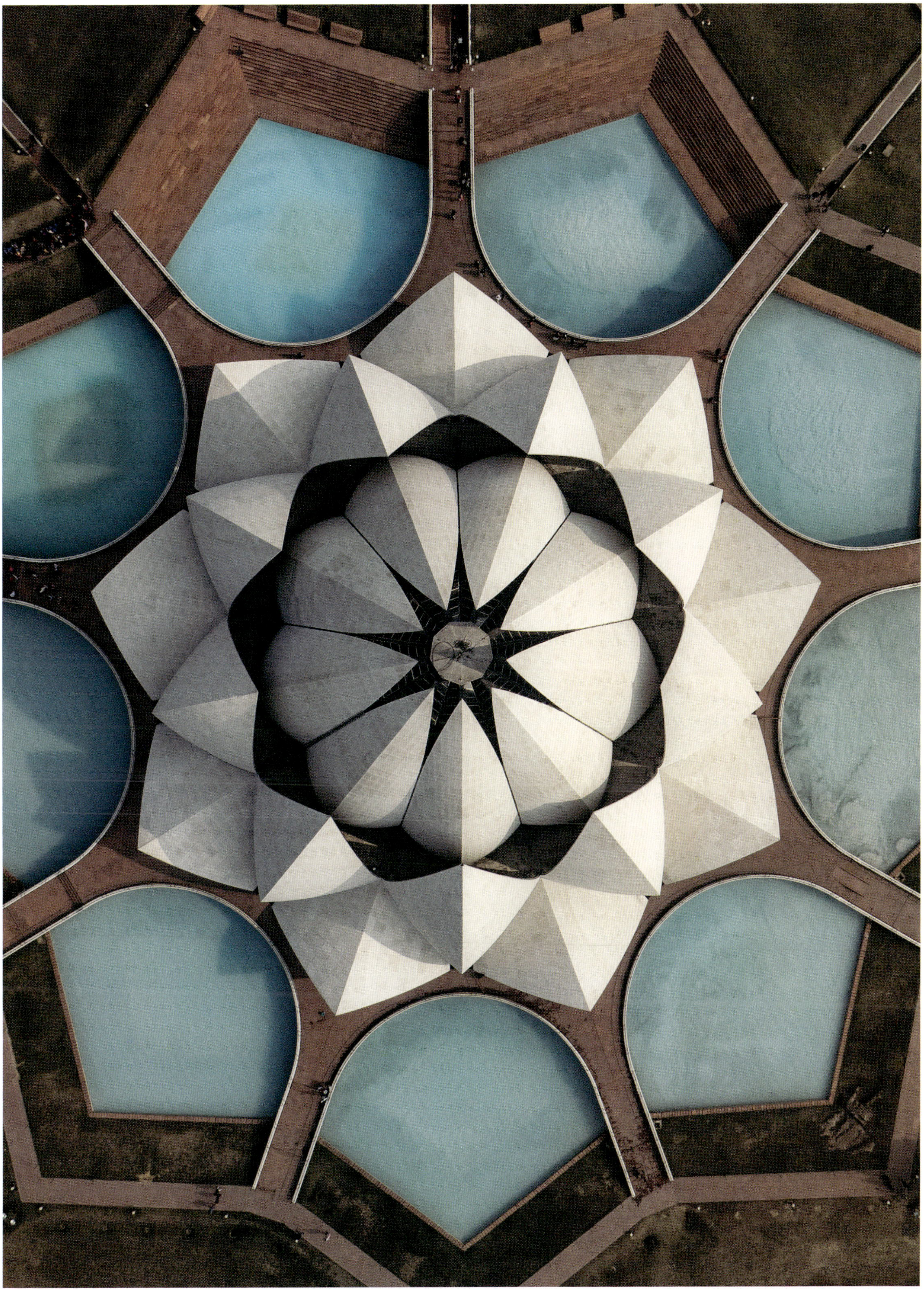

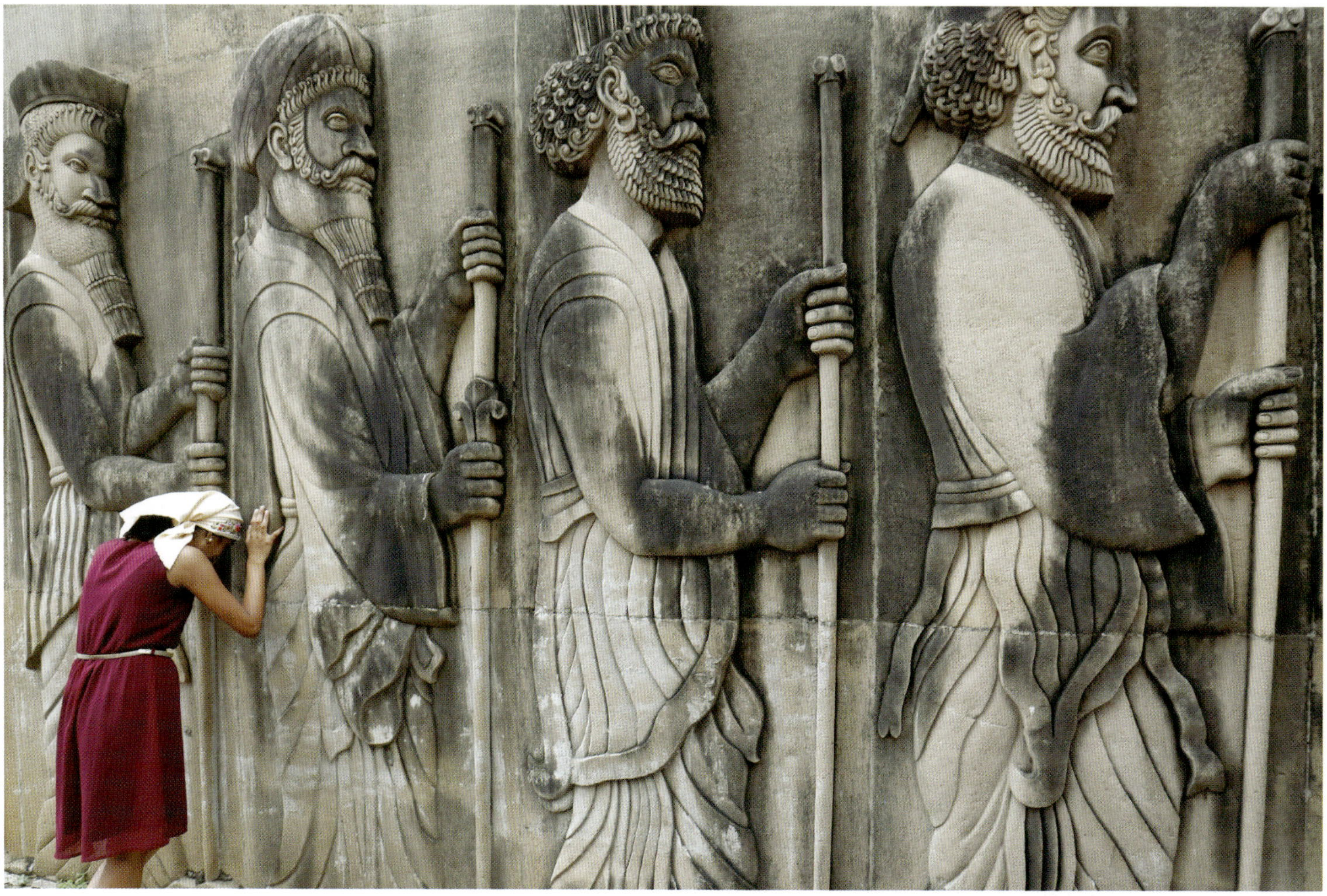

ABOVE, RIGHT AND OPPOSITE:

Maneckji Seth Agiary, Parsi Temple, Mumbai

A woman touches the talismanic relief of knights guarding the entrance to Mumbai's second-oldest Parsi Temple, built in 1735. It is protected too by Iamassu – sphinx-like figures – but with bulls' rather than lions' bodies, whose origins lie lost in Mesopotamian tradition. The examples here are clearly modelled on those to be found at imperial Persia's ancient capital, Persepolis, so proclaim the Parsis' pride in their ancestral origins.

So-called for these roots, the Parsis came to India as refugees from their home country, now Iran, after it was invaded by the Muslim Arabs in the seventh century. They brought with them their Zoroastrian religion and established a thriving community in Mumbai.

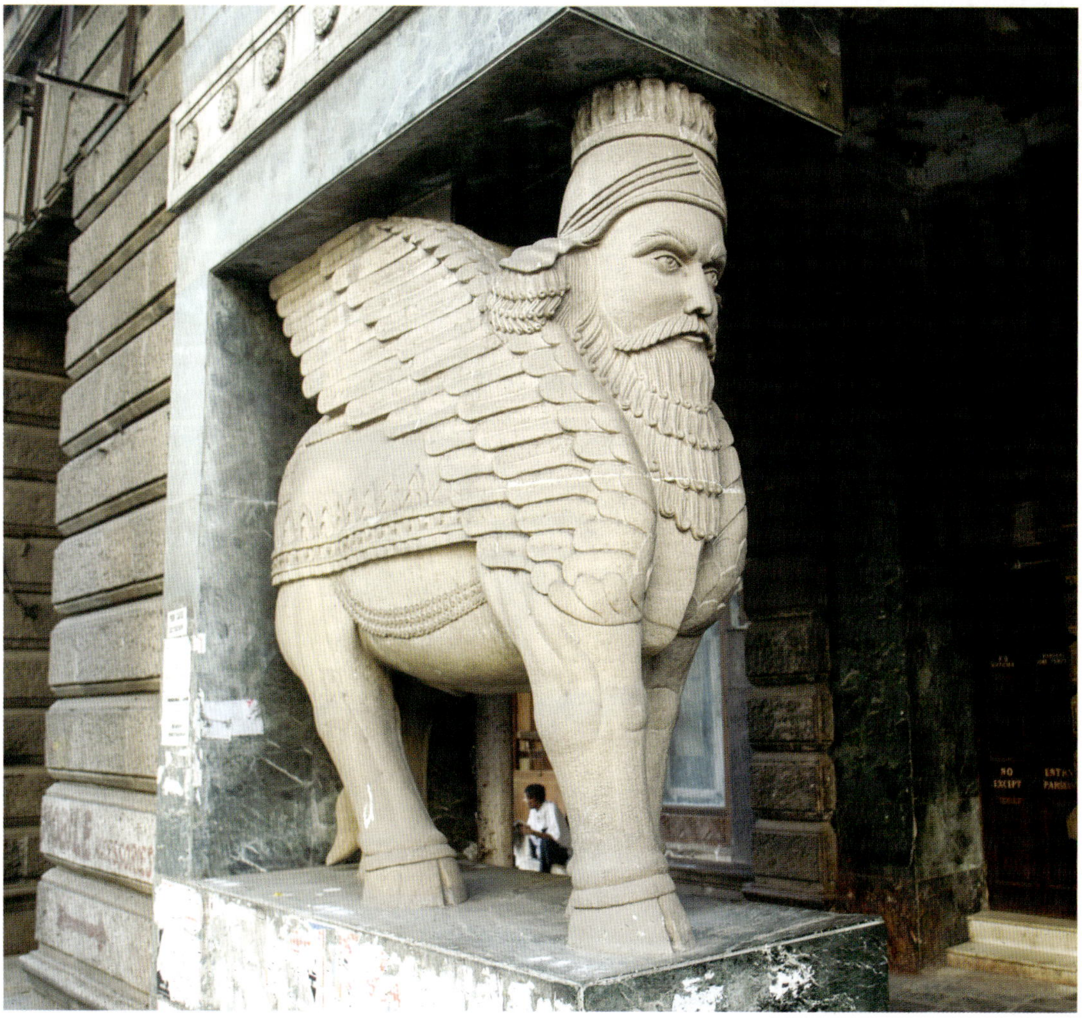

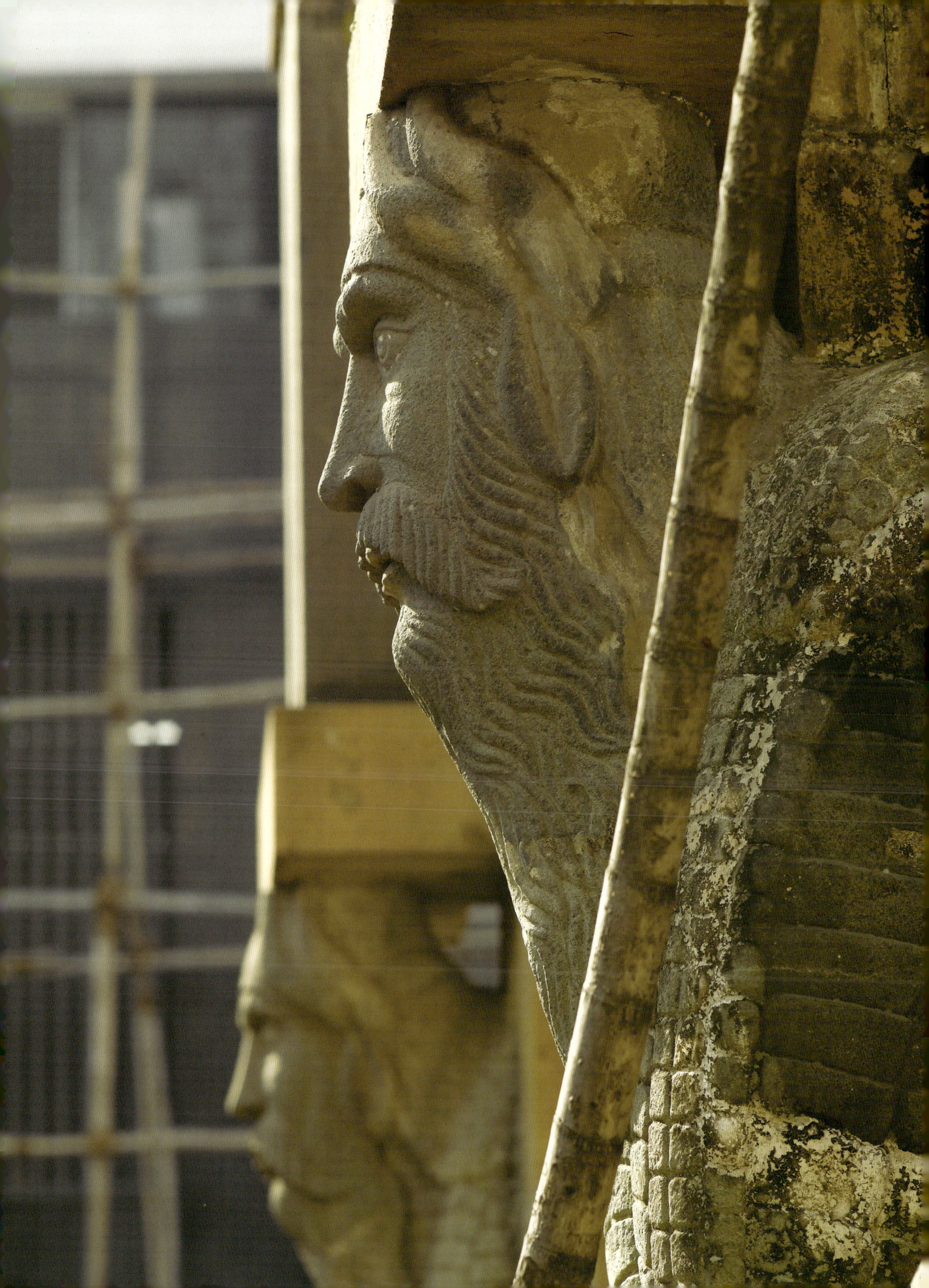

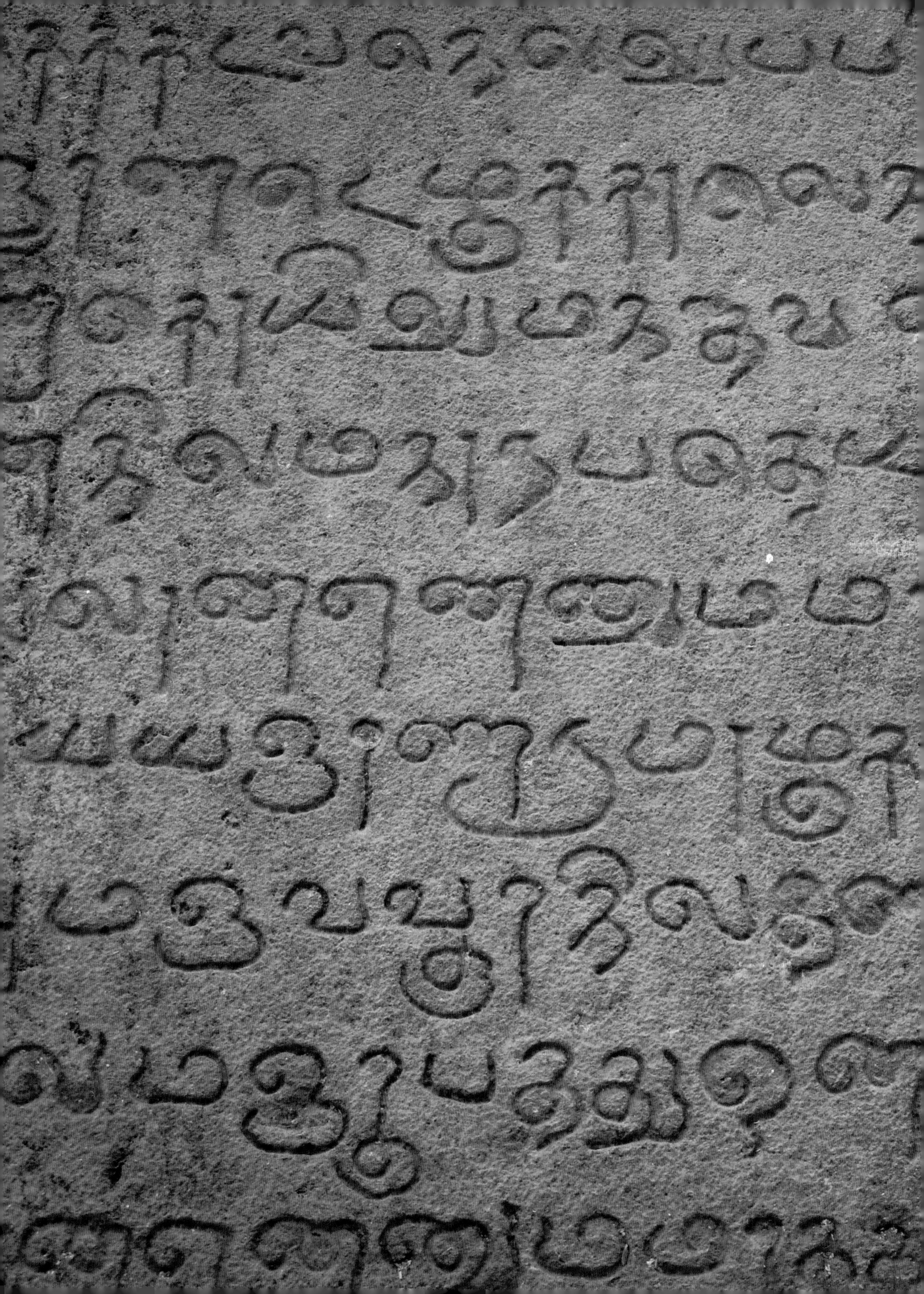

OPPOSITE:

Brihadishwara Temple, Tanjore, Tamil Nadhu, India

The kings of the Chola dynasty ruled this part of southern India from the third century BCE to the thirteenth century CE. They left behind a string of splendid temples. Magnificent as this one is, its most arresting feature is the way its walls are so densely covered with thousand-year-old Tamil and Sanskrit inscriptions. These record the affairs and personnel of what seems not to have been so much a shrine as a small city. A major temple was as much an economic as a spiritual centre, a place where tribute was brought and taxes paid.

RIGHT AND BELOW:

Bodh Gaya, Bihar, India

It was here, it's said, that after six years of wandering vainly in search of spiritual enlightenment, Gautama Siddhartha, resolved instead to start seeking it inside himself. He sat down beneath a tree to rest and meditate, struggling as the forces of evil hurled down lightning bolts – which fell as blossoms from the tree, thanks to the calming effects his peaceful presence had. Three nights later, he stood up and set out again, his state of holiness achieved, his message formulated: 'Cease to do evil; learn to do good, and purify your heart.' A great temple – and a massive statue – were erected here.

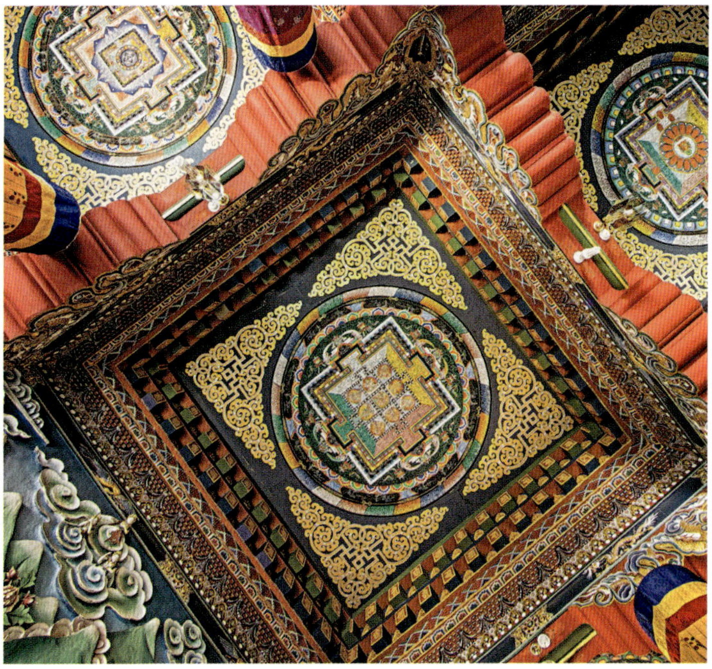

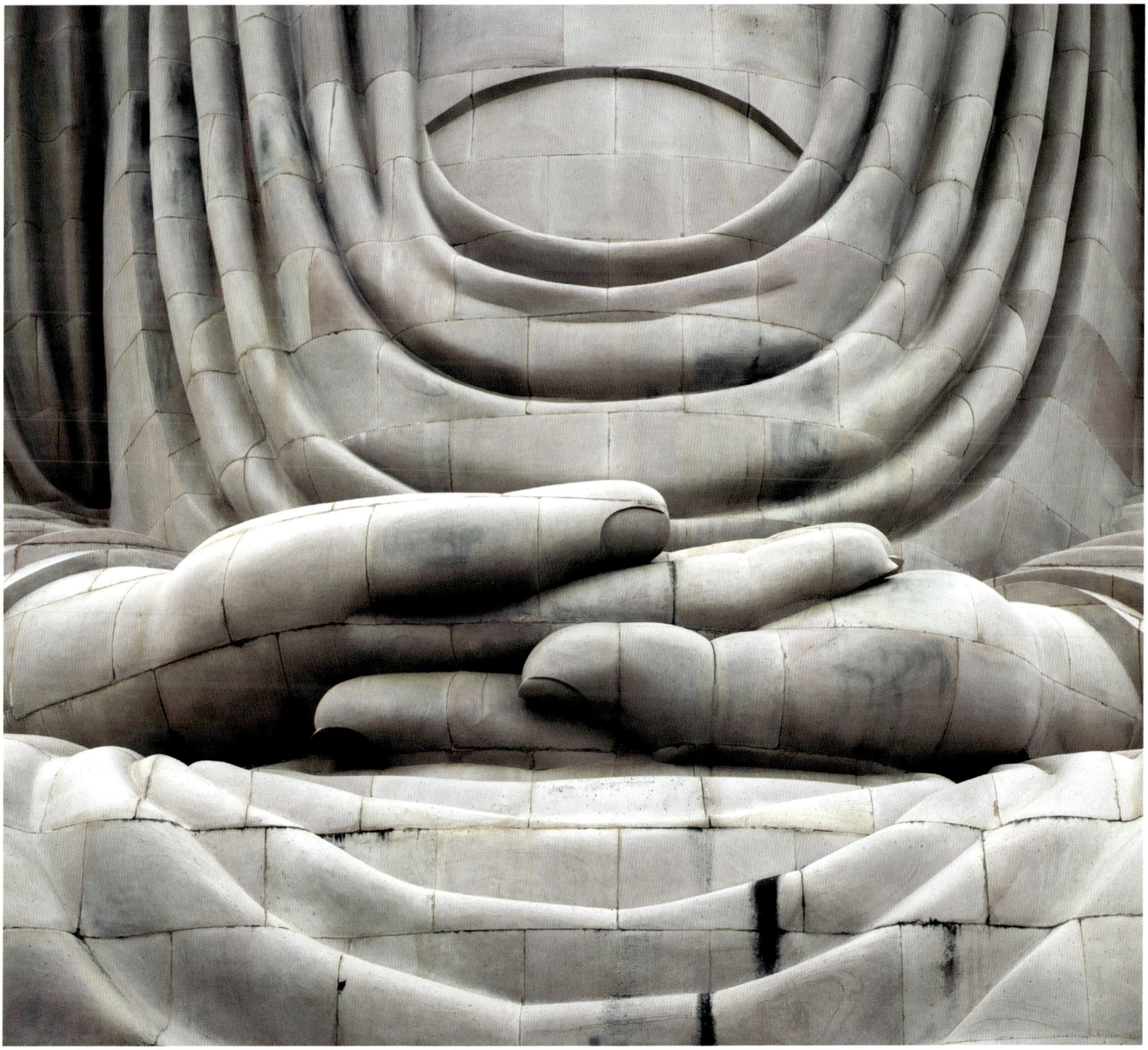

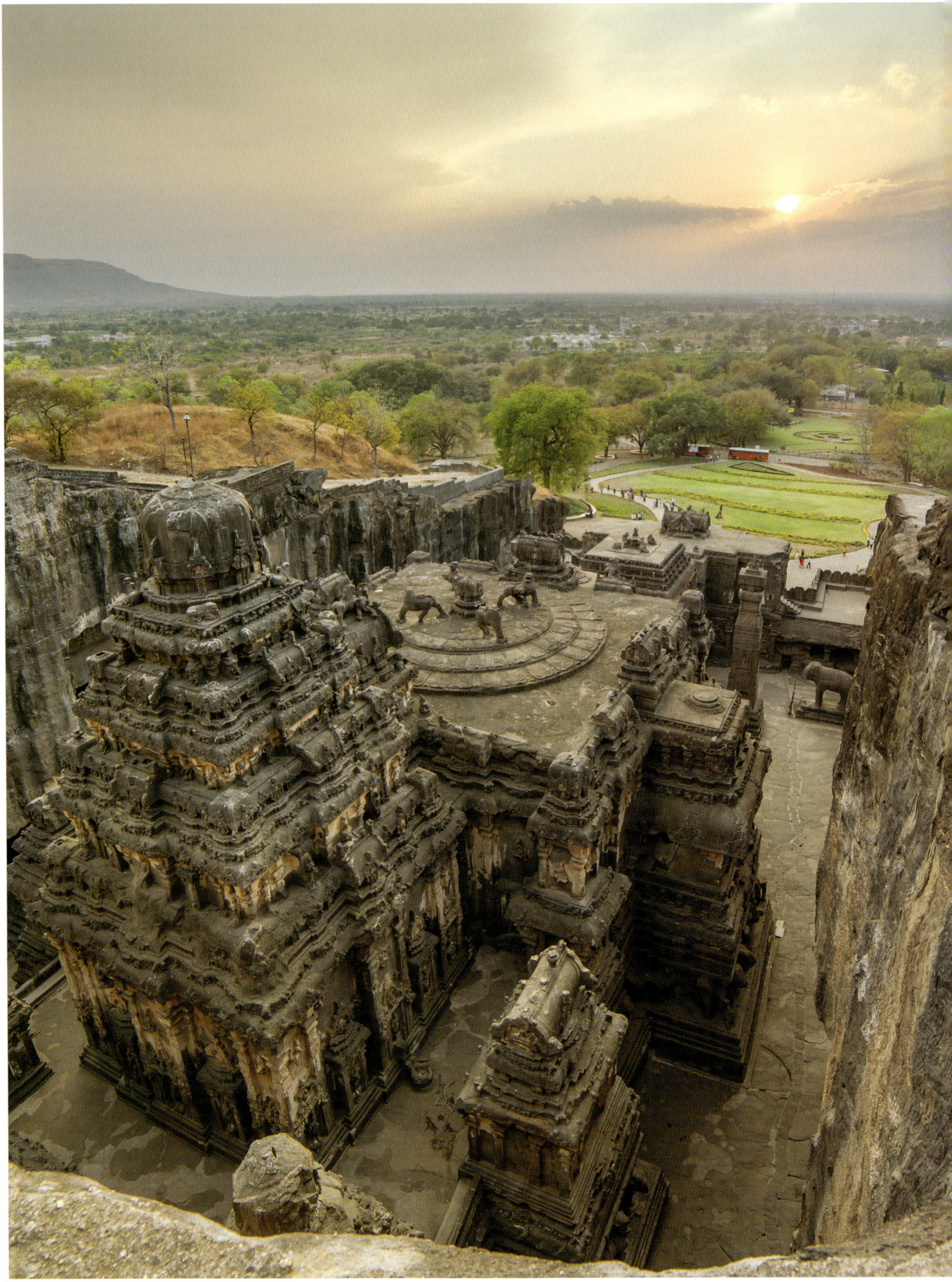

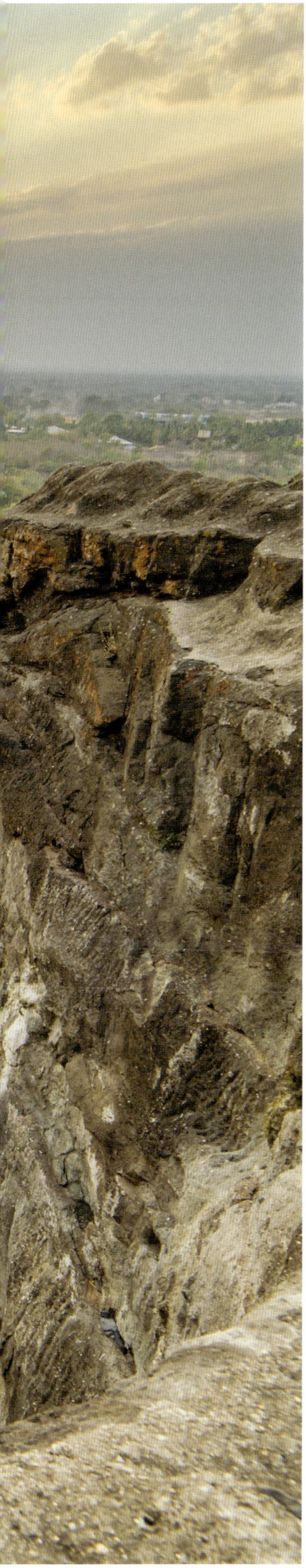

ALL PHOTOGRAPHS ON THESE PAGES:

Ellora Caves, Maharashtra, India

Not 'constructed' as such but carved directly from the rock of western India's Maharashtra province, north of Aurangabad, this temple complex – sacred to Hindus and Buddhists (as well as Jains) – dates from the latter part of the first millennium CE. Both Hindu carvings (*below top*) and Buddhist iconography (*below bottom*) can be found here.

OVERLEAF:

Surya Deula temple, Konark, India

This sun temple's richly-carved wheels don't just suggest the sun itself but mark the months of the Hindu calendar. They also evoke the spirit of samsara – the endless cycle of birth, death and rebirth that makes the Indian universe go round.

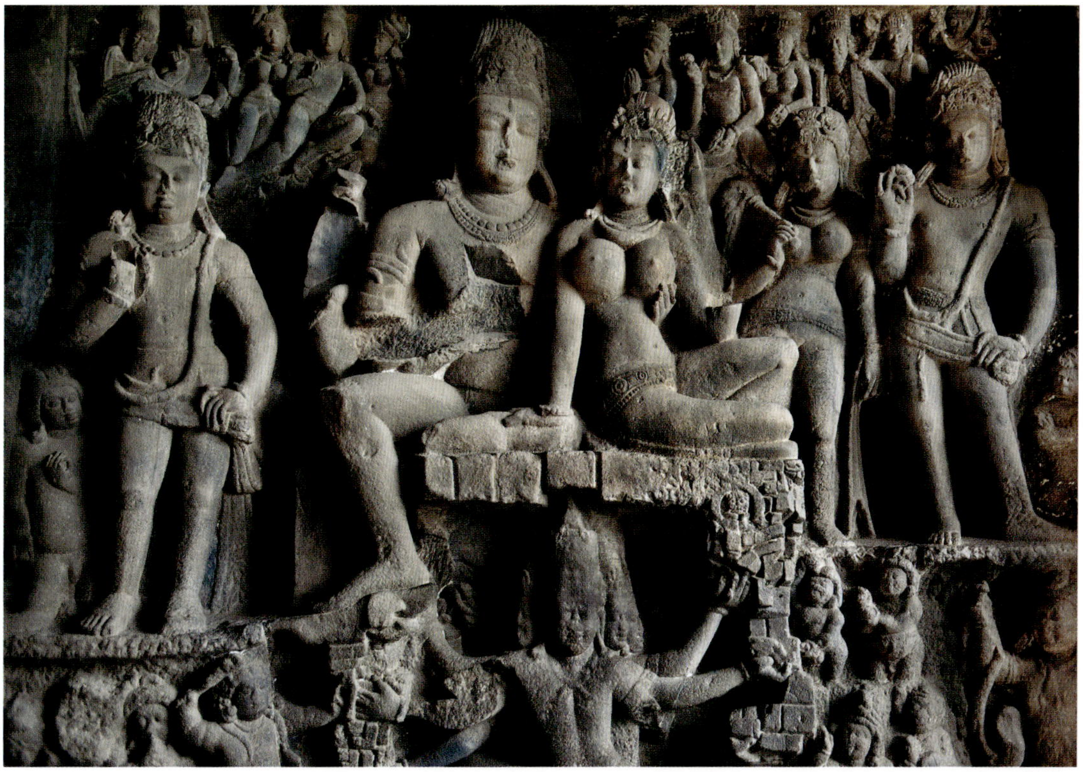

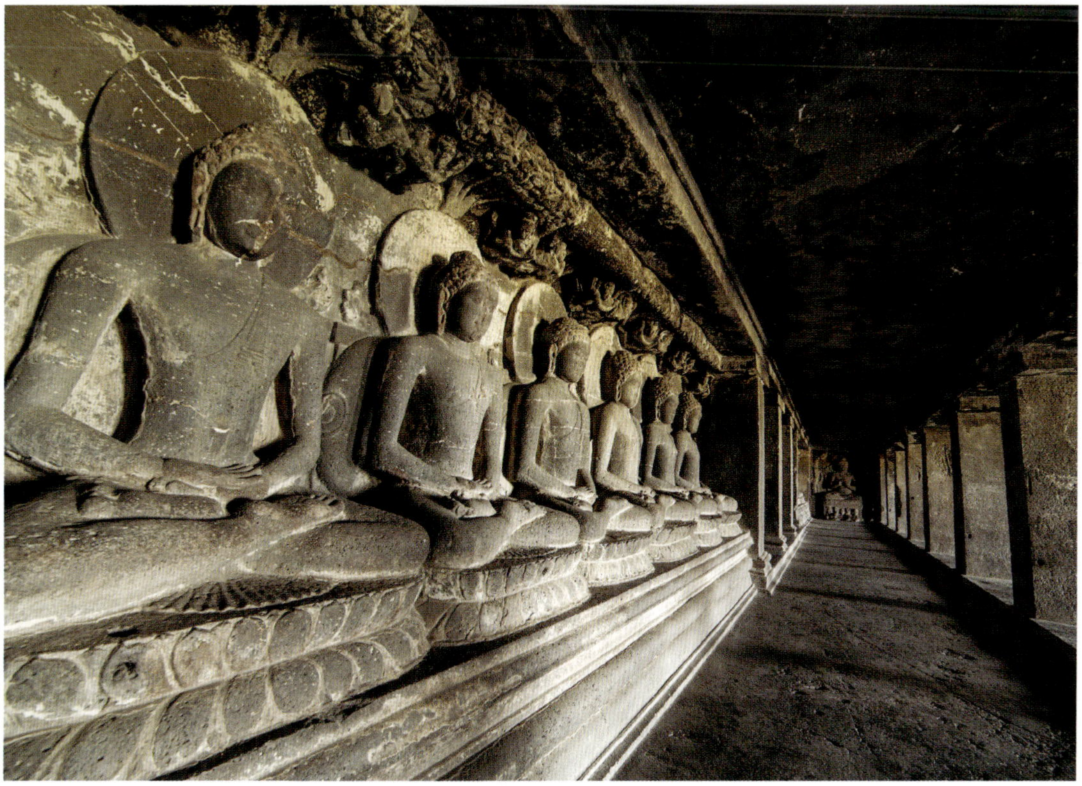

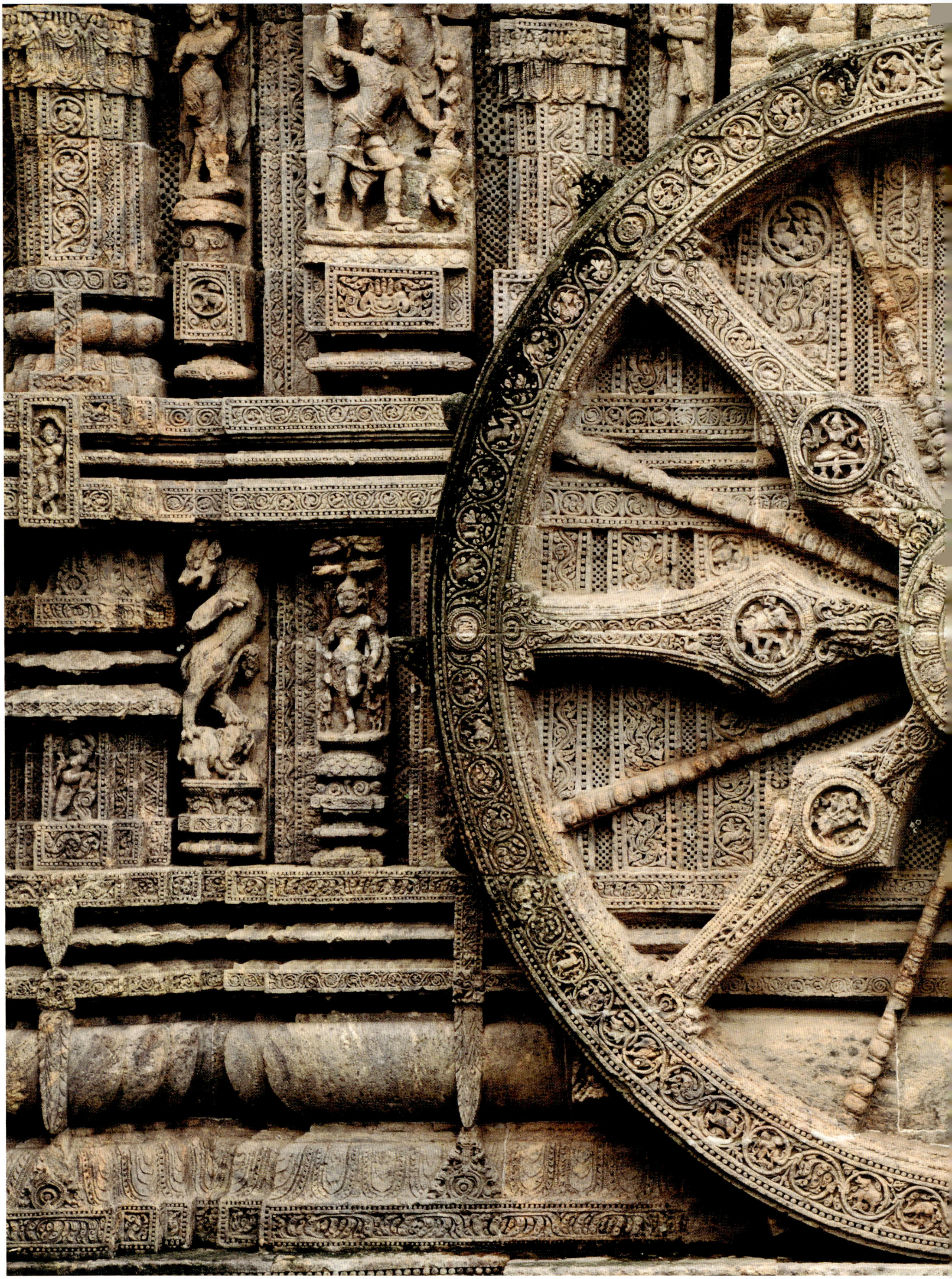

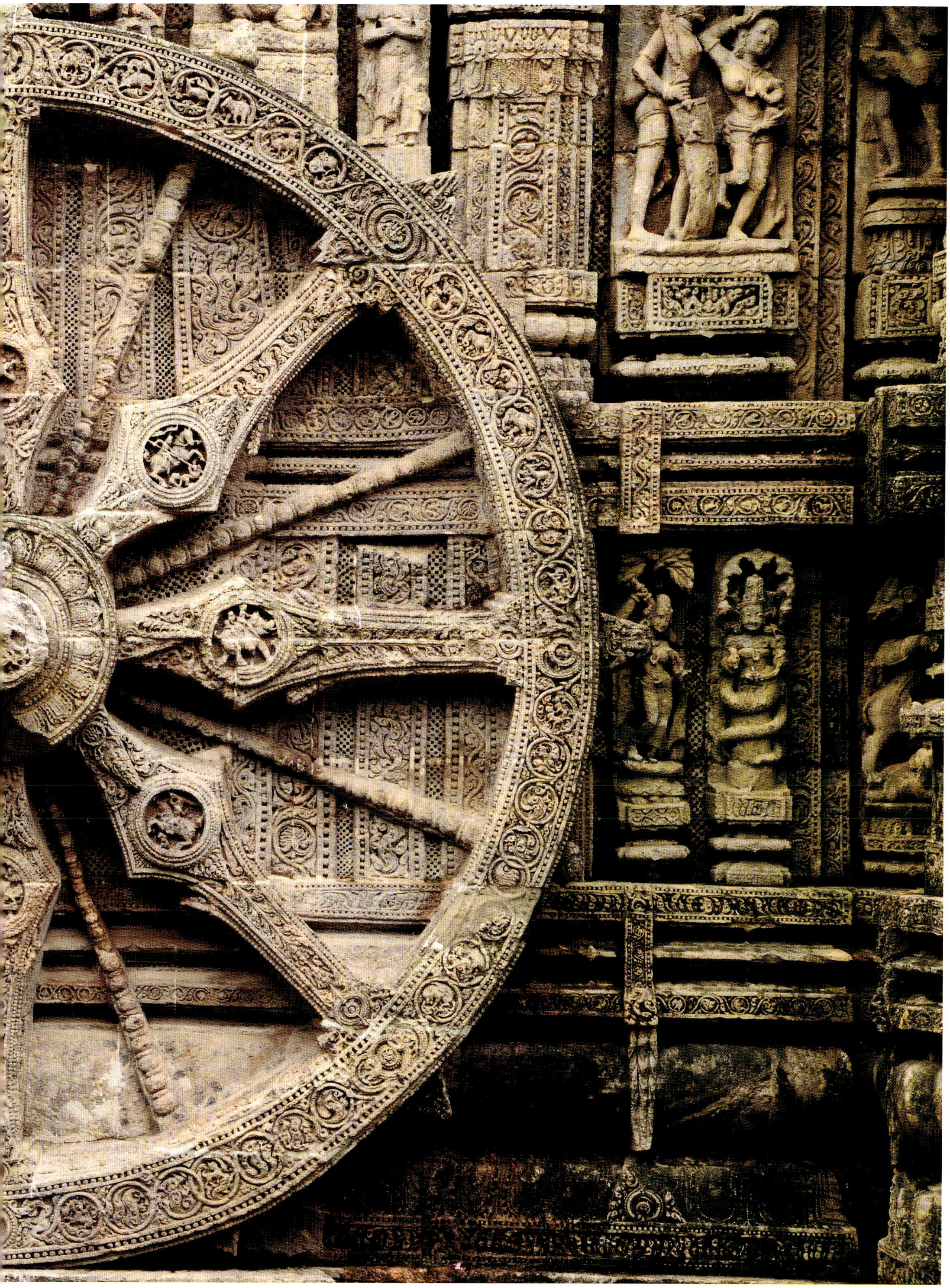

Japanese Peace Pagoda, Unawatuna, Sri Lanka
Built by Buddhist monks from Japan in 2005, this monument is one of several score built around the world in commemoration of the Hiroshima and Nagasaki bombings (1945). But stupas like this have been built in India and beyond since ancient times. Believed to be (among other things) a stylized representation of Mount Meru, the ancient world-mountain – around which we all live and towards whose exalted summit we strive to make our way – the stupa clearly brings together maternal and male phallic symbolism, too.

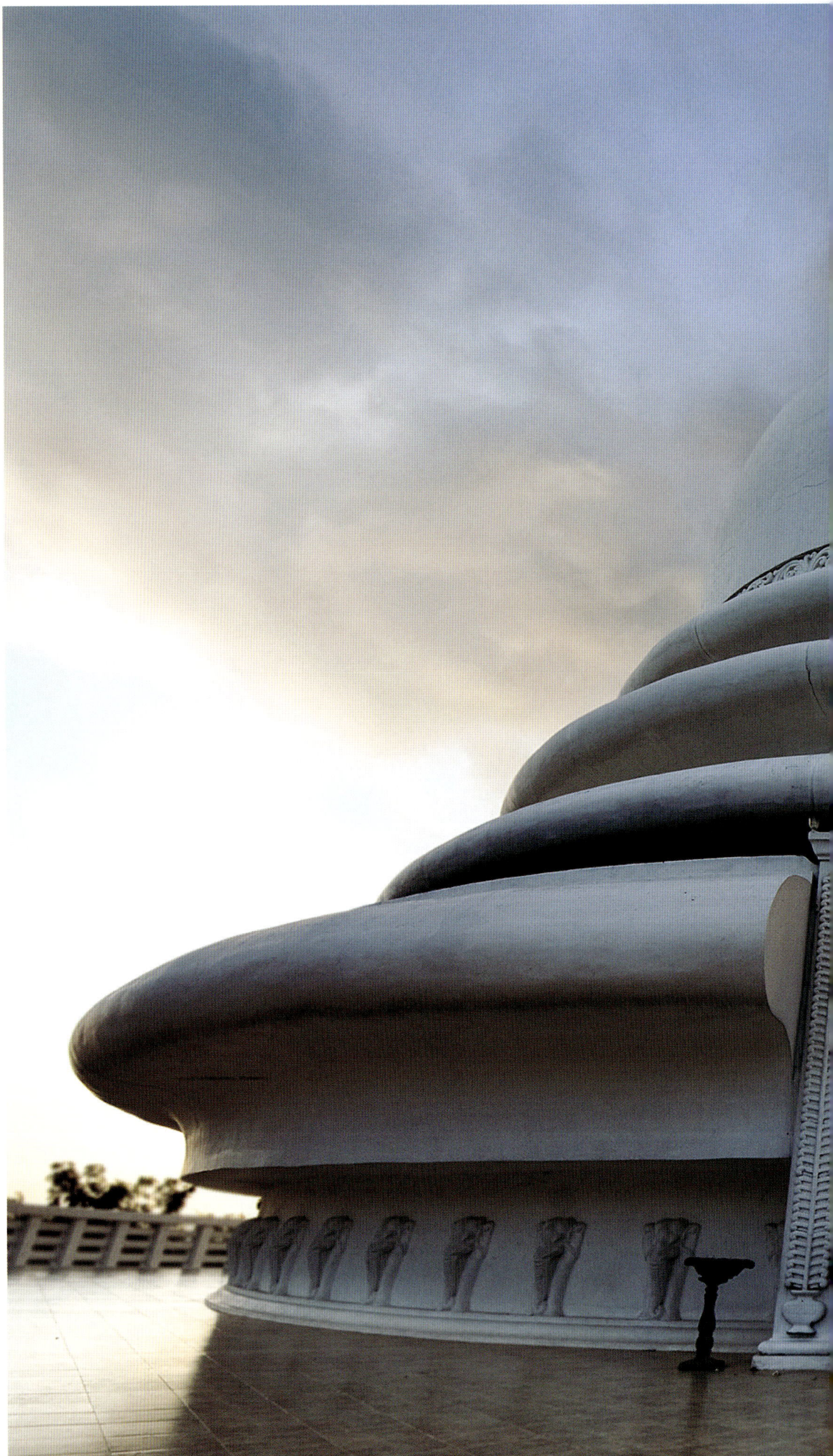

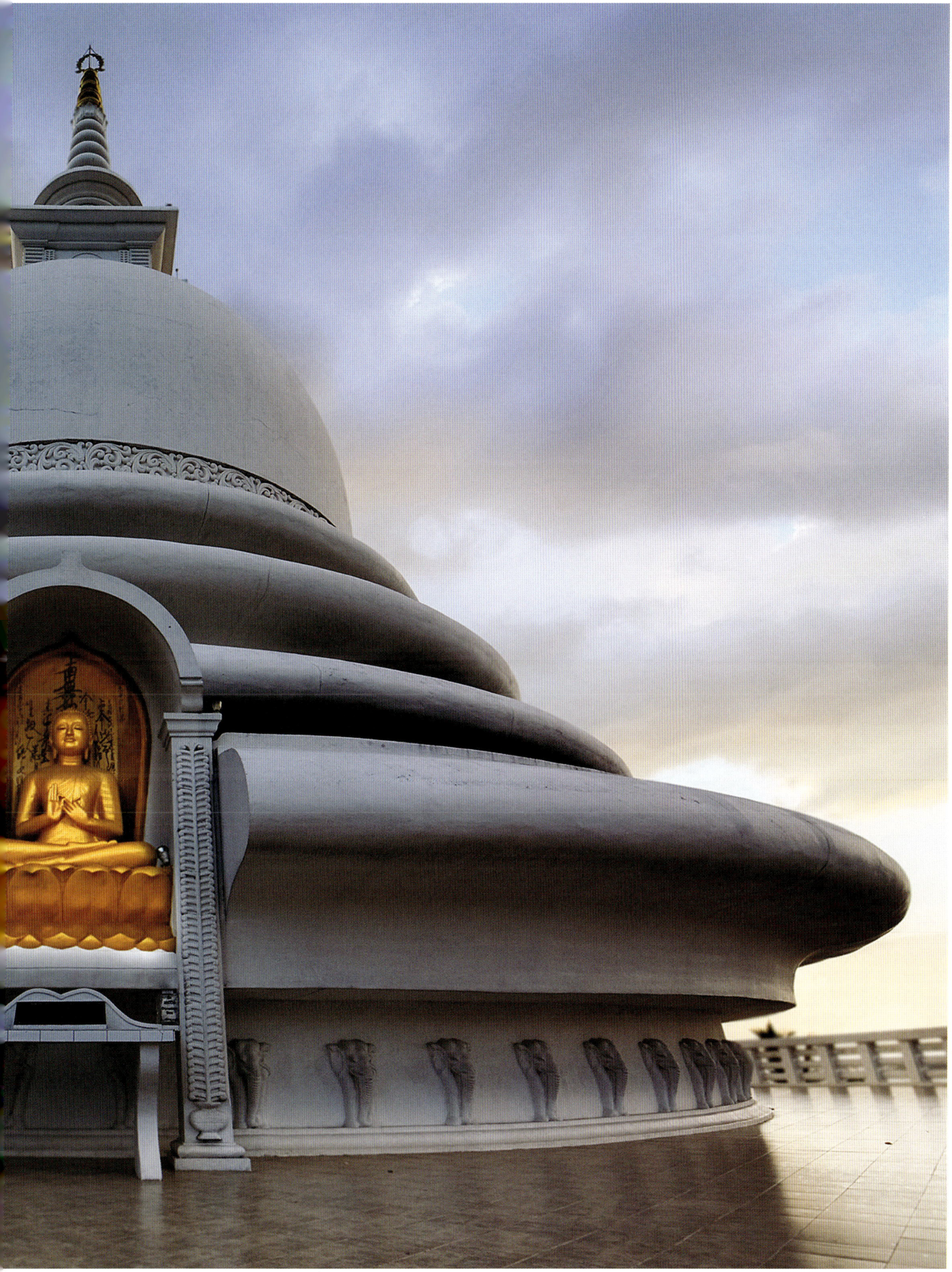

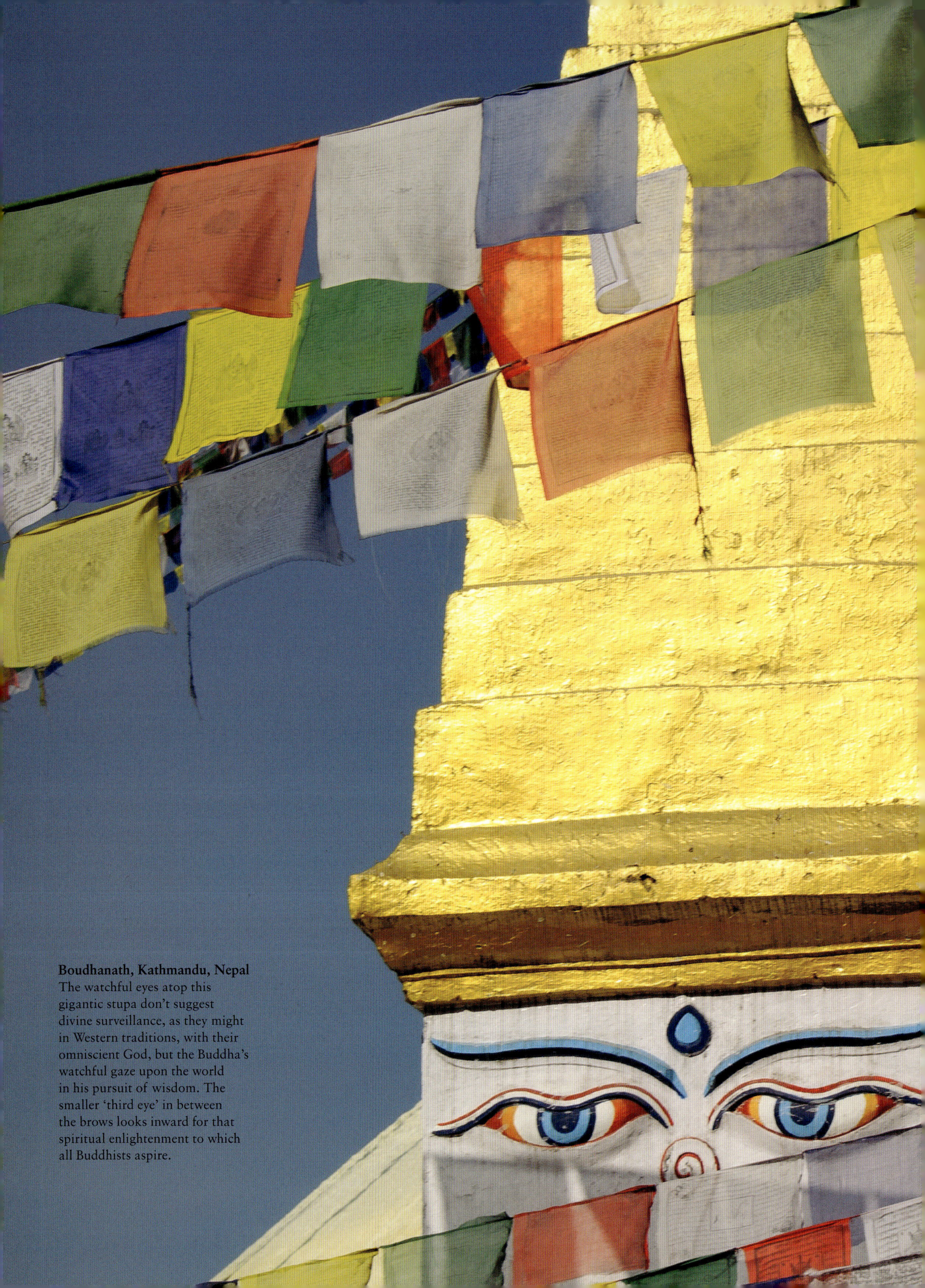

Boudhanath, Kathmandu, Nepal
The watchful eyes atop this gigantic stupa don't suggest divine surveillance, as they might in Western traditions, with their omniscient God, but the Buddha's watchful gaze upon the world in his pursuit of wisdom. The smaller 'third eye' in between the brows looks inward for that spiritual enlightenment to which all Buddhists aspire.

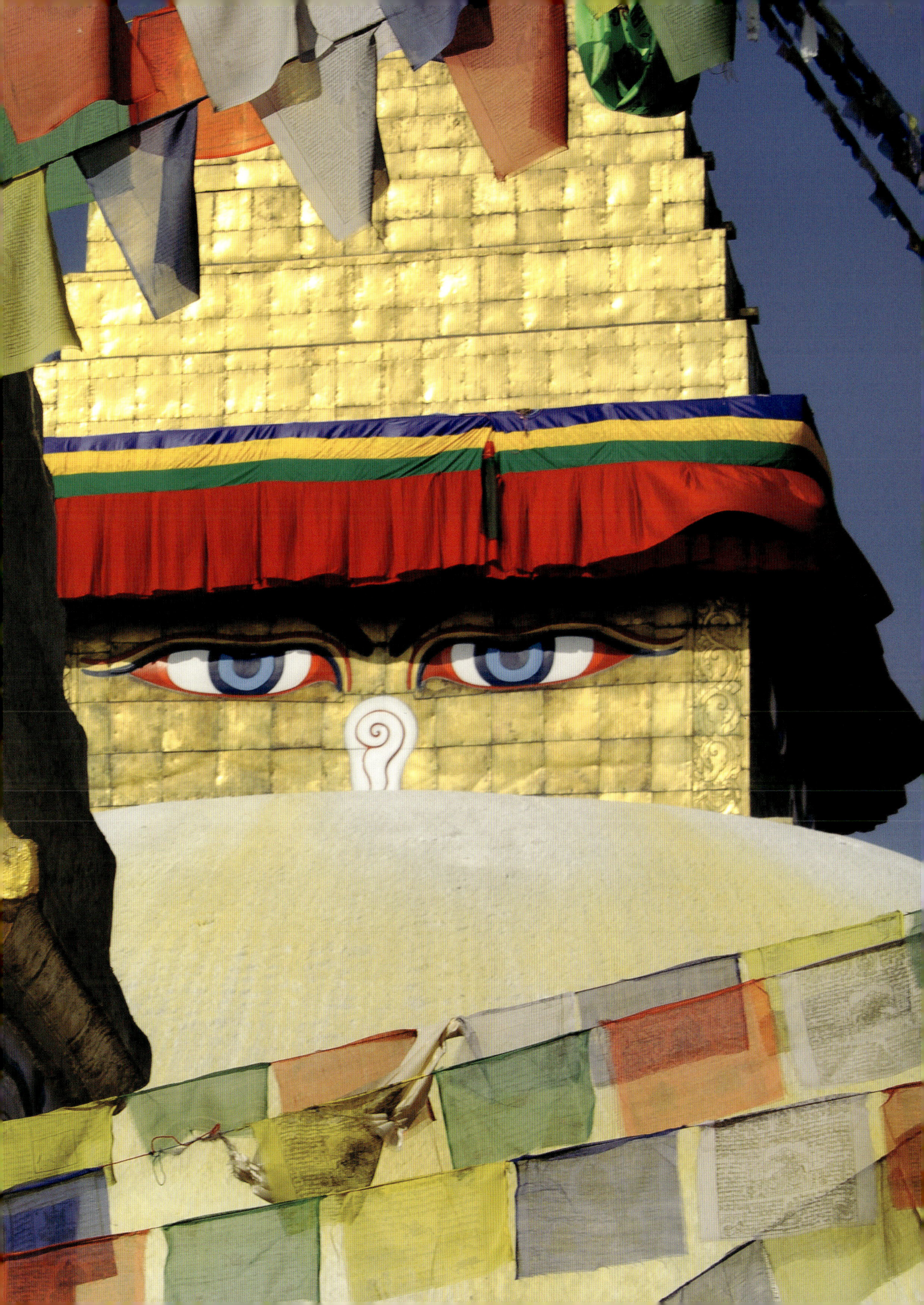

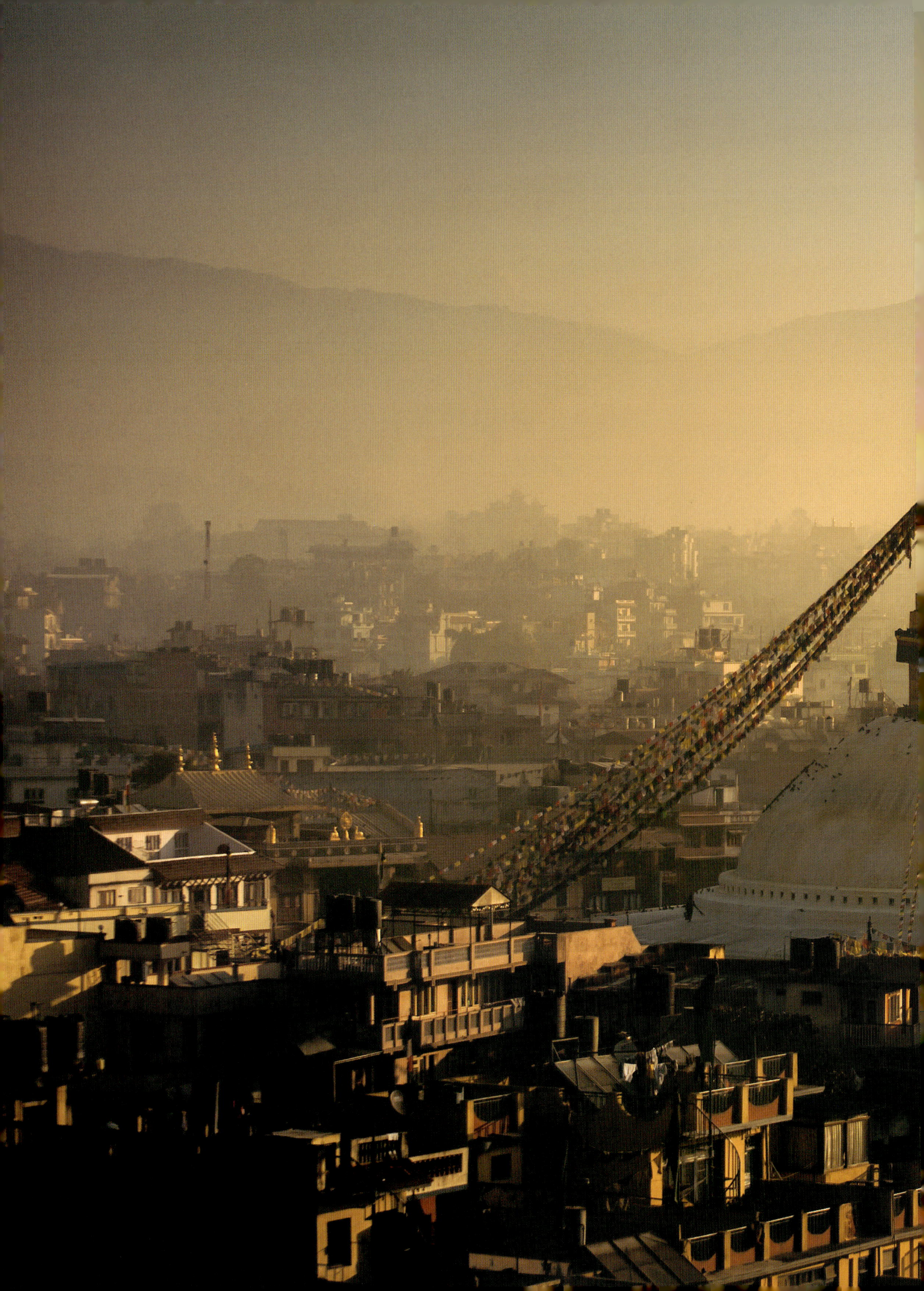

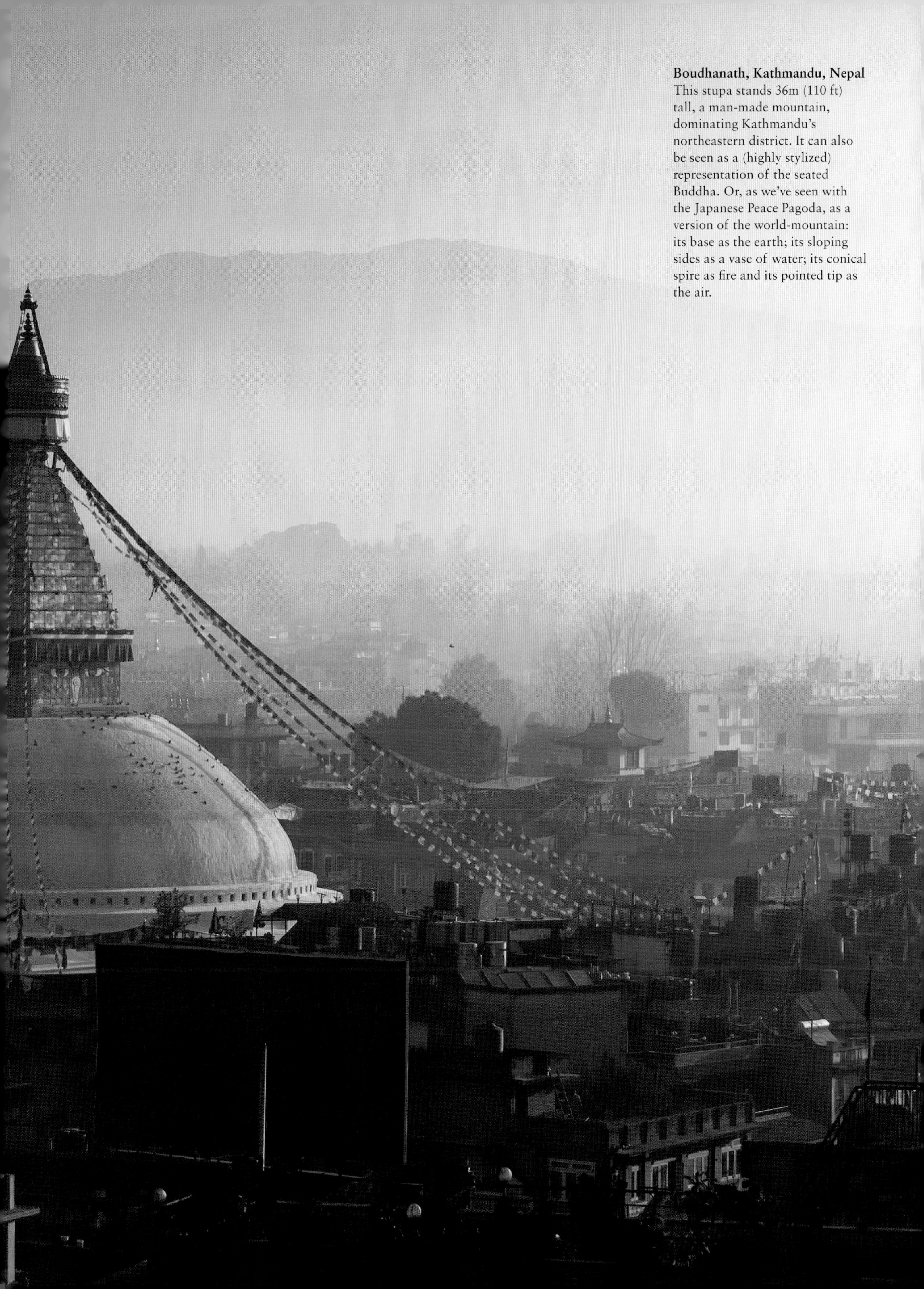

Boudhanath, Kathmandu, Nepal
This stupa stands 36m (110 ft) tall, a man-made mountain, dominating Kathmandu's northeastern district. It can also be seen as a (highly stylized) representation of the seated Buddha. Or, as we've seen with the Japanese Peace Pagoda, as a version of the world-mountain: its base as the earth; its sloping sides as a vase of water; its conical spire as fire and its pointed tip as the air.

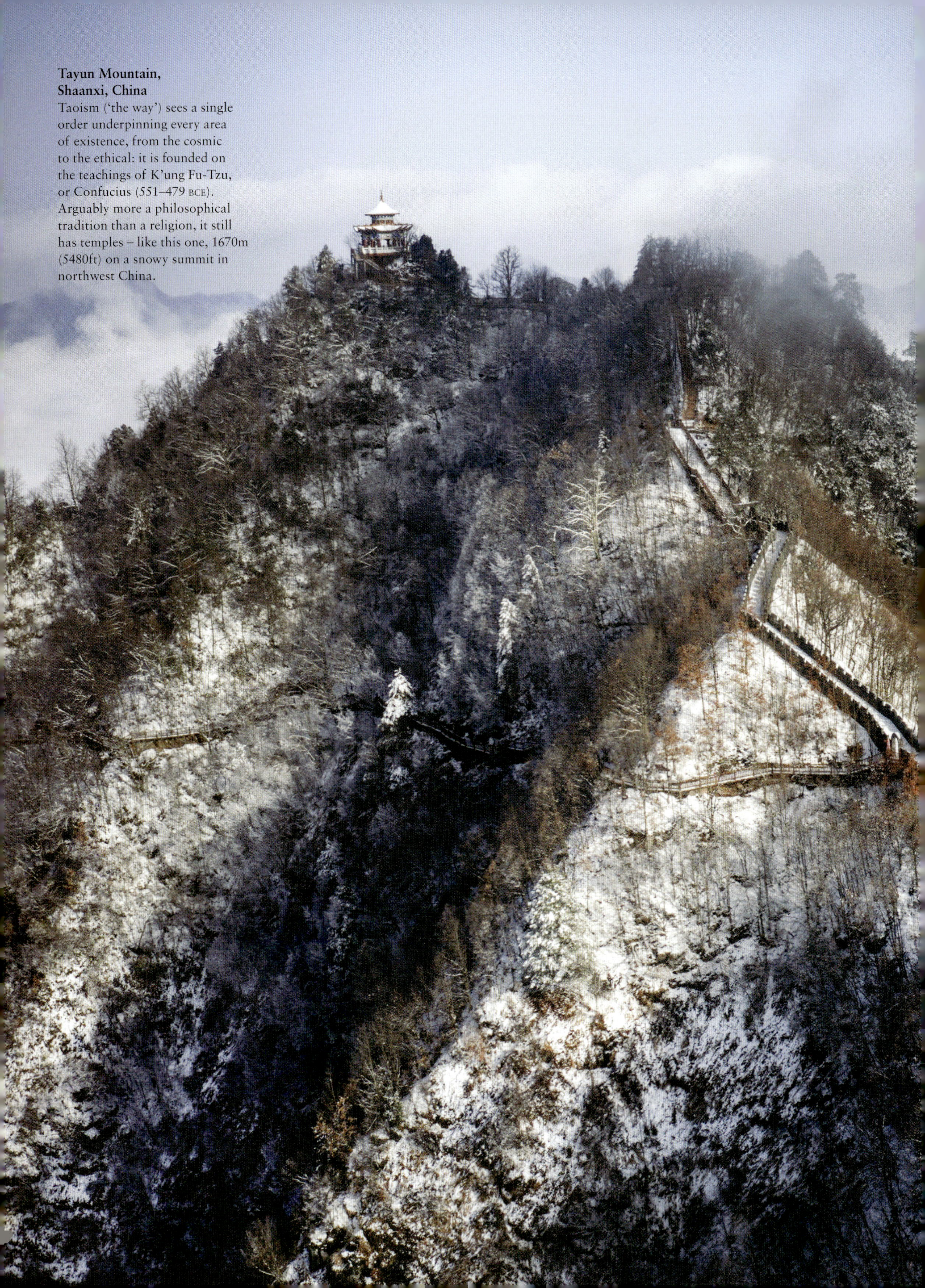

Tayun Mountain, Shaanxi, China

Taoism ('the way') sees a single order underpinning every area of existence, from the cosmic to the ethical: it is founded on the teachings of K'ung Fu-Tzu, or Confucius (551–479 BCE). Arguably more a philosophical tradition than a religion, it still has temples – like this one, 1670m (5480ft) on a snowy summit in northwest China.

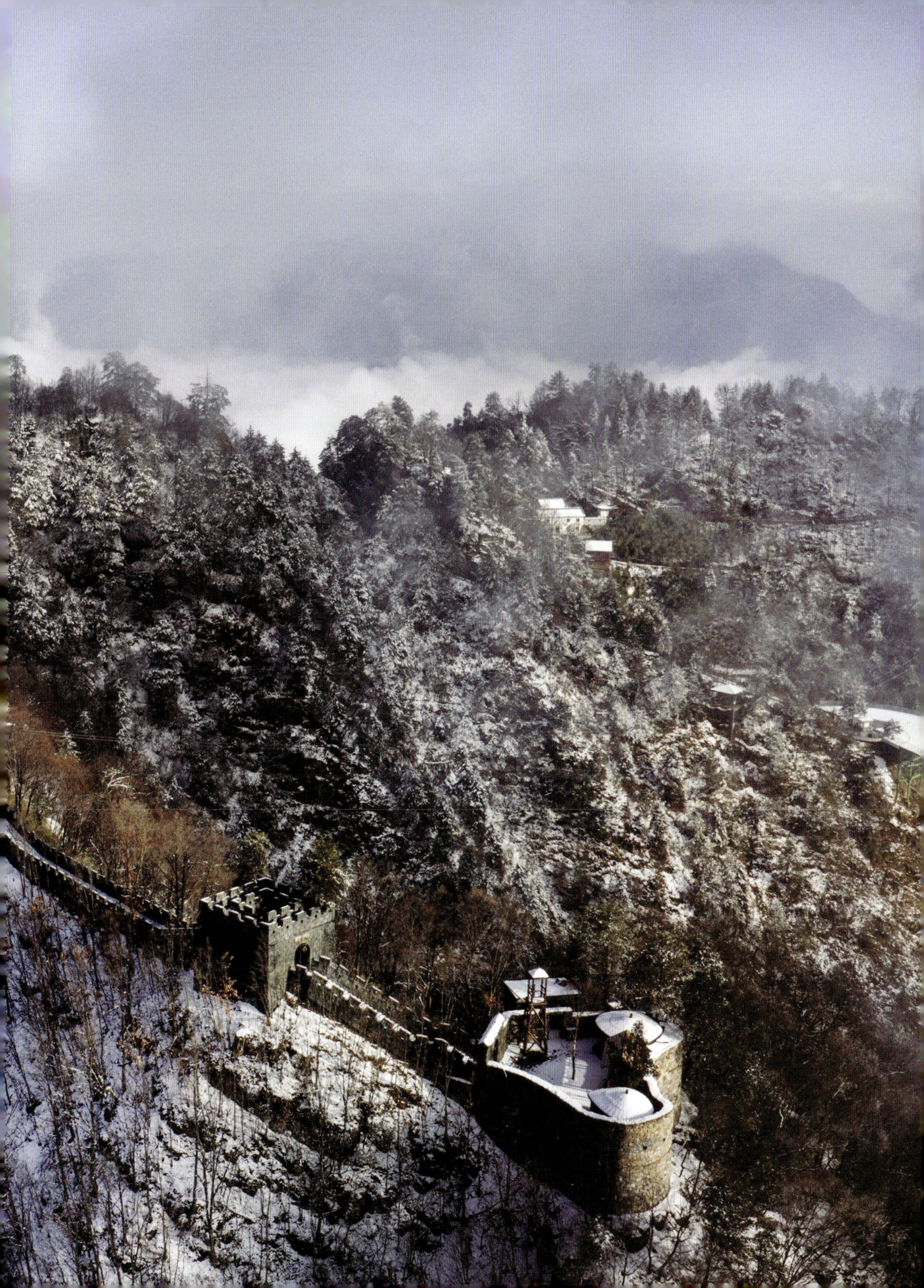

Qingyang Palace, Sichuan, China
One of China's most famous temples, Chengdu's Qingyang Palace is celebrated for its sumptuous statuary – most notably this magnificent bronze goat. This animal was traditionally prized for its purity and beauty, its mild manner and its pleasant flesh (a warming *yang* food). It was also seen as a powerful symbol of filial piety, supposedly from the way the young kid was seen to 'kneel' as it suckled from its mother.

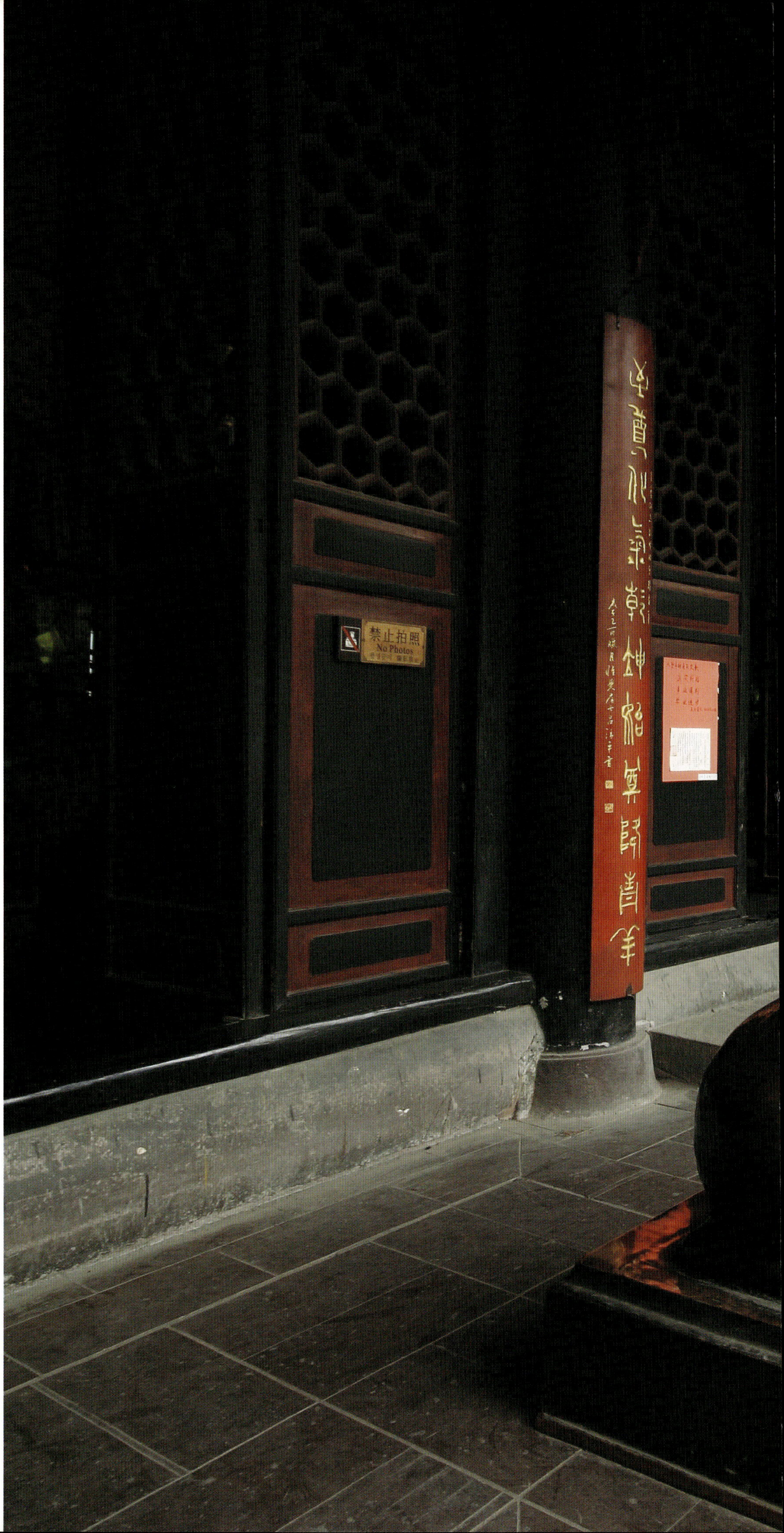

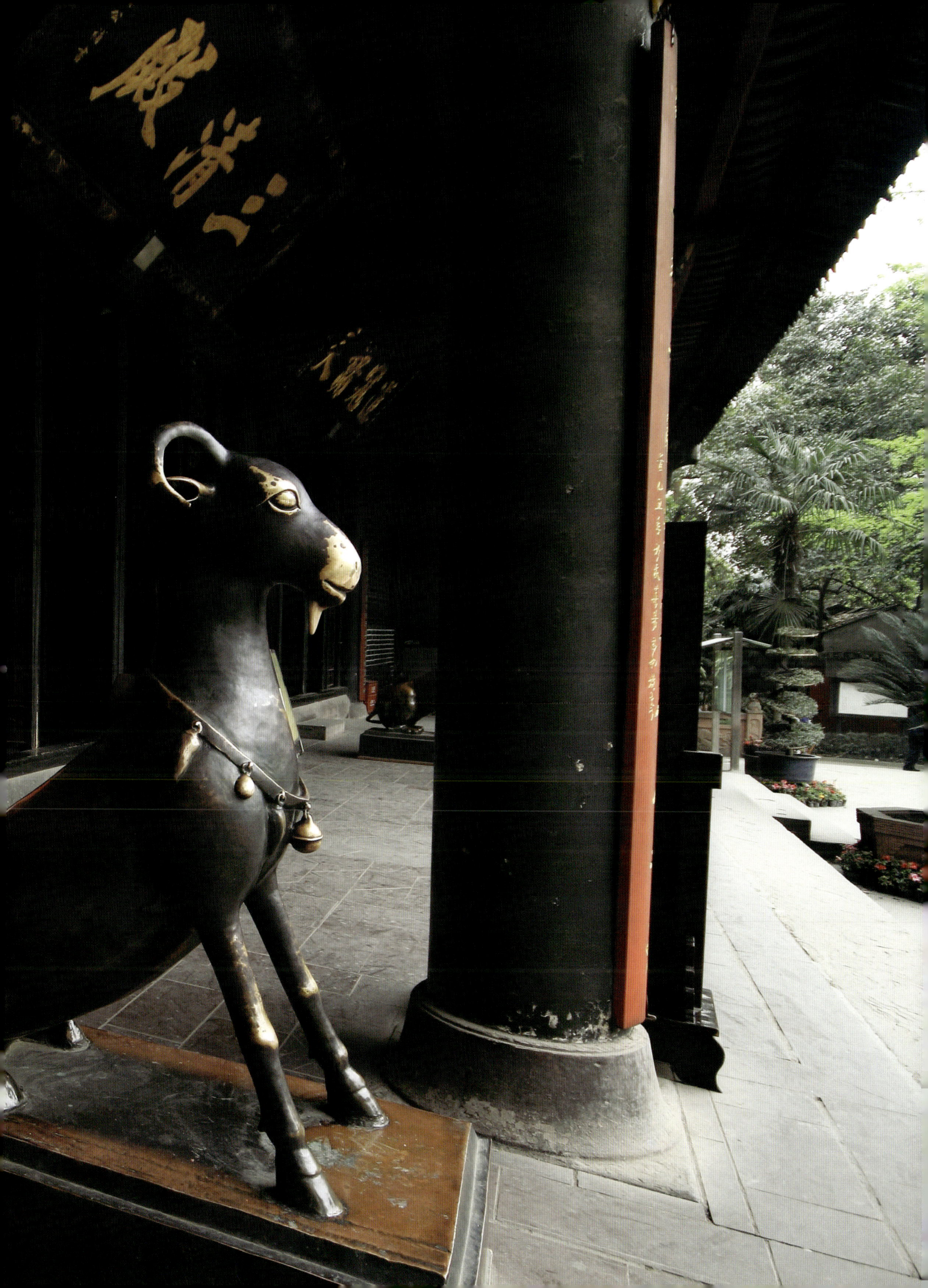

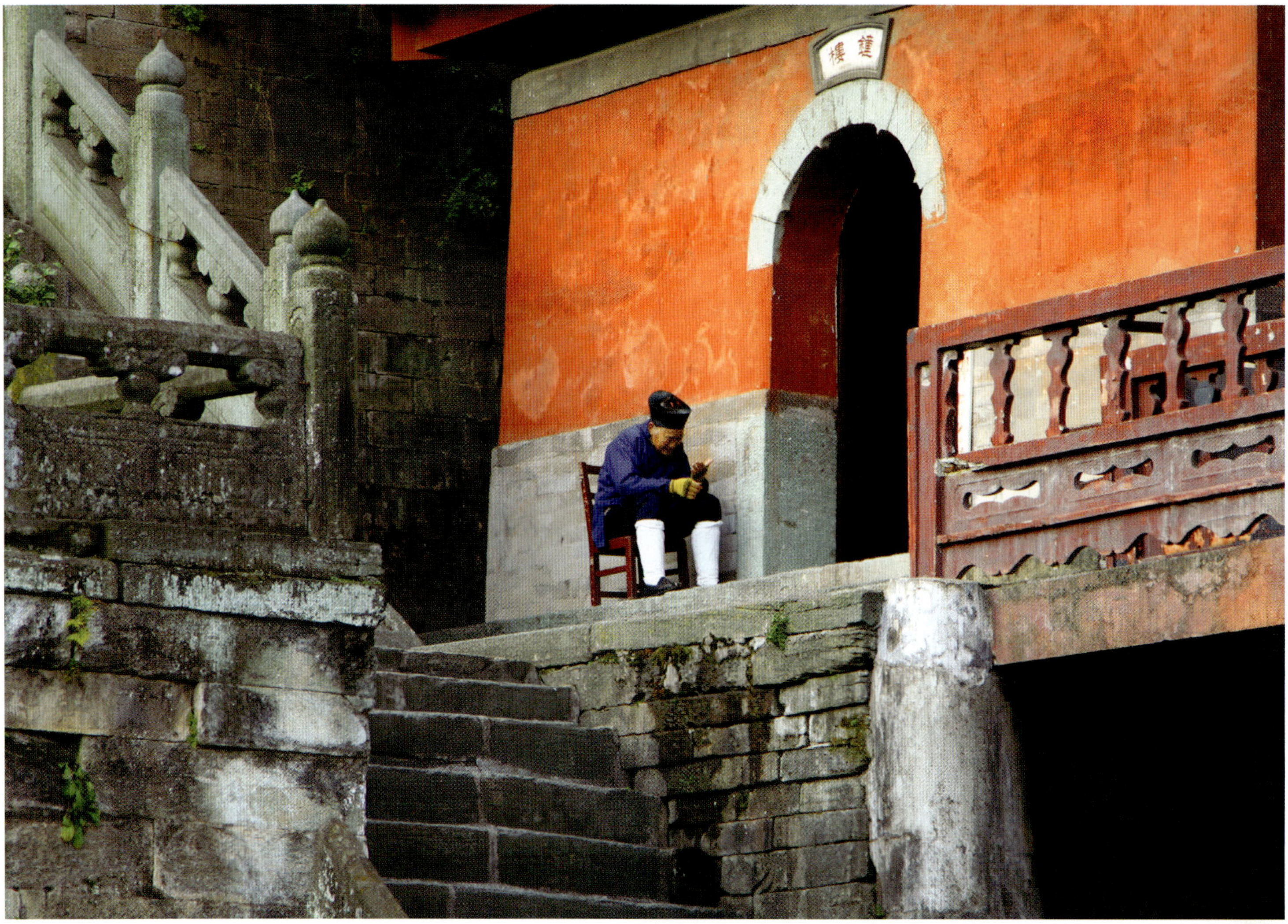

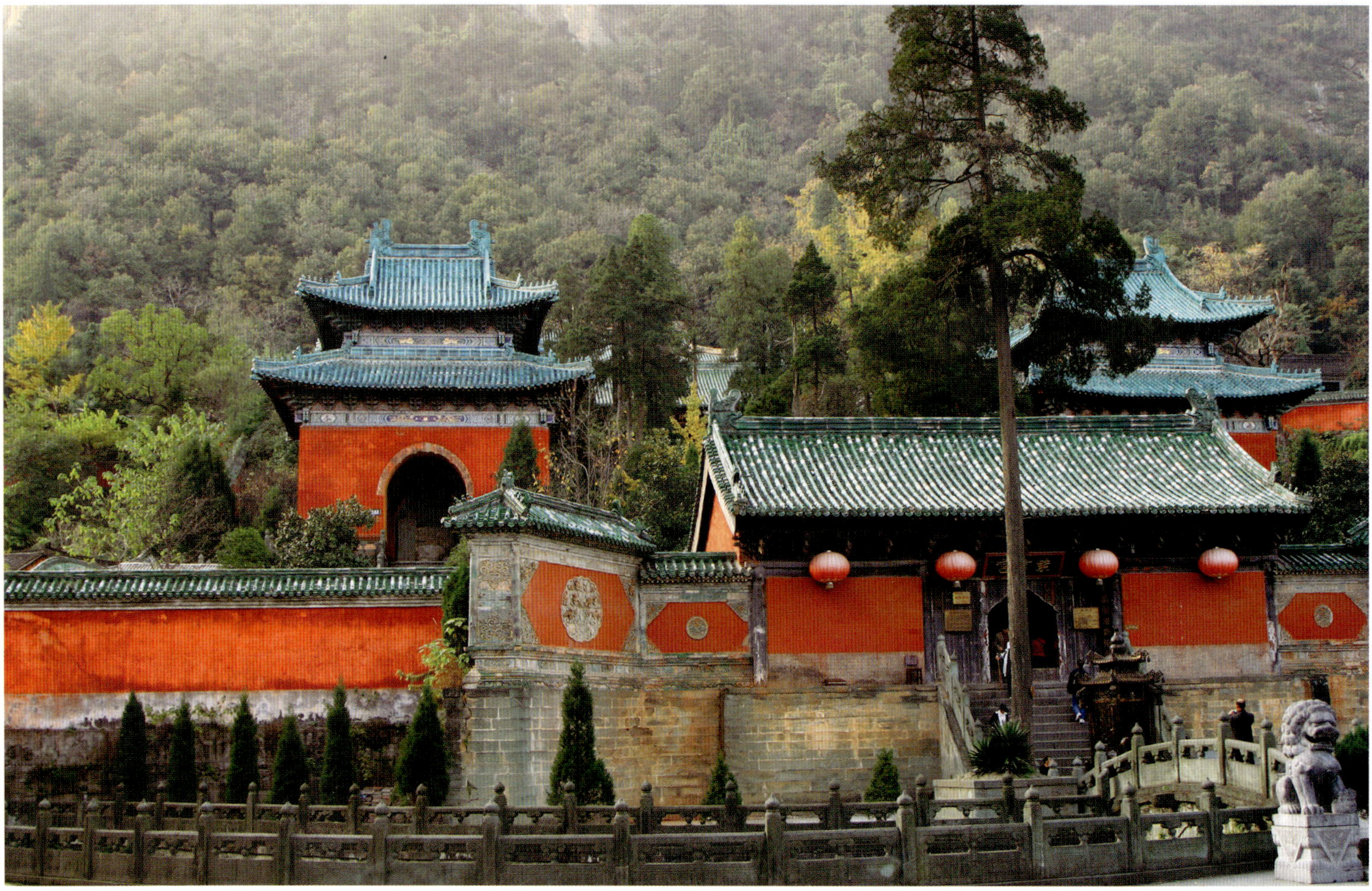

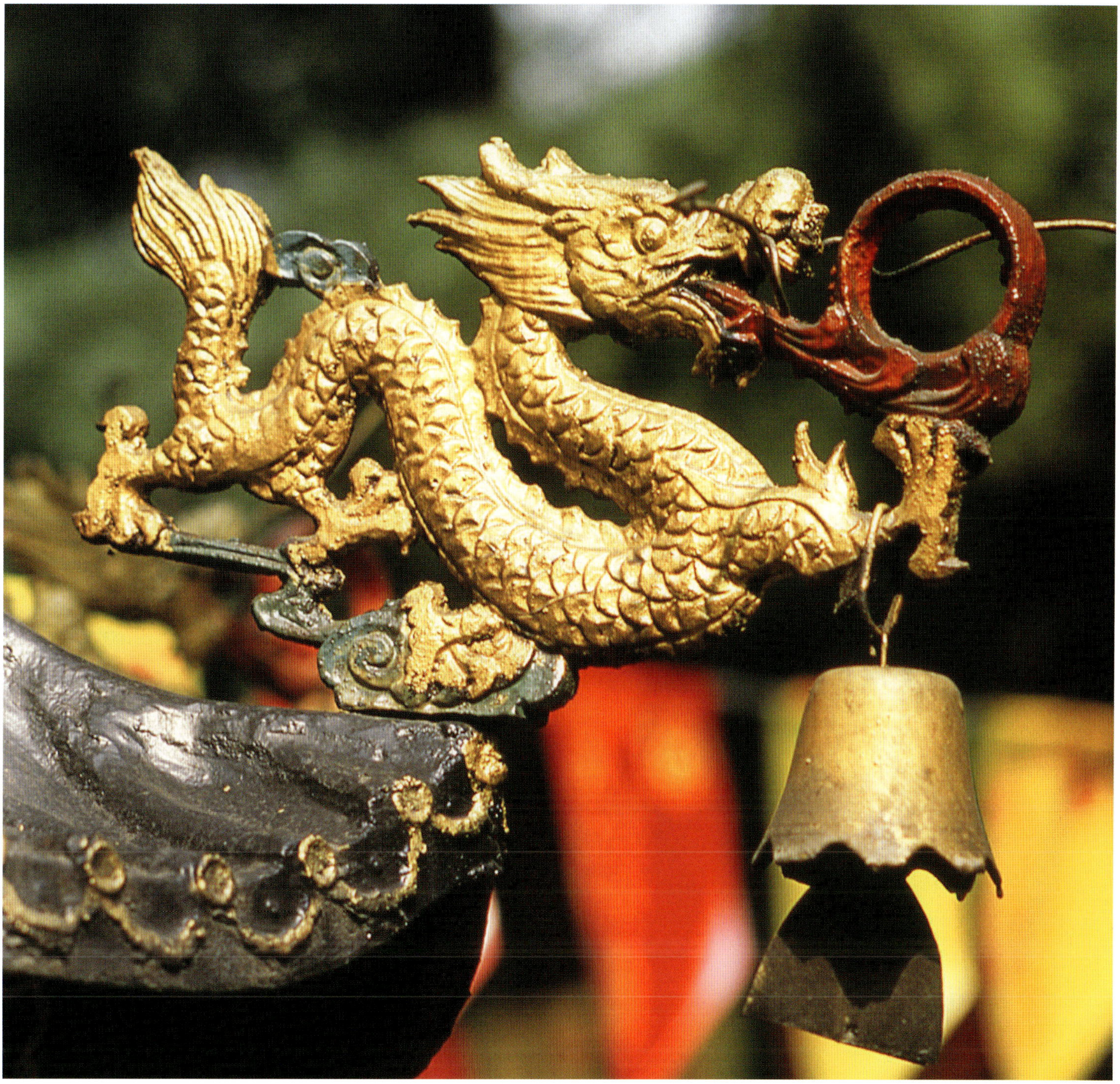

OPPOSITE, BOTH PHOTOGRAPHS:
Purple Cloud Temple, Wudang Mountains, China
Taoism does have deities, though theological scholars are at pains to point out that they're more personified principles than beings in their own right. (There's no strong sense of a 'Creation', for example: the Taoist universe has always existed; no 'divine will' was needed to bring it into being.) First established in the twelfth century, this great monastic complex is dedicated to Xuan Wu, the 'Black Emperor', a cunning sorcerer who can control the weather and a wrathful warrior who can bring his devotees success in battle.

ABOVE:
Qingyang Palace, Sichuan, China
Taoist temple architecture aimed to reflect that universal equilibrium most famously associated with the symbols of *yin* and *yang*, representing complementary principles of masculine and feminine, fire and water. The Chinese dragon doesn't generally breathe fire the way its Western equivalent does. With its undulating, phallic form it symbolizes water and fertility. When it does breathe flames, as here, it seems to reconcile important oppositions, to embody that crucial balance between *yin* and *yang*.

OVERLEAF:
White Cloud Temple, Beijing, China
Symmetry and space are sacred here. Much has been made in the West in recent years of the Chinese tradition of *feng shui* – the idea that with the right arrangement of our furniture we can access 'energies' from our environment and establish harmony. Such discussion may have been largely nonsense, but there is no doubt that, for centuries, Chinese thinking has seen architecture and interior design as a way of curating the relationship between living space and landscape – and the wider order of the universe.

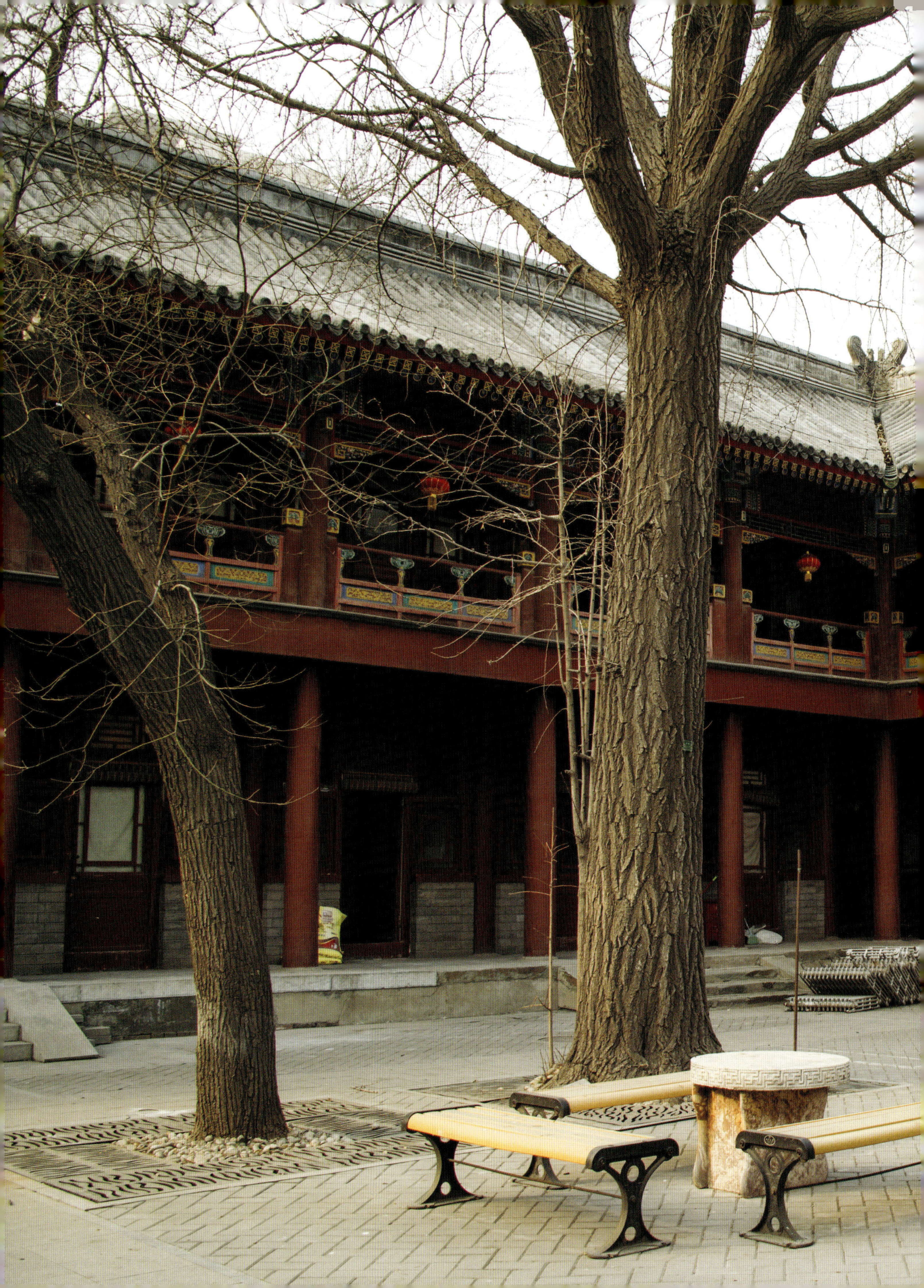

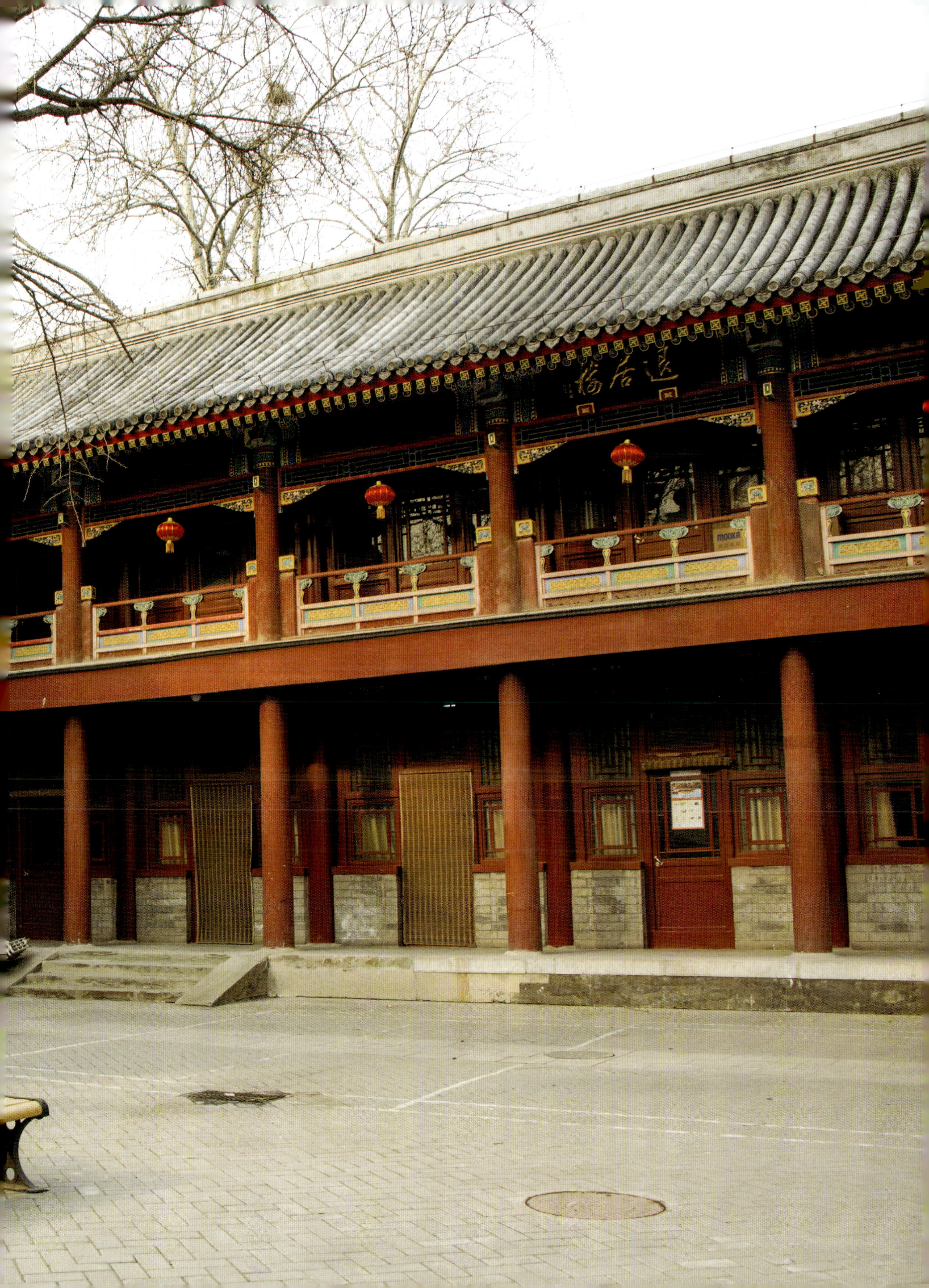

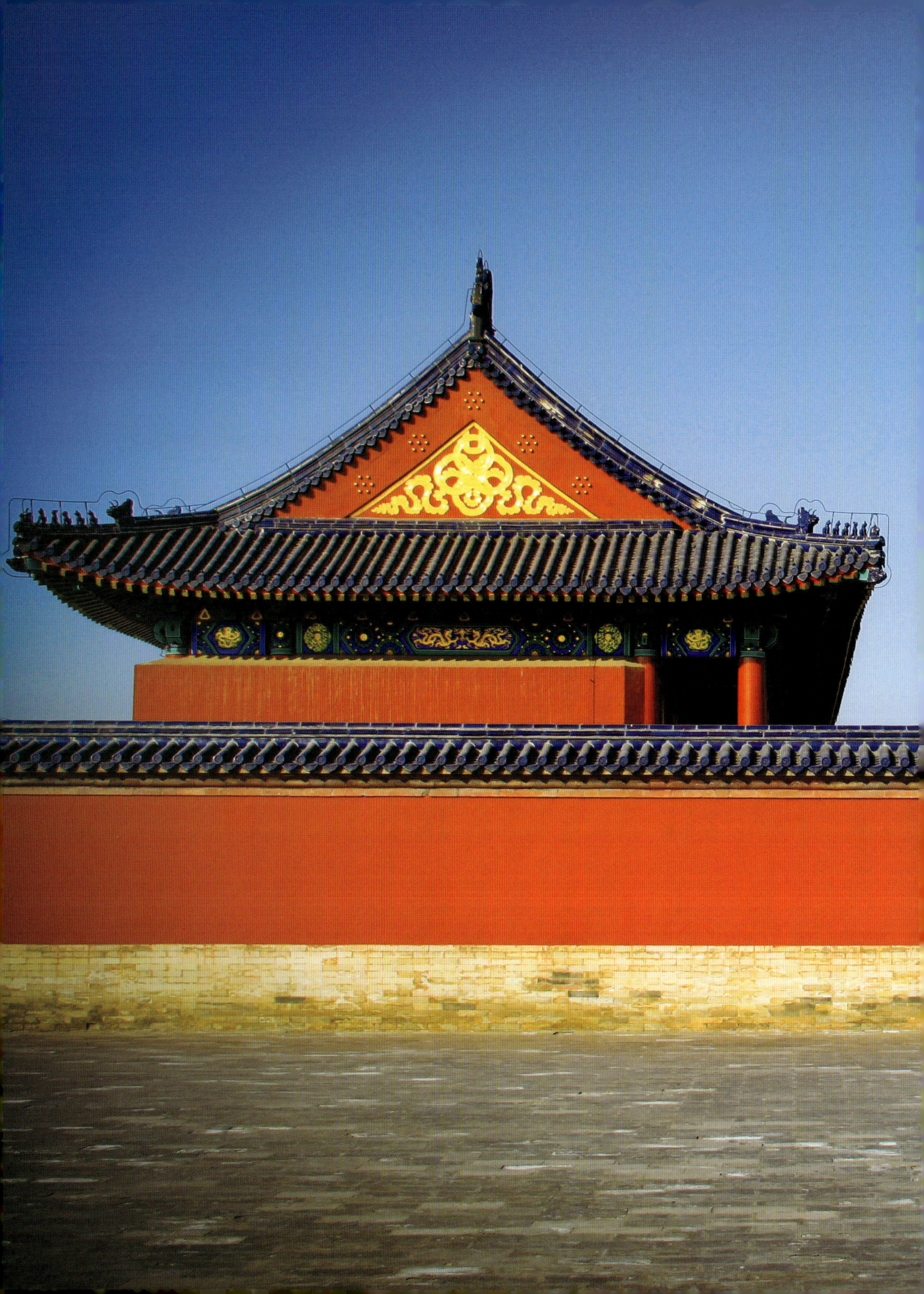

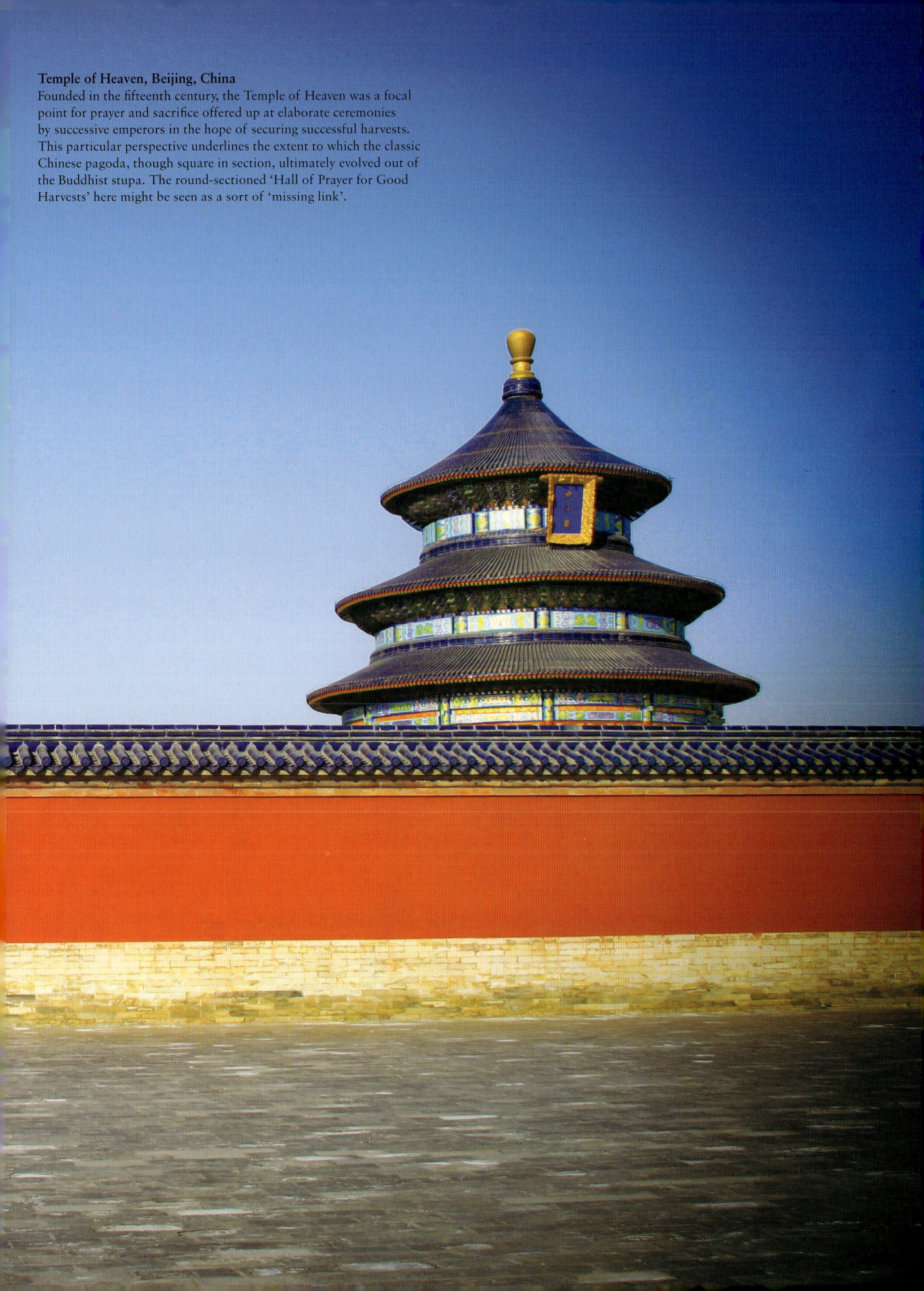

Temple of Heaven, Beijing, China

Founded in the fifteenth century, the Temple of Heaven was a focal point for prayer and sacrifice offered up at elaborate ceremonies by successive emperors in the hope of securing successful harvests. This particular perspective underlines the extent to which the classic Chinese pagoda, though square in section, ultimately evolved out of the Buddhist stupa. The round-sectioned 'Hall of Prayer for Good Harvests' here might be seen as a sort of 'missing link'.

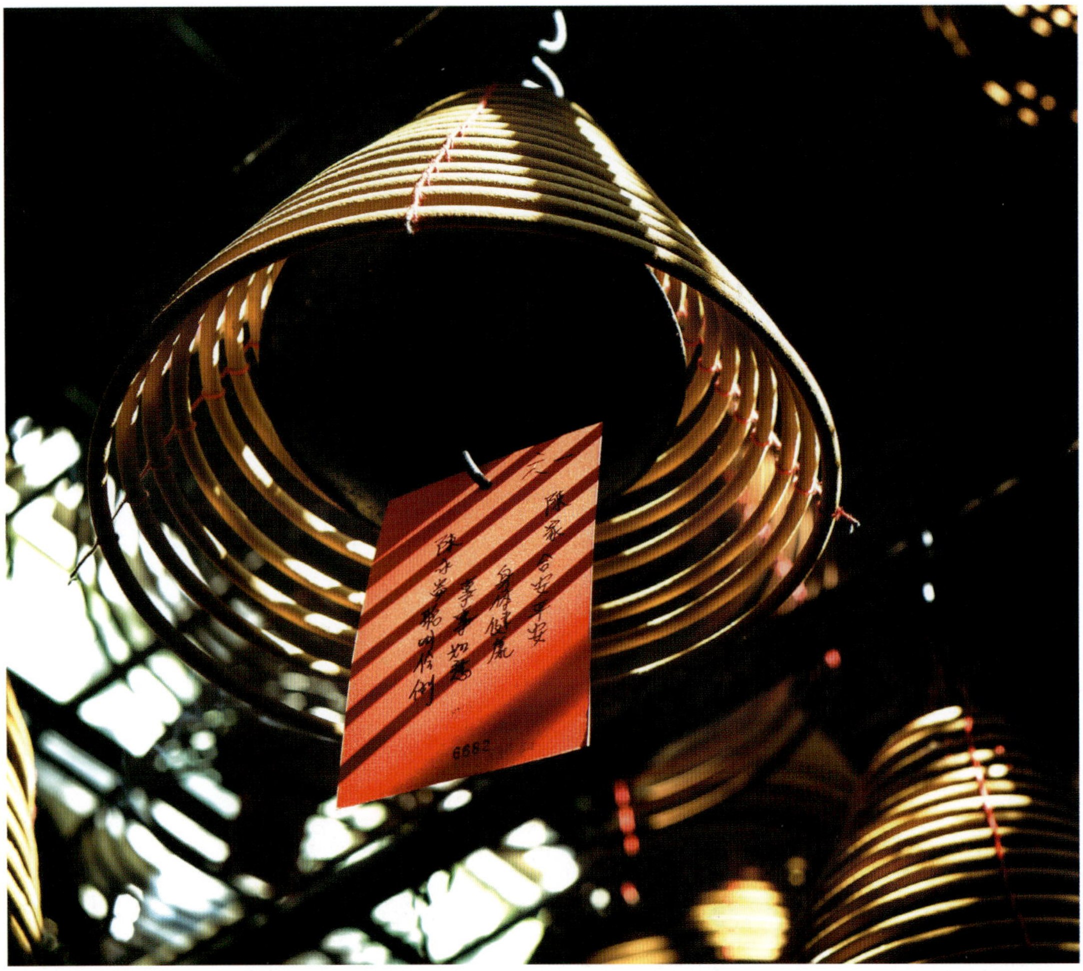

LEFT:
Man Mo Miu, Hong Kong
The lantern is of course a powerful symbol of enlightenment in Tao tradition. Man Cheong, to whom this shrine was dedicated, stood for civility and culture. A temple to Kwan Tai, the god of martial arts, stands nearby.

BELOW:
Fo Guang Shan Temple, Taiwan
The name of this temple means 'Buddha's Light Mountain' and since 1967 it has been the headquarters of an international monastic order dedicated to the diffusion of Buddhist principles into everyday life.

OPPOSITE:
Haeinsa, South Gyeongsang Province, South Korea
The home of Korean Buddhism, this monastery is especially remarkable for its library, the Tripitaka Koreana, which keeps the Buddhist scriptures, in the form not of books but wooden printing-blocks, carved between the eleventh and thirteenth centuries.

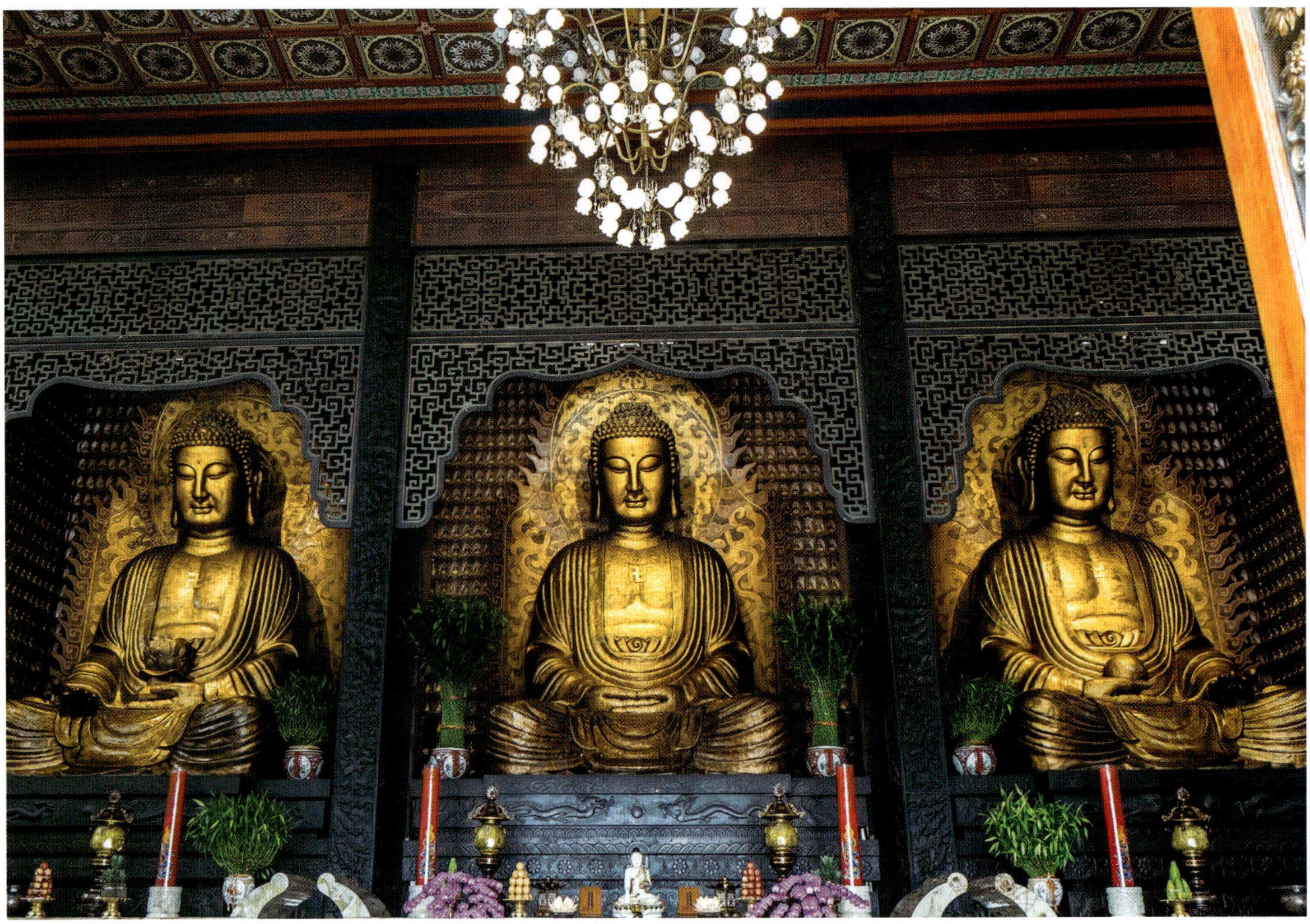

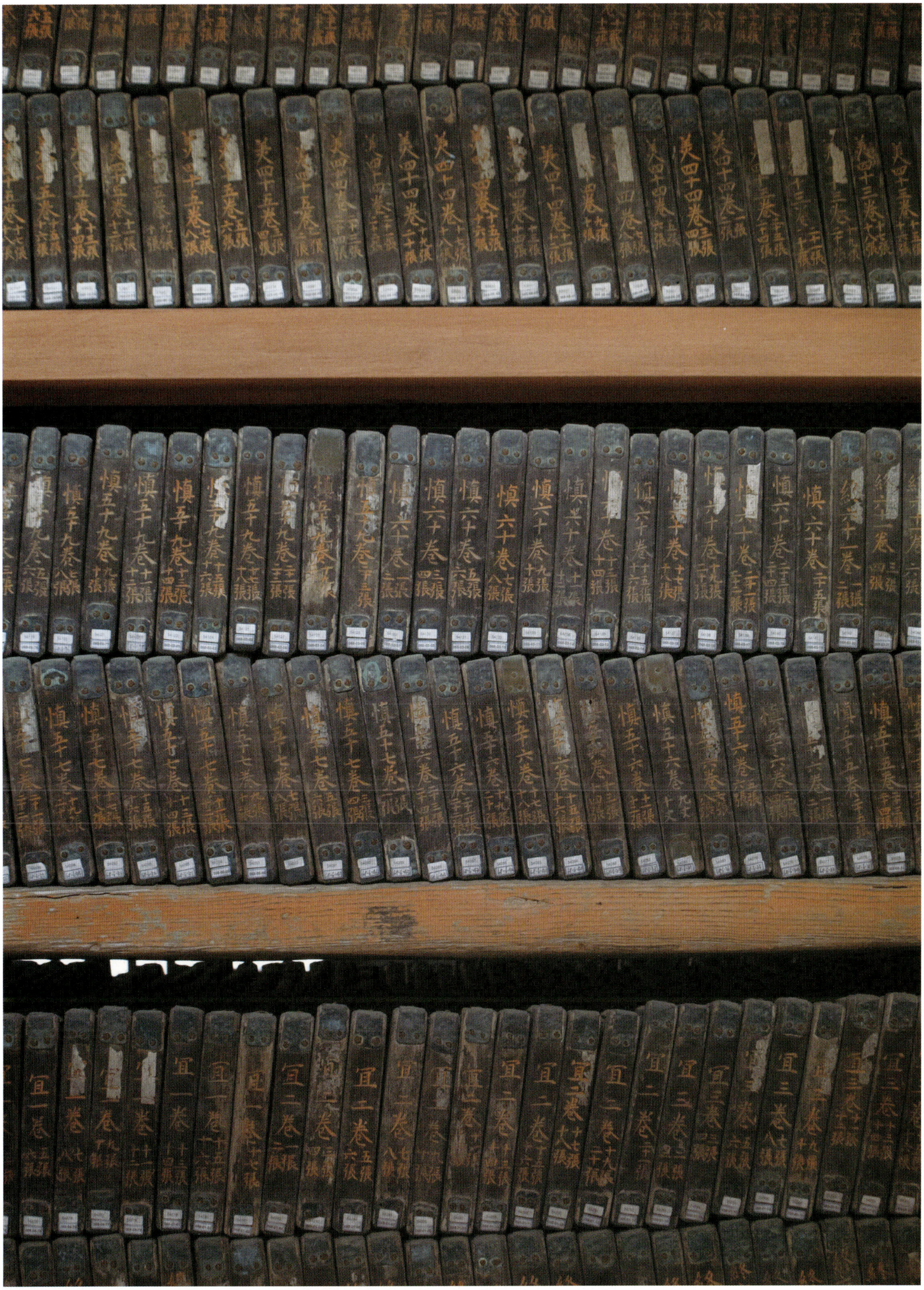

Tofuku-ji, Higashiyama-ku, Kyoto, Japan
In Asian cultural traditions, landscape and garden design have been of a piece with architecture, never really seen as separate – let alone dismissed as incidental. This vision of fresh greenery, viewed from the window of one of Japan's most venerable Buddhist shrines, doesn't just celebrate the earth's fecundity: it exemplifies the order and harmony of the natural world within the wider universe.

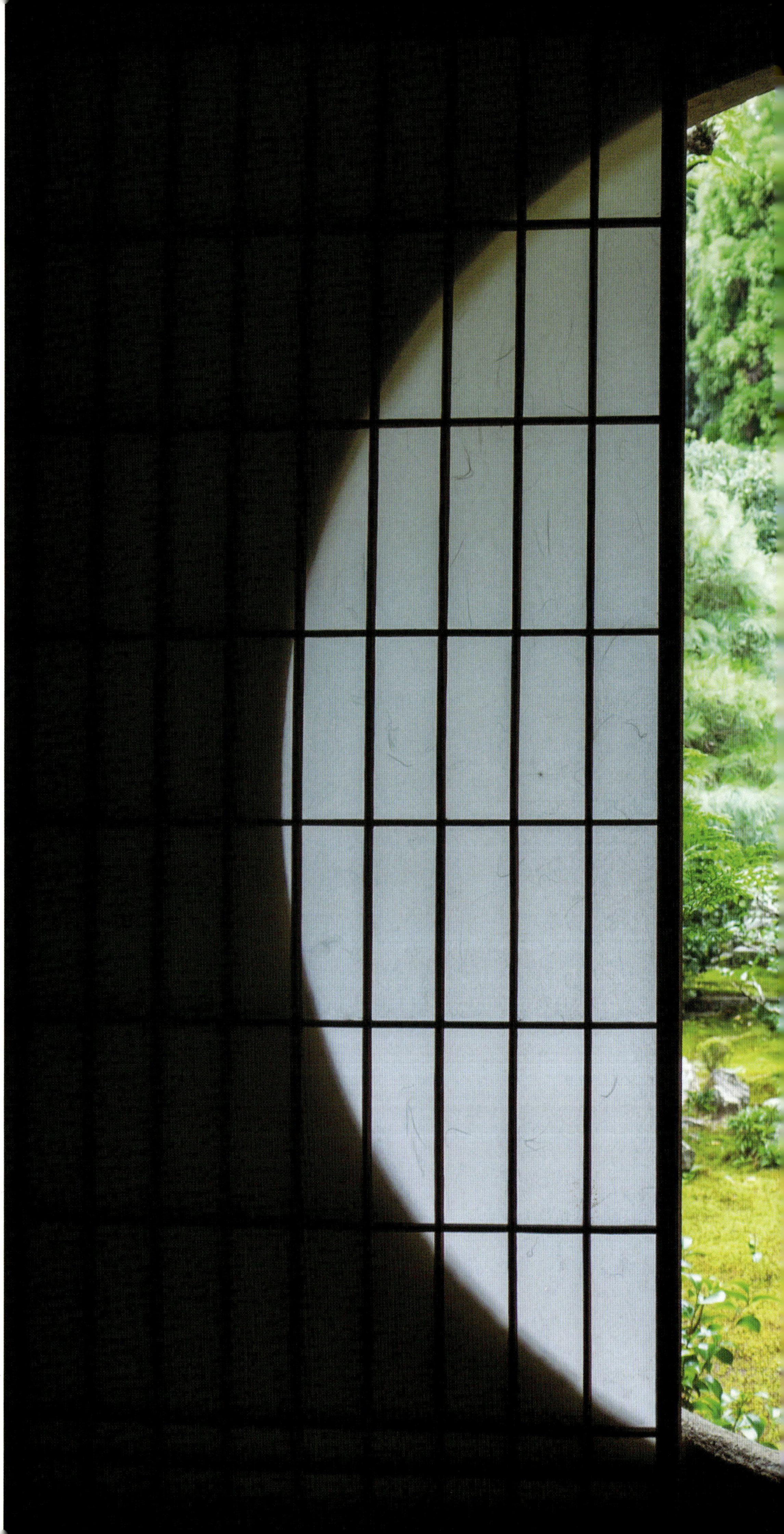

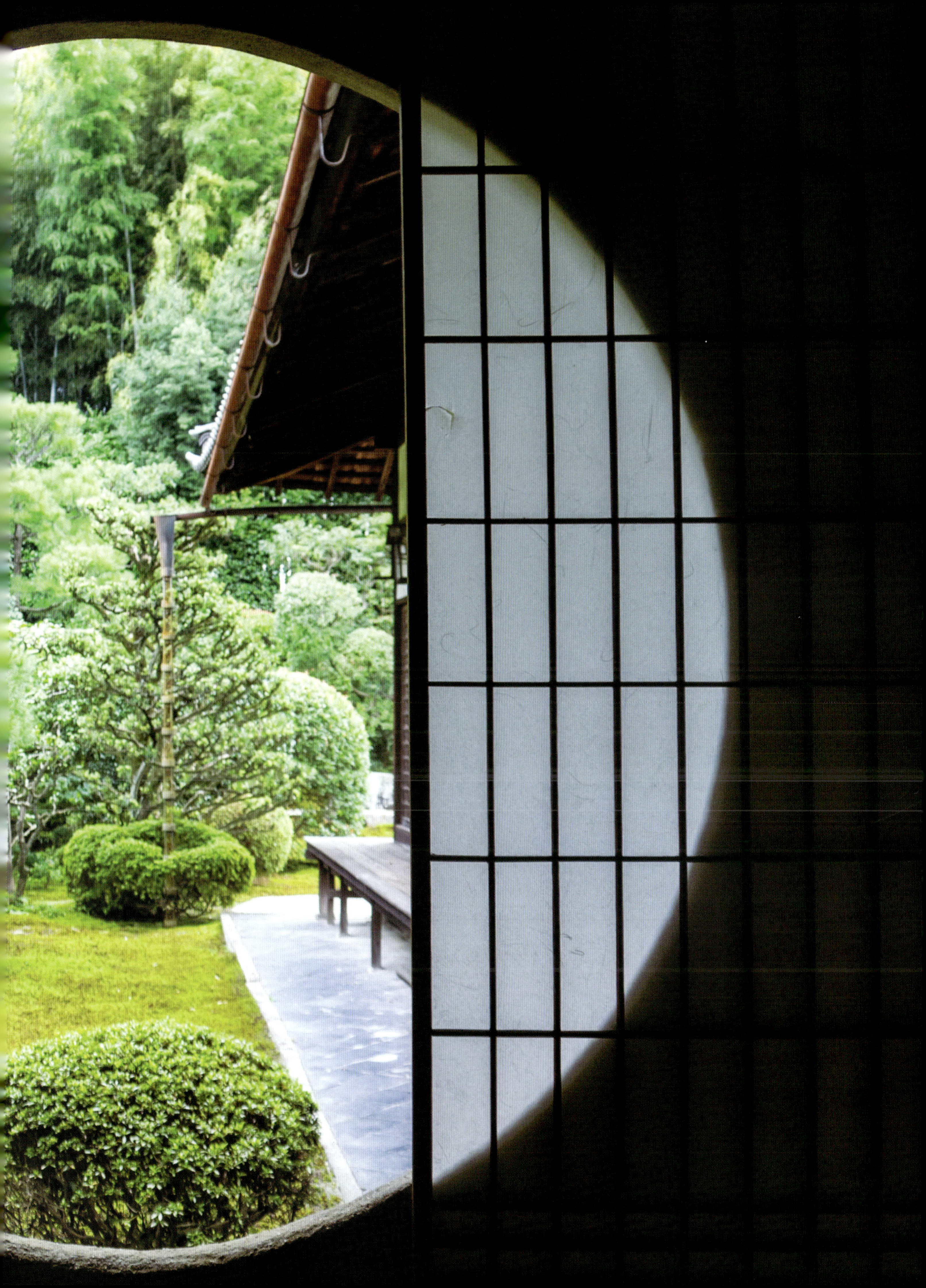

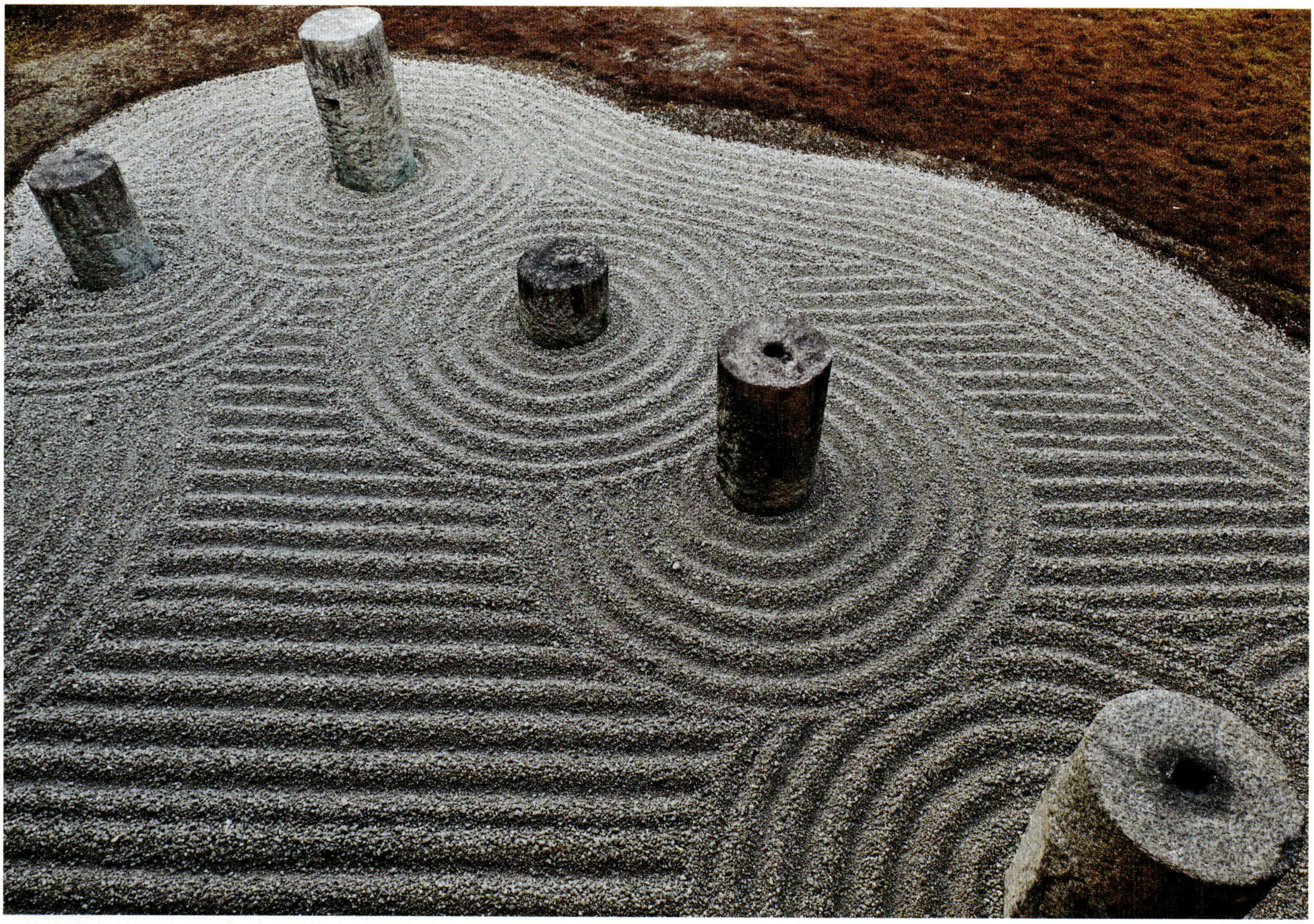

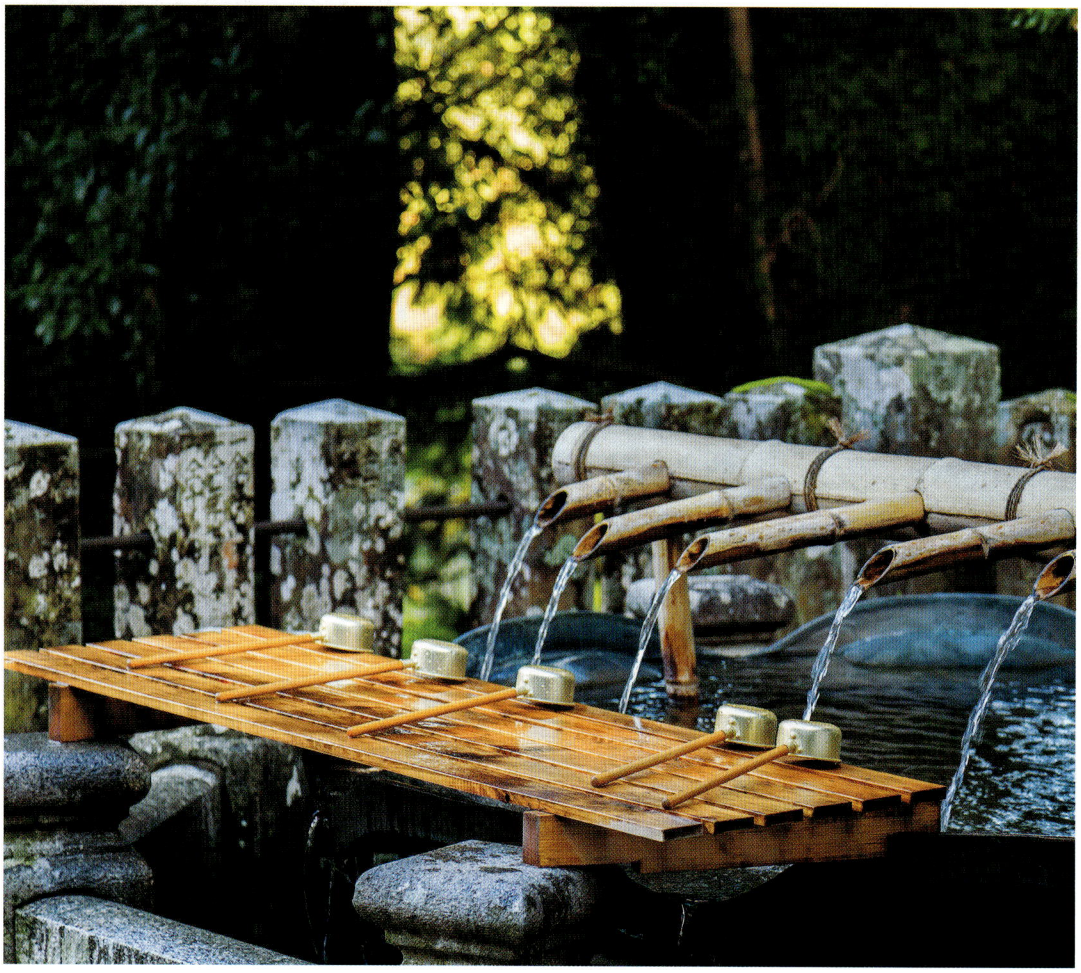

ABOVE:
Tofuku-ji, Higashiyama-ku, Kyoto, Japan
A stylized representation of natural forms in sand and stone, the 'dry garden' is a feature of Zen Buddhism. The spiral swirls here offer a way for the mind in meditation to find its focus, moving gradually inward, dismissing distractions as it goes.

LEFT:
Seiganto-ji, Wakayama Prefecture, Japan
Perpetually in motion, eternally self-replenishing, the waterfall has been a powerful spiritual symbol for centuries. These characteristics are reproduced in miniature in this sculpture from the Buddhist temple at Seiganto-ji, established beside natural rapids in the fourth century.

OPPOSITE:
Todai-ji, Nara, Japan
The Buddha is all peace and calm, of course – hence his need to be accompanied (many of his followers felt) by warrior-companions or *nio*, like this irascible-looking fellow here.

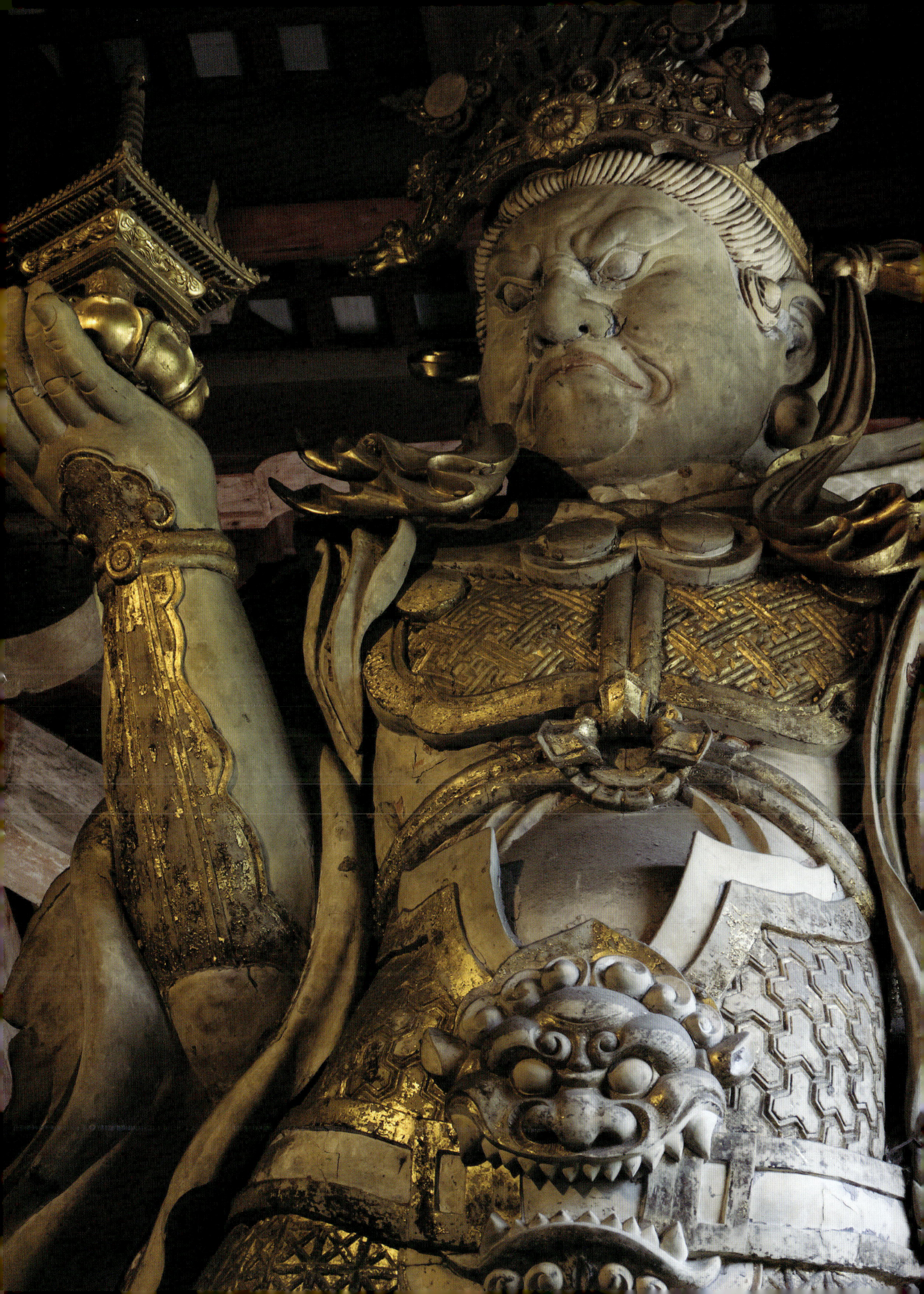

Nanzen-ji, Kyoto, Japan
Golden dragons cavort across the ceiling of a sumptuously-decorated wooden hall. The *hondo* (main hall) is the architectural heart and spiritual soul of any Japanese Buddhist temple. This one at Nanzen-ji is particularly stunning. This important temple complex was originally founded towards the end of the fourteenth century, but it's been destroyed by fire and had to be constructed several times since then.

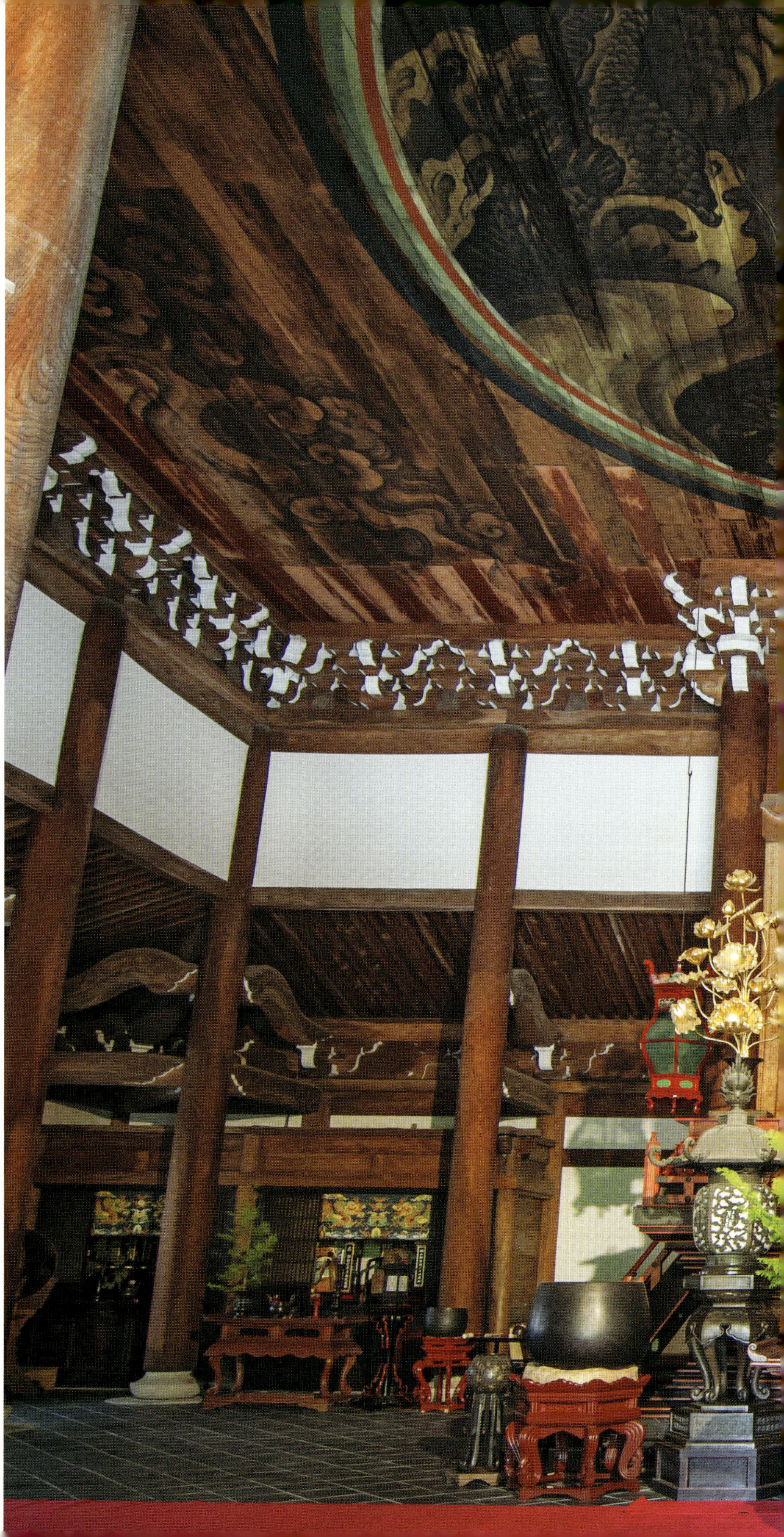

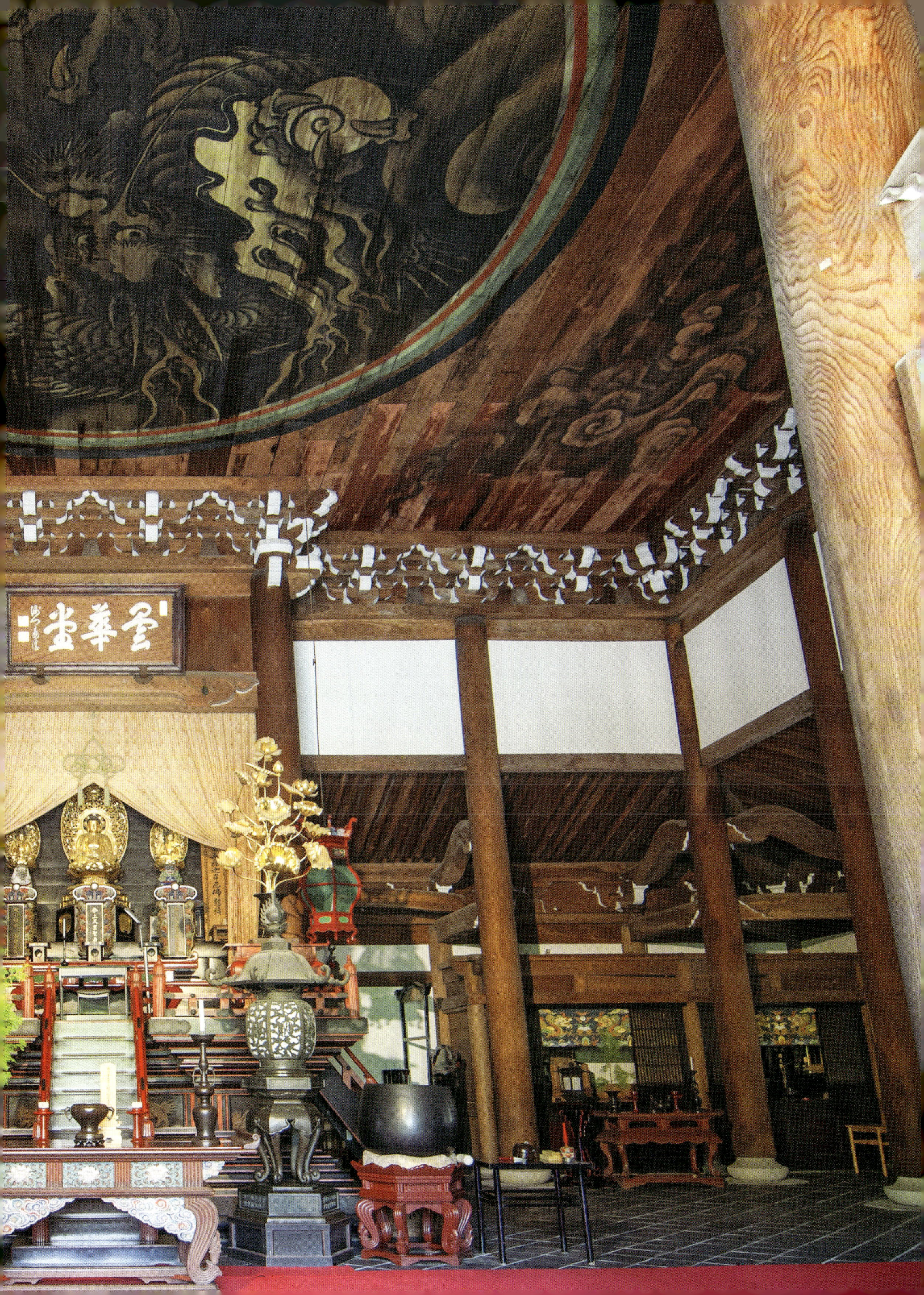

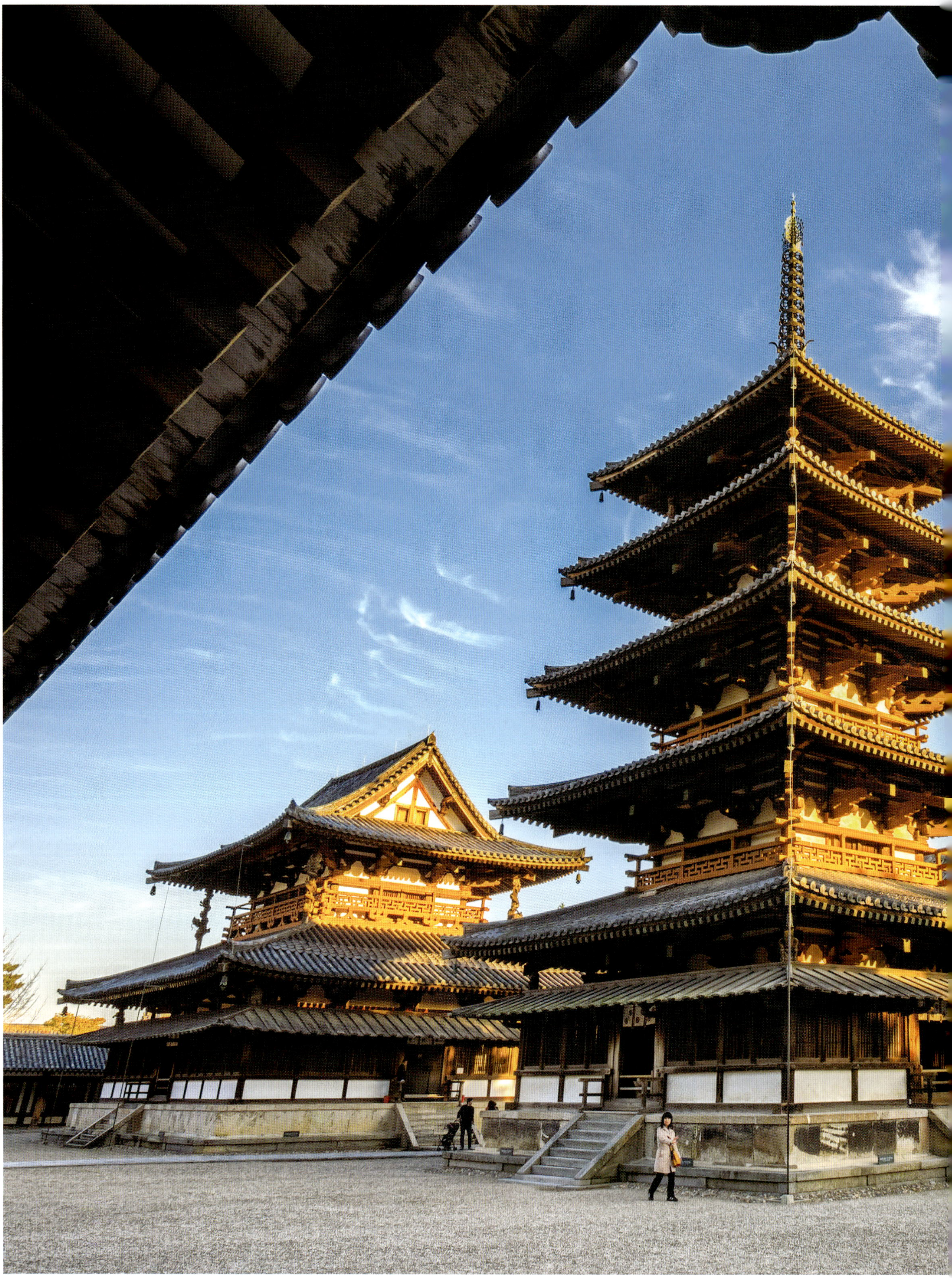

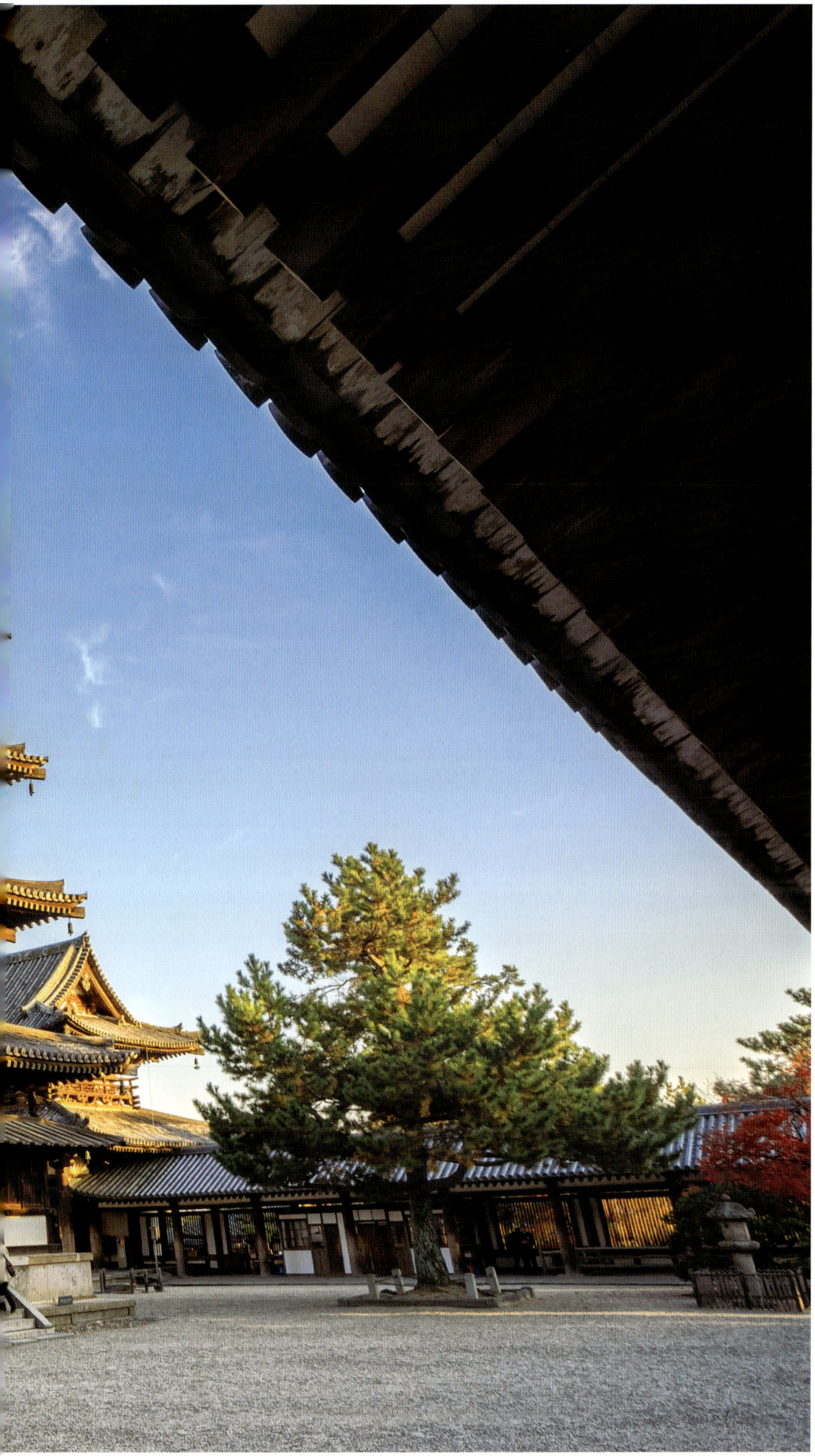

Horyu-ji, Nara, Japan
Standing just over 32m (122 ft) tall, this magnificent pagoda has been dated to the end of the seventh century, which firmly places it among the oldest wooden structures in the world. The gatehouse and *hondo* (hall) beside it aren't too much younger. Tradition has it that Prince Shotoku (574–622) first founded a temple here in 607; his (largely legendary) life and works are still commemorated here.

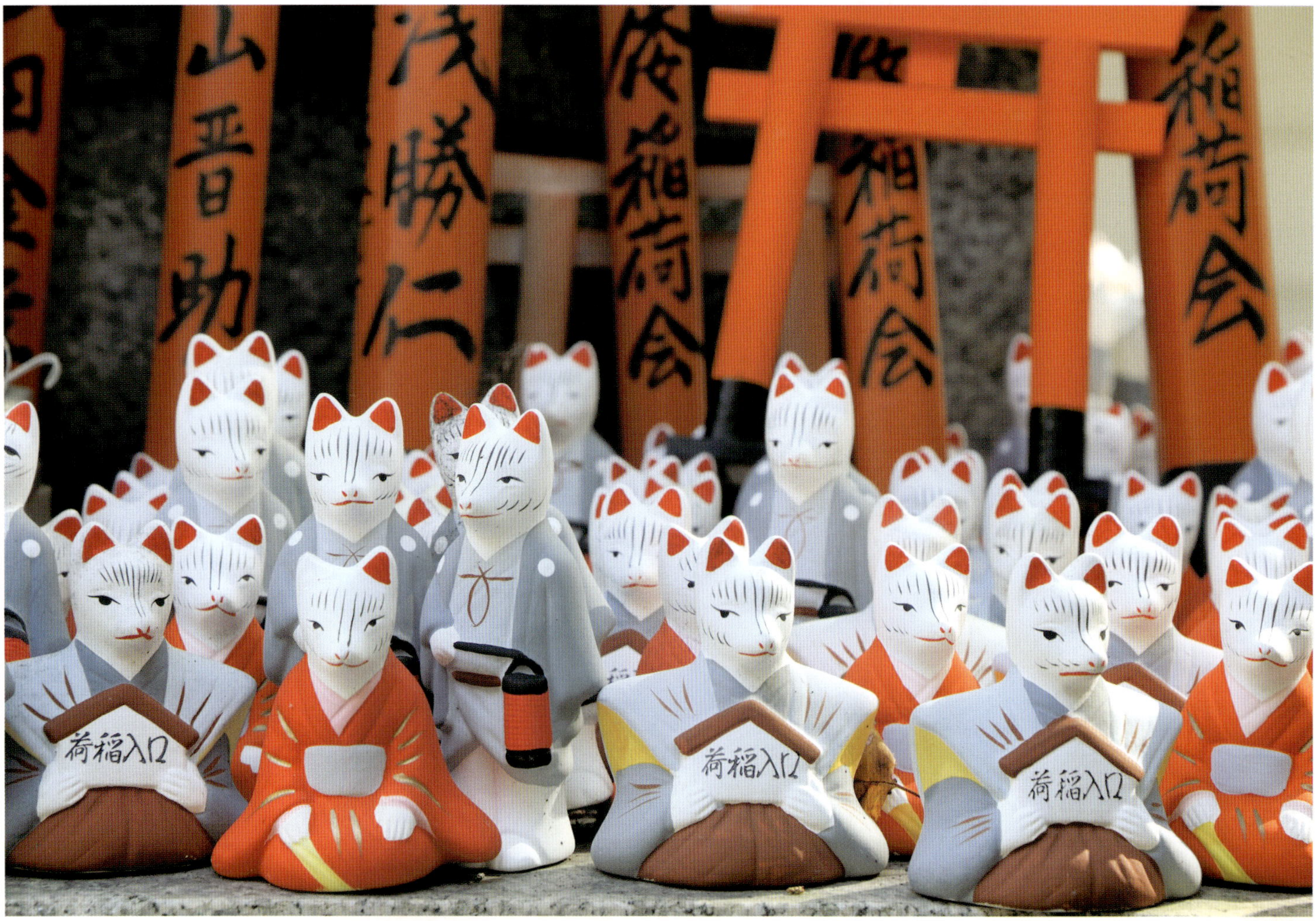

ALL PHOTOGRAPHS:
Fushimi Inari-taisha, Kyoto, Japan
Japan's home-grown religion, Shinto is difficult to define, not least because it is so profoundly local. Anarchic alike in institutional structures and doctrines, it centres on place-specific pagan practices and beliefs and is consequently different everywhere. The deity or *kami* honoured at this shrine is associated with Inari, a god of rice and agriculture – and, nowadays, of success in business too.

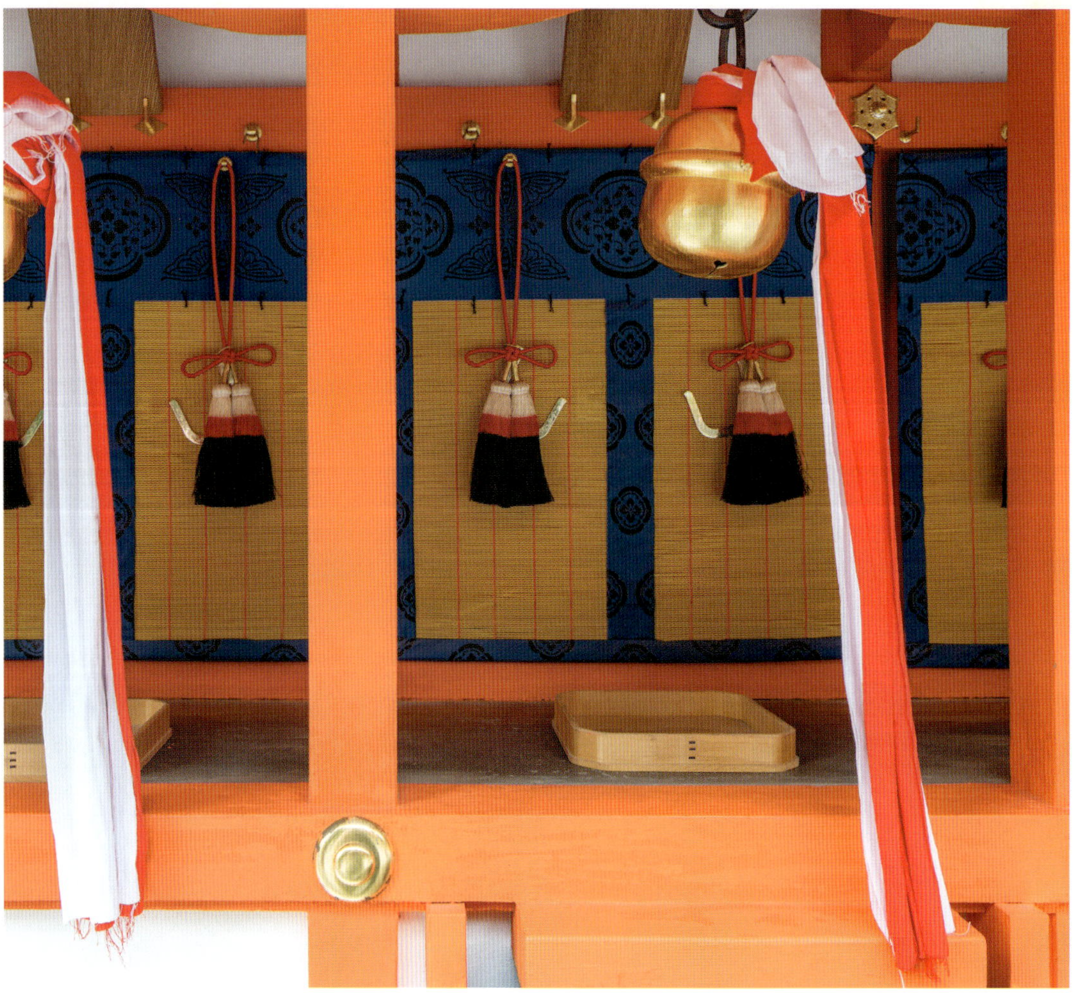

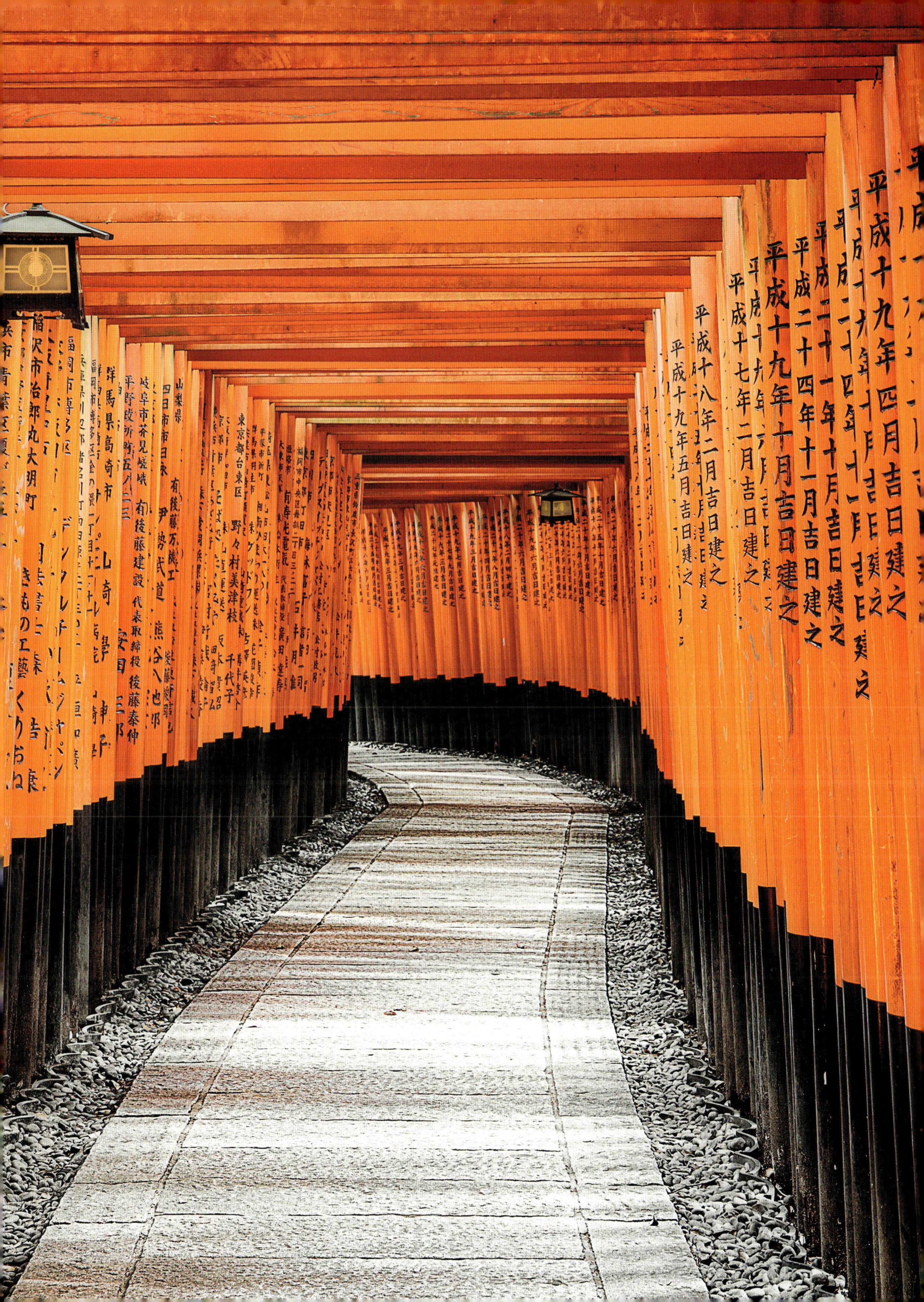
平成十九年四月吉日建之
平成二十四年十一月吉日建之
平成十九年十一月吉日建之
平成十七年二月吉日建之
平成十八年二月吉日建之
平成十九年五月吉日建之
群馬県高崎市
東京都台東区
野々村美津枝

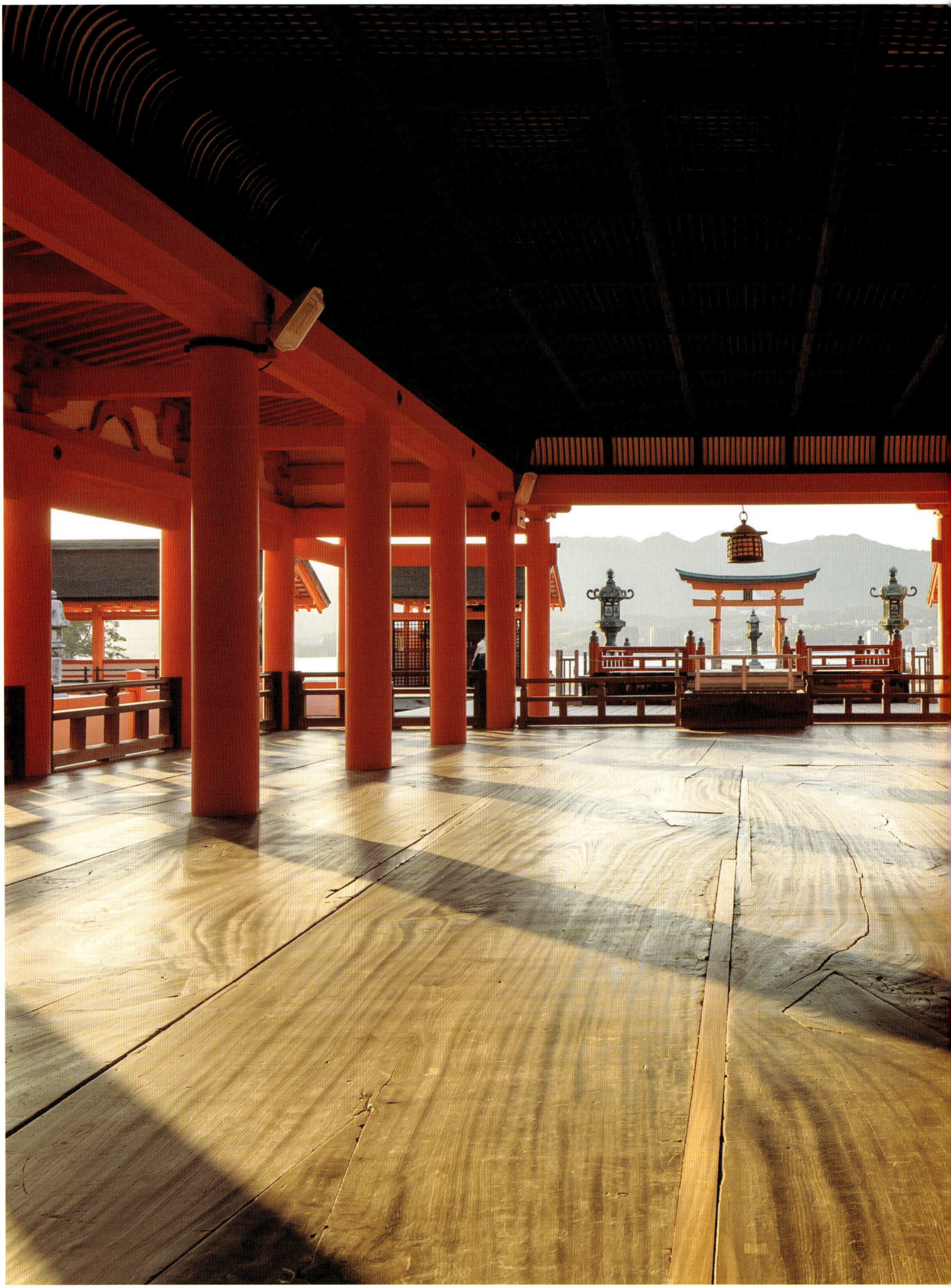

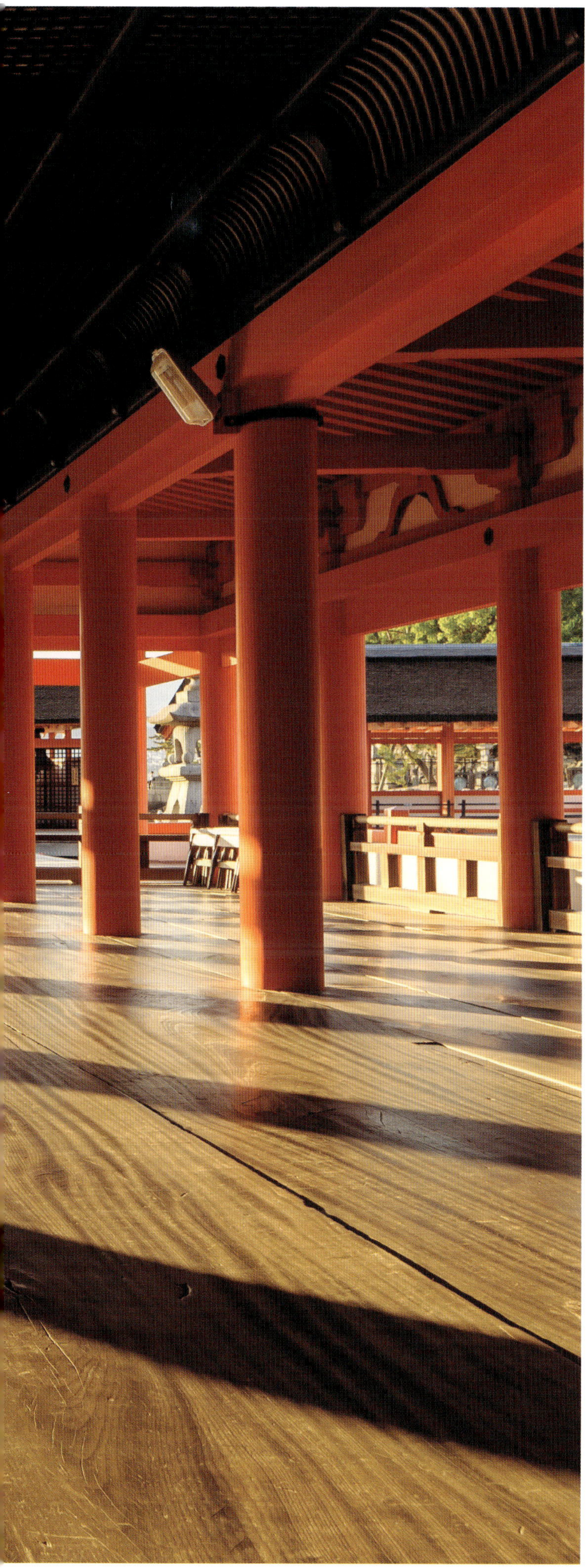

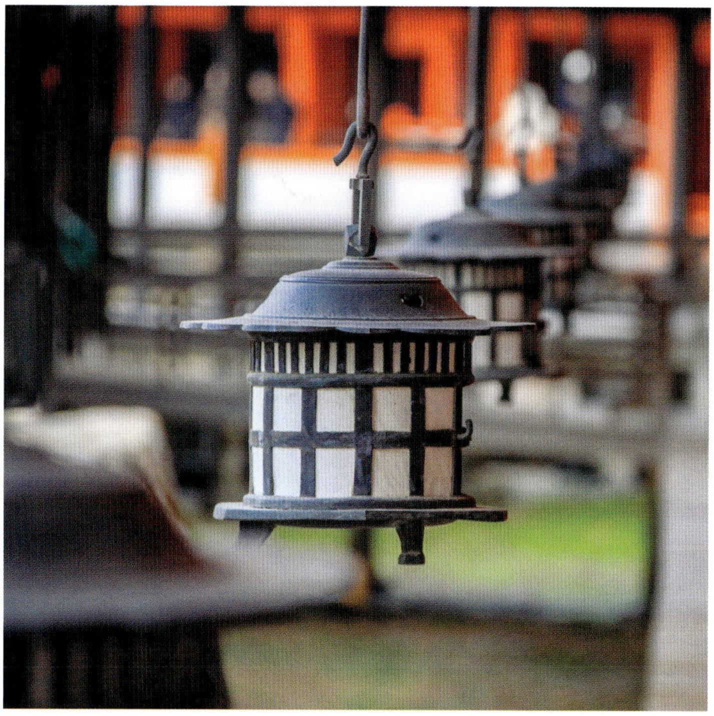

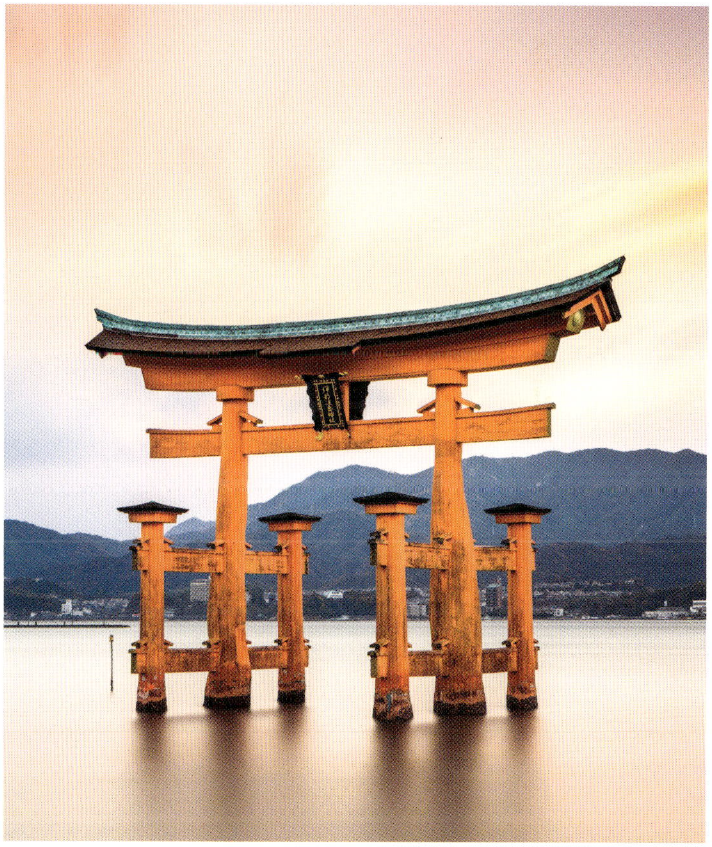

ALL PHOTOGRAPHS:
Itsukushima Shrine, Hatsukaichi, Japan
Three goddesses, patrons of the sea and storms, the so-called *Sanjoshin*, are worshipped at this Shinto temple, which stands on a lovely little island in Hiroshima Bay. It is famous for its *torii* gate, which marks out the entrance to the sacred precincts of the shrine, and at any but the lowest tide appears to float. Itsukushima Shrine was reputedly founded by Taira no Kiyomori, a semi-legendary twelfth-century warlord.

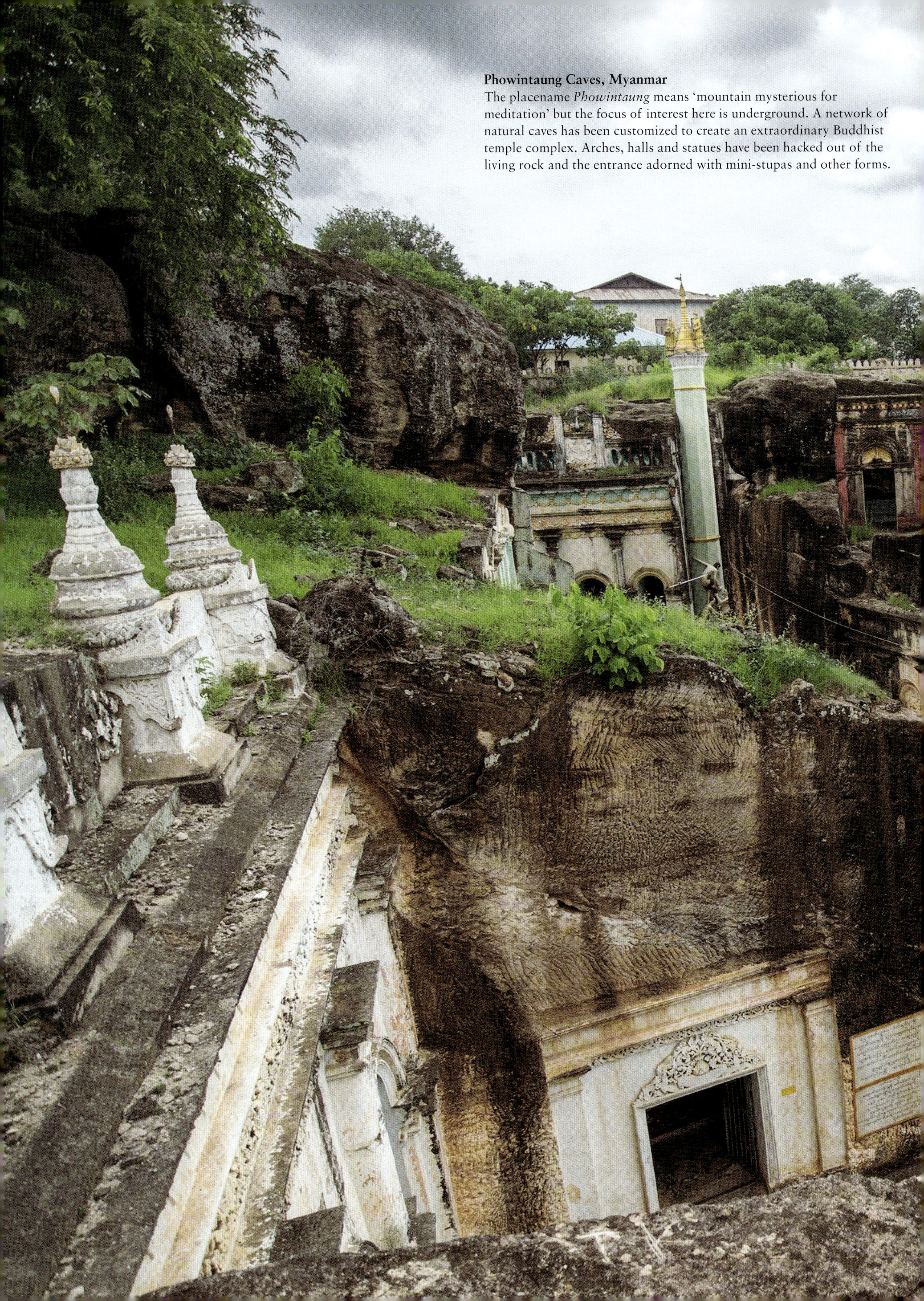

Phowintaung Caves, Myanmar
The placename *Phowintaung* means 'mountain mysterious for meditation' but the focus of interest here is underground. A network of natural caves has been customized to create an extraordinary Buddhist temple complex. Arches, halls and statues have been hacked out of the living rock and the entrance adorned with mini-stupas and other forms.

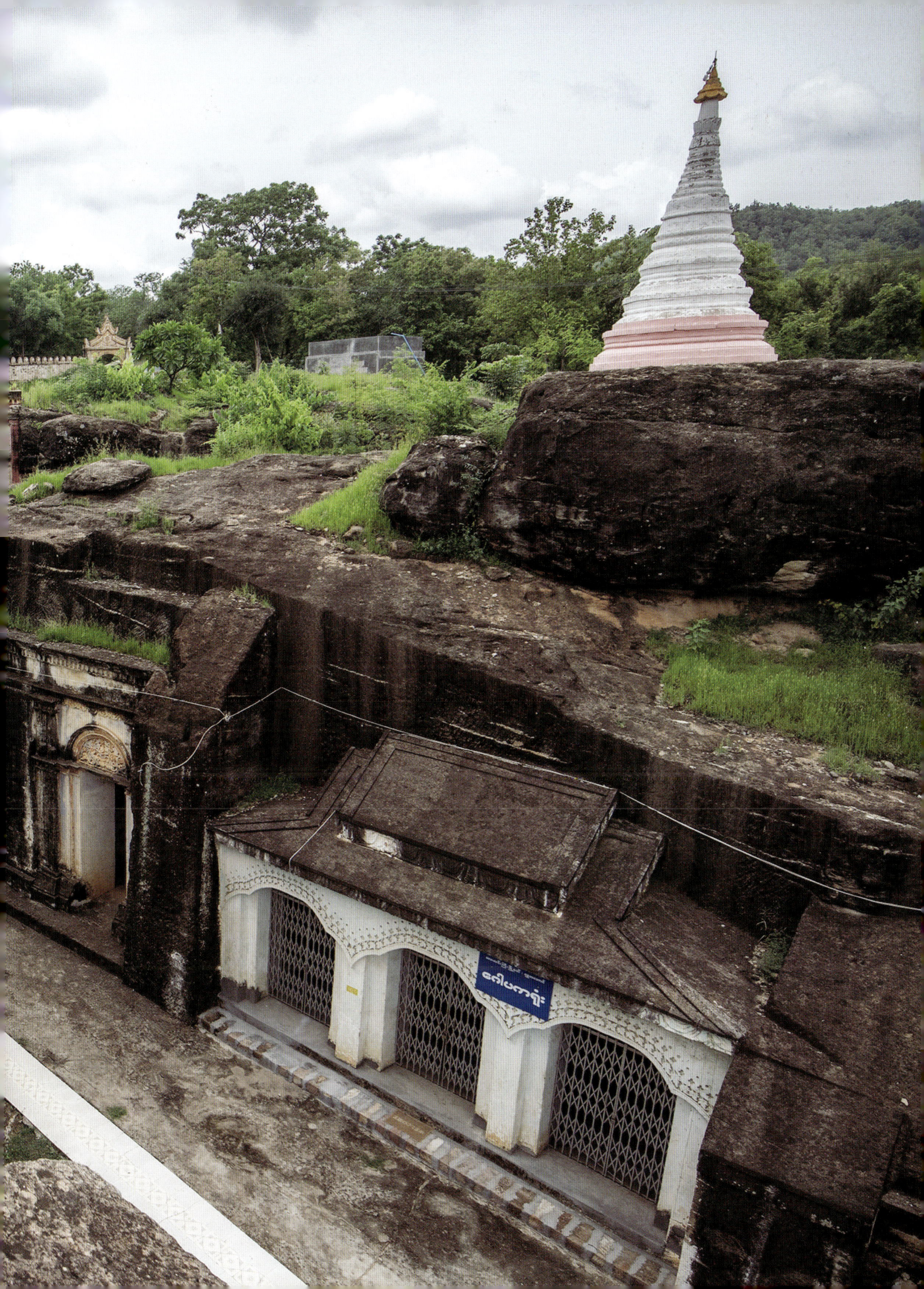

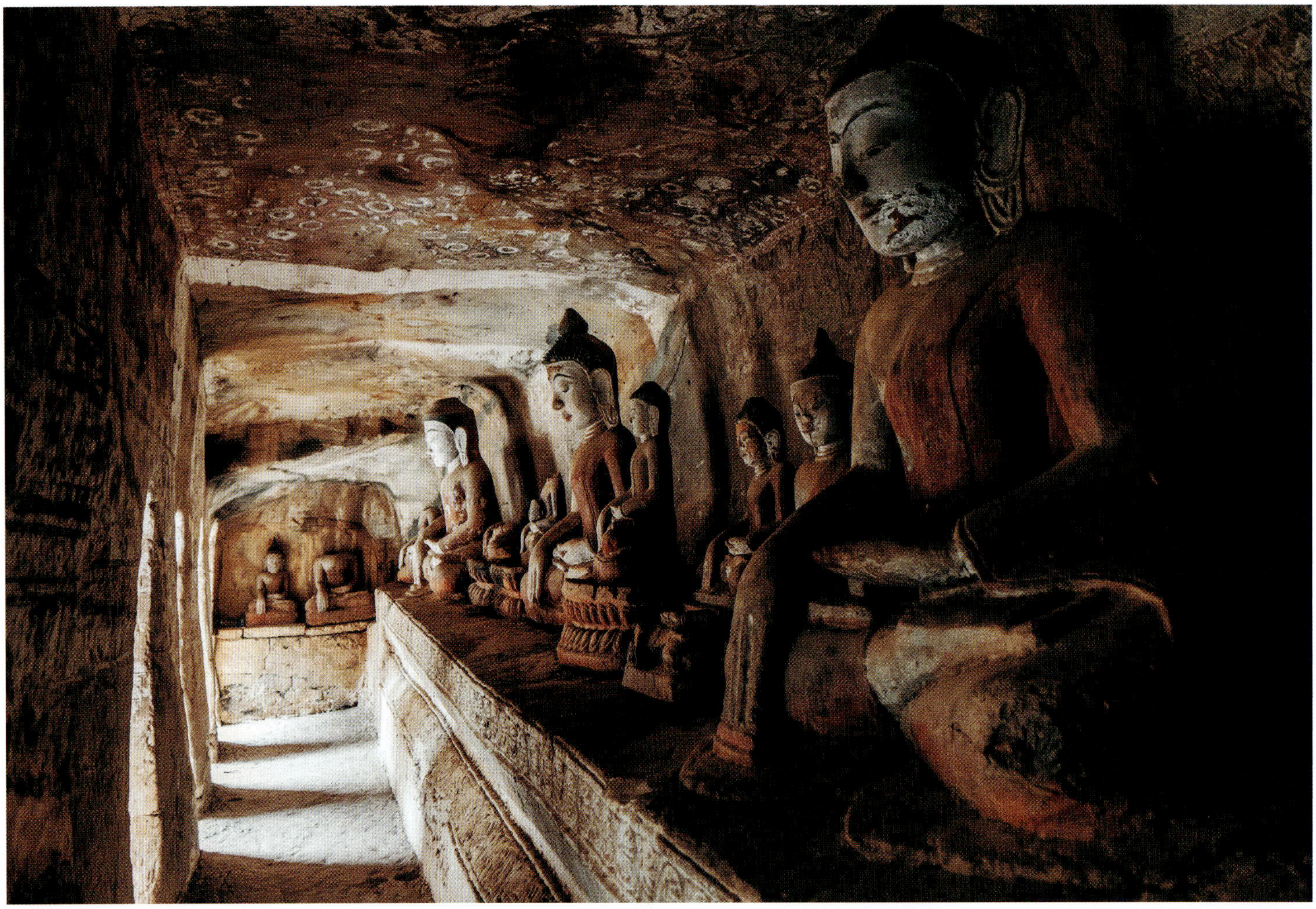

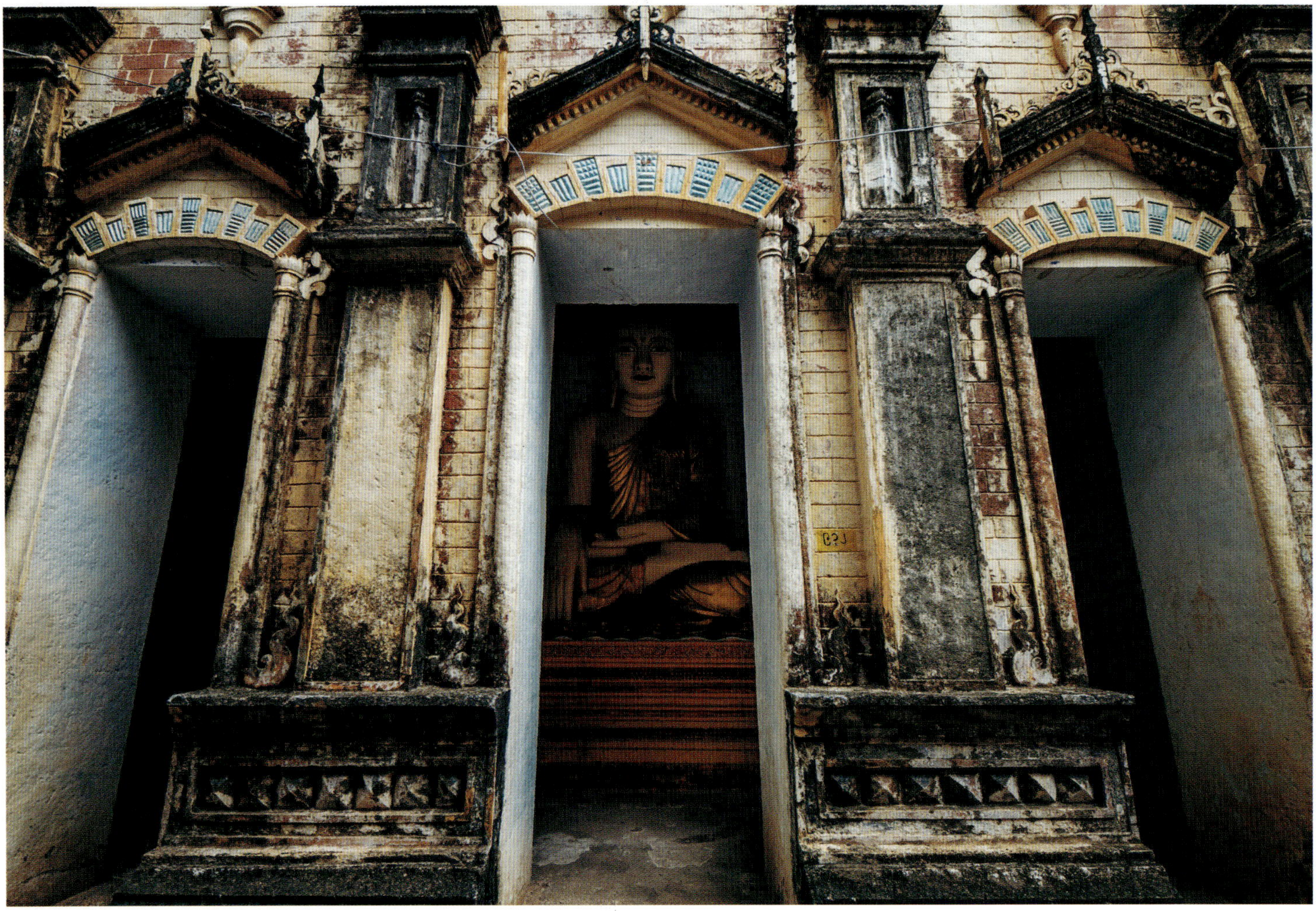

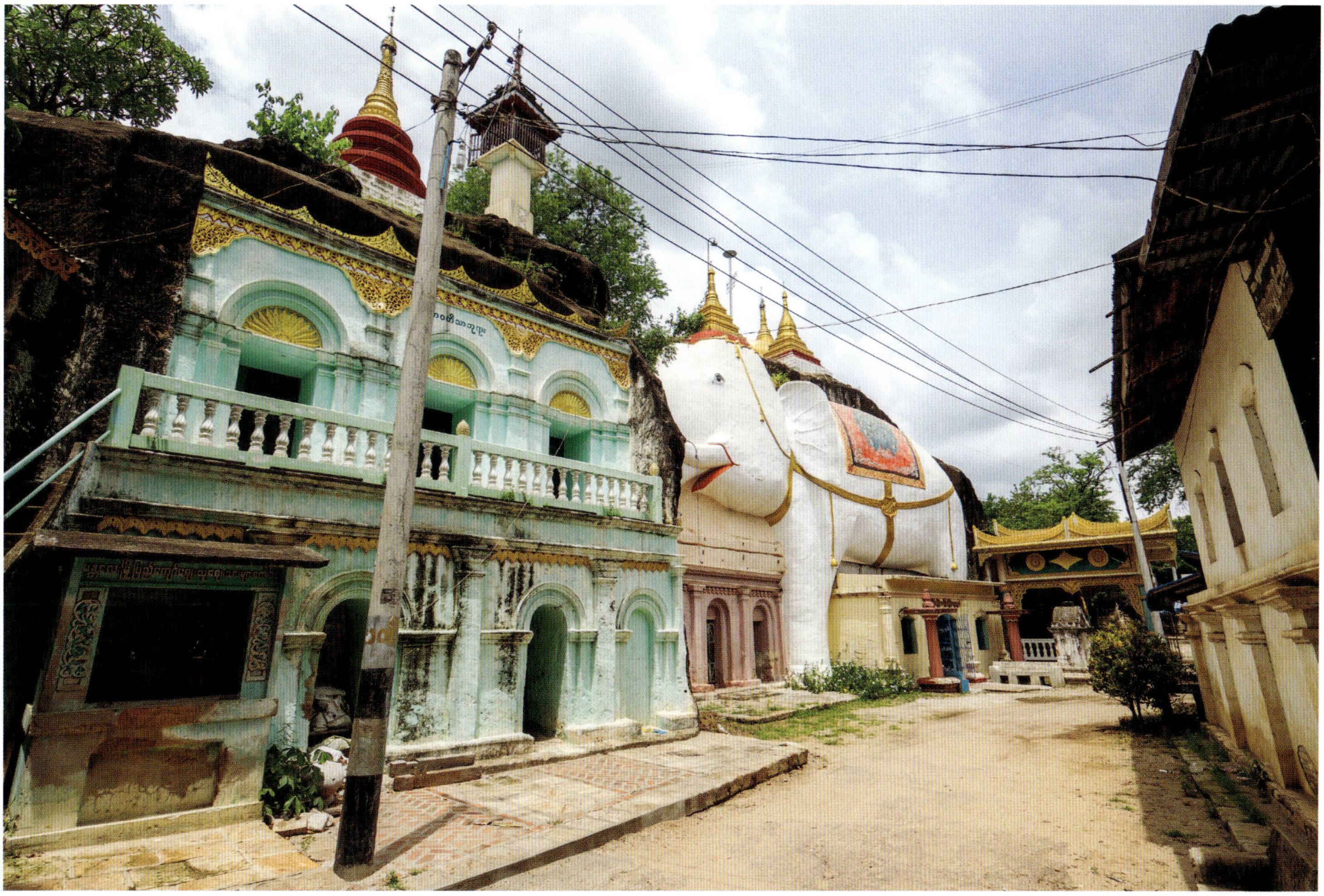

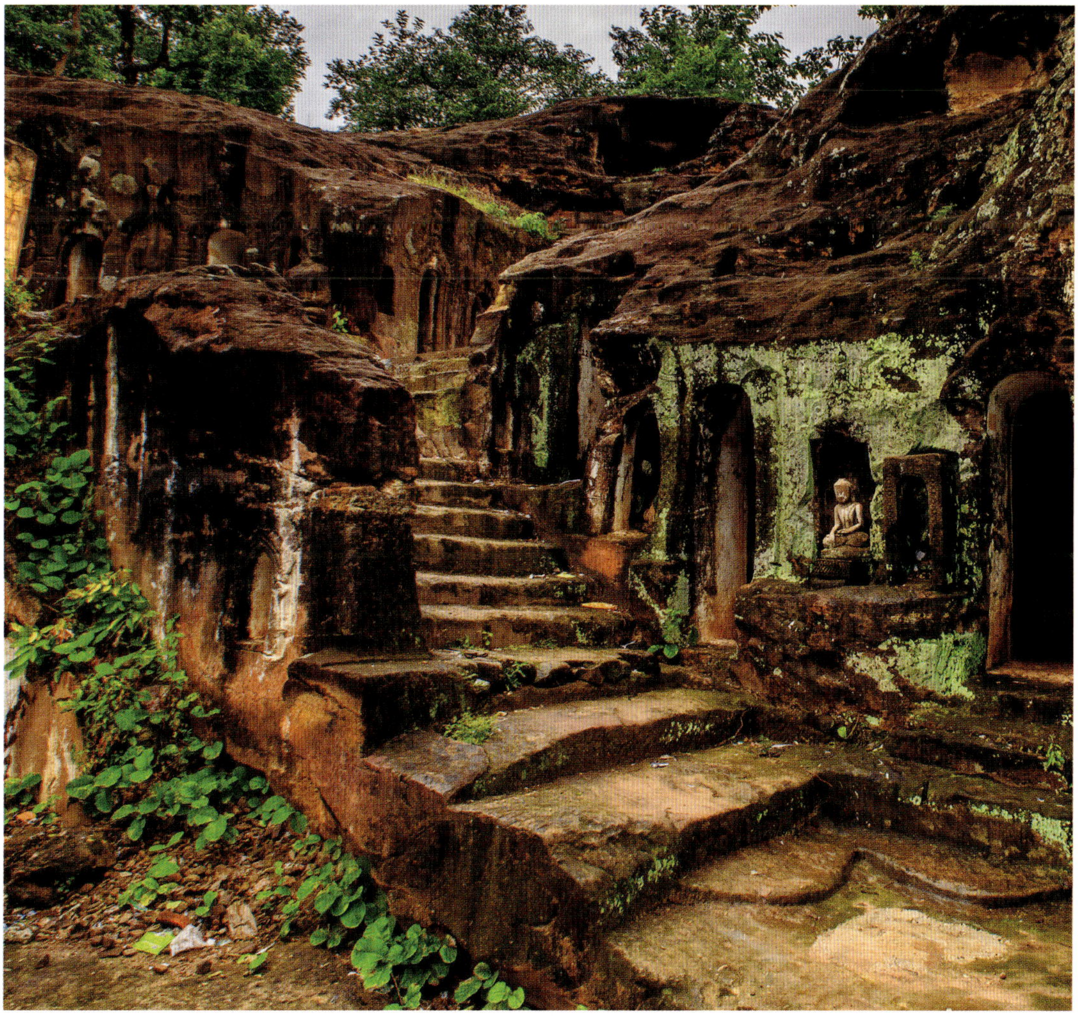

ALL PHOTOGRAPHS:

Phowintaung Caves, Myanmar

A visit to this most eerily atmospheric of shrines is unforgettable. There's a mystic thrill about walking these halls beneath the earth. Where they aren't a-shimmer with sacred murals, their walls are bristling with Buddha statues.

There are believed to be in the region of half a million images all told. Most were donated by pious pilgrims in the seventeenth and eighteenth centuries, but some date back to the fourteenth century – perhaps considerably before. The dating process is complicated by the fact that efforts were made to restore and redecorate from early on, making it difficult to establish a clear chronology for all these works.

The Phowintaung system is large and labyrinthine – there may be as many as 900 distinct caves in total: fresh galleries were being opened up and decorated well into the twentieth century.

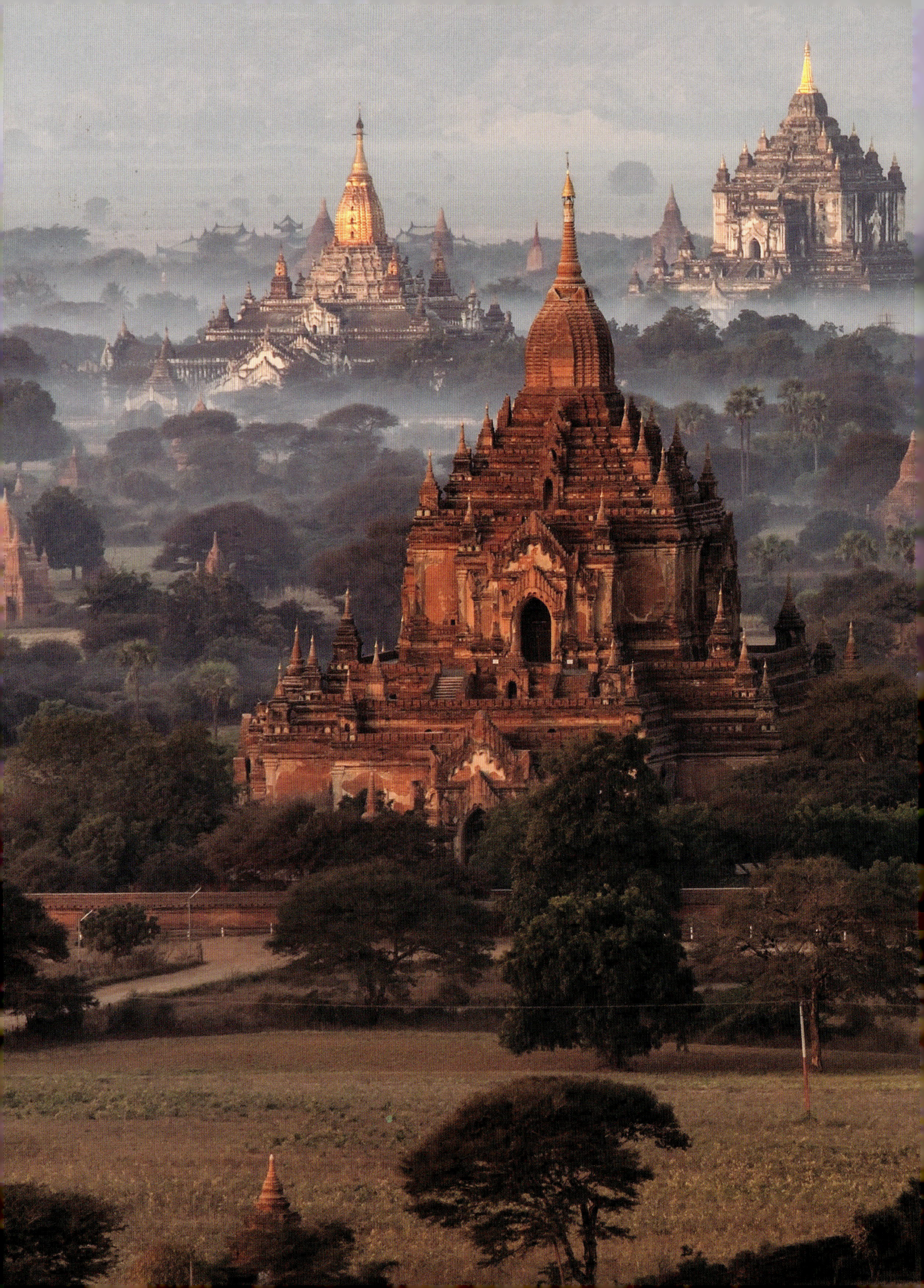

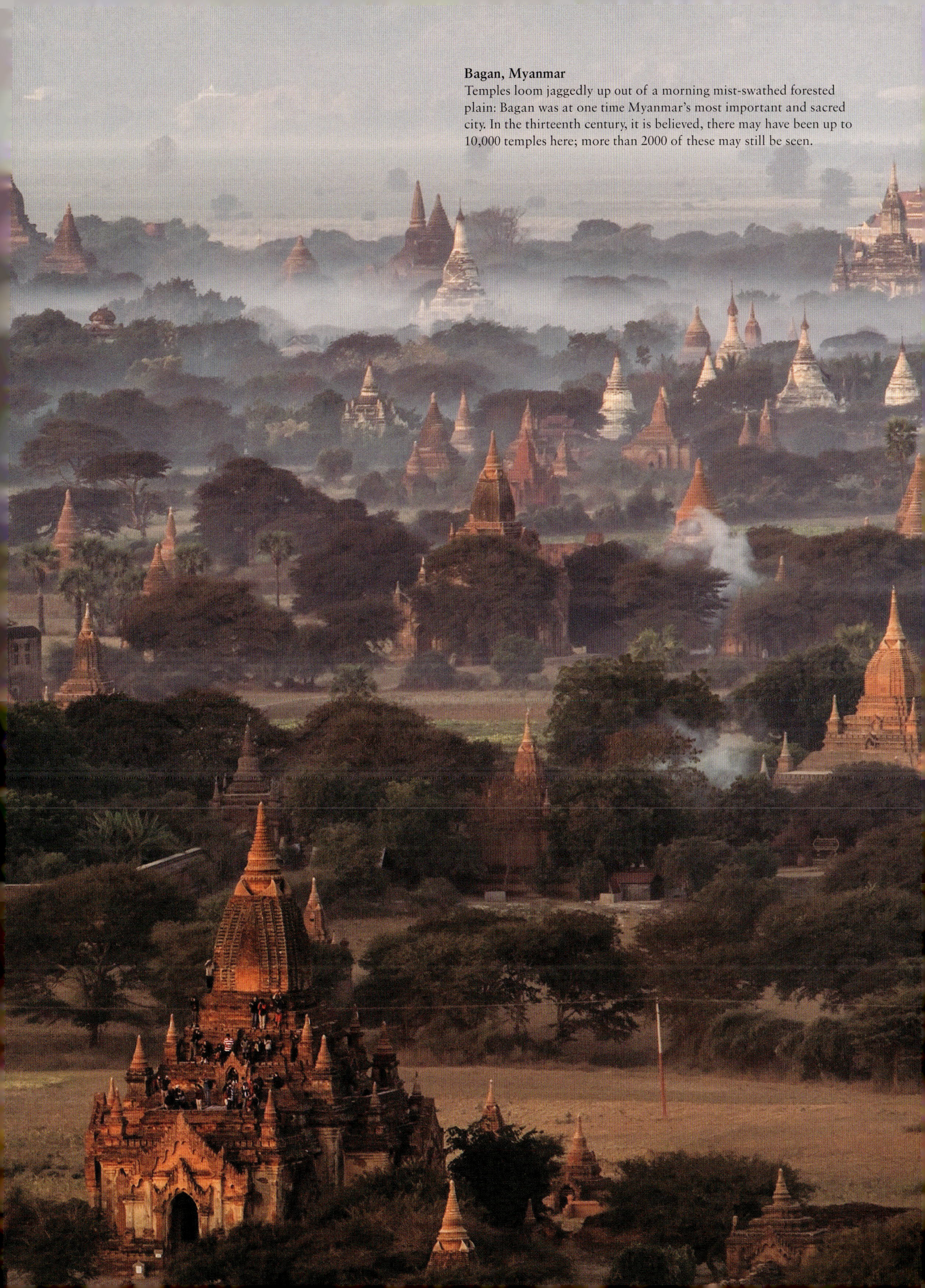

Bagan, Myanmar
Temples loom jaggedly up out of a morning mist-swathed forested plain: Bagan was at one time Myanmar's most important and sacred city. In the thirteenth century, it is believed, there may have been up to 10,000 temples here; more than 2000 of these may still be seen.

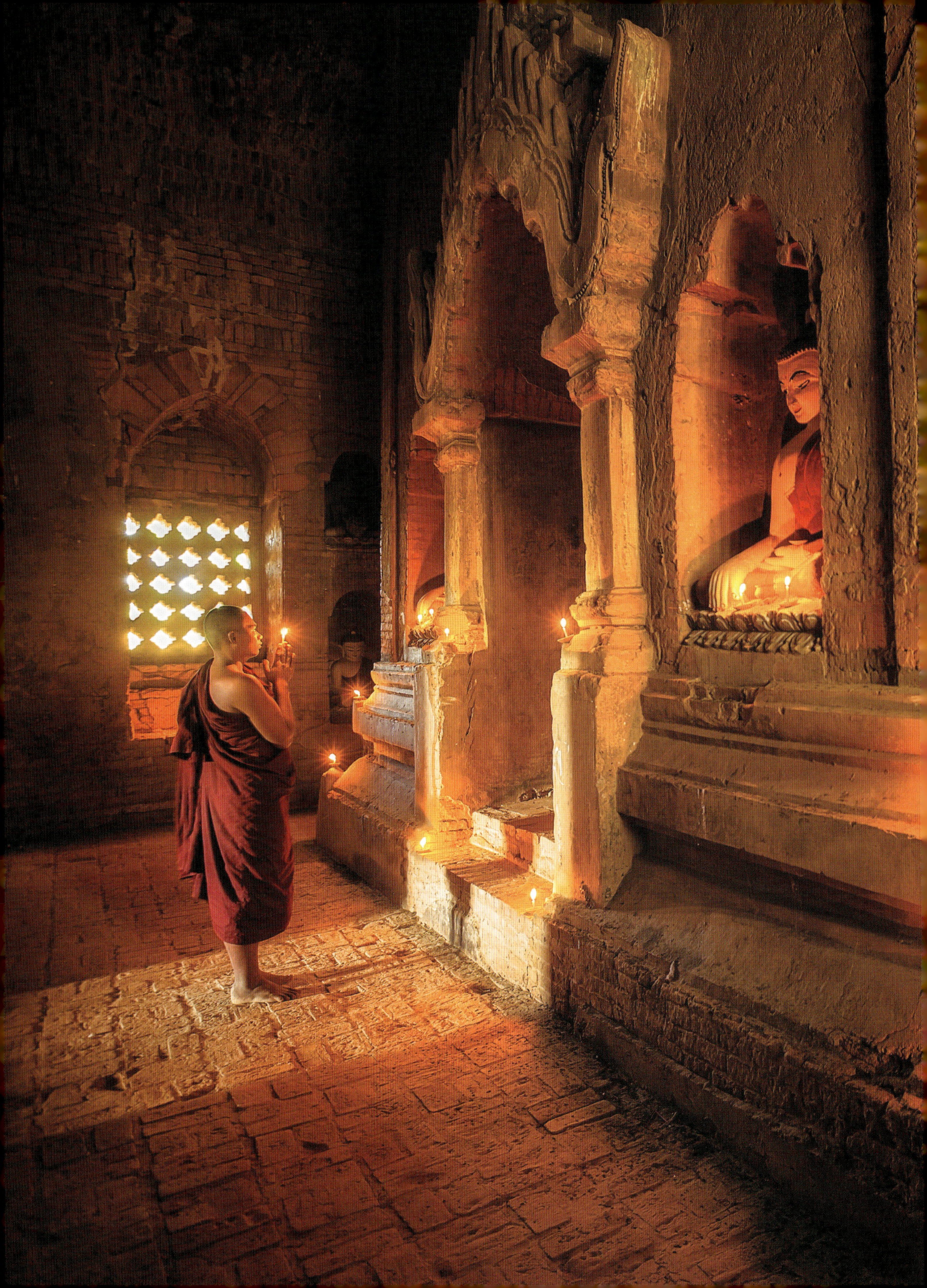

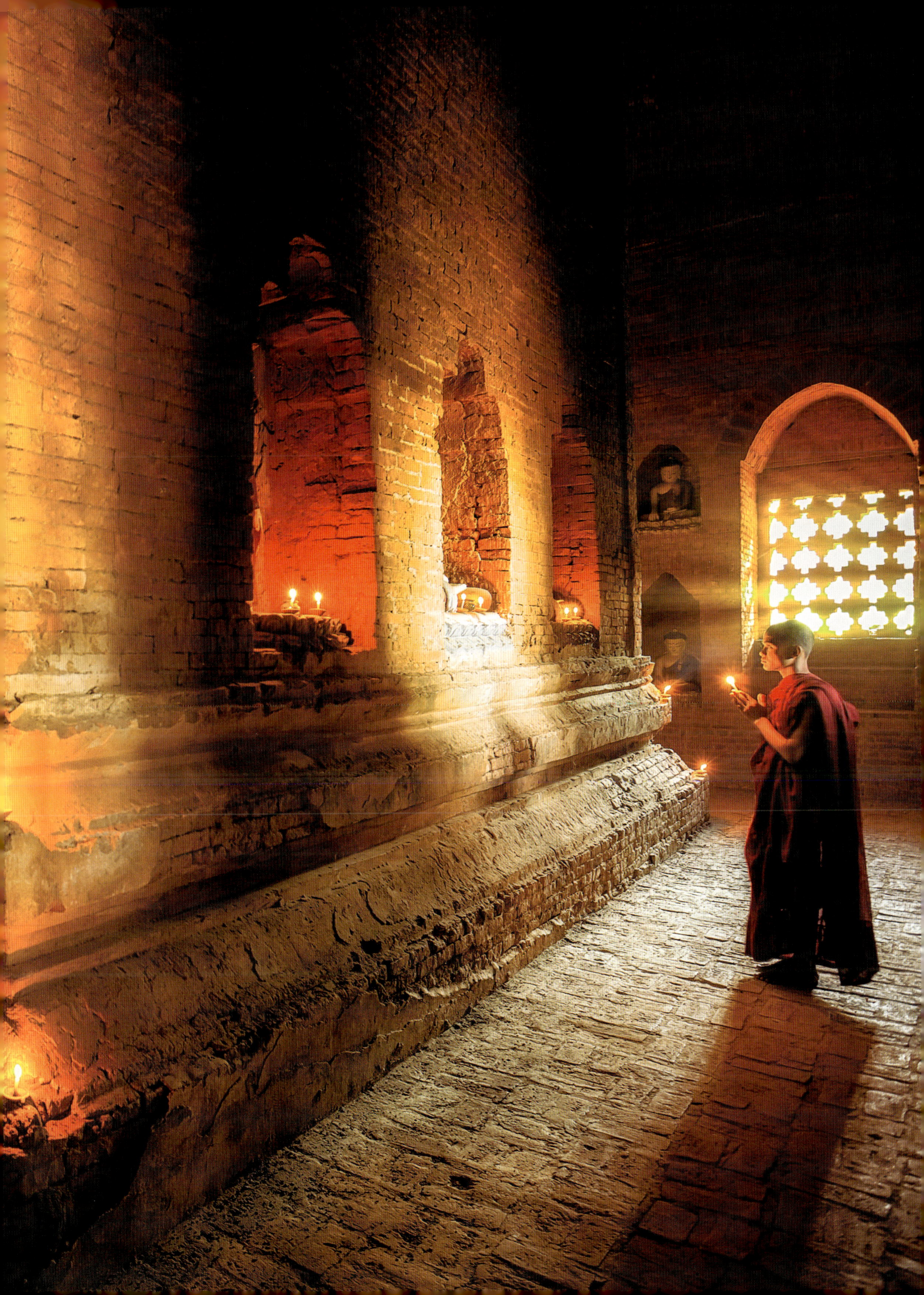

PREVIOUS PAGES:

Bagan (pagoda interior), Myanmar

In the 1990s, with an eye on opening up the tourist trade, Myanmar's military government ordered refurbishments on hundreds of ruined pagodas here. In their crass insensitivity and headlong haste, however, these efforts marred as many monuments as they 'restored'. Even so, there are places of enormous interest and spiritual resonance to be found at Bagan.

RIGHT:

Wat Xieng Thong, Laos

Built in the middle of the sixteenth century by King Setthathirath (1534–71), this lovely temple is a jewel in Laos's cultural crown, with its gilded raking wooden roofs, its ornate golden stencilling and sumptuous sculptures and extraordinary mosaic-patterned walls, like the one shown here. This picture presents a scene of bustling life, with brightly-coloured trees and an assortment of animals, wild and domestic; growing crops, praying priests and sailing boats.

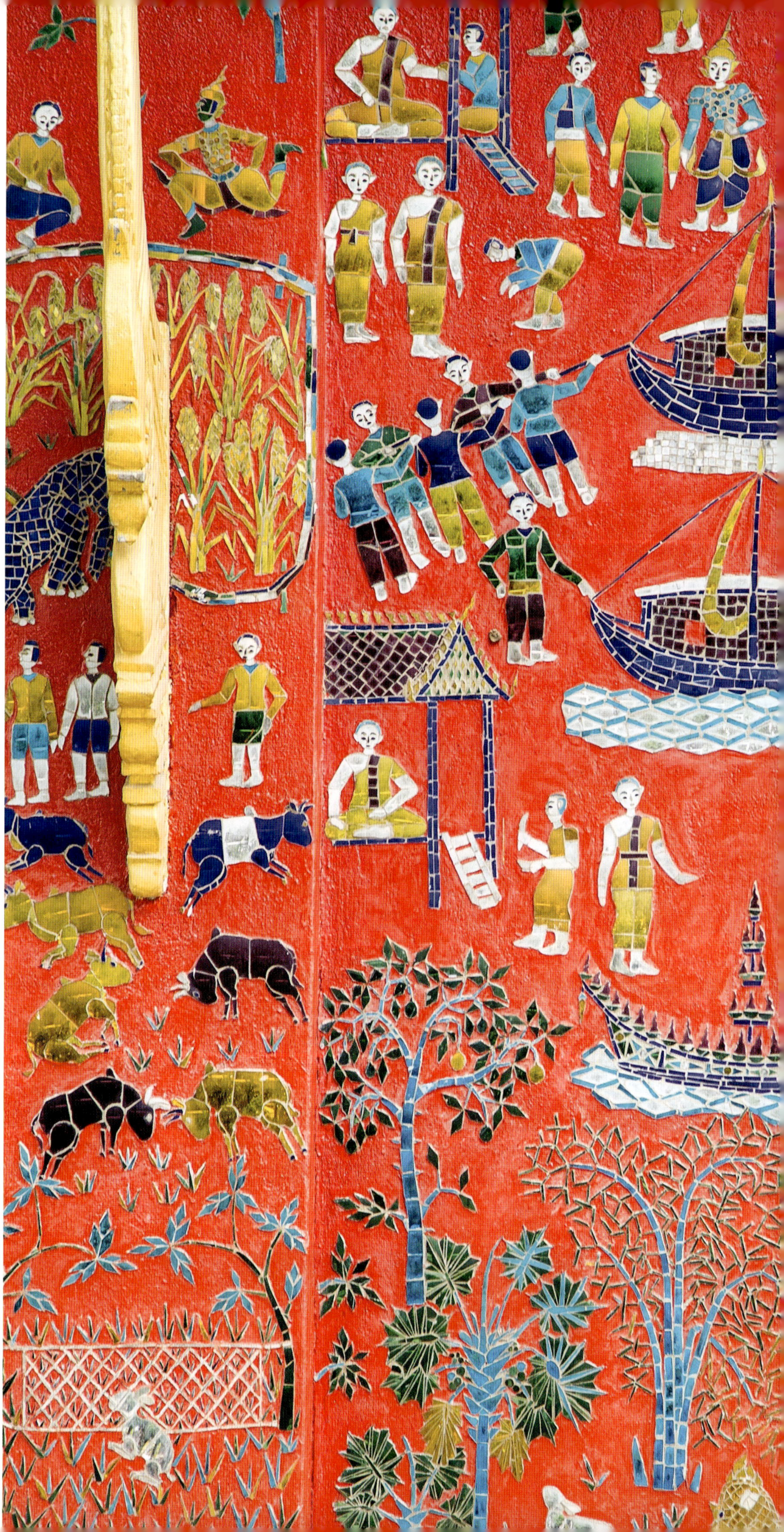

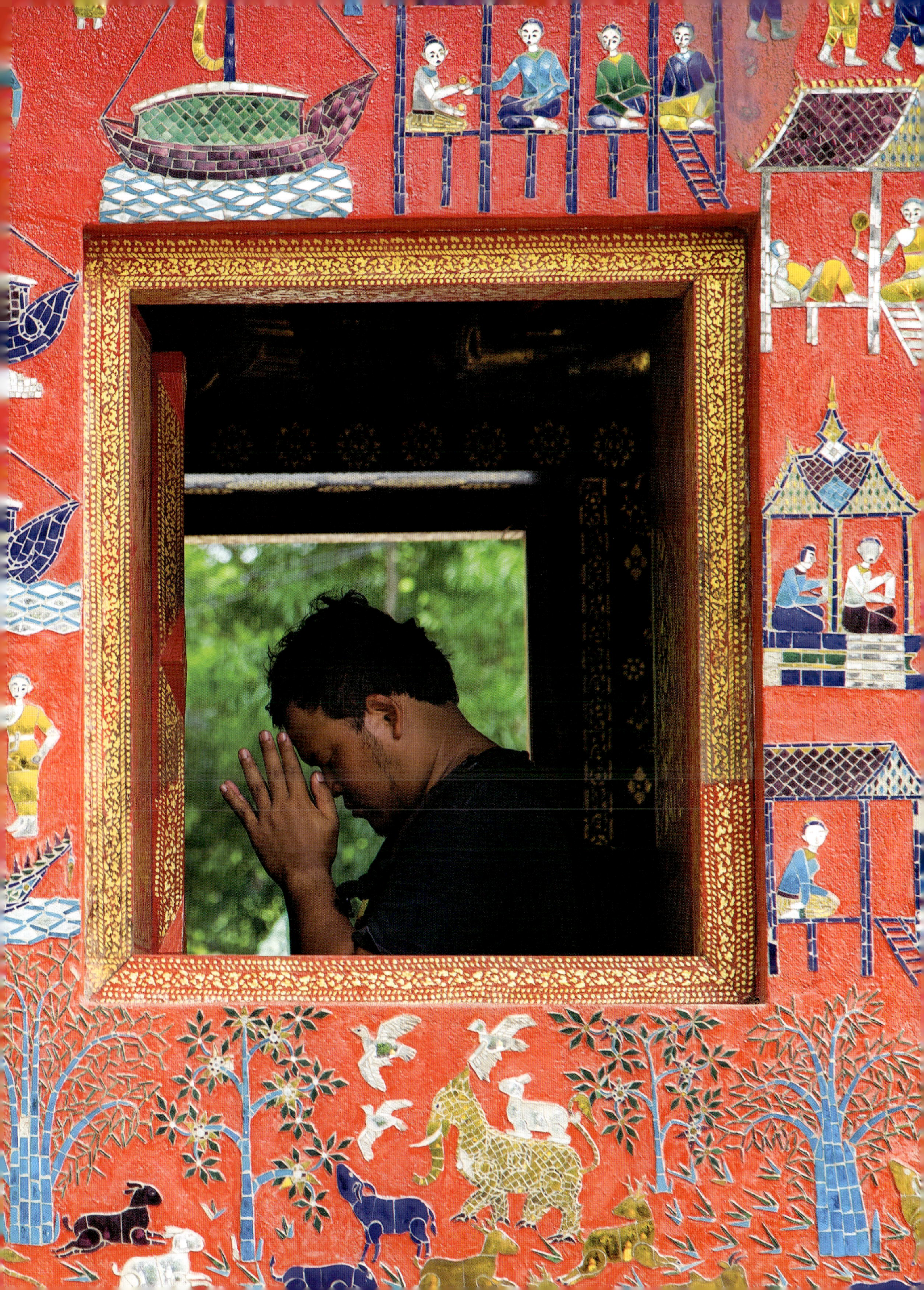

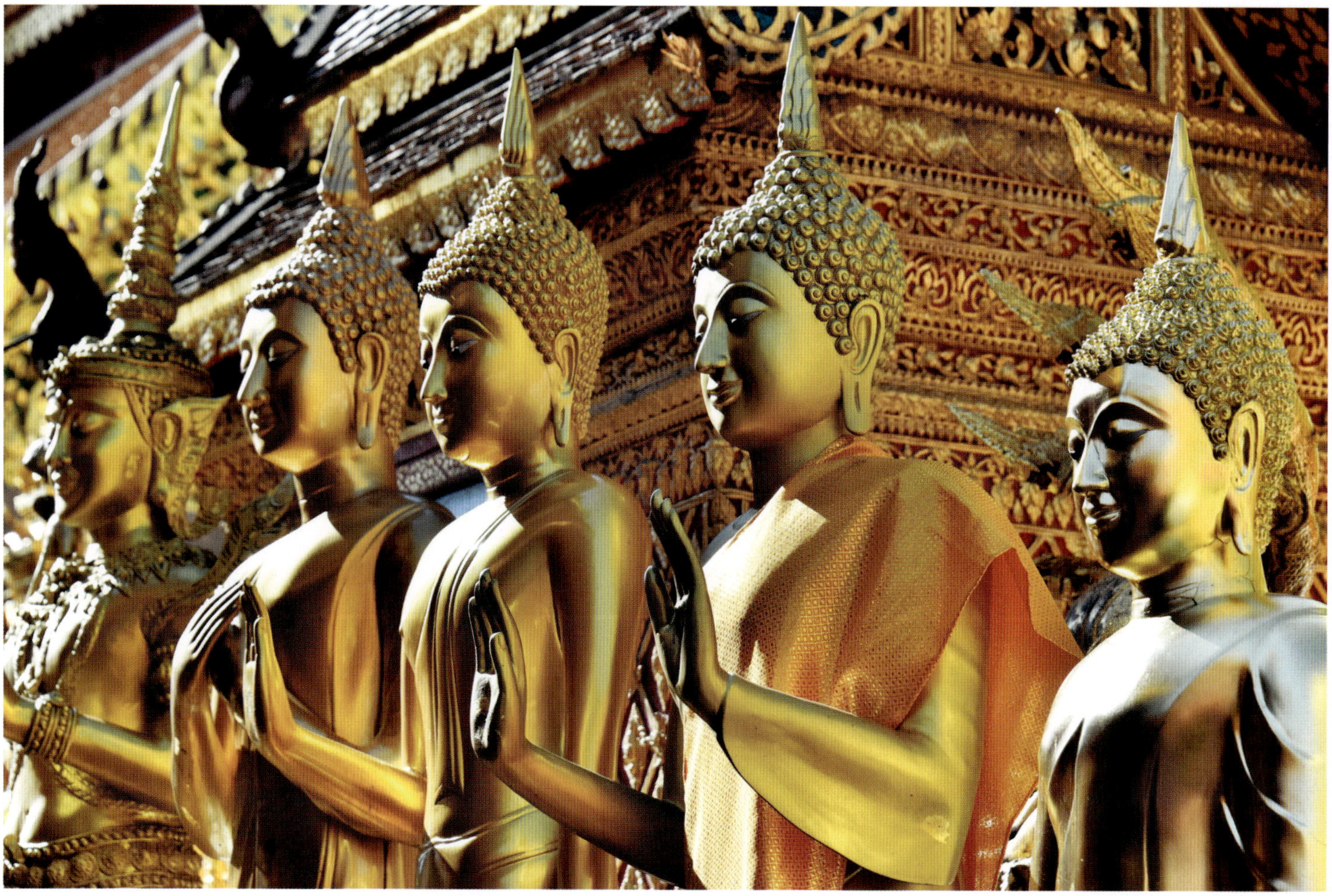

ABOVE AND RIGHT:

Wat Phra That Doi Suthep, Chiang Mai Province, Thailand

This gold-decorated temple stands 1000m (3300 ft) up in the mountains of Chiang Mai. It is said to have been founded in the fourteenth century. Inspired by the dream of a monk named Sumanathera, a sacred relic was set on the back of a white elephant, the story goes: the monk was to follow where it led. It made its way up the mountainside where it trumpeted three times and then fell dead – Sumanathera's signal to build his temple on this site.

OPPOSITE:

Pha That Luang, Vientiane, Laos

King Setthathirath set up his royal seat here in 1560. His role in the construction of modern Laos is seen as key. He founded Pha That Luang temple, too – hence this statue, erected in the 1960s at a time when the country's governing elite was eager to establish their legitimacy. The richly-gilded central stupa of this temple, serried round by gleaming needle-spires, stands out against the skyline of the Laotian capital.

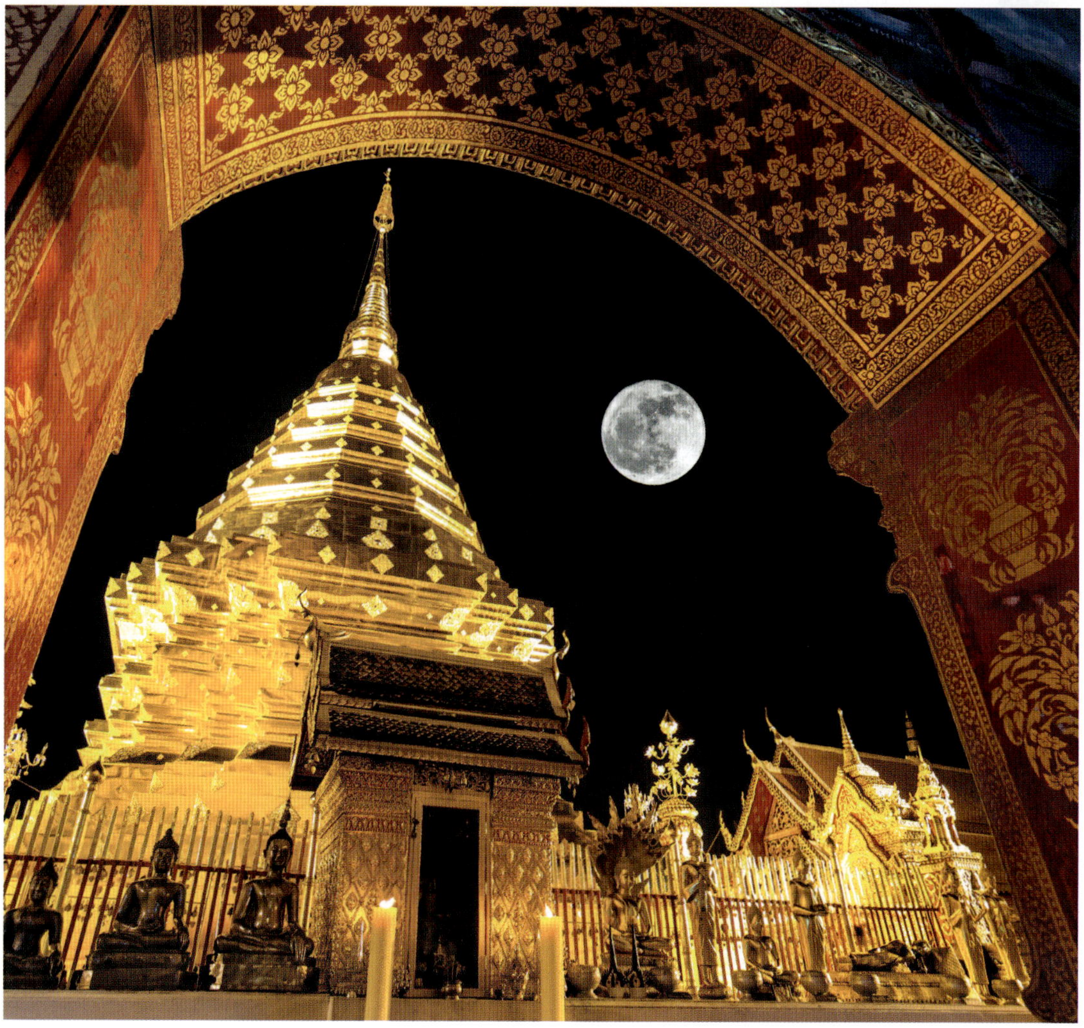

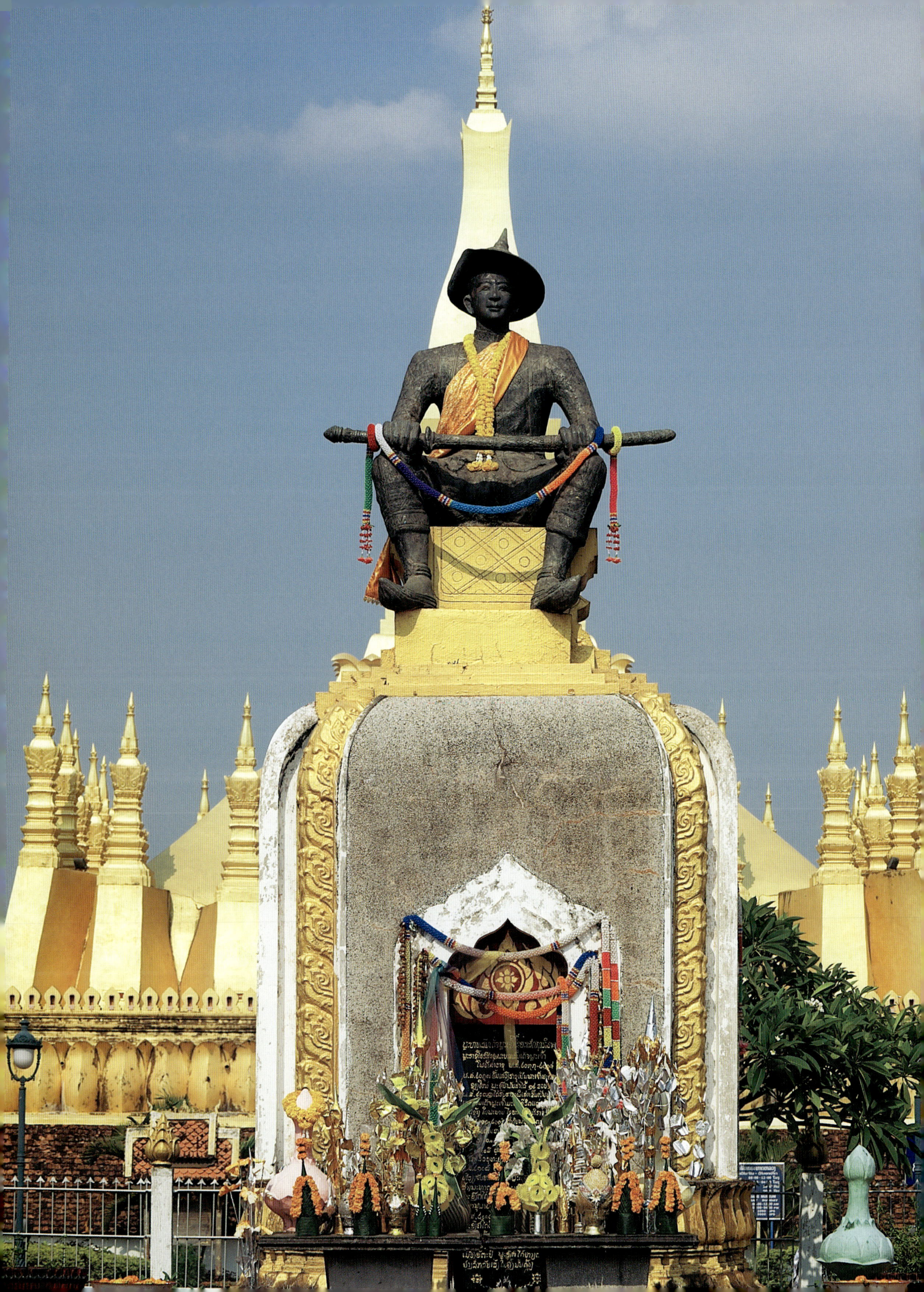

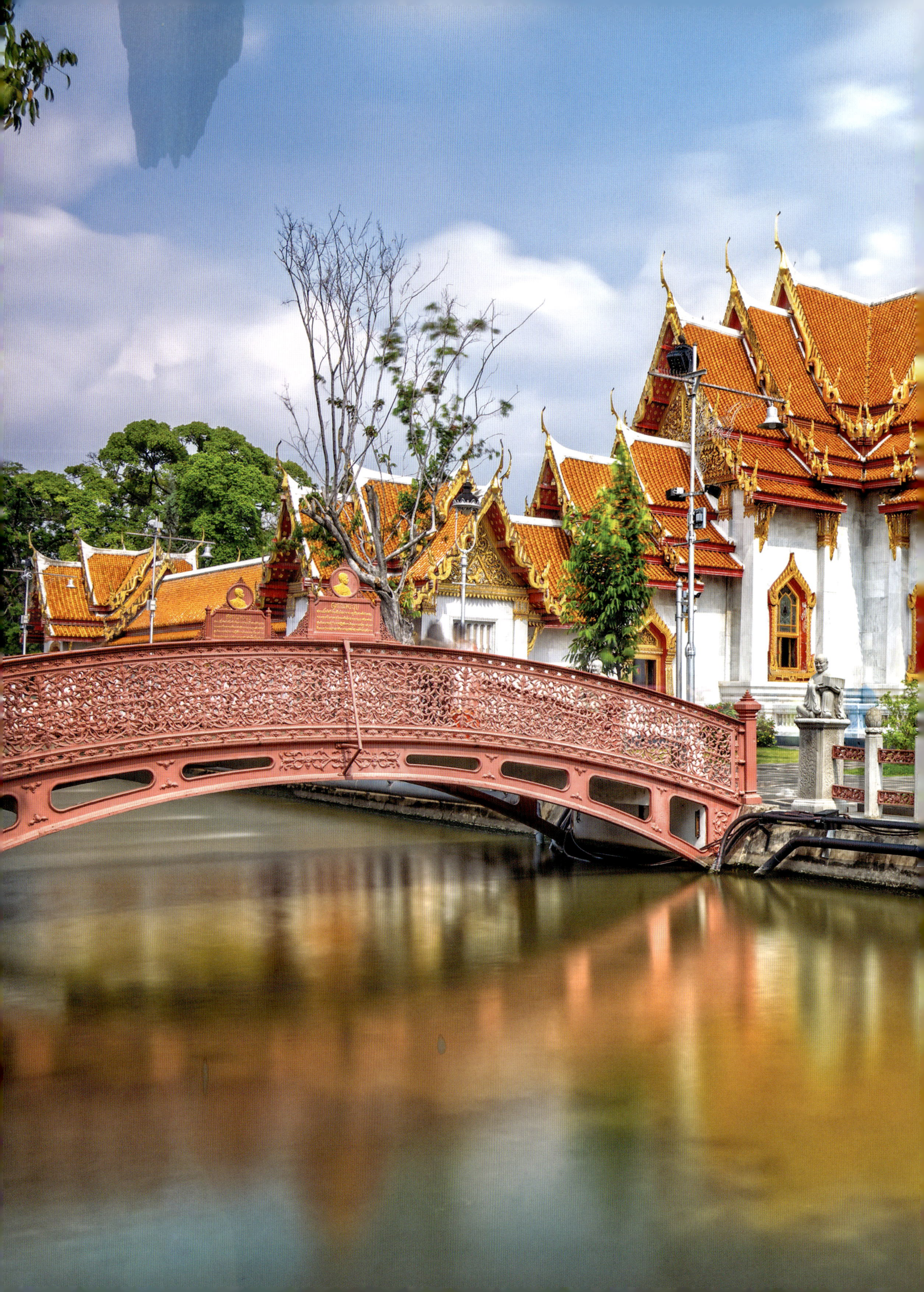

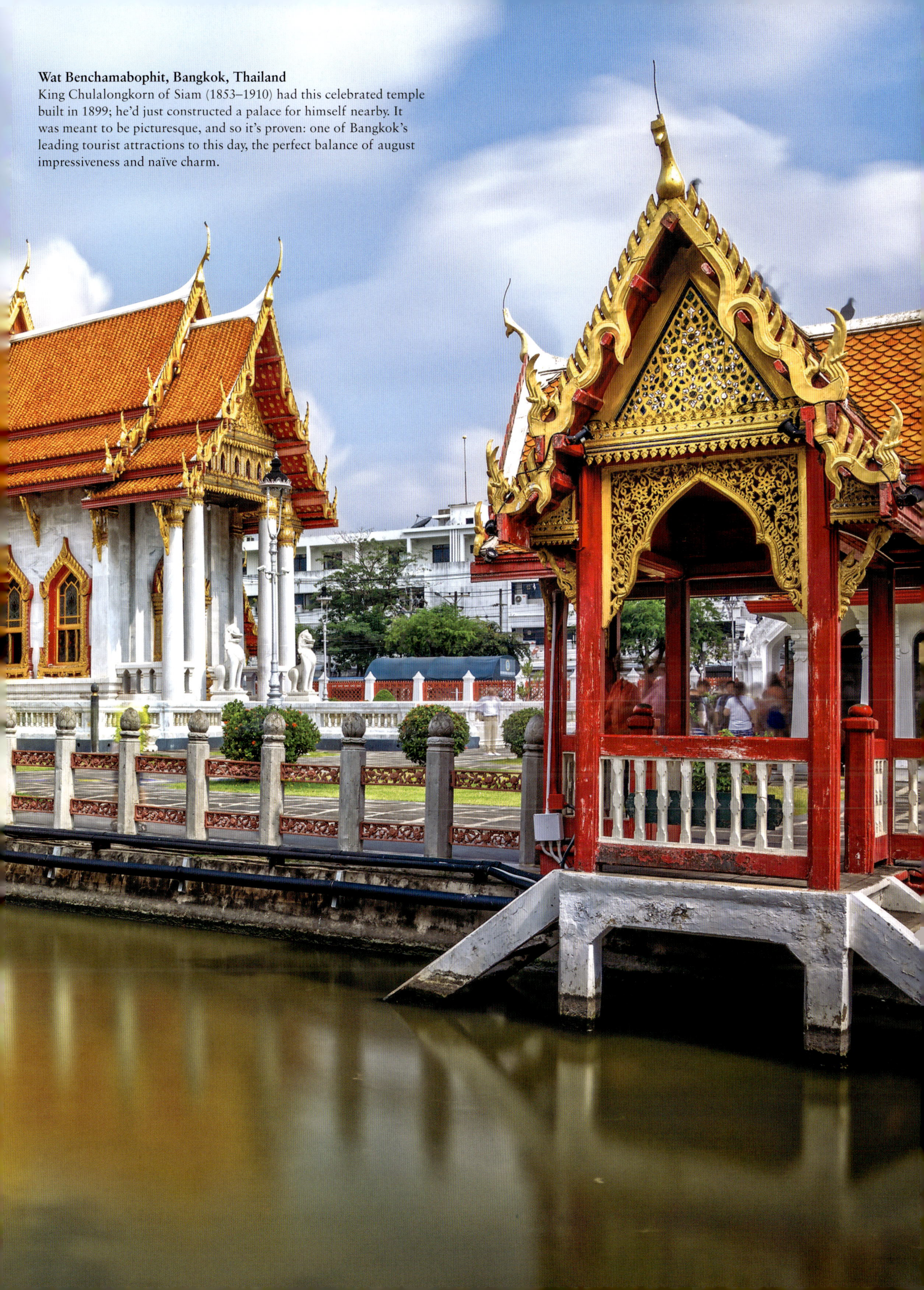

Wat Benchamabophit, Bangkok, Thailand

King Chulalongkorn of Siam (1853–1910) had this celebrated temple built in 1899; he'd just constructed a palace for himself nearby. It was meant to be picturesque, and so it's proven: one of Bangkok's leading tourist attractions to this day, the perfect balance of august impressiveness and naïve charm.

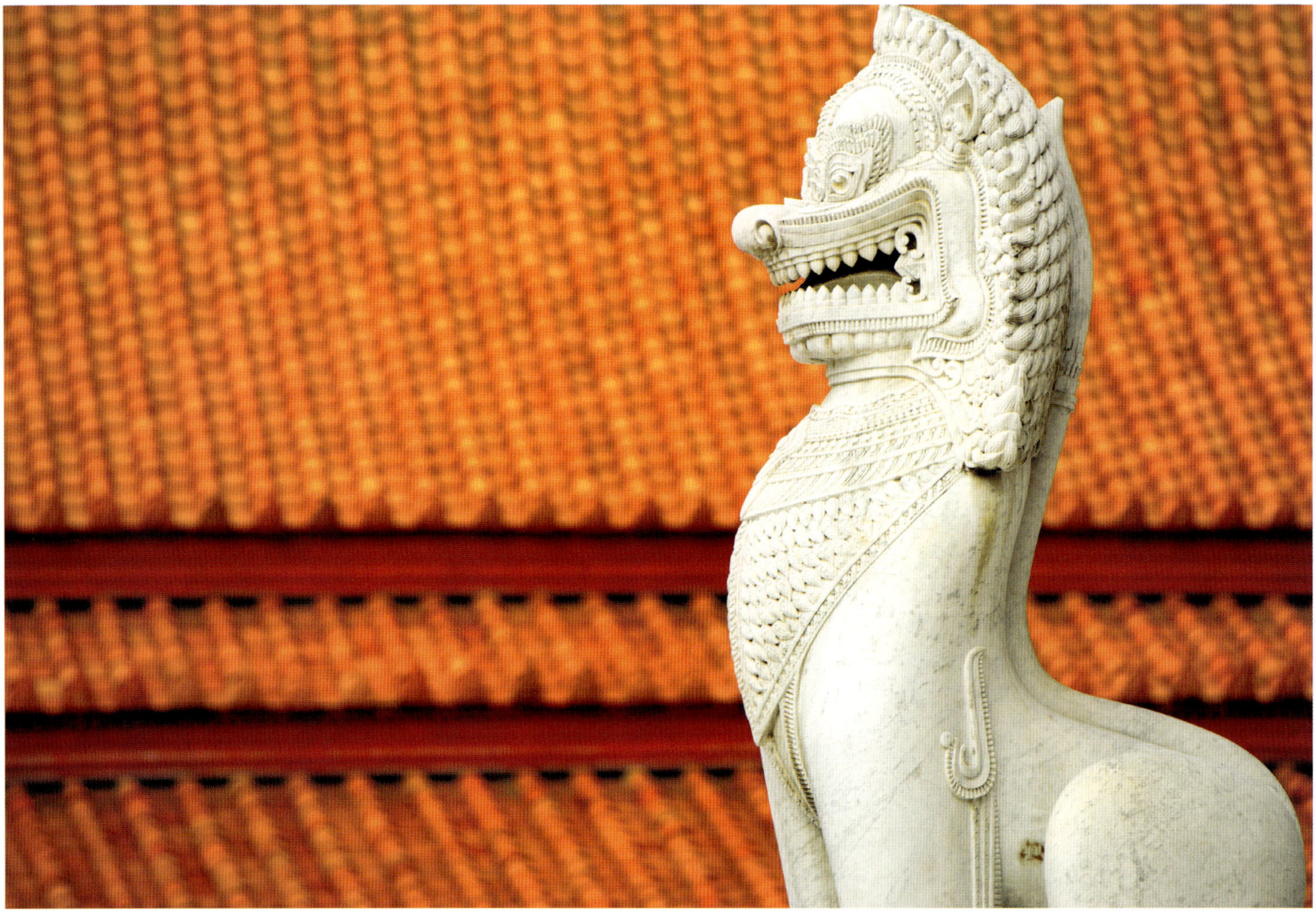

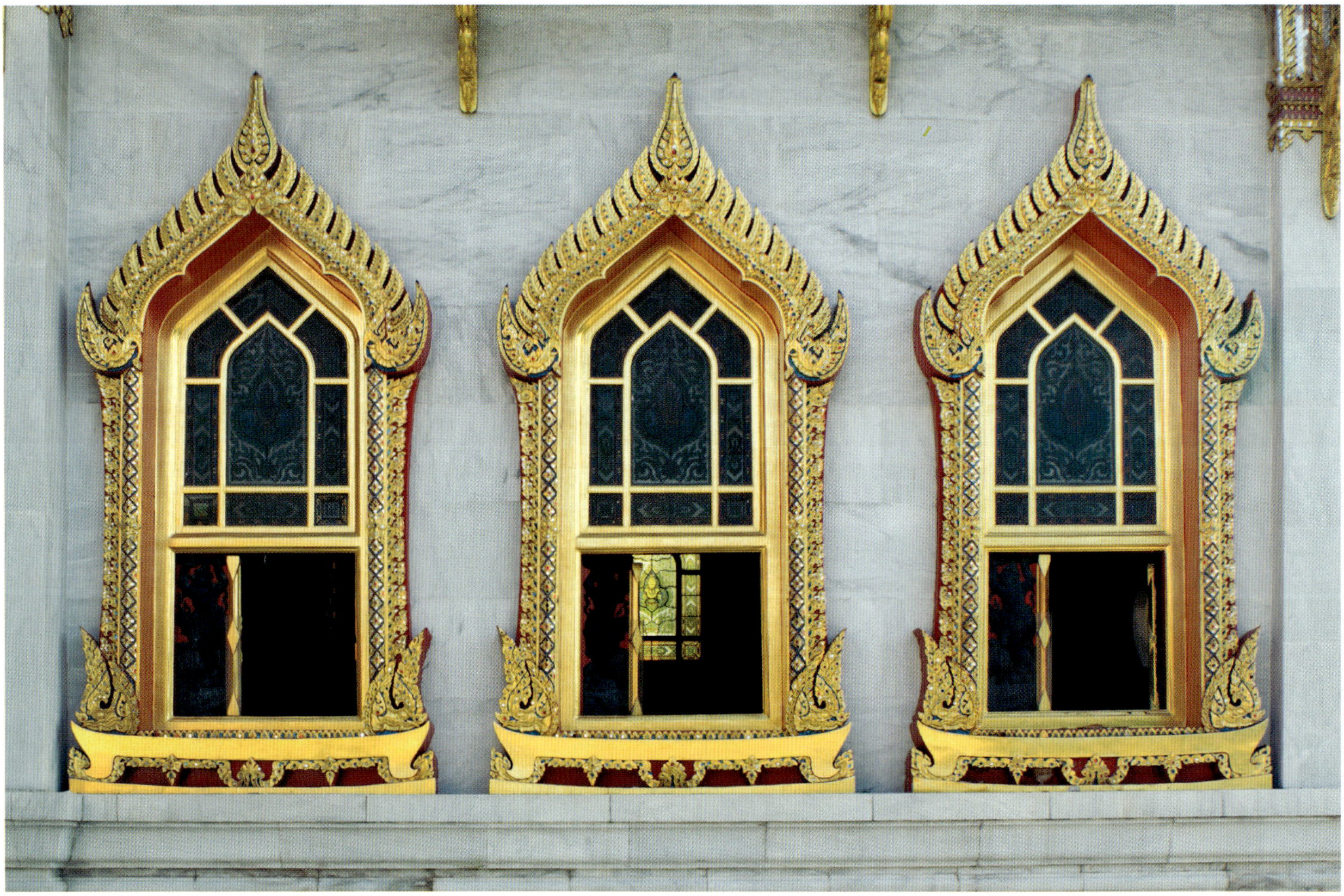

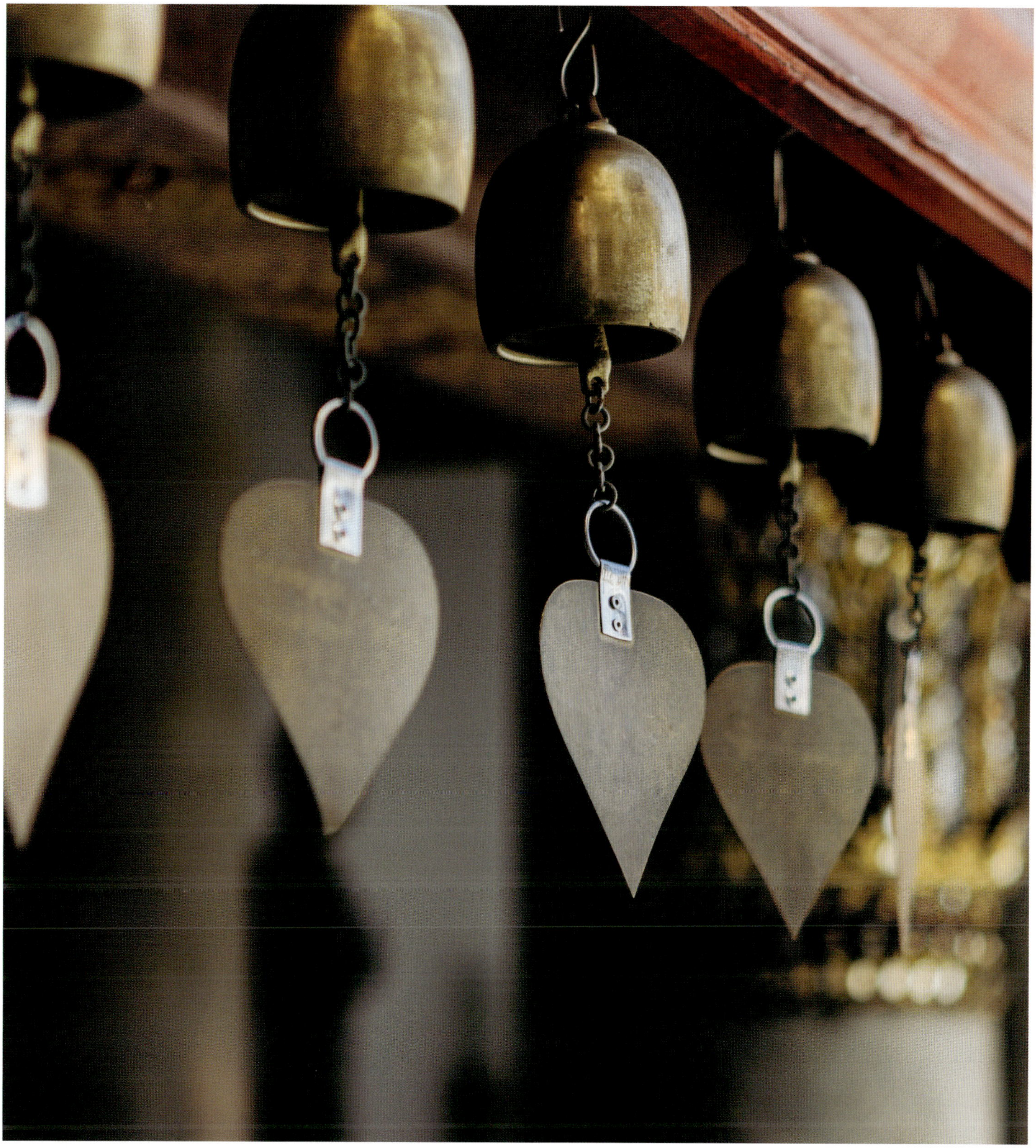

ALL PHOTOGRAPHS:

Wat Benchamabophit, Bangkok, Thailand

This temple is indisputably beautiful, but at the same time, it is unmistakably (not to say unabashedly) hybrid in its inspiration. In this, it exemplifies the ambivalence of the monarchy of Siam. At a time when both the British and the French were bent on expansionism in Southeast Asia, the country's ruling house had striven to find a pathway between reaching an accommodation with Western imperialism and being swallowed whole. Or, perhaps, to put it more cynically, Chulalongkorn's family had come to look to the Western powers for strategic and political protection even as they claimed legitimacy from their local pedigree.

Though widely referred to as the 'Marble Temple' for the Italian stone imported to build and clad its walls and columns, Wat Benchamabophit also boasts a host of traditional Thai details as well as a series of murals showing the stupas of important temples from the length and breadth of Thailand.

Wat Phra That Lampang Luang, Lampang Province, Thailand
The title *Buddha* means 'awakened one': Gautama Siddhartha was the first of several sages to earn this title. In any case, Thai Buddhists have always been happy to have similar statues in their temples, taking the view that the more divine energy, the merrier the shrine. Wat Phra That Lampang Luang was built atop a raised foundation and ringed around by high defensive walls.

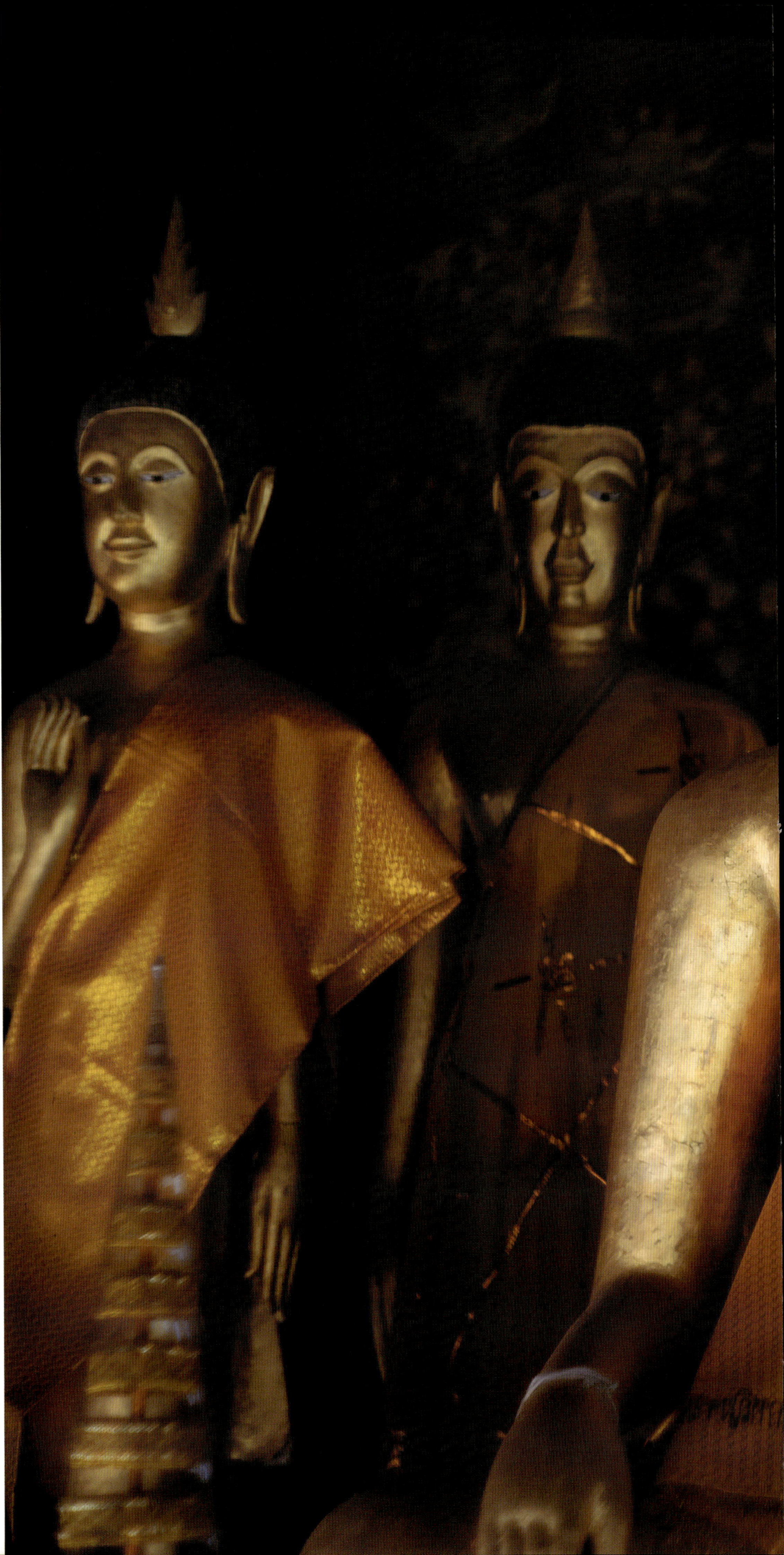

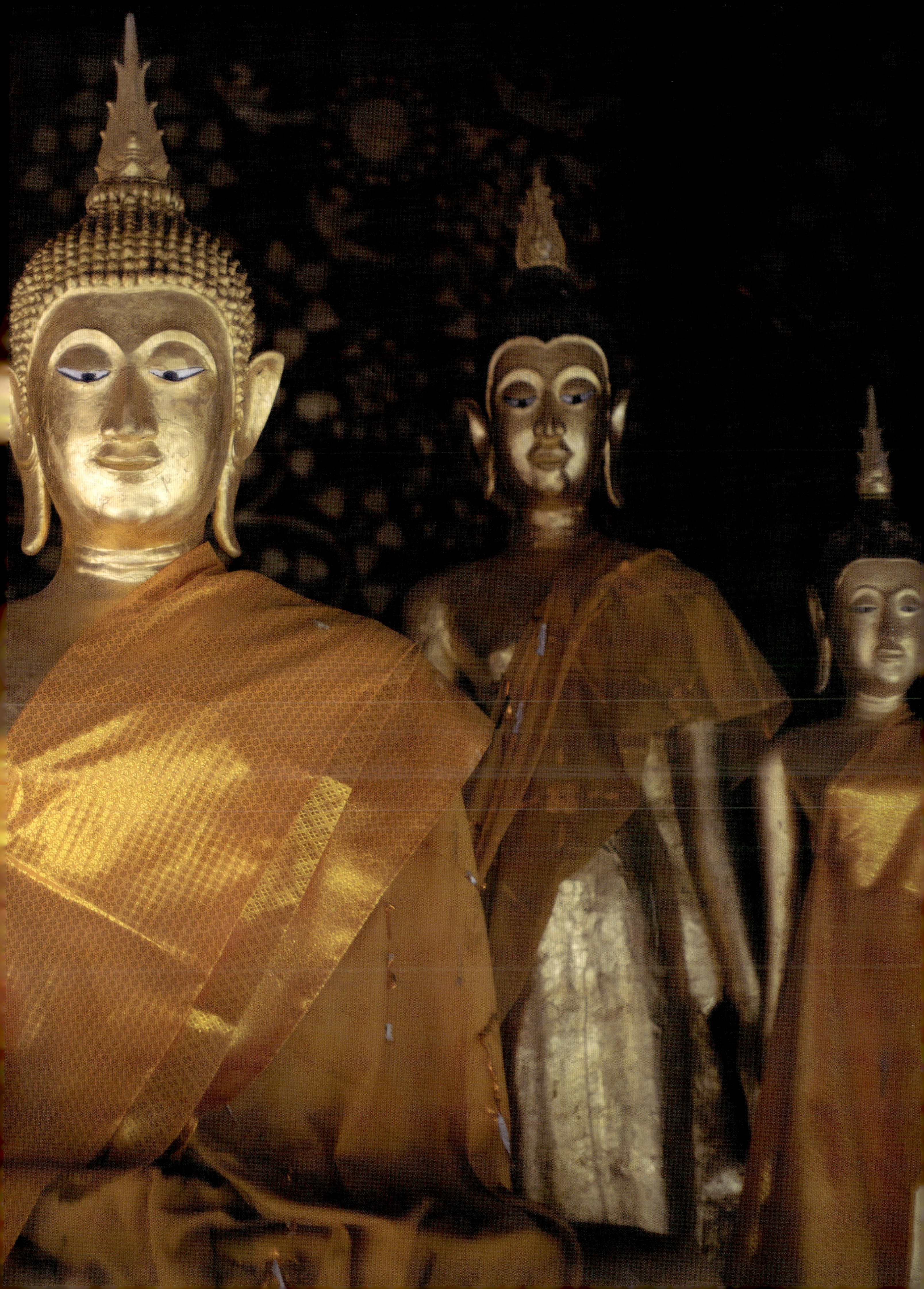

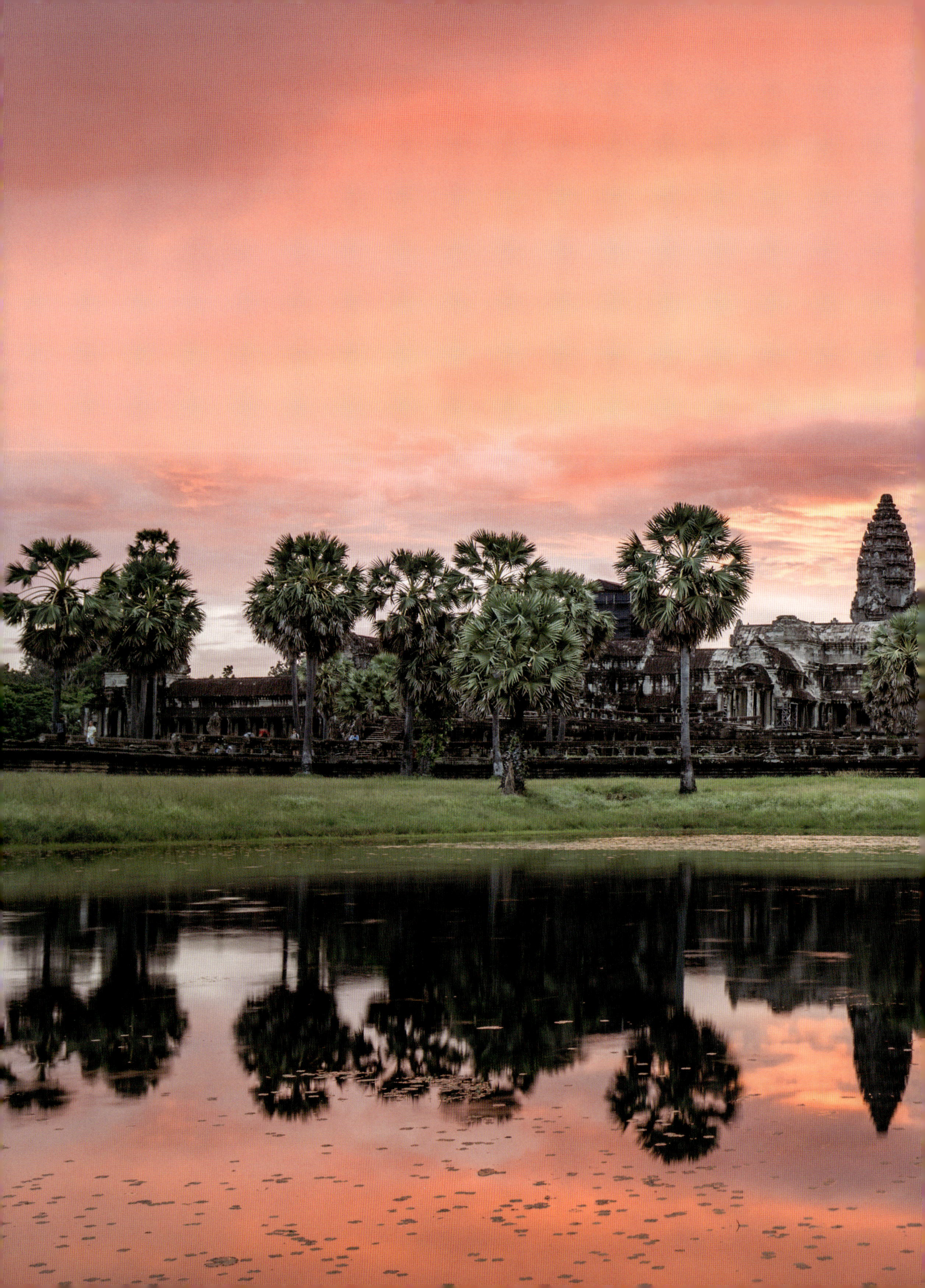

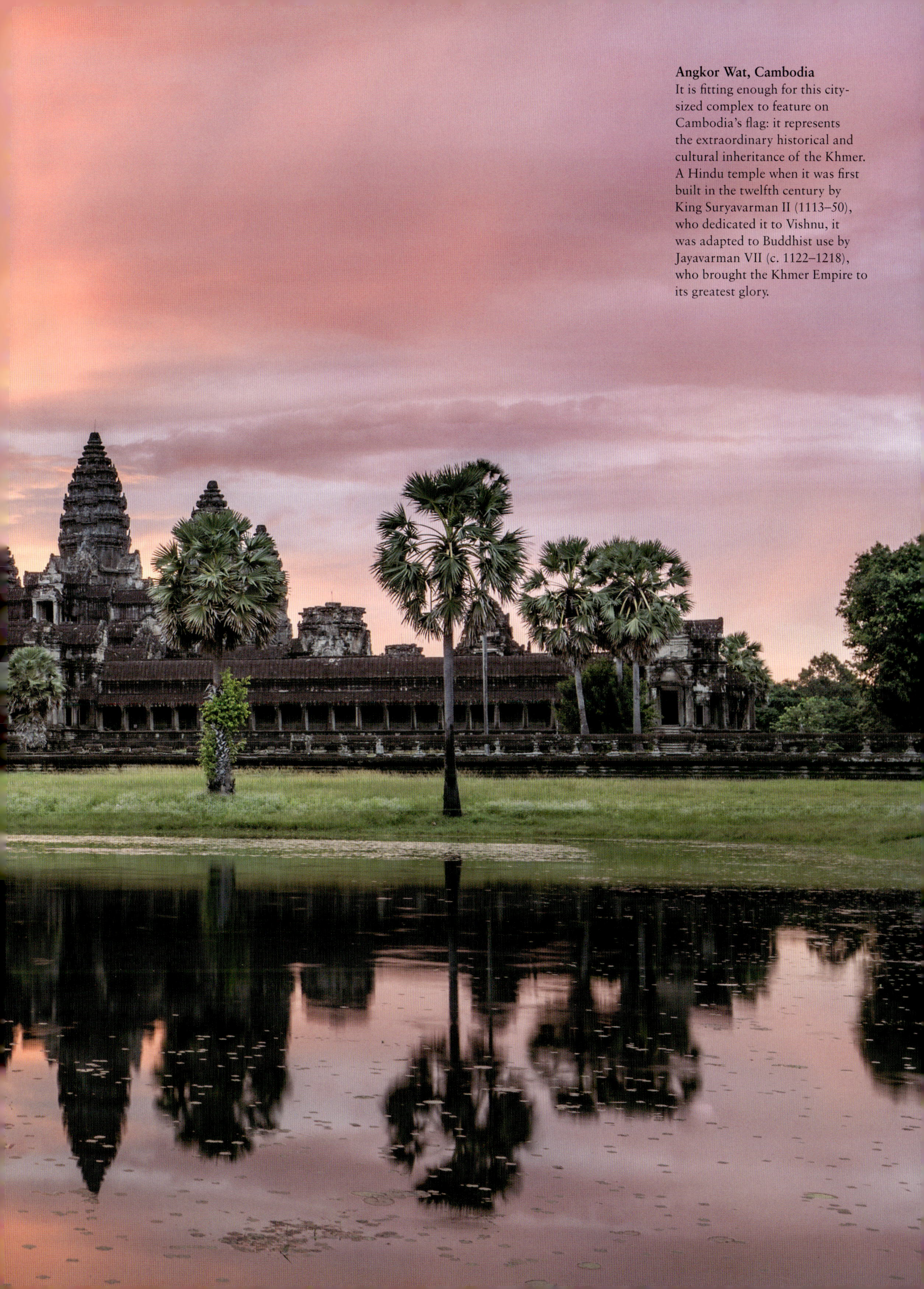

Angkor Wat, Cambodia
It is fitting enough for this city-sized complex to feature on Cambodia's flag: it represents the extraordinary historical and cultural inheritance of the Khmer. A Hindu temple when it was first built in the twelfth century by King Suryavarman II (1113–50), who dedicated it to Vishnu, it was adapted to Buddhist use by Jayavarman VII (c. 1122–1218), who brought the Khmer Empire to its greatest glory.

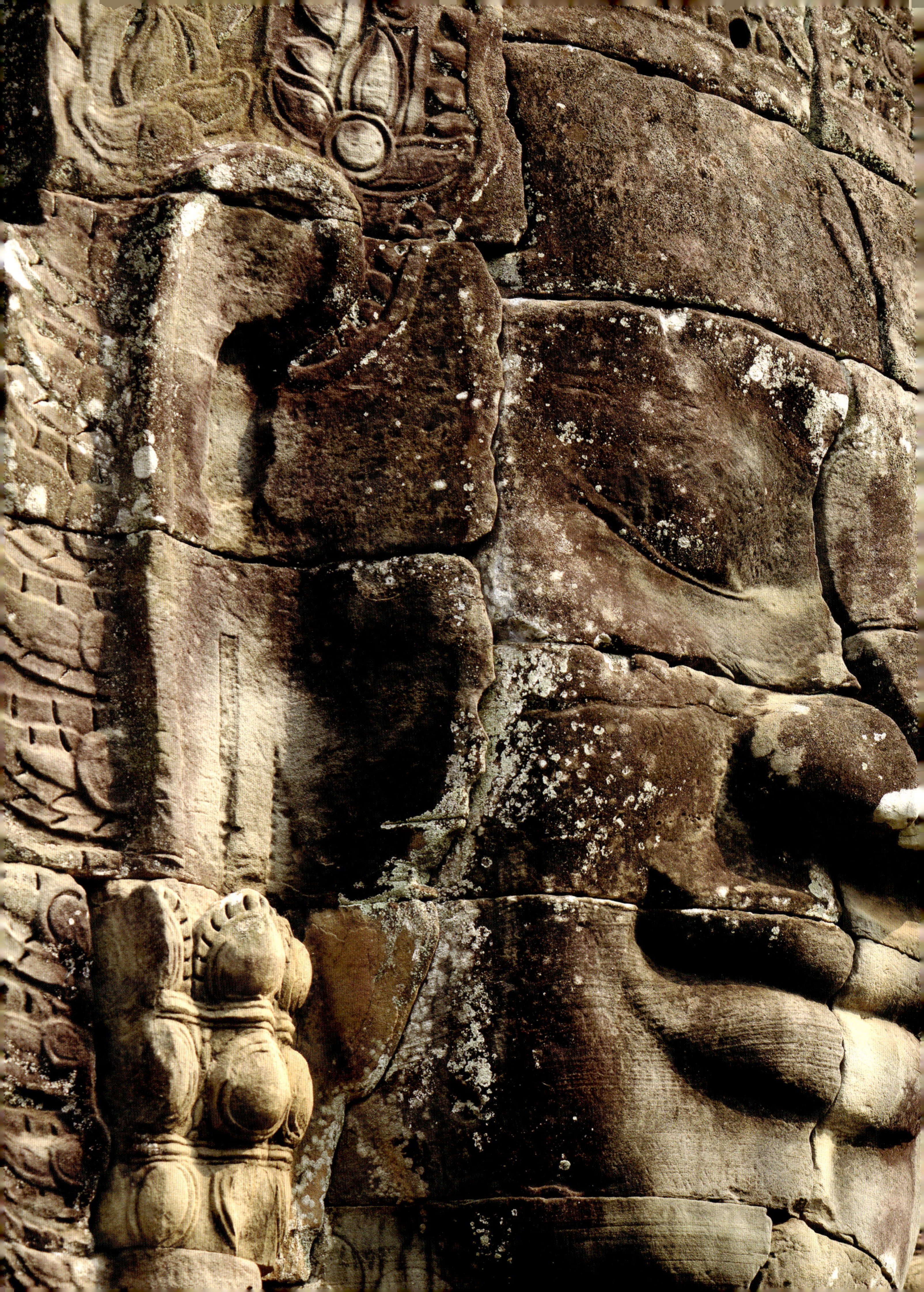

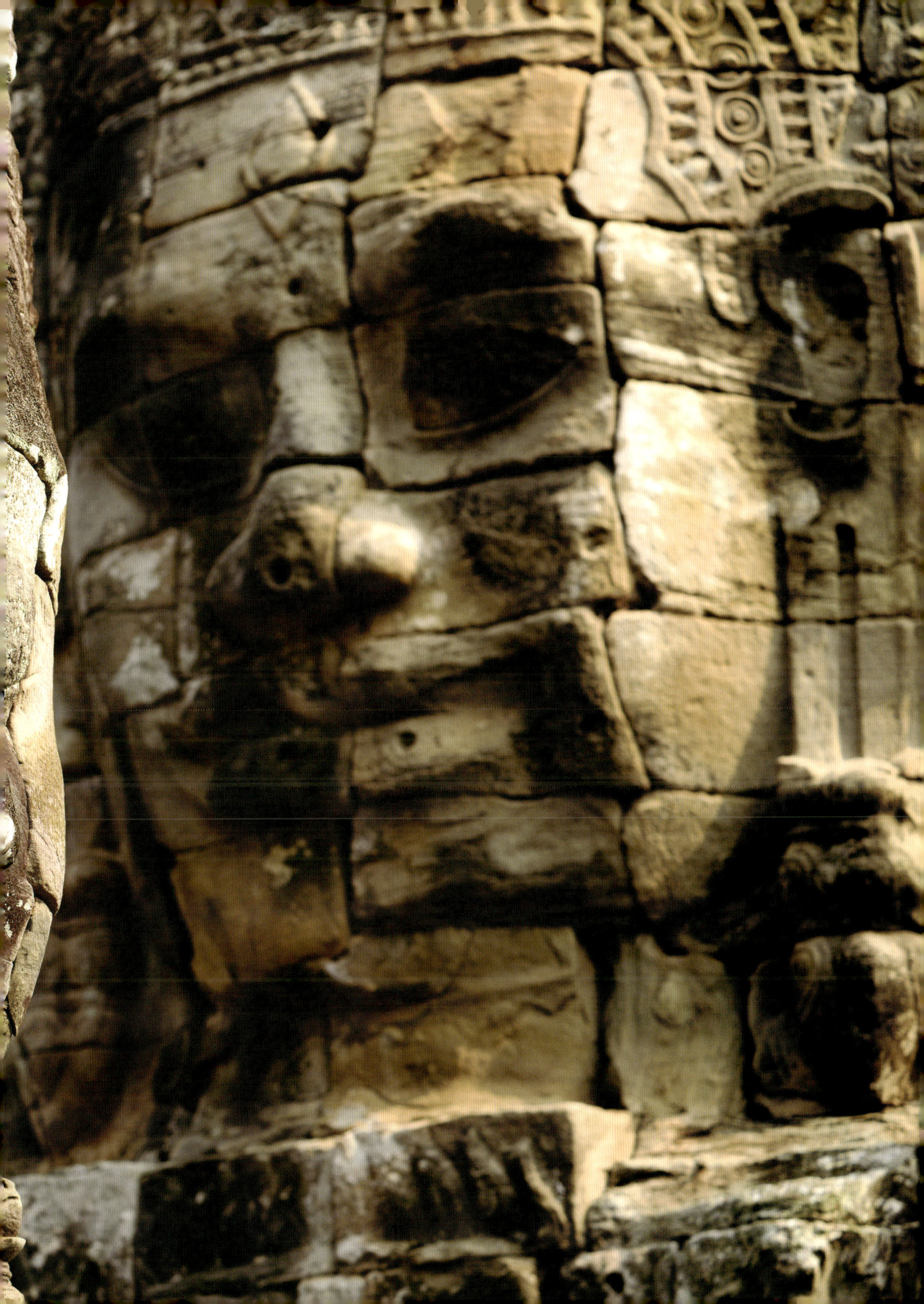

PREVIOUS PAGES:

Bayon Temple, Angkor Thom, Cambodia

Just beyond the precincts of Angkor Wat itself stand the ruins of Jayavarman VII's Bayon or state temple at the centre of the old city of Angkor Thom. This is famous for its massive stone sculptures – which include these monolithic Mona Lisas with their secret smiles.

RIGHT:

Ta Prohm, Cambodia

Long reclaimed by nature, this twelfth-century Buddhist temple makes an atmospheric sight. It was once the heart of a major monastery and university. Along with the other buildings at Angkor, the Ta Prohm temple was uncovered and excavated in the twentieth century, and the giant tree roots that envelop the structure were carefully managed to avoid further damage to the ancient stonework.

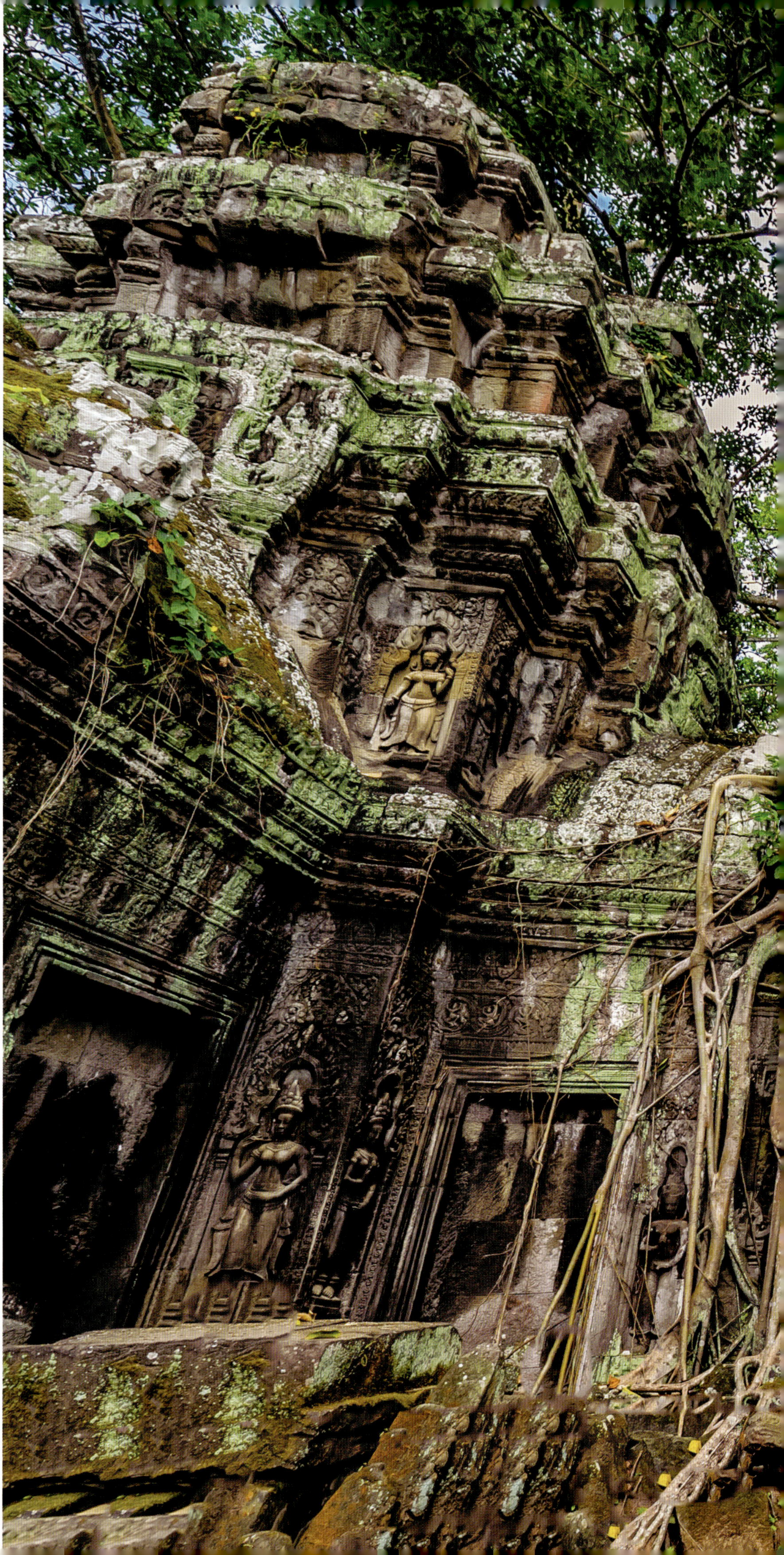

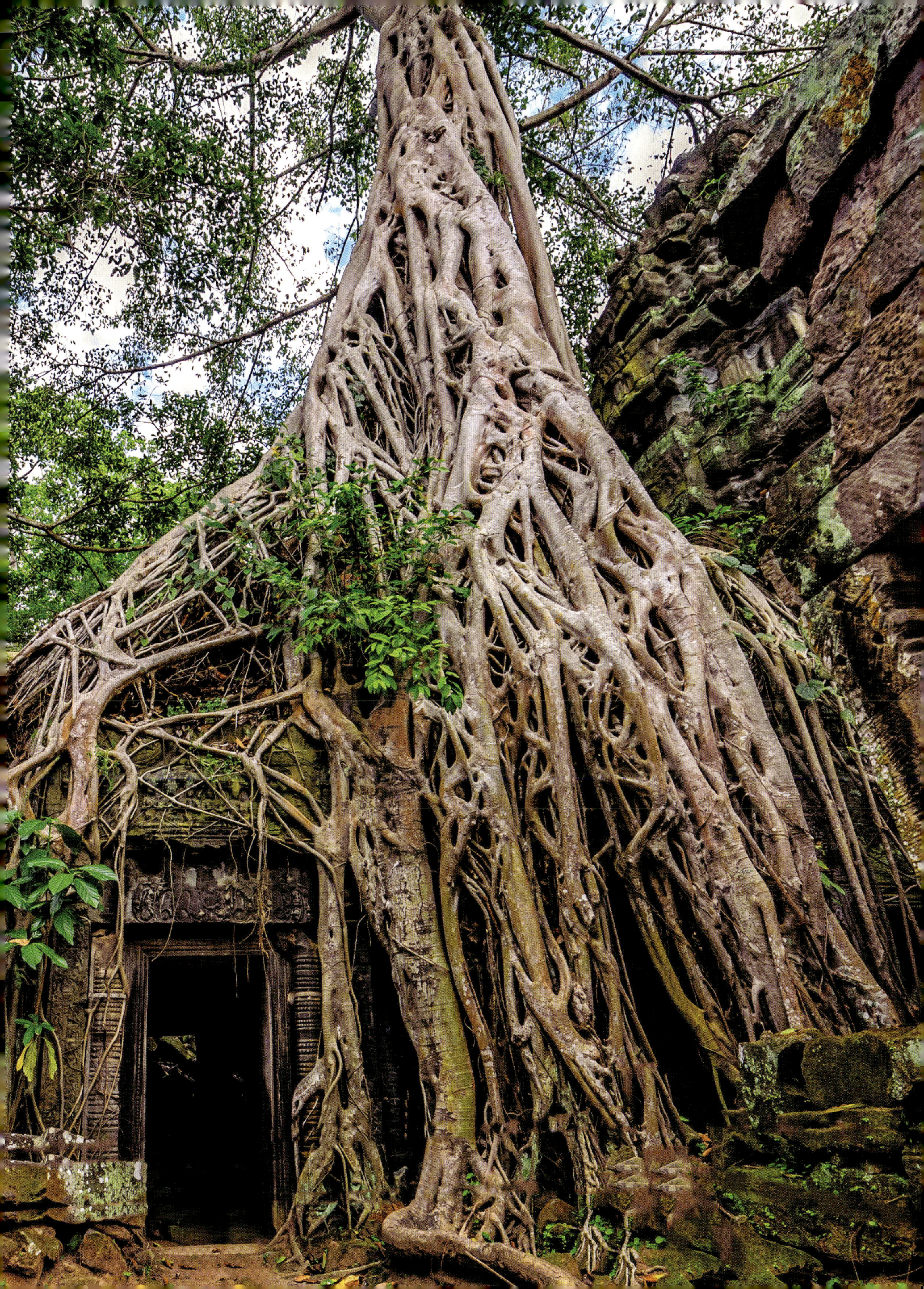

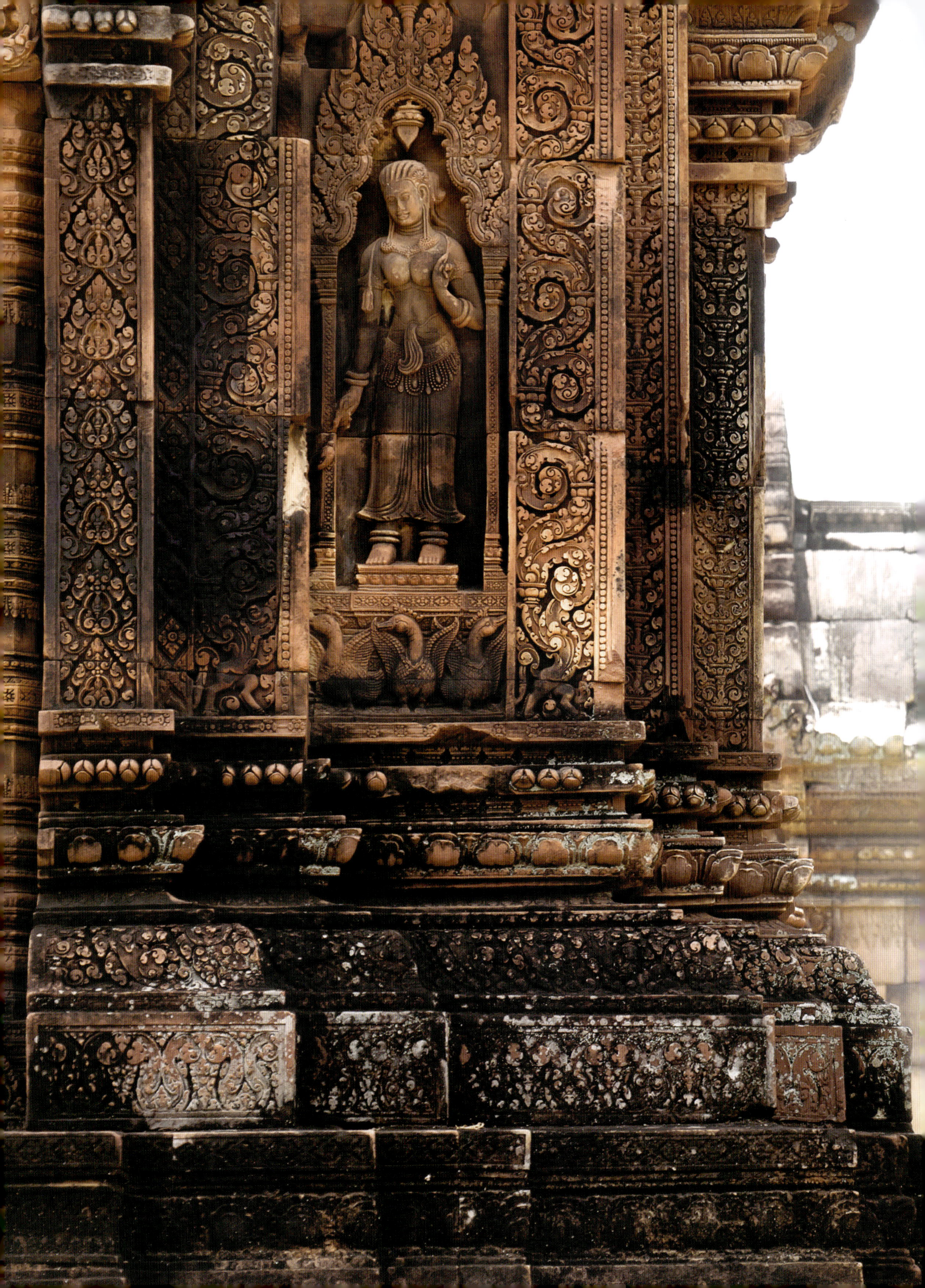

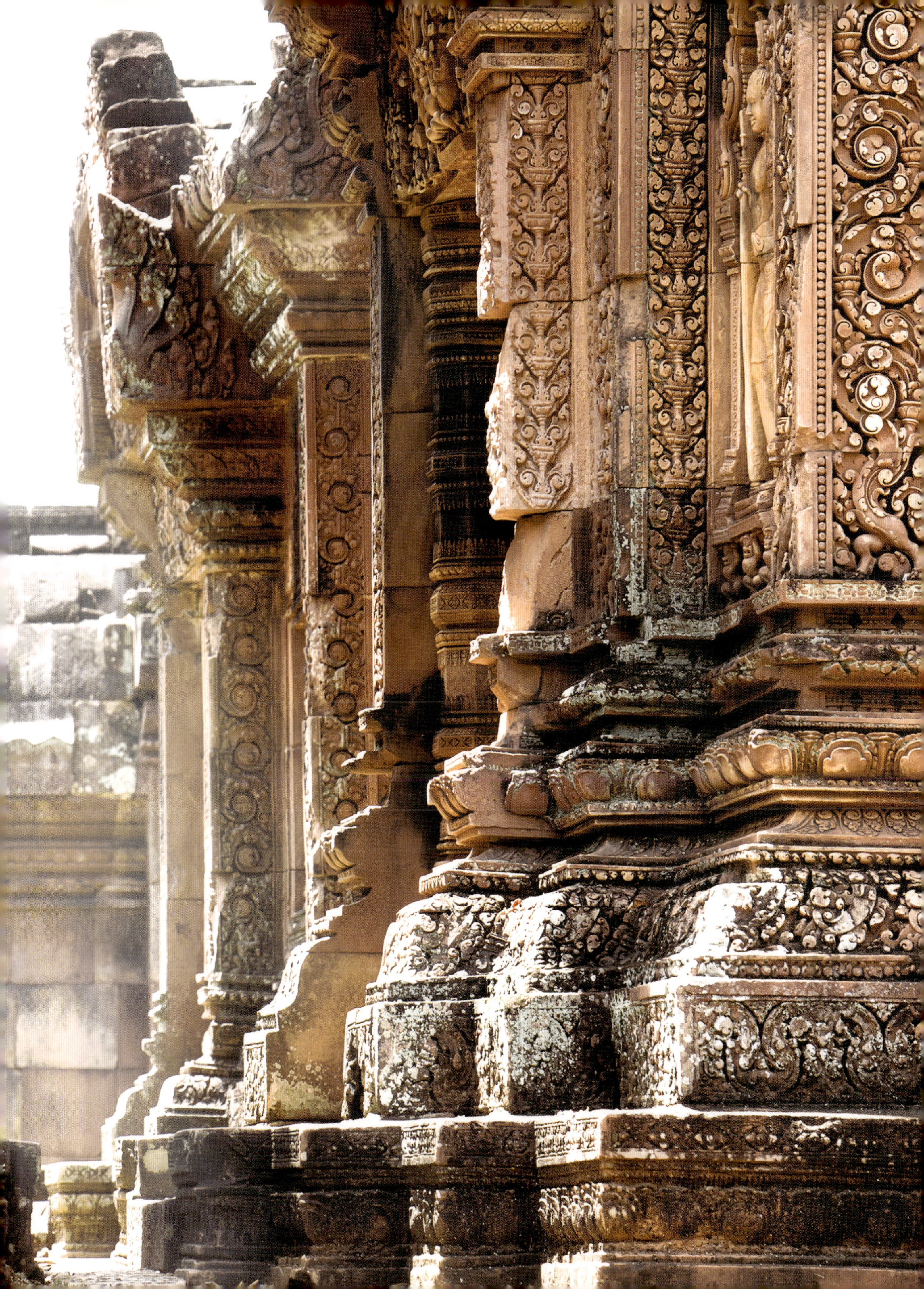

PREVIOUS PAGES:

Banteay Srei, Cambodia

The Khmer name *Banteay Srei* translates as 'citadel of women' – and certainly the stone friezes that surround this lovely little temple feature any number of beauteous female forms. Originally, however, it was called *Tribhuvanamahesvara*, which means 'great lord of the threefold world', a title that was given to the great Hindu deity, Lord Shiva.

RIGHT:

Trán Quóc Pagoda, Hanoi, Vietnam

Standing on an island in Hanoi's West Lake, the Trán Quóc complex is seen to best advantage across the water. There has been a Buddhist temple here since the sixth century, though the structures we see now date from the seventeenth century and after. A Bodhi tree in the grounds was grown from a cutting of the original at Bodh Gaya given to the temple by the Indian government in 1959.

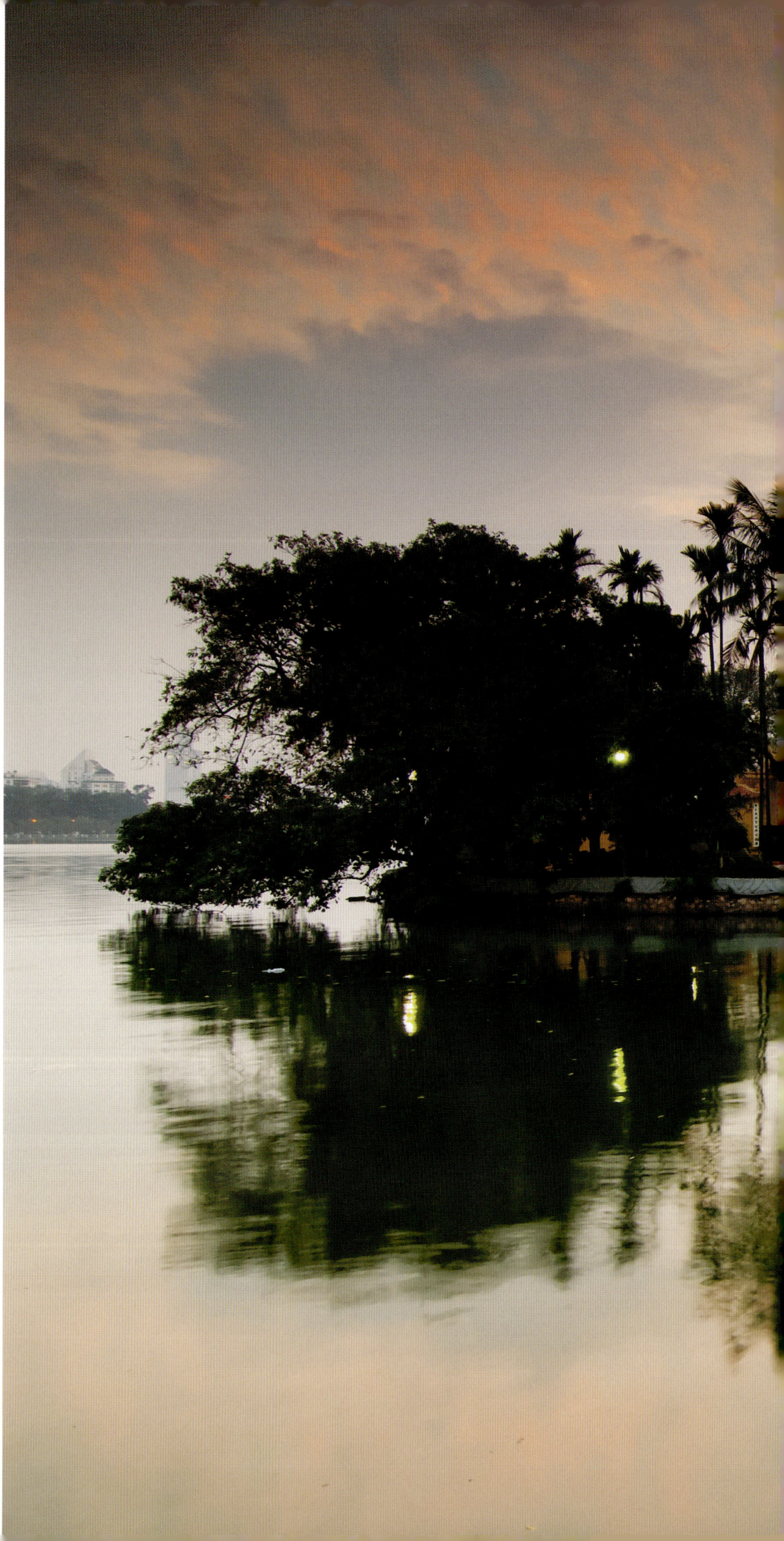

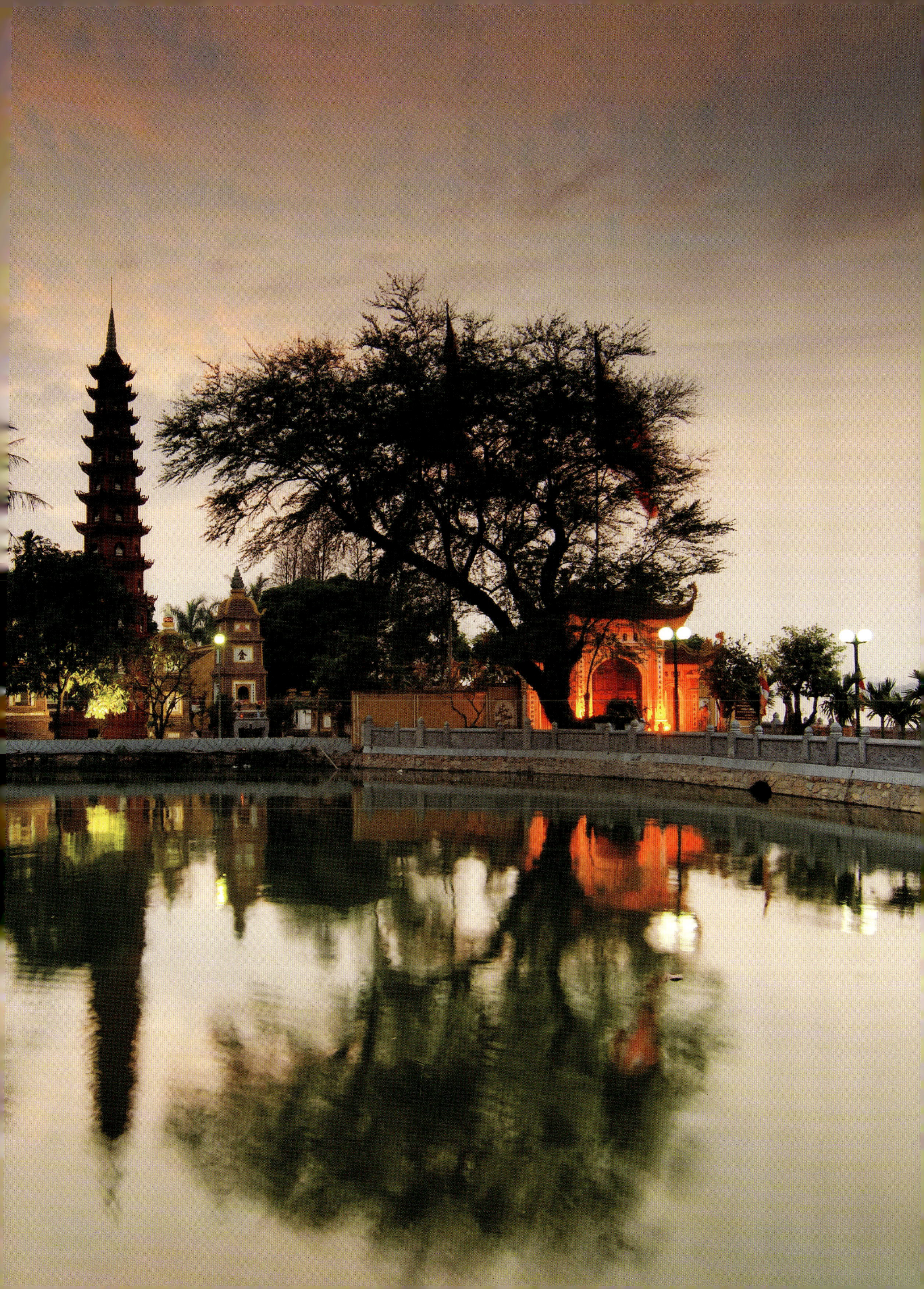

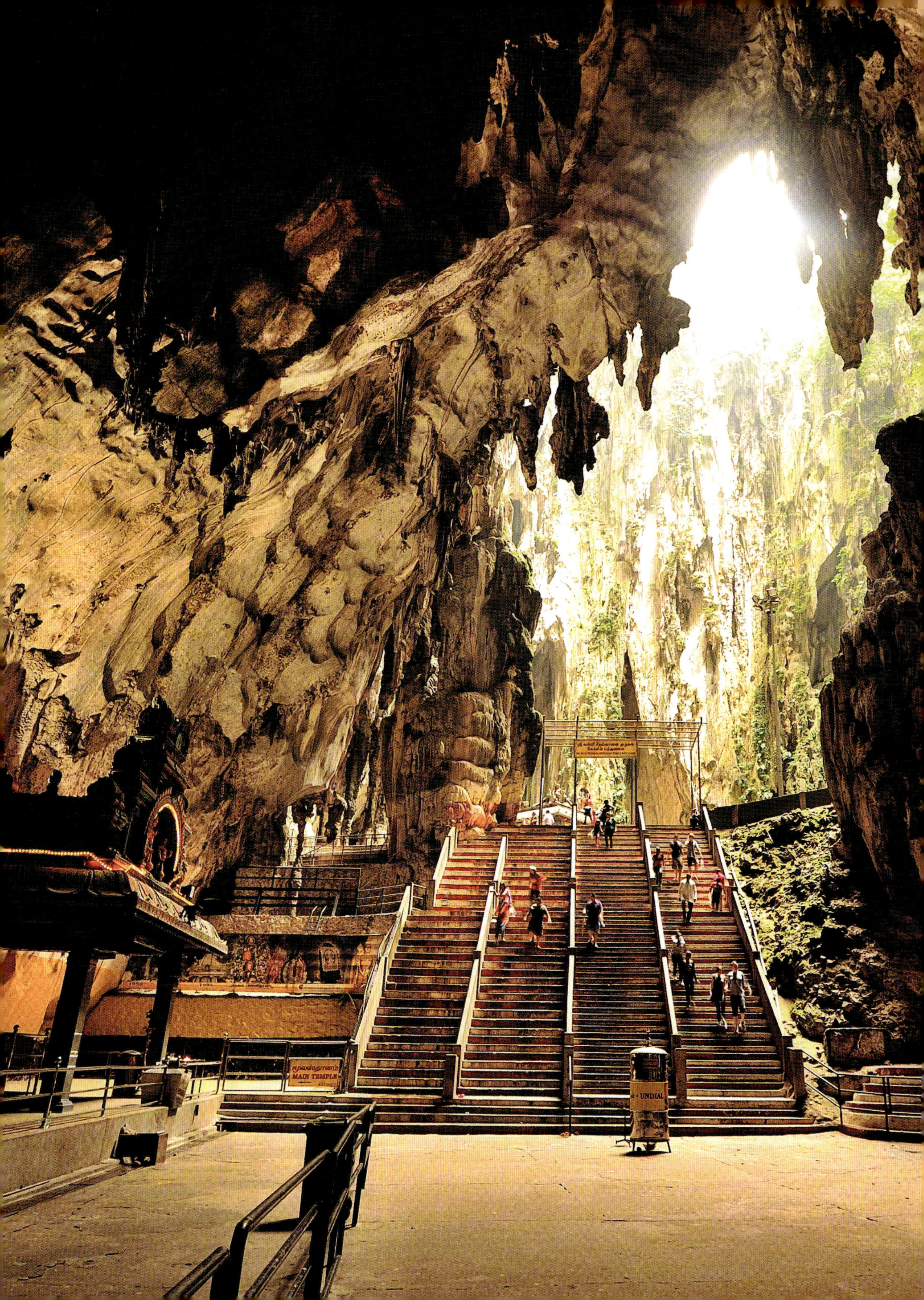
MAIN TEMPLE
UNDIAL

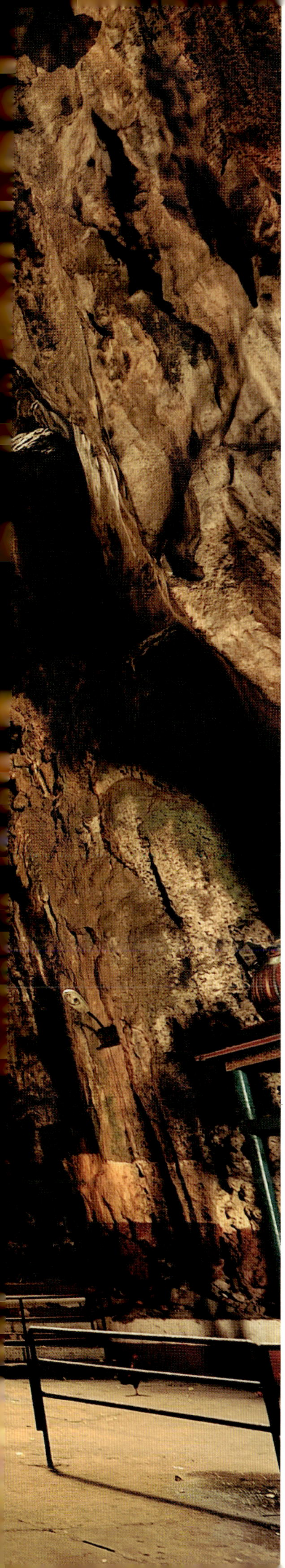

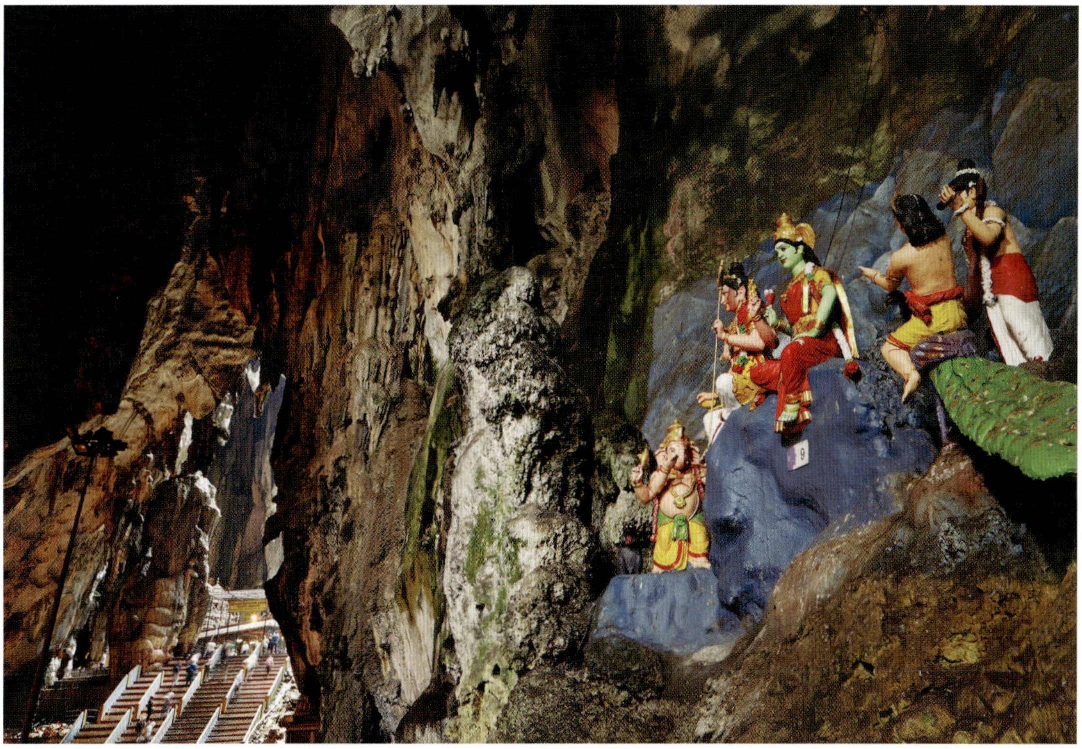

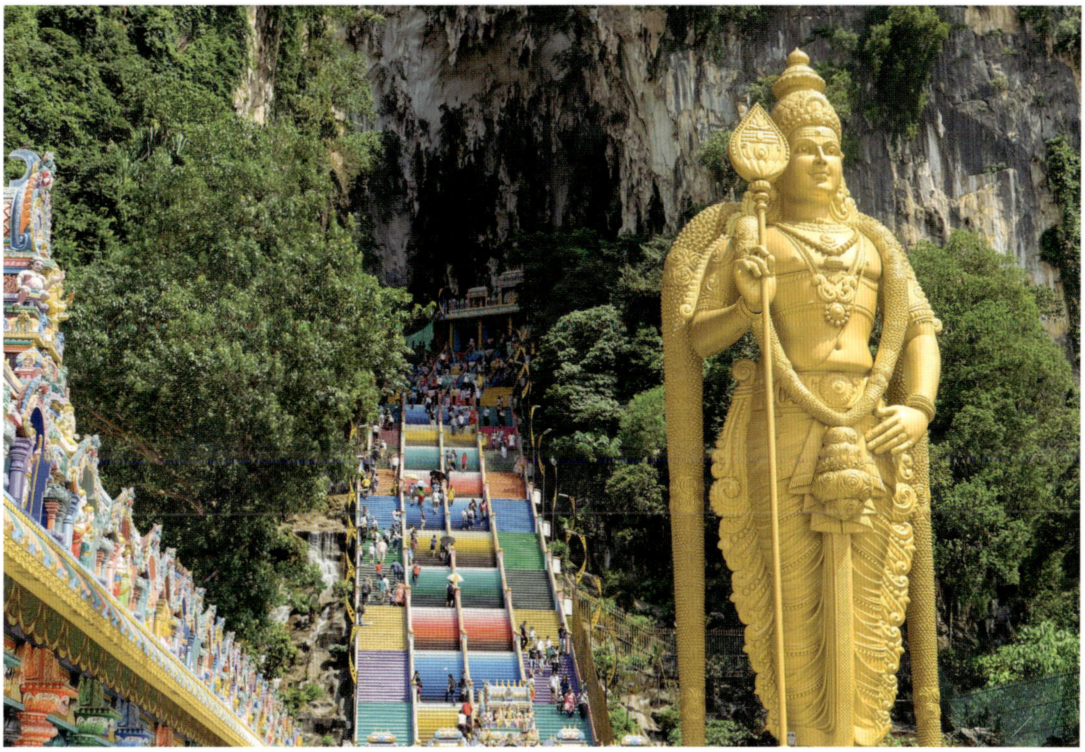

ALL PHOTOGRAPHS:
Batu Caves, Gombak, Selangor, Malaysia
Dedicated to Murugan, Hindu god of war, whose giant 42m (140 ft) gilded statue stands outside, these caves have been used as a place of worship since the 1890s. Though occupied by humans on and off from paleolithic through to early-modern times, they weren't seriously developed until the Malaysian-Tamil trader K. Thamboosamy Pillay (1850–1902) was taken both by the presence of what amounted to a hall in a hillside and by the resemblance he saw in the shape of the cave's entrance aperture to the *vel* (Murugan's sacred javelin-point). He was inspired to create a temple here. There are other caves – and other, smaller shrines: some dedicated to Murugan's more specific exploits; some to other deities. There is one for Lord Rama and another for his companion Hanuman, for example. Further caves have been made into more general museums of Hindu art and sculpture.

Climbing the 272 multicoloured concrete steps is popular among worshippers and tourists today.

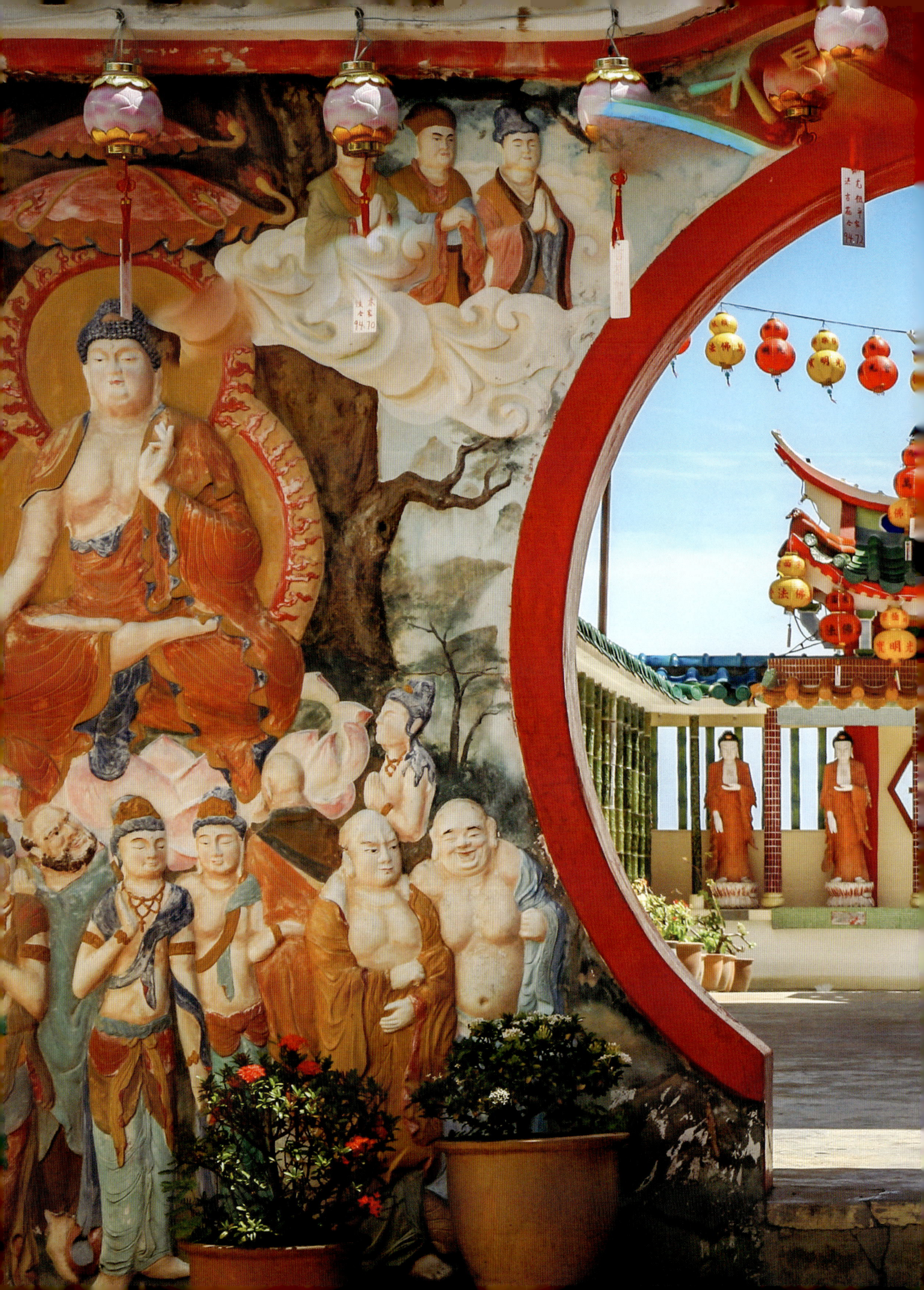

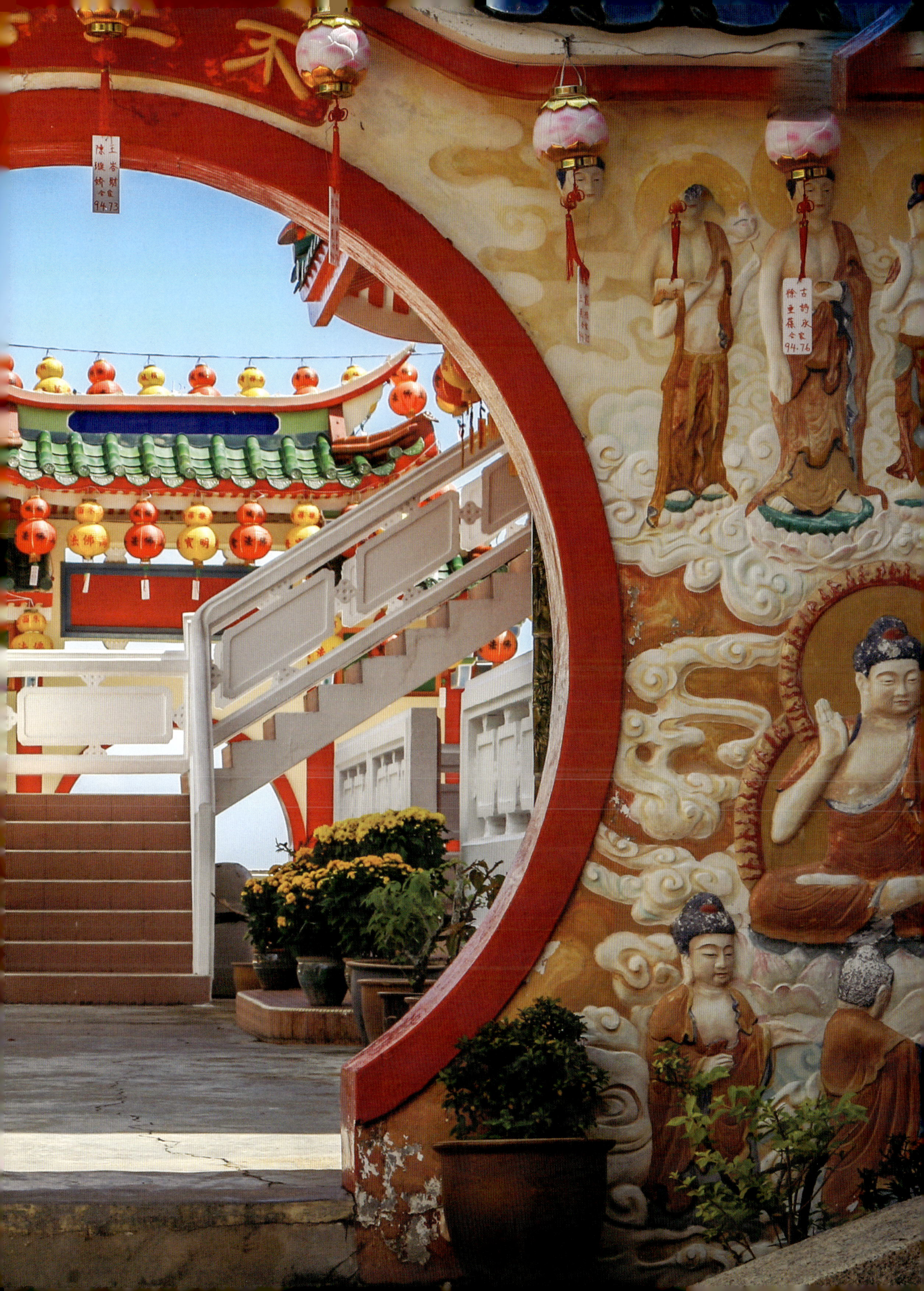

PREVIOUS PAGES:

Kek Lok Si Temple, Penang, Malaysia

Pilgrims flock to Air Itam, Penang, from every part of Southeast Asia to visit this most popular of Buddhist shrines. It's easy to see why: the mood's upbeat; the colours bright; the emphasis not on sobriety but celebration; not on understated subtlety but sheer excess. The Pagoda of Rama VI here is reputed to have 10,000 statues of the Buddha alone.

RIGHT:

Leong San See, Singapore

This, the 'Temple of the Mountain Dragon', was built in the early twentieth century by a Buddhist monk who brought a statue of Guanyin with him from his native Fujian. A Chinese *bodhisattva* (a saint or holy person), Guanyin was especially celebrated as the goddess of compassion, in keeping with which this Singapore shrine plays host not just to Buddhists, but to Taoists too.

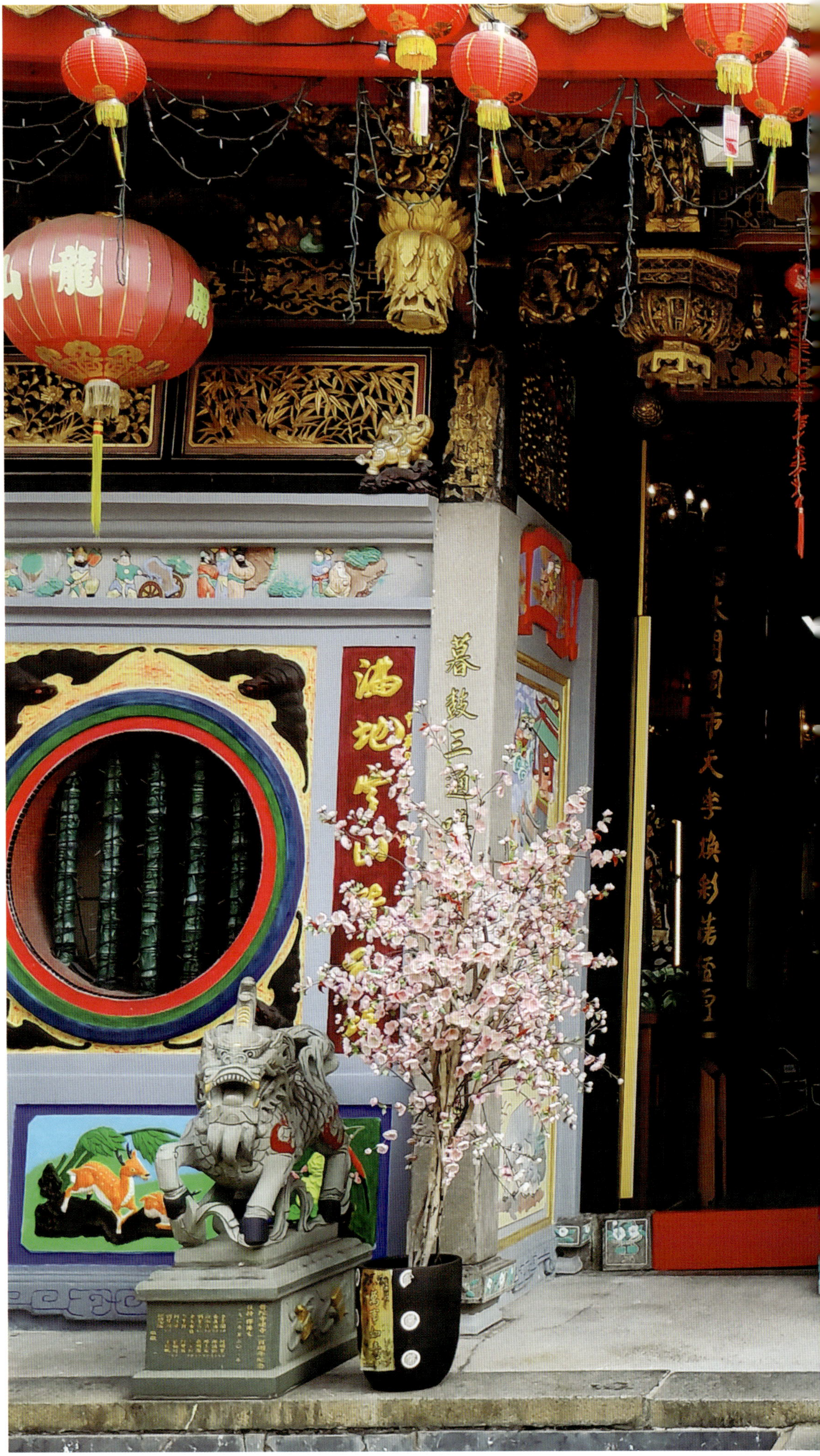

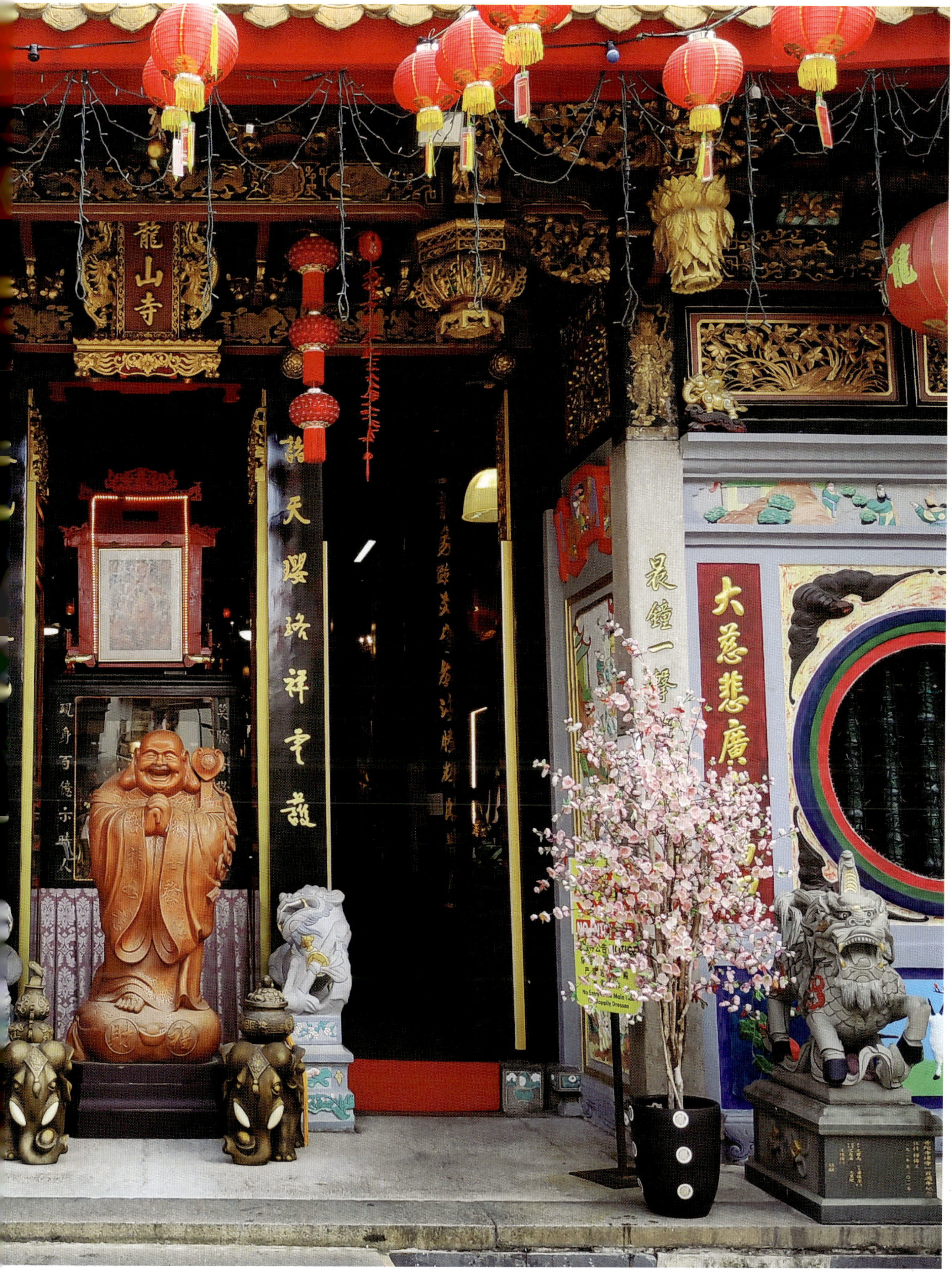
龍山寺
諸天瓔珞祥雲護
大慈悲廣

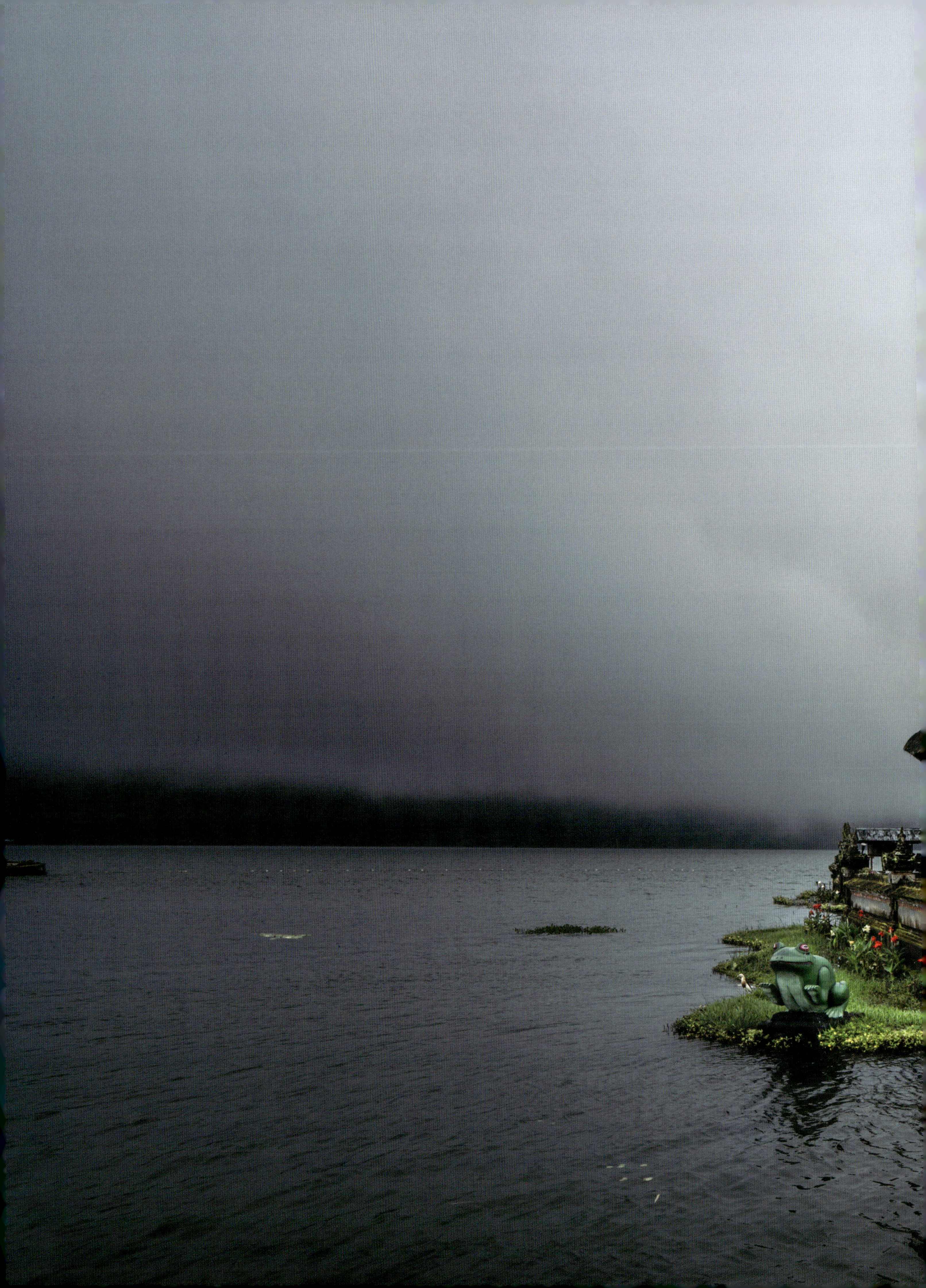

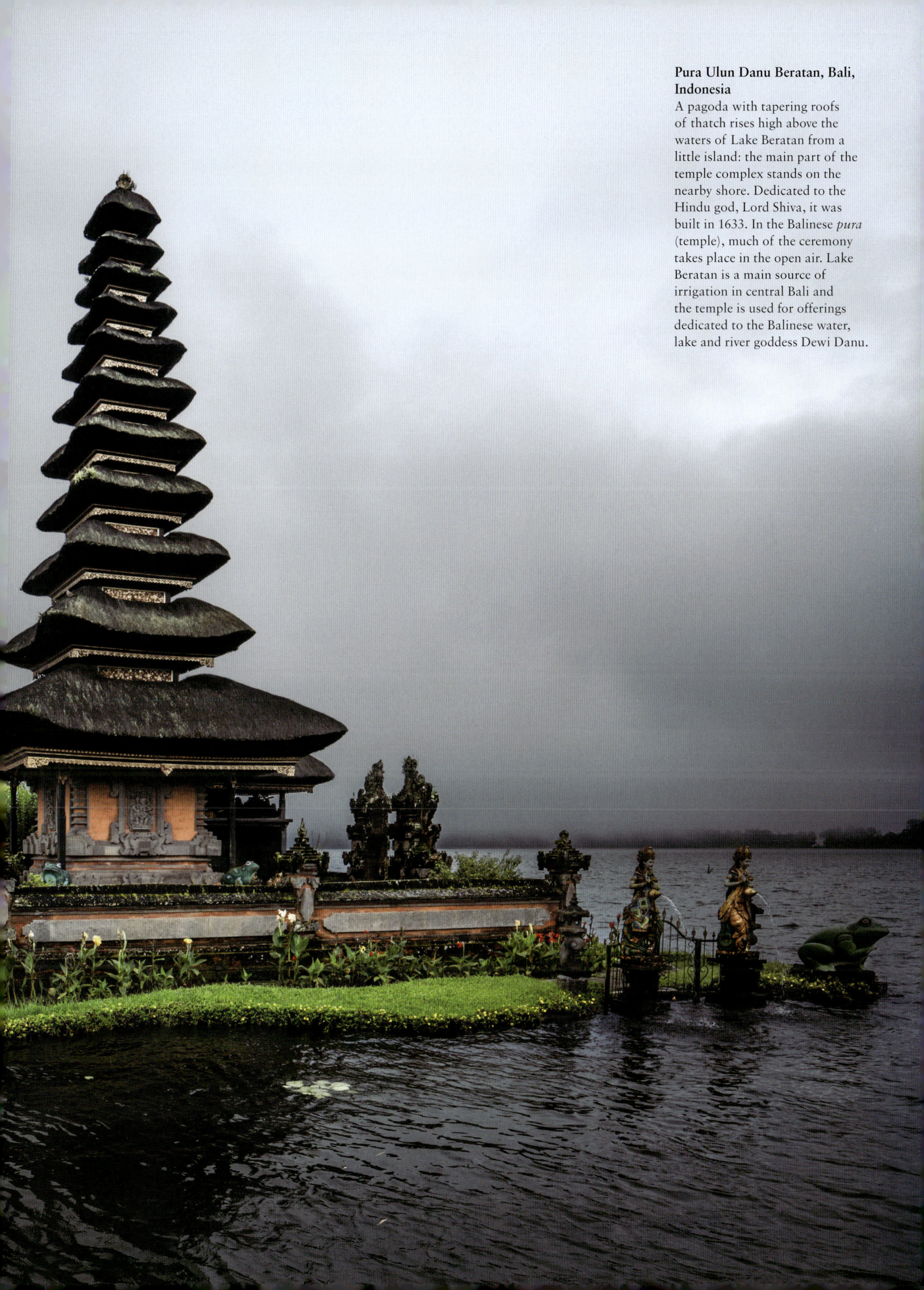

Pura Ulun Danu Beratan, Bali, Indonesia
A pagoda with tapering roofs of thatch rises high above the waters of Lake Beratan from a little island: the main part of the temple complex stands on the nearby shore. Dedicated to the Hindu god, Lord Shiva, it was built in 1633. In the Balinese *pura* (temple), much of the ceremony takes place in the open air. Lake Beratan is a main source of irrigation in central Bali and the temple is used for offerings dedicated to the Balinese water, lake and river goddess Dewi Danu.

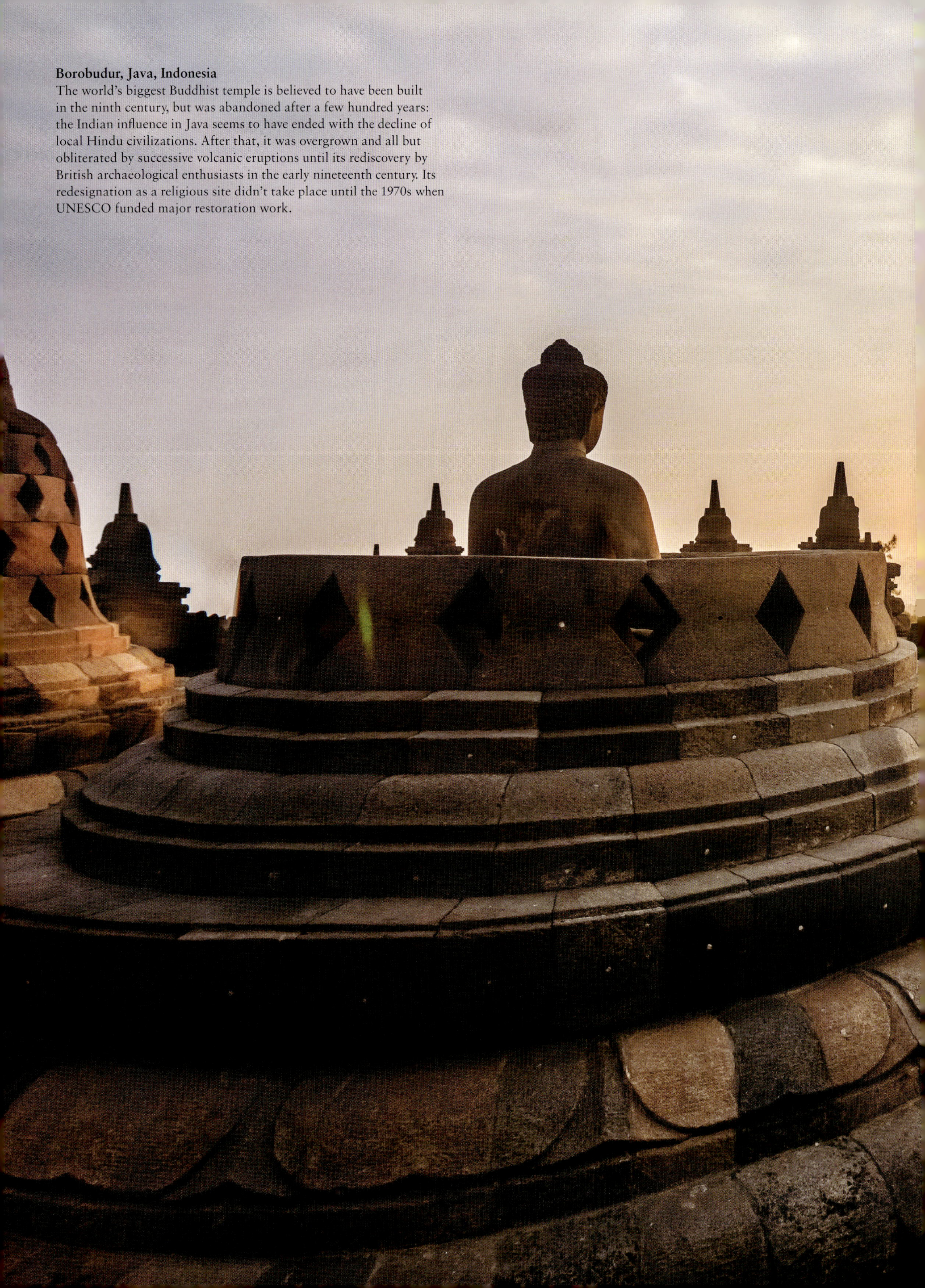

Borobudur, Java, Indonesia
The world's biggest Buddhist temple is believed to have been built in the ninth century, but was abandoned after a few hundred years: the Indian influence in Java seems to have ended with the decline of local Hindu civilizations. After that, it was overgrown and all but obliterated by successive volcanic eruptions until its rediscovery by British archaeological enthusiasts in the early nineteenth century. Its redesignation as a religious site didn't take place until the 1970s when UNESCO funded major restoration work.

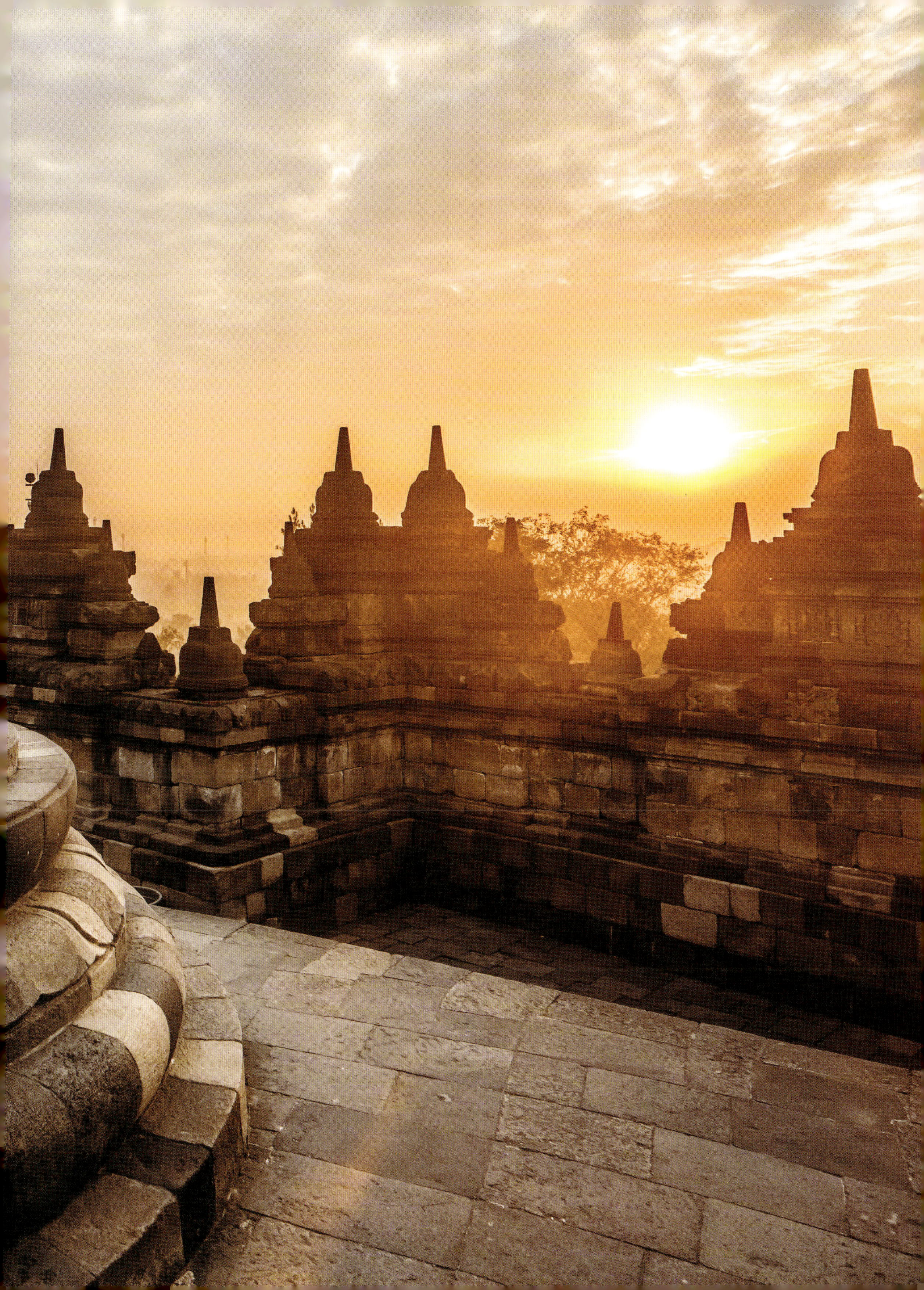

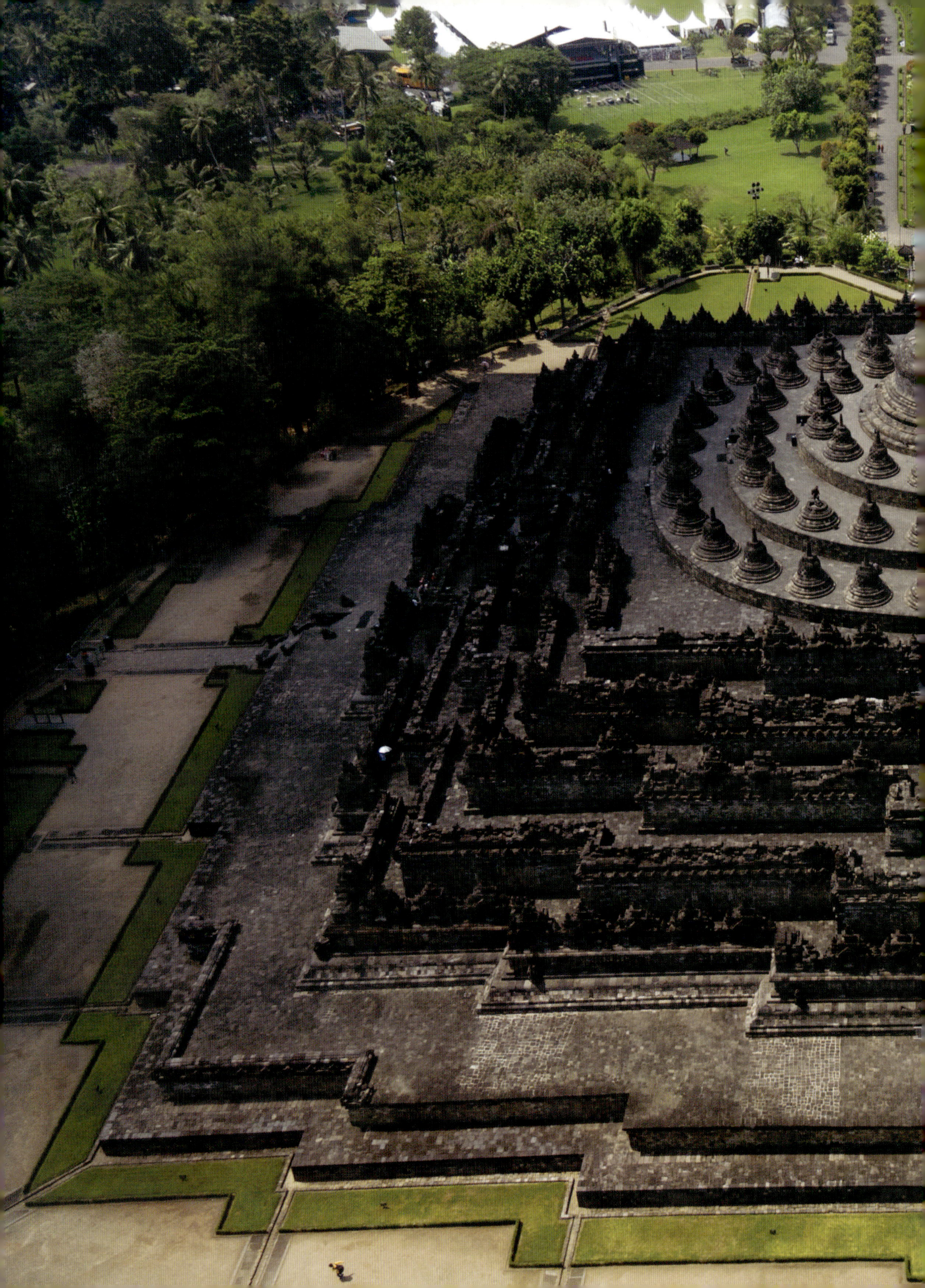

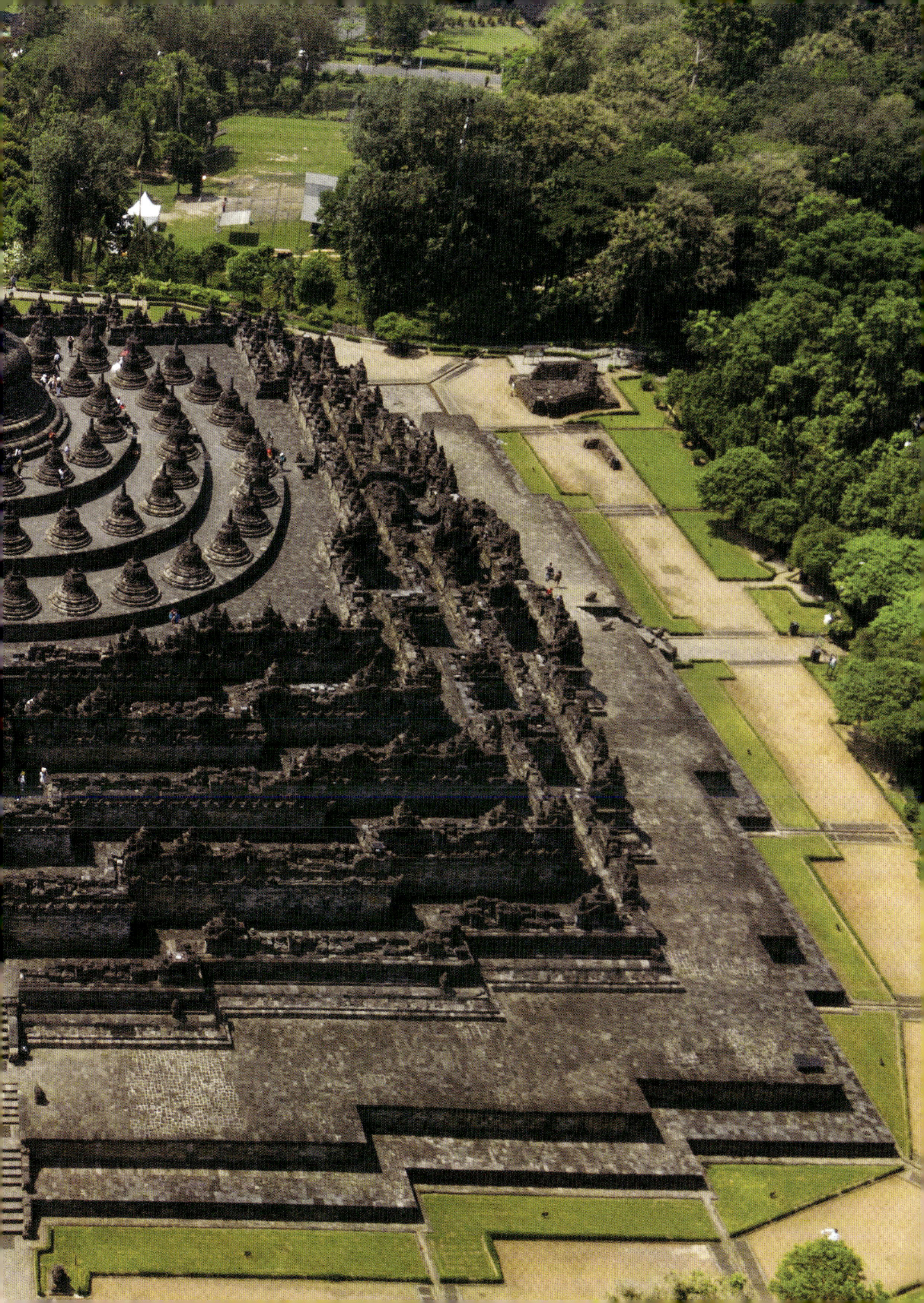

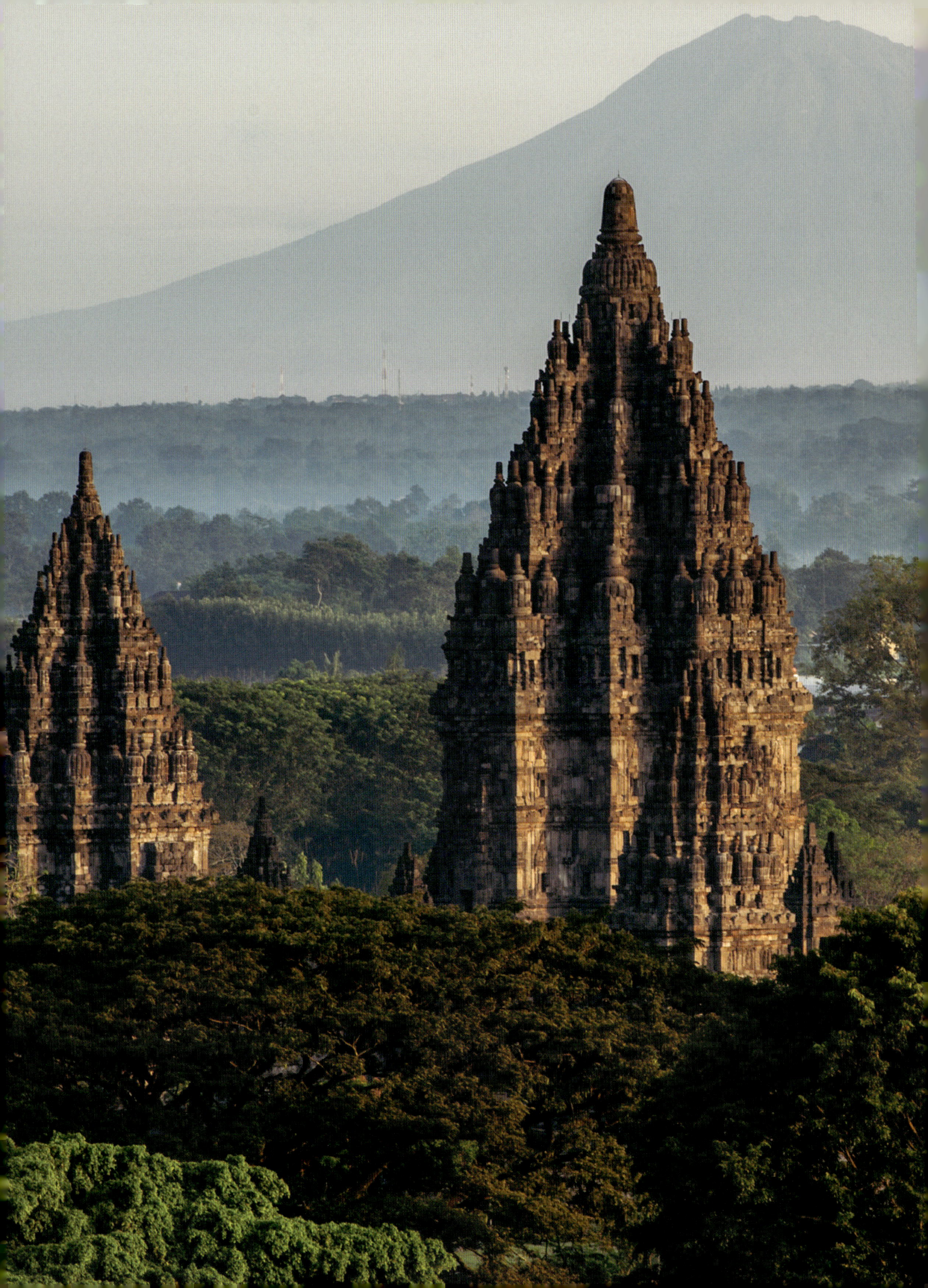

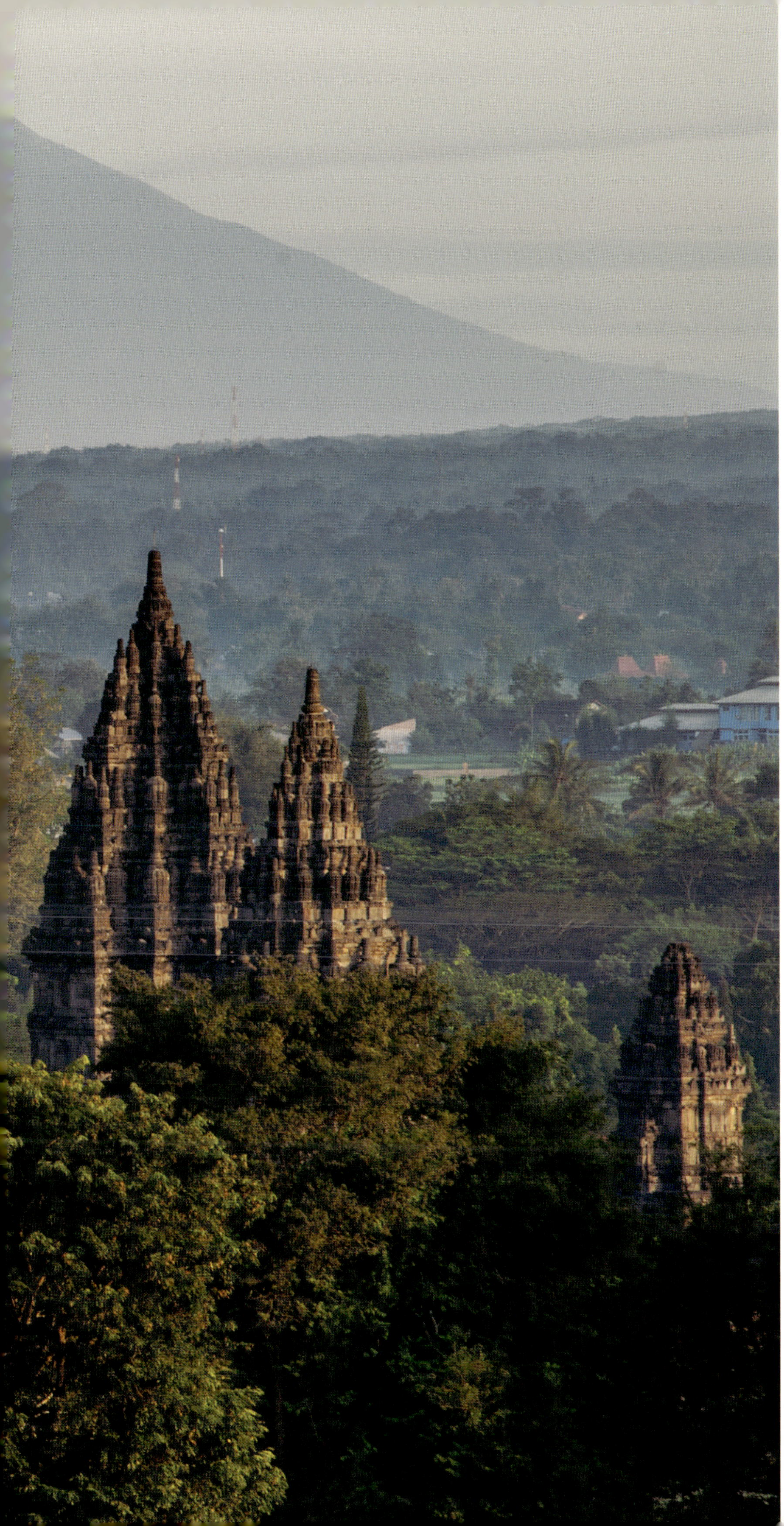

PREVIOUS PAGES:

Borobudur, Java, Indonesia

In its tiered design, the main temple at Borobudur may be seen as another man-made Mount Meru. Pilgrims are encouraged to see the parallels. A step pyramid structure, the temple has nine platforms, decorated with more than 500 statues and more than 2500 relief panels. The sculpted stone reliefs add to the aesthetic and spiritual impact of the ascent from the world of down-to-earth desire to the summit of enlightenment.

LEFT:

Prambanan, Java, Indonesia

Indonesia's largest Hindu temple encompasses over 200 separate shrines, a stupendous monument to the age of Indian ascendancy across this region. The complex was constructed on an ambitious scale, its main tower standing 47m (154 ft) high. Like Borobudur, Prambanan was built in the ninth century but subsequently abandoned, only to be rediscovered and restored in modern times.

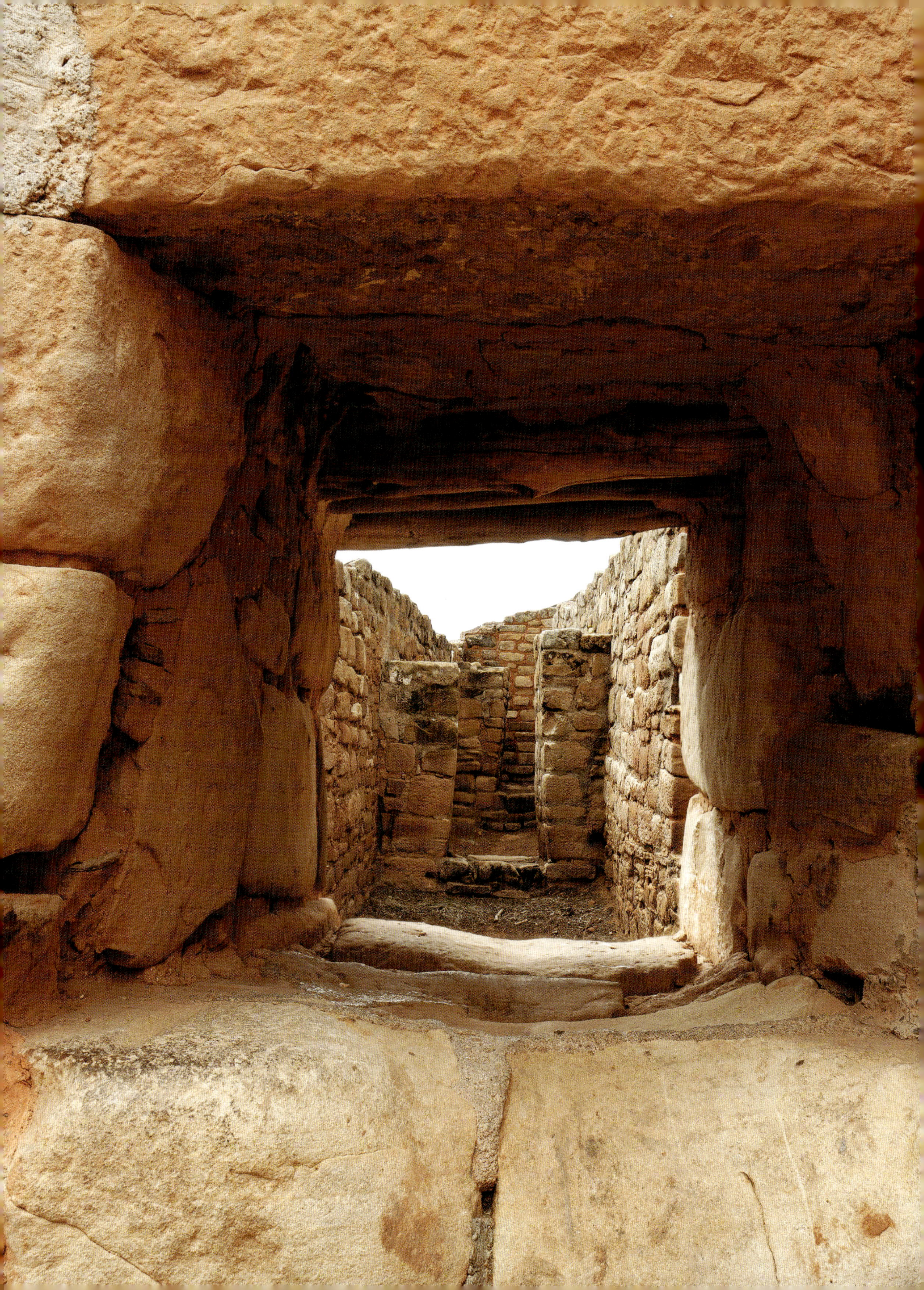

North and South America

A Hindu temple was never of course intended to be 'exotic'; Buddhist spirituality might have been mystic, but it wasn't 'strange' – not in its original context, at least. As these creeds were exported around the world they naturally acquired an alien aura – appealing or otherwise.

The arrival of European adventurers in the colonial era caused indigenous cultures to be pushed aside, displaced and, with the introduction of a Christian order, relegated to a lower status. The conquered peoples were still there, though, their communities oppressed but still coherent; their religious traditions remembered, if not actually observed. Unfortunately, the most immediate and enduring effect of the European presence in the Americas was the virtual annihilation of existing populations. While thousands were killed or condemned to starve after being driven from their lands, millions more were wiped out inadvertently, stricken by Old World illnesses to which they weren't immune.

It meant over a century, the wholesale Christianization of the Americas by English Protestants in the north, and Spanish and Portuguese Catholics further south. Lots of lovely churches appeared – but little sign of what went before. Today the temples of the Americas' first inhabitants have come to seem every bit as alien as those of its most recent ones.

OPPOSITE:
Sun Temple, Mesa Verde National Park, Colorado, USA
The first rays of the rising sun at its winter solstice could be observed from here each year; the first reassurance that the darkening and chilling of the earth would be reversed. 'Paleo-Indians' were living here from the tenth century BCE, but the earliest stone-built settlements (*pueblos*, as the Spanish called them) date from the seventh century CE.

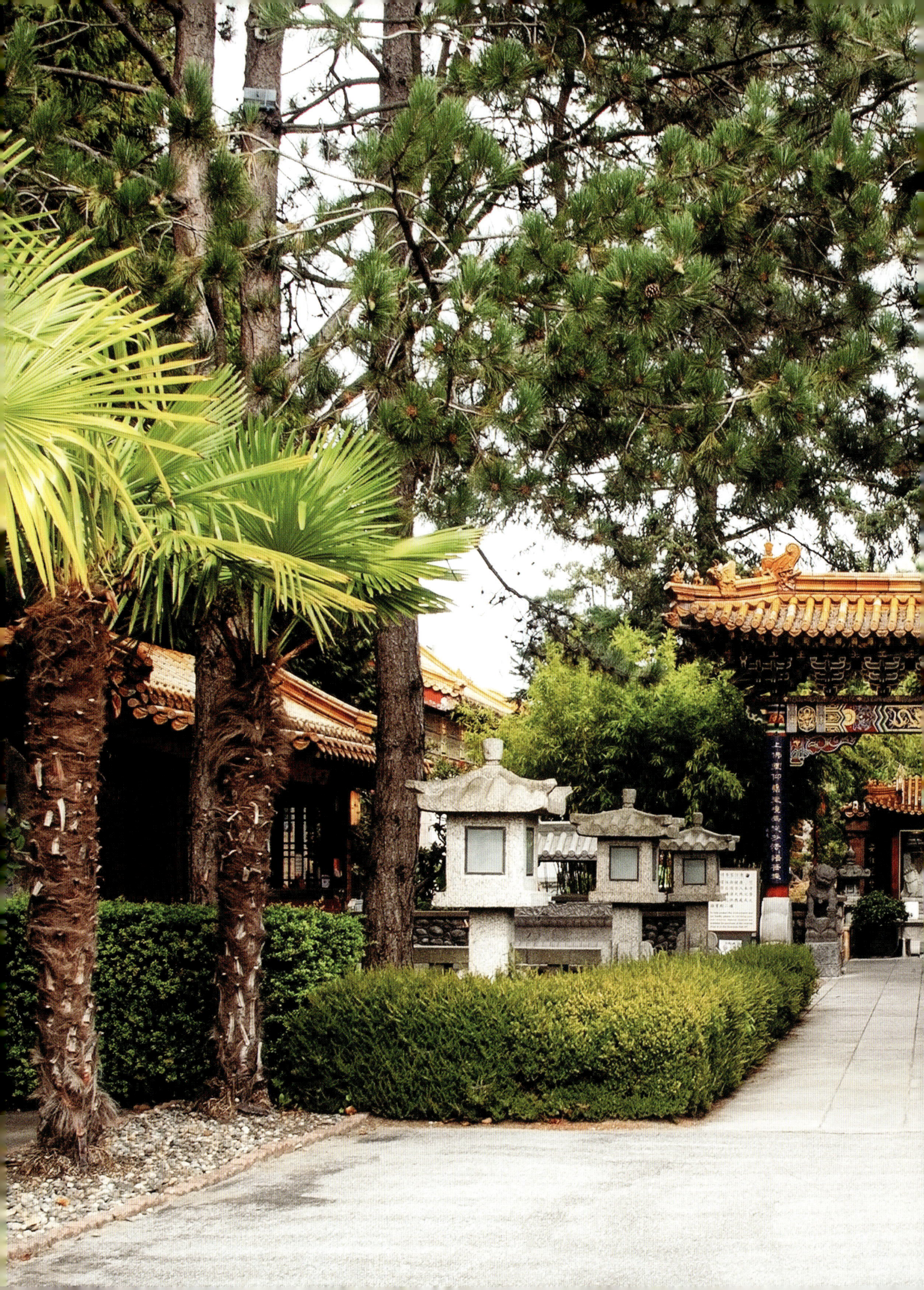

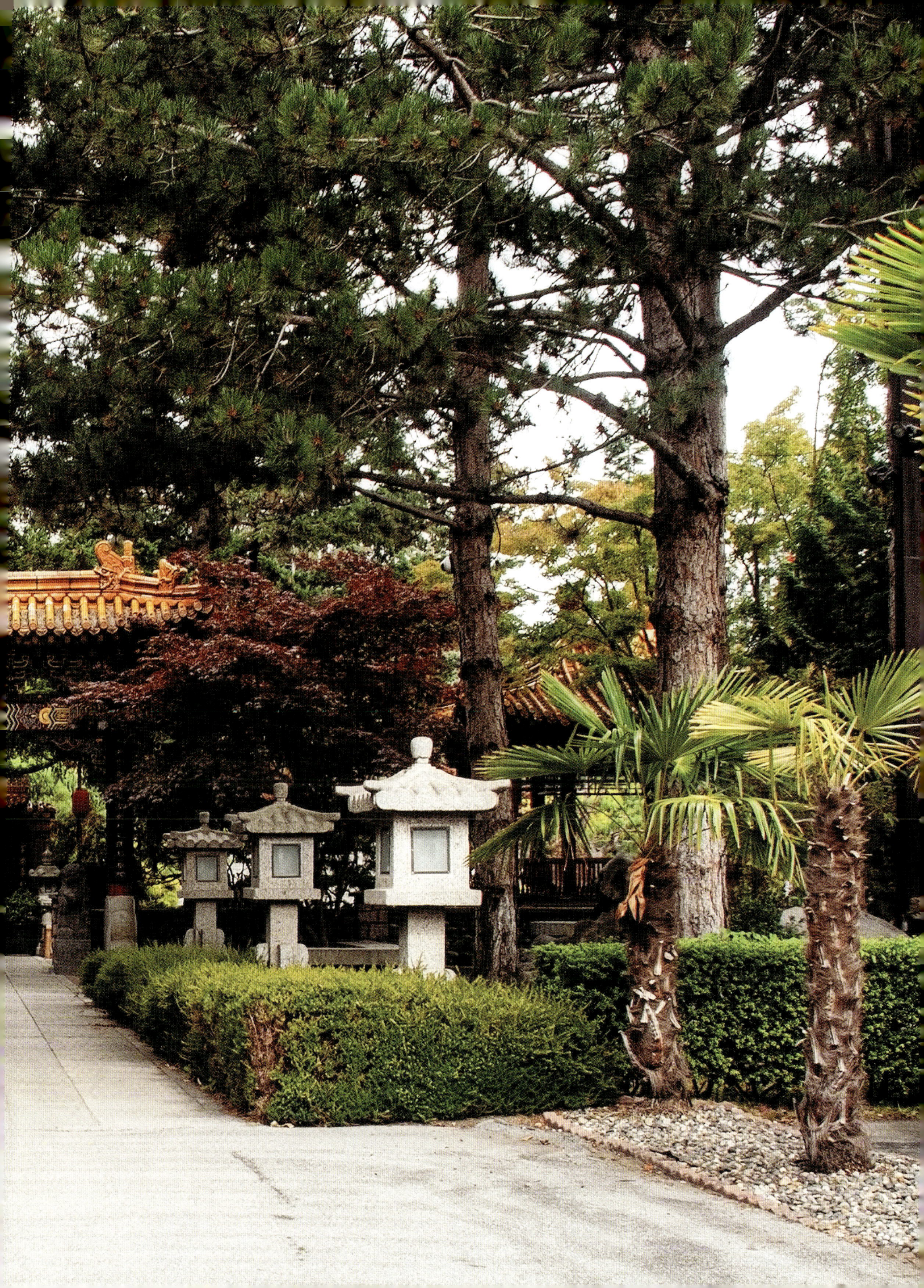

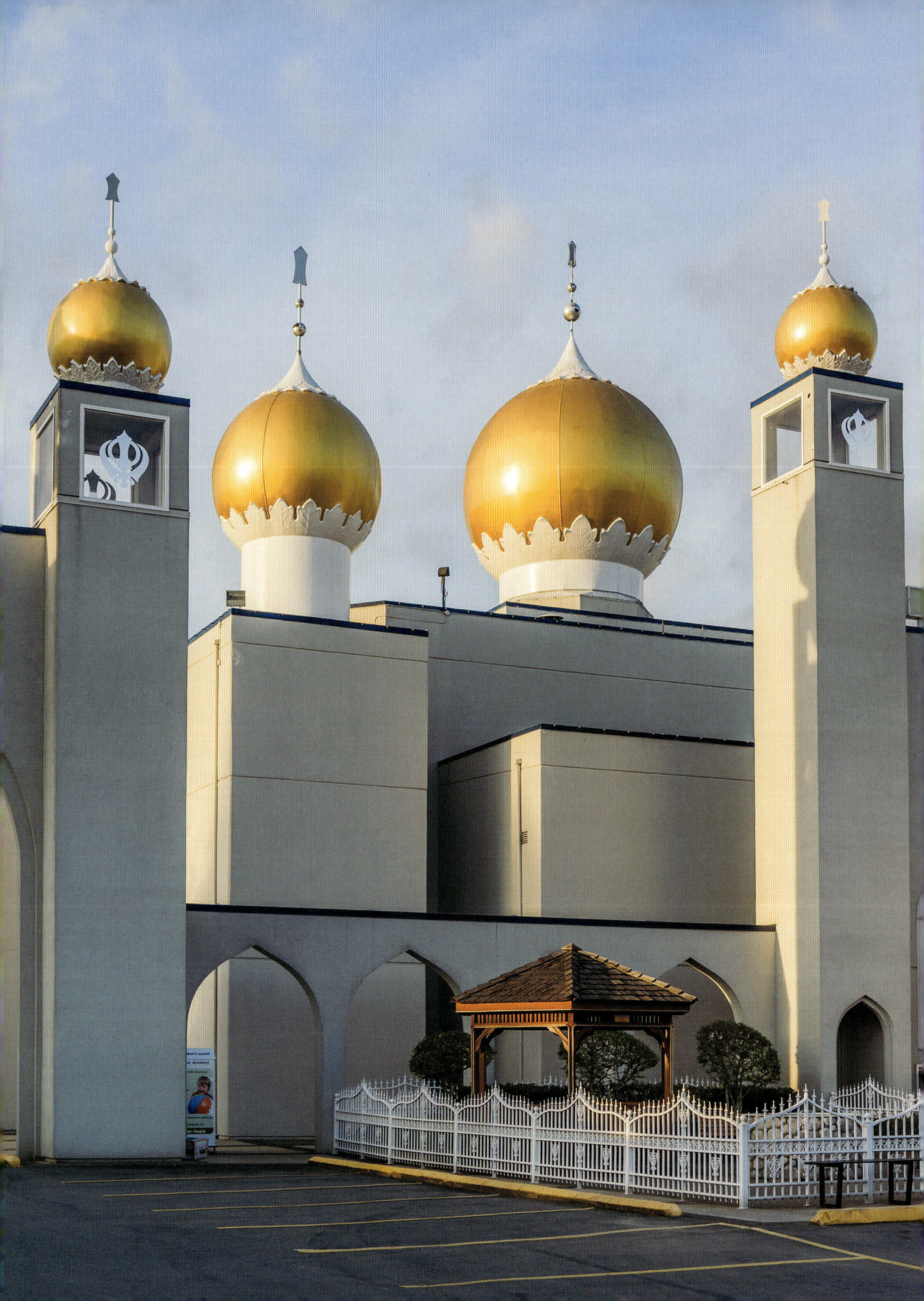

PREVIOUS PAGES, RIGHT AND BELOW:

Goddess of Mercy Temple, Richmond, Vancouver, Canada

The suburb of Richmond lies in Vancouver's southern outskirts. There was nothing much here in the 1970s. Since that time, it has been rapidly and massively developed, as home to a fast-growing Chinese immigrant community. Built primarily to serve them, but also to raise interest among Western converts, this 'International Buddhist Temple' is colourfully-designed and stands in a leafy setting.

OPPOSITE:

Akali Singh Sikh Temple, Vancouver, Canada

Vancouver's Sikh community first set up in an abandoned church in the east of the city in the 1950s. Their wealth and confidence growing as they became more firmly established in Canadian life, by the 1980s they were able to build this magnificent gurdwara, its design evidently referencing that of the Golden Temple of Amritsar in Punjab.

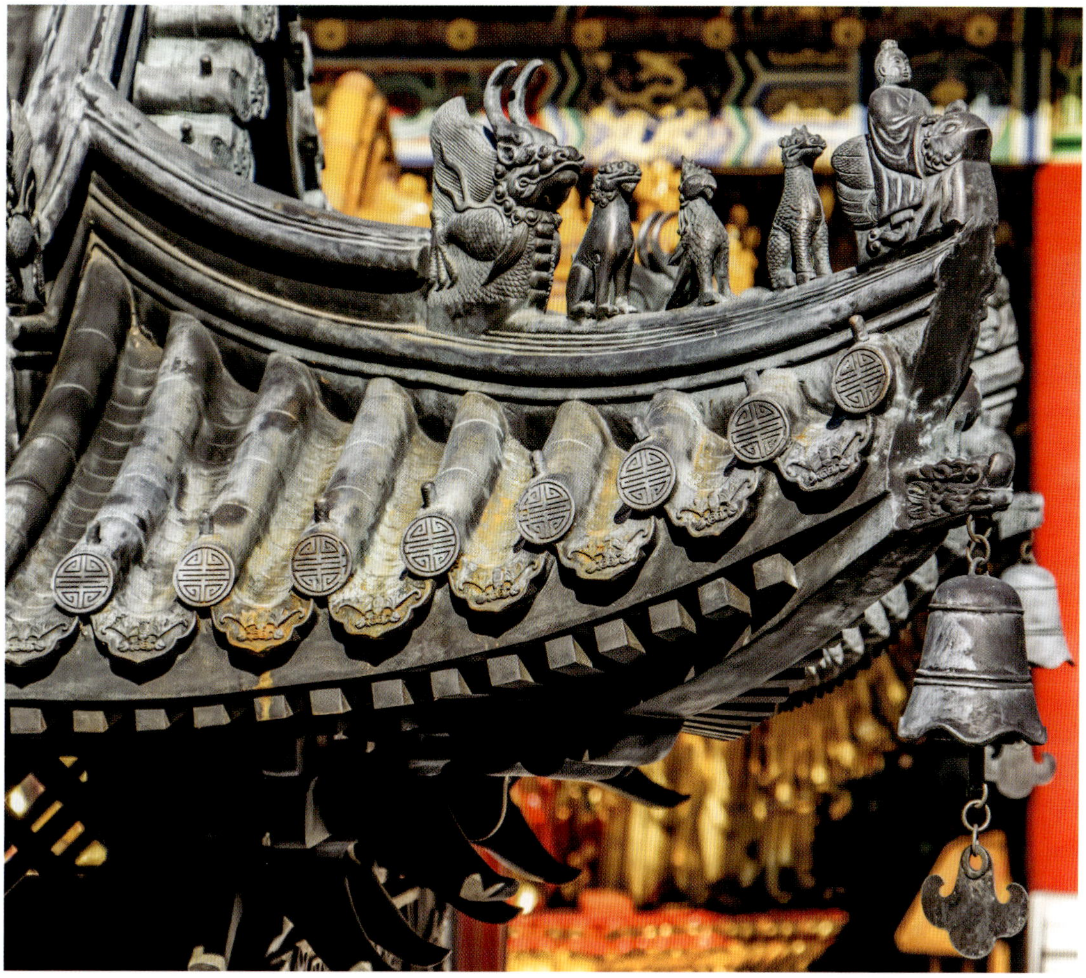

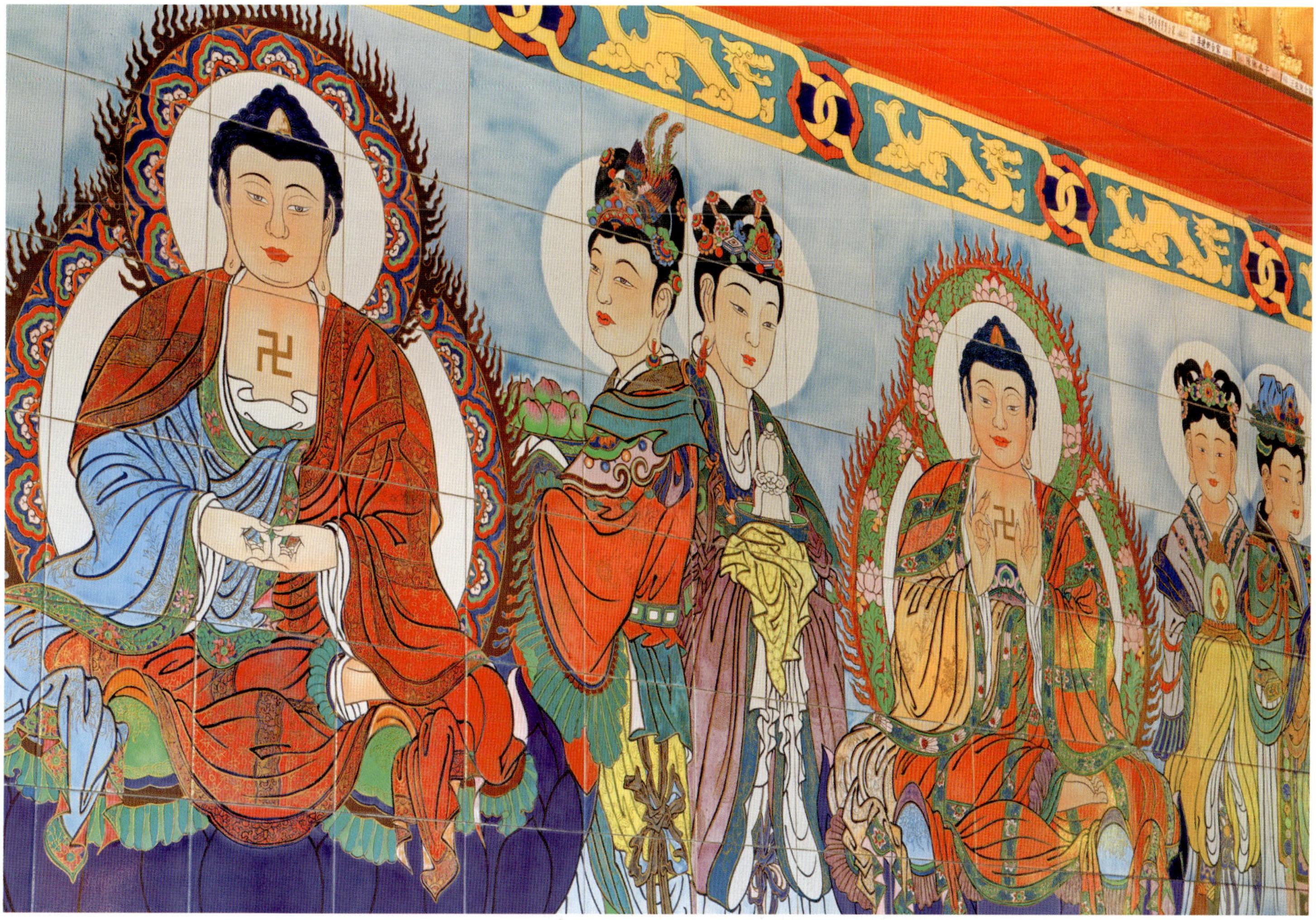

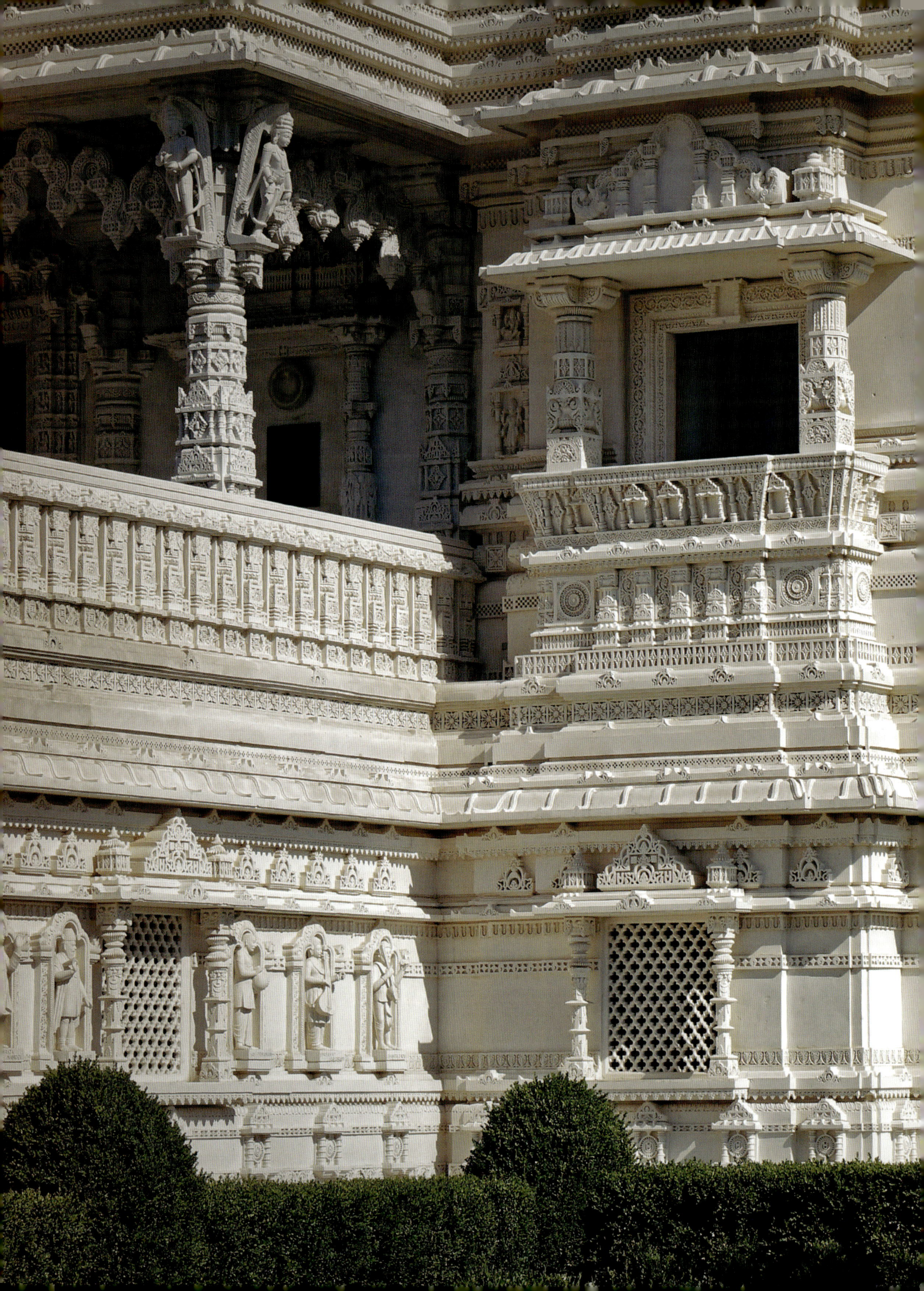

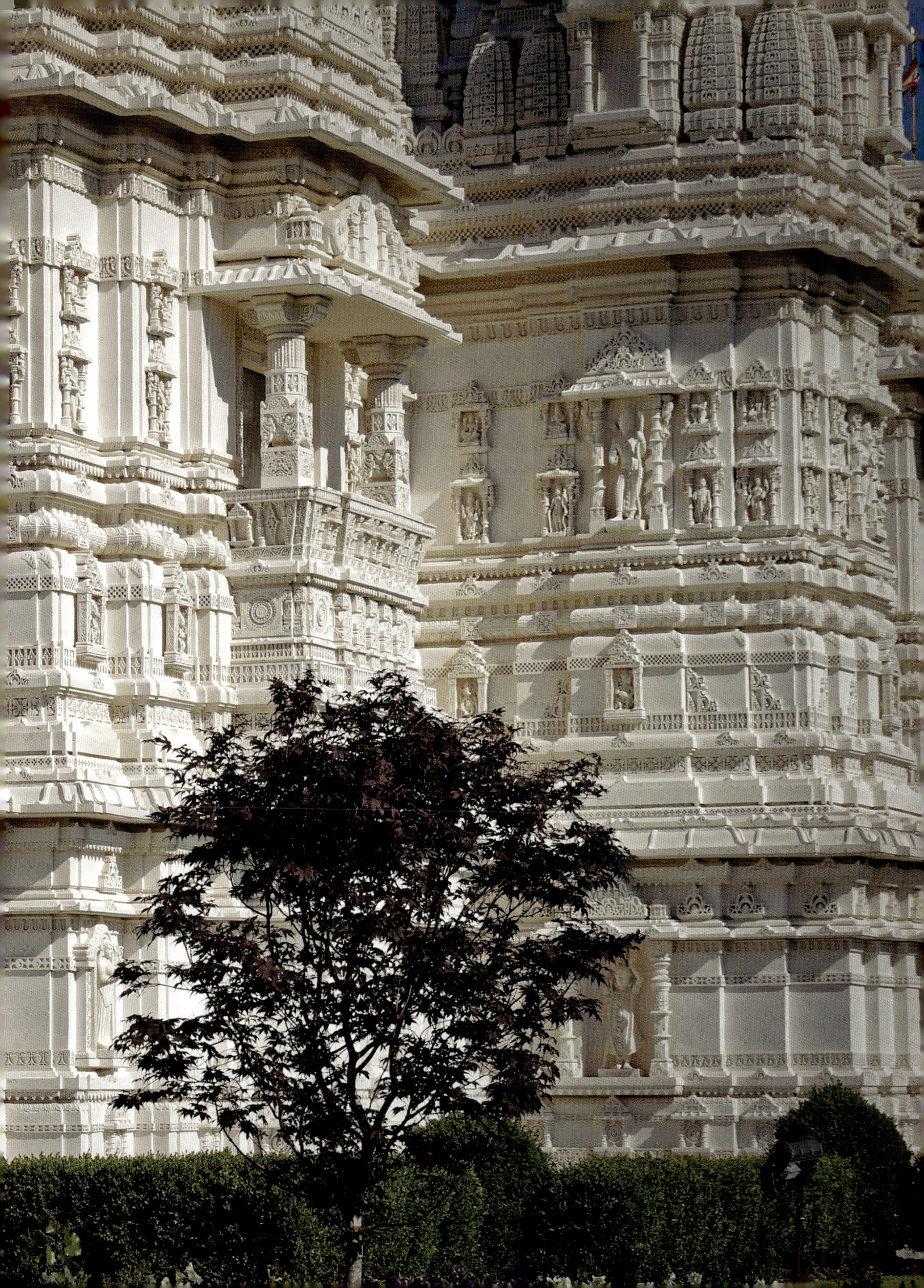

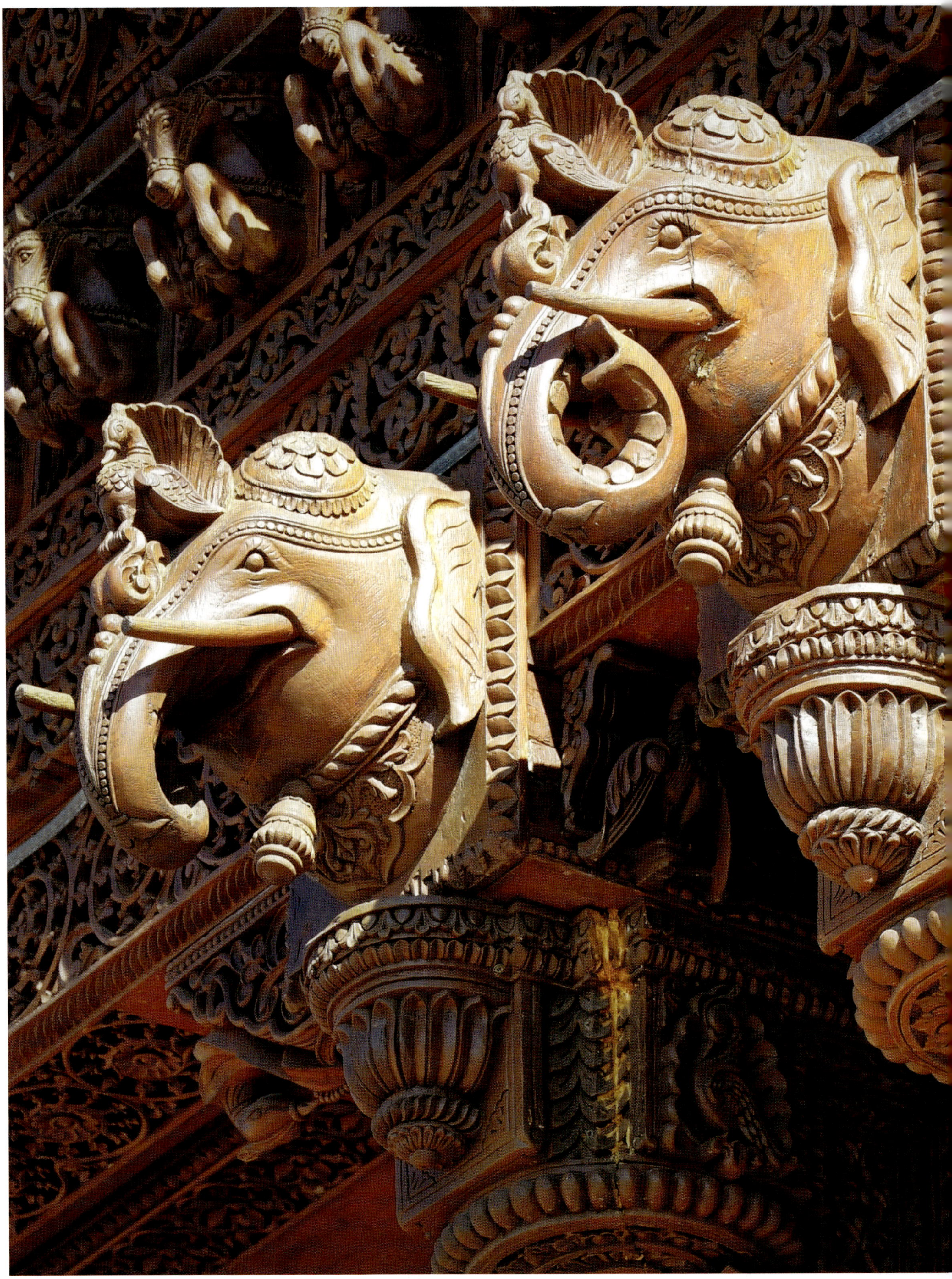

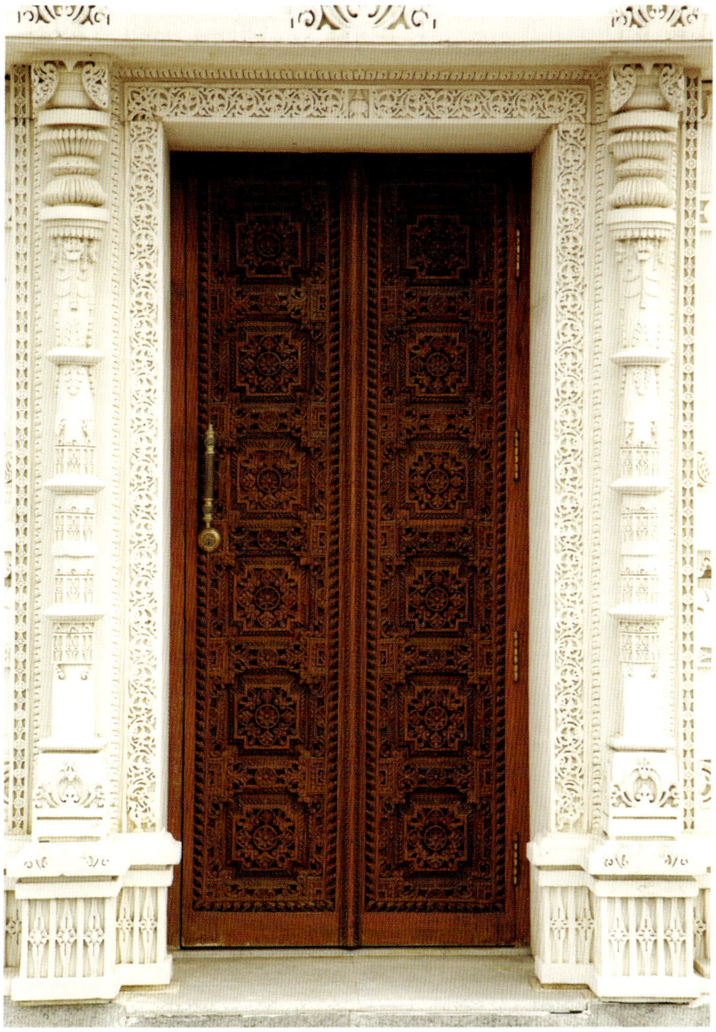

PREVIOUS PAGES AND ALL PHOTOGRAPHS ON THESE PAGES:

Shri Swaminarayan Mandir, Toronto, Canada

This flagship temple was opened in 2007, just over a decade after its sister shrine in London whose history it closely follows. Here, too, a massive fundraising effort allowed a community of Indian immigrants to make its presence felt emphatically in an adoptive homeland which hadn't fully acknowledged its importance yet.

OVERLEAF:

Eldridge Street Synagogue, New York, USA

Since this synagogue was built in 1887, this section of Manhattan has greatly changed: Eldridge Street is now in the heart of Chinatown. It remains in use, but its congregants are few, and feel more comfortable in a smaller room – once the *beth midrash*, the school for boys. The rest of the building has been made into a museum.

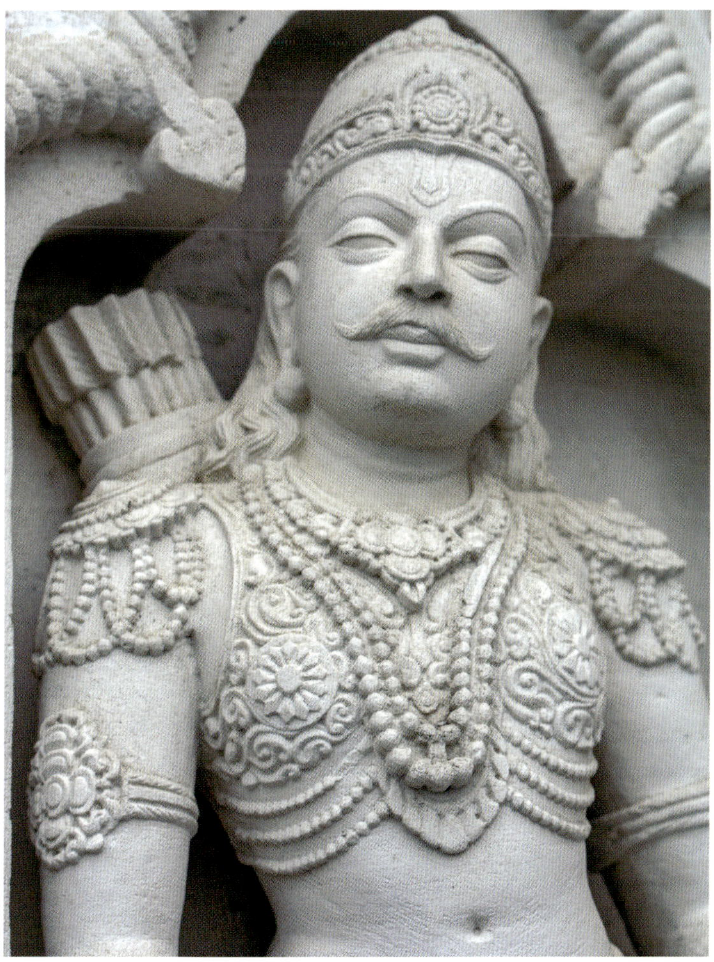

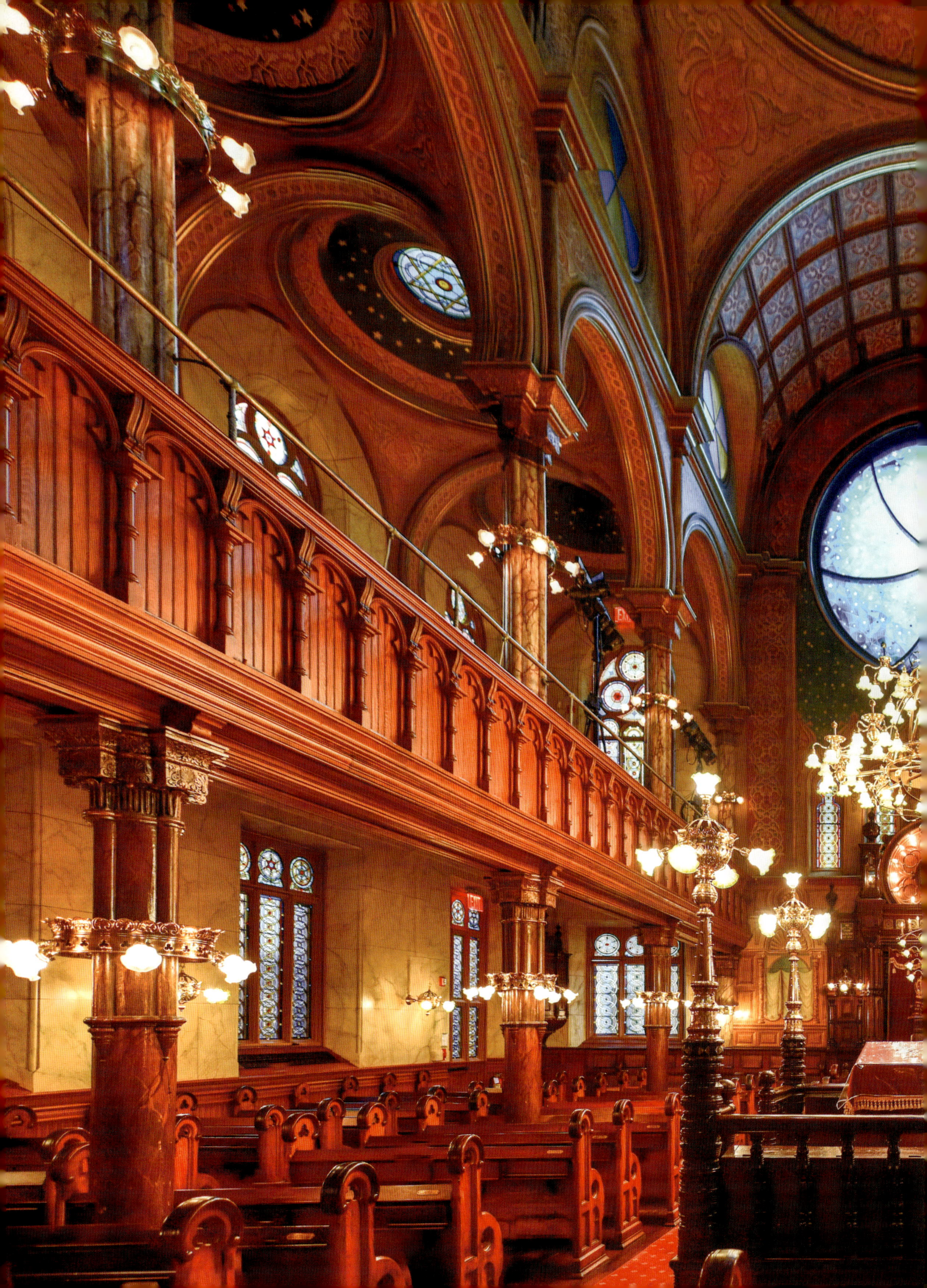

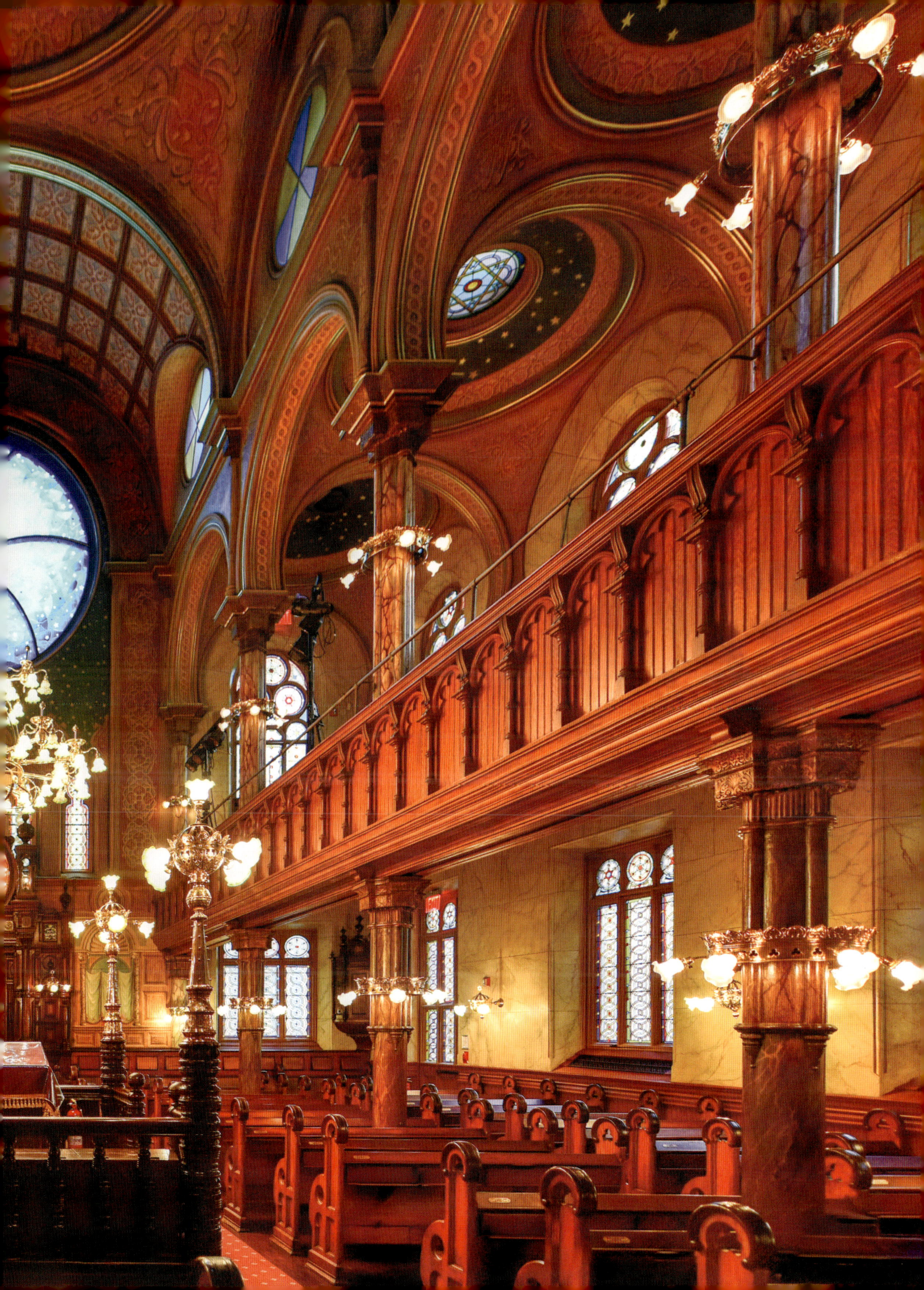

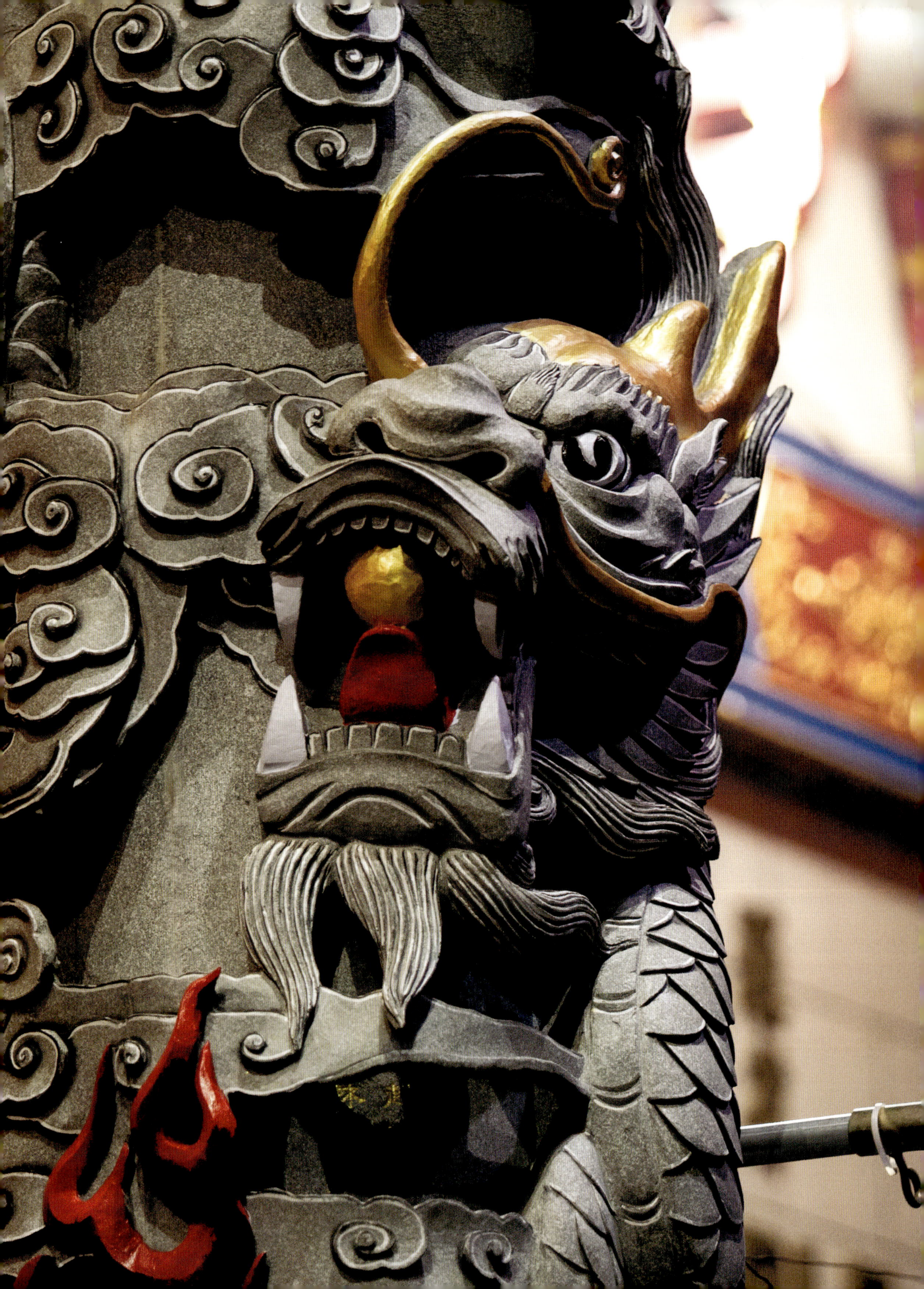

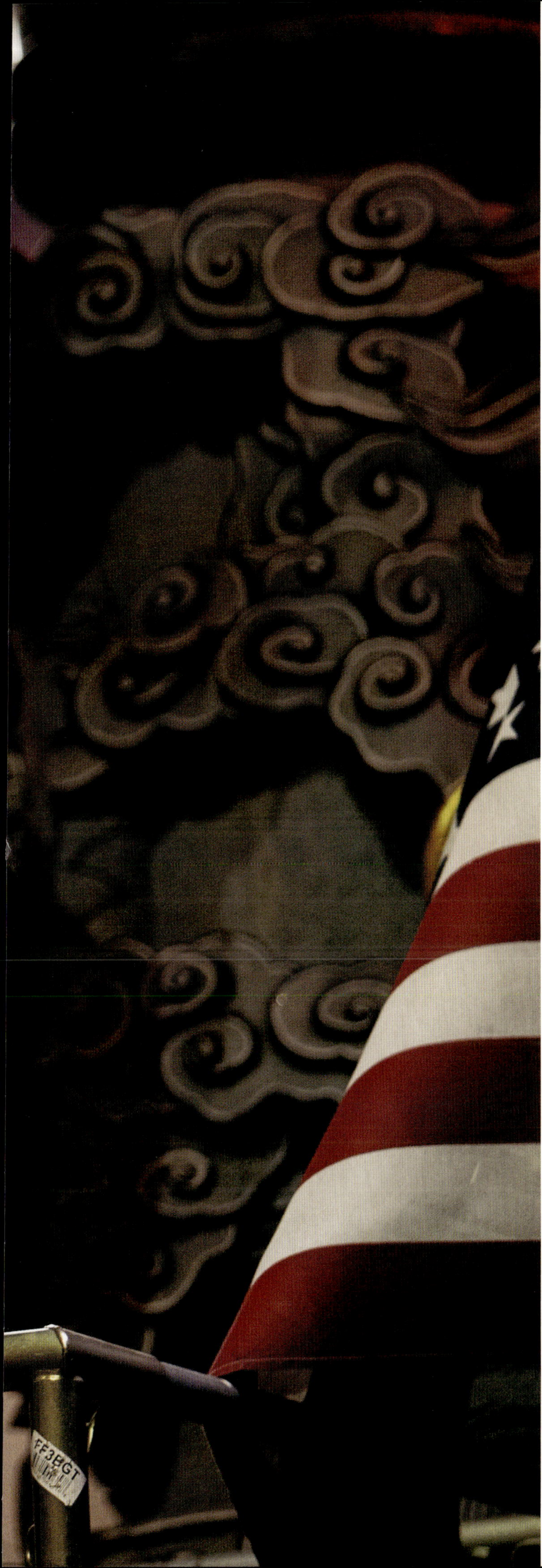

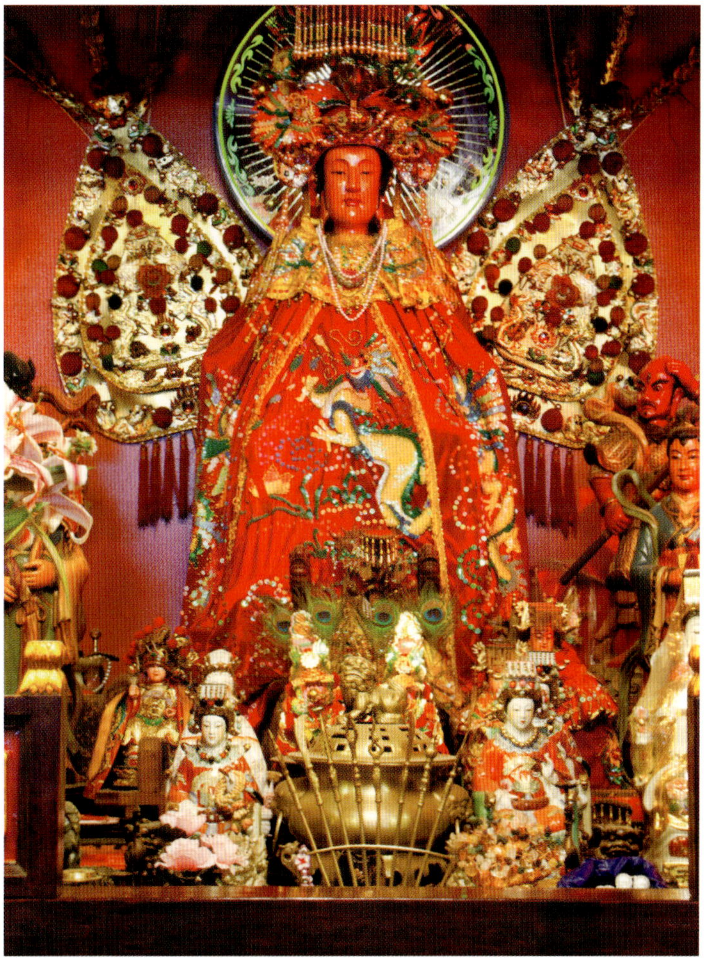

LEFT AND ABOVE:

Thien Hau Temple, Los Angeles, California, USA

The appearance of temples in North American cities may be seen as a mark of the progress immigrant communities have made in recent years. You'd never guess now that much of LA's Chinatown was until comparatively recently its 'Little Italy' – or that until the 1980s this celebrated temple was once a Catholic Church. It is now an important centre for Taoist worship, drawing people from Chinese communities across southern California.

Their religious function apart, temples are every bit as important to the communities they serve as Christian churches. The more so maybe, now once-isolated European groups have so successfully integrated into American life. Italian-, Irish- and Polish-Americans don't have to rely so much on each other for support. That baton has been passed to more recently-arrived communities – with rich dividends for American cultural and social life. The T'ien Hau Temple has added immeasurably to the liveliness of the LA scene and been a bright and colourful draw for tourists, too.

Gurdwara Sahib, San Jose, California, USA

California's first Sikh immigrants arrived from Punjab in the nineteenth century. Overwhelmingly unlettered and unskilled, they moved straight inland to labour on farms. Like other Asian communities, they grasped growing educational opportunities with both hands: soon they were city dwellers, their sons and daughters prospering, but still aspiring. Now they are well-represented in some of America's most important and forward-looking industries. Hence the need for a place of worship and a social and cultural centre in San Jose, the urban heart of Silicon Valley, where so many Sikhs have now come to live and work.

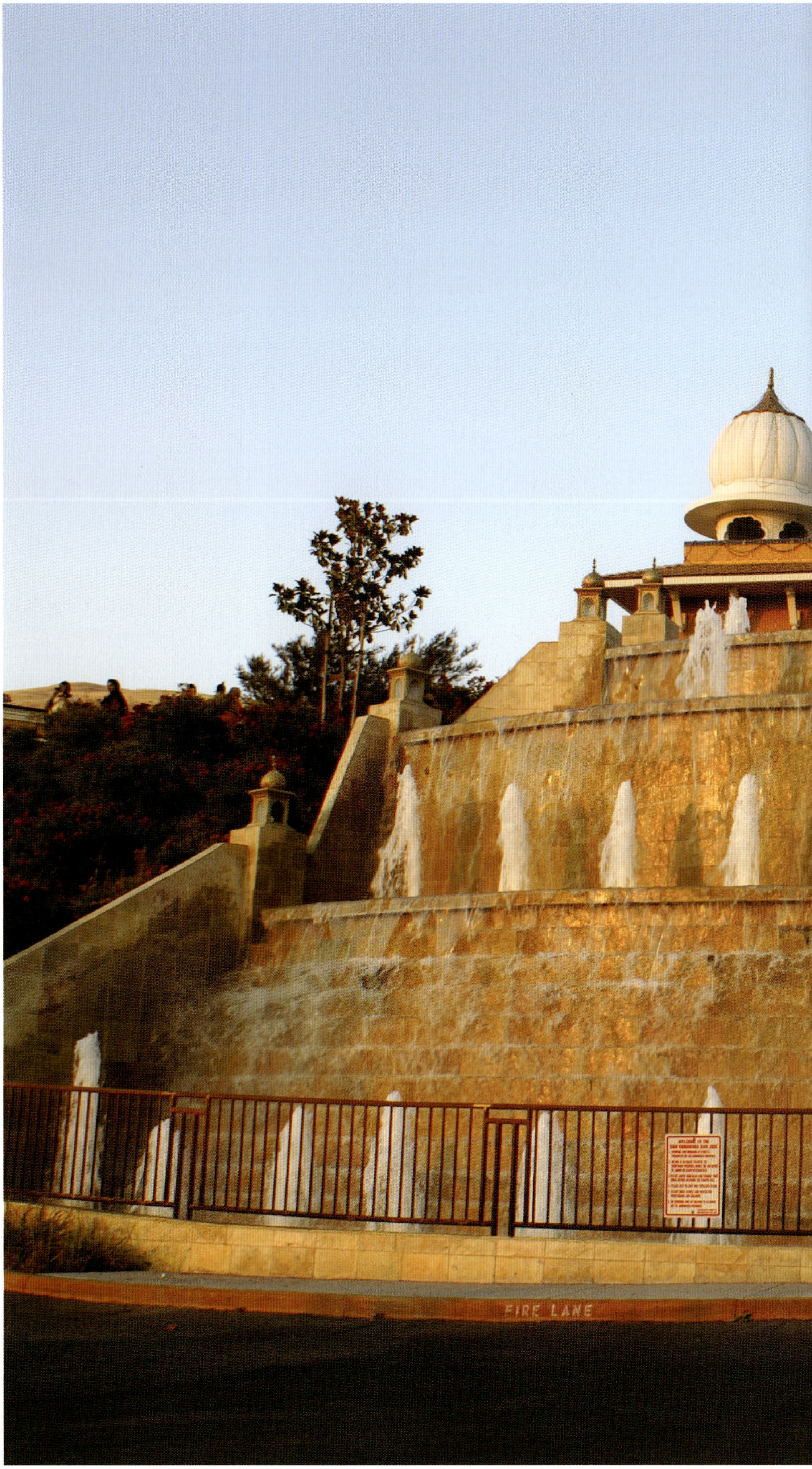

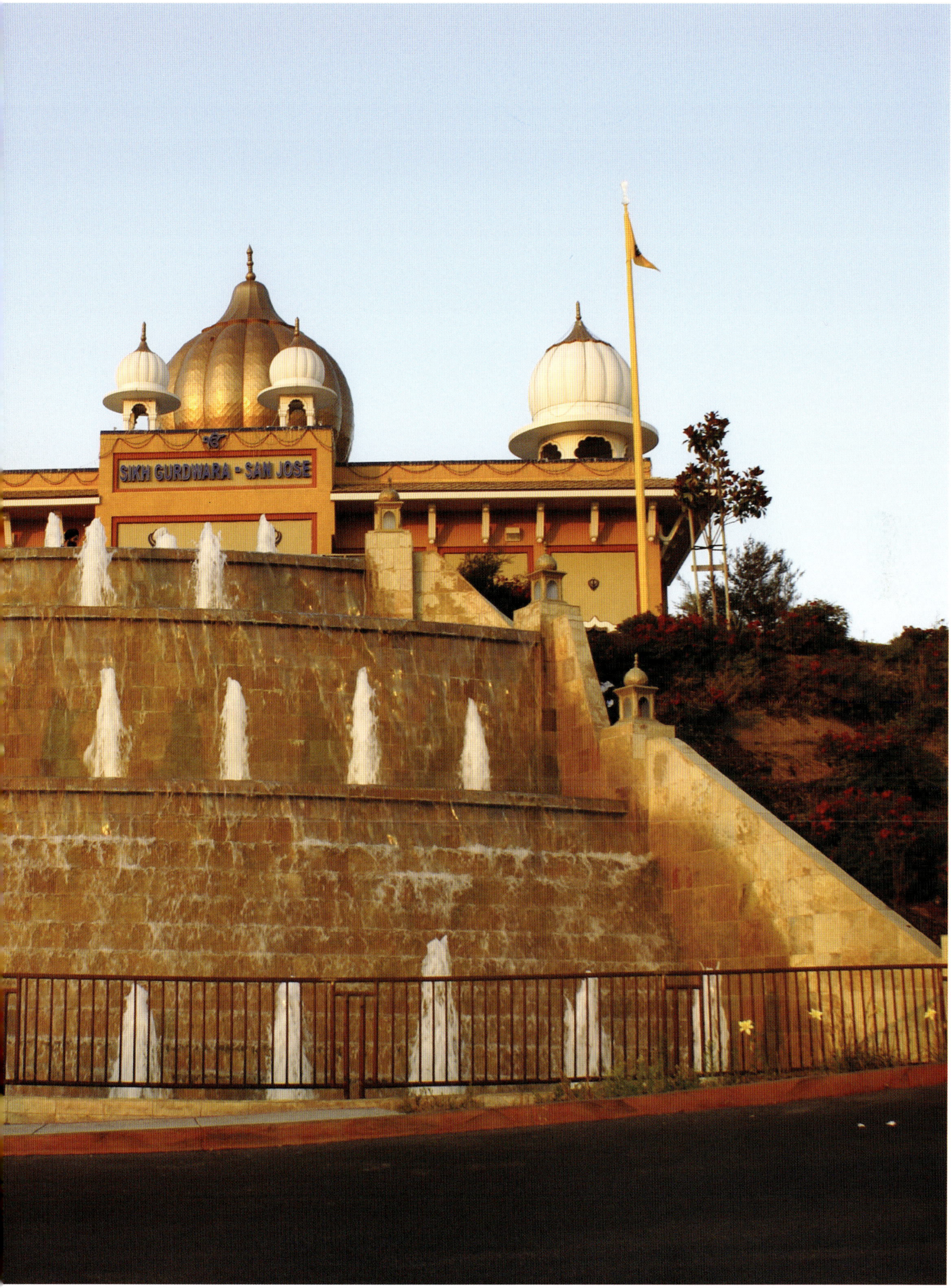
SIKH GURDWARA - SAN JOSE

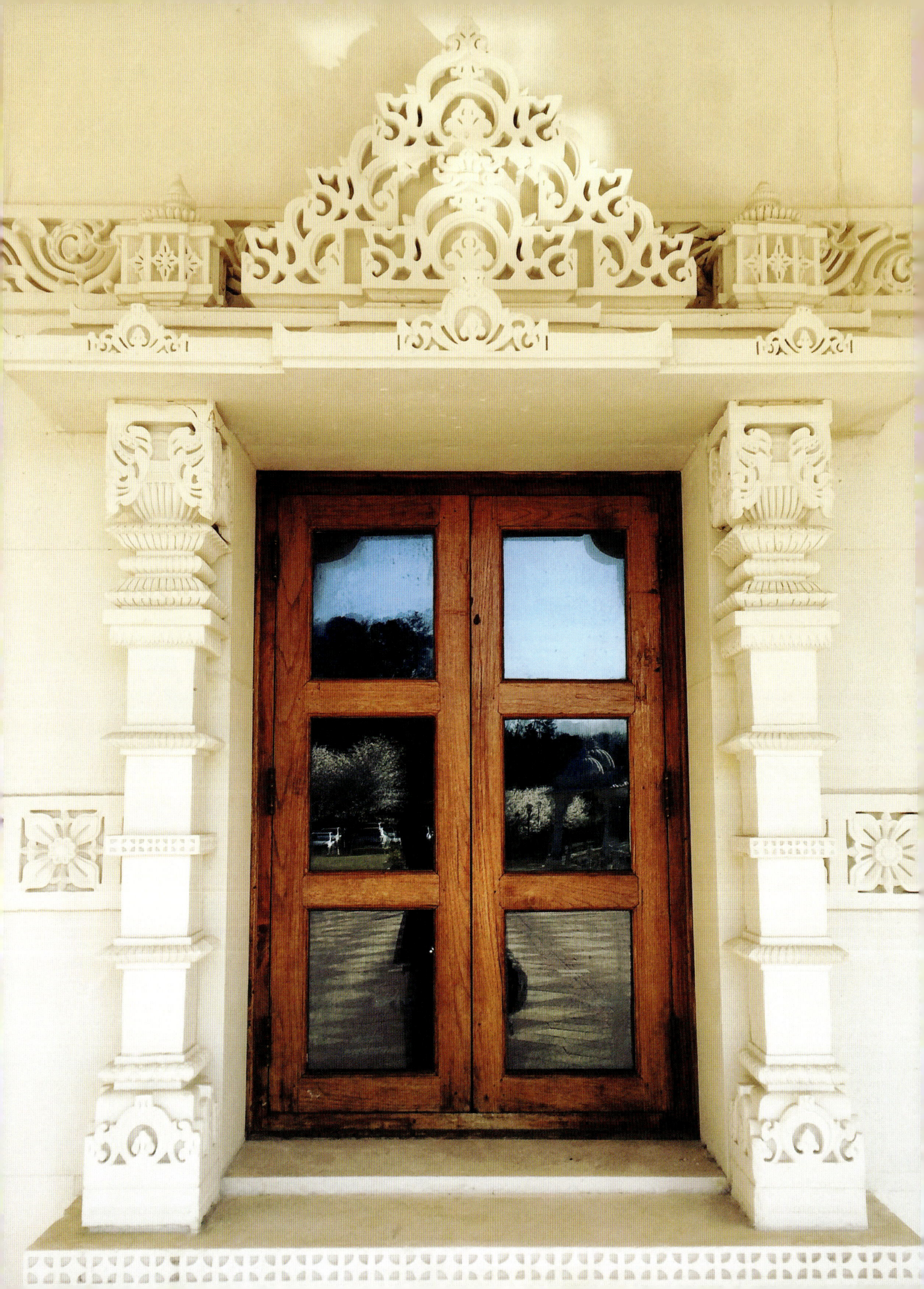

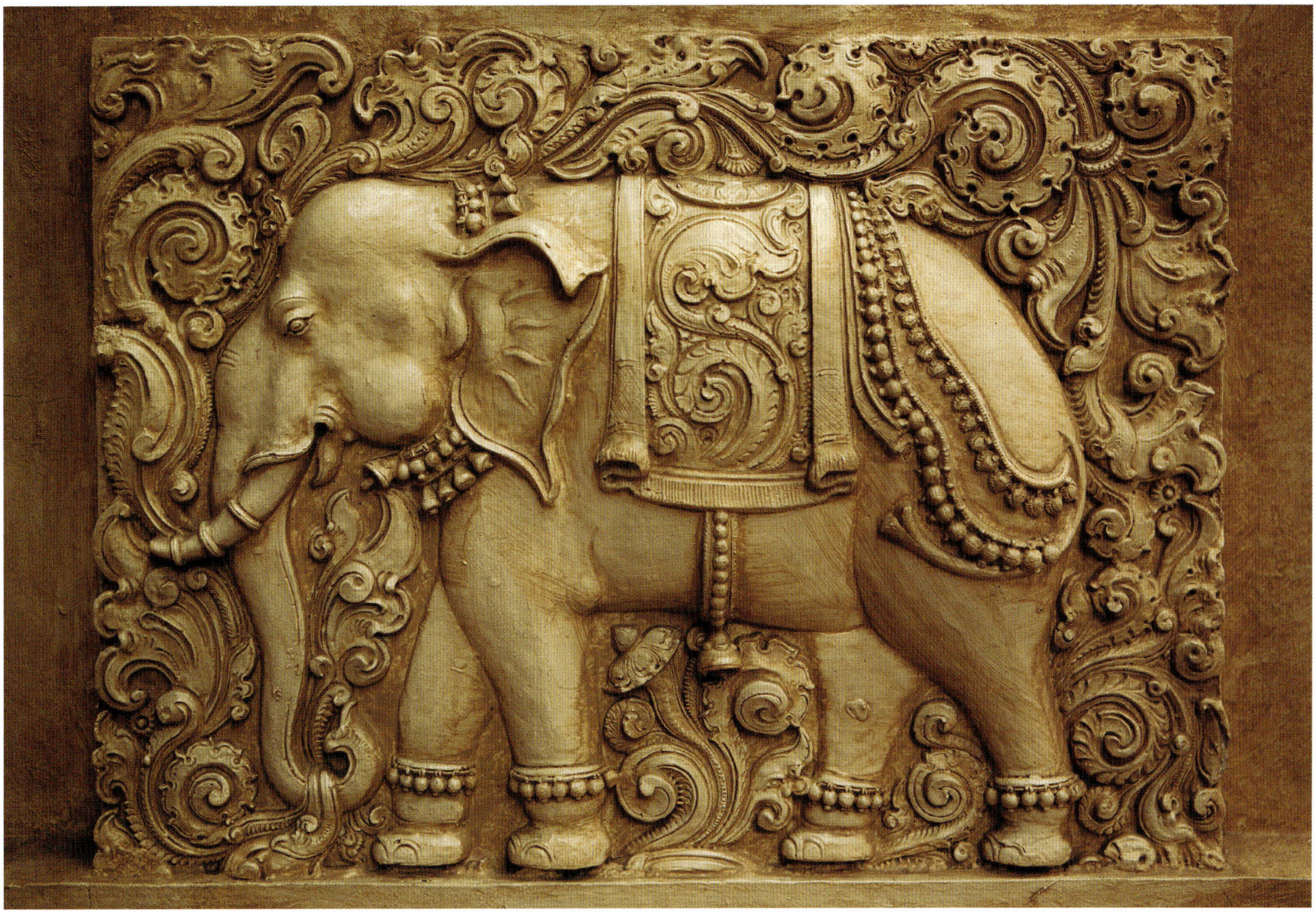

OPPOSITE:
Swaminarayan Mandir, Georgia, USA
This lovely temple was opened in 2007. Though built on a smaller scale than its equivalents in Toronto and London, it was constructed in the same way, incorporating Indian craftsmanship from the motherland.

ABOVE AND RIGHT:
Malibu Hindu Temple, California, USA
This temple was built in 1981 to honour Lord Venkateswara. A form of Vishnu, the supreme being, this Hindu deity is especially associated with the southern part of India whose architectural styles have been clearly influential here. Much more than a place of worship, the Malibu Hindu Temple is important as a social centre for California's Hindus and a place of 'cultural outreach' for other communities in the region.

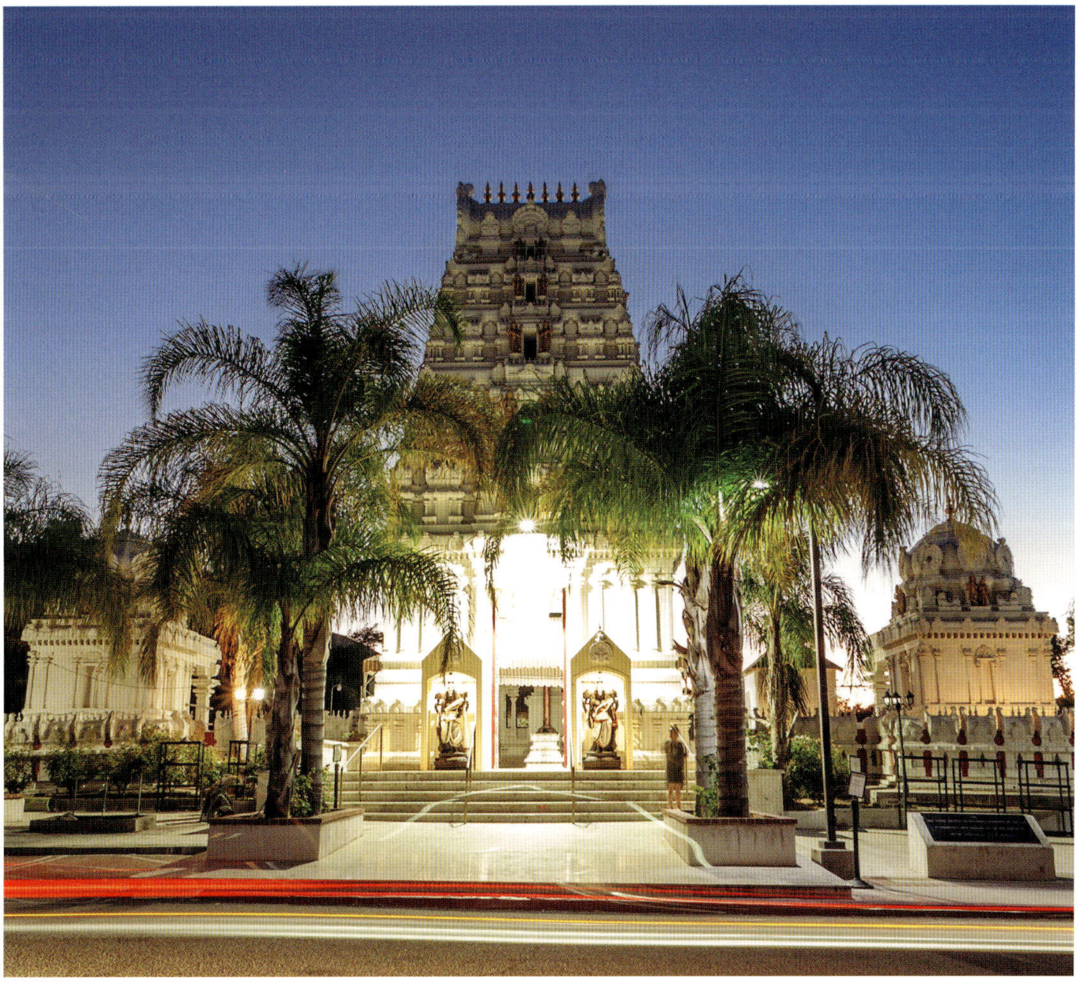

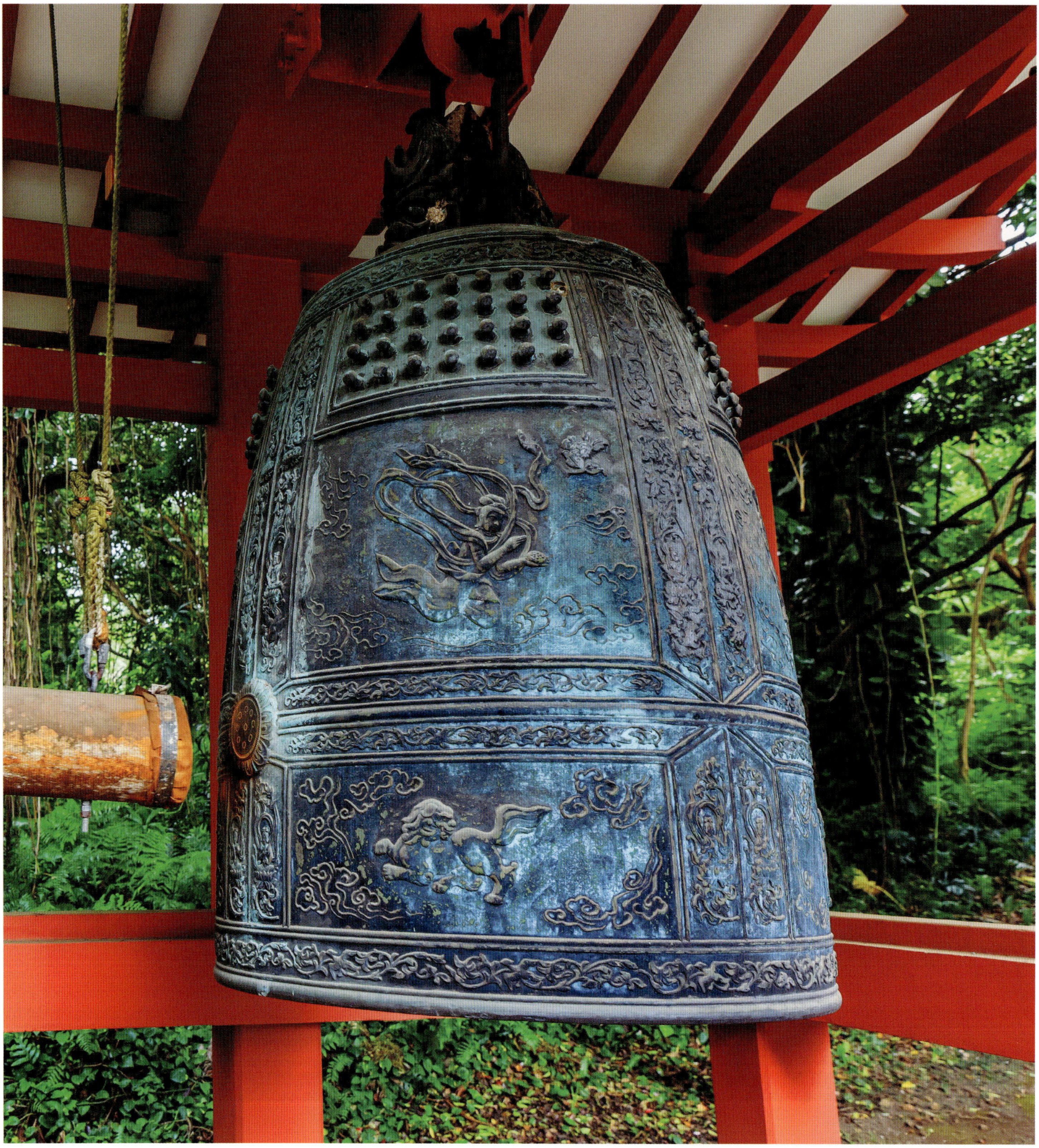

ABOVE AND OPPOSITE:

Byodo-In Temple, Hawaii, USA

The original Byodo-in Buddhist temple is in Japan, at Uji in the Kyoto Prefecture, and was built approximately 900 years ago. This one was built in 1968 to mark the centenary of the first Japanese immigrants in Hawaii. It is fair to say that the hundred years between had seen steady decades of grinding poverty along with some violent vicissitudes – the Pearl Harbor attack of 1941; the internment of Japanese Americans.

This temple was built in a spirit of friendship and with a sense of belonging, it stands in O'ahu's 'Valley of the Temples Memorial Park', near Kane-ohe. Here too are places of worship (and burial) for Protestant and Catholic Christians, as well as for adherents of the Buddhist and the Shinto faiths.

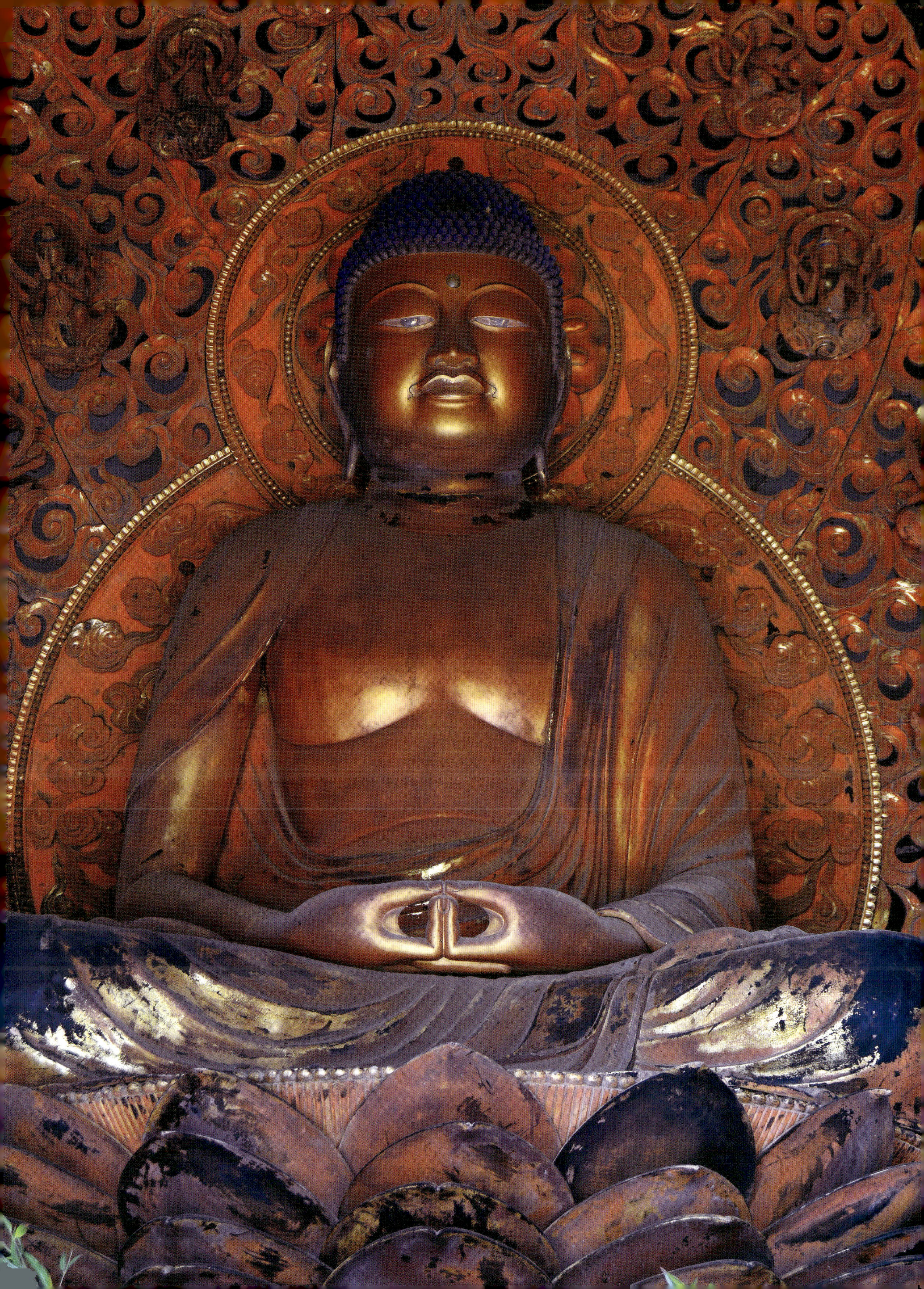

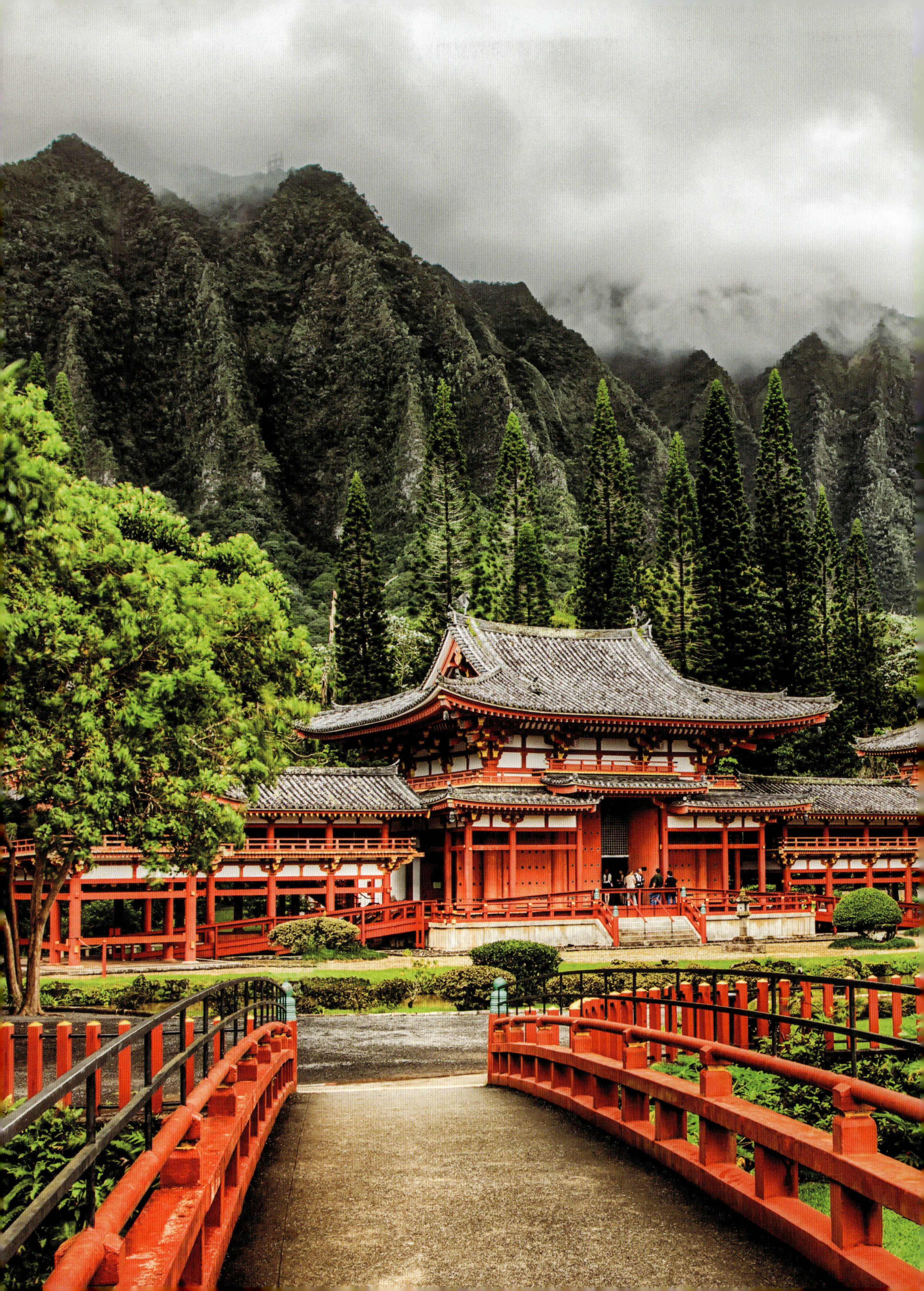

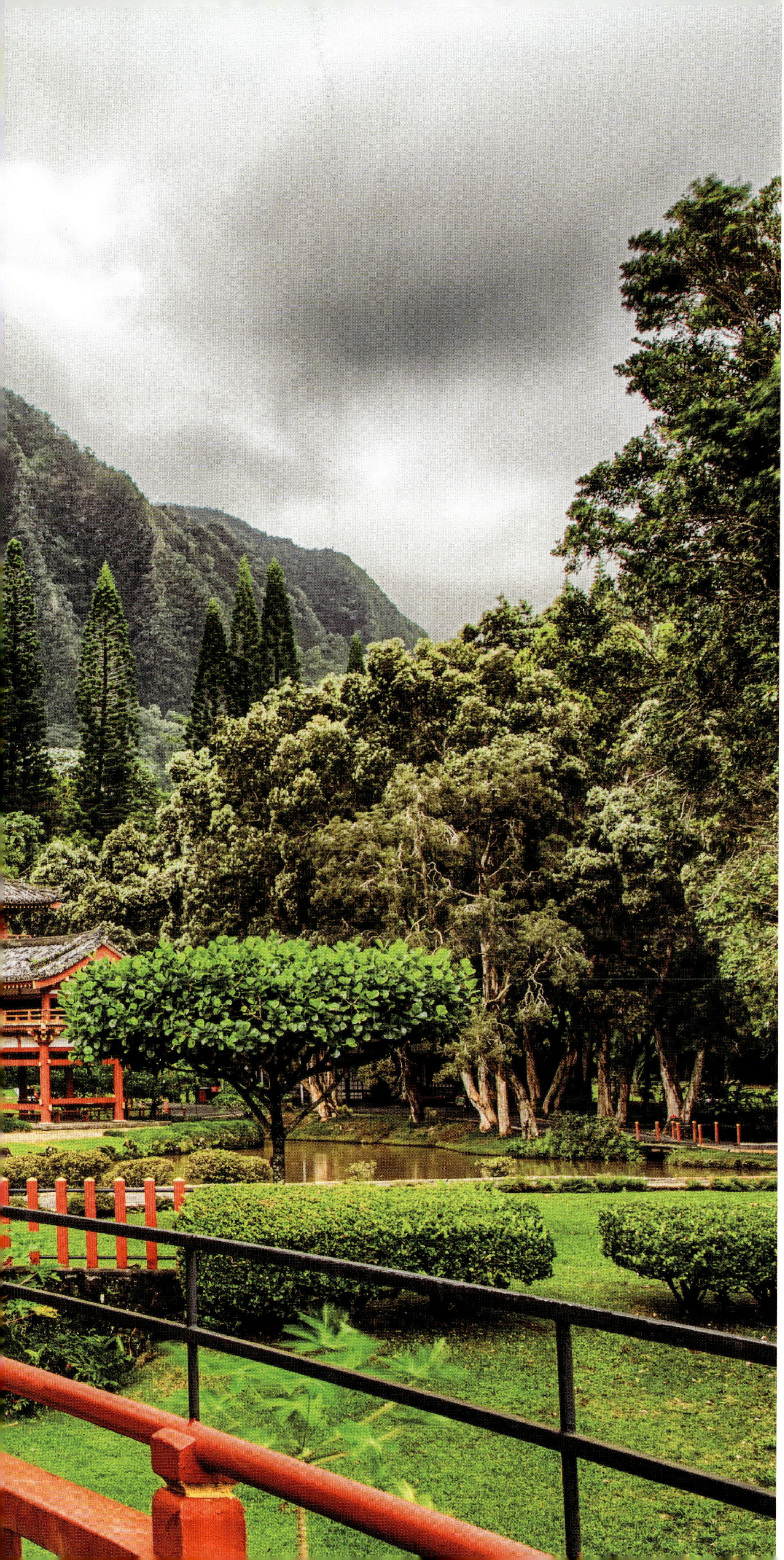

Byodo-In Temple, Hawaii, USA
O'ahu's Byodo-In Temple is essentially a replica of its Japanese original, and there is no disputing that it looks the part. Nor that it fits in beautifully to its dramatic island setting, backed by volcanic mountains and ringed with green. Strictly speaking, though, it cannot truly be counted as a 'temple' given that it is used for occasional gatherings and has neither a regular congregation nor a community of monks.

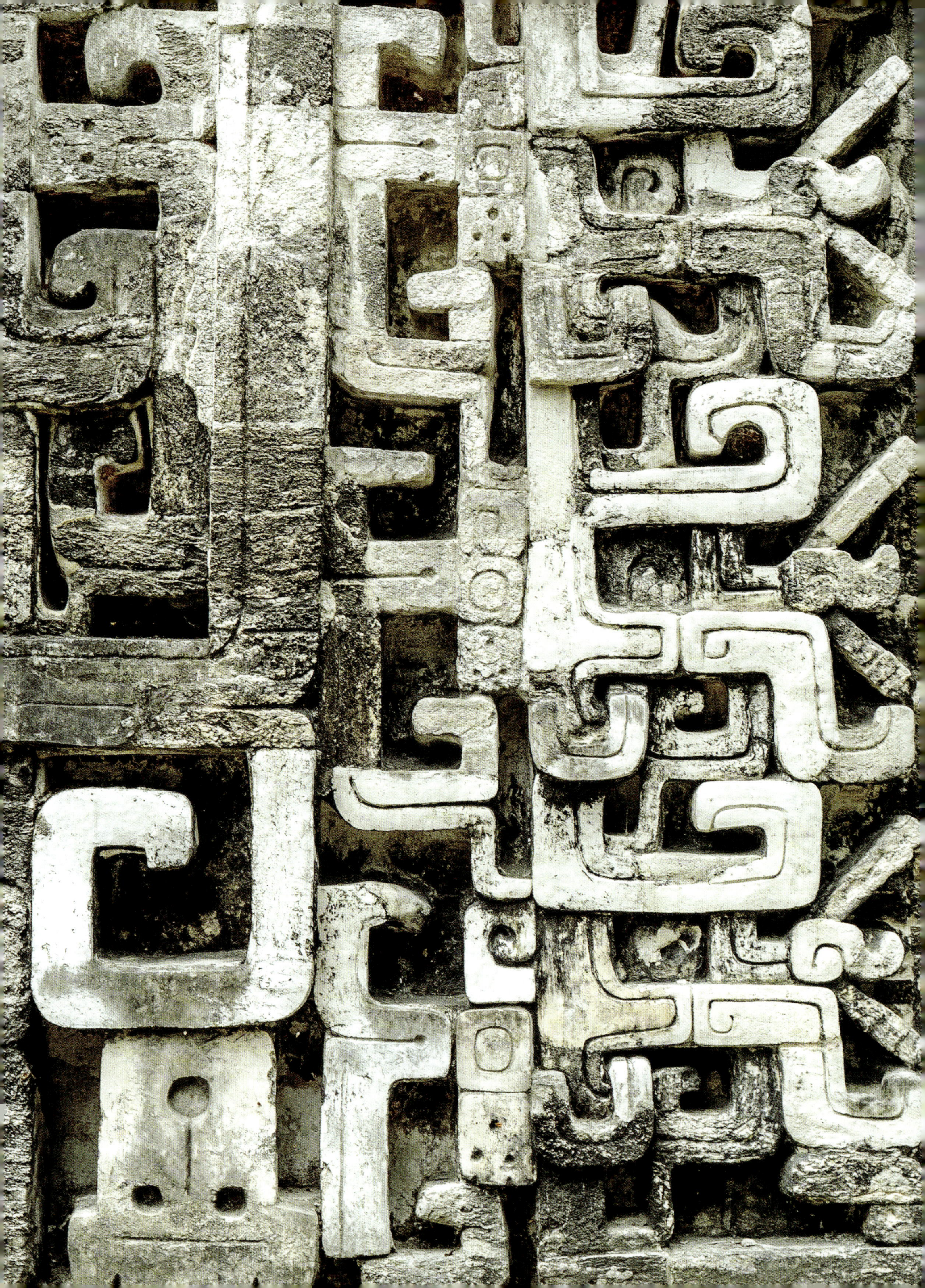

OPPOSITE, BELOW AND OVERLEAF:

Calakmul, Mexico

Looming up abruptly out of the endless greenery of the tropical rainforest, this massive structure in stark grey stone was once the religious and ceremonial centre of a substantial city. Over 50,000 people lived here by the end of the eighth century, at the height of Mesoamerica's Mayan civilization. Now its stunning stelae (sculpted standing stones) are for the most part mysterious to us, yet the sense of sanctity is inescapable.

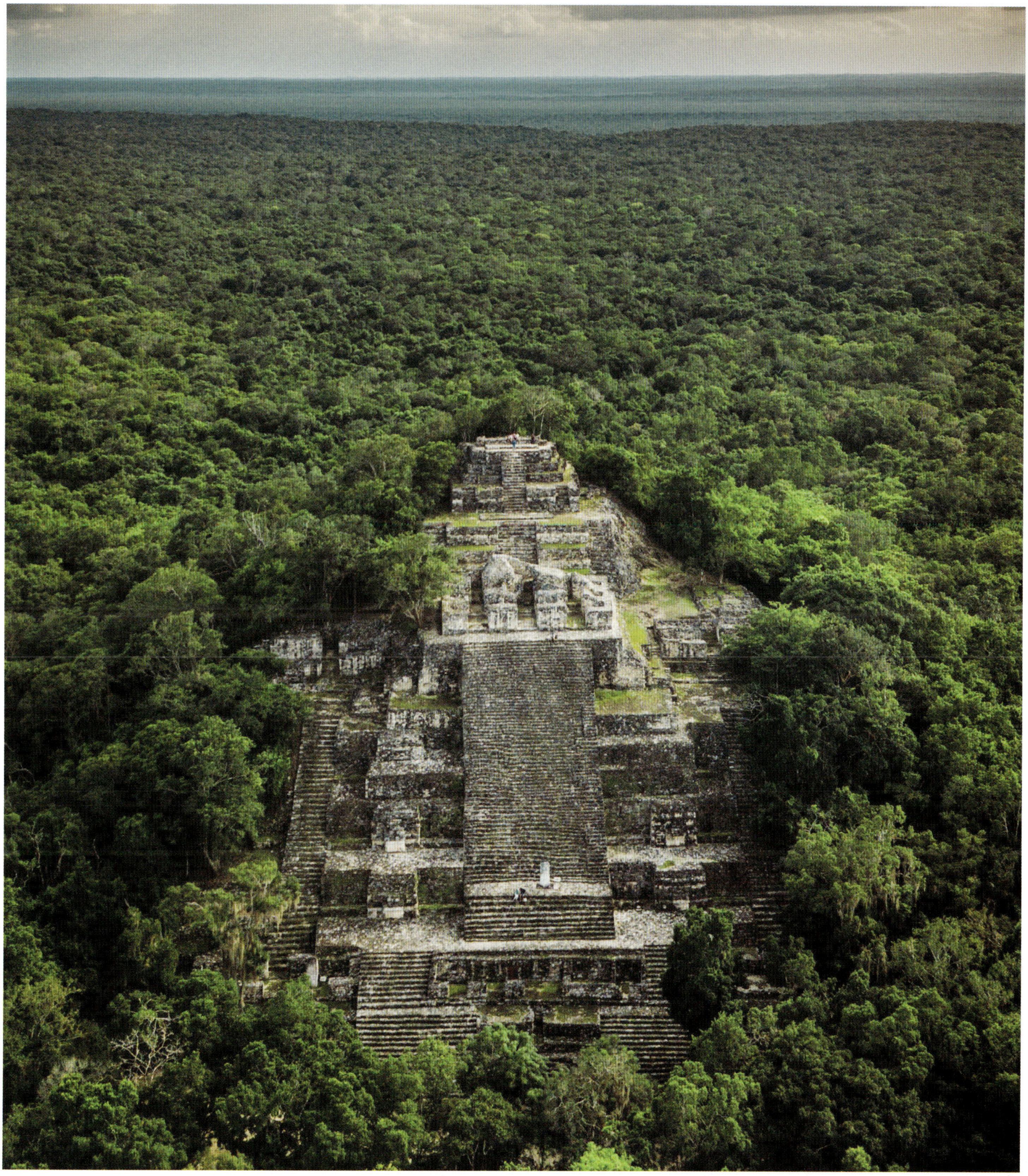

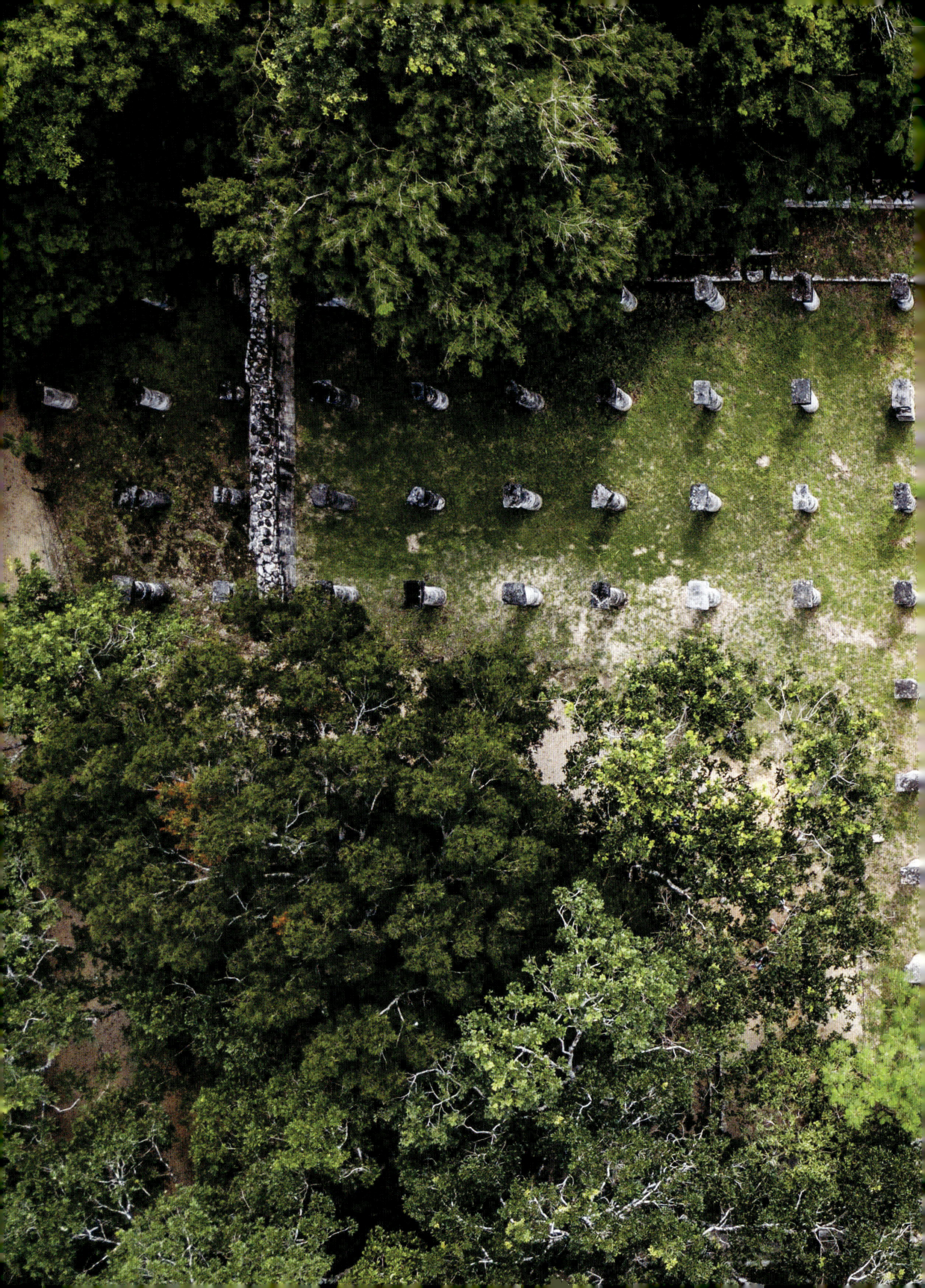

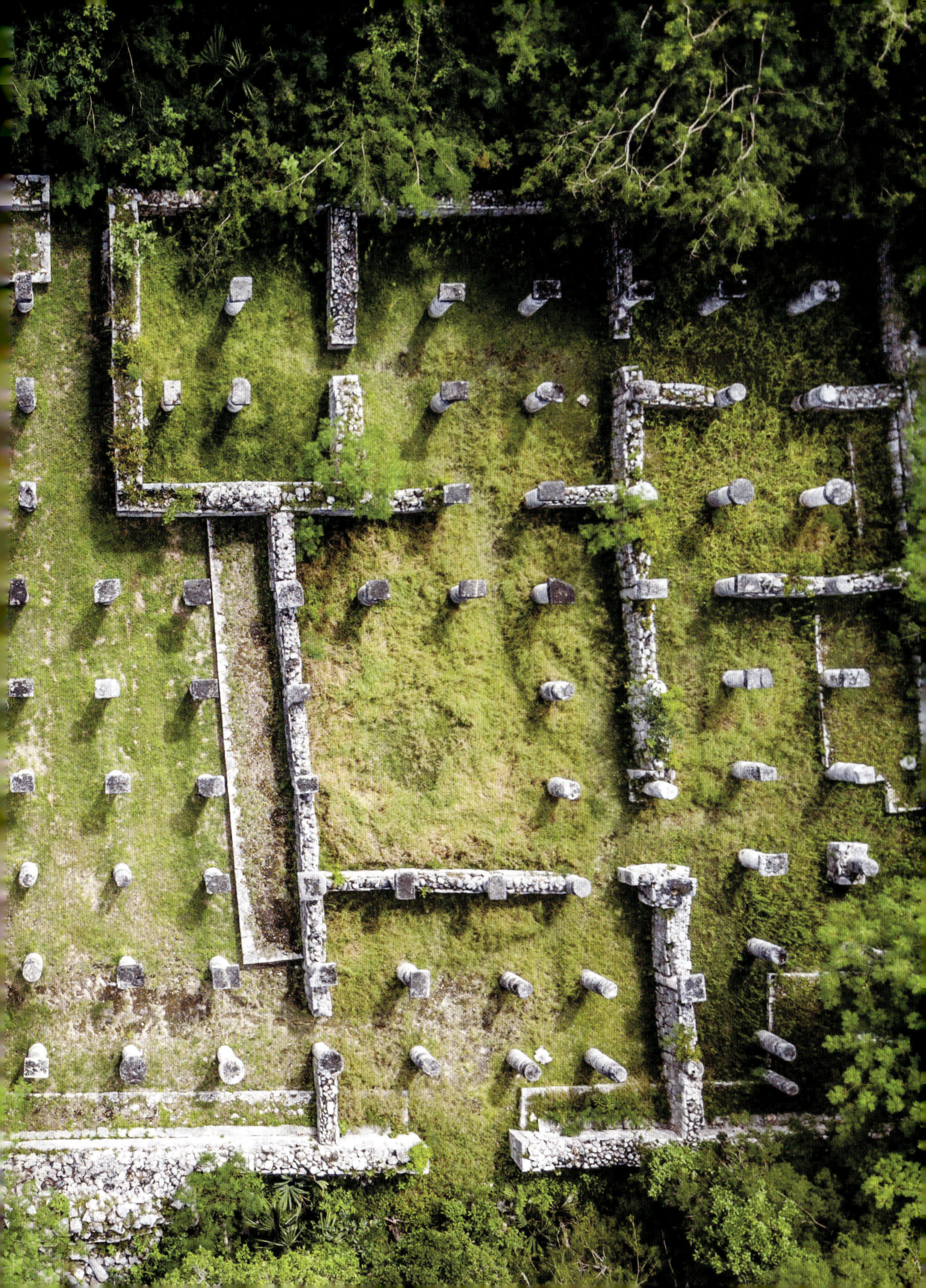

ALL PHOTOGRAPHS ON THESE PAGES AND OVERLEAF:

Pyramid of the Moon, Teotihuacán, Mexico

The massive temple complex here was so important that an actual city arose alongside it. Its ruins are still prominent, just outside the modern metropolis of Mexico City. This central part of Mexico is now thought of as Aztec country, but it remains unknown who Teotihuacán's constructors were. A processional route, the 'Avenue of the Dead', linked this majestic monument with an even larger one, the Pyramid of the Sun.

Mesoamerican pyramids weren't tombs in the way that those of Egypt were. Rather, they appear to have been platforms for worship, straining up towards the skies.

Even so, archaeologists working on sites like this have been having to adjust to the possibility that what lies beneath ground might be as important as what is built above. A number of concealed tunnels have recently been discovered at Teotihuacán (see below) – symbolic 'secret passages' to the Underworld, it would seem.

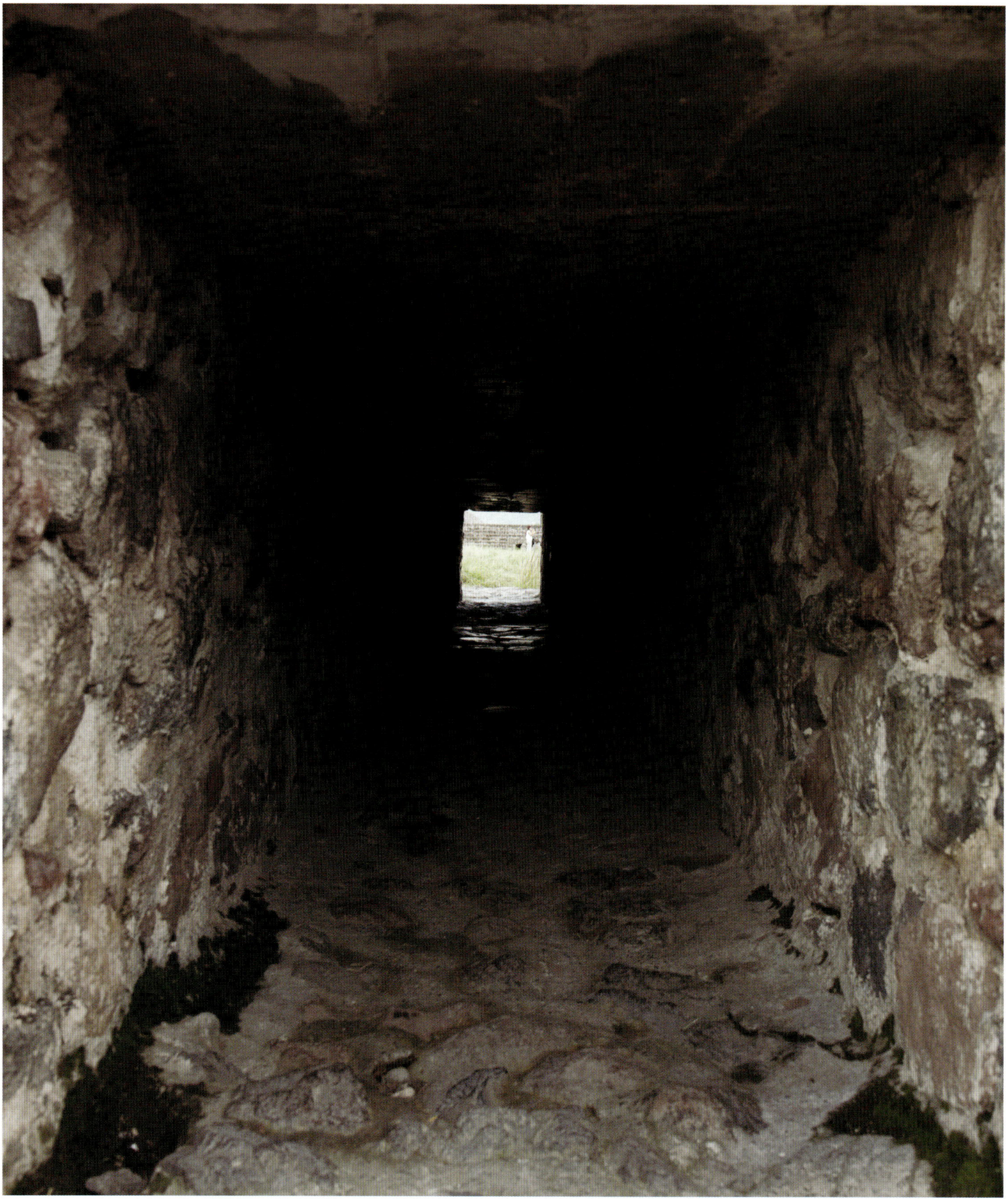

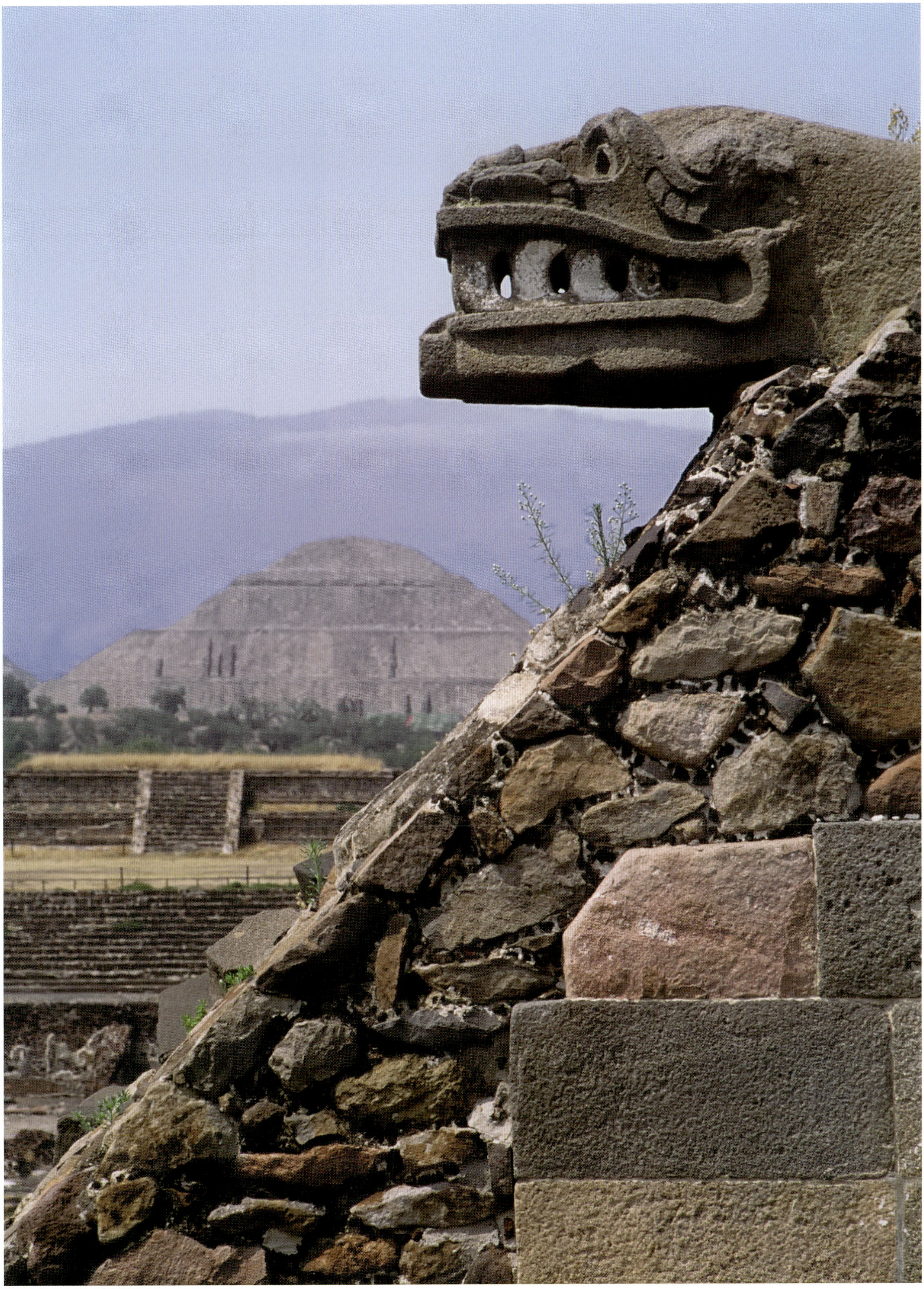

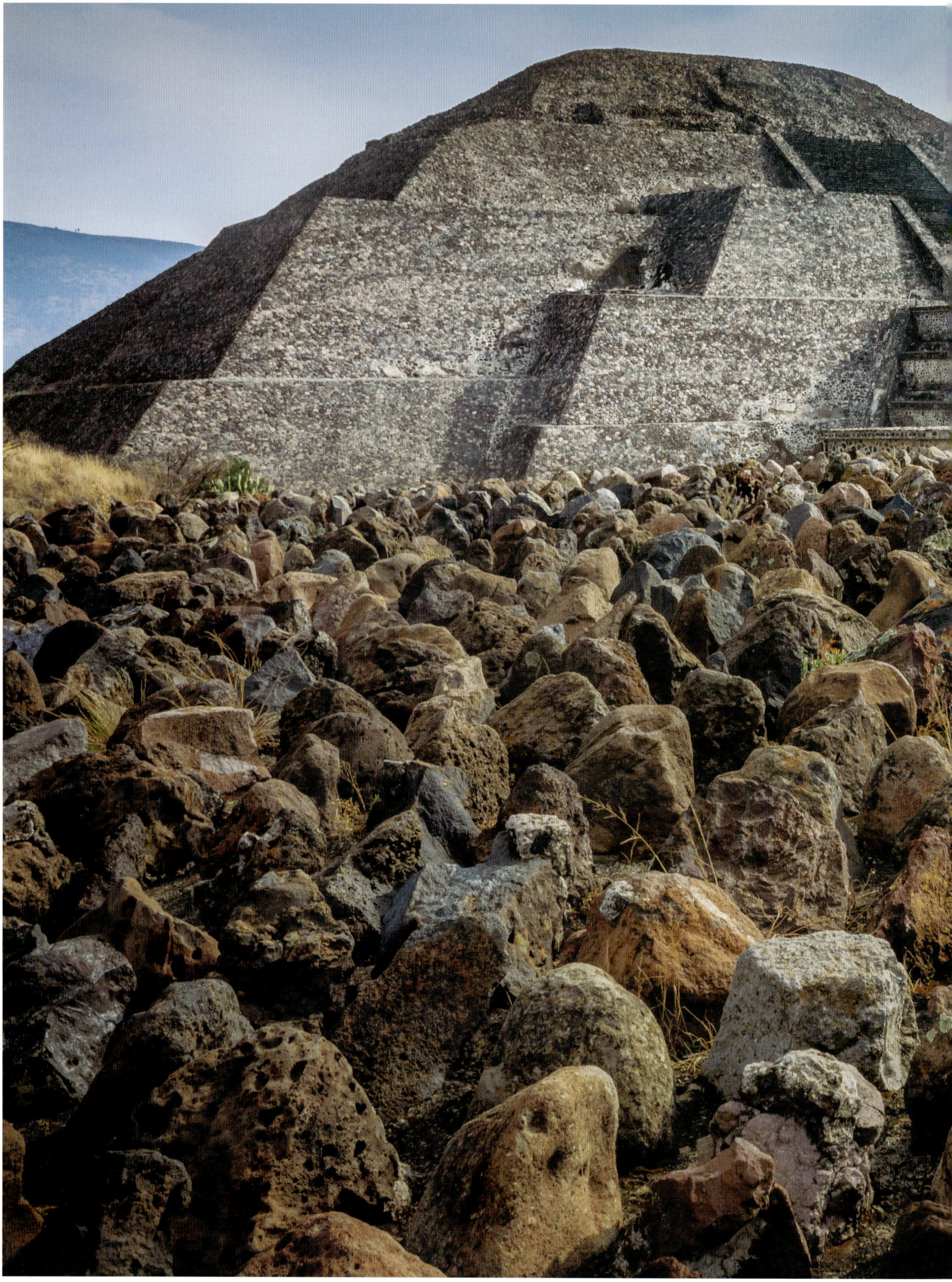

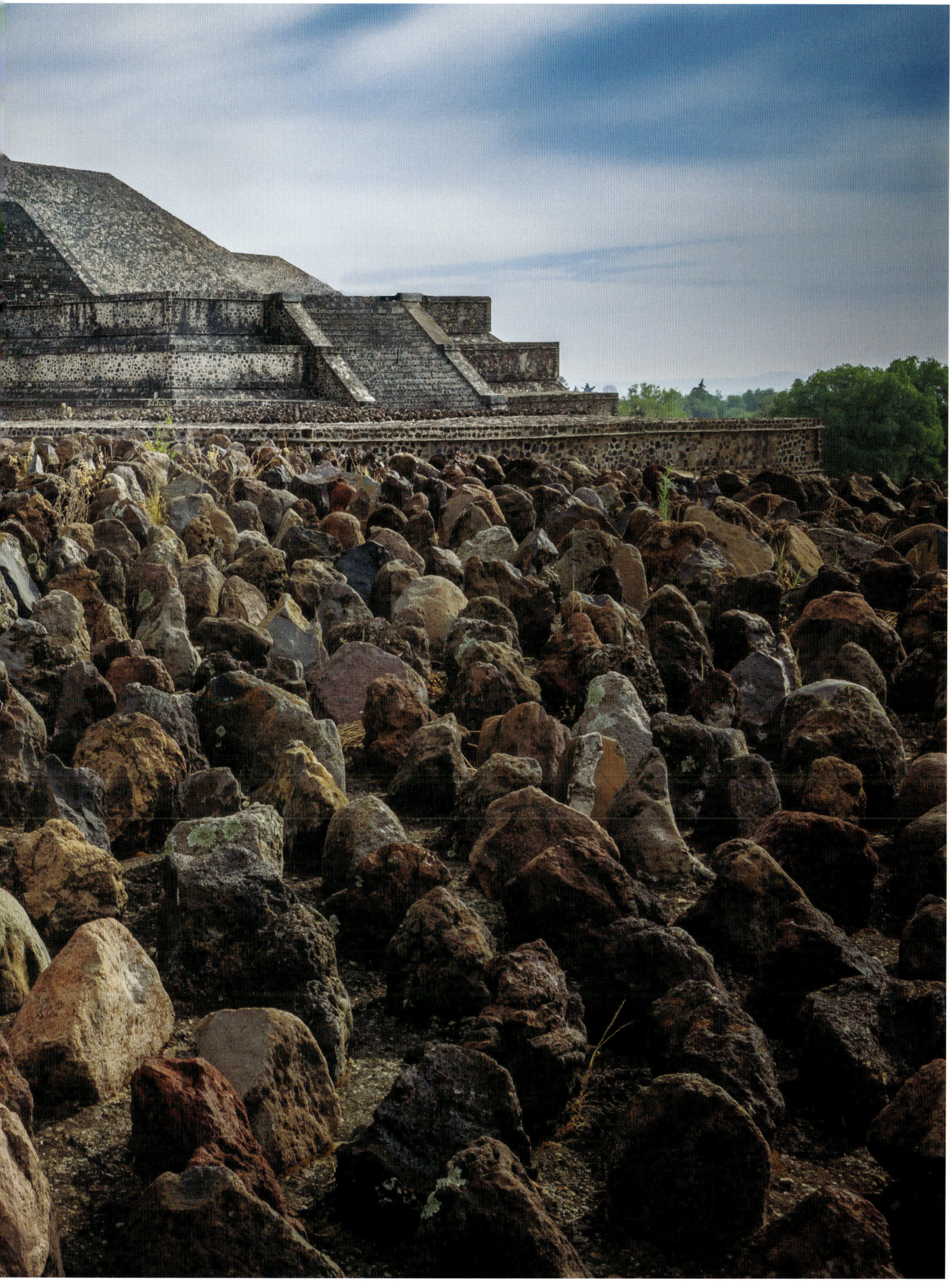

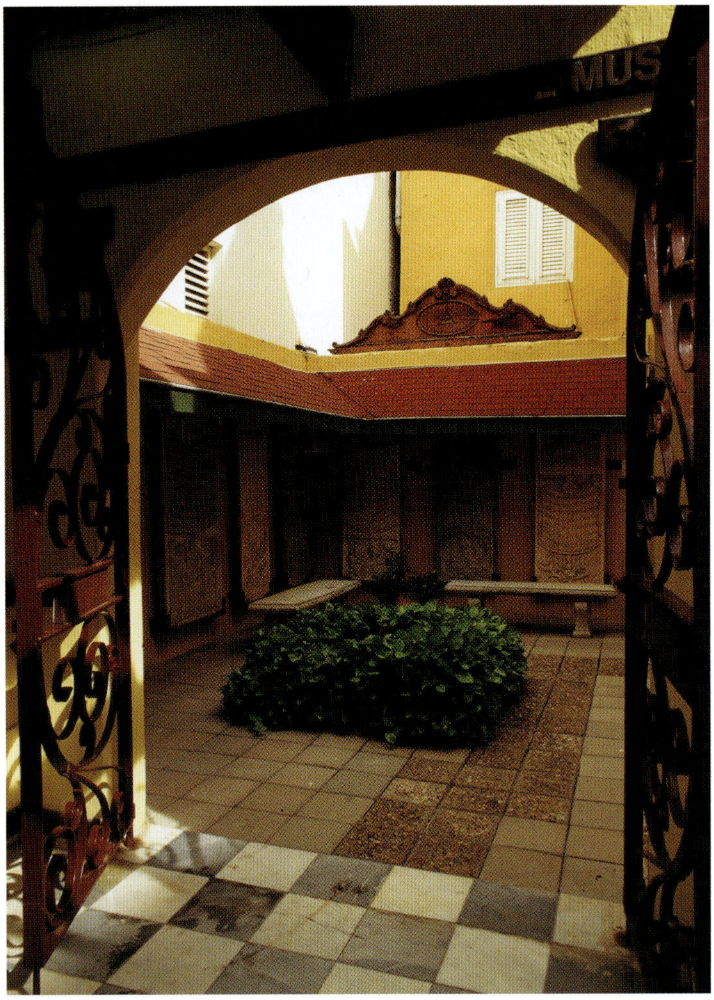

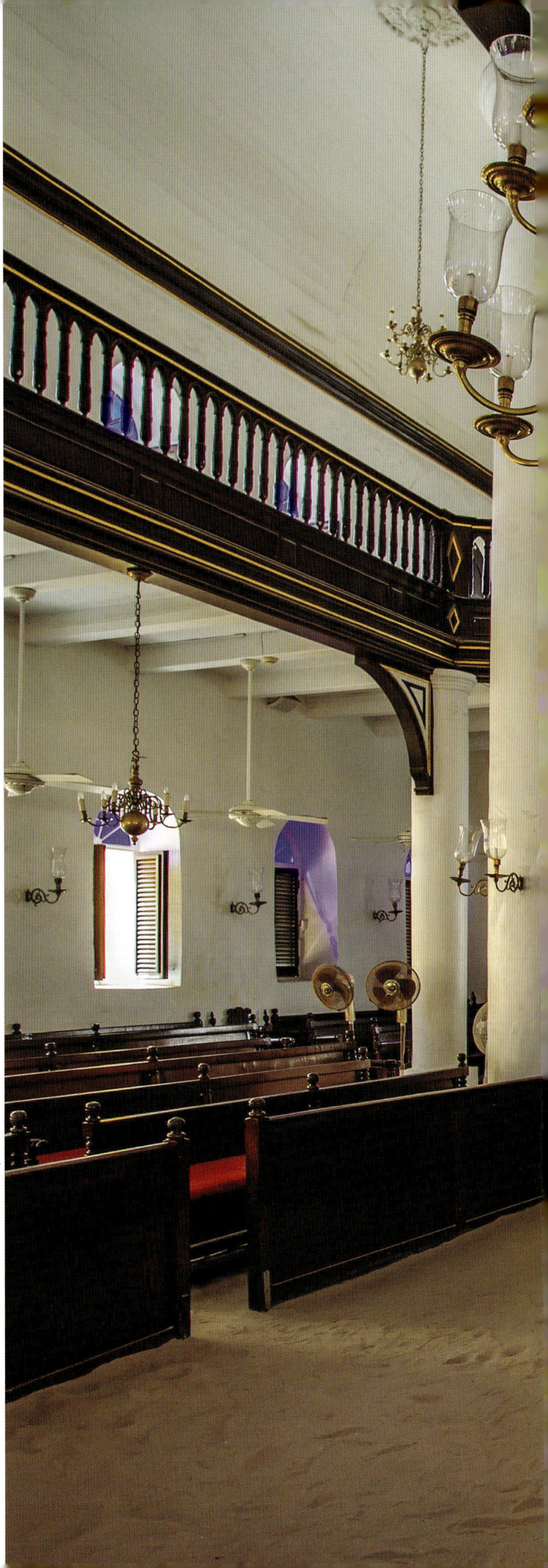

ABOVE AND RIGHT:

Mikvé Israel-Emanuel Synagogue, Willemstad, Curaçao

The oldest synagogue in the Americas dates from 1730, though there had been a Jewish community in this Dutch colony for as long as it has existed. Like so much of the New World, the Lesser Antilles was colonized by the Spanish in the sixteenth century.

At that stage, as it happened, the Spanish ruled most of the European Netherlands, too. The Dutch Revolt against them went on for 80 years. From 1634, the newly-liberated Dutch set about securing a trading empire. It must have been satisfying that this was to be partly at Spain's expense.

Even so, the years of Spanish domination had cast a cultural shadow. Ironically, the sanded floor around the *bima*, the platform from which the Torah was read and the rabbi addressed his congregants, followed the practice of Jews in Iberia. Meeting in secret, they had done this to muffle the sound of footsteps.

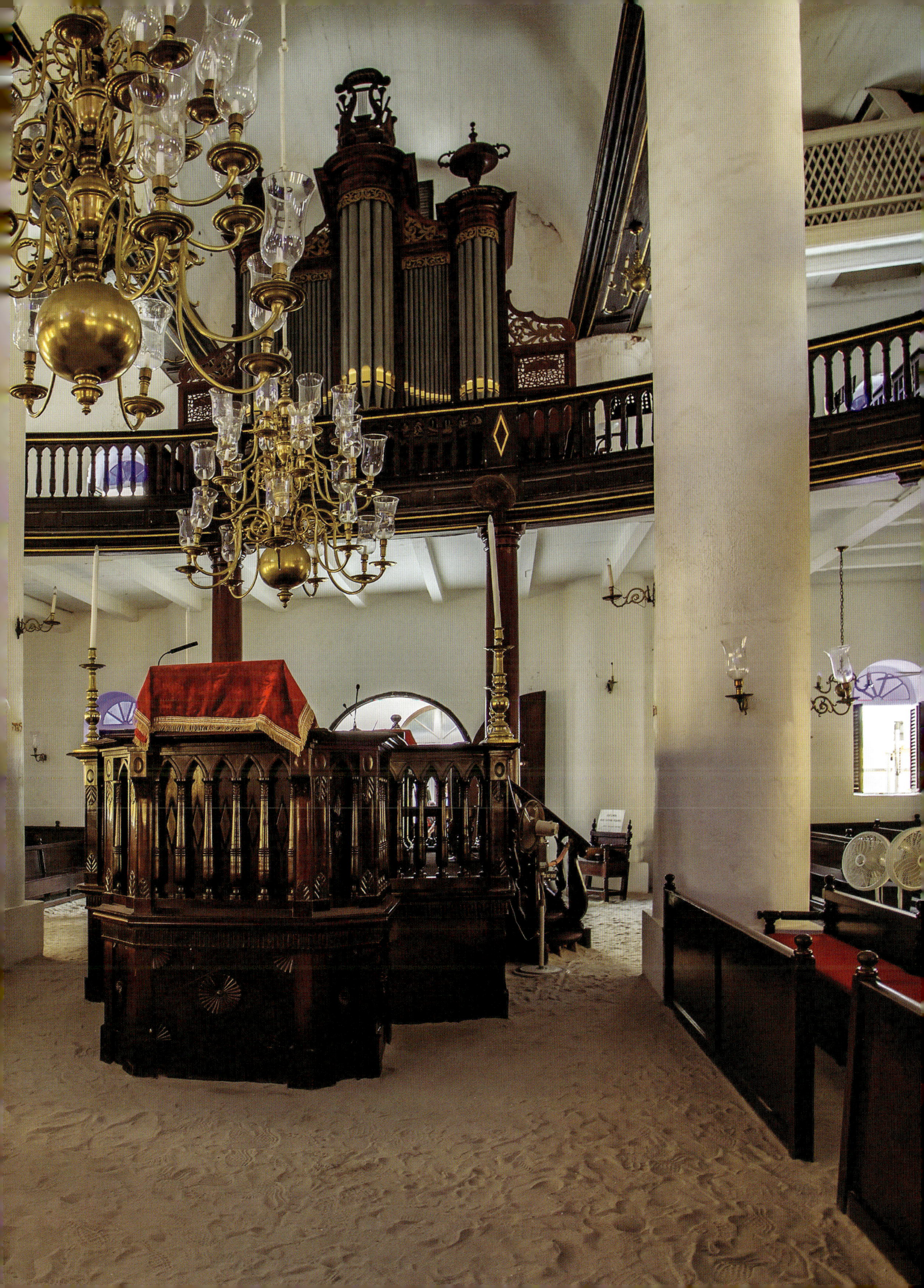

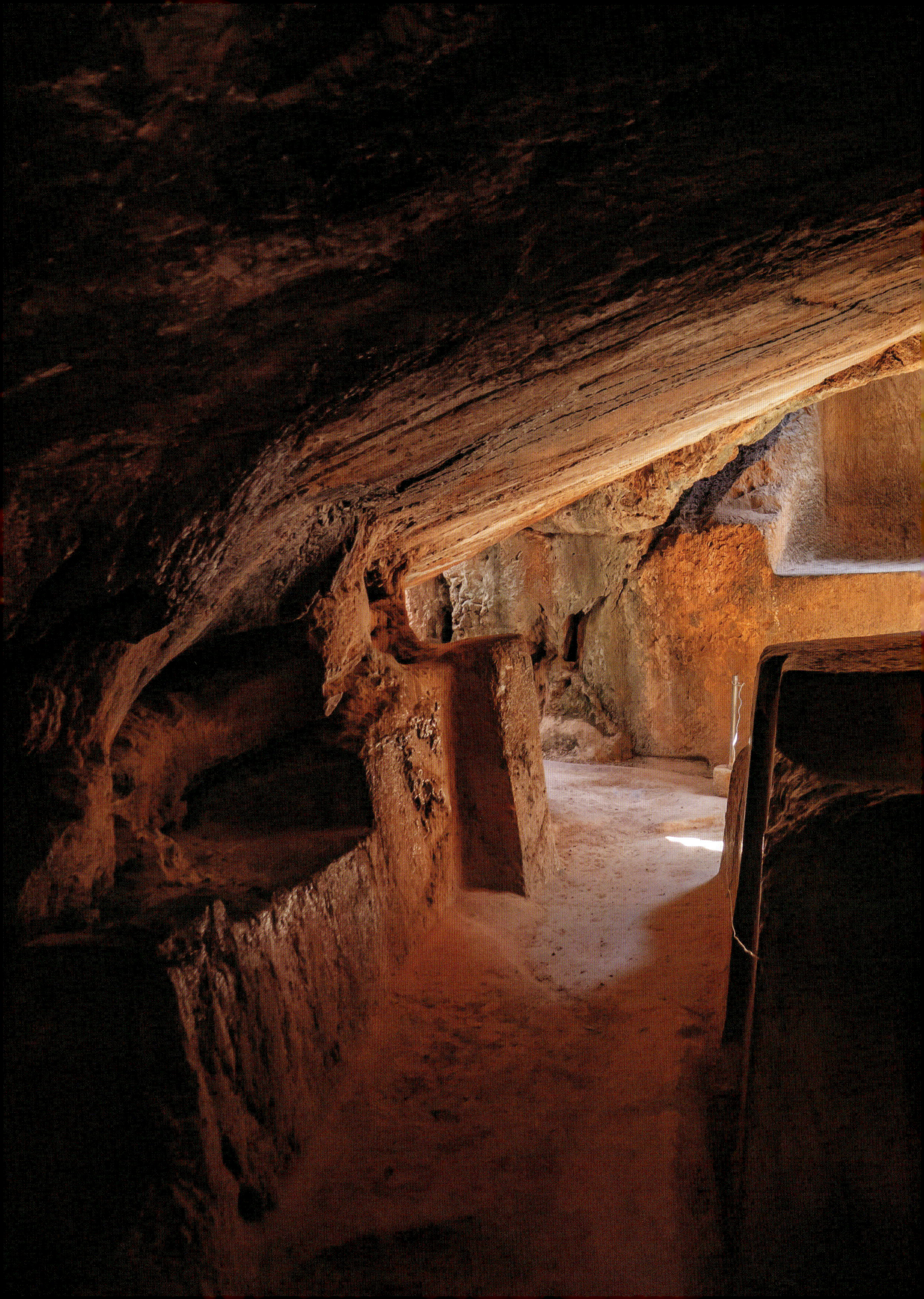

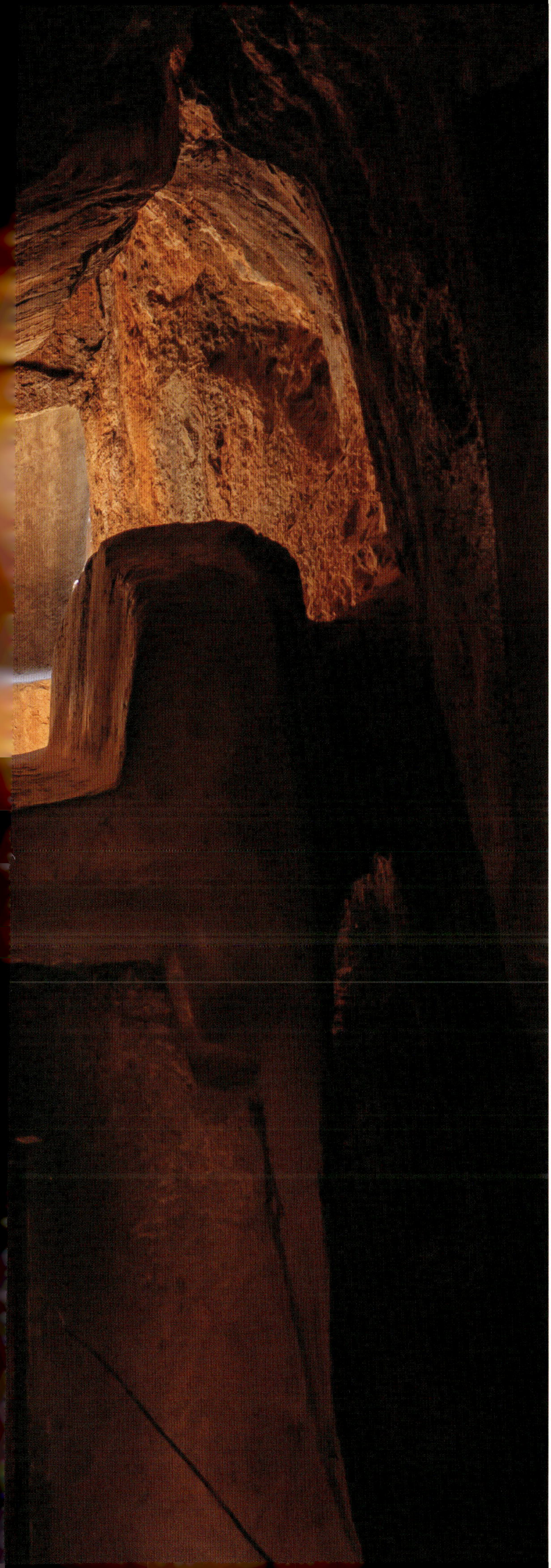

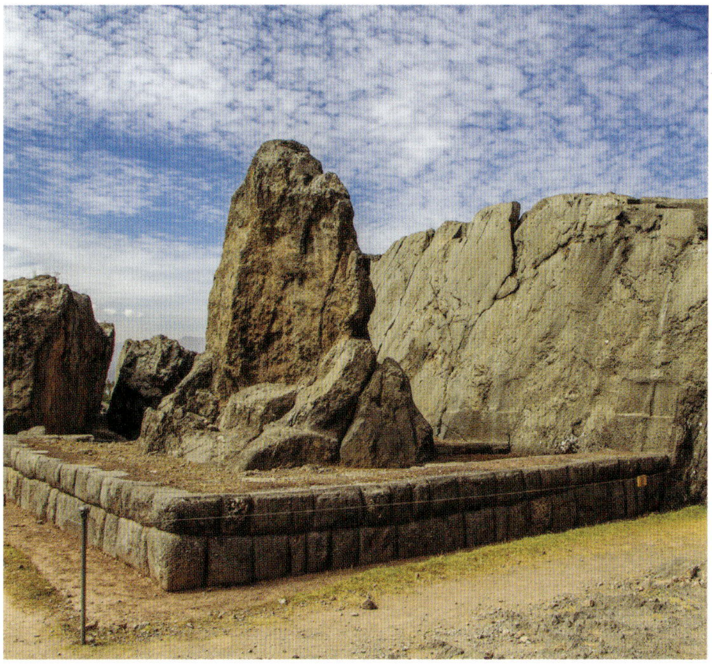

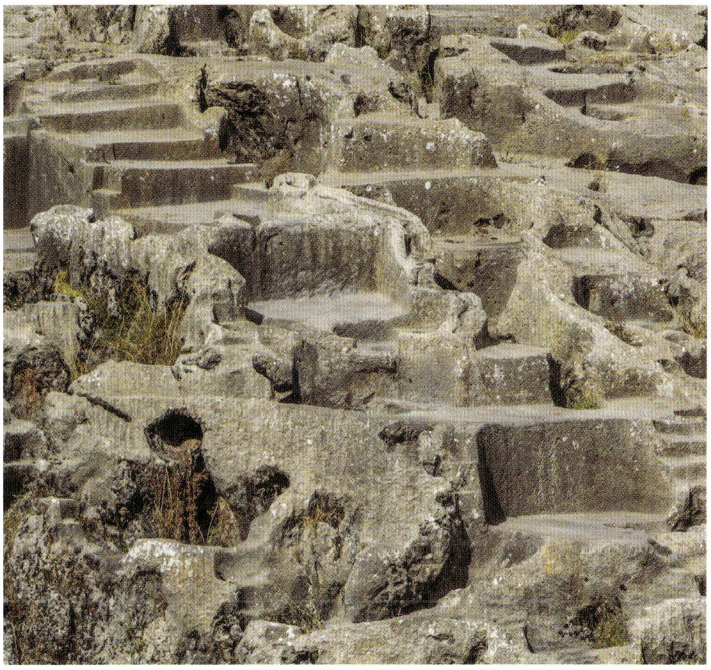

ALL PHOTOGRAPHS:

Qenqo, Cusco, Peru

Natural cavern or constructed chamber? The Incas of Peru could never be in any doubt that the Andes were the great unalterable of their existence. Is this why their craftsmen so often went 'with the grain' of the rock they worked in? Many of their *huacas* ('holy places') were wholly natural formations. Others, like this one – constructed sometime between 1000 and 1400 CE – were only subtly modified.

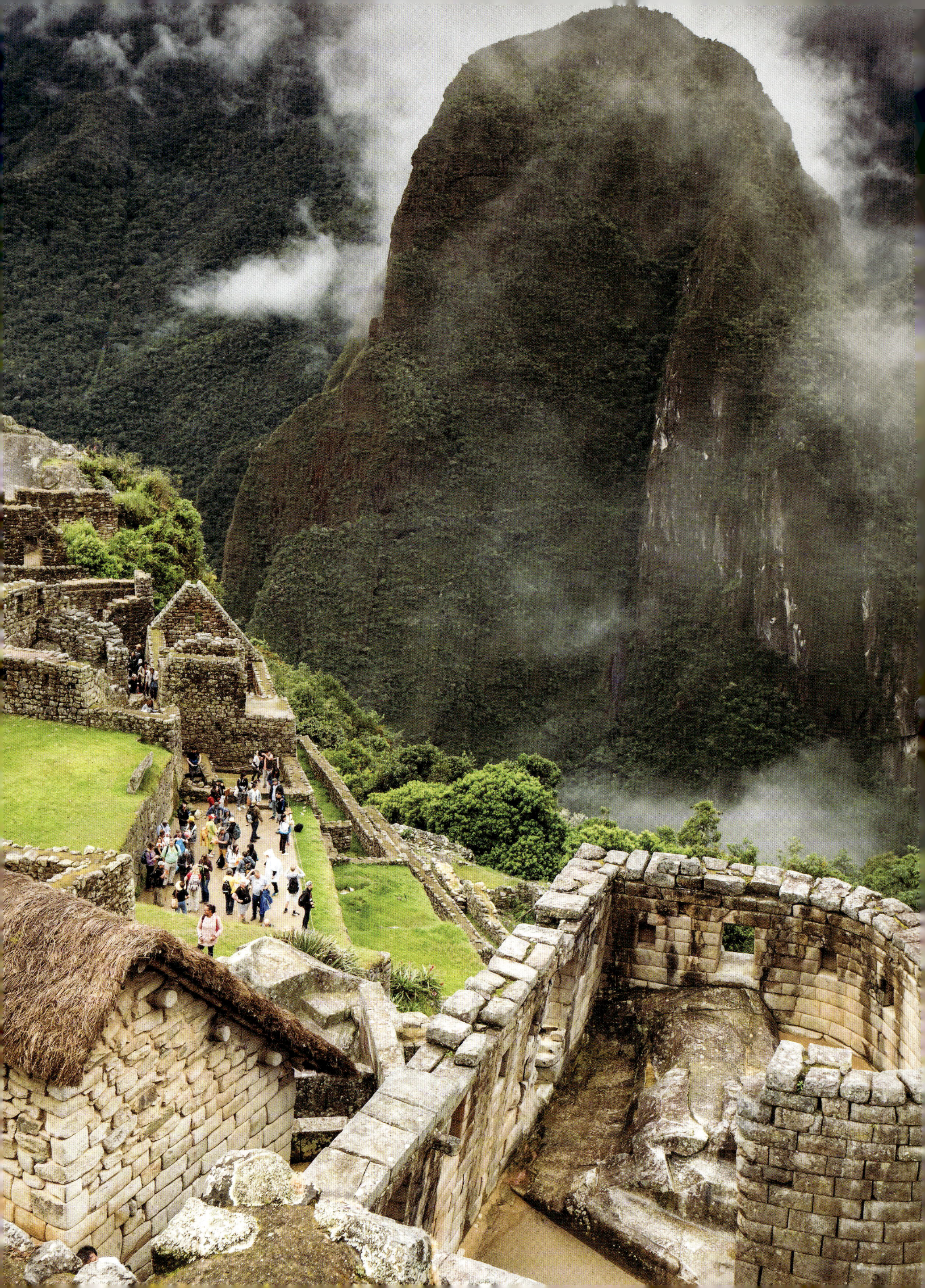

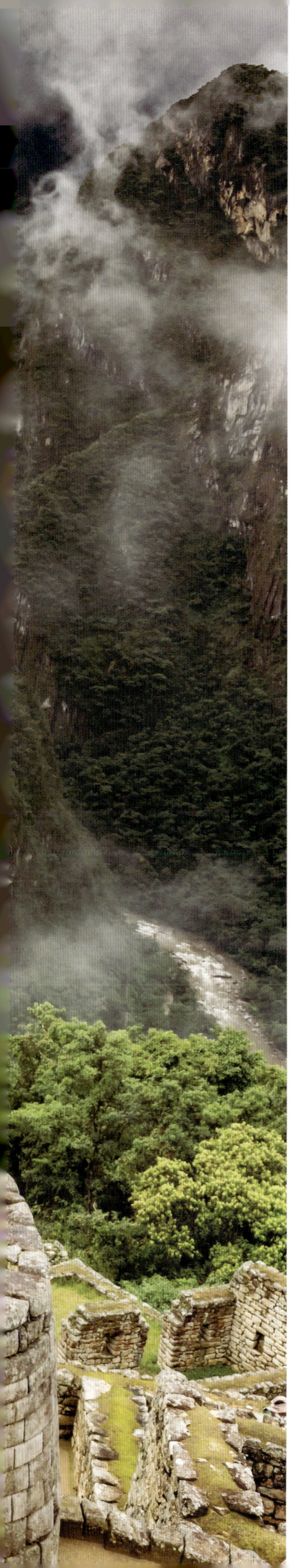

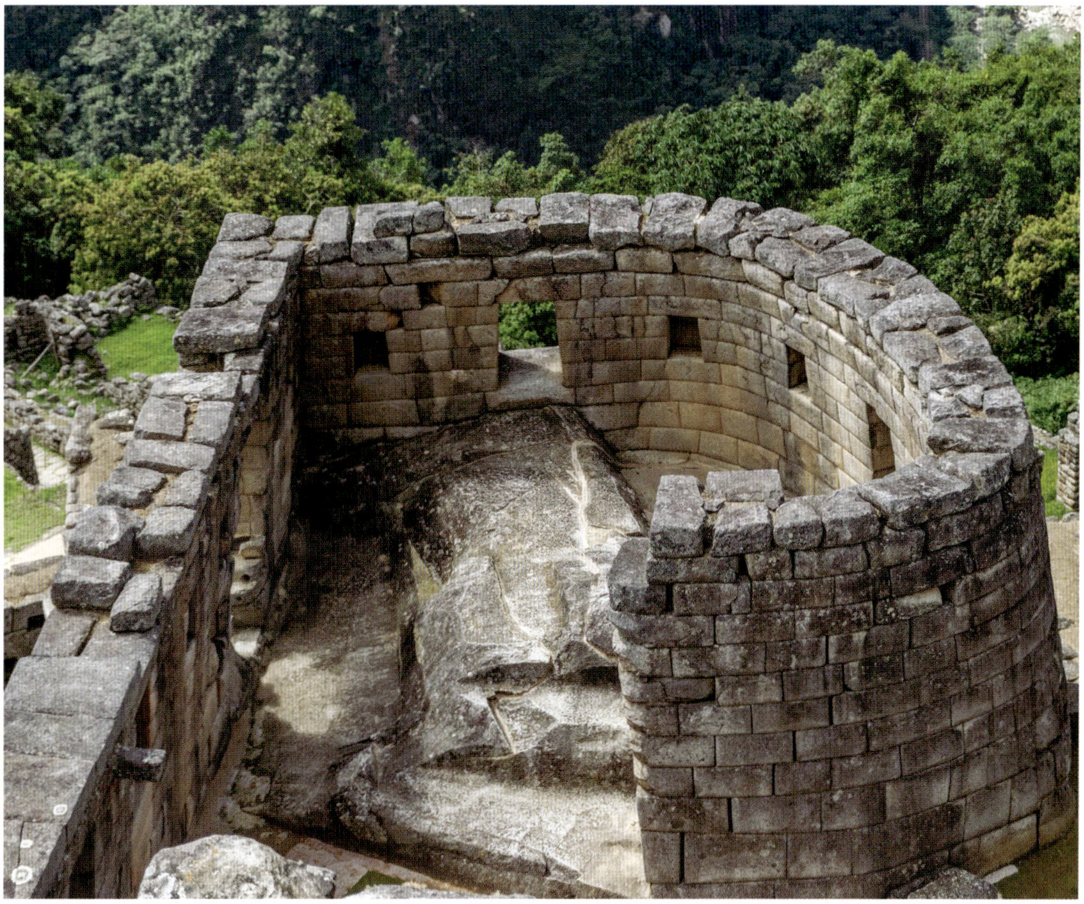

ALL PHOTOGRAPHS:
Temple of the Sun, Machu Picchu, Peru
One of the world's most celebrated archaeological sites is also among its most mysterious. We can only guess at Machu Picchu's original purpose, but it seems more likely to have been a temple complex than the 'Lost City' of the tourist guides. As at Qenqo, we see the Incas carefully accommodating the contours of the land – not just the rocky outcrop that the little tower (the so-called 'Observatory') sits on (*see above and right*), but also the nearby peak that it mirrors.

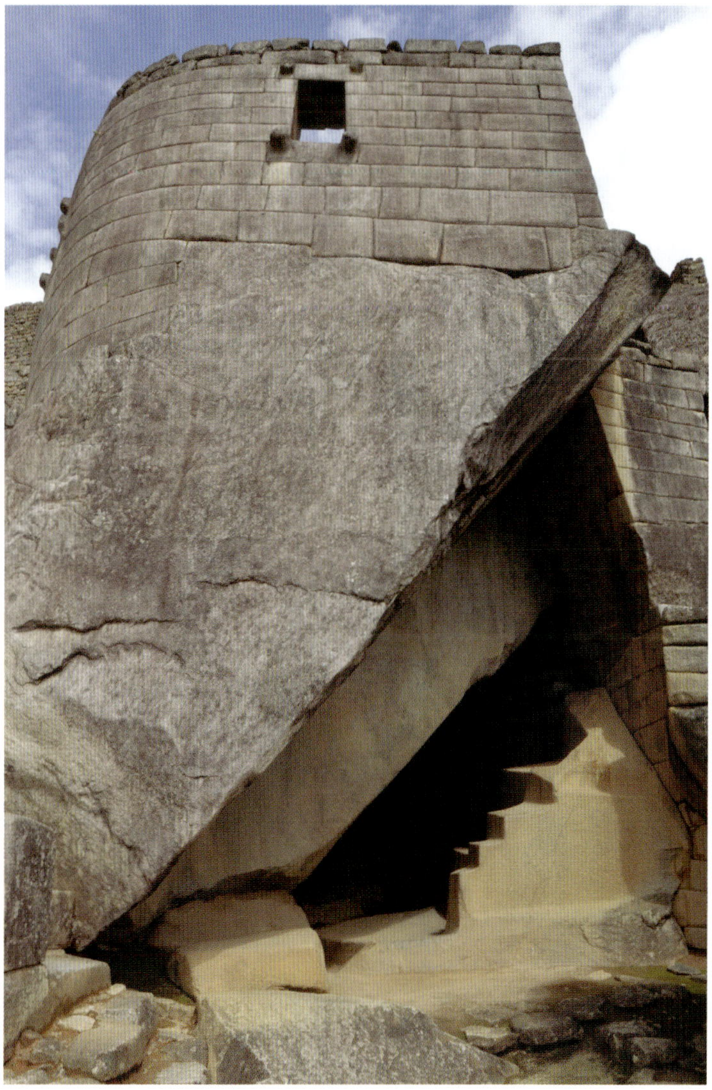

Picture Credits

Alamy: 76/77 (V Dorosz), 86/87 (Jan Wlodarczyk), 91 (Robert Preston Photography), 94 (Juan Carlos Munoz), 108 top (Reuters), 108 bottom (Paul Quayle), 109 (Viren Desai), 122/123 (Xinhua), 127 (CPA Media Pte), 134/135 (directphoto.bz), 136 top (Zaact gf/Tuul and Bruno Morandi), 188 (Images by T.O.K), 192 (Michael Wheatley), 193 top (Design Pics Inc), 193 bottom (Richard Cummins), 201 (LHB Photo), 204 (sep120/Stockimo), 205 bottom (aureliadumontphotography), 214 (EDU Vision), 216/217 (Inge Johnsson), 218 (Danita Delimont)

Dreamstime: 7 (Rolf52), 8 (Slawek Kozakiewicz), 12 top & 13 (I Wei Huang), 12 bottom (Kevin Eleady Cole), 14 (Kovalenkov Petr), 15 top (Catherinelprod Catherine), 15 bottom (Njarvis5), 20/21 (Hel080808), 32/33 (Wibaimages), 34 bottom (Steve Lovegrove), 35 & 36/37 (Krzysztof Janczewski), 38 top (Jorgefelix), 40/41 (Tomas1111), 44/45 (Scaliger), 46 top (Sven Hansche), 47 (Isabel Dubert), 48/49 & 50/51 (Sven Hansche), 54/55 (Alberto Zamorano), 58/59 (Elena Svetleyshaya), 60 & 61 (Nenad Nedomacki), 68/69 (79mtk), 74/75 (Narda Gongora), 78 top (Richard Billingham), 81 bottom (Dan Grytsku), 95 (Hakan Can Yalcin), 106 bottom (Anna Artamonova), 114/115 (Gaurav Masand), 118/119 (Burachet), 124/125 (Liang Wei), 126 top (Katoosha), 128/129 (Zjm7100), 132 top (StrippedPixel), 133 (Tommy Song), 137 (Pipa100), 138/139 (Cezary Wojtkowski), 140/141 (Luciano Mortula), 154/155 (Banky405), 157 (Dmitry Chulov), 174 (Ravindran John Smith), 175 top (Jaromir Chalabala), 178/179 (Tang90246), 184/185 (Untukbikinipaypal), 194/195 & 196 (Vadim Rodnev), 198/199 (Demerzel21), 202/203 (Westhimal), 206 (Madrabothair), 207 (James Kirkikis), 208/209 (paulacobleigh), 223 top (Legacy1995), 223 bottom (Simontgom65)

Getty Images: 10/11 (Peter Dazeley)

Shutterstock: 6 (Wead), 16/17 (Santi Rodriguez), 18 (Robert Paul Van Beets), 19 (Alex Ragen), 22/23 (Ugis Riba), 24/25 (S Vidal), 26/27 (Matej Kastelic), 28/29 (Leonid Sorokin), 30/31 (Tito Slack), 34 top (Kiev.Victor), 38 bottom (Phant), 39 top (Per-Boge), 39 bottom (Aerial-motion), 42/43 (Miruna Iona), 46 bottom (Lambros Kazan), 52/53 (Maziarz), 56/57 (Martchan), 62/63 (Telia), 64/65 (Ungvari Attila), 66/67 (Shchipkova Elena), 70 (Akimov Konstantin), 72/73 (Gimas), 79 bottom (Styre Reineck), 79 (JJ Millan), 80 (Tanya Keisha), 81 top (PenskyMonkey), 82/83 (Akimov Konstanin), 84/85 (Dmitri Kalvan), 88/89 (Tsuchi), 90 top (AlexelA), 90 bottom (Vadim Nefedoff), 92/93 (Bildagentur Zoonar), 96 (M Khebra), 97 top (Michael De Plaen), 97 bottom (Canyalcin), 98 (Uwe Bergitz), 100/101 (Boris Stroujko), 102/103 (Joolyann), 104/105, 106 (nomads.team), 107 (MBL1), 110 (Elamaran Elaa Photography), 111 top & bottom (RM Nunes), 112 & 113 bottom (Mazur Travel), 113 top (Aleksandra H Kossowska), 116/117 (Saman Weeratunga), 120/121 (Nitipol Temprim), 126 bottom (Katoosha), 130/131 (Lukas Hlavac), 132 bottom (Vatchara Ruttikul), 136 bottom (Cowardlion), 142 top (Robert Paul Van Beets), 142 bottom (Lee Yiung Tung), 143 (Dr_Flash), 144 (Tsuchi), 145 top (Ole A), 145 bottom (Sean Pavone), 146/147-149 top (John Chica), 149 bottom (Anton-Ivanov), 150/151 (Steve Allen), 152/153 (Anek Soowannaphoom), 156 top (Monticello), 156 bottom (Punya Family), 158/159 (Luciano Mortula-LGM), 160 top (Pumidol), 160 bottom (Blacknote), 161 (ArtRomanov), 162/163 (Art789), 164/165 (Sean Kruger), 166/167 (dangdumrong), 168/169 (Jixin Yu), 170/171 (Andrew Lam), 172/173 (Jimmy Tran), 175 bottom (OceanEye Studio), 176/177 (Pav-Pro Photography Ltd), 180/181 (Iakov Kalimin), 182/183 (Merabet Hichem), 186/187 (Widayat_f), 190/191 (Blaze986), 197 top (AnjelikaGr), 197 bottom (Mirjana Simeunovich), 200 (Rommel Canlas), 205 top (David Olivera), 210 (ahau1969), 211 (Alfredo Matus), 212/213 (Aksenovden), 215 (Gordon Galbraith), 219 (Carlos Yudica), 220 (Videobuzzing), 211 top & bottom (obscur), 222 (Terri Butler Photography)